THE MANUAL

The Definitive Book
On Parenting
and
The Causal Theory

By Faye Snyder, PsyD

Edited by Robyn Buehler

Copyright © April 2012 by S. Faye Snyder, PsyD.

All rights reserved. No portion of this book may be reproduced – mechanically, electronically, or by any other means, including photocopying – without the permission of the publisher.

Includes index
ISBN 978-0-9854714-2-2 (paperback)

Cover Design: Lisa Wiscombe
Color Photo: Jim Warren

Clifton Legacy Publishing
Los Angeles, California

Printed in the United States of America
First printing April 2012

*To the memory of my mother.
I wish she were here to talk.*

Acknowledgements

I have been supported by a small band of detail-oriented women who have donated their editing skills to this book as their very own cause. I don't know what I would have done without them. They enabled me to finish in my lifetime. Robyn Buehler laid out this manuscript in such a way that it has become beautiful to behold; she makes me look good. Nearly a year ago when I was ready to start wrapping this up, Stephanie Rydall gave my manuscript a once-over for glaring issues and to her I am so grateful. It's a big book to read, much less edit. I would like to thank Mary Jane Julius for taking on the role of citation editor, insuring sufficiency and correctness of references. My dearest friend and colleague, Reenie Sklar, reviewed my words with a fine-tooth comb, scrutinizing every nuance from the point of view of the reader. She also recruited her science-minded sister, Sheila Forrette, to help proofread for credibility and her academic daughter, Billie Soo, to proofread for any remaining grammar and punctuation problems. Thank you, ladies. Thank you.

I also want to acknowledge the uncompromising scientists and clinician's upon whose work mine stands. For more information about any of the following authors, please see the index and references. Initially, I want to acknowledge the pioneers of attachment researchers Rene Spitz and Harry Harlow. I especially want to acknowledge the Father of Attachment Theory, John Bowlby, a scientist and theoretician of the first order, whose work has withstood heat, scrutiny and time. He studied attachment issues, wrote model theory and spawned magnificent researchers, Mary Ainsworth and her protégé Mary Main, who have demonstrated the long-term critical importance of attachment in the formation of personality. While attachments are difficult to assess, they have been able to develop the necessary criteria to produce results that were not only meaningful but profound. Jay Belsky is another researcher who has dared to confront the status quo by producing attachment research, which documents the traumatic impact of day care on the very young child as well as the long-lasting symptoms to follow.

Peter Breggin, the "Conscience of American Psychiatry," has challenged the pharmaceutical industry for producing bad theory, faulty research results and dangerous drugs. Standing with him against drugging children are author Richard DeGrandpre and clinicians Howard Glasser and Robert Whitaker, who also report other explanations and treatments for disruptive or disturbing behavior, reasons to suspect misrepresentation by the drug industry and the harmful results of pharmaceuticals. Scientists who have confronted the myth that genes explain behavior include Richard Lewontin, Ruth Hubbard, Jay Joseph, Elliot Valenstein, Stuart Kaplan and Richard Bentall. Bruce Lipton is another researcher who writes about the role of genes and the significant but frequently discounted role of cell membranes in biological responses to environment.

I am grateful to all of the researchers who have believed in the original integrity of the child, the impact of experience and the significance of symptoms as indicators of past experiences. A number of researcher-clinicians have specialized in the effects of trauma, thereby taking on the genetic explanations of behavior as misleading. Bessel van der Kolk, Colin Ross and Alvin Pam, supported by their colleagues, have scrutinized and exposed bad research that has passed for good, illuminating the trend. Van der Kolk has been searching for more effective treatments of trauma, perhaps such as those described herein. Ross, a theoretician himself, has studied the lifelong effects of untreated trauma and proposed that the diagnostic criteria of this field has been a way of disguising the multiple and overlapping symptoms of trauma. He offers his Trauma Model for understanding various clusters of symptoms. Their studies and the work of consummate researcher Allan Schore and researcher-clinician Daniel Siegel have provided ample non-genetic explanations for healthy and symptomatic behaviors. The field is replete with heroes like Martin Teicher and Joseph LeDoux who have studied the impact of trauma on the brain and how the body remembers trauma.

Psychiatrist Bruce Perry is another researcher who has worked hard with the support of his teams to educate the field as well as the public about the actual role of the brain, trauma and genes in the development of human beings, clarifying what genes *don't* do. Additionally, van der Kolk, Ross and Charles Whitfield tackled the "false memory" debate in their research, in their books and in the court. Van der Kolk triumphed in the court over a so-called forensic expert who could be had for a high price. She consistently argues false memories when a grown child reports their parent for incest. Van der Kolk proved to the satisfaction of one judge that a recovered memory is as good as any memory. Other clinicians and researchers have pioneered in the field of domestic violence, so many to mention, not the least of whom is Donald Dutton, who dared to propose and write that perpetrators were once abused and neglected children. Psychologists Jennifer Freyd and Robert Fleiss were brave contributors to this issue, as their parents were professionals who stood against the grown child on the issue of incest. Freyd and Fleiss dared to speak up about their own experiences of incest by these parents.

There is another group of renegades I need to acknowledge: the watchdogs and critics of the politics within our field. They confront the myriad of false representations that descend from our training institutes, department directors, professional organizations and licensing magnates. They confront conventional and popular bad theory. These critics include psychology's own ethicist Kenneth Pope, as well as clinicians Ty Colbert and Robert Whitaker. The greatest of these is recently deceased Alice Miller, who wrote vociferously about the harm our field has done to its patients in the name of Analytic and Behavioral Theory. I so had hoped to finish my work in time to earn her favor.

Disclaimer

The contents of this book are intended to span every important issue in the formation of personality so the reader can assess his or her life's issues and make educated choices in parenting, self-care, ethics and selection and pursuit of relationships. All of the contents of this book cannot pertain to all people at all times, so it is up to the reader to make reasonable use of this book.

If the reader is unsure about how to interpret and apply any of this information, they should seek their own therapist or guide to help them sort out a healthy application of the contents herein. If you feel certain you know how to apply the contents of this book, perhaps you too should check yourself. A little uncertainty will probably promote better self-reflection and more careful consideration of the passages within. Additionally, the author requests that if a parent has difficulty with making healthy choices then the reader would do well to seek therapy to work these barriers through. The author believes that until you have healed yourself, it is difficult to perceive clearly and make healthy choices.

The Manual is written with an understanding that each reader shall take full responsibility for their interpretation and application of the material within these pages. For example, a parent who is prone to neglect must not take the chapter on Faith Parenting as permission to further neglect or place their child at risk. The chapter on Discipline must never be interpreted as a method of rejecting their child because we are reminded to love, honor and respect our child as much as we correct her.

Sometimes I have been redundant because I have wanted to be careful how I am understood. I am not advocating that you cease to take your medication because that can be a dangerous move without medical or psychiatric supervision. If you wish to heal naturally in order to get off medication, you must find a cooperating psychiatrist and therapist to help you do this. Nothing in the contents of this book is specific permission for you or any person to follow without professional guidance, and one of the most important tenants of building a healthy personality is the assumption of all responsibilities for your choices. Therefore, if you embark upon the application of the information herein, you have consented to take full responsibility for your choices.

Lastly, as this is a patchwork of my life's lessons and the concepts I have learned along the way from experts before me, I fear I have not credited everyone who deserves it. I could even have heard ideas in a lecture that I thought of later myself, without realizing I had been influenced. Even if I never heard of your work, if you pioneered in areas I represented as my own ideas, I will be happy to give you credit for your work. As a matter of fact, the last leg of writing this book has been one of looking for sources to validate my assertions. The truth is there is nothing new under the sun because all insights are built upon previous experiences and information. Giving credit only makes me look smarter and healthier.

This edition is a shakedown cruise and the next edition will entail corrections. If you take issue with this book and you wish to express yourself, I will be happy to listen and respond if at all reasonably possible, given you use relationship skills with me. You can contact me through my website, drfayesnyder.com. I am also open to public debate.

PREFACE

This is my life's work. It is a user's manual to the human being and a parenting book. I believe it offers the most comprehensive account of human behavior and human personality to-date. It is a map of human development as it takes place from the inside out, including how to make a personality, how to undo and heal disorders and how to be the best you can be.

It will help you to understand how your parents came to be who they were, why they chose to raise you the way they did and how those choices manifest in your behavior every day. It is a chance to understand killers and saints, yourself and your baby, your friends and your lovers, and even your dog. The information in this manual is observable, verifiable, replicable and consistent. It is the science of character.

So far, we seem not to afford ourselves the ability to treat our psyches and minds as we would any other area of nature, where every cause has an effect and every effect causes something else. We look for the easy answers that aren't really answers at all: He was a bad seed. She's got the vengeance gene. His chemicals are imbalanced. She was born talented.

In every other area of science from weather to illness to physics, the things we used to think of as "mysterious" were simply once unknown. They were only unknown. Operating under the assumption that things could someday be understood, we began to find the answers.

Yet when it came to souls and psyches, we had a bad habit of mistaking the unknown for the unknowable and we ignored the causes and effects right in front of us. The reasons for this choice to give up our point of view and our capacity to see will be discussed in this book. But for now, I propose that most of us arrive into adulthood more blind than we know.

In the field of psychology we have had many ways of not finding the truth. We have purported that the causes of these changes can never be known and represented, that the causes are within a metaphorical black box that cannot be opened (Behavioral Theory) or perhaps *shouldn't* be opened. We have fathomed that traits are inborn (most analytic theories) with a myriad of explanations from original sin to bad seed, pretending we are on the trail of the actual genes that account for behavior.

Social sciences have fathomed that these differences were racial and then cultural. More modern versions of this sociology have represented that different cultures reach different levels of awareness up a ladder of consciousness, leaving transcendence to the minority and overlooking parenting as a way of catapulting social consciousness forward. New sages seem to evidence a high level of enlightenment in their theories, yet regretfully they have the same blind spots. With emphasis on meditation and transcendence, they too rule out environmental cause. Even most social workers appear to operate from the view that children are abused and neglected by parents who are, at least in part, products of bad genes. All but a few anthropologists and psychotherapists recognize the essential role of the parent-child relationship in the evolution of human consciousness.

Unfortunately, every generation has a group of authorities at the top that retains the power of definition. These gatekeepers welcome information that further supports the going theory. They either ignore or ridicule information that challenges conventional wisdom. This bias is especially activated if it points toward parenting as the primary vehicle for the evolution of consciousness. For thousands of years, parents have been both protected and vindicated at the high cost of awareness. Ironically, most of them would rather have had the information and the clarity.

Our bar is too low and we have settled for the idea that our personalities are a roll of the dice. In fact, I think we find the assumption comforting, especially if we think we are gifted and even more so if our character becomes our identity, something we think is inborn. However, those of us with low self-worth experience such ideology as a form of damnation and abandonment, even though they accept their fate with resolve, like the untouchables in India.

Psychology is a soft science that could be harder. It could also be less political and corruptible.

We could come much closer to a true science if we weren't serving so many masters. This theory, The Causal Theory, proposes a tangible way of understanding behavior that is grounded in reality.

This book isn't a marvel of modern science or communication and it was never funded by anything but my own pocket. Only in part is it a product of my education and to a great degree, it survived my education. It seems to be born of a series of insights and blessings. The first blessing was a handicap, or so I thought. I was born with my left eye turned out, which I suppose made it very difficult for my mother to gaze into my eyes, a key ingredient of attachment. Before I turned four, I had two eye surgeries to straighten out my wall-eyed look. When I entered adolescence, my eyes began to trouble me again as it became painful to read. If I pushed forward, I would get migraines. This is still true. It slowed down my education and I became addicted to opiates at one point. I have developed a third eye, one that enables me to skim a book to get the author's bottom line, surmise her motives, agenda and the ramifications of her thinking. This helped me become a good listener, especially to teachers. I developed the ability to visualize. Somehow this led me to see people's ideas as ideas that were not written in stone, and I think it also helped me to see myself in others.

My father, Paul Stoyle Means, worked hard so my mother could stay home. My bonding with my mother, Kathleen Clifton Means, bonding was sufficient to provide me the necessary strength to speak up when I believe something is wrong, while inadequate enough that I am driven to speak on behalf of babies everywhere. As the result of a difficult childhood, I had an additional need to make sense of things. I had parents I loved, who loved me but didn't know how to parent. My mother was the intellectual daughter of a farmer who taught his children to labor and to ask good questions. My mom was a tough woman who set me to work at age five, yet she best related to me through ideas. I became a good student to please her and my favorite moments in my childhood were when we talked philosophically.

I remember having to pick the switch from the backyard tree she would use to punish me. My worst memories were of her whipping my bare legs while cackling the words, "Dance, dance, dance!" But she never asked me to repress my feelings. I was free to cry if I needed to cry, something I have since learned was redeeming. The abuse made me think she enjoyed hurting me. I never remember thinking that it was for my own good and it gave me the impression that she didn't know what she was doing, my second blessing.

Even though I grew up believing that authority was not necessarily authoritative, I have always been in search of good authority and when I find it I am a humble student. When I find the appearance of authority without good theory, I am reviled and indignant. I have never felt timid about confronting bad thinking. As a matter of fact, when I encounter bad thinking, I can barely contain myself.

I am concerned that my engine is so stoked that I may forget to acknowledge that there are gems of sparkling light amongst us. There are rigorous scientists who cannot be bought. There are therapists who seek state-of-the-art information and live authentic lives. There are leaders in the field who have one foot in research and the other in the therapy office. My field has no shortage of heroes.

I have imagined myself as a witness to great historical dialogues over the centuries, having an eye for great thinkers and contempt for arrogant and ignorant leaders. I promised myself if I was ever in the presence of greatness, I wouldn't miss it or take it for granted. After living in the South I vowed I would never end up on the wrong side of history. I was in my prime during the sixties and seventies, identifying with the oppressed and with liberation movements. I related to people who felt dominated and exploited. I realized that just as my mother regularly seemed to inaccurately define what was right and true, so had dictators, religious leaders and politicians. Too much wrong was going on in the name of what was right.

I helped integrate Fat Boys Barbeque with a few friends in Cocoa, Florida. I participated in a sit-in and went to jail to defend academic freedom and teachers who were fired for challenging the status quo. I studied under a great theorist, Joseph Waller, who was also a black nationalist, from whom I learned that we can actually re-define things to preserve the truth and to best represent reality as it really is. He was a charismatic leader who was also a facile theoretician substantially teaching me, among others, how to think and question. I liked to watch white people interact with him. I noticed that most did not realize they were in the presence of genius.

I devoted myself completely to the left and I was purged from two national left-wing organizations for questioning theory, my third blessing. Over the next few years, I worked a single magnificent koan of sorts: historical and dialectical materialism, a shorthand Zen-like description of The Way of reality. I couldn't see it, but I looked and looked until I gave up. It was then that I "saw" the chain of events preceding all things, developing out of an interaction of opposites. Unfortunately, seeing didn't make me feel better back then. I actually became lonelier.

I attended the State University of New York at Stony Brook. I majored in political science, but also studied law, philosophy and economics. I wanted to be a lawyer for the misunderstood. I didn't know yet that my eyes weren't going to let me do that.

As a young woman, finding good therapy was not easy. The more my therapists sat in front of me nodding knowingly while keeping their thoughts to themselves, the worse I got. It seemed as if they were judging me and withholding their wisdom, like my mother withheld her guidance and faith in me, although I couldn't see the correlation at the time. Whatever was wrong with me seemed permanent and I felt like a specimen. I stuck it out with eleven therapists for at least one year and with others for less than that, because I didn't want to quit before the magic. Sometimes I wondered whether my inability to find good therapy for sixteen diligent years was, to some extent, just an unlucky run of improbable bad odds. In any case, I was unstable, getting progressively worse, my fourth blessing. Time seemed to be wasting.

When I finally found one good therapist, Michael Lilienfeld, I knew I'd hit "pay dirt," as my mother would say about striking gold, but I did challenge him some in the beginning. I thought he was like the devil, tempting me to be selfish and put myself first. I told him that such intentions were wrong. He asked me to give him six months and then I could go back to my old beliefs if I wanted. I did. I surrendered. I paid attention to him and myself, all the while wondering why the therapists before him didn't seem to know what he knew. He guided me and taught me what my mother did not, the things healthy kids learn from their mothers in childhood. When our work was done, I kept what I wanted, which was most of it, and threw out the ideas from my past that made me sick. The collection of good theory about my past, good theory for the present and good theory toward my future served me well.

My questions were answered. I worked hard on myself. I learned what I wished to know and what I wished that my mother knew. Once a very dysfunctional person, I had come a very long way, observing myself all the while. It was time to meet my husband, Ron, who was very peaceful and comfortable with himself. He was highly interested in Zen Buddhism, practicing many of the precepts as a lifestyle on his own, and he took a deep interest in my insights, recommending that I read *Zen Flesh, Zen Bones* by Paul Reps and works by Alan Watts. He also turned me onto *Varieties of Religious Experiences* by William James. I was in love. We married. When I was in labor with my one and only late-in-life child, my husband read D.T. Suzuki to me.

I was sure that how we would raised our child would determine what kind of character he would develop. I wanted his name to be predictive of his abilities so I started thinking aloud about the meaning of names or his initials, but my husband had no grandiose plans for his son. "I just want him to be moral and love his life," Ron insisted. So I engineered his initials to mean success, Scott Clifton Snyder, and kept the meaning to myself for more than 20 years. For the most part, we have always been on the same page when it came to parenting, even though he never came to my class or read a word I wrote.

In working so hard on myself, despite my problems with my eyes, I was rewarded with some clear sight and insight. Imagine that; there's more than one way to see. I became perceptive. The more one heals oneself, the smarter and more authentic one becomes. Apparently the work never ends, but insights get better and better. I found the process to be an adventure, the adventure that gives purpose to our lives. I learned that healing includes working both ends. I had learned how to heal myself from the inside out, but I lacked a role model. I took a little from Joseph Waller, a little from Michael Lilienfeld and a little from my husband. But I continued to be awkward. I tried to teach my insights to others and my husband overheard me. He said, "Perhaps you will write books, but you will never teach." I was so ashamed that I learned to give up thinking of myself as a teacher.

I continued to have a burning desire to understand why it took so long to get the help I needed. My hunger for clarity was so strong that I ended up in graduate school partially because I wanted to become a therapist myself and truly see what was wrong with the theory and training that wasted so many expensive years of the prime of my life. I found a small school in West Los Angeles, California Graduate Institute, which had a good enough reputation even though it wasn't accredited. It was a good enough school for me because I was critical of conventional theories and practices anyway. If my credentials appear lacking, let me say that we were taught the same material as any other school because we all had to pass the same licensing exam. Some information was quite valuable and some of it was a shame even though it was conventional wisdom for training therapists.

I was angry that bad ideas would be given so much credibility. I had a burning awareness that so much was at stake and children were suffering because therapists and parents were kept ignorant of how important they were to their children. I thought therapists and the public were significantly misinformed. First, do no harm. No wonder my therapy took so long.

After one year in graduate school, my son was born and fortunately I had already learned about Attachment Theory. I tested different theories on him as I nurtured and adored him, rejecting a great deal of what I was learning and embracing other information as long as it worked well. I was amazed to discover that raising a child could be so fulfilling and so much fun. I became the mother I wished I'd had.

In school I asked a lot of questions and some of my instructors reported that I was an odd student with odd ideas. After experiencing a worm's eye and bird's eye view of what therapists are taught, I was ready to formulate my own theory. The most disconcerting thing I learned in graduate school was the almost invisible role parenting takes in the creation of personality and behavior. It seemed like the white elephant in the living room no one discussed. I also noticed that there was a great deal of presumption that behavior and pathology are inborn. That seemed to be the reason to me that I'd wasted years in therapy with therapists treating me more like a fragile object than an educable person who just needed guidance.

I wrote the outline for *The Manual* the year I graduated, inspired by a friend, Karen Sontag and her baby, Lindsay. My goal was to teach new parents what babies and children need from them, how personalities and behaviors come into being as a result of good and bad parenting and how one needs to undo those adaptations and replace them with healthy skills in order to heal. I assumed that this would be sort of a corrective parenting process, where clients would be told the truth about how childhood was supposed to be and taught how to self-correct with the guidance their parents never gave them, guidance for which I waited so very long. I was soon to discover that not all clients in therapy want it as bad as I did.

With help from Karen, I founded The Institute for Professional Parenting (TIPP) in 1988. I taught from a course outline that I shared with my students. The skeleton is the same today, including the eight chapters in the same order, but split into two versions, a sparser version for *The*

Handbook, the supplemental guide to *The Miracle Child Parenting Series* and also this text. *The Manual* still has remnants of the first bullet points because sometimes people just need the bottom line. In other areas, I have also written directly to you about what I know are issues on people's minds. I answer all the questions I have heard over the years and I write to the recurrent lament I hear from parents, "But my child didn't come with a manual." This is true. It is a confusing time in human history where parents have needed a manual as we have abandoned our evolutionary design for child rearing. We are trying to re-invent the roles of women, men and parents for many good reasons, but sometimes we set ourselves up for failure as we try to figure out a better formula for these exploding times rather than refining the one nature evolved for us. Human babies need to be born "sooner" than other mammals because our heads are bigger. That means we need to spend more time outside the womb close to our mothers. Human babies are not ready to separate for at least three years. They need to stay close to their very own mom.

May it be now that children do come with a manual. Perhaps *The Manual* is the best shower gift a new mommy can get. The sixteen-hour, eight-week lecture series is available live in some locations. We are considering presenting it over an extended weekend in various locations around the country to students who have already listened to the series once on CD or watched the series once on DVD. The lecture series has more stories and examples as it is presented in a more narrative form and, of course, it accommodates questions and answers.

You may want to simply look up a particular topic in this book like "evil" or "resilience," but I have always been reluctant to talk about any concept out of context. *The Manual* is laid out strategically. If you look up "resilience" or "attachment" before you have read the foundations of these, or any concepts herein, you may reject the information you initially find. They are in the index so you can quickly find them again for reference, but I trust you will read from cover to cover first. If I use any psychobabble, I will explain concepts as I go. I have also included a glossary at the end.

The Manual is the product of a relatively bad childhood, a frustrating journey into therapy, a long-awaited experience with good therapy, a decent education and experience raising a child late in life. It definitely helped that I gave birth to an ever-so-wanted child while I was in school and I was able to test different theories as he grew. I have always said he was my laboratory as well as my evidence.

Ironically, many of the famous theorists in psychology were poor parents and their flaws in theory were apparent in their parenting and ultimately in their children. I would insist that anyone who coached me would be living what they teach and their lives would be models of their theory.

My views have been considered controversial from the time I discovered it was taboo to criticize a person's parents for their parenting, so I am still frequently challenged to provide scientific proof that it's all about parenting. Gradually I began looking for evidence to support my experiences, intuition and position. Slowly, the research and the references appeared. As I reviewed the data and its interpretations, I discovered major discrepancies and contradictions and I began to see a "War of the Researchers" as I have come to call it. I discovered that not only was one side of my field pro-parent and the other side was pro-child, but the researchers appeared to be polarized as well. The pro-parent researchers seemed to be willing to do whatever it took to prove that it's not about parents, and they had the loudest voices. More and more I was discovering why it took so long to find good therapy. The corruption that infiltrated the world of my earlier political life was apparent in my ivory tower too. Here it was again in the profession of helping, healing and compassion, infiltrating theory and practice. I now found deliberate obfuscation of information. I became even more aware that this might be a difficult path, and hoped that someone would do some trail blazing for clinicians and parents.

I took some necessary time to develop a compatible practice to go with what I came to call

The Causal Theory, which led me to learn some things the hard way. I learned that many clients don't want to be told that their parents made the mistakes that account for their present symptoms. Some would rather believe they are genetically defective than acknowledge and process parental errors from their childhood. I could see them twisting and turning under a mandate not to betray their parents under any circumstances. This was a shocker to me. It somewhat justified and explained the inverted theories I had studied that seemed to side-step laws of cause and effect. I began to understand the major inclinations of therapists to avoid dealing honestly and directly with the histories behind symptoms, lest clients get up and leave. I began to understand why many therapists are so withholding of information and take it so slowly, as if money was not valuable and time was not priceless.

I essentially solved that problem by creating my parenting class, *The Miracle Child Parenting Series*, now simply called *The Parenting Class* or *The Class*. I asked my clients to take the class first before coming to see me. I found that sitting in a chair amongst many and listening to an academic lecture gave clients the freedom to silently try on the truth of the concepts without feeling as if they were betraying their parents. After sixteen lecture hours over eight weeks, most had dropped their resistance to reflecting on childhood experiences. Most participants became better parents almost overnight and many realized they needed to work on themselves in order to parent better. Some decided I was not the therapist for them and I imagine, in those cases, we both were relieved to have learned we were not a good fit before beginning the work. Most, however, came to therapy ready to address their childhood issues. They arrived having already diagnosed themselves and were prepared to share why they chose the diagnosis they did and how it most fit with the childhood they had. Usually, they were correct. They became respected partners in the work. They collaborated with me in their assessments and goals. Other times, if their assessments seemed off, I would dialogue with them until they had a more accurate appraisal of their adult traits and causes. I have found that when a diagnosis is accurate, people embrace it as long as it means they get to transcend it too. Additionally, in this process, my clients have actually contributed to the theory. I have listened to avowed passive-aggressive students talk to one another about how they didn't want to act until they understood their feelings, a variation of "until they felt like it."

Over the years, I've had thousands of students and hundreds of clients. Every client had a diagnosis that matched up his or her childhood with his or her personality. If not, the diagnosis was suspended, at least temporarily. This is to say that I have been observing the accuracy of The Causal Theory almost daily for about twenty-five years. When you have completed *The Manual*, you will too. You will see how understanding traits and their causes makes it easier to see people clearly. Nevertheless, we never ever try to fit a square peg into a round hole. A diagnosis that doesn't explain behavior is useless.

My next problem was that "talk" therapy did not seem to get to the root of most issues quickly or deeply enough, and self-awareness, self-reflection and self-discovery were important in my opinion. It's one reason I utilize Behavioral Theory as an adjunct, but I don't depend on it to create mental health. A friend of mine introduced me to a Reichian process of extended deep breathing which yields buried memories and emotions without any suggestion from the therapist. I treated myself to one session of this work. I got it. Gradually, I began to introduce it to my clients where there seemed to be repressed material. Ultimately it became a staple of my work as I realized how profound and effective it was with nearly everyone. Even my healthier clients had insights about themselves from the work. Most clients had unsolicited body memories, even from their first year of life. Incredible as this may sound these memories are supported by recent neurological research.

"In fact, psychologists and neuroscientists have discovered that babies not only learn more, but imagine more, care more, and experience more than we would have ever thought possible.

In some ways, young children are smarter, more imaginative, more caring, and even more conscious than adults are" (Gopnik, 2009, p.5).

Amazingly, most of the time my clients would find those early memories verified by siblings, uncles and aunts, even their parents. I was in awe of the human design. We have something in our make-up that enables us to heal trauma and become more deeply self-aware. It seems like an accelerated form of meditation and it is so internal that Causal Therapists cannot be accused of planting memories. Couchwork clears us of our emotional drives to act out the impact of trauma, if we are willing to revisit the experience one last time in the safety of an office with a compassionate therapist who has done the same work.

Another problem developed. People could have great insight, theory and healing, but it did not give them new skills to replace their bad habits. So I began to include my Relationship Skills Workshops as part of the transcendent process. Anyone who worked with me privately became required to attend the workshops, while anyone who took the parenting class could take the workshop. In other words, a client could invite a partner to come take the workshop with them who has not committed to doing the private therapy. In these groups that met for four hours twice monthly, they would listen to each other process issues incorrectly and then correctly. I ultimately developed a highly successful format for retraining people to have good relationship skills and healthy ethics. I discovered that when you replace unhealthy relationship skills with healthy ones, it's almost impossible to have a personality disorder anymore.

I increased my sessions to an hour-and-a-half so there would always be time for both "couchwork" and "talk" therapy. This reduced the number of sessions whenever possible. I usually met twice monthly for private sessions and the workshops met twice monthly for four hours each, unless of course the client had insurance and we had to fit into the standard insurance formula of shorter weekly sessions. Couchwork was rich in formative memories and clients began to heal two to three times faster when they took the class, attended private sessions with couchwork and participated in a relationship skills workshop. Occasionally, clients would attempt to opt out of one of the ingredients, but I stood firm in their participation in all three aspects of treatment to lead them most effectively to healing. I called this three-pronged approach "The Magic Formula."

I nearly had my own out of body experiences watching my clients intelligently interview one another and connect their childhoods with their symptoms. To have a theory pan out again and again before my eyes has been amazing.

Guest therapists have come to these groups and my students have questioned them for apparent characteristics, many of which were learned in their training. I have witnessed my students give feedback to many of these visitors that they seemed defensive, withholding, superior, inauthentic and even judgmental. Witnessing this too has convinced me that this theory and technique serves therapists too, especially the ones who take the feedback and self correct. Additionally, I have seen therapists who feared that dropping their defenses would be unprofessional become convinced that they sacrificed nothing and gained credibility when they were freed to model authenticity. Honestly, my students teach me and make me proud.

The evolution of this theory and its practice has been swift as it has included a relentless kind of scrutiny, requiring problem solving at every turn in my office and at home. I've watched the results of my actions as consciously as possible.

I knew of the disturbing history of parenting experts whose children grew up to disapprove of their parent's parenting, some of whom are discussed in this book (Dr. Daniel Gottlieb Moritz Schreber, Dr. John Watson, Dr. Sigmund Freud and Dr. Melanie Kline). I had more fun parenting than I've had any other time in my life. I was betting that my attitude toward raising Scott would make the difference. He was not an object. He was consciousness in a warm body with a point of view.

Today, I often sit in disbelief over how well it works and I have to try not to stare at my own grown child in awe, now making his way in this world as Scott Clifton. Other times, I wish I could have one more shot at raising him. I know what I would have done differently, all of which is included within the following pages. Actually, he has told me what he thinks I should have done differently. I believe him. That he can tell me so freely and clearly is another success to me. That I can listen with interest and care is more evidence of how healthy I have become.

After I completed a thorough representation of my theory and technique, I allowed myself to visit a Zen center in Santa Monica, where I knew I would find my first real role model. I was actually frightened and excited. I anticipated complete inferiority. I loved the ceremony, the bells and the incense and I wore the legacy of centuries past and future. I wanted to pinch myself. It was perhaps the most exciting thing I have ever done. I studied my Roshi, Bill *Yoshin* Jordan, to see what someone so disciplined and self-aware would be like. He wore the mantle of his forbearers with dignity. He appeared ethical. He held a high bar and didn't ask anything of anyone that he didn't ask of himself. He was both loving and confronting. I saw him get outraged and angry once, which seemed to be exactly what the situation called for. He was fully alive. He seemed conscious and strong, at the same time humble, down-to-earth, playful, natural and loving. Truth be told, he had a warrior's heart to which I related. I think his background is conservative and mine remains liberal. He taught me to hold two opposite truths simultaneously. His mind was bright and I wished I could talk to him forever. I loved to bow to him. I took him in. I found my role model, which was the second-to-last piece I needed to presume to contribute to the field of psychology and reach out to the world of parents.

I attended a Ropes Sesshin, a sort of endurance process of many days facilitated by *Yoshin*, Roshi. The ordeal led us to become clear about to what we wanted to commit and complete in this short life. No more rationalizing. No more futility. I saw clearly that my age and my eyes were no excuse. I had to finish my job, and I would have to leave the Santa Monica Zen Center to do it because time was of the essence. That was the final piece. By the time I left, I was ready to be a real teacher and to blaze a trail. I bowed and took my leave, although my heart is still there.

In this book, I critique my Roshi and my sangha (Zen community). I want to be absolutely clear that I hold my Zen master in the highest possible regard. It is my reverence for him and them that allows me to do so, just as my son can critique my parenting of him. I intend this to be a model to my readers that they, too, can respectfully critique their parents, mentors and leaders. They can also examine their own beliefs and assumptions to see clearly. Question and allow yourself to be questioned. Everyone grows. The goal is to see the influences of your beliefs as clearly as possible and how beliefs, projections and assumptions affect our ability to perceive cleanly.

Often when I am sitting without purpose, the thought pops into my head that thousands, perhaps millions, of children are suffering right now as a result of bad theory. I had believed I wasn't qualified to muster an assault on conventional wisdom. The Ropes Sesshin and my driving need to take this theory as far as I could sent me back to college to attain a doctorate. I picked another little school in Los Angeles named after a Zen priest, Ryokan, because it was a relatively inexpensive and small school. I was warned that if I went to such an obscure school, I would never get to teach in a university. It was the best education I have received, including my studies at the State University of New York at Stony Brook and New York University.

Since I have received my best education from these small schools, I suspect America Psychological Association politics are at hand, impeding the accreditation of small schools even though a greater percentage of graduates of approved but unaccredited schools obtain licenses than graduates of accredited schools. It appears to me that the authorities at the top are supporting a monopoly of big expensive schools with the myth that they are better. Until theory is corrected, none of them are good enough. Since I never had any aspirations to teach at a university, it didn't matter to me when I was told that I would not be accepted at colleges as a professor. Ironically, a few years ago, I was invited to guest lecture at the California State University, Northridge. After I spoke, I was invited to apply to teach. I told the woman, "I can't. They wouldn't accept me." She said they would because of my theory. I enjoyed working for a while as a part-time professor at CSUN, and I absolutely loved teaching college. Now I want to open a college.

This is the leg of my journey where I deliver this Causal Theory and create a treatment structure and a better legacy for parents. Our students at TIPP, now the Parenting and Relationship Counseling Foundation, or PaRC, span a spectrum in mental health. They range from referrals by the Department of Children and Family Services to children of very high functioning parents who want to raise a Miracle Child. They all sit in the same class alongside therapists in training.

I used the term "Miracle Child" in order to effectively drive home an important point. The human baby is so perfectly "designed" that she has potential far beyond the children we are raising today. Every child could reach the level of a Mozart, Cezanne, The Buddha, Jesus, Gorbachev or Oprah with the right parenting. Right parenting isn't like playing the lottery. You can plan it and have a wonderful, magical time raising a Miracle Child, one who is charismatic, self-motivated, humble, enchanted, ethical, brilliantly artistic, problem solving and low-maintenance. I use the term "faith parenting" to remind parents to have faith in their child because most parents over-control and suffocate the greatness out of their children, missing some of the most profound dialogues of a lifetime. I talk about the "Transcendent Child," referring to children and adults who do the work to heal; it's never too late to transcend tragic events or a bad childhood. When we do the work, the results are so wonderful they seem transcendent and enlightened. I wanted a term that measured up to Miracle Child since I believe Transcendent Children are actually more gifted than Miracle Children in terms of insight, having seen reality through two significantly different lenses. I have chosen language designed to inspire us to focus our sights on potential. I have heard criticism of "cult" resulting from the language, which is unfortunate because I want to use professional language to describe the indescribable potential in a child. (I don't know of a cult that teaches the students how to challenge authority, including me, with relationship skills.)

The structure at PaRC is more like a Zen center than a clinic and I have been told that I am more of a Jedi than a therapist. All my coaches, interns and therapists have done the hard work themselves and practice the precepts on a daily basis, so they are able to truly guide. Since we have anywhere from coaches to therapists, we are able to provide help at all levels of ability to pay. I teach my team to be the parents, mentors and resources our clients never had. Sometimes we have referred to The Causal Theory as "The Theory" to simply abbreviate words. Sometimes we refer to Causal Theory as CTT because it includes Causal Theory & Treatment (thereby also distinguishing it from Cognitive Therapy). The complete name and acronym is Snyder Causal Theory & Treatment (SCTT) ☺. We are teaching people to practice a specific lifestyle according to a specific theory that we ask them to learn well. Sometimes we use the term "The Work" to refer to the hard work that has to be done to attain the desired results and sometimes we use the term "The Community" amongst ourselves to refer to the good company we keep.

We could have been normal and healthy if we hadn't been taught otherwise, but even though most of us were not raised for optimal mental health, we can still learn new values and practices that will someday simply be normal. Introducing off-putting terminology seems to be a necessity to communicate essential concepts. The trick is to make the terminology user-friendly. Other theories use terms like "object relations" to describe how a child relates to people (analytic theory) or "conservation" to represent how a child learns that a given amount of water is the same in different shaped vessels (cognitive theory). There are too many terms that are elitist, erudite and misleading in this field.

I seek to introduce The Causal Theory simultaneously to parents as well as the profession. This is because parents create the personalities which the professionals later treat. Hence, *The Manual* is written to professionals and parents alike. At times it is academic and at times it is casual (as distinguished from causal). I am casting a wide net and I expect that I may attract criticism from readerships at both ends of the spectrum for trying to appeal to both worlds; I hope to reach all who are open.

TABLE OF CONTENTS

CHAPTER 1: CREATING A PERSONALITY 1
Sensitivity to Our Environment 2
Universal Genetic Instruction 3
The Brain and Environment 5
Inborn Knowledge or Inevitable Lessons 7
How Inevitable Lessons Work in Societies 11
EVOLUTION OF SOCIAL SCIENCES 13
COMPETING CONTEMPORARY THEORIES 22
Pro-Parent vs. Pro-Child Ramifications 26
Players in Making or Breaking a Theory 27
Assessing a Theory 28
Types of Therapy by Philosophy 29
Pro-Parent Bias 31
About My Bias: First the Child 35
What If I Am Wrong? 35
Other Popular Outlooks 36
Confronting Standards of Enlightenment 41
The Causal Theory 42
OVERVIEW OF THIS BOOK 44
FAMILY SYSTEMS 45
A Healthy Family System 45
Unhealthy Family Systems 46
DEVELOPMENT OF SELF IN TWO STAGES 48
Stage I of Bonding and Attachment: The Core Self 48
Stage II of Separation & Discipline: The Personality 49
TRAUMA 49
Mitigating Trauma 51
True Parent 51
Consolation 53
Behind Closed Doors 54
MY VISION 55

CHAPTER 2: PREVENTIVE DIAGNOSIS 57
WHEN DIAGNOSIS ENABLES PREVENTION 59
WHEN DIAGNOSIS ENABLES PREDICTION 64
INTRODUCTION TO PERSONALITY DIAGNOSIS CHARTS 72
MAP OF THE PERSONALITY DIAGNOSIS CHARTS 74
PERSONALITY DIAGNOSIS CHARTS 77
Healthy 78
Passive-Aggressive 79
Dependent 81
Obsessive-Compulsive 83
Histrionic 90
Narcissistic 93
Borderline 99
Avoidant 109
Approach-Avoidant 111
Schizoid 114

- *Schizotypal* 116
- *Schizophrenic* 118
- *Dysthymic or Cyclothymic Disorder* 120
- *Bipolar* 121
- *Dissociative Identity Disorder (Multiple Personality Disorder)* 122
- *Paranoid* 123
- *Antisocial* 126
- *Sociopath* 128
- *Psychopath* 132
- *Rapist* 134
- *Mass Murderer* 135
- *Serial Killer* 136
- POSITIVE TRAITS OF PERSONALITIES 138

CHAPTER 3: HEALING 141

- RESPONSES TO INJURY 142
- FOUR TRAITS NECESSARY FOR HEALING 148
  - *Courage* 148
  - *Love of Truth* 148
  - *Self-Observation without Judgment* 148
  - *Surrender of Ego* 149
- STEPS FOR HEALING 150
  - *Pick Your Therapist* 150
  - *Choose Your Teacher* 151
  - *Face Your Shadow* 152
- THE CTT MODALITY 155
  - *1: Theory* 155
  - *2: Treating Trauma* 155
  - *3: Relationship Skills* 159
- BECOMING A HEALER 162
  - *Couchwork* 162
  - *Healing the Child* 164
  - *Containing* 165
  - *Healing Your RAD Child* 167
  - *Healing Your Grown Child* 170
- HEALING PERSONALITIES 173
- A NOTE ABOUT IDENTITY 181
- RECOMMENDED READING FOR HEALING 182

CHAPTER 4: STAGES & AGES OF DEVELOPMENT 183

- FEMINISM AND CHILDREN 183
- THE FIRST YEAR: BONDING AND ATTACHMENT 188
- BONDING BECOMES ATTACHMENT 191
- THE SECOND YEAR ON: FREEDOM & DISCIPLINE 206
- LATENCY (GRAMMAR SCHOOL YEARS) 240
- ADOLESCENCE 246
- REVIEW OF DEVELOPMENTAL SYMPTOMS 253

CHAPTER 5: IMPRINTING 255

- LOVE, THEN DISCIPLINE, THE DOMINANT IMPRINT 255

IMPRINTS BECOME AND DETERMINE DRIVES	256
READING ACTING-OUT BEHAVIOR	262
EVIL: WHEN TRAUMA IS DENIED	269
BULLYING	274
HOW TO BREAK THE CYCLE OF ABUSE	277
CONFRONTING BAD SEED THEORY AND RESEARCH	278
Misrepresentation by the So-Called Experts	*278*
The War of the Researchers	*279*
Business of Science	*281*
Research Fraud	*282*

CHAPTER 6: FAITH PARENTING 287

OVER-CONTROL	288
FAITH PARENTING DEFINED	289
STAGES & AGES OF FAITH PARENTING	292
FAITH *VS.* NEGATIVE PROJECTIONS	295

CHAPTER 7: DISCIPLINE 299

LIMITS AND CLARITY	300
WHY WE DISCIPLINE	302
BASIC DISCIPLINE GUIDELINES	304
Set and Maintain Personal Boundaries	*304*
Set and Enforce Limits	*305*
Discipline Rationally	*305*
MAJOR FAILURES FROM OVER-DISCIPLINE/ABUSE	307
MAJOR FAILURES FROM UNDER-DISCIPLINE/NEGLECT	311
ETHICS	317
CONSEQUENCES	320
AGE-RELATED DISCIPLINE ISSUES	326
DISCIPLINING RAD KIDS	330

CHAPTER 8: RELATIONSHIP SKILLS 341

HOW TO CHOOSE A FRIEND, MATE & PARTNER	341
RESOLVING INCOMPATIBLE SEX DRIVES	349
RELATIONSHIP SKILLS WORKSHOP (RSW)	352
Goals and Guidelines	*353*
The Rules	*357*
The Four Skills of Interaction (based on The Change Model)	*360*
How to Have an Issue	*362*
Ethics/Issues that Arise in Workshop	*365*
Terminating	*376*
SUMMARY OF RELATIONSHIP SKILLS	377
ENDINGS	379
DYING AND DEATH	380
CONCLUSION	381

APPENDIX 383

CHAPTER 1

Creating a Personality

"Though the laws of the internal evolution…are at the moment undiscovered, …if it were possible to find them, the rate and direction of all other cultural change could be explained."
-- Lloyd deMause

This is a parenting manual and it is also about The Causal Theory, which is a theory of developmental psychology that explains how we become who we are without consideration of invisible forces, especially genes. Thus, it is a guide to understanding ourselves as well the kind of information that will enable us to avoid major and even smaller mistakes in raising a child. The bonus is that this theory helps us raise an extraordinary child from scratch or heal the injuries we might have suffered or inadvertently made. You can jump in at any time, but the sooner the better.

My goal within these pages is to improve your ability to perceive. In order to see more clearly you may need to question some of the things you have always believed to be true. Throughout this manual I poke at sacred cows, including my own. I imagine that every reader will sooner or later become offended in reading this text. I want to encourage you to let yourself be challenged and to try not to throw the baby out with the bathwater. You don't have to accept all of the information in this book to appreciate some of it. However, if you fathom new explanations of behavior and question older ones for even a few seconds, you will become a sharper thinker and a more perceptive person.

Most of us are individually and collectively attached to the notion that our traits and personalities are inborn. When we think this way, we write off available information about how someone is doing. This book challenges superior seed and bad seed theories and any theories that place the blame for personality on the child, including gene association, original sin, reincarnation (that babies choose their parents) or astrology.

There is no inborn genetic temperament or predisposition in you or your child or anyone for that matter. There is no inherited Attention Deficit Hyperactivity

Disorder. There is no schizophrenia running in families, at least not via genes. There is no inherited depression or intelligence. This is both the bad news and the good news.

It is bad news because as of today, you know that how your children turn out is up to you. There has been no other time in your personal history during which your actions will have created as many profound and lasting results rippling into future generations. You are responsible for the quality of another human soul and with it, your legacy. You can create amazing children who leave the world a better place or, depending on the amounts and types of neglect, selfishness, meanness and thoughtlessness, you can create any disorder from ADHD to schizophrenia, with different formulas for each of course.

This is good news because, other than physical traits and socio-economic conditions, there is no such thing as "luck of the draw." Parenting is a game of chess, not craps. Depending on how clearly you see the game board and how thoughtfully you respond to surprises, you can raise a winner. When you get off to the right start, your child will be low-maintenance by the age of three or four. If you follow the basics in this book, you will rear what I have been calling a Miracle Child: one who is resilient, in love with life, inspired, creative, problem-solving, ethical, charismatic, good natured, confident yet humble and ethical. You can raise a child for greatness with less effort than you would raise an average child without any guidance from this theory. Your efforts will be an adventure, not a sacrifice. Many parents have set out intuitively to accomplish this and some have succeeded. Now you too can succeed, with *The Manual*.

If you're repairing problems that have already developed, this information can help you learn from your mistakes and heal your child from past parenting errors. A child who has derailed can be turned around and become what I call a Transcendent Child. The child who successfully corrects is wiser than the Miracle Child, just as the adult who does therapy and corrects is wiser than the adult who never had to develop that kind of self-awareness. Children are so much easier to correct and heal than grown-ups, but this theory works for adults too, including you. In fact, the ideal path is where the entire family works to self-correct.

The key to being a good parent is learning to truly see your children, read their behaviors, accept their authentic feelings, hold a high bar for ethics and goals, and coach them. If you believe what you see is inborn, you cannot read all the messages they are sending you. These messages are to guide you, indicating how you are doing as a parent and how they're doing in your care. These messages in your children's behavior are essential for you to read so you can correct the course of your child's path. When they are young this is easy to do. Likewise, you need to pay attention to yourself and make your own self-corrections along the way.

An essential perspective in this theory is that we never beat ourselves up for what we didn't know or do correctly in our past. That was then and this is now. We are all heir to something and we start from where we start. That is just the way it is for each of us. From wherever you are beginning this journey, I'm glad you made it to this moment. Most people never get this far. Whatever you have to undo or redo, this manual will help you with your adventure. Self-loathing and guilt are impediments. "Woops" is good. From wherever you start, let go of self-judgment or denial and put on your seatbelt. Do your best. After that, feel good about yourself for doing just that.

Sensitivity to Our Environment

We are exquisitely sensitive to our environment, especially the social aspect. This sensitivity begins at birth, as I will explain herein. How infants are treated determines who they think they are and how much they conclude they are worth. However, in order to drive this point home, I offer you some adult references.

We are all aware of the agony we experience when someone we love betrays us or chooses someone else. Breakups and divorces can be devastating for us, so you can imagine how a young child feels about being left behind, especially when they cannot understand your reasoning.

I notice that when I have enough money to pay my bills I feel differently than when I do not. When the money comes in I notice that a safe or comfortable feeling of relief washes over me and the flowers in my garden look lovelier.

I have had the good fortune of staying at five star hotels a few times. I've marveled at the way I was treated and the accompanying feeling of worth that surrounded me like a golden mirror. That wonderfully comfortable assumption of regard is the feeling we all want 24/7, so a goal of mental health and raising babies is to achieve a secure, though not superior, feeling inside where ever we are.

It's the same type of experience that gang members offer one another. This social regard within the gang makes rehabilitation difficult because rehab means giving up the unconditional acceptance and replacing it with requirements such as getting sober, finding a job and showing up for appointments on time. These new behaviors are authority-set, foreign and not hard-wired, so the gang member might not want to sacrifice that feeling of regard for the sense of inadequacy that comes with learning to meet social expectations. They aren't so sure they want to leave that safe feeling for a feeling of inadequacy.

That said, I believe that the best reassurance of self-worth, if we didn't get it in early childhood, is learning a skill that will take care of us for the rest of our lives. Expertise solves so many problems, at least for a while.

Our sensitivity to how other people see us tends to define us, usually incorrectly. While a goal in mental health is to be above or free of these invisible definitions, know this: How we treat one another is beyond measure. How we learn to feel about ourselves no matter what people think of us is also beyond measure. Read this book with an awareness of this sensitivity and your understanding of the words within will run deeper.

Universal Genetic Instruction

All babies are born aware and present to their experiences. Even though they have little frame of reference, they know they need our care. They look to us to satisfy their urges and needs such as hunger, warmth, loving, holding, touching and protection. They are born needing to see how important or valuable they are to us, their parents. They perceive in a highly aware state of powerlessness and they get their answers about who they are in the way we treat them. If we don't understand how much our view of our child matters we are more likely to raise difficult children.

Children perceive us from their original selves. They are actually more perceptive in this regard than most adults are. This uncontaminated window of awareness is who they are until they learn to avoid evidence that we don't see them or that we see them negatively. They can learn to pretend and repress what they see and feel or they may accept completely what we appear to believe about them. They take their ideas of the world from what they see, hear and feel from us. This angelic and exquisite state of awareness has no personality as yet because personality will develop around experiences and input as a way of coping. What these infants have is more wonderful than personality. They have purity: purity of being and purity of seeing.

John Colombo, psychologist at the University of Kansas notes, "Adults can follow directions and focus, and that's great. But children, it turns out, are much better at picking up on all extraneous stuff that's going on...And this makes sense: If you don't know how the world works, then how do you know what to focus on? You should try to take everything in" (Lehner, 2009, p.3).

Some people need to see personality to see the infant. Some people cannot love without connecting to a personality. Some believe that the infant is empty, dull or has little to love until it has a personality, so they wait for it to develop before engaging. This is a mistake. The infant is fully present and alert to the parents, so if emptiness and dullness is what you're modeling by waiting or superficially engaging with your child, the child may become empty and dull as a result.

We need to see the true infant rather than projections of personality. Let it not be the personality we seek, but the infant's core self we see. Mother Teresa said, "When you look into the eyes of another cleanly, you can see God." Perhaps you can see God in your baby's eyes. How you see your child influences who they become, not the other way around. When you gaze into her eyes and interact with her, neurons in her brain connect too (Siegel, 1999). These neurons anticipate future interactions of the same kind and organize around new experiences. Your baby looks forward to your gaze. You are co-creating your child's fragile personality and you will not be the best parent you can be if you are tied into the passive notion of pre-existing behavioral genes, giftedness, superiority, inferiority and other predispositions you wait to see unfold. No waiting allowed. Be part of the miracle.

Genes drive the formation of the human physiology from the inside out and the bottom up, resembling the evolution of life on this planet from microorganisms to the aging adult and dying human being. They direct the formation of the brain in a cascade up from the spine to the brainstem where automatic functions keep us alive, and ultimately to the frontal lobes where reasoning takes place (Perry, 2000). There, genes build a drive to attach. We inherit an un-programmed yet curious brain with temporary reflexes for the first few months of life. Our genetic design prepares newborns with a built-in capacity to recognize emotions and attitude, especially in parents. Additionally, we are gifted at birth with mirror neurons (Society For Neuroscience, 2007) ready to record and internalize how we are treated. What we record now will replay later. This helps us adapt to the particular environment into which we were born. With these inborn capacities we come prepared at birth to learn how to respond in the uniqueness of our personal world.

Universal genetic instructions urge us to seek nurturing, touch, gazing, loving, approval, limits and other developmental adventures toward universal human milestones. Genes direct the unfolding of the body to seek satisfaction for its built-in needs. The environment addresses our needs positively or negatively in distinctive ways that create unique personalities. Genes create the body. Environment (including physical traits and disabilities) impacts and creates personality according to experiences, especially patterns or regular, repeating types of experiences.

The Causal Theory holds that there are two biologically driven stages in development: one of attachment and the other of separation. The rest of the stages are actually inevitable lessons and not stages at all. Thus, the self is like a piano and its player. A piano is nothing without a pianist, and a pianist is not a pianist, really, without a piano. If you sit down to play a piano without the experience of lessons, the piano will not play beautiful music. And not even the most practiced pianist could make beautiful music on a coffee table.

The Brain and Environment

The earliest and most critical events for a human being are the ones of interaction with their caregivers, the most important people in our lives. Babies and small children marvelously adapt to the way they are treated as if the world will always be similar, even after they've grown. Of course this is a handicap if their childhood environment does not prepare them to go for greatness or become people in love with life. Every event is recorded in the brain and in the body and most events are taken in total. **Neural connections** are made as experiences take place, and other neurons die away in a process called "**pruning**" when these neurons are not used (Siegel, 1999). The more positive a child's experiences before the age of three, the more brilliant, inspired and healthy the child will be. The fewer nurturing and supportive experiences a child has before the age of three, the duller will be her intellect and the more injured will be her personality. Neglected and abused children have underdeveloped brains that will shrivel even though their hypervigilant attitude may make them appear "smart." Thus, the first three years of life are critical because it is during these first three years that ninety percent of the child's brain and personality develop (Perry, 1997; Perry, 2000a; Szalavitz & Perry, 2010). She prepares to represent a unique and even logical perspective on the universe based upon all the experiences that come with her life.

The younger we are, the more profound each and every event is for the developing personality. Birth may be one of the major disposition-forming events of our lives, including how we are received shortly thereafter. This is because the impact of these early events creates moods, and our grownups may begin to treat us as if these moods are our **temperament**. These projections by our parents can become self-fulfilling prophecies when our caregivers don't try to address our moods responsively or can't figure out how to satisfy our needs. Thus, the more these recursive events repeat themselves, the more they determine what others will confirm as our temperament, which is still just a temporary mood continuing due to ongoing conditions or treatment. Without changes in parental responsiveness, this mood turns into a pervasive attitude. Soon enough our family labels us with this or that temperament.

Babies are genetically designed to seek contact, touch and essentially to love and be loved. They have a need to cuddle and gaze into the eyes of their mother at the breast. Babies' right brains are highly developed at birth, for the most part, to understand emotions and to understand things in terms of **emotions**. Not only do they intuitively recognize happiness, they recognize aggression and anger. Babies instantly understand emotions and feelings and have the capacity to anticipate or dread them. How children understand themselves and others is determined by how their parents respond to their feelings (Schore, 1996 and Siegel, 1999). If something creates good feelings it is good. If something creates bad feelings then negative thoughts or beliefs form from the event. If a parent responds to a difficult moment in life with empathy for their child's painful feelings, mental health is in the making. Their child has had the experience of feeling seen and understood, which is something that creates resilience, a positive outlook and an appreciation of how communication works. The child has now experienced empathy and will one day be able to give it.

Babies are hypersensitive and nothing gets past them. These little blobs know when mommy and daddy fight. They know when mom doesn't feel like changing a diaper but does it anyway. They know when daddy is jealous of mommy's attention to the baby or when mommy can't handle crying. They are pre-wired to see and record. They seek understanding of their world. Whatever they experience goes into their internal map of what's out there and who they are and what they are worth. Each baby experiences different things and each baby makes different internal maps. Some babies will learn trust and others will learn mistrust while still others will learn jealousy or judgment.

On rare occasions, children have been raised in the wild by animals and deemed as "feral children." It is next to impossible to reverse the influences of their early years, much less completely civilize them after a certain age. While non-human species are acknowledged by developmental psychologists to have a **critical period** of development during their early years, they overlook the same urgency in humans and demote the name of the same stage to **sensitive period**. Instead they only apply the term critical period in humans to the physical events that occur during gestation.

Our critical periods are perhaps longer than other species, but during these stages more damage can be done or more resilience can be created than in just the physical events of gestation. The results in humans may not be as obvious, but they are definitely as profound as the results in animals. If we acknowledge this, we become more aware of the influences of neglect and abuse during critical periods. These experiences have the greatest impact on the personality during younger years. For example, Clayton Chad was a child who was once loved in his early childhood, then locked in a closet at age six for nearly a year (Oprah, April 15, 2011). He was able to have a far better result than a child who was left in a crib most of his first year of life, which could conceivably lead to symptoms of autism. In another example of a critical period, an infant who is rocked may be a calmer adult (Barker, 2000; Prescott, 2000). One could consider that there is either a critical or a sensitive period for rocking depending upon whether or not one believes that a lifetime of unnecessary anxiety and edginess is tragic. If an older child is rocked, the long-term result will not be as significant as if the child had been rocked as an infant, even though results would still be better than if the child had never been rocked at all. When the "age of rocking" passes, I do not know. That study has not been made to my knowledge.

Instincts or Reflexes

Human beings are the first and only animals that have escaped having **instincts.** Instincts create restricted responses. We could not be as adaptive and intelligent if we had limiting inborn instructions. Lack of instincts frees us up for learning, thinking and solving problems. Learning, adapting, and reflecting are the primary traits that allow human beings to play the role of the superior species.

Even though we have no instincts, we do arrive with some inborn **reflexes** for the first few months of life. These reflexive behaviors include the Babinsky Reflex to flex our toes when the bottoms of our feet are touched; the Moro Reflex to relax and throw out our arms when thrown or falling; a reflex to crawl and walk; and the reflex to suck (Cole, *et al.*, 2005). I have been told a story of a baby born in the wild to a sick mother who crawled up her body and began to nurse. I have also heard a story from a Leboyer Childbirth Coach of a midwife who gave birth and asked that the attending midwife not touch her baby. They reportedly videotaped this baby. When mom did not move, the infant crawled up her mother's body and began to nurse. I was not able to get a copy of the video. I did however get a copy of a baby born in a Leboyer bath or tub. Leboyer births are more elaborate and nurturing to mothers than Lamaze, although both prepare a mother for childbirth. While the baby was crowning, the mother stroked the top of her infant's head. After the baby was born she lifted her head to make eye contact with her mom.

Inborn Knowledge or Inevitable Lessons

All these reflexes die away and are replaced by learned behaviors, many of which are discovered in sequences according to the unfolding abilities of our body and our inherited personal environment. In the beginning babies learn about the properties of things with their mouth. Early on, we learn orally as we wave our rattles around our heads until we can bring them in to taste and feel. In a short amount of time, we learn to crawl, cruise, stand, walk and then run, in the order in which our bodies can unfold and cooperate. So as we are able to do more, we are able to learn about those things we can now discover.

Unfortunately, a great deal of speculation about innate information resulting from internal genetic instruction demonstrates our lack of insight into the **inevitable learning** that must take place as the human body unfolds in a given order. The body grows sequentially, from tiny to adult and young to old. This physical growth is predetermined genetically, but the universal order of growth is prescribed for all developing humans. To be absolutely clear, how the body unfolds is predetermined, but the information it acquires is not predetermined, though sometimes inevitable. Some lessons are inevitable for *all* of us, while others are inevitable for *some of us*, depending upon our environment. Barring disabilities, learning to walk and talk is inevitable for all of us. Learning to speak Spanish is inevitable for children born in Spanish speaking countries. Learning to fear vulnerability is not inevitable at all, unless a baby remains unattached or is abandoned.

Some say that all human beings are prone to jealousy and other primitive emotions that remind us that we descended from the Neanderthal strain of human evolution. I propose that jealousy results when a baby, toddler or child has experiences of deprivation associated with injustice. If a child has not been sufficiently loved, held and reinforced by his mother in infancy or even the toddler stage, then he may feel deprived. But if he witnesses his mother give affection to another child, especially a younger sibling, while he is left feeling empty, he may develop jealousy. Jealousy is an inevitable attitude in the face of scarcity and no commodities are more precious in our formation than motherly nurturing and fatherly protection.

The under-nurtured child may even regress to acting like an infant, wetting his bed, hoping to be held some more. Yet there remain inevitable lessons he must eventually learn. He will discover that even when he thinks smaller, his body keeps on growing. He cannot become small enough again to return to her breast. Thoughts such as these are not inborn. They are inevitable consequences of growth and specific experiences and they may become reenacted in adult relationships when the lesson is not fully learned. I would hold and rock the child every day for a while to try to fulfill his emotional longing. (See Chapter 3: Healing.)

Psychology students may be taught about the cognitive developmental stages identified by **Jean Piaget**. Learning and education facilitates these stages, but students are commonly left with an impression that these stages are inborn. The instruction does not teach students that what the child discovers is inevitable and can be learned sooner than later with instruction. Instead, for example, students are taught that the child discovers object permanence—that things do not disappear when out of sight—between the ages of eight and twelve months. The common application of this principle is the placing of the baby's rattle under a blanket. When he has object permanence, he will seek the rattle. When he does not yet have object permanence, he will not. He just assumes the rattle disappears, according to Piaget.

I worked with two six-month old babies on this issue. Both were passive when I put the toy under the blanket, just as they were dependent on just about everything. They did not have sufficient motor skills to be adventurous enough to remove the blanket, and they were both in that stage of infancy where they assume the grownups do everything and the babies wait. They just watched the mother, in one case me, put the toy under the blanket, accepting it as if to think, "I wonder why she did that." I felt like a tease taking away the child's toy. In both cases I taught the baby to lift the blanket and get the toy. Of course, we only learn what we experience and we don't know yet what we don't know yet.

Psychology students may be taught what **Melanie Klein** hypothesized: that babies think of mom as the good breast or the bad breast, as if babies only relate to nursing and as if the baby projects that each of her breasts will be thought to be good or bad. Klein was another researcher who looked at babies, including her own, as objects that developed independently of how they were treated. To me her theory of the good breast and the bad breast indicates that she did not enjoy gazing into her child's face and interacting lovingly and playfully. How Klein's baby thought of mom was believed to be the product of the baby's inner wiring or inborn drives, not the mom's success or failure to relate to her own child. Interestingly, Klein's daughter did not attend her mother's funeral but reportedly wore a pair of special red shoes that day (Grosskurth, 1985). John Bowlby, the father of Attachment Theory, studied under Klein at one time and was reported to have exclaimed during a lecture, "There are bad mothers, you know" (Wallin, 2002).

Primitive childhood needs and fears result from how we are guided through life's lessons. As the body grows more and more, inevitable lessons appear. As the child learns to crawl and walk, she will not only discover the world, but also how her parents think of the world, how much of it they will let her take on and at what peril. To this end she will test limits and she will discover whether or how they stop her, how and for what.

Parental **projections**, like expectations, may lead to self-fulfilling prophecies rather than parental self-corrections or modifications. Sometimes our parents interfere with the way we are allowed to understand and record experiences. In other words, there is pressure on us to believe things did happen that didn't happen, or things that happened didn't happen, or things were not what we experienced them to be. This is a formidable pressure and the brain is designed to accept and adapt to these pressures for a price. The brain can revise the truth for us and these revisions can become the misleading operating systems that we take to the bank and upon which we will stake our lives.

Some children with ADHD are stuck with thoughts of unresolved issues from home that either they can't process because they have no healthy model for airing thoughts and feelings or they are not allowed to process in a healthy, honest and expressive way. And in some cases, if not most, they have learned that what they think and feel about their life is irrelevant anyway since they will be going to day care no matter what. Children who have **repressed thoughts and feelings** can be prone to hyperactivity, simply bouncing off the walls, because they are not allowed to know what they know or express what they feel. By the time the subject is open to them, they have buried and forgotten what they are not supposed to know or feel, even though it still kicks them around inside.

We are also born with an ability to dissociate from trauma in order to survive (van der Kolk, 1994). Additionally, we can **repress trauma** if we learn that reporting the experience would put us in greater jeopardy. We can "split off" from memories of painful moments and thoughts in order to avoid them and even find a way to enjoy new experiences. Finally, we can accept "replacement" thoughts given to us in order to bury what we learned and felt. I think we can do these things to varying degrees, depending on how much positive material we can find to bury ourselves and how much material we are expected to take on as fact in lieu of our own experiences.

The very same conflict infects my field as well as the patients we treat. All of our clinicians are children who had to grow up. Clinicians and researchers have two opposing ways of thinking, which I call the War of the Researchers. I have referred to these two camps elsewhere in *The Manual* as the **Pro-Child Advocates** and the **Pro-Parent Advocates**. For now, I would like to expand this epistemology beyond the field of mental health, as it appears important to apply this observation to professionals who hold the power of definition in the judicial, political, research and religious arenas. To simplify matters for the reader, I would have loved to call a religious leader pro-parent or pro-child. I would have loved to refer to lawyers and judges as pro-parent or pro-child. But when I began to write it I became concerned that the terms wouldn't fly in those arenas because many of these people do not think at all in terms of psychology or developmental origins of thought. As a matter of fact, they often attribute their opposing views to other causes, such as religious and economic influences. As such, I have decided to use the terms Type A and Type B Thinkers instead, to represent pro-parent and pro-child biases. I am identifying the first philosophy ever formed by a human as pro-parent. A child has to evolve his awareness from a pro-parent bias to consider his parents objectively or even that any parent may be wrong or unethical and their immoral behaviors must not be defended. This pro-child perspective is a hard insight to achieve, and sometimes the multiple pressures against this insight are more than a human can entertain. Thus, these are the most intrinsic-seeming beliefs of all beliefs, and they seem to almost be embedded in our genes.

I have encountered numerous situations in which a grandparent molested a child, but the child's parents' empathy went to the perpetrator instead of the victim. It is possible to talk to these parents about why they cry for their parent but not for their child and they usually acknowledge that they know it is illogical and even wrong, but they can't help it. To see their parents shamed or humbled is unbearable to them. While all their reflexes go toward rationalizing for their parent, anyone else in the world that committed the same offense would be held just as accountable as the next guy. Ironically, sometimes we will even identify more with the next guy if his victim was his own child, or we will have less tolerance for a child who stands up to their parent for abusing them.

All of this is to say that we are raised to protect parents against children's accusations or complaints. When such issues show up in church or court or the classroom or the political arena, ministers may scold children for seducing their parent; lawyers, judges and juries may disbelieve a child; principals may believe the teacher; and mothers may reflexively protect their mate over their child. So I am now referring to these defenses as Type A Thinking. I am referring to the ability to rise above these biases as Type B Thinking. I have hope that my readers and witnesses to this invisible war will be better trained to understand and appraise the real issue: whether to hide or uncover parental causes behind behaviors.

Type A Thinkers (pro-parent) may not be conscious of the origin of their blinding philosophy. Type A Thinkers in general want to excuse or immunize the behaviors of parents, but ironically, they want to excessively punish all others for doing what they do. Type A Thinkers appear to hate any attempt to understand or interpret behavior. They may refer to "the abuse excuse" or "psychobabble." They may act very threatened by such endeavors to understand what is behind behavior. They may seem disgusted, repulsed and downright contemptuous of such inquisitions or hypotheses.

It appears to me that **Type A Thinkers have a propensity to abuse their power**, as if seeking to eliminate the Type B Thinkers one by one. Many such examples will follow in this chapter. I have witnessed numerous events and cases where Type A Thinkers were in positions of authority as evaluators over Type B Thinkers. For years I continued to be shocked over the numbers of psychologists, researchers or attorneys who would officially annihilate the thinking of a psychologist or psychotherapist who interpreted behavior. I have watched these Type A Thinkers critique Type B thought as if they had no responsibility to accept such thinking as valid, when a whole school of psychology, training and licensure recognizes the behavior speaks volumes about the past. Their bias may be so palpable that they may discredit a professional, her point of view and the half of the field she represents by finding her wrong. On he other hand, Type A Thinkers may interpret behavior without any basis whatsoever. The investigating detective and prosecuting attorney in the Amanda Knox case virtually invented a persona that could never have existed given Amanda's history (Amanda was accused in the 2007 murder of her female roommate while studying abroad in Italy). On the other hand, Pamela Bozanich, who prosecuted the Menendez Brothers (for murdering their parents in 1989), the judge and the jury could not see how all the experiences reported by the two young men pointed to the ending.

Type B Thinkers want to get to the issue of cause and shine a flashlight on ingredients leading up to a situation. Type A Thinkers want to cover it up. Ironically, they have no problem projecting motives onto people who they seek either to punish or immunize. Their projections are comparable to "evil" or "sinister" on one hand and "infallible" or perfectly "appropriate" on the other. To put it another way, Type A Thinkers project guilt or innocence without logical cause while Type B Thinkers perceive what is, in search of explanation. So Type A Thinkers have projections over reality while Type B Thinkers exercise perception. Projection is about seeing what isn't and perception is about seeing what is.

I hope the reader develops an ability to understand what is behind the disagreements and what is at stake. These heated debates are about hiding or punishing *vs.* understanding. Type A Thinkers are often emotional beyond the content because grown children who learned in childhood to immunize their parents are recruited for life and they will defend their parents and all parents as if defending themselves. Once they grow up, there will still be a conflict between what they know and what they get to know, even as these children become behavioral psychologists, biogeneticists, prosecuting attorneys, politicians or religious zealots.

Conversely, the more a child is allowed and even encouraged to represent his own senses and experiences, the more **intelligence** he will develop. Human curiosity is in place at birth and lasts until pro-parent mandates shut it down. Sometimes children are free to be curious about some things and expected to tow the party line about other things. In such cases, it is better they develop expertise where they are allowed to be curious and employ critical thinking. While Albert Einstein was not nurtured into interactive dialogues at home, he was encouraged to wonder about the nature of physics when his father bought him a compass and his uncle asked him to contemplate how butterflies can fly.

Our brains really want to make sense of things, people and events. We have a drive to perceive and seek to understand the properties of objects so we can anticipate their actions. We have a need to organize what we experience in terms of cause and effect. The better able we are to do this, the more intelligent we are. Some parents encourage development of **curiosity** and others block it with their own agendas. Thus, children who are repressed are less intelligent, unless they have an outlet that is not censored. As we grow, we encounter our inevitable lessons, as I have said. When we are free to observe The Tao of Nature, absent distracting instructions from our parents and culture, we enjoy more advanced insights. The more cleanly we observe the more intelligent we become as we begin to develop internal holograms of the universe and how it works in our Mind's Eye. These internal models can be sorted, modified, rewound and fast-forwarded. We can use them to prophesy. The more accurate our perceptions are, the more accurate our holograms. These four-dimensional right brain pictures can be modified. With the best observations we are able to more accurately hold a sense of The Way of the universe, especially including physics. We can come to see that all things share similar properties and like everything else in the universe we are interrelated and interdependent with one another.

How Inevitable Lessons Work in Societies

Some highly recognized thinkers of our time, from psychology to sociology to neuroscience, write about inborn or evolutionary predispositions of human beings. Some have represented inborn behavior in terms of developmental stages and others in terms of genetically driven social proclivities. Yet others speak of the collective unconscious (Carl Jung). In truth, people and societies have varied and prospered to unique extremes as a result of our abilities to **adapt**.

The body provides the perspective and the events provide the point of view. Real evidence about how personalities are formed by experiences is available, and the jury is in. Those who *need* to prove behaviors result from genes, in whole or in part, as a species or as unique personalities, will not necessarily give up. They may even try harder, and, as a matter of fact, they do. Researchers have been willing to skew the results of research as a matter of course in an arrogant attempt to redefine reality for their own agendas (Ross & Pam, 1995; Valenstein, 1998; Leo, 2000; Lewontin, 2000; Whitaker, 2002; Galves, 2002; Joseph, 2004; Scott, 2006). The redefining of reality in the field of psychology for monetary and power-seeking agendas is not new to this decade or even this century.

> History provides us with examples of the ongoing battle between those who want to claim the right to define mental health and true scientists. – Reenie Sklar, LMFT

Cooperation and competition are inevitable lessons that stem from adequate and inadequate mothering and fathering and emulate interactive and interrelated laws of the universe. These forces of interactive opposites (*i.e.*, from the largest vibration in the universe, the Big Bang, to the finest vibrations of the human brain) tend to develop from rough to fine, from chaos to order, and from violent to harmonious and from ugly to beautiful. Societies, like all patterns in nature, are formed around competition and/or cooperation, often led by leaders who share similar outlooks. Where parenting practices tend to produce more fearful children and adults, societies will tend to band together against perceived or projected external threats, often creating self-fulfilling prophecies. Where societies produce more secure children and adults, they tend to organize more around cooperative ventures amongst themselves while opening up to trade and cooperation with outsiders. The more barbaric the parenting practices the more competitive or suspicious the adult ideology and the more nurturing the parenting practices, the more humane and cooperative the culture. Of course, competition has forwarded technology and enterprise, but cooperation has advanced humanity. Cultures that support competition within ethical guidelines may be the ideal end goal.

There appears to be a correlation between culturally supported abuse and neglect with political aggression and economic exploitation defended by religious ideologies, where a punishing god offers forgiveness and rewards for obedience and sacrifices. These religious, political and economic goals come to reflect practices of dominance and subservience. On the other hand, where nurturing parenting practices are widespread enough to become a cultural value, there seems to be corresponding socioeconomic and political practices of acceptance, cooperation and creativity mirrored by harmonious values of acceptance, tolerance and ethics. Lastly, there appears to be a common endeavor of people who were insufficiently nurtured to seek the protection and solace of a loving, nurturing, seeing and understanding Parent named God. All of this, of course is an over-generalization, but I am suggesting that we need to begin to understand cultures and religions in terms of parenting practices as well as heritage. It seems to me that there are two root forces driving society, which are parenting and economics, while religion and cultural values tend to mirror and affirm these conditions. Interestingly, there appear to be upcoming atheist voices that are challenging all religions to step up their ethical and moral values.

Nazi Germany had ruthless parenting practices recommended to and accepted by Christian parents. It had aggressive goals to dominate the world with a self-issued license to commit genocide against millions of its own citizens. At the other end of the spectrum, history has presented passive Buddhist religions, Quakers, Episcopalians, reformed Jews, Unitarians, Muslims and Protestant sects that focus on personal development or charity. I suspect there may be evidence that these sects have healthier parenting styles.

While people tend to follow in the religion of their heritage, many opt for variations that reflect their childhood conditioning or needs. Thus, some variations of Christianity, Judaism and Islam are stricter, while others are more tolerant. I believe studies can be done to show the correlation between these stricter and harsher religious sects with followers who had more painful childhoods as well as more tolerant and open sects with believers who either seek safety or who had healthier childhoods.

Nevertheless, Type A Thinkers throughout the social sciences continue to suggest that some behaviors are inborn. Ethicist and atheist neurobiologist Sam Harris ironically leans toward the educability of humans, but gives excessive lip service to possible inborn traits when compassionately trying to cover all the bases of any given behavior. He talks about our brain's alleged predisposition toward religiosity or magical thinking over the last 100,000 years, however varied the permutations (2010). I would bet he knows better, but he seems committed to giving different biogeneticists their due. In my opinion genes have nothing to do with any predisposition to religious thinking and every culture deals uniquely with its dependency on nature and especially its dependence on parents. How nature and parents meet these needs and how well we do or do not understand cause and effect informs our beliefs.

To sum up, **inborn traits** include abilities to recognize emotions and perceive treatment; a drive to seek love, nurturing and protection; a drive to imprint and re-enact; curiosity about causation in the world, others and our selves; and a need to grow and learn inevitable lessons. How parents address these drives in our childhood determines our type of thinking and the endeavors of our adulthood and our society.

Evolution of Social Sciences

The history of my field seems to be one of measuring success by how well one eliminates symptoms. But for some, the elimination of symptoms has nothing to do with their cause.

Insane Asylums and Workhouses

In Europe in the 15th and 16th centuries, the broken and "mad" of the cities and towns were believed to be less than human and impervious to the weather, so clothing was often unnecessary. They were fed with rotten food, kept in chains in cold, dark and rat-infested dungeons, often lying naked in their own excrement on beds of rotten straw until they died.

Improvements in medicine brought "insane asylums" or "general hospitals" to remove indigents from the streets. They were incarcerated until they became sober and industrious citizens. Only those who were able to provide for themselves were allowed to return to society. The insane were predominantly considered unreachable and uneducable and thus, were rarely released.

The work ethic had become paramount to the extent that it applied to indigent children. In John Locke's 17th century Treatise, he advocated that masters of workhouses (also known as "houses of correction") make them into "sweated labor manufacturing establishments or forced labor establishments." In 1679, he wrote for England's Commission on Trade to answer against the "relaxation of discipline and corruption of manners." Children of the unemployed "above the age of three" should not unnecessarily "become a burden on the nation and should be set to work and made to earn their keep" (MacPherson, p. 64).

Moral Management

Around the time of the American Revolution or the late 1700s, the conditions of asylums were at their worst. Two reformers, Philippe Pinel of France and William Tuke of England, developed therapeutic programs known as the Moral Management Model, through which they achieved considerable success. "Moral," perhaps like "morale" connoted "zeal, hope, spirit and confidence. It also had to do with custom, conduct, way of life and inner meaning" (1977), explains J.F. Calhoun.

The mentally ill were invited to retreat into peaceful settings on quiet rural estates, one of which was named York Retreat of England. They had volunteer companions who would listen and talk with them. They were encouraged to take walks through the rose gardens and the countryside, work, pray or rest until they felt ready to leave.

These Moral Management retreats were so successful that 71% recovered and left within one year, never to return again. Funding became available in the United States, England and France for more of these retreats, at which point, in the middle of the 18th century, medical doctors showed an interest in appropriating these funds as the new "experts in insanity."

Psychohistorian Ty Colbert wrote, "After the takeover by the medical profession, overcrowding became the norm, and asylum living conditions gradually deteriorated once again to pre-moral management levels" (2000, p. 34).

Transition to Medicine

"By the end of the 19th century, when scientific psychiatry was supposedly making great strides, discharge rates had dropped to 20-30%" (p.37), wrote Colbert. The medical community established jurisdiction over the insane by defining insanity as a "medical disease" (p. 37). As a result of lobbying by the Royal College of Physicians, England's 1774 Vagrancy Act mandated that only licensed medical doctors could approve the confinement of the insane.

Initially the moral managers refuted the claim that lunacy was a medical disease. Physicians struggled against reformers, fearing that the moral management institutions would remain in the hands of lay people, thereby excluding or diminishing the role of doctors. "Their income, prestige and medical theories were all threatened" (Bynum, p. 325). In order to completely take healing away from lay people, the medical profession knew they would have to develop a vocabulary for their publications that lay people couldn't understand. Further, a newly formed Association for Medical Superintendents of American Institutions for the Insane (AMSAII) published the American Journal of Insanity. According to R.T. Fancher in his book Cultures of Healing, "...the AMSAII undertook a vigorous, effective—and, we may fairly say, fraudulent—campaign to promote medical control over asylums and to ensure that their own views of care would be promulgated among the public and followed in other asylums" (Francher, 2009, p. 59). Fancher went on to relate that superintendents published annual reports replete with "consciously manipulated statistics...boasting grossly about inflated cure rates...producing a campaign of fraudulent materials...which were then distributed to libraries, policymakers and journalists" (*Ibid*).

In the hurry to establish expertise over the insane, doctors believed they had to establish dominance and dominion. They approached this by dominating the mentally ill into submission in order to destroy the symptoms. Further, they considered insolence or rebellious behavior against the doctors to be a form of mental illness. Acting as if inmates were biologically sick, microscopes became a standard part of asylum equipment. Drugs were increasingly used to sedate inmates. Cold baths and showers, isolation, electric shock, rotating chairs and purging procedures replaced the successful treatments of the moral managers. "It is important to understand that psychiatry, at this time, was able to establish itself as a medical profession—not because it identified any true diseases—but because it medicalized a highly successful non-medical program" (Colbert, 2000, p. 37).

The roots of patriarchal medicine were political, arrogant, insensitive and devoid of intuition and empathy. According to Colbert, Dr. Benjamin Rush, a signer of the Declaration of Independence and the designated Father of American Psychiatry, treated George Washington by draining his blood, causing his death, hence the saying, "The father of American psychiatry killed the father of America" (1996, p. 20).

Rush invented the tranquilizing chair: "I have contrived a chair and introduced it to your Hospital to assist in curing madness. It binds and confines every part of the body. By keeping the trunk erect, it lessens the impetus of blood toward the brain. Its effects have been truly delightful to me. It acts as a sedative to the tongue and temper as well as to the blood vessels. In twenty-four, twelve, six and in some cases in four hours, the most refractory patients have been composed. I have called it a Tranquillizer" (p. 19-20).

Rush also invented the gyrator. It was a device that constituted a long board that rotated from the center. The patient was fastened to the board with her head pointing out. She was spun at high speed so her blood would rush to her head. Rush said the tortures he proudly invented, as if he were a great innovator, resulted from his compassion. He asserted that patients had to be dominated and compliant if they were to be successfully treated. He interchanged "punishments" and "treatment" in his terminology. He took terminology seriously, writing a dictionary of sorts that redefined nearly all traits and reactions of a patient in medical terms as well as all the responses of doctors, to include occasional use of the lash for self-defense (Szasz, 1970).

Dr. Emil Kræpelin wrote a medical text in 1883 called *Textbook on Psychiatry* about techniques of his time: "Tobacco smoke was administered in the form of an enema by a special machine in severe cases of imbecility and melancholia attonia [depression] (p. 60)." Kræpelin used other techniques to include "harnessing and tying the patient in a standing position and with arms outstretched for eight to ten hours. This was supposed to mitigate delirious outbursts, encourage fatigue and sleep, render the patient harmless and obedient and awaken in him a feeling of respect for the doctor (Kræpelin, p. 86)." Kræpelin experimented on a catatonic schizophrenic patient, pricking above her eye and all the way through her tongue. He noted: "She does not generally react at all when spoken to or pricked with a needle, but resists violently if you try to take her hand or pour water on her. She obeys no kind of orders" (p. 23).

It must be specifically said that the way psychiatrists historically treated their patients was schizogenic. In other words, if a parent treated her child the way psychiatrists treated their patients, the child would have become psychotic. As you will later read, the way to induce schizophrenia is to acutely or chronically injure a child, to then negatively and intrusively redefine that injury and his resulting feelings and thoughts so that the suffering was not suffering after all and the treatment was said to be humane. The child will never be allowed to recall the truth of what actually happened or express his authentic feelings. Feelings and memories are forever forbidden in order to protect the identity and interests of the abuser.

Medicine did evolve, becoming more scientific even though funding often went to experiments that were whimsical, heartless or mercenary. Nonetheless, medicine improved. Dr. Louis Pasteur discovered germs. Milk became pasteurized. The public cleaned up better. Medical procedures became more sanitary. Life spans got longer. Other progress was made in medicine, but much of medicine remained inhumane and patriarchal until recent years. As late as 1982, doctors were commonly performing surgery on infants without anesthesia because they didn't think infants felt pain (Hall, p. 72).

The medical model became the basis for psychiatric medicine: Anything that reduced symptoms could be considered a cure as long as an "approved" doctor developed it. When England passed its Divorce Act of 1857, divorce became popular for women. Dr. Isaac Baker Brown concluded that wanting a divorce was a biologically based mental disease that somehow correlated with having a defective clitoris. He developed a procedure as an antidote to this trend, performing clitorectomies to cure the problem. "After the operation, they humbly returned to their husbands and there was no recurrence of the disease after surgery" (Colbert, 1996, p. 21).

Creating Nazis

In the mid to late 1860s, Dr. Daniel Gottlieb Moritz Schreber became Germany's version of America's 1950s parenting expert, Dr. Spock. He was a Christian orthopedist whose daughter and sons were born shortly before he published his treatise on how to raise children. He believed that his fellow Germans were soft and he saw a need for a stronger breed. He offered a way to develop a better race. To make the change, parents needed to submit their children to ruthless parental authority once and forever. He recommended corporal punishment on newborns and infants in order to destroy their soul-sucking tendencies so they could become productive and robust citizens. Schreber taught Christian parents to use contraptions to correct children's postures. He produced drawings of these structures in which children were to sit, eat and sleep. He had another such devise to keep adolescents from masturbating. In child-rearing pamphlets written by Dr. Schreber, some of his parenting recommendations included putting three-month-old infants into baths of ice cubes. His advice was so popular that 40 editions have been traced including several translations (Schatzman, 1973).

Dr. Schreber's techniques did not raise robust children, rather his daughter was reportedly mentally ill, his oldest son committed suicide, and his second son, Daniel Paul Schreber, known in his adulthood as "The Hanging Judge" and "The Paranoid Judge," died in an asylum. While hospitalized, Judge Schreber wrote *Memoirs of My Nervous Illness* in which he described a series of tortures he had to endure. Not only was he tormented, but he was taught that his sufferings were "miracles," in my experience a perfect recipe for schizophrenia (lack of touch + intrusive parenting + extreme mental abuse + repression = schizophrenia). In the case of the Judge Schreber, torture was included in the recipe as well, resulting in a paranoid schizophrenic (hence "The Paranoid Judge" nickname). Judge Schreber wrote of his childhood experiences as if he had survived these tortures by holding completely still for extended periods of time, performing mental tricks and achieving states of dissociation or "out of body" experiences. We can hear the effects on his mind as he tries to recall these "miracles" of torture in a positive light, even though they were unbearable to the child he once was. We can follow him holding his stomach in until it didn't exist. We can see how he thought he didn't breathe. We can see that he convinced himself that parts of his body disappeared during the trials. He remembered the freezing and the wooden prisons into which his body was strapped for long periods of time (Santner, 1966).

"I remember that I once had a different heart... On the other hand my lungs were for a long time the object of violent and very threatening attacks... At about the same time some of my ribs were sometimes temporarily smashed, always with the result that what had been destroyed was re-formed after a time. One of the most horrifying miracles was the so-called compression-of-the-chest-miracle, which I endured at least several dozen times; it consisted in the whole chest wall being compressed, so that the state of compression caused by the lack of breath was transmitted to my whole body... I existed frequently without a stomach... Of other internal organs I will only mention the gullet and intestines, which were torn out or vanished repeatedly, further pharynx, which I partly ate. Those miracles always appeared most threatening to me, which were in one way or another directed against my reason. These concerned first my head; secondly also the spinal cord...finally the seminal cord, against which very painful miracles were directed... All my muscles were (and still are) the object of miracles for the purpose of preventing all movements and every occupation I am about to undertake... My eyes and the muscles of the lids which serve to open and close them were an almost uninterrupted target for miracles... This was perhaps the most abominable of all miracles – next to the compression-of-the-chest miracle; the expression used for it if I remember correctly was 'the head-compression-machine.' In consequence of the many flights of rays, etc., there had appeared in my skull a deep cleft or dent roughly along the middle, which probably was not visible from the outside but was from inside...compressed my head as though in a vice by turning a kind of screw, causing my head temporarily to assume an elongated almost pear-shaped form... Manifold miracles were also directed against my skeleton, apart from those against my ribs and skull... In the foot

bones particularly in the region of the heel, caries was often caused by the miracle causing me considerable pain... A similar miracle was the so-called coccyx miracle. This was an extremely painful, caries-like state of the lowest vertebrae. Its purpose was to make sitting and lying down impossible..." (Santner, 1966, p. 64-65)

Many of the techniques suggested by Dr. Schreber were apparent in the judge's recollections, yet slightly distorted as a traumatized child might imagine. Judge Schreber mentioned the "freezing miracle" as well, which seemed to correspond with the experience he likely had as an infant of being placed and left in freezing water.

Judge Schreber was confined to an asylum when he started hearing voices and feeling suicidal. In these pages Judge Schreber described threats by his physician-neurologist, Dr. Paul Emil Flechsig, of homosexual advances (Schreber, p. 99), which Freud assessed as fantasies born of a longing for his beloved father (further explored in the following sections on Freud).

We will never know if Flechsig actually made advances on the judge, but at least one unknown source reported that Dr. Flechsig was said to be cyclothymic and may actually have been bipolar. Flechsig reportedly spent years working ceaselessly on his projects and would fall into long stretches of severe depression, becoming "irritable, arrogant, intolerant and tyrannical" (encyclopedia.com).

Freud Struggles with Theory

In his early days Sigmund Freud enjoyed collaboration with his eminent friend and physiologist, Joseph Breuer. The two of them were pioneering in the actual treatment of psychological trauma. They discovered that under hypnosis, patients could review earlier traumatic experiences that they had blocked from conscious awareness. Freud and Breuer did not doubt the recollections of their hysterical patients and it's believed that the patients experienced therapeutic results. Breuer termed the healing process abreaction while Freud called it catharsis. Freud observed that repressing trauma seemed to affect the physiology of the body, which many current day trauma theorists (*e.g.*, Allan Schore, Martin Teicher, Alice Miller, John Read, Peter Breggin, Bruce Perry, Bessel van der Kolk) also believe. In his own office, Freud discovered that many of these types of repressed events could also be recalled consciously through the process of free association.

Breuer and Freud began to drift apart as the discovery of repressed trauma tended more and more to indicate parental culprits. Breuer was not up for blaming parents.

Freud developed another close professional relationship with the rather delusional Dr. Wilhelm Fliess, who came to play an important role in Freud's life as a father figure. Fliess somewhat took an interest in his theories when no one else did. He was not a warm man, but Freud believed he was an extraordinary human being, which may have been rather delusional of Freud.

In 1893, Freud treated a twenty-year-old patient, Emma Eckstein, during which time he continued to regularly consult Fliess. Although Freud's background was in neurology and he was motivated to study the unconscious, his mentor-colleague was developing a medical theory or "exact biology" of mental illness called Reflex Neurosis that was based on a "complex set of clinical entities that flowed from the nose" (Colbert, 1996. p. 109).

Freud introduced Emma to Dr. Fliess around Christmas in 1894. Emma's symptoms included stomach ailments, problems with her menstruation, masturbation and difficulty walking. Fliess persuaded Freud, surely against his own causal intuitions, to refer Emma to him for nose surgery, believing that unwed women who masturbated suffered from dysmenorrhea (painful menstruation) and that the only cure was a nose operation to "help them give up this bad practice" (Masson, 1998, p. 57).

In 1895, Fliess operated on Emma using only cocaine to anesthetize her and cauterized spots in her inner nose using a wire heated by a galvanic current. Severe complications developed following the operation and Freud had to call in another doctor when he couldn't reach Fliess. Freud informed Fliess of the gravity of Emma's condition, reporting that he had removed two bowls of pus from her nose and had to call in another doctor who inserted a drainage tube in Emma's nose and suggested further surgery may be necessary. Freud wrote a letter to Fliess about two to three months after the surgery that ended with, "Please send me your authoritative advice. I am not looking forward to new surgery on this girl (Masson, p. 61)." A few days later, yet another doctor was called in to treat profuse bleeding. This doctor pulled out twenty inches of gauze that Fliess had erroneously left in. Freud again wrote to Fliess, confessing he believed Emma was not abnormal for masturbating, strongly implying that she didn't need the operation in the first place and stating they had both done her an injustice.

Nevertheless, Freud began to recant his disrespect toward Fliess, his father figure. He began to modify his own theories on mental illness, in part to protect Fliess and in part to assuage his own guilt, as he sensed Fliess pulling away. He began to blame Emma for her hemorrhaging and to reassure Fliess. He wrote, "It's now time that you forgave yourself for the minimal oversight [of leaving in the gauze]" (p. 68). Freud had begun to explain away his own bad conscience.

Emma's situation worsened and it looked like she might die. She underwent another surgery that left her face permanently disfigured. "I am very shaken that such a mishap could have arisen from the operation which was purported to be harmless," wrote Freud. In another letter he wrote, "Eckstein once again is in pain; where will she be bleeding next?" On May 4, Freud wrote, "So far I know only that she bled out of longing [for attention from me]" (p. 100). Freud's exchange with Fliess revealed his constant internal conflict with the truth and his deep need for validation. His struggle with blaming Fliess was as likely as anxiety-producing as blaming a parent. He struggled with his own conscience, whether to take responsibility for Emma's conditions and what that would mean to their identities as doctors. He struggled with countertransference, including anger toward Emma who seemed to be putting them through such suffering. Who was to blame for Emma's original symptoms, the patient or the parent? Who was to blame, the patient or the doctor? Or was it the biology or the experience? What to heal, the body or the memory?

Freud was torn between acknowledging the truth and protecting his mentor, who refused to take any responsibility for his malpractice. He appeared to need Fliess and Fliess' acceptance. A healthy Freud would have challenged Fliess' lack of ethics.

As a pioneer in the observation of cause and effect in psychology, compelling evidence unfolded before him that trauma was the source of psychopathology. First, he told Fliess about his "Seduction Theory" regarding incest trauma, which held that hysteria results from childhood incest. He wrote to Fliess that he had reason to believe that his own father had been "perverse" with his brother and younger sisters. Fliess reportedly responded that he believed something similar had happened in his home (Miller, 1990, p. 56).

In early April 1896, about a year after Emma's surgery, Freud wrote to Fliess with excited anticipation of formally presenting his Seduction Theory to his colleagues. On April 21, 1896, he presented his paper to the Society for Psychiatry and Neurology in Vienna, Austria, proposing that psychological symptoms resulted from childhood trauma in the home and specifically, that hysteria was rooted in incest. Convinced he was about to unveil one of the greatest discoveries in history, the amazing Dr. Freud began his speech, "Gentlemen, stones do speak. I have discovered the source of the Nile of neuropathology. I have discovered the origin of human misery..." (Ellenberger, p. 488). He went on to explain how symptoms of hysteria made sense when understood as symptoms of repressed childhood sexual abuse.

Freud was not well received. His peers rejected him and his theory with a cold shoulder. It devastated him. In a letter to Fliess, he wrote, "Word was given out to abandon me, for a void is forming all around me" (Masson, 1985, p. 185). His colleagues soundly banished him and his proposition that an alarming number of their patients had been molested. They rebuffed the implication that psychiatrists should take on parents and their secrets. Two weeks after the devastating rejection of his paper, Freud began to formulate and explain his new theory about Emma to Fliess, a theory that would completely exonerate Fliess (p. 186). Robert, Fliess' son, who grew up to become a psychologist, revealed later in his life that his father began to molest him during this time period (Miller, 1990, p. 56). It was one month later in a letter dated June 4, 1896 that Freud wrote to Fliess, "Her story is becoming even clearer; there is no doubt that her hemorrhages were due to wishes." Nearly six months after his colleagues rebuked him, Freud's father died. The night after the funeral, Freud dreamt that a notice was posted on his front door that read, "One is requested to shut the eyes" (Ellenberger, p. 445). In a remarkable pro-parent blindness, the otherwise brilliant Dr. Freud interpreted his own dream to mean that he had carried unreasonable hostility toward his father for far too long. By contrast, a pro-child interpretation would have suggested that both the all-powerful peer group, Society of Physicians, and Freud's father, whose secrets he kept, had requested, demanded and decreed that he shut the eyes. Bad theory yields bad insight.

A little more than a year after the debut of his Seduction Theory and a year after his father died, Freud shut the eyes. He recanted his Seduction Theory in a letter to Fliess dated September 21, 1897, but he did not begin work on a replacement theory for another seven years. He was ostracized for many years but continued to develop his pro-parent theory over the next forty-plus years, explaining, however farfetched, that sexual fantasies were inborn and resulted from an Oedipal Complex or Electra Complex for the parent of the opposite sex. He presented that it was normal for children to desire their parents sexually or to at least compete with their same sex parent for attention and affection. He also presented a theory of inborn internal drives that propel us away from destruction toward pleasure (rather than the drives to act out denied trauma). Fortunately, he preserved common valuable concepts employed today, such as defense mechanisms, resistance, and repression. In formulating a theory of internal causation to replace the one of childhood trauma, Freud turned "from the repressed to the repressing" (Ellenberger, p. 517).

Geniuses are not always heroes.

> In questions of science, the authority of a thousand is not worth the humble reasoning of a single individual. – Galileo Galilei

Freud Gets Another Opportunity

In 1911, fourteen years after recanting the Seduction Theory and six years after proposing the Internal Drive Theory, Freud was challenged to evaluate Judge Daniel Paul Schreber via his memoirs.

After Judge Schreber published his

memoirs, Freud was presented with an opportunity to regain the acceptance of his peers by evaluating Schreber. In effect, he was being tested. Freud accepted the challenge, apparently as an opportunity to prove to his colleagues that he had abandoned his Seduction Theory. He assessed Judge Schreber, applying his famous new theories on internal drive and fantasy and some new theory he was formulating on the universality of bisexuality. Freud's greatest proof that he had abandoned his Seduction Theory was his apparent indifference to the long-term effects from a childhood history of torture that Schreber endured, focusing solely on symptoms as inborn fantasy.

Freud wrongly evaluated the judge to be a paranoid homosexual who projected his repressed sexual desires for his beloved father onto Flechsig as a father figure, thus vindicating Flechsig. In other words, he hypothesized the judge was fixated on unresolved childhood pleasure-bound fantasies of having sex with his father in order to be closer to him. Freud did not consider that the paranoia was born of extreme childhood trauma, possibly including molestation, rather than a longing for his father. Neither did he consider that the Paranoid Judge had actually been sexually accosted by his symptomatic doctor (whonamedit.com) or both.

If Freud had dared to investigate Judge Schreber's childhood he would have discovered that his father was a prestigious physician and popular parenting pedagogue who advised Christian parents throughout Germany to torture their children, cruelly requiring respectful obedience and emotional repression. He might have been moved to expose Dr. Schreber, discredit his theory and warn German parents. He might have made his case for his Seduction Theory by way of a sister theory on paranoid personality, thus exposing the long-term effects of emotional and physical trauma instead of hiding behind his new Internal Drive Theory that blamed the victim or the victim's constitution. Yes, he might have further jeopardized his professional standing but he would have left a greater legacy for himself with vindication to follow. He might have prevented the rearing of a whole second generation of German-born Schreber children who had to grow up without empathy or conscience and a drive to scapegoat, as apparently Judge Schreber had. He might have prevented the genocide of millions of Jews. Instead, Freud crumbled under the pressure to see what he was expected to see and to overlook what he was forbidden to see, a choice many of us understand.

Freud had a number of disciples and friends over the course of his career. One of them was Sandor Ferenczi who befriended Freud during his painful exile at the same time that Dr. Schreber's theory was bearing fruit. Over the years in his own practice Ferenczi became more convinced that there was something to Freud's original premise that sexual abuse underlay certain types of symptoms. The closer Ferenczi got to this abandoned conclusion, the more Freud distanced from him. Ultimately Freud's biographer characterized Ferenczi as mentally ill and he reportedly died alone in exile, another casualty of causal theory.

Adolph Hitler, the Child

Hitler's father, Alois, was the bastard son of a Protestant maid who had lain with her employer, a Jewish businessman who reportedly paid her child support. She eventually married and the family made an attempt to alter the church birth records to disguise the origins of Alois' paternity and give him Protestant legitimacy. That Alois was the bastard son of a Jew was a great disgrace to him and a major family secret. He became a rigid, humorless perfectionist, apparently trying to make up for his imposed feelings of shame and inadequacy. He was a clerk-bureaucrat by profession who wore a starched shirt and suit every day while taking his position most seriously (Miller, 1983).

Alois followed the teachings of Dr. Schreber, but preferred daily whippings. It appeared that there was nothing his son could do to escape these beatings. Hitler got the worst of it among his siblings as the family's scapegoat. He later boasted that he had developed the capacity to bear the lash without screaming or crying, something I have called the "sociopathic decision," because choosing pride in how well one can bear the lash with stoicism is bound to produce a drive to scapegoat. We cannot repress trauma without scapegoating others for it.

Hitler later revealed that the worst moment in his childhood was one night when he was trying to run away. He had to slip through an opening so tight he had to remove his clothes. Alois came to whip young Hitler, who jumped out of the open winter window to flee down the freezing fire escape. Alois looked down upon his son, stark naked, shivering under a street lamp in the snow, and laughed and jeered at him (as if it would rid Alois of his own childhood shame).

Hitler had been raised to show nothing but complete respect for his tormenting father so he had to find a place to put his rage. He resolved his dilemma by hating Jews as he consciously or unconsciously understood the source of his father's shame was his Jewish parentage. Hitler's resulting hatred and scapegoating of Jews may have been a way of hating his father indirectly and safely, or it may have been a way of trying to defend him.

Alice Miller (1983) reports that when Hitler became Fuehrer he had his parentage investigated. Shortly after that, he took action and ordered tanks to desecrate the Jewish cemetery where his Jewish grandfather lay buried. Then Hitler's first decree as Fuehrer was to declare that German Jews were the enemy within and anyone of Jewish decent by less than three generations would be included. Ironically, Hitler should have been included in his own roundup. Ultimately, he sent millions of shivering Jews naked to their deaths, symbolically recapitulating his worst trauma and scapegoating millions.

At his bidding Hitler found millions of willing German Christians who had been likewise raised by their parents to scapegoat others. (See Chapter 5: Imprinting.) They too had made the "sociopathic decision" and learned to bear the abuse by burying the truth of their experiences for the sake of the abuser (their parents).

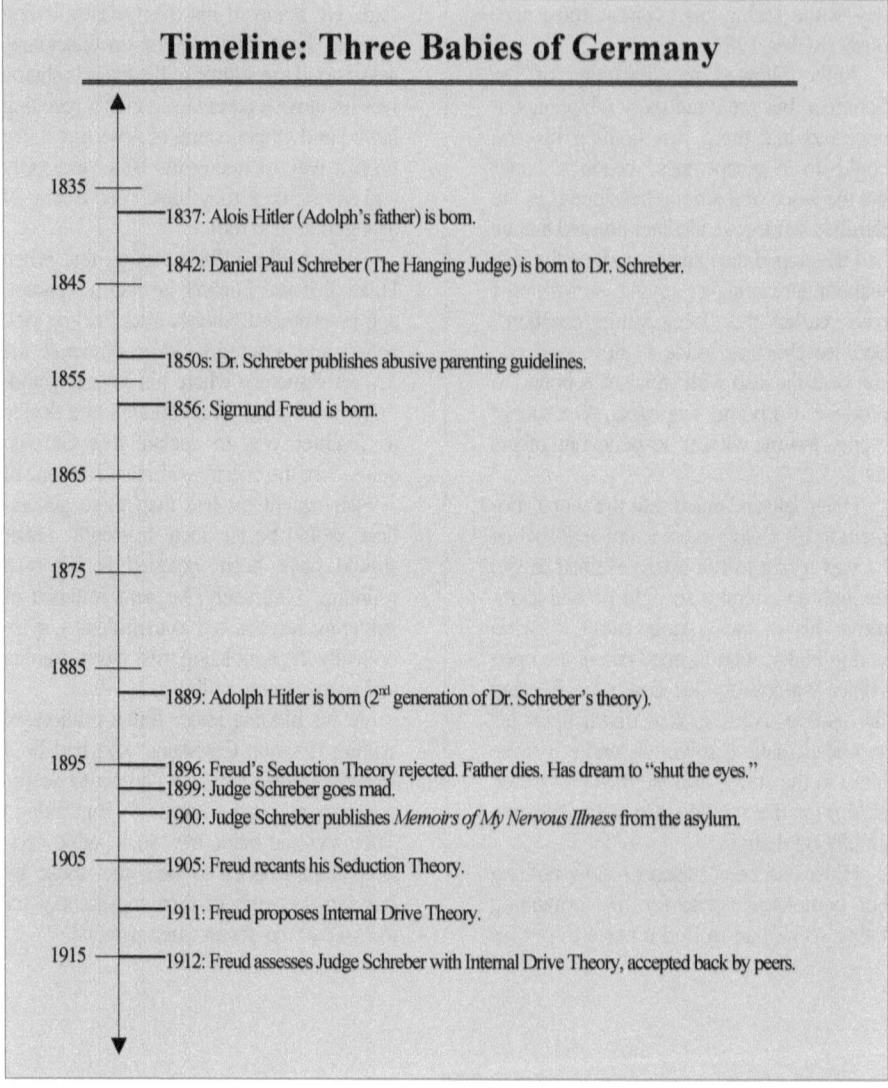

Competing Contemporary Theories

John Watson, Father of American Behavioral Psychology

While Analytic Theory ultimately came to hold that the source of behavior is inborn drives from within (thereby blaming the child), Behavioral Theory held that all of us are born a "blank slate" and each of us can be fashioned by parents if only they have the right recipe for conditioning. The father of American Behavioral Theory, John Watson, pioneered some early experiments with a young orphan, known as Little Albert, who he taught to be afraid of all things with white fuzz or fur when he had no such phobias before the work began. This proved that children can be taught all their fears by parents. Unfortunately, the child was adopted before Watson could reverse the conditioning.

It was also unfortunate that Watson did not detect the importance of bonding and attachment before he introduced his theories. As you shall see his blindness may have resulted from too much mothering of some sort in his own childhood.

Watson's father abandoned his mother and him, which is almost the only thing I know at this point about his childhood. They lived on a poor farm in South Carolina. Before the end of his life he destroyed all his notes, journaling and personal correspondence, so we cannot say he was an open man (Nance, 1970). From reading his book on childrearing I have developed a few hypotheses about his personality as well as his childhood. He wrote about parenting as if he was trying to protect the child. He was as adamant about the role of parents in the creation of personality as I am. He had high regard for infants and children. He attributed nothing to inborn traits. He was clear that children should be treated with respect and never be hit. He did not think masturbation was unnatural. He advocated regular conversations between parent and child. Yet he wanted to protect the child from too much affection, which he held in visceral contempt to the extent that he nearly suggested that we replace mothers with professional nannies.

All children need more affection than he realized so his advice admonishing mothers to relinquish kissing, hugging and holding their infants was actually harmful advice since most children already don't get enough nurturing. I speculate that little John Watson got too little affection or too much affection. Too little affection could cause him to develop Reactive Attachment Disorder, leaving him averse to affection, vulnerability and intimacy. Too much affection could be suffocating and unbearable if the child comes to feel responsible for the mother's feelings. Either extreme would create a child who was vigorously against affection, leaving him defensive for a lifetime against minimal affection and intimacy. He could have been a parentified child, stuck in an emotional role as his mother's friend-in-need or her surrogate husband. It's possible that his mother molested him. In any event, it looks as if we will never know the causes behind his adverse reaction to maternal affection. What I suspect is that he suffered substantial feelings of suffocation and that tender maternal gestures came to revolt him and he projected those revulsions onto nearly all the dynamics between mother and child. He saw these dynamics as retarding the growth of children and thought that if women really loved their children, they would let them be. Watson became a prime example of why untreated theorists should not write theory.

I found some wonderful quotes from Watson's book, first printed in 1928, postdating Dr. Schreber's theory by sixty years. He proposed to parents that they could have "a doctor, lawyer, artist, merchant chief and yes, even a beggar-man or thief, depending on how they raised a child" (p. 6). Watson truly seemed to be pro-child. He dedicated his book "to the first mother who brings up a happy child," and it seems clear that this was not his mother. "When the 25 million American homes come to realize that the child has a right to a separate room and adequate psychological care, there will not be nearly so many children born" (p. 8).

Sometimes he seemed like a trailblazer. He wrote, "[I have hope] that some day the importance of the first two years of infancy will be fully realized" (p. 9). He considered parenting a cherished profession. "The oldest profession of the race today is facing failure. This profession is parenthood. Many thousands of mothers do not even know that parenthood should be numbered among the professions. They do not realize that there are any special problems involved in rearing children. For them, all the age-old belief that all children need is food as often as they call for it, warm clothes and a roof over their heads at night is enough. 'Nature' does the rest almost unaided. They argue that parents have been rearing children for a great many centuries, therefore, why bother about learning anything new" (p. 11)? It seemed as if I could have said these words myself.

"No one today knows enough to raise a child" (p. 12), Watson argued. He sometimes spoke like a scientist, "Will you believe the almost astounding truth that no well trained man or woman has ever watched the complete and daily development of a single child from its birth to its third year? Plants and animals we know about because we have studied them, but the human child until very recently has been a mystery" (p. 13). Attempting to persuade mothers, he wrote, "This awakening is beginning to show itself in mothers who ask themselves the question, 'Am I not almost wholly responsible for the way my child grows up? Isn't it just possible that almost nothing is given in heredity and that practically the whole course of development of the child is due to the way I raise it" (p. 15)?

Watson, the researcher, proposed that the only two things that infants naturally fear are loud noises and falling or being unsupported. All the rest we learn by experiences with our parents. "There are no instincts," Watson asserted. "We build in at an early age everything that is later to appear" (p. 38). "Children's fears are home grown just like their loves and temper outbursts. The parents do the emotional planting and cultivating. At three years of age the child's whole emotional life plan has been laid down and his emotional disposition set" (p. 45). As if he was advocating Faith Parenting (explored indepth in Chapter 6), Watson said, "The parents' 'don't' is the most potent factor of all in producing both fear and negative responses. Have you as a parent ever stopped to consider how many times a day you use 'don't'" (p. 57)?

"A certain amount of affectionate response is socially necessary but few parents realize how easily they can overtrain the child in this direction. It may tear the heartstrings a bit, this thought of stopping the tender outward demonstration of your love for your children or their love for you. But if you are convinced that this is best for the child, aren't you willing to stifle a few pangs" (p. 44)? asked Watson, as he delivered very bad advice. "Mothers just don't know, when they kiss their children and pick them up and rock them, caress them and jiggle them upon their knee that they are slowly building a human being totally unable to cope with the world it must later live in" (p. 44).

Watson observed the symptoms of broken attachments, or Reactive Attachment Disorder, but did not correctly understand what he saw because his bias was so strong. "Some of the most tormented moments come when the parents have had to be away from their nine-month old baby for a stretch of three weeks. When they part from it, the child gurgles, coos, holds out its arms and shows every evidence of deepest parental love. Three weeks later when they return the child turns to the attendant who has in the interim fondled and petted it and put the bottle to the sensitive lips. The infant child loves anyone who strokes and feeds it" (p. 73). Watson did not know he was describing the clues that a child's attachment has been broken and the child will not trust his parents no matter how much they take over his feeding and petting. He will guard his heart for the rest of his life and he will fear abandonment by anyone he ever lets get close to him. Watson did not recognize a broken heart when he described this fickle child. Neither did he observe that the child would never coo and gurgle in his parents' arms again.

Perhaps the most disturbing words Watson wrote were these: "How about its loves – its affectionate behavior? Isn't that 'natural?' Do you mean to say the child doesn't 'instinctively' love its mother" (p.

43)? Answering, he says, "Only one thing will bring out a love response in the child – stroking and touching its skin, lips, sex organs and the like. It doesn't matter at first who strokes it. It will 'love' the stroker. This is the clay out of which all love – maternal, paternal, wifely or husbandly – is made. Hard to believe? But true. A certain amount of affectionate response is socially necessary but few parents realize how easily they can over-train the child in this direction" (p. 43).

While I believe touch is critical in the formation of personality, it is not the only thing, and implicit in this paragraph is permission for a mother to stroke her child's genitals in the name of love. If it is not what Watson meant, it is certainly something that could be interpreted that way by readers. It is also a reason why I threw in the possibility that Watson had been molested in the above speculation about why he hated suffocation. I had two clients who became sex addicts because their mothers either stroked or manipulated their genitals to keep them from crying. Both feared their own emotions and masturbated to quell their feelings. I have also known mothers who admitted to me that they couldn't stand their child crying, so they knew a way to stop him. I have heard too many references to this harmful technique. I wonder how much the permission, if not the recommendation, that Watson gave mothers was advice to do something they otherwise might not have contemplated.

Watson went on to recommend an "ideal formula" for raising children that was not ideal at all. He advocated molding human behavior by strict scientific control, beginning with firm four-hour feeding and sleep schedules, no matter how hungry or tired the child. He said that children must be toilet trained early, that six months was not too early and may have even been too late.

"Forbid pacifiers, thumb sucking and other forms of coddling. Employ strict discipline at all times. And above all, show no displays of affection. Babies and children can and should be left alone...Never kiss or hug your children. Remember that mother love is a dangerous instrument which can destroy your children's future happiness" (p. 81).

Behavioral Theory came to hold that within the consciousness of a human being is a "black box" that contains the material that influences formation of personality. Unfortunately, Watson, who was over-controlled himself and over-controlling, had a caveat that protected parents as well as analytic theory protected them. He postulated that the material within the black box can never be known. The notion of investigating its contents through reporting forbidden memories or self-examination was considered an inaccurate waste of time and when he destroyed his papers, he suggested something else, possibly his own aversion to self-disclosure or personal histories. Behavioral Theory simply recommends that the way to change the contents of the black box is to simply recondition behavior without bothering to understand from whence it came.

Theodore Reich

One of Freud's protégés was a man named Theodore Reich, another admitted victim of incest. He discovered and introduced breathwork. However, like most other theorists, he too was in denial about the source of behavior, especially his own. To Reich, acting out sexually was healthy. His speculations were validated by the social attitudes of people at the time that feared honest and healthy expressions of sexuality.

Because he was so blind to his own history, Reich avoided any acknowledgement of the meaning of the memories that would surface when he did his labored breathing. He had recall but rather than recognize that these memories were traumatic, he insisted they were positive memories of buried sexual feelings that led to his sexual freedom of expression. He believed that these memories were evidence that the breathing led to sexual openness rather than traumatic memories he needed to address for their influence on his present thinking. His denial of the impact that his own abuse seemed to have on him led to rationalizations that ultimately drove him to insanity. He died in prison of syphilis believing he was a political prisoner advocating for truth and sexual liberation. In fact, he was in prison for defrauding the public by selling his "Orgone Box," a contraption he devised that he told buyers would cure a wide range of psychological ailments, including frigidity (Levy & Orlans, 1998, p. 270).

Pro-Parent *vs.* Pro-Child Ramifications

Different theories of psychology have been developed with the issue of parental responsibility in mind. Thus many theories are designed to spare parents' embarrassment and others are designed to rescue children in crisis.

Pro-Parent Ramifications	Pro-Child Ramifications
Repression Ethic	Expression Ethic
Buck-up philosophy	Let-it-out philosophy
Swallow feelings to protect parents	Require remorse of parents before forgiveness
We are the way we are	We change through self-awareness
Healing is harder, if not impossible	Healing is possible and takes place
Heal through affirmations, denial ethic, ignoring feelings and moving on	Heal through revisiting, releasing pain, and owning the truth
Medication and conditioning	Revisit past hurts and correct
Fear of feelings	Value on feelings
Parent has primacy	Child has primacy
Parental immunity	Parental responsibility
Challenging parents is threatening	Confronting parents is a right
Parents are fragile	Children are fragile
Better to defend parents' feelings than allow child to heal	Better to heal child or grown child than protect parents' feelings
Parents' feelings matter more	Child's feelings matter more
Don't blame parents	Don't blame child's genes
Protect parents ethic	Protect-the-child ethic, like a detective
Advocate parents' point of view even to exclusion of child's	Desire to see and perceive child and child's point of view
Resistance to excavating childhood	Willingness to excavate childhood
Let parents continue to injure child or grown child	Hold parents to a responsible and respectful standard
Cool to parent education	Warm to parent education
Bonding/attachment can be done by many	Quality and continuous attachment pursued
Lack of curiosity	Curiosity
Blindness problems	Good at seeing
Assessment problems	Good at assessing
Less concern about whether child is ok	More awareness/concern for child's feelings
Prevention is pointless	Prevention is possible
Bad Seed Theory	Everyone-Born-Good Theory
Gene Association	Causal theory of some sort
What was good enough for me is good enough for my child	My child can have better parenting and a better outcome than me
Personalities are inauthentic, rigged, and rigid	Personalities are more authentic, enlightened and spontaneous
Fear of emotions and intimacy, or very emotional and fears loss of intimacy	Ease with emotions, intimacy and ability to leave an abusive or unethical person
More fear of death	Less fear of death

Players in Making or Breaking a Theory

As I have said before, the contributors to psychological theory can be narrowed to two camps, one pro-parent and the other pro-child. Sometimes battles over theory arise as revisions develop. Other battles erupt over territory. Most battles take place behind the scenes. These attempts to establish a position are meaningful, with long-range ramifications that affect the wellbeing of millions of people. There are four general contributing groups within the pro-parent and pro-child camps. The broad field of psychology must be understood in terms of its players.

Theoreticians. The theoreticians try to describe how reality works and what practices are most effective, but they don't operate in a void. They seek the recognition of clinicians. They seek the research of scientists to support or to help correct their theories and they hope to pass the gatekeepers who preserve the status quo.

Clinicians. Just as in the old days, today's clinicians are a faction of the contributors with a minority voice. Many clinicians have been sold on genetic theory and Behavioral Theory and resist the thought that parents have anything to do with symptoms. Others with true powers of observation suspect error and follow the pro-child researchers, many of whom have been listed in my Acknowledgements. A clinician's effectiveness depends on the correctness of her theoretical strategy as well as her capacity to perceive and empathize. It includes her mental health, values and ability to self-reflect. Even though they are bombarded with evidence that genes play a role in psychopathology, many of these aware clinicians have reservations and may welcome The Causal Theory for the answers it provides.

To a large extent it is the practicing clinician who adopts applications of the going theories and makes unpublished discoveries of her own. The clinicians are the players who implement theory, effectively or not, and sometimes like Alice Miller and Jeffrey Masson, it is the clinician who ends up critiquing bad theory.

Scientists. The role of our scientists is to prove and disprove theories. They are the examiners or triers of fact. They are the judges who develop and weigh evidence. They carry our sacred trust, and we count on them to be objective. To find out that scientists are human with biases and can actually be bought is shocking, but true. To me, it is as if I found out that the Supreme Court is corrupt. When our researchers are credible, they provide the foundation for solid theory. When they betray our trust by letting themselves become co-opted, they are like spies on the wrong side of history.

To my mind the heroes and villains in this field are the researchers. They have the best credentials, especially those who are also clinicians. I have never had such regard for anyone as I have for the researchers who demonstrate the truth or falsehood of going theories, and I have never had such disdain as I have for the scientists who sell out, whoring themselves and their "results" for a price.

So, to be clear, when I am accusing some theoreticians of inaccuracy, I do not mean all of them, especially the researchers and critics who have done the most impeccable work in our field.

Usually, players in the development of schools of thought operate in more than one role. Often researchers are also theoreticians, such as John Watson. We clearly saw how Freud modified his theory to clear the gatekeepers. It appears to be a common practice to this day. The ideal mix is when the researchers or the critics are also clinicians or take clinicians into account.

Gatekeepers. Today the gatekeepers include licensing boards, accredited colleges and professional associations, and they usually operate on a bias, which includes whether the theory is sufficiently medical or whether it benefits the powers that be. For example, Freud introduced a posture of the aloof psychiatrist, a doctor who did not reveal anything of himself or even to offer advice, while his patients remained in the role of the helpless specimen. This type of pose validated the role of the medical professional in stark contrast to the historical roles of mentors and shamans who walked amongst their students, modeling what they taught. Today, it is more important for a psychotherapist to act professional than to be authentic.

Gatekeepers now include marketing complexes funded by pharmaceutical corporations. These strategies include press conferences announcing new discoveries that have yet to be replicated, putting the spin on the research necessary for further self-validation. They include pharmaceutical representatives who wine and dine psychiatrists. There is a new push by the pharmaceutical industry for some psychologists to hold a license to prescribe medication.

Gatekeepers also include accredited colleges, the course content and books students will be assigned and the items they must know to pass the licensing exams. Two great critics of contemporary theory and practice of our time, John Bradshaw and Alice Miller, were scarcely recognized by these gatekeepers, so the public barely got to know them. On the other hand licensing exams, as well as television ads, are flooded with a bias toward psychotropic medications.

Students who want to become psychologists or marriage and family therapist in the State of California must learn an excessive amount of pro-parent theory, including more and more deference to psychiatry and medical doctors, results of fraudulent genetic research, false memory theory and brief therapy techniques for Health Maintenance Organizations (HMOs). Additionally, Behavioral Theory, which is pro-parent theory, has taken over the preferred treatment for Post Traumatic Stress Disorder and is now the recommended treatment for most disorders in the state exams.

The California Board of Psychology has a policy that they will not accept any applicants from unaccredited colleges, unless they were approved by the state before 1999. Only graduates of accredited schools are accepted. At first glance, this looks like consumer protection. At second glance, it is clearly an attempt to insulate existing colleges from competition and new competing schools of thought. In other words, if this policy continues, there will be no new colleges of psychology in California. The cap is on.

Additionally, the Western Association of Secondary Schools, WASC, no longer offers financial aid to approved schools, only older accredited schools. Yet, it is the approved, but not yet accredited, schools that are most likely to offer groundbreaking theory and more innovative approaches to education, smaller classes, more personal attention, more flexible hours for working students and significantly lower tuition.

Today there is another push in the direction of Behavioral Theory because its practices can be easily studied and it skips the review of childhood experiences. Evidence-Based Practice is a new and cherished criterion held by the gatekeepers and many of the Health Maintenance Organizations of our day, which puts a high premium on simple problem-solving approaches. HMOs are businesses designed to cut overhead in expenses on patients, so they too want to get patients in and get them out, without concern for the origins of pathology or treating its roots.

Assessing a Theory

The best theory will be the one that represents the way of reality most accurately. If two theories represent reality well, the simplest theory would be the best one. A measure of a theory is how it instructs practice, action or behavior. Because theories do instruct practice, the unspoken measures are the **ramifications** of that theory or what its impact will become if put into practice. It is important for anyone assessing a theory to consider the **motives of the theoretician** or scientist who developed it. This is perhaps the hardest to assess because people are often unaware of their own motives or they may not want others to know them. It is common for a theoretician to wear one motive externally while implementing another internally. Lastly, we should learn about how the theoretician lives and how he treats his mate, students and most of all, his children.

The Causal Theory is very sensitive to motives, and it is my belief that theoreticians, clinicians and scientists are just as likely to be acting out as anyone else. In order to become aware of our unconscious motives, we must be willing to look at how we were reared. A theory that discourages this sort of self-reflection has an investment in keeping a taboo against scrutinizing our parents' impact on us. Sometimes scientists and theoreticians reveal these motives during unguarded moments. Sometimes you can identify the motives of a theoretician by the company she keeps. Often those with similar motives share the same beliefs.

This is The Causal Theory. That means that everything throughout this manual is understood in terms of cause and effect. For that reason, I have somewhat digressed into the histories of pre-existing theories. Every piece of conventional wisdom has a genesis that is a chain reaction leading to now. The causative factors in the history of a thing are often invisible to us, having become our assumptions. Reviewing history makes motives conscious. That is the reason I have presented some historical content. To understand a thing, you have to know its history and motive as well as the opposing forces that propelled its development.

I dare say that there is some virtue and some truth in every theory. While some truths may be illuminated, some truths may be concealed behind comfortable falsehoods. All the major developmental and parenting theories to date have holes in them and most have instructions that are downright wrong. We can take the best of the different parenting and developmental theories and forgive their shortfalls with eyes wide open, but we need to know what to discard.

When we listen to a theory, we need to question. Can you identify motives behind the theory? Who does this theory serve? What are the ramifications of this theory? What is the life of the theorist like? What are her children like? It is our job to identify the most truth possible and let go of aspects of theory that seem unsupported by science or reality. I dare say that anything less is malpractice. We must let go of the liberal, politically correct position that all theories can be simultaneously correct. They can't. They aren't.

Types of Therapy by Philosophy

I have found that most of the great theoreticians who contribute to this field have had deep childhood injuries that influenced their theories both positively and negatively. The ones who contributed the most seemed to have the biggest blind spots requiring the most exposure. At the root of these theoretical flaws are the drives to cover up to protect parents in a host of innovative ways. Below, I attempt to illuminate the positives and negatives of each theory.

Freudian Theory/Isolated Mind Theories. Late Freud theorized that the source of pathology is held to be inborn internal drives. Healing can take place by insight gained from a blank-screen therapist who deflects content back onto the patient to facilitate insight or resolution. This process takes years and is very expensive. There may or may not be clarity about the source of dysfunction. There are no replacement skills modeled (Taylor, 1996).

Cognitive or Behavioral Theory. The child is born good or blank. He or she can be conditioned in any direction. Behavior is not created by any internal drive, but by outside conditioning. However, understanding behavior is thought to be a waste of time. The mind is a "black box" which can never be opened or understood. There is presumed to be no correlation between trauma and behavior, although you can condition behavior with experiences of reward and punishment. The point is to condition behavior; empathy is essentially irrelevant, other than the formation of a "therapeutic alliance." Catharsis (emotional release) is thought to represent inappropriate behaviors and loss of control. (This belief about emotions and catharsis often shows up in the parents of children with Attention Deficit Hyperactivity Disorder (ADHD) and even their therapists.)

**Object Relations Theory/
Self Psychology/Relational Model.** The psychoanalytic tradition of Freud originally held that drives were born of repressed trauma. After Freud succumbed to social pressure, he revised his theory to hold that the origins of pathology are inborn. However, the more recent development of object relations theory, influenced by Bowlby, Winnicott, Kohut, Ainsworth and Spitz, among others, has given birth to a new kind of psychoanalysis intended to expose and release or purge the repressed emotions and destructive drives born of thoughtless or harmful experiences, especially parenting.

The child is born pristine or good. He develops drives according to how he is treated during critical, early years of childhood. Healing is a function of expressing up and out the emotions of repressed trauma. That is, we don't get to just feel the emotions, we need to cry, rage or scream in a pillow. We need to express feelings out of our body in the form they would normally leave as much as possible. Ideally, we do this in the presence of a therapist, thereby creating the "corrective emotional experience," as our therapist offers us empathy for sharing our feelings, like our mother or father was supposed to do.

Pathology is not the result of trauma itself; it is the result of repressed trauma. The repression is usually needed, modeled, expected, taught or mandated by the parent, and so it requires a parent figure or therapist to invite expression and thus, unlock, authorize and authenticate it. Your therapist signed on for that honor.

Attachment Theory. Attachment Theory recognizes that some children and adults chose at the moment of an attachment break or trauma never to be vulnerable again. They repress emotions on their own accord due to a total lack of trust and a resulting fear of losing control. Other dynamics of parenting such as discipline or trauma are not sufficiently explored.

Attachment Parenting. Introduced by pediatritrian William Sears, parents are encouraged to maintain a continuity of attachment through kindergarten. Mothers and fathers "wear" the baby with slings and may have a family bed. Mothers may nurse until the child is five years old or older. Even though Sears encourages parents not to indulge these children, attachment parents often set weak limits and the children seem entitled.

Interpersonal Therapy. IPT is a treatment that focuses on attachment injuries in adults with a focus on interpersonal relations with the therapist and an exploration into relationships. Delving into early childhood truths is not considered necessary. It is symptom reduction orientated. It's all here and now.

Family Systems Theory. The family is an organism of interdependent dynamics. Everyone in the family plays a role in how the others in the family turn out. Change the family dynamics, and you change the individuals. No one is the "identified patient," especially children. When parents bring a child to therapy to be fixed, it is generally the parents who need fixing rather than the child, especially one child designated as the "identified patient."

Reichian Therapy. Founded by Theodore Reich, a protégé of Freud, this approach is based on Reich's discovery of the power of breath in resurfacing trauma. This technique utilizes a natural, built–in method for releasing buried trauma. Unfortunately, the technique may not be supplemented sufficiently by replacement skills or good developmental theory.

Psychohistory/Psychogeneology. The science of "evolution of the psyche" from generation to generation is defined as the science of evolution of parent-child relations as the basic cause of personality. This is offered as more social science or the study of how cultures treat their children, *en masse*, and is very educational.

Trauma Theory. Trauma Theory is the search, study and recommendation of the best ways to treat victims of trauma. These specialists work with patients who have Post Traumatic Stress Disorder, dissociation and recovered memories. (Most recovered memories are not of sexual abuse, by the way.) Some theorists recommend emersion in and catharsis of the original memory. Others recommend avoiding the memory. Another, Eye Movement Desensitization and Reprocessing (EMDR) takes the patient into the memory without re-experiencing it fully. Marion Soloman (Healing Trauma, 2003) recommends helping the patient identify the beginning and ending of their original trauma, so they can see how it won't reappear out of the blue, often laying the memory to rest.

The Causal Theory. The child is born innocent, good, divine, or blank without personality, even though the child is highly observant and susceptible to formative treatment techniques. Quality of attachment is especially important, followed by safe separation. Respect and discipline with natural consequences are ingredients that make up healthy human beings. Experiences fashion personalities. Coping mechanisms are adaptations that may later become dysfunctional interaction patterns or personality structures, if not disorders. Shedding these coping styles entails revisiting the injuries, dissolving resistances and defenses (whether born of repression for parents' sake or attachment trauma), catharting the relevant emotions and replacing old reflexive habits with healthy communication and interactive skills, similar to CBT. Behaviors speak of injuries and imprinting. Specific injuries predict specific behaviors or traits. The Causal Theory invests in prevention and especially focuses on interpreting and treating children via the parents and correcting the parents so they can correct or heal their children. Parents are the best healers of their own children once they learn how to truly see and hear them, honoring their feelings.

The Snyder Causal Theory & Treatment (SCTT) includes aspects of analytic theory from Object Relations or Early Freud (*vs.* Late Freud), Cognitive and Behavioral Theory, Family Systems Theory, Attachment Theory and Trauma Theory.

Pro-Parent Bias

The pervasive advice against holding parents responsible for abuse or neglect is, "Get over it. Stop blaming your parents for your own shortcomings. Spare me the psychobabble." We look at the parents as the ones whose egos and identities need protection, not the children.

On Mother's Day 2010, my friend Karin Gottheiner, a family law attorney, sent me this email: "I was in the car listening to AM talk radio. I was shocked to hear their Mother's Day news blurb (which was repeatedly played throughout the day), which told moms not to worry so much about always doing the right thing for their kids. It said to ignore the nonsense that they may hear, that everything they do to/with their child will have an effect on the child. It went on to say that moms should not feel guilty if they do the wrong things and they should not worry that doing the wrong things will in some unknown way affect their child for life. It ended by saying that kids will be 'just fine' whether the moms do the right thing or the wrong thing, so moms should give themselves a break from feeling guilty and enjoy their Mother's Day!"

Recently, I watched a brilliant YouTube rant my son sent me entitled "But They Did the Best They Could: A Moral Examination of Historical Parenting," by an empiricist identified as Stefbot, who asked the viewer to hold a higher standard for parents. Interestingly, one of the viewer comments was (copied verbatim), "what about those how have problem with their parents? what do you suggest to them? go to work? Separate from parents? Kill them? Or be with them and use this stuff to abuse them for their mistakes? you do not have answer to these questions you only make the situation worse than it is. you put the parents and children against each other as enemies. you do not solve anything in this context." (Stefbot, video uploaded 2010)

This is not just one person's unconscious fear. Most of us who need to protect our parents share this fear. We do not want to end up enemies of our parents. To hold parents responsible for abusing children would be almost equivalent to killing them. Yes, we see parents as weaker than children and hold children to the higher standard, or perhaps, more accurately, we sacrifice children to protect our parents' good humor or fragile identities. We are afraid of hurting them or pissing them off, so much so that we don't see them capable of an ethical conversation in which we could say, "Dad, when you beat me it really hurt and I thought you didn't love me," with Dad responding, "Son, I was a fool to do that to you. I am so sorry."

Any inclination to sort out the truth is often met with contempt or ridicule. I am on delicate ground here because what I am saying is socially forbidden. Never before has this philosophy to protect parents become so economically important. It protects industrial enterprise because wages can be lower when both parents work and because the market is flooded with two parents working and buying. It feeds the feminist movement thereby necessitating a thriving day care industry. The cause behind symptoms resulting from children losing their parents too young are symptoms born of a child's unmet need to be with her parent. These symptoms then become attributed to a child's genes, which is a relief to most parents and a blow to the child's identity. We are invited to medicate our children so their symptoms don't disturb us and so we can feel comfortable about our choices to leave our children too young.

This is not just my theory. This is not just my idea. We were evolved to need and require a secure attachment and the natural and obvious one was with mother. This is our human and genetic design. I didn't make it up to frustrate mothers or collude with fathers or the ruling class. I didn't make it up to be a bad sport about parents. I am reporting it as a witness. I am just the messenger. It is simply the truth of cause and effect and human development. It would be great if it were not the truth. We could have it both ways. Unfortunately, when I look at the way nature is set up (actually evolved), I see there is no free lunch - not amazing children, not healing, not friends, not mates and not character.

We have to earn our way to everything worthwhile.

The following grid is designed to illuminate the agendas behind the different theories of psychology that appear to be at odds. Some polarize over causality, with some arguing that Nature is the primary or sole cause of behavior while others argue that only environment fashions behavior and personality. Other disciplines focus on ways to treat patients by skipping childhood and heading straight for the here and now. Others assert that true healing requires the exploration and release of childhood injuries. The chart is laid out with each theory/discipline represented in one of the broad theoretical categories: Nature-Based and Pro-Parent; Nature-Based and Pro-Child; Nurture-Based and Pro-Parent; and Nurture-Based and Pro-Child.

War of the Researchers and Theoreticians Grid
Nature vs. Nurture Theory and Pro-Parent vs. Pro-Child Theory

	Nature-Based, Pro-Parent	Nature-Based, Pro-Child
Philosophers/ Believers:	Neo-Freudian Theory (internal drives, inborn fantasies), AMA medical model, pharmaceutical industry	Social workers, pediatric nurses, pediatricians, teachers.
Motive:	Protect parents. Build labor force, pharmaceutical industry, AMA and day care.	Protect child, AMA, labor force and status quo with compassion.
Premise:	Parents are not cause of child's personality and behavior. No need to explore childhood. Causes are inborn, more final.	Bad things can happen to children but won't create personality or behavior because personality is inborn.
Practice:	Denial/repression ethic. These theorists see poorly and are blind to trauma, causes and clues, not believing in identifying original cause. Fear of feelings. Medicate symptoms and/or pray.	Rescue, protect and punish abuse, but don't blame parents for child's behavior, especially adult child's behavior.
Manifestation:	Gene Association, Bad/Good Seed Theory, "chip off the ol' block." Luck of the draw. Astrology. Baptism. God's will. Reincarnation.	"Poor thing."
Ramifications:	Bad parenting goes unnoticed, causes of pathology unseen, including effects of premature separation. Unhealthy society.	Cause of pathology not identified. No boats rocked. Blaming the victim or his genes.
	Nurture-Based, Pro-Parent	**♦ Nurture-Based, Pro-Child ♦**
Philosophers/ Believers:	Behavioral Theory, Cognitive Theory, Zen Buddhism	Freud's Seduction Theory, Reichian Breathwork, Attachment & Trauma Theory, Systems Theory, Object Relations Theory, Self Psychology, Psychogeneology or Psychohistory, ♦ CAUSAL THEORY ♦
Motive:	Don't blame parents or genes, but propose discipline and conditioning techniques and cognitive behavioral treatments.	Prevent unnecessary suffering. Identify real causes. Teach parents how to raise amazing children. Recognize how healing works & ways of deep healing. Protect society from criminals & mentally ill.
Premise:	No bad seed. Can't see into the "black box" of someone's unconscious. Can act only to reinforce good and punish bad acts. Behaviors are learned.	Quality of attachment determines personality. Bad behaviors driven by trauma.
Practice:	REPRESSION ETHIC. Work on the here and now, Avoid childhood. No point making parents feel bad. Practice positive thinking and affirmations.	EXPRESSION ETHIC. Revisit causes to treat destructive drives. Observe and express feelings. Release (with empathy) heals and creates insight. Learn new coping skills.
Manifestation:	"Spare the rod, spoil the child."	"There, but for the Grace of God, go I."
Ramifications:	Superficial treatments, some of which can occasionally work.	Clearer seeing. Healthier society.

About My Bias: First the Child

To place the responsibility on the child to honor parents without requiring their mutual honor and protection is an old bias against children. It is so old and pervasive that we find it hard to separate it out of our assumptions. We grant parental immunity for something we would punish in another, but defend in our parents. This leaves us free on an unconscious level to continue the legacy of treating our children, without guilt, the way we were treated. We think someday our grown children will "understand" so they can enjoy the same privileges. It's sort of like hazing in a fraternity: because it was done to us we get to do it to our children. This can continue through generations for millennia until someone self-reflects and raises a healthy child or two. In carrying on this legacy of thoughtlessness, neglect and abuse, not only do we harm our children psychologically, we set a low bar for what they are to become. We "dumb them down," then look at what's left and call it personality by genetic design. Instead of taking this approach, I look to see what could have been and seek to make it right.

I believe the highest functioning people among us are the grown Miracle Children who were raised correctly from birth and the Transcendent Children who have healed and self-corrected. Our most conscious and nurturing parents are the ones who parent our Miracle Children, raised according to their design, not against it. The Miracle Child is more enchanted and less encumbered than the Transcendent Child, who has to do the work to unlearn and relearn. However, for those parents who regret learning this theory too late to raise a Miracle Child, if you invest in healing your child, especially dropping all defenses, you can have a Transcendent Child who may be even wiser than the Miracle Child. Often our highest functioning citizens are the Transcendent Children who once suffered but did the work to self-correct. When one does the work to self-reflect and break the spell defining what to see and believe, they achieve an additional perspective or a second world-view. These are people who used to see through their parents' eyes, but have come to see through their own eyes and experience significant enlightenment. This enlightenment experience renders them even wiser than the Miracle Child because the Miracle Child never had to unlearn and relearn to live a functional and problem-solving life.

What If I Am Wrong?

A fairly popular question that some religious followers pose to non-believers is, "What if you are wrong?" usually followed by the suggestion to get saved, just in case. It's actually a logical question worth pondering. So I ask my skeptics now: What if you are wrong?

Will you suspend your disbelief until you have finished this book? Can my readers suspend their beliefs in genes as the origin of personality, their defensiveness for parents or their positive-thinking ethic long enough to finish this book?

What if others would suffer for my wrong choices or if more harm than good results from my choices? When it comes to parenting, the consequences to our children and to others may ripple through future generations. Couldn't we measure all our choices by their possible ramifications?

I want to leave the world a better place and I would hate to be wrong about such things that matter. I would hate to have lived in the South before the Civil War and thoughtlessly adopted a belief that some human beings are inferior, causing my heirs to remember me for my ignorance and racism. Likewise I would hate to have been a Nazi who persecuted Jews, leaving a legacy of shame and dishonor. I'd hate to have been someone in the Inquisition who ignorantly burned witches solely because that was how people thought at that time. I would hate, now, to oppose gay marriage or do anything that diminishes the "aliveness of another" (*Yoshin* Roshi) because I couldn't see my way out of my own conditioning and bias. I would hate to project onto *anyone* that they are less worthy than they are. I would hate to die on the wrong side of history.

If I think global warming is a hoax and I am wrong, the consequences for living thoughtlessly are dire and they implicate me. Likewise, if I believe that genes cause behavior and thus see my children's traits and choices as inborn, I will most probably injure them, regardless of whether I love them. How long will each one of us hold out in the face of evidence? If my religious belief or disbelief is wrong and I have to spend eternity in Hell, at least it doesn't hurt anyone else but me.

The way to ensure our choices are right is to live morally and consider others. If I can't find any reason for believing in God, including the atrocities I see in the name of religion, I can live safely by always being ethical, in case there is, in fact, an ethical God that regards ethical people. Even if we are wrong about varying beliefs, if we live ethically we protect ourselves. Further, in the process we will diminish the impact of beliefs that were formulated and perpetuated to permit unethical choices; such unethical beliefs are designed to give us comfort for our cooperation.

One of my former college students, Nicole Lampson, spoke out to other students about the Causal Theory, "What is the problem? What's the harm in this theory that simply asks us to treat children well? It's all win-win." Will students trade their pro-parent theory for a pro-child theory when the evidence for pro-child theory is thoroughly convincing? Those who hold out will be holding out to protect their parents, not for science.

If I were convinced sufficiently by highly credible scientists that all my other treasured sources were wrong and that genes do cause some or all behaviors, then apparently I would have to change my thinking. Then I would be free to believe it is acceptable to let other people raise our babies and drug our children. I would be free to defend myself if I abused my children or animals and I wouldn't have to self-correct. What a relief that might be!

Would I then tell students and clients that genes, not specific interactions, cause their behaviors? No, I would continue to operate in absolute faith that there is nothing inherently wrong with them and they can grow and improve, if not heal, by doing the work. I never want anyone to believe there is anything intrinsically wrong with them. Likewise, if I believe it is too late to save the planet, do I quit trying? No, I continue to live my best life and I persist in trying to leave the world a better place because it is the right thing to do.

Other Popular Outlooks

The Stern Christian Father. If we "spare the rod," we "spoil the child" is another belief advocating possible abuse, assuming a child is bad until you hurt him or her into behaving. To be fair, even though this Biblical philosophy assumes children are born bad, at least it also acknowledges the role of parenting in the formation of character. Wherever we see Michael Jackson's father interviewed, we can find him defending his right as a dutiful father to give his children their whippings.

The Feminist Mother. Another belief, which can be an impediment to good parenting, is the feminist belief that it is the equal right of women to have careers and that to be sentenced to parenting at home once we have given birth is sexist. Children need a good role model, they say. It is good for children to see their mothers with successful careers. This one breaks my heart. I was a true blue feminist and never realized that this theory took me away from my sisters until feminists drove me off my radio show. So I am forced to say that feminism, as such, is another belief that blinds us to the true needs of our children. This theory asks mothers to make the sacrifice for at least the first three years, ideally the first five. It is all right for the father to take the role of mother, or even a nanny, as long as everyone understands that whoever is raising the child is the mother and the child cannot tolerate abandonment from him or her either. Nannies need to not be fired, not take weekends away from the child or go on vacations separate from the family.

The Pharmaceutical Industry. The special interests of the drug industry are supported by the American Medical Association, the American Psychiatric Association and the American Psychological Association, who write the required theory for therapists-in-training to learn, believe and regurgitate. These customary values of our field are harmful standards for therapists to support. In order to become licensed, we have to know and tow the party line to pass the licensing exam. The drug industry produces the research it needs to supply the uncritical members of our boards of psychology and behavior sciences. They hold press releases for parents to read about claims to have found the gene for any given behavior. Therapists learn what to believe to pass exams and support the propaganda.

In my own review of the studies that claim a genetic link for behavior, I have never found an instance where these studies were successfully replicated after the press conference was over and everyone went home. Drug companies hire scientists to prove on a regular basis that genes cause behavior, no matter what they have to do to prove it. In our desire to believe the genetic explanation, we collude against our children and ultimately our great society, which will soon no longer be great because the quality of children and the adults they become has begun to decline.

The Day Care Industry. Day care is a booming industry that serves industry itself. It has freed up both parents to join the workplace, so wages have been driven down. The day care industry is invested in its perpetuation and parents are invested in believing professionals can do as good a job or better taking care of their children.

Schools and Teachers. Schools need to diagnose students with disabilities to get more money. Rather than identify the specific hole in the child's education and fill it, they diagnose learning disabilities. (See Chapter 4: Stages & Ages of Development.) Teachers prefer the disruptive children to be diagnosed and medicated because they have to get along with the parents and they want a classroom of students they can control.

Reincarnation. Belief in reincarnation was a feudal religion at one time, which served the ruling class by convincing the faithful that if they accepted their lot in life, they would enjoy a higher status in the next life. This was an efficient form of social control as people no longer had to be managed with cumbersome tools like shackles and guards. They lived their one and only life accepting their circumstances in anticipation of the next life, for which no evidence existed, believing they would be rewarded for such good subservient behavior.

Some people who believe in reincarnation believe that the baby's soul from the previous life picks his parents so he can work through his issues from that previous life. That puts full responsibility on the baby and growing child for having picked the parents, no matter how they treat him, since he "knew" how they would treat him. Maybe it helps the child not take the injuries of his parent so personally.

Reincarnation was an archaic ideology, but it did accurately teach us that how we act comes back to us. In more contemporary theory, we understand that natural consequences come to us in this lifetime.

This more accurate notion of karma is valuable: the results of your actions come back to you, since with every action, there is an equal and opposite reaction.

At PaRC we believe reincarnation functions as a pro-parent philosophy (explained in depth at the end of Chapter 1: Creating a Personality).

Astrology. Many students who never understood science or history seem to be attracted to astrology in order to understand causation. One premise of astrology is that personality results from the alignment of the stars. When someone asks your sign they have no idea what you're about. Their ability to witness traits in people has been replaced by an ideology that blinds them to cause and effect.

Positive Thinking. Positive thinking has its place, but it can be harmful to the healing process. It is excellent for people who have not had healthy coaching in their childhood, but who otherwise do not carry excessive buried pain. For those of us who have honored our parents to the exclusion of a healthy self, we cannot think positively over buried trauma. It is not a shortcut for healing. In order to heal, we need to manifest our own courage and character to go into the injury, acknowledge it and let the feelings out. To do so is to address the core self and to change or normalize the body's chemistry. Following a cathartic healing, there will be epiphanies that are far more valuable than positive thinking exercises. With epiphanies come clarity. With clarity, we become enchanted with what is. Positive thinking is a cheap second to enlightenment, insight and clarity. We are far more genuinely positive when it comes from healing old injuries so that we may finally discover what is, in the present.

Meditation, Here & Now. Meditation is rather a non-philosophical philosophy. It is a technique that enables us to cut through our programs, assumptions, fears, expectations and other projections we employ over reality, blinding us to what is. By focusing on our breath or by counting, we can develop a sense of awareness of our own program that will enable us to gradually replace projections with perception. This chapter has been dedicated to contemporary philosophies, which instruct us in what to see.

I am in love with Now and What Is. What keeps us from being in the moment is our internal dialogue. The more we become aware of our ongoing internal dialogue, the healthier we get. From there, we want to discover the content of this internal dialogue because it's on a loop replaying itself and tripping us up while we miss out on what's really happening.

We can meditate to witness our thoughts with an eye for what beliefs place a screen between reality and us, usually taking form as assumption. Often we see reality through a veil by comparing ourselves, whether judging or feeling judged. Some of us see with an eye for threats, rejection or impediments. Still others are tinted with impatience or chronically disappointed by expectation. We all have a different take on what is and most of us are wrong a fair amount of the time.

Perhaps we suffered things in our early life that we had to deny, or we simply learned to believe things that weren't true, whether about the world, others or ourselves. Maybe we have been guided by these wrong beliefs and thoughts. The way out is to consciously unravel the delusions to see clearly. We have to be willing to see that we have been lying to ourselves, if not working against ourselves.

Paranoids see differently than narcissists, and borderlines see differently than dependent personalities. We can create self-fulfilling prophecies, collecting evidence for our theory, when we take what we see to the bank. Even so, there is so much we don't see that Is.

When we see ourselves driven by misinformation from the past, we can follow the invisible thread of our projection back in time to the original truth and then feel and express old emotions out of our body. Learning how to be present can never be to the exclusion of a buried past. I don't think we get to realistically enjoy the miracle of reality until we address the unfinished misinformation, injuries or injustices of our childhood.

We can only process so much at one time, so after our body exhausts from crying or raging or simply seeing, we can return to the rest of our day and tune in to the present possibly better than ever. Later, we return again to look at more.

We can practice being in the present with curiosity, paying attention and listening. What fascinates me is that most of the great sages who have managed to clear away the cobwebs report having seen the same thing. That's why there are so many Zen sayings for the Zen Calendar, many of which were not said by Zen Buddhists. They show up everywhere, brilliantly reporting on the same material that's out there and in here. The claims about What Is that don't match up need to be eliminated. For example, nearly every sage throughout time encourages us to be humble because ego or identity is an illusion. Beware of an arrogant "sage." The great ones point out that we are all the same in the final analysis. They report on the interconnectedness and interrelatedness of things. These are insights we get to have once we work through our competitive illusions.

Good books help. *The Passionate Mind* by Joel Kramer and *Zen Flesh, Zen Bones* edited by Paul Reps gave me keys to replace projections and expectations with perception and acceptance. They are rather perfect philosophies that free us to be present.

Meditation is an excellent tool for becoming self-aware. It is similar to prayer, absent beliefs. The goal of meditation is to be able to see the world and ourselves without beliefs coloring what we see. To be able to purely see What Is is as good as it gets.

Most instructors of meditation teach us to chant, count breath, focus on breathing or do something to keep ourselves from thinking so we get the message we should try to stop thinking. These techniques are tried and true.

Many of my students have told me that they have difficulty with meditation, revealing that they think they are supposed to be learning how to sit without thought and "just can't do it."

I tell my frustrated students to sit in a lotus position if they can or with their legs simply crossed facing the wall staring at a spot, or they can simply sit on a chair, even an easy chair, or lie down if they don't think they will fall asleep.

It is not my goal to be without thought, *per se*. Yet it is my goal to see clearly without thoughts and beliefs in the way. To see clearly I want to become aware of my thoughts, see how they are not "me" and how they are misleading. Some, or perhaps most, of my thoughts are not even correct. Some of them are automatic and reflexive. Some of them are old and primitive. Some are defensive. Some are based on seeing myself as separate from others. Some are based on concern for how I am being perceived to the degree that others give me identity. The question is, who (about myself) am I? Who am I defending? Why am I defending? What do I believe about myself that I have all this mental armor?

For me, stopping myself from thinking (as if I could) would sort of skip a step. As I said, I see my meditation with a dual approach and a dual purpose. First, I want to self-observe, so I can see my own compulsive thinking, assumptions and what is driving my reflexive choices. Self-observation leads to exposing these primitive voices that form projections or screens over reality and objective truth. So at times when I am sitting, I pay attention to my thoughts using my third eye.

With self-observation we can use our

third eye or mind's eye to observe ourselves thinking and see how we separate ourselves from others. To think of ourselves as separate from others is an illusion. We can dismantle our projections and automatic thoughts one reflexive board at a time.

Second, I begin meditation with a view of the result, where there is no greater clarity than to see without thought. I know what it is like to sit in a room, aware of the room, without thought. You do too. It's like being tuned in to anything, whether television, your lover's eyes or your baby's laughter or that cute thing your dog just did before you decided to put it into words. The difference is that becoming aware of the room may not seem at first like a wonderful thing or anywhere near as entertaining. You might even think it's boring, which is another way we dumb ourselves down. But see if you can put your awareness on the room with all its majesty in the miracle of being alive, here and now, perhaps as if it is the last thing you will ever see. Maybe you can hold this moment for one second.

So when I meditate, I sit quietly. I choose a neutral, meaningless spot upon which to place my gaze, while actually taking in the entire room. I like to see if I can hold the entire room in my awareness for even a single second while simultaneously being aware of myself as part of the room.

I accept that my internal dialogue will be rushing in any second now. I intend to watch and observe my thoughts as they arrive in the next second or the one after that.

Along the way, I observe my thoughts enough that they are thinning out a bit, so it gets easier to take in the room again with me in it.

Let's take in the room again. Now hold it. Oops, I see myself thinking, "Hold it." And so it goes. I am interested in what thought actually rushes in. Usually it is a commentary on how long it/I lasted or how well I did or didn't do. I then give up judgment and return to the spot. I will seek to pay attention from an alive awareness of myself in the room again between my interrupting thoughts. Seeing what thoughts come between pure perception and me is important information to me.

I go back to sitting and allowing myself to think whatever comes into my head so I can see what wants to run my show. After I observe my intrusive thoughts for another while, I actually give myself permission to consider something, like a problem or a koan.

After awhile, I try the room again. I go back to see if I can have another second or two or three of being one with the spot and all that surrounds and forms me, without ambition. I notice that it is easier toward the end of sitting than at the beginning.

The more I do this work, things become less personal and I make choices that are more effective. My own state of mind becomes calmer and I can actually feel wonderfully present and maybe even competent. I feel at the top of my game when I am more responsive than contemplative.

New ways of understanding come to me. I discover that I can take this neutral awareness and connectedness into my day. When my ego takes precedence, I lose my sense of connectedness, becoming "important" again, separate and in a state of opposition. I can wake myself up, see what I am doing and return to myself in my day, like returning to the spot. I think the fastest way back is to find my humility. Thus I have a third goal for meditation, my ultimate goal, which is to live my day as if I were meditating, seeing and connecting from a humble place.

When I can do this, the projections and judgments seem to lift away from my view of things so I can see more clearly What Is. Having discovered that we cannot perceive while we are thinking, I have learned that the more accurately we perceive, the wiser we are. The more defensive we feel and think, the crazier we are.

In this way, I can go through my day in this natural interest and curiosity about What Is. It is that state of mind I seek of self-awareness and interrelatedness with everything. It's like meditating all day.

Of course it comes and goes, but my reason for sitting is so that when I am walking and meeting others, I see clearly. When I see clearly, I respond wisely. We all do. We don't have to think of what to say like we did in the past. Now we just respond when we have something to say. My favorite meditation is doing the day itself. Having discovered that my ego and identity are completely irrelevant, I get to enjoy my very unique vantage point on the universe and for a very brief time, even a few seconds, I can become the eyes and ears of God to see what I have made today.

Confronting Standards of Enlightenment

I am disturbed that recognized enlightened people, including the Dalai Lama, don't seem to get the primacy of childhood. Ken Wilbur with his Integrative Theory and Clare W. Graves and Don Beck, the two founders of Spiral Dynamics, all overlook parenting as the primary cause of personality and awareness, or lack thereof. Even our most enlightened leaders seem to have a blind spot around children. They mostly assume normal parenting. There is just so little mention of childhood that it's as if we all were somewhat parented the same: fairly well.

In Zen we learn to get on with forgiving our parents. My own community at the Santa Monica Zen Center seemed prone, as a possible result, to granting parental immunity to all parents everywhere, as if unaware that bad parenting leaves its legacy in the minds and behaviors of the grown children, especially criminals and the mentally ill. My roshi at the Santa Monica Zen Center facilitated work on childhood issues, something not done in any other religion known to me. But then it's sort of supposed to be over. Zen students by all rights should not have much baggage compared to most religions, so letting it go is an excellent idea and possibility. Unfortunately, I think they may not know that what is good or true for them is not true for everyone. On the other hand, not just anyone in therapy can take the Santa Monica Zen Training, Erhard Seminar Training (EST) or The Landmark Forum; they must have permission from their therapist.

Still, when I listen to leaders and followers of the "get over it" theory, they seem to be in denial. I don't hear the acknowledgement or the enlightened awareness that who children become is a direct product of their parenting, that there really is bad parenting out there, all around us, and that matters. I am not trying to turn the pursuit of enlightenment into a parenting theory. I am saying that some supposedly enlightened people say the damnedest, most ignorant things. Of course, often times this is for effect to teach, but it seems there is still a hole in enlightenment.

Finally, I am concerned that the Zen Buddhists I have met do not understand that the mentally ill and the most violent criminals that we may love to hate have been so neglected or traumatized that their brains have been dramatically affected, often shrunken. Healing can take place to greater or lesser degrees, but it will require remembering and seeing ourselves once innocent at the hands of perpetrating parents. It will require more than fifty times the nurturing interaction and compassion to reverse childhood trauma than if we did it right in the first place. The most violent and insane among us are too damaged and too far gone to heal. But it sure would be nice if we held in our discussions about them an awareness that they suffered more than we will ever know at the most tender ages. Had we been there, we would have rushed in to protect them. Zen Buddhists understand these people are not qualified to do the work, but I think it behooves us not to brush them off thoughtlessly or arrogantly, as if we can't see that horrible things happened to them, still live in their minds and they don't know how to transcend. They are the most injured among us. I believe if my roshi did a survey of his students, he would find that most of them are not aware that criminals and the insane are the victims of the worst abuse. If they know it, I still say they know it intellectually, not operationally. I have heard too much intolerance.

I don't think Zen students generally make it a priority to hold parents as accountable as they do the criminals that parents create. I don't think they are as clear about this cause and effect as they are about all the labors from where their food comes. I get that students learn to think that no matter how bad the parenting, people can work it out if they want to. It's sort of a "let-them-eat-cake" attitude, wherein Marie Antoinette offered a thoughtless solution to hunger without understanding the problem. Likewise, it appears Zen students offer little consideration to understanding the origins of severe pathology. While Zen Buddhists may be the cream of consciousness and self-awareness, I ask that they be conscious and compassionate where it counts, for abused and neglected children.

The Causal Theory

Until now, no text has been available to offer a comprehensive developmental theory of psychology. When I decided to develop and write the Snyder Causal Theory and Treatment, aka SCTT, I did so in major frustration with the pieces of theories that were available. These theories were often incomplete and, in my opinion, incorrect to varying degrees, and it seemed that there was a great deal of contradiction between the mini-theories. Recently, researchers have begun to investigate which theories stand up under scrutiny, but scientists are not properly evaluating some theories. Behavioral practice is easier to study and insight oriented theories are more difficult to measure and assess, so biases are being formed around the superiority and efficiency of behavioral theories in this field, especially since funding sources seek to steer us in the direction of the medical model, quick fixes and pharmaceuticals.

Mini-theories offer different observations and approaches for different problems, yet it seems researchers do not hold the big picture. They fail to take into account what is known about overlapping areas. Many theories appear to have huge holes in them. There was no complete theory explaining behaviors or how to raise a healthy, resilient child who could flourish like a miracle. For some time I didn't understand why obvious issues were not addressed. I finally compiled the best concepts from the available theories and filled in the missing pieces myself because I had no need to see anything as I wished it to be. Rather, I wished to see what actually was and how it worked. I wrote this theory to fill a void.

I spoke with a psychologist who said, "The amazing thing about your theory is that you deal with ethics." I appreciated her insight and it's true. It appears to me that there is no mental health without ethics. Show me a case of suffering and I will show you bad ethics, and if you change the ethics, you get mental health.

- The Causal Theory is groundbreaking first because it holds an overview. It is a comprehensive theory of developmental psychology.
- This theory also accounts for personality without the genetic assumption. It explains human development, temperament, predispositions, mood disorders, insanity, character, behavior and traits without the genetic assumption.
- This theory places Attachment Theory at the very heart of psychology.

- This theory places responsibility for character squarely on the parent and has techniques for enfolding parents who were once children too, as we correct them.
- This theory includes a theory of resilience.
- This theory confronts other theories that fail to address root causes. It takes on mini-theories, including cognitive behavioral theories or cognitive restructuring initiatives, which often fail to address root causes and don't go any deeper than challenging wrong thoughts. These theories, like positive thinking ethics, create their own barriers to self-awareness.
- This theory teaches diagnosis to parents with the intention of prevention, correction and understanding. It proposes how each personality disorder is created so they know what not to do. It is also a tool for them to reconsider assumptions about their own childhoods, facilitating their own inventory of their own past and how they are affected now. By teaching parents how to create symptoms, it teaches parents how to read behavior and to recognize that symptoms are clues to one's past. When one understands what's behind behavior, reversals are deeper and more efficient. Further, insight into the behavior of others enables us to receive others' behaviors with more compassion rather than taking them personally.
- This theory uses our children's behavior as a feedback system. It prepares parents to self-reflect in the mirror of their children's behaviors, using the child's actions as a feedback system. It makes sense of their seemingly irrational actions.
- This theory identifies trauma, including its impact on behavior in almost all its forms and offers a profound yet natural technique for healing trauma.
- This theory requires students who want to heal or achieve wisdom or greatness to first find humility, honesty and the capacity to surrender. It identifies the necessary traits for healing to take place. The Causal Theory teaches students how healing works and how to self-observe. It teaches parents how to see and heal their children and therapists how to see and heal their clients.
- This theory deals with people's faulty cognitions, but from a Zen perspective, and assumes the Original Self is divine. It addresses the notion of identity and self-esteem building as a potential waste of time because humility is key; we are already divine and only need to tease out our separateness, the negative messages and ego.
- This theory accounts for drives and the uniqueness of personality through imprinting, something barely recognized in the field. It recognizes the chain reaction of imprinting from generation to generation, a non-genetic explanation for behavior and personality.
- This theory teaches parents a special technique on raising their children for greatness if all the other developmental needs have been properly met, especially attachment needs. PaRC Foundation encourages parents to Faith Parent, relieving their children of worrisome projections born of their parents' own childhoods.
- This theory teaches how to discipline with natural consequences and what to discipline, with personal values being the most important concern. The Causal Theory sets a high bar for ethics and asserts that there is no mental health without ethics. This theory takes a practical look at the reality of evil and its ingredients.
- This theory doesn't see most students as fragile like the rest of the mental health field does. It assumes students can take feedback and correction directly. This theory acknowledges that children took a lot when they were most fragile and survived. Correction cannot be *that*

threatening when handled correctly. However, corrective feedback requires a respectful presentation. The technique is often direct yet soft because we are to some extent re-parenting our students. When parents give wrong information or model poorly for their children, then who is going to correct the grown adults? Other times we are soft and we certainly give more strokes than corrective feedback. One reason for this book and the taped lectures is that parents can learn without being singled out. This is not to say that we don't recognize defenses and resistance, but we do understand what they are about. Protecting and building ego is a waste of time in this theory, as the true self is plenty good enough and humility is one of the highest virtues, not to be confused with shame or low self-worth. On the other hand, devaluing self-concepts must be addressed as lies that we internalized.

- This theory tends to create a community of like-thinking, mutually supportive, mutually reinforcing students that has come to be called PaRC or The PaRC Community.
- While we offer confidentiality, we encourage expressiveness and openness as a measure of mental health. Causal Therapists seek to be transparent (although too much openness is seen as boundary confusion). Our students understand each other in classes and groups because they talk somewhat freely about their issues. This creates intimacy and reinforces the feeling that we are all in this adventure of life together. When self-disclosure is problematic for a client, we help them design appropriate discrete responses, so they become otherwise more able to drop their walls.
- This theory teaches relationship skills and ethics so students may learn what healthy people know. This theory looks at relationship skills and ethics as the antithesis of the dysfunctional coping skills of personality disorders. When students learn the new skills, the disorders tend to fall away, especially when they are also processing trauma in private sessions. That's why we start these interactive groups as young as possible, beginning with Infant Group.
- This theory deals with personal responsibility and assessment while teaching not to judge or blame.

> **All babies are born G∞d.
> There are no bad seeds.**

Overview of this Book

This Chapter 1 is now about to explore the primary ingredients in the formation of a personality. Some of these staples will have their own chapters, but some will be specifically detailed in this chapter, to include the elements of family systems and resilience. From here forward, I will detail the ingredients of the Causal Theory of Developmental Psychology.

Chapter 2: Preventive Diagnosis is designed to throw evidence at you, attempting to convince you that this theory works and is predictive. It teaches you how to create every possible personality disorder by parenting. Now all you have to do is look at your own life and the lives of others to see the cause and effect of the Causal Theory. Your evidence will become personal. You will see the truth of Preventive Diagnosis; the proof is all around you.

Chapter 3: Healing is about the way of transcendence and it is placed strategically for relief, teaching you how to heal whatever parenting creates. It clarifies the ways that trauma manifests into behaviors. This chapter helps you understand how healing works and that the process can be implemented at any time, even for old wounds. It teaches you how we developed techniques for keeping our trauma buried and how this backfires on us every day until we deal with it. In this chapter, parents also learn how to heal their own children, ideally with the assistance of a therapist coach.

Chapter 4: Stages & Ages of Development gets down to basics and explains the developmental milestones of childhood in the unfolding and growing human mind and body and what the biology of a child requires from parents to obtain maximum expression. Funny, it's not that hard to meet these needs and when you do what you're supposed to do, it becomes the most fun you've ever had.

Chapter 5: Imprinting describes the ways we internalize and re-enact how we have been treated. While the body unfolds the same way for every infant and child ever born, it also has a different mechanism for uniqueness. The brain-body has a special drive to internalize the events of our lives. This internalizing process stores experiences in the brain in exquisite detail. We learn how the tiniest events shape our uniqueness. When these unique events are harmful, however, we may become harmful to others. A technique for transcending negative imprints is offered.

Chapter 6: Faith Parenting is about how to raise a Miracle Child. It's for parents who have a securely attached child as clarified in Chapter 4. This is for parents and children who are ready to go for greatness. To faith parent a child who is insecurely attached needs to be done judiciously, if at all.

Chapter 7: Discipline is the long-awaited chapter on how to respond to bad or self-defeating behavior. I have refused to teach discipline until I know that parents understand how to read behavior and take responsibility for what they are disciplining. Once parents understand that their child's behavior is the parents' own guidance system telling parents how they are doing, they can "smash the mirror" and correct the behavior. This is a chapter on disciplining with natural consequences or assisted cause and effect.

Finally, Chapter 8: Relationship Skills is written to explain our rights and responsibilities in relationships because how we treat our mates and others will show up on the playground. Children who have good social and relationship skills can become pioneers and charismatic leaders.

Family Systems

A Healthy Family System

There is no judgment in healthy families. There may be assessment and feedback, but no one is treated as if any trait is permanent. No one is rejected, per se. Instead, problem-solving takes place to facilitate or even force growth. There is faith in one another's abilities to learn and grow, with minimal controlling and domineering parenting, thereby allowing learning through natural consequences. Parents model problem-solving, personal responsibility, moral choices, family values, and standards (Peck, 1978). Parents become consultants for the most part. The child is taught from the beginning a vocabulary to express his or her own feelings, needs, and experiences. The child learns that it is okay to say and use words to define and express feelings. (Siegel, 1999)

Build a Repertoire for Self-Expression:
- Hungry?... Nurse?... Baby wants to nurse?... Mommy's baby wants to nurse?
- Bottle?... Bottle of milk... Bottle empty.

- All gone?... Juice all gone... Jesse's bottle of juice is empty.
- Sad?... Are you Sad?
- Angry?... Angry... I see you feel angry.
- Hurt?... Mommy's baby feels hurt... Mommy's baby looks hurt.
- Boo-boo... Ohhh. Did you hurt yourself?
- It's okay... You're okay.
- Ball.... Ball up... Ball away.
- I feel hurt (*vs.* I am hurt.) I feel mad. I feel sad. I feel scared. I feel angry when you... I don't like... I hate you. I love you. I resent... It bothers me when...

Unhealthy Family Systems

Alternatively, where we find a dysfunctional child, an unhealthy family system will most likely be found. There are different types, the most common of which are:

Pseudo Mutuality (*vs.* Pseudo Hostility). Qualities: pseudo (fake) mutuality is a good show with no depth, and may even be fraudulent, whereas pseudo hostility, which looks like pretend fighting or bantering, may in fact be a loving, playful relationship. Examples:
- evil family: the Menendez family father Jose said, "I've always thought it far better, Roger, to be feared than loved." (from Roger R. Smith, Jose's business associate and witness at the Menendez trial, *Court TV*, October 30, 1993)
- fake/hypocritical: attending PTA or church to support the image of being a 'good Christian' or 'good parent'. These parents can be pillars of the community and a danger to their children (Peck, 1983)
- pretending intimacy and health: looking good for outsiders, but behind closed doors there may be alcoholism, addiction, violence, rage, abuse, etc.
- lack of empathy: treating the child as a possession who must obey at all costs

- parents as priority: parents who leave young children while they vacation, parents who return to work because they're bored or need more things (they value material acquisitions and lifestyle above the child's need for a primary caregiver)

Disengaged Family System with no family boundary (Minuchin, 1974). Qualities: No one cares. No cohesiveness, no communication, no honesty, no sharing, no one knows anyone else because they don't talk about feelings or what is really happening, indifference, superficial relationships, family loyalty. Secrecy may be required despite disengagement and explosions *i.e.,* the rampage at Columbine High School.

Enmeshed Family System is too close (Minuchin, 1974). Qualities: parent has suffocating relationships with children and lives vicariously through children or is overly intrusive); children encouraged to spy and tell on one another; family members judge, blame, and gossip; implosions, such as suicide, self-destruction and insanity. Adult child still seeks parents' permission and approval.

Closed Family System. Qualities: major secrecy ethic, often hiding one or more major family secrets like incest, alcoholism, *etc.*, not open to new information, would be highly resistant to a parenting class or therapy

Family Projection Process (Bowen, 1988). Qualities: parents project different identities or roles onto each child; therefore, each child has "different parents" and each child forms a "different personality." Examples: hero, scapegoat (black sheep or bad child), clown, lost/invisible child (withdrawn), star/performer, helper/good child (people pleaser)

Addict/Enabler System. Examples: Addict/Enabler, Obsessive/Co-dependent, Incompetent/Nag, Infidel/Missionary (AA Model)

Family Secrets (deadly repression). Examples: incest, physical abuse, alcoholism, homosexuality, infidelity, adoption, parental identity secrets

> If ethics are the issue, side with ethics, not people. If ethics are not the issue, when asked to which family you should be loyal, you must pick your mate and children over your parents. Likewise, pick your children over your mate.

The Four Parental Sins

Abuse. As serious and harmful as it is, abuse is often the least damaging of the parental sins, depending on what kind of abuse, how often it occurred, the length of time suffered, and the child's ability to cry or express feelings. The point is not that abuse is tolerable for children. It is not. They suffer injuries to their bodies and souls. The point is to tell you that where there is physical abuse, there are almost always also other types of abuse that bring injury to the personality for a lifetime.

Types of abuse:
- physical
- sexual
- verbal (name calling, belittling, yelling)
- emotional – (ridiculing emotions of child, shaming, raging, sarcasm)
- mixed messages ("mind-fucking")
- religious (often found in the most severely damaged: serial killers, schizophrenics, dissociative identities (multiple personalities), *i.e.,* God will get you, you're going to hell, God sees how evil you are, get down on your knees and pray that God will forgive you for seducing me.)

Neglect.
- failure to bond or maintain a bond in first year
- physical neglect (parent does not provide adequate food, shelter, clothing, cleanliness)
- emotional neglect (parent has little interaction with child)

Abandonment. Attachment trauma, separation trauma and abandonment cut to the core. These injuries are the deepest and the hardest to heal. The younger the child the deeper the injury. Types of abandonment:
- permanent (*e.g.,* death, relinquishment of child)
- short-term, but chronic (*e.g.,* both parents work, leave child in day care). Tends to result in a diagnosis of ADHD
- once, but for too long (*e.g.,* hospitalization or vacation during first year). Tends to result in withdrawal, clinginess, or Reactive Attachment Disorder (RAD)
- chronic disregard (*e.g.,* ignores child for adult interests, leaves child with babysitters, lets kids fend for themselves)
- rejection (*e.g.,* I never wanted you. You look just like your father/mother.)

Repression. None of the aforementioned injuries can be repaired if there is continued repression. Trauma must be expressed to heal (further explored in Chapter 3: Healing). Buried trauma festers but creates telltale symptoms. The worst part about sexual abuse is that the child cannot tell anyone. The worst part about any family dysfunction is denial. Examples of repressive statements:
- Ssshhhh, don't cry.
- Eat this, it'll make you feel better.
- I will wash your mouth out with soap.
- I can't handle it when you cry.
- Cheer up; look at the bright side.
- I don't know how you could feel that way because I love you.
- If you don't stop crying, I'll really give you something to cry about.
- What did I do to deserve this?

- Don't you dare talk back to me.
- What the hell is wrong with you?
- That's a stupid thing to cry about.
- Big boys (or girls) don't cry.
- You're ugly when you cry.
- Don't you dare tell anyone, or I won't love you anymore.

- If you tell anyone, I'll kill you.
- If you tell anyone, your mother will die.
- I don't believe you.
- How could you say something like that?
- You're lying.
- I better not hear that you uttered a word about this to anyone.

Development of Self in Two Stages

There are two stages that form a personality. One involves two primary developmental stages, attachment and separation, and the qualitative way we pass through them (.4: Stages & Ages of Development.) The other is imprinting: the unique impact on our personality that each of us internalizes from our individual experiences with our parents and family. (See Chapter 5: Imprinting.) Put another way, a person's 'self' develops in two life stages: The First Year is where attachment and bonding are established, which create the core of a personality. The Second-Year-On is where freedom and discipline are balanced, building the structure of a personality. Needless to say, the first stage folds into the second stage with an overlap that lasts into the fourth or fifth year or even a lifetime if early needs are not met.

Stage I of Bonding and Attachment: The Core Self

For healthy development, from day one and throughout the first year and on, the baby needs to see in the mirror of the parent's eyes that he/she is loved, adored, cared for with empathy and enjoyed. From mirroring comes her sense of identity. From one continuous caregiver, he/she develops a sense of trust and a sense of security.

Healthy parent messages give her more identity and include: I love you. I see you. I hear you. You are special. I'll take care of you. I'll protect you. You amaze me. You can trust me. I believe in you.

	Cause and Effect: First Year	
	If the baby gets this in the first year...	**...this is what he'll have in his core.**
Healthy	bonding, attachment, symbiosis, oneness, warmth, empathy, mirroring, parents who see and adore their baby	self worth, positive identity, fullness, wholeness and the abilities to merge, trust and be intimate
Unhealthy	lack of bonding, inconsistent attachments, parental detachment, emotional neglect, deprivation, lack of nurturing, emptiness, coldness	emotional starvation, feeling of deprivation, feeling of being cheated, lack of trust, lack of identity, difficulty with intimacy, insecurity, desperate behavior, feelings of emptiness, overeating, substance abuse, worthlessness

Stage II of Separation & Discipline: The Personality

For healthy development, from the second year forward, the child needs to separate, individuate and be free to explore, discover, make mistakes, learn, have feelings and feel safe. The child needs to learn self-discipline and have strong, protective parents who can see him/her. She needs to have a few limits that are enforced with zero or one warning because, almost always, the child already knows and nature does not warn. She needs clear boundaries. From her parents' messages, the child learns more about herself and choices.

Healthy parent messages include: You can talk to me about how you feel. I believe in you. I will always be there for you. (Don't say this to a child you're putting in day care. Don't say it unless you mean it.) I love you, but you may not hurt other people. I see you are angry, so let's try to figure this out. I love you for who you are, but not always for what you do. When I tell you no, it is to protect and take care of you. I will not tolerate bad or mean-spirited behavior. Do the right thing, even when it is the more difficult option.

	Cause and Effect: Second Year On	
	If the child gets this from the second year on...	**...this is what his personality will include.**
Healthy	separation and individuation with a sense of safety, freedom within limits, respect, autonomy, communication	initiative, cohesiveness, innovation, pioneering, calculated risk-taking, leadership, ability to problem-solve
Unhealthy	forced dependence or independence, shame, neglect, authoritarianism, required blind obedience, guilt-tripping, physical or sexual abuse, domineering parenting	defiance, anxiety, compulsivity, reactivity, irrationality, abusiveness, fragmentation, false self, absent-mindedness, scapegoating, conforming, people-pleasing

When we are little and out of power, we imprint the unique forces and styles our parents employ into our individual personalities. Later, we treat people weaker than us the way we were treated as children. What goes in must come out. Abused children grow to abuse. Nurtured children grow to nurture. What does not go in cannot come out. Neglected children grow to neglect. Un-empowered children don't empower others.

The most impactful imprints we experience are in the Second Stage of Development, the Stage of Individuation. In this stage our parents attempt to modify our behavior many ways as we try out the world, mostly with discipline. We continue imprinting, but the imprints are much more global and personality-forming when it comes to discipline. I have dedicated whole chapters to Imprinting and Discipline. The harshest and most devastating of all imprints is trauma.

Trauma

When trauma takes place young enough or is severe enough, the child learns to dissociate from the traumatic occurrence while it is taking place and may even be able to leave it out of awareness in order to go on with his life. The more trauma the child experienced, the more the child lives in a sort of out of body state or can quickly de-realize or de-personalize when feeling threatened. It's like going into shock. The young child may have a habit of bumping into things. He may seem to live in a bubble, sort of chronically dissociated. He may not be in touch with his feelings. His eyes may look very big on his face, somewhat similar to the eyes of Charles Manson, who shows symptoms of major shock and de-realization.

Sometimes these symptoms develop in an infant who has suffered a major attachment break. When babies feel abandoned, they may resort to head banging in order to survive their unbearable suffering. Sometimes the symptoms develop in a child who is physically abused. Since our personalities are pretty well established by age five and our brains are fairly well organized by age ten, the earlier we address childhood trauma, the easier it is to treat. Attachment trauma has the most pervasive and long-term effects of any trauma. The younger the child, the more successful the therapy will be with less effort (Perry, 1997).

According to major trauma researcher and clinician Bessel van der Kolk, soldiers and other adults who suffer from Post Traumatic Stress Disorder usually had it when they were young, which makes them more fragile and susceptible as adults. The more PTSD a child suffered in childhood, the more fragile the soldier. Soldiers with secure childhood attachments are less prone to PTSD even though their wartime traumas may be equal or even worse than the next soldier (1996). According to Colin Ross, who introduced the Trauma Model, all pathology stems from trauma (1995). Donald Dutton (1998) tells us how these are the seeds of the abusive personality.

According to researcher Martin Teicher, neglecting an infant creates abnormalities in the cerebellar vermis, which leads to dissociative symptoms including disorders such as bipolar disorder (manic-depressive illness), schizophrenia, autism and ADHD (2002). Even adults cannot handle sensory deprivation, which is what neglect of an infant is, without developing difficulties assessing their physical circumstances or reality. In the 1960s, sensory deprivation tanks produced hallucinations similar to hallucinogenic drugs.

Teicher says exposure to various forms of mistreatment in the earliest years of life do not show changes in the brain when the victim is a child, but by the time the same child is an adult, his limbic system (specifically the hippocampus and the amygdala) may be 8 to 16% smaller than the adult who was not treated badly as a child. The hippocampus is responsible for storage and retrieval of verbal and emotional memories. There seems to be a correlation between a smaller hippocampus and severity of dissociative symptoms and there is evidence that when trauma is stored in these areas of the brain, the brain growth "freezes" or stops developing. The amygdala stores emotional content relating to fear and aggression, and when the subject is threatened in similar ways as an adult, his responses are sudden and either fearful or rageful, depending on the nature of his childhood experiences. According to Joseph LeDoux, "The amygdala never forgets (1998, p. 179)." It is the part of the brain that holds "body memories" and the part of the brain that is accessed in couchwork. (See Chapter 3: Healing.)

When a child experiences abuse at a young age, the brain stores the unexpressed feelings of fear and rage, particularly in the amygdala. No matter how young the child is, the amygdala records the experience at a visceral level so the body remembers. The amygdala stores feelings of fear and rage that can be triggered by objects or events that are reminders. Trauma tends to introduce dissociative symptoms or flashbacks, whether from neglect or abuse. Dissociation seems to be a way of surviving or coping with traumatic events, while flashbacks seem to be opportunities to remember and process buried feelings in safe moments.

The gift of dissociation may come predominantly from the hippocampus, which normally stores long-term memory, as well as the cerebellar vermis, which normally physically orients us and may kick in during traumatic events to create a mental distance from the trauma. The ability to dissociate protects children from trauma, but leaves them prone to cope with stress and triggers by de-realization, depersonalization, splitting off and other evidence that the brain has put up walls and now lacks integration between mind and body. This can lead to a child whose head is in the clouds or a child who is clumsy.

The earlier a child learns to dissociate and endure subsequent trauma, the more expert the child becomes at dissociation. Some children can easily access the altered state while others may opt to live in it. This creates some interesting developments in exhilarating experiences of protection as well as magical thinking. Some victims of trauma come to believe they are "special," that they have special powers or that God talks to them. Dissociation experiences can actually rescue a child and care for her. It's a wonderful consolation prize for the traumatized child. The problem is when the child comes to take these experiences as true and real, insanity begins and their ability to interact proficiently with reality is impaired.

Mitigating Trauma

Rocking. James W. Prescott (2000) redefined "maternal-social deprivation" as Somatosensory Affectional Deprivation (SAD). According to Prescott, rocking an infant can go a long way toward correcting otherwise neglectful mothering. Infants who have been rocked will be less violent than infants who were not rocked. Drs. William Mason and Gershon Berkson conducted a study on the mitigating effects of rocking on deprived and otherwise violent monkeys. The researchers found that monkeys that were ordinarily shown to become violent from being raised in isolation did not become violent when provided "fabricated swinging" mother monkeys. What is not clear is how much of a difference the rocking "mother" made compared to the cloth mother of other studies.

Animals. I have known people whose abuse was so cruel that they should have turned out much worse than they did, but for one thing. They bonded with pets. If a child is neglected or abused, but she has a pet to comfort her and to comfort in return, a part of her humanity that wants to go away stays for the pet. A child who never experienced empathy from a parent, but gets it from an animal, has been redeemed. So, I believe animals have healing power.

On the other hand, I have seen children abusive to animals and who do not yet deserve this privilege until they prove that they can be kind and responsible to a pet.

Enlightened Witness. A concept introduced by Alice Miller in *For Your Own Good* and *Thou Shall Not Be Aware* is the Enlightened Witness. Just one grown-up who bears witness to the abuse or neglect and dares to acknowledge aloud to the child that it's not fair, it's wrong, or it's not about the child, can make the difference between a pathological killer *vs.* a functioning artist, or a suicide *vs.* a seeker of help. Of course, the more acknowledgement from an enlightened witness a child gets, the better. A stranger in the supermarket who lets the child know the way he is being treated is wrong can completely leave an impression of another perspective to last a lifetime. I have had clients who should have been much more symptomatic, but they had an Enlightened Witness they remembered vividly.

True Parent

A woman asked after class, "Is there anything I can do to repair the damage I've done to my children? I'm a single mother of four girls, and I whipped them and locked them in closets to try to keep them under control." I asked, "Would you be willing to let them whip you back?" The woman answered, "Yes." This is a true parent.

A true parent has made mistakes, even the worst ones, yet she owns them, evidencing parental responsibility. A true parent is one who will do anything to reverse the mistakes she's made. A false parent may have made fewer mistakes, but won't want to own what they have done and may demand parental immunity. A false parent is willing to let the child take a label and a diagnosis rather than acknowledge responsibility for her mistakes in parenting. Only a true parent can heal their child.

For the true parent, it's the child who matters most. The true parent will do whatever it takes to heal the child, including apologizing or even being willing to allow the child to hit them back, if necessary. This is allowed through a process we call "containment." (See Chapter 3: Healing.) The willingness rather than the actual act may be the point. In order to heal, we have to give our pain back to our parents, directly or symbolically (*e.g.*, couchwork, unsent letters, [talking to the] empty chair work and rage work with a therapist). An apology should never be a way of heading off the child telling us how he feels (which is a necessary part of healing).

I am not recommending that a parent apologize for the little things like losing our temper, even though we usually shouldn't. If we have gone too far, the process of making ourselves wrong when the child behaved badly is often not helpful either. But in clear-cut cases of abuse or neglect, it is essential for a parent to apologize if it won't happen again. If a parent is an alcoholic parent who apologizes the morning after on a regular basis, that makes apologies worthless. If a parent apologizes for abandoning a child then continues his behavior, then that is worthless too.

The false parent seeks reasons to blame the child and make excuses for bad parenting decisions or actions. Given a choice of self-correction or blaming the child or the child's "condition," these parents seek psychiatrists who medicate or behaviorists who won't look for causes of the child's problems. They don't seek family therapists or serious parenting experts. Jeffrey Dahmer's mother disappeared for an extended period while his father picked the evaluators that could not assess his parenting (behaviorists), even for his son's sake. Lionel Dahmer wrote *A Father's Story*, contributing to the myth that some killers have normal childhoods. To be fair, Lionel seemed to love Jeffrey from afar and seemed to be in denial. He seemed somewhat curious, but given what is socially acceptable, he never was able to grasp that while he was gone his son was starving for touch, physical affection and attention.

I watched and listened to most of Jeffrey Dahmer's Sanity Hearing on Court TV. Behavioral Psychologist Judith Becker, PhD, couldn't interpret his dream, childhood or explain his favorite song or quote from the Bible. Nearly all of his evaluators were behavioral psychologists and all seven of them saw his symptoms of emotional starvation differently. Each had a different assessment and diagnosis (Court TV, February 1992).

I treated a man from an upper middle class family who had gone to good schools and had all his material needs met. He was a heroin addict and his younger brother was already institutionalized. When I asked his mother to come in and dialogue with her son about some of his memories, she said, "I've already done my part. He's your problem now." This is a false parent.

False parents blame and make excuses such as:
- "I did the best I could."
- "That's the way you were born."
- "You were always this way."
- "There was nothing wrong with your childhood."

False parents suggest it's the grown child's problem and has nothing to do with them:
- "Why don't you just let the past be the past?"
- "Forgive and forget."
- "Why do you want to bring these things up now?"
- "I never did that."
- "I don't remember."
- "Maybe you shouldn't be in therapy."
- "Get over it."
- "Why do you want to hurt me?"

Consolation

Sometimes parents have to make difficult decisions between bad and better. My husband wanted to circumcise our child. I thought it would be traumatic. However, I knew if I took a stand, I could run the risk of damaging a strong father-son bond. I wasn't even sure it was my call. As a matter of fact, I took a position that it was between the two of them. He took his ten-day-old son in for the procedure. When Ron brought Scott home there was a lot of crying, consoling to be done, and bandages to be changed. I listened to the sound of my child in pain and did not move. I believed that if Ron handled his pain, especially since Ron was the one who took him to get the injury, they would be closer. At first Ron looked at me rather surprised at what may have seemed like a lack of maternal commitment, like I was cold, not willing to go to my son. It wasn't easy for me to do, but within seconds my husband had to run to comfort his son. He sat with him the whole night as if he was trying to make it right.

People ask me sometimes what my stand is on circumcision. I think the child suffers. But I believe the bond between a father and son is more important than the trauma if there's a choice to be made. This is one of those issues about which I am not necessarily the expert, but it is a matter of important consideration. The point is, when you have to put your child through a surgery to straighten a leg, or turn an eye, or repair a hernia, it is critical that you are there to console. We cannot protect our children from life's pains. But we owe them consolation and understanding.

Resilience

I cannot tell you the number of times I have heard that there is no accounting for resilience. According to the Diathesis-Stress Model, quite popular at California State University, Northridge, "Some babies are just more resilient than others, as are children" (Kring, et al., 1992), suggests that a genetically fragile child may be able to withstand less trauma while a child of strong genetic stock can handle more trauma. But this is one way of hiding a traumatized child from our view by leaving open the possibility that the symptoms we see result from weak genes rather than neglect or trauma. We don't have to think the parenting is necessarily bad or something is wrong in the child's life if we accept the Diathesis-Stress Model.

When we already understand that no two children have the same experiences or even the same parents in the same family (because parents treat each child differently), we can understand that no two people have the same environment or history. As children differ in a family, it makes no sense to blame it on genes when their different backgrounds can account for everything.

The Resiliency Spectrum: Two Brothers

"Good" Brother	"Bad" Brother
Healthy birth for mother and child	Birth trauma or complications after
Good bonding from the first minutes	Poor, bad or interrupted bonding
Continuous attachment	Broken attachment at young ages
Nurtured	Neglected
Protected	Unprotected, overprotected or parentified
Appropriate and gradual separation	Multiple, premature separations (childcare, preschool)
Rocking	No rocking
Parents "see" child	Parents don't "see" child or project onto child
Allowed to express negative feelings, even to parents (parental responsibility)	Required or expected to repress feelings for parents' sake (parental immunity)
No secrets	Keeps secrets to protect adults, especially hurtful ones or ones about harmful events
Not abused	Abused, with no avenue to vent after discipline
Child had enlightened witness	Child had no enlightened witness
Intimacy available from loving caregivers	Intimacy only available with negative influences or abusive caregivers
Good projections	Negative projections
Hero child	Scapegoat child
Parents enjoy rewarding child	Parents have drive to blame or punish child
Good projection gets better (twice-blessed)	Bad projection gets worse (double-damned)
Good modeling of good values	Parents make and model selfish choices
Parents discipline consistently and with natural consequences	Parents discipline erratically if at all or parents discipline brutally
Pets	No pets
Child has ethical and/or religious training	Child has no ethical training or extreme religious training
Creativity encouraged	No creative outlet
No head trauma	Head trauma
Child has had no previous trauma	Child has had previous trauma
Parent forgives after discipline	Parent holds grudge, even after discipline

Behind Closed Doors

There is a great deal of secret neglect and abuse. Mothers with postpartum depression often neglect the baby, leaving her in the crib while the father is at work and when they hear his car, get up and act as if they have been with the child all day.

Some mothers were not allowed to cry as infants or small children and now can't bear the sound of their own baby crying. Some may train their baby not to cry, as they were trained, and may even hold her nostrils and lips closed until the child faints (and ceases to cry). Others put a pillow over their child's face until he stops crying. Some mothers drug their babies so they can sleep. Some of these children may learn to cope with the silent rejection by bonding with things, by head banging or rocking to focus on physical pain over the emotional pain that is unbearable. Some parents play with their baby's genitals until they stop crying, leaving children who have to masturbate to self-sooth. Whichever technique is employed to stop the crying, it's a secret.

Some parents secretly torture their child to ensure obedience, believing if they hurt her enough, she will comply. Some burn their child with cigarettes; pull them out of bed in a dead sleep for a whipping; have them wait down the hall with their drawers dropped for hours; or some just pinch them so no one can see, threatening them with more abuse if they tell. Some parents cannot handle the slightest bit of defiance so they train their child to obey above all else. When the child forgets to obey, the abuse is swift, violent and private with promises not to tell lest the abuse escalate. It's a secret.

Other forms of emotional abuse or neglect are more invisible and even more painful and could be practiced right under our noses without our detection. Early day care is one such practice. Babies or toddlers left in day care may resort to head banging or rocking. That means they are suffering pain worse than torture, for there is no pain more horrible than the pain born of rejection. Some mothers believe their babies will turn out the way they will turn out whether or not the parents are the ones caring for them, whether or not they're abused and whether or not they're neglected.

There are also stay-at-home moms who are preoccupied with themselves and their lives so they ignore the child. Some do it thoughtlessly. Others are premeditated. Still others are in too much pain to nurture. Most still haven't any idea that what they are doing is harmful. These moms and dads necessarily believe in predetermination or genes as the origin of personality. These parents don't know that their child's personality and skills develop according to how their child is treated. Their children languish in neglect and withdraw more and more, shriveling as they become invisible while imprinting neglect as a way of relating from their parents. Their child's intelligence never develops to potential. Many never even make it to average. Or, perhaps when the children are grown, they'll think it is normal to have shallow and distracted relationships. They will begin to feel violated by normal warmth and intimacy, developing a need to dilute it or defend against it.

We all frequently meet children who have been secretly neglected and abused. There are several in every class your child attends. We look at them like they are strange children. It rarely occurs to us that these children are suffering or there is a problem with the parents. May it be from this page forward that we never look upon a troubled child again as if there is more wrong with the child than the parents. May we realize that disturbed parenting is a red flag that the parent is in trouble and needs help if they are only open. Do we risk offending the adult in hopes they will respond, or do we become a child's enlightened witness who she will never forget? If we cannot believe that what we see is evidence of parenting issues, at least let us wonder. May we be open to the possibility that the child's symptoms are cries for help so that we remain curious.

My Vision

If only one parent who has been blind to the needs of children seriously considers the content of this manual in the raising of her two children who each have two children, then writing this book will have been worth it all. For these seven anonymous souls I have pushed forward every day to leave my message, determined to make a difference that I can only imagine.

Truth be told, I see a difference in lives almost daily, so my imagination often takes flight to grandiose possibilities that leave me intoxicated with hope. If my book could show up in one-half of the baby showers in the United States, all parents would become influenced by its contents. Childhood disorders, including ADHD, would be all but eradicated, and those left would be swiftly identified and treated before their symptoms become handicaps. Schools would once again become places where children were safe to study and learn.

The rise in mental health would become epidemic and what now appears to be a decline in civilization would become the renaissance of future generations. Populations would shrink in prisons and mental hospitals. There would be fewer and fewer homeless people on our streets. Alas, my own field would place a premium on good parenting theory and require that all therapists learn how pathology is created and how to practice and teach good relationship skills.

We would enter an era of problem-solving, sufficient to undo the dilemmas we have set for ourselves and creativity would abound. I can imagine a society where nearly all our people are not only capable of greatness, but we daily astound one another with humor, acceptance, intelligence, insight, humility, courage, honesty and works of art. Greatness would actually become commonplace but never ordinary and our bar would be set at new levels while we revel in daily acts of daring and kindness. Many of us would seek and achieve our potential. Most of us would feel safe in our homes and at work and we would be inspired by every new day, even if we only chose to just do our part, which would be good enough. Our citizens would become icons of mental health and perhaps the rest of the world would inherit translations and join us. Of course, I will never know how many brave parents I might ultimately reach, but I can imagine the worst and the best. In the meantime, I keep my expectations low and write to my imagined seven, one of which is you.

CHAPTER 2

Preventive Diagnosis

> "Throughout the work I have concentrated on problems of aetiology and psychopathology, believing that it will only be when we have a good grasp of what the causes are of psychiatric disorder and how they operate that we shall be in a position to develop effective measures either for their treatment or for their prevention."
> --John Bowlby, Father of Attachment Theory,
> *Attachment, Separation and Loss*

It is perhaps more than revolutionary to present diagnostic information to the general public; it may be downright insurgent. We psychotherapists are trained that we should not diagnose anyone who has not requested an assessment in a professional context. We are also trained not to diagnose children with adult diagnoses. Of course we may think it. That doesn't mean we actually dissociate from what we know. There is, generally speaking, no need to openly assess someone with whom we interface in our private lives. For me, when I'm off duty, I simply like to just be and let the other person just be. However, it appears that some of us are actually walking around with blinders on. While those of us who see more clearly must pretend not to see what we see, it is an easier mandate to obey when one does not see cause and effect in behavior. It is easier to obey when one does not believe that the causes of symptoms are childhood experiences.

We psychotherapists are instructed only to diagnose in the sanctity of our office, but our venue does not make us any wiser. Yes, there are assessment instruments that facilitate a diagnosis, but when one sees clearly enough, there is usually no need to test a patient to get a diagnosis. Symptoms are symptoms. We see what we see and we know what we know regardless of our location. Presenting issues are usually a pattern of behaviors with a common history. The best diagnosis is the one that includes a correlation between history and symptoms. Unfortunately, many if not most diagnoses are wrong or incomplete due in part to expedience without considering histories.

I have recently been involved in a case where I needed to assess whether a person I learned about in my personal life could have done something that would have put her children at risk, if the rumor was true. I had no way of knowing whether the rumor was true, but I did have accurate information about other things she had done as a lifestyle. Those other things led me to a reasonable suspicion that the rumor was worthy of investigation by the Department of Children and Family Services, if they so deemed. Without the other information about how she conducted herself in her public life, I would have doubted the rumor. The other information was key. When asked by officials to explain myself, I discovered that I was expected to do so without reporting on the patterns of behavior that influenced my decision to call. I was expected to justify my DCFS report without explaining my reasoning because to describe her documented actions was to diagnose. In the same moment, I was both commanded and forbidden to say what I thought. The ban on diagnosing was stretched to the point where I was considered wrong for having even reported patterns of behavior. I was sent a message that one should shut the eyes. The truth was that if I had met with the woman in my office, I would have had far less information than was otherwise available to me. I suspect that the facts learned out of the office offered more information than she would have revealed in the office.

I have on my shelf a book entitled *Bush on the Couch: Inside the Mind of the President* (Frank, 2004). It is a book in which a psychiatrist brilliantly evaluates the childhood and choices of former President George W. Bush. I am a member of the International Psychohistory Association and subscribe to the *Journal of Psychohistory*, where histories are repeatedly reported and interpreted. Some of the players are still alive and their actions are interpreted by professionals and lay people alike. I believe the more knowledge we have about the causes of behavior, the better we will understand one another. Alice Miller did a wonderful job explaining the behaviors of famous and infamous people based upon their childhood and corresponding adult choices throughout her generous catalog of published works.

I have been asked if I would interpret the behaviors of famous people for a reality show. I would be willing to interpret based upon the information provided in the show, as if we were interpreting a vignette, but the interpretation would only be as accurate as the information provided. It would demonstrate cause and effect more than claim actual accuracy. Assessment should be a life skill for all of us because people often tell us things that don't match their actions. We need to understand a person by their history and also learn about them through their actions and words. It is clear that diagnosis belongs to professionals alone and under strict guidelines for good reasons. However, when one actually believes as I do that the creation of personality disorders is in the home, it becomes apparent that the information about how personality and behaviors are created must be shared with parents. It is by telling parents the effects of their parenting that they become self-conscious, self-aware, responsible and mindful of the importance of their actions. By teaching parents this information they become more perceptive and aware of what to look for and how to see more clearly. The following information must be used judiciously, never ever to hurt people, only to understand them, especially yourself.

We've learned over the years at PaRC that the more cause and effect information that's shared with students and clients, the more power it has to inspire growth, dissolve denial and resistance to healing, improve social awareness and most importantly, prevent parents from doing the same things their parents did that they might otherwise believe were okay to do because they "survived." In deterring parents from repeating the mistakes of their parents, we prevent the creation of more personality disorders. The more parents understand about how pathology is created, the more likely they'll refine their practices in the interest of their child's well-being.

Our experience has been that most students relish the information they learn in this chapter. It sets them free and helps them make sense of their lives. However, it's imperative to note that personality and behavioral labels are not permanent.

Personality structures and disorders are simply descriptions of different combinations of coping mechanisms and interaction skills from childhood. These learned systems developed and served us in the context of our families of origin, but out in the rest of the world where people are unlike our families, these coping mechanisms and interaction patterns are outmoded, sometimes inappropriate, and need to be replaced. As students, one of our main purposes in life is to unlearn what was "normal" for us and replace it with healthy interaction skills, the ones we were supposed to learn originally. To do this takes great self-awareness, courage, love of truth and humility. We choose how we want to be, do the work to become it and authenticate our true or original selves in the process. Our reward is finally seeing clearly that to which we've always been blind. This clear seeing creates insight, if not enlightenment.

When Diagnosis Enables Prevention

There's no doubt this approach may be one of the first (if not the first) attempts to assemble a cohesive theory that includes the causes of all the personality disorders and structures. Preventive Diagnosis identifies personality disorders as coping patterns used to adapt to childhood conditions. The three courses I took in graduate school on diagnosis scarcely taught anything about the origins of these disorders, only how to recognize them. I have since borrowed from various observations of different professionals as well as my own. As the years go by, more and more research supports my Causal Theory. Suggestions by professional observers of behavior are invited and welcome to improve on this theory. In the meantime, I will continue to use my classroom and clinical observations as a forum for testing and refining the hypothesis behind each and every personality disorder to follow.

I hope therapists will want to learn more about Preventive Diagnosis and the entire Causal Theory because I believe they will discover that it greatly informs and accelerates treatment.

I hope that the following critical component of the Causal Theory, "Preventive Diagnosis," will inspire volumes of research. In the meantime, do your own research. Look for cause whenever you observe effect as a pattern. Look to see the effects of experiences. Cause and effect will relate to one another in the most apparent ways. One wonders, "Why didn't I see that before?" When we presume effects are simply inborn character traits, we fail to look for cause. We don't see as clearly and we don't have as much faith in healing.

Diagnosis: Road Map or Offensive Label?

The view amongst clinicians that laypeople can't handle diagnostic information reflects the common belief in the psychology field that pathology is probably genetic, not created (nature vs. nurture). Many psychologists, psychiatrists, psychoanalysts and other psychotherapists have thus agreed to keep diagnostic information to themselves and from the public because they have believed it would be hurtful, if not dangerous information in the hands of laypeople. This stems in large part from a belief that these personalities are not only genetic, but relatively immutable, especially if there is no plan as to how to heal the patient other than pharmaceuticals. Under these conditions it is reasonable to say that labeling would further injure fragile identities.

Other therapists do not believe in labeling and believe people can change. It makes perfect sense to me that they would then be opposed to labeling and even be revolted by it. Until now, labeling tended to become a permanent stamp. Labeling without any redeeming value or without instructions on what we are specifically attempting to correct is offensive. Thus, out of empathy they make a choice to ignore disorders and perhaps pretend they do not exist.

Unfortunately, by ignoring diagnosis, we miss a priceless opportunity to get at the heart of cause. Until now, there was no suggestion that the various constellations of symptoms would actually inform us about what types of experiences create which types of symptoms.

As critical as I am of the medical model, I find that it is useful in getting to cause, now that I have a working theory that correlates causes with results or formative injuries with personality structures or disorders.

I am hoping that empathic therapists are open to the reasoning behind using labels as a faster method of identifying related symptoms and for getting to the heart of the injury, especially when our goal is to eliminate the disorders with techniques that can do just that.

For the most part, laypeople commonly dismiss one another with ideations of judgment and develop philosophies on inherent worth and worthlessness. Laypeople often look at traits as indelible and their carriers as deserving of adoration or rejection.

Thus, most professionals believe that diagnoses in the hands of lay people could be hurtful or even abusive. I actually heard one myopic graduate student exclaim when he heard that I teach diagnosis to parents, "What if they use the information to create a personality disorder or a killer!" Of course, I have yet to meet or even hear of a parent who deliberately wants to create a monster.

It is generally assumed that it is professionally irresponsible to inform patients of their diagnosis or to give laypeople enough information to diagnose themselves and others. However, given that there are disorders created by particular types of experiences and treatable by techniques that address those types of experiences, it is important to identify and treat.

Secrecy regarding diagnosis may indicate that the field does not have a clear understanding from whence pathology comes, how pathology is healed or how diagnosis informs treatment. I believe the patient can pick up on that futility.

Given that there is cause and effect in parenting, withholding diagnostic information from the public could be paternalistic, territorial or faithless. It could be tantamount to conspiring to preserve the disease in order to protect parents, patients or the value of the profession as much as Freud's peers and paterfamilias did. I am proposing that it could even be unethical and immoral to withhold this information from parents, given that parents create the diagnoses and could prevent them, as well. Of course, that's how strongly I believe that personality is created in the home. It is also a reflection of something I notice in myself. I take advice and change my behavior when I understand its origin.

Theory Informs Practice

When the client has studied the Causal Theory before entering therapy, Preventive Diagnosis allows therapy to get to the point much faster. As a Causal Therapist, I get to have all the faith I need that a person can be more quickly and deeply healed if we can identify what happened. I am therefore not afraid to tread on sacred parental ground, as I know the answer lies within the grown child.

Early on, in the context of a parenting or theory class, the client/student is relieved of the responsibility of protecting parents. The client relaxes, listens and takes it in, putting two and two together without self-consciousness or defensiveness.

Soon, in our private session, the client and I share a premise that what is wrong was not inborn. She would not have made the appointment if she didn't embrace The Causal Theory she just learned. We both appreciate the chance to dive in. We move quickly together, collaborating. Let's get to the cause so we can reverse it.

Following a false cause, by the way, will not reverse a symptom. My client and I know that acting out tends to point to the types of experiences they repressed, so we begin putting together their existing memories with their family's attitudes and systems of interaction along with how they "act out" today. It's like prospecting for gold when you know it's there. It's like putting together a puzzle when you know you have all the pieces. I get to be clear that what's in the way of healing is repression, not the client's genes. When the client and I are on the same page regarding the Causal Theory, I can more readily point out the resistance to "going there," and then we can talk about it. I am also relieved of having to cajole a client and treat him like he is fragile, unless it is clear he is. What children endured in their childhood was far worse than the quest for truth we will share together.

On the other hand, I don't plant the suggestion of a particular type of memory. This is one reason for clients taking our parenting and theory class that covers all the bases. They recognize the correlation between experiences and symptoms. They know what fits before they get to see me. I follow their lead.

Essentially, Causal Theory gives clients permission to own their original innocent self, to remember what is there to be remembered and to grasp that we are whittling away wrong messages and wrong generalizations to get to their original self. I find that people are so affected by their childhood and so loyal to their families of origin that it is extremely unlikely that someone will make up something against a parent – against anyone else perhaps, but not against a parent. If anything, they will fight a memory because "It can't be; it must be my imagination."

For example, I may have an arrogant client who idealizes his parents but has a general contempt for authority. My first suspicion based on the pattern I've seen again and again is that his parents were weak and could not handle his emotions or effectively discipline him. Yet he idolizes them and has a drive to scapegoat other authority for being too weak to teach him anything. I don't present this hypothesis. I simply hold the line that even my own child does not idolize his mother, that where a grown child claims his parents did nothing wrong, there is denial and his arrogance must be serving some purpose. Gradually, with that mirror, he comes to confess his own disappointments with having had to care for their feelings at the expense of his own. That's the worst-case scenario. After having taken this class, a similar client is more likely to come see me, reporting from our first meeting that he sees he got his narcissism from his parents being too weak, "But I still don't quite see how to deal with it." The dialogue has been jump-started.

As another example, we may have a parent who is driven to rage at his children. By now he has diagnosed himself as borderline. He understands his rage is not inborn, but is the result of abuse by his own father (or mother). We will not waste time coming to this discovery. We can begin to explore his buried anger. Ironically, once it is explored and expressed in session, he will be free to love his father more genuinely and will have learned constructive ways to relate without blame.

If theory informs practice, we need to always remember that the only good reason for a diagnosis is that it can inform the corrective process. It helps lead the way to the work that must be done. There is no point in diagnosing if there is no goal to heal or conviction that the problem can be solved.

The Joy of an Informed Client

Preventive Diagnosis makes therapy a cooperative venture, and we can go deeper faster. It allows for the patient to be an expert on the problem. The client comes to therapy understanding what needs to take place and why we explore what we explore. I have found that most people love diagnosing themselves because they are comforted to find an explanation for their problem and a path to its cure. Often it's a relief, an Aha! moment. I love it when a client comes to me after taking the class, with a hypothesis on what went wrong for her. I enjoy the intuition of an informed client versus playing the role of an all-knowing expert who keeps her trade secrets to herself, thereby preserving her position of mystery and authority. Mostly, I find that I am repeatedly rewarded by this approach to healing. Like a scientist who tests and retests her hypothesis, I enjoy profound and rapid results that continuously affirm this theory. Ultimately, I am a more effective therapist with a willing and informed client.

Resistance Busting

With this information, we can cut to the chase when it comes to healing the effects of our childhood. The only things in the way of healing are resistance (defending our parents) and denial. As a matter of fact, once we are out of denial, then only resistance is in the way of healing. The wound is never too awful to heal. It is only the strength of the resistance that keeps us unhealed. We can know our resistance by our loyalty to our parents. The more we defend our parent's treatment of us in childhood, the more resistance we have to healing ourselves. People who have a high degree of resistance to this process may describe it with phrases like "psycho babble," "parent bashing," and "abuse excuse," and advocate that you "get on with your life." Others may argue that our "parents did the best they could" or even that they "feel disloyal" talking badly about them. Yet others feel bad for their parents to the exclusion of themselves, while still others are afraid to cry or complain even though it would help them heal.

Preventive Diagnosis helps most people acknowledge their childhood treatment without feeling they have betrayed their parents. In the anonymity of a classroom or the quiet of reading *The Manual*, they naturally match up the childhood and adult traits that seem most like theirs. If they can't find them, they may not exist. I find teaching Preventive Diagnosis cuts one to two years off therapy, saving a great deal of time and money. Good, fast, deep work is enabled.

Usually at the core of resistance is the conviction that we should not explore any history that may impugn our parents. A therapist who endeavors to "go there" is at risk of losing the patient, which is the main reason therapy takes so long. Some therapists have even found ways to appear to treat pathology without "going there." These therapists are often popular because they are so good at steering clear of the issue and helping you feel it was the right thing to do.

Once a person reads *The Manual* or takes The Miracle Child Parenting Series (a live or taped lecture series based on *The Manual*), they are significantly more prepared to give up protecting their parents in order to heal and transcend their internalized limitations. They are willing to do this because they can see how healing is ultimately not "blaming the parent" but rather allowing old childhood feelings, often repressed for the parents' sake, to come up to the surface and be resolved. They can see how confronting feelings in the privacy of therapy, without their parents ever experiencing a "betrayal" is possible. They can see how their parents were victims of their own childhoods too. Thus, Preventive Diagnosis cuts through resistance.

Preventive Diagnosis and Social Awareness

Preventive Diagnosis also helps us realize that how others treat us may not be about us, may be something we don't need to take personally and, in fact may be something we can understand and forgive. It might inform us how to communicate better with different types of people. It will lead us to realize how profoundly important it is to prevent abuse, neglect, abandonment and repression.

Checks and Double Checks

Preventive Diagnosis requires us to check and double-check our theory. We suggest laypeople apply the highest standards for diagnosing themselves or anyone. You must have a match between childhood experience and the predictable adult traits such an experience reveals. Therefore, there is no diagnosis unless there is a match between the childhood and adult traits. Sometimes, when memory is vague, it might be helpful to investigate the parenting style under which you were raised by inquiring into how and when you were toilet-trained, anecdotes regarding what kind of baby you were and other tales of how you were parented that could come from parents, siblings, extended family, photos, baby albums, etc. An investigation into parenting style may reveal further the parents' consciousness and how they perceived their children.

Responsible Use of this Information

At first there is a tendency to want to go around diagnosing everyone you meet, a byproduct of the education. Only use it to inform yourself how to respond to the person you are assessing, not to try to change them. How they are is none of your business unless they are your children or you think they are a threat to someone. Understanding them, however, improves you and the world. Recognizing symptoms as they develop may help us self-correct and prevent our children from developing structures or disorders.

The information contained in Chapter 2: Preventive Diagnosis, Chapter 3: Healing and Chapter 8: Relationship Skills, gives you more responsibility for your choices in people and relationships. While you may understand someone who continues to make choices that hurt themselves or others, with this understanding comes the responsibility to not remain with them or give comfort or support unless they are actively working to heal.

Therapists are not allowed to diagnose anyone who is not their client. That does not mean that we stop seeing when we are not with clients. It is just that we understand we must use diagnostic criteria responsibly. Students of the Causal Theory may use diagnosis for understanding themselves as well as others. You may ask someone else who is doing this work in the relationship skills workshop what diagnosis they gave themselves. Almost always, these students enjoy the question and the discussion. However, you must not use this information to label another person, especially in the world at large. That is as serious as name-calling and it may actually become misused. To label someone with a diagnosis without invitation is arrogant, abusive and intrusive.

Prevention

One of the best inspirations to change is to understand the consequences of one's actions. I believe that to prevent these disorders, we need to bring the information to those who inadvertently create them and give them the opportunity to head them off. Preventive Diagnosis helps a parent resist the strong, internalized predisposition or drive to pass on to their children the hurtful parenting they received with its resulting personality disorder or structure.

As I have said, giving this information to the lay population may raise eyebrows by my licensing boards, to say the least. But the problem is deeper. I want to teach parents how to identify personality disorders in the making. For this reason, I have provided every diagnosis with lay terminology to describe how the child will look as the child is taking on patterns to cope that will backfire later in life if not addressed earlier. This is why I refer to a child who is, for example, becoming narcissistic as a "demeaning child," or the "fake positive" child. I would say, "Your child is learning to be demeaning. How do you think this is happening?" I might say, "I see your little boy is already learning to fake positive feelings when he's in need of your attention. Do you have an idea how we can correct that?" "I see your child has the symptoms of the betrayed child. Do you know what happened?" This way, we can describe the child's behavior and demeanor without formal diagnoses. That's all we need to prevent and predict.

Perhaps a more relevant approach for children is simply improving awareness of red-flag symptoms. I have comprised an incomplete list of symptoms that often suggest further investigation in a chart to follow entitled "Common Coping Mechanisms."

When Diagnosis Enables Prediction

One of my favorite aspects of theory building is forensics: profiling and predicting behavior. The template that informs how a killer became a killer given the sum total of his experiences is the same template that explains how a saint or a great leader in history became or had to become great and couldn't turn out any other way, given her history.

I devised a template for my college students to account for the behavior of a notorious criminal or exceptional leader. I asked them to especially look at the two primary stages of life and rate them, starting with the most common milestones. It facilitates an initial, temporary hypothesis, which all data would prove or disprove, as the resulting hypothesis becomes more and more confirmed. This approach has served me well over the years and the temporary measurement is no more than my attempt to try to share how I think when I read people, seeing if their childhoods foretold their behaviors. When I ask a student to fill it out for someone, it becomes a quick way to discover whether we are seeing eye to eye about someone or if they are missing key considerations. I suspect that trauma researcher and clinician Colin Ross might agree with the premise of the Trauma Predictor Scale, which attributes and somewhat measures nearly all pathology by trauma (Ross, 1995) while it measures resilience and mental health by nurturing, forgiving and protective parenting (Schore, 2003).

I would expect the perfectly average childhood to create a perfectly average child, who would be scored 0. I would expect a great leader to score about 75 or higher. I would expect a menace to our society to score -75 or lower. Abuse of substances at the time of acting out can put a person below -100, while meditation, high-quality prayer or self-reflection and therapy can put a person over 100, so I have line items for Substance Use and Other Circumstances. Richard Ramirez's substance abuse was pervasive (Carlo, 1996) but not as bad as Jeffrey Dahmer's (Norris, 1992). Methamphetamine abuse can make a normal person a monster. On the other hand, therapy or meditation can be profound, radically improving the quality of one's life. An injured child and a Miracle Child can still be raised up 70 points, maybe even more. I also have other considerations in the form to follow, as extenuating occurrences may impact us for better or worse.

Below is a sampling of how I would rate some people's childhoods, not their deeds, *per se*, but they are rough approximations, because no one will ever know exactly how a childhood was. Even so, rough approximations may be good enough to improve understanding. The bonding/attachment stage is primarily a measure of the first year, breakable in the first, second and third year. Attunement and coaching by parents become more and more important in the development of intelligence before kindergarten. Separation-individuation takes place during the discipline years where consequences for "wrong" choices can be issued with guidance or brutality and everything in between.

Einstein was not so emotionally healthy or socialized, but he channeled his loneliness into curiosity, something his uncle taught him to do. Richard Ramirez went to day care as an infant and had a father who violently beat all his sons, often causing head trauma (Carlo, 1996). Many Americans have suffered such a fate and not turned into serial killers. However, Ramirez became particularly violent because the first adult who truly paid attention to him was his uncle, a Vietnam Vet who showed him photographs of people he tortured and killed, and who premeditatedly killed his wife within feet of Richard and told Richard not to tell anyone. Shortly after that, Richard began using drugs (Carlo, 1996). His childhood had been bad, but it was this trauma during his adolescent surge of hormones, the loss of his mentor, combined with drugs that put him over the edge. On the other hand, while Hitler's mother was somewhat loving and consistent, she passively allowed her husband to beat and ridicule her son daily. As bad as the beatings were, it was probably the failure of his mother to protect him and the ridicule that put him over the edge, especially since he knew his "loving" mother wouldn't rescue him.

In order to form a theory that is reflective of reality and justice, I would say anyone who scores below -50 on the following scale falls into the realm of insanity because no one raised with childhood mistreatment causing a score that low can do any better as an adult without major therapeutic intervention. I would say that these scores indicate Insanity by Parenting. The more we call behavior as it is, how it came to be and what it could not otherwise be, the more we become personally responsible for allowing these travesties against children. If this information does not become common knowledge, then we can expect more and more killers among us.

We have no problem holding violently abused children responsible for their actions as adults. We must take responsibility too for the safety of our young. As we executed Aileen Wuornos for killing multiple would-be male perpetrators who wouldn't take "No" for an answer (*Monster*), we needed to apologize to her for allowing her to suffer all the way through her childhood. When her family kicked her out of the house at age 15, after all the incest and physical abuse had been done, she was allowed by the State of Florida to live in the woods in cardboard boxes. The crimes we want to combat will be reduced when parents and the state are held accountable for allowing children to suffer so terribly. When we see a disturbed child, we need to assume it is not genetic. We need to investigate. We need to heed the warning signs and the cry for help. Ignoring these children is criminal. Aileen Wuornos was Insane by Parenting. We wouldn't even have to try the parents to find out if it were true or not. No one turns out this damaged without severe childhood trauma in the care of their parents, no one. Whether or not she could have been rehabilitated is another issue and I would trade life in prison or even condone execution if we could all agree that these monsters were victims of the worst child abuse amongst us.

Trauma Predictor Charts

Example: Jesus of Nazareth

Prenatal Assaults (*i.e.,* violence, toxins) *vs.* Warm Parental Anticipation (-5 to +5)	5
Bonding/Attachment	
Insecure Attachment *vs.* Quality Attachment (-15 to +15)	15
Broken Attachment *vs.* Continuous Attachment (*i.e.,* day care) (-20 to +20)	20
Separation-Individuation	
Physical Abuse *vs.* Karmic Discipline	
Age (lower score for early age) (-5 to +5)	5
Severity (lower score for degree and frequency) (-5 to +5)	5
Sexual Abuse *vs.* Safe Affection	
Age (lower score for early age) (-5 to +5)	5
Severity (lower score for degree and frequency) (-5 to +5)	5
Emotional Abuse *vs.* Identity & Confidence Building	
Age (lower score for early age) (-5 to +5)	5
Severity (lower score for degree and frequency) (-5 to +5)	5
Ethics	
Repression *vs.* Expression (-15 to +15)	15
Blaming/Judging *vs.* Personal Responsibility (-15 to +15)	15
Substance Use *vs.* Therapy, Meditation, *etc.* (-50 to +50)	50
Other Circumstances	
TOTAL	150

Example: The Buddha

Prenatal Assaults (*i.e.,* violence, toxins) *vs.* Warm Parental Anticipation (-5 to +5)	5
Bonding/Attachment	
Insecure Attachment *vs.* Quality Attachment (-15 to +15)	15
Broken Attachment *vs.* Continuous Attachment (*i.e.,* day care) (-20 to +20)	20
Separation-Individuation	
Physical Abuse *vs.* Karmic Discipline	
Age (lower score for early age) (-5 to +5)	5
Severity (lower score for degree and frequency) (-5 to +5)	5
Sexual Abuse *vs.* Safe Affection	
Age (lower score for early age) (-5 to +5)	5
Severity (lower score for degree and frequency) (-5 to +5)	5
Emotional Abuse *vs.* Identity & Confidence Building	
Age (lower score for early age) (-5 to +5)	5
Severity (lower score for degree and frequency) (-5 to +5)	5
Ethics	
Repression *vs.* Expression (-15 to +15)	10
Blaming/Judging *vs.* Personal Responsibility (-15 to +15)	10
Substance Use *vs.* Therapy, Meditation, *etc.* (-50 to +50) *meditation under the Bodhi Tree*	50
Other Circumstances	
TOTAL	140

Trauma Predictor Charts, cont'd

Example: Mother Teresa

Prenatal Assaults (*i.e.,* violence, toxins) *vs.* Warm Parental Anticipation (-5 to +5)	5
Bonding/Attachment	
Insecure Attachment *vs.* Quality Attachment (-15 to +15)	15
Broken Attachment *vs.* Continuous Attachment (*i.e.,* day care) (-20 to +20)	20
Separation-Individuation	
Physical Abuse *vs.* Karmic Discipline	
Age (lower score for early age) (-5 to +5)	5
Severity (lower score for degree and frequency) (-5 to +5)	5
Sexual Abuse *vs.* Safe Affection	
Age (lower score for early age) (-5 to +5)	5
Severity (lower score for degree and frequency) (-5 to +5)	5
Emotional Abuse *vs.* Identity & Confidence Building	
Age (lower score for early age) (-5 to +5)	5
Severity (lower score for degree and frequency) (-5 to +5)	5
Ethics	
Repression *vs.* Expression (-15 to +15)	5
Blaming/Judging *vs.* Personal Responsibility (-15 to +15)	15
Substance Use *vs.* Therapy, Meditation, *etc.* (-50 to +50)	35
Other Circumstances indoctrination, lack of critical thinking	-5
TOTAL	120

Example: President Barack Obama

Prenatal Assaults (*i.e.,* violence, toxins) *vs.* Warm Parental Anticipation (-5 to +5)	5
Bonding/Attachment	
Insecure Attachment *vs.* Quality Attachment (-15 to +15)	10
Broken Attachment *vs.* Continuous Attachment (*i.e.,* day care) (-20 to +20)	15
Separation-Individuation	
Physical Abuse *vs.* Karmic Discipline	
Age (lower score for early age) (-5 to +5)	5
Severity (lower score for degree and frequency) (-5 to +5)	5
Sexual Abuse *vs.* Safe Affection	
Age (lower score for early age) (-5 to +5)	5
Severity (lower score for degree and frequency) (-5 to +5)	5
Emotional Abuse *vs.* Identity & Confidence Building	
Age (lower score for early age) (-5 to +5)	5
Severity (lower score for degree and frequency) (-5 to +5)	5
Ethics	
Repression *vs.* Expression (-15 to +15)	15
Blaming/Judging *vs.* Personal Responsibility (-15 to +15)	15
Substance Use *vs.* Therapy, Meditation, *etc.* (-50 to +50)	
Other Circumstances sought to resolve identity issues	10
TOTAL	100

Trauma Predictor Charts, cont'd

Example: Richard Ramirez (Night Stalker)

Prenatal Assaults (*i.e.,* violence, toxins) *vs.* Warm Parental Anticipation (-5 to +5)	-5
Bonding/Attachment	
Insecure Attachment *vs.* Quality Attachment (-15 to +15)	-15
Broken Attachment *vs.* Continuous Attachment (*i.e.*, day care) (-20 to +20)	-20
Separation-Individuation	
Physical Abuse *vs.* Karmic Discipline	
Age (lower score for early age) (-5 to +5)	-5
Severity (lower score for degree and frequency) (-5 to +5)	-5
Sexual Abuse *vs.* Safe Affection	
Age (lower score for early age) (-5 to +5)	-5
Severity (lower score for degree and frequency) (-5 to +5)	-5
Emotional Abuse *vs.* Identity & Confidence Building	
Age (lower score for early age) (-5 to +5)	0
Severity (lower score for degree and frequency) (-5 to +5)	0
Ethics	
Repression *vs.* Expression (-15 to +15)	-15
Blaming/Judging *vs.* Personal Responsibility (-15 to +15)	-15
Substance Use *vs.* Therapy, Meditation, *etc.* (-50 to +50) *drugs*	-20
Other Circumstances witnessed violent murder, coached by murderer, multiple head traumas	-30
TOTAL	-140

Example: Jeffrey Dahmer

Prenatal Assaults (*i.e.,* violence, toxins) *vs.* Warm Parental Anticipation (-5 to +5)	-5
Bonding/Attachment	
Insecure Attachment *vs.* Quality Attachment (-15 to +15)	-15
Broken Attachment *vs.* Continuous Attachment (*i.e.*, day care) (-20 to +20)	-20
Separation-Individuation	
Physical Abuse *vs.* Karmic Discipline	
Age (lower score for early age) (-5 to +5)	0
Severity (lower score for degree and frequency) (-5 to +5)	0
Sexual Abuse *vs.* Safe Affection	
Age (lower score for early age) (-5 to +5)	-5
Severity (lower score for degree and frequency) (-5 to +5)	-5
Emotional Abuse *vs.* Identity & Confidence Building	
Age (lower score for early age) (-5 to +5)	-5
Severity (lower score for degree and frequency) (-5 to +5)	-5
Ethics	
Repression *vs.* Expression (-15 to +15)	-15
Blaming/Judging *vs.* Personal Responsibility (-15 to +15)	-15
Substance Use *vs.* Therapy, Meditation, *etc.* (-50 to +50)	-30
Other Circumstances barely touched as an infant	-20
TOTAL	-140

Trauma Predictor Sample Outcomes

150	Jesus
140	The Buddha
130	Galileo
120	Mother Teresa, Nelson Mandela
110	Michelangelo, Albert Einstein, Zen Masters
100	Mikhail Gorbachev, Barack Obama, Oprah, Sam Harris, Peter Breggin, Phil Donahue
90	Great careers, good marriages, good parents. Matt Damon, Lady Gaga, Bob Dylan, Bill Gates, Dwight Eisenhower, Barry Goldwater, Eleanor Roosevelt
80	Greatness with some self-defeating traits. Bill Clinton, Steve Jobs, Jane Fonda, Joan of Arc
70	Constructive & critical thinking, persistence.
60	Focus on education with some self-reflection and values.
50	Great character, average or normal goals.
40	Self-defeating behavior despite great talent. Michael Jackson, Whitney Houston
30	Hard worker, possible personality structures.
20	Superstitious belief in luck, lack of cause and effect thinking, otherwise decent character.
10	Admires good or talented people but sees them as different.
0	Average person, relationships, career, parent, ethics.
-10	Dependent, obsessive-compulsive personalities.
-20	Depression, anxiety.
-30	Loyalty ethics without values or courage.
-40	Secrets, infidelity, lack of problem-solving and ethics.
-50	Avoidant, schizoid personalities.
-60	Narcissistic, borderline and paranoid personalities.
-70	Schizophrenia, suicidality, terrorist, gang members.
-80	Lack of self-reflection, empathy or conscience.
-90	Sociopathic crimes, exploiting and cheating. Bernie Madoff
-100	Major domestic violence perpetrator.
-110	Rapist, child molester, child abuser, child abuse secret keeper. Dr. Schreber
-120	Killers. Charles Manson, Jared Loughner
-130	Adolph Hitler, Saddam Hussein, Joseph Stalin
-140	Richard Ramirez, Jeffrey Dahmer
-150	John Wayne Gacy

Common Coping Mechanisms

Abandonment Trauma
- Child refuses eye contact with parent while being held by that parent.
- Infant or child makes a permanent decision never to love or be vulnerable again.
- Infant learns to change the subject, pointing away, when people get too personal or intimate.
- Child dissociates and sees self from outside himself, even in dreams.
- Child bangs head.
- Child bonds only with strangers.
- Child develops rage.
- Child forgets or "can't remember" his childhood.
- Child mistrusts.

Separation Anxiety
- Child clings.
- Child acts hyper.
- Child is distractible.
- Child fears parents will be abducted.

Mother's Postpartum Depression
- Child learns to bond with objects over people.
- Child repeats behaviors she knows are safe or acceptable.
- Child repeats behavior that discharges energy, but has no social meaning.
- Child focuses on petting objects and fabrics that remind her of skin.
- Child rocks to self-sooth.
- Child relates to objects.
- Child withdraws.
- Child dumbs down.

Domestic Violence
- Child learns to solve issues with violence.
- Child learns to defend self with blame.
- Child develops drive to scapegoat, beginning with toys.
- Child dissociates and sees self from outside himself, even in dreams.
- Child thinks she can't feel her feelings.
- Child can't remember his childhood.
- Child develops rage.

Trauma
- Child learns to change the subject when people get too personal or intimate.
- Child dissociates.
- Child is clumsy due to preoccupation.
- Child thinks she can't feel her feelings.
- Older child cuts to feel.
- Older child cuts to disguise emotional pain.
- Older child cuts to communicate pain.
- Child may have hallucinatory, out of body experiences.

Mental Abuse
- Child denies reality is real.
- Child buries the memory of the truth.
- Child repeatedly asks questions he knows are safe.
- Child stutters in fear of expressing himself.
- Child avoids the parent and ultimately others.
- Child mistrusts.
- Child criticizes self before others can.

Emotional Abuse
- Child fears crying and represses feelings.
- Child makes up words and sounds that won't enrage parents or that safely have no known meaning.
- Child avoids the parent and ultimately others.
- Child repeatedly asks questions he knows are safe.
- Child chooses harmful people over healthy people.

Emotional Neglect
- Child steals to compensate self for feeling cheated out of nurturing.
- Child chases after feedback.
- Child is susceptible to sexual abuse.
- Child overeats.
- Child doubts her own experience.
- Child doubts his own existence.
- Child chases after reassurance.
- Child has shallow dialogue.
- Child will maintain a childlike intellect.

Physical Neglect
- Child has bad manners, bad grammar and poor hygiene.
- Child may have a less than average intelligence quotient.

Sexual Abuse
- Child becomes hypersexual and re-enacts sexual abuse.
- Child wets bed past four or five years of age.
- Child thinks her parents aren't her real parents.

Controlling and Intrusive Parenting
- Child organizes belongings.
- Child imagines parent reads his mind and thinks he can read minds.
- Child fears and avoids germs or dirt.
- Child watches parents for cues on what to say.

Over-Burdened Child
- Child wets bed past four or five years of age.
- Child acts uncommonly mature.

Repression
- Child keeps dialogue shallow.
- Child gasps when he cries.
- Child looks to her parent for the safe answer.
- Child has stereotyped dialogue, often independent of meaning.
- Child defends the parent.
- Child shuts down.
- Child overeats.
- Child doubts her own experience.
- Child stutters in fear of expression himself.
- Child abandons curiosity and natural intelligence.

Weak Parenting
- Child devalues adults.
- Child becomes a positive, reassuring mirror for others and fears negative feedback.
- Child worries about the welfare of the parent.

Custody Dispute
- Child attaches, but will not stay attached.
- Child feels guilty or corrupt for loving the other parent.
- Child becomes secretive and withholding.
- Child wants to be where he is not.
- Child learns to play people against each other.
- Child learns to tell people what they want to hear.

Introduction to Personality Diagnosis Charts

First Year of Life

The first year of life is a significant determinant in the formation of personality, as this is when bonding occurs, or should occur. The borderline has erratic bonding. The schizoid has flat, absent "bonding." The paranoid possibly had traumatic bonding. The dependent personality and the passive-aggressive personality may have had healthy bonding. In more severe cases they had less than healthy bonding. Every personality disorder or structure is minimized or exacerbated by the quality of attachment in the first year. Yet attachment theorists are recently forming hypotheses predicting adult behavior based on quality of attachment. Many different terms are used by different theorists, but they boil down to (1) Secure, (2) Ambivalent, (3) Avoidant and (4) Disorganized. I have tried to match these up with personality disorders, but I still intuitively believe that how the child is treated in the Second Year On (the discipline and individuation stage of personality development) complicates a retrospective view of what kind of attachment a person had. On the other hand, the way we were treated in the separation/discipline process may actually reaffirm attachment styles in most cases.

I'm excited that other theorists are so interested in attachment and its importance. I'm excited that they have their own causal theory. I'm so appreciative of their work that I'm trying to reconcile it with mine. Nevertheless, one can at best use the following material as a guide for thinking and assessing, rather than as rules of personality formation.

Second Year On

The specific traits, whether amounting to structure or disorder, tend to come from Second Year On parenting control techniques. For example, part of what makes a borderline personality is the minimal, erratic or suffocating bonding of the first year, but another part of what makes a borderline is the domineering and/or neglectful parenting of the Second Year On. Thus the family system is both neglectful and intrusive. This style tends to lead to abusive parenting "for one's own good." Parents may be hot headed, rageful or borderline themselves. So, in order to appreciate cause and effect and severity in a diagnosis, you may need to appreciate the treatment of the second year as distinct from the first year, as the discipline and control techniques will determine the personality disorder or coping style. See if you can surmise which types of childhood events most likely correlate to which adult traits.

Paradox

Notice that in almost every diagnosis, as in life, nature has a paradox. There appear to be two ways to make each diagnosis. For example, you can under-nurture or over-nurture a borderline. Both will crave and fear intimacy because in a funny way the suffocated borderline never got enough intimacy, as she was too busy defending against too much of it.

Controlling parents who try to potty train too early may produce an obsessive-compulsive personality two different ways: one child responds by being frightened into over-cooperation; another child rebels against over-control by refusing to poop and "holding it in."

Fragile, weak mothers can create "dark" narcissists (coined by Scott at age 8). By setting weak or inconsistent limits, they create these dark narcissists who disregard and devalue adults and all others. Vain and insecure mothers can create "light" narcissists. In having an insecure identity, they may create a light narcissist who is always responsible for holding up a positive mirror to mom and eventually to all others, sacrificing his own authentic feelings for a false self. The fragile mother is still a selfish mother because she sucks more empathy than she offers, leaving a child who cannot offer empathy, only positive thinking. By the way, mothers who idealize their children out of denial are also weak mothers who not only don't perceive their child's need for limits but project entitlement into their child. On the other hand, hard, cold, critical, judgmental, rejecting mothers or fathers can model dark narcissism for their child.

Organizing Personalities

The remainder of this chapter will focus mainly on personality disorders and their causes. These are the same disorders detailed in the *Diagnostic and Statistical Manual of Mental Disorders, Fourth Edition-Text Revision (DSM-IV-TR)*, which is the therapists' bible of psychiatric diagnoses. In *The Manual*, I have decided to offer more user friendly descriptions and stories, as well as causal experiences that create personality. You might find that personalities don't fit into exact categories and rather exist on a continuum. The chapter goes into sufficient detail so that you can picture the child, the childhood and the resulting adult behaviors. At the end of each specific personality section, I have included a brief description by Gerry Grossman, who is the founder of Gerry Grossman Training Seminars. I find his short descriptions used to train therapists are both accurate and succinct.

We've arranged the personalities in *The Manual* from mildest to most severe in a social context. That said, theoretically, the most severe Passive-Aggressive can do more damage than the least severe Antisocial since every personality disorder in its extreme is harmful, toxic and even violent or murderous. Here are a few other differences between *The Manual* and the *DSM-IV-TR*:

- Passive-Aggressive was removed from the *DSM-IV-TR*, but we have kept it in *The Manual* because Passive-Aggressive personalities play a significant and provocative role in stressing a relationship. They often like to imagine their innocence because the other party is becoming so enraged at their disengaged lack of cooperation and communication. Their aloof lack of proactive commitment to a relationship is problematic and, in my opinion, needs to be highlighted as a personality type or dysfunction, with which it is difficult to contend.
- I've added a personality disorder of my own, the Approach-Avoidant. I see them created in childhood and the symptoms continue into adulthood. I borrowed from developmental terminology to give this personality type a label.
- I have further broken down the Antisocial Personality into three separate personalities: Antisocial (overtly violent and angry), Sociopathic (charming while covertly committing criminal acts under our very noses) and Psychopathic (profoundly out of touch with reality due to the worst abuse of all). Millon, one of the leading authors of the *DSM-IV-TR*, wanted to include the Sociopath as distinct from the Antisocial Personality (Millon, 1993). I can't figure why there is no diagnosis for a Psychopathic Personality in the *DSM-IV-TR*. Maybe it's because they cannot be healed, but at least they can be diagnosed.

Disorder vs. Structure

A personality disorder will generally include 70-80% of the cluster of traits outlined. If you have at least one-half of the traits, you may have a personality structure, which is milder than a personality disorder and therefore easier to heal.

To our clinicians in training, diagnoses

often have a secondary diagnosis to account for overlap. We call these secondary diagnoses "features." Borderline is the personality that most often has multiple diagnoses within and a specialty (the secondary diagnosis). Borderlines had parents who practiced most of the worst parenting mistakes and therefore created most of the personality structures as part of the disorder. In other words, borderlines often also have obsessive compulsive, paranoid, narcissistic, dependent or histrionic traits within the borderline diagnosis. But, they usually specialize in one. So, to characterize a person who is appearing borderline I would seek to identify a secondary diagnosis. For example, you may say a person has a borderline personality structure with obsessive-compulsive features. Therefore, the diagnosis may be "Borderline structure with Obsessive-Compulsive Features" or a "Borderline Personality with Narcissistic Features."

Usually there is quite a bit of overlap. I have found this clarifier useful for almost any diagnosis. Clients find it helpful to identify the traits they want to reverse the most.

Map of the Personality Diagnosis Charts

Following is a Map of the Personality Charts, which helps you understand the layout of the personality charts. Following that is the Preventive Diagnosis Cheat Sheet, which may make it easier to remember and track personalities. I begin my series with a description of the Healthy Personality.

CAUSE (How Parents Make the Personality)

Attachment	Describes the nature of the child's attachment.
Second Year On	This section describes the parenting style from the Second Year On, during the discipline phase of development. This includes behaviors, words and attitudes of parents.

EFFECT (How the Child Reveals the Personality He Is Developing)

Infant/ Toddler	INNER THOUGHTS: This section hypothesizes on the infant's **interior world** that develops as a result of parental bonding and attachment behavior in the first year. These inner thoughts include **false beliefs, fears, needs, desires, motives, drives** and **agendas**.
Older Child	This section describes the child's responses to the parenting style of the Second Year On, in terms of appearance and behavior. (Possible or allowable existing childhood diagnosis)
	INNER THOUGHTS: This section describes the child's interior world resulting from the second-year-on parenting style: false beliefs, fears, needs, desires, motives, drives and agendas.
Adult	This section describes the **grown child** – the adult personality **traits** resulting from the parenting errors described above. This section may or may not be divided into attachment issues and second-year-on issues.
	ATTACHMENT ISSUES: Adult traits resulting from attachment failures.
	SECOND-YEAR-ON ISSUES AND INTERACTION STYLE: Adult traits resulting from second-year-on discipline and parenting mistakes.

Preventive Diagnosis Cheat Sheet

Personality	Attachment	Individuation
Passive-Aggressive	maybe normal	guilt, sarcasm about feelings
Dependent	maybe normal	either too early or too late
Obsessive-Compulsive	normal or obsessive care	potty training: comply (anxious) or defy (avoidant)
Histrionic	positive or neglectful care	incest or over-stimulating touch
Narcissist	weak or cold mother	mother needs a happy face, has weak limit setting, superiority ethic or cold rules
Clinging Borderline	erratic bonding, frequent abandonments	**overpowered** (domineering parents) or unprotected
Distancing Borderline	**intrusive** bonding	either suffocated or alienated
Avoidant	mother is present but neglectful	ruthless **punishment of failures** and/or **brief idealization of child after neglect**
Approach-Avoidant	stigmatized, child expected to match mom's projections	abusive/rejecting for leaving mom or complaining to mom, then mom gives conflicting messages: come close then get away
Schizoid	mechanical, aloof, **insufficient touch**	mechanical
Schizotypal	insufficient touch	threats of god or spirits, other-worldly reasoning
Schizophrenic	insufficient touch, inappropriate response to infant's needs	incorrect yet strong ascription of motive (**projections**), "double-bind" (**mixed messages**), inappropriate parental responses, possible abuse
Dissociative Disorder (Mult.Pers.)	mother may sometimes be nurturing and other times abusive	radically **diverse experiences** including positive and horrible, **cruel** tortures, usually includes religious and sexual abuse
Paranoid	erratic care, possibly threatening	severe physical or emotional **abuse out of the blue**
Antisocial	erratic, possibly threatening chronic abandonment and/or major attachment breaks	often lower socioeconomic background, major **neglect**, **cruel** punishments, chronic rejection, shaming, sexual abuse, imprinting of destructive choices
Sociopath	**no attachment**, or **cold** or **severe** attachment break(s)	**upper-class** or rigid training for appropriateness or discipline to **perform with superiority**, appropriateness, deception, and **retribution**; imprinting
Psychopath	**infant abuse and/or lack of empathy**, rare warmth, major attachment breaks	torture, **cruel**, erratic, vicious discipline or **mind-warping experiences**
Rapist	lack of maternal empathy, mother may despise child	**mother tortures son** and/or ridicules his masculinity, mother sets up molestation or abuse by male and **refuses to protect**
Mass Murderer	attachment break(s), repression of infant	**cruel**, **critical father**, huge loyalty and repression ethic
Serial Killer	**cruel or absent mother**, repression ethic	**cruel &/or unprotective mother**, repression ethic, hidden family secrets, absolute loyalty

Personality Diagnosis Charts

HEALTHY

How to raise a Miracle Child. This child is adored from birth and so becomes adorable. People warm to her as a matter of course and she is accustomed to winning. As an adult, she is charismatic, charming, ethical, clear-thinking and clear-speaking. She attracts people like a magnet with her humble self-worth and good humor. She was cherished as a child, and she will be revered as an adult. She is twice-blessed.

Twice-Blessed or Miracle Child: Derived from Good Parenting

CAUSE

Attachment	**Secure attachment.** Mother and father are overjoyed with their new arrival. The parents gaze deeply into their child's eyes. The bonding is **tender, empathic and responsive.** The caregiving is **continuous,** without breaks of more than a few hours at the most here or there. **There are no rotating caregivers.**
Second Year On	Parents **delight** in the child's unfolding as much as ever. Parents **allow** the child to **express anger** and other emotions freely, especially when injured, but no judgment or name-calling is allowed. Parents **trust** the child to explore and try things out freely within limits. Child is encouraged to have adventures, to communicate, to self-reflect and to try new things. Parents **nurture independence.** Parents show visceral disapproval for mean or selfish behaviors. Limits and boundaries are set frequently with **natural consequences** and no more than one warning, but parents don't over-parent. When parents take a stand, they follow through and keep their word. Parents **model morals, ethics and values.** Parents teach their child how to speak up diplomatically in confrontations – parents **model relationship skills.**

EFFECT

Infant/ Toddler	The baby learns to **smile** right away. The baby responds to a deep loving gaze with **alertness** and a look of intelligence. The baby looks happy and contented. The baby is so much fun to hold that people don't want to put her down. INNER THOUGHTS: The baby develops **deep trust** and never even considers that he/she might be left alone prematurely. "I love life. I love my mommy and daddy. I love people. I love the world. Wow! Wow! Wow!"
Child	This is a low-maintenance, mellow, warm, easy-going, good-natured, thoughtful, considerate, happy, creative, intelligent, moral and ethical child. This child attracts compliments galore. He is already a natural leader and everybody who knows him wants to be with him as much as they can. People are drawn to him. He's distinctively different than the other children. INNER THOUGHTS: "I can't wait to walk! I want to discover everything. I feel brave. I like talking and thinking. I love learning." (Brilliant)
Adult	ATTACHMENT ISSUES: Able to perceive and gently reject potential unhealthy mates and attract a **healthy mate.** Capable of and enjoys all forms of **intimacy:** physical, emotional, spiritual. Is tender, romantic, thoughtful. SECOND-YEAR-ON INTERACTION STYLE: **Self-disciplined, self-motivated, very high functioning.** Questions ideas and wants to understand the nature of things. **Interested** in philosophy, justice, creativity, ground-breaking discoveries and other forms of pioneering and leadership. Stands up for what is right and fair and does the right thing, even when it's difficult to do. Examples: Mother Teresa, Jesus, The Buddha, Moses, Phil Donahue, Mikhail Gorbachev.

PASSIVE-AGGRESSIVE

This is the healthiest-appearing diagnostic category. In the grown child, dysfunction appears in the form of avoidance. In relating to a PA in a disagreement, it's hard to get a handle on what their issue is.

Secretly Angry Child:
Derived from Diminishing Child's Feelings

CAUSE

Attachment	**Secure or avoidant attachment.** Possibly normal bonding. Possibly excellent bonding.
Second Year On	Parents set few limits. Parents discipline/control this child by either **sarcasm** or **guilt** or both. Parent may **criticize through innuendo**. Mother may be weak, even dependent. Parent models passiveness in problem-solving and relationship skills. Parent may give numerous **mixed messages** where actions don't match words. Some fathers may be physically or **emotionally absent**. Parental affections may have been given to another favored child. Older siblings may be responsible for parents' feelings. **Parents' feelings supersede** child's feelings.

EFFECT

Infant/ Toddler	Infant looks normal. INNER THOUGHTS: "Life is good. I love my mommy and daddy."
Child	This child looks smart, but **inward**. The content of his inner world is not available to the parent or other adults. He is not a great striver. He contests little and **avoids** a lot. INNER THOUGHTS: Child **fears** that straight-on expression of independent or negative feelings will cause catastrophe, **rejection**, **abandonment**, **criticism** or sarcasm. Child craves a strong parent to make them act on their own behalf. "The less I expose myself (disagree, express my feelings or commit), the less I will be subjected to guilt-tripping or sarcasm."
Adult	ATTACHMENT ISSUES: Usually has great eye contact, a warm manner and comfortable countenance. Likeable. SECOND-YEAR-ON ISSUES AND INTERACTION STYLE: **Fears confrontation**. **Fears commitment**. Experiences difficulty identifying **feelings**. Believes has to understand feelings first before making **choices**. **Avoids problem-solving** or acting on obvious imperatives. Is forgetful and **procrastinates**, feeling both obligated and rebellious. Offered insights, they say, "yes, but..." Is negativistic. May resent requests or pressure to act on ideas that are not their own. May drift through life. Scorns those in power. May agree to do what someone wants and then continue to do what he/she intended to do in the first place. May be highly **unreliable**, making others very angry. They are not known for honor or keeping their word. Has a humble ethic. Feels misunderstood. Tends to underachieve. Underestimates opportunities. Secretly wishes that a strong person would read his/her mind and take care of him/her. Is **indirect** with wants or anger. Handles disagreements by quitting, walking out or refusing to talk. Is two-faced. A common misunderstanding is that Passive-Aggressive types vacillate from passive to aggressive. This is not true. Their version of aggression is refusing to keep their word and refusing to cooperate. That is a very substantial expression of aggression. It can be very difficult to deal with this personality type in a relationship or group.

PASSIVE-AGGRESSIVE, cont'd
Anecdotal Application
When I was learning diagnosis in my first class I believed I recognized every diagnosis except passive-aggressive. I thought to myself, "I've never met a passive-aggressive before." Lo and behold, my business partner was passive-aggressive and my husband was passive-aggressive. They were right under my nose and I didn't even know it.

You don't think there is anything wrong with them at first because they are so easy-going, mellow and good-natured. Yet they can be uncooperative and won't tell you if they have an issue with you. It is very possible they'll even disappear on you. If they don't disappear on you, they may sabotage a cooperative venture. They may agree to go camping with you, then complain about everything and want to go home. Or they may offer to do your laundry because you have an important meeting the next day, then "forget" to do it. But they didn't really forget. Instead they were mad at you for something else and kept saying, "I'll get to it. I'll get to it," and pushing it to the bottom of their priorities until they ran out of time to do it.

Passive-Aggressive Personality Disorder as defined in Gerry Grossman Seminars MFT license exam prep materials:
This diagnostic category is characterized by being aggressive by not doing things: procrastinating, "forgetting," not doing jobs or chores correctly, whining when asked to do something. People with Passive-Aggressive Personality Disorder don't want to hear suggestions on how to do things better and resent authority.

DEPENDENT

The adults never get to grow up because they were either held back or forced to grow up too soon. Subtypes (2): Infantilized Child: Princess Baby/Baby Prince and Parentified Child: Baby Mom/Little Man.

Infantilized Child: Princess Baby or Baby Prince: Derived from Holding Child Back

CAUSE

Attachment	Bonding could be good or not. Mother is getting positive identity for mothering. Mother is self-invested.
Second Year On	The child is **kept young**, infantilized. The child is a possession. Parents restrict child's initiative and exploring. Parents worry excessively over child. Parents try to keep baby from growing up. Parents make life too easy through over-protectiveness. Parents talk down to her like she's a baby, even after she's well into grammar school. Parents dress her in "cutesy" outfits, especially with ruffles and bows. The child is rescued from her feelings.

EFFECT

Princess Baby	**Separation Anxiety**, but not from separation trauma (unless she experiences both causes of separation anxiety), but from being denied normal separation. This little girl will act like a **baby** and will do "baby talk" to engage an adult. She may even throw tantrums like a baby and act inappropriately in public places or she will act "darling."
	INNER THOUGHTS: This child **knows that she is not really being seen**, that she's stuck in a projection and can't get out. She throws her tantrums to get out of the projection and to be seen. She's craving that her parents will demand she get off it, treat her with higher expectations and according to her age.
Baby Prince	**Separation Anxiety.** This child looks likes a **mama's boy**. He may even have classical features of ruddy complexion, pudgy body or scrawny body. He's probably a whiner, complainer. He's a weak-acting, over-protected, awkward boy.
	INNER THOUGHTS: He's begun to be **embarrassed** that his mother infantilizes him, but he doesn't know what to do. He needs his father to move in and help him separate and do more manly things.
Adult	These traits primarily result from being kept from individuating out of the bonding and attachment stage.
	Princess Baby: Copes by being cute and helpless. Acts like a little girl, especially noticeable in voice, dress, actions and helplessness. Some simply ensure their caretaking by holding onto their helplessness. They choose mates upon whom they can depend.
	Baby Prince: Not a go-getter. Somewhat paralyzed and dependent upon instructions or instructors. He falls into relationships where someone will take care of him.

DEPENDENT, cont'd

Parentified Child: Baby Mom or Little Man: Derived from Too Much Responsibility

CAUSE

Attachment	Bonding could be good or not. **Under-nurturing** mother or nurturing mother needs help. Mother may be depressed. Mother may be dependent herself. New infant comes along too soon.
Second Year On	Parents may be alcoholic, dependent or disabled. Child is parentified and forced to grow up too soon, which taps into first-year internal gains. Child is placed in role of **caretaker**. **Child's feelings don't matter**. Only parent's feelings matter.

EFFECT

Infant/ Toddler	**Separation Anxiety**. The child worries about taking care of mommy. Will she be alright if I leave? The child wets the bed for years after she/he should be dry. The child is secretly an infant over-his-head in responsibility. Normal until child can walk. **Prematurely** starts to take care of mother and help her. The child will look **responsible** for the parent. Grown-ups often admire this child. INNER THOUGHTS: "Mommy needs me."
Child	Separation Anxiety. Enuresis. Starts with **sparing mother's feelings**, helping mommy too much and "being strong for mommy." People will think this child is the *best* child. She or he will be a consummate caretaker, maybe caring for younger children. She will act incredibly **mature, helpful** and **thoughtful**. INNER THOUGHTS: She is hoping/believing that if she takes care of mommy enough, someday mommy will take care of her.
Adult	ATTACHMENT ISSUES: (These traits are primarily a result of not finishing being a baby before being required to grow up.) **Helplessness** and **weakness** will come as an eventual surprise to their mate, who has been nurtured from the beginning of the relationship. SECOND-YEAR-ON ISSUES AND INTERACTION STYLE: Copes by winning people over with **caretaking**. As a child they heard how grown-up they were. As a grownup they are **underfueled**, wishing to be a child again or to find a caretaking mate. Nevertheless, they may become the caretaker, hoping they can earn or design a caretaker in their own image.

Anecdotal Application

I know a young man whose mother had twelve miscarriages before he was born, so when she finally had him she was excessively over-protective. When he got into high school the coach of the football team invited him to try out. He was thrilled and couldn't wait to get home. "Mom, you'll never guess what happened! The coach asked me to try out for football!" "Oh no," she said, "No way, I don't want anything to happen to you." When he was an adult I had a project with him. When I went to get lunch, he sat there and waited for me. When he went to get lunch, I kept working. He was always waiting for someone to tell him what to do next.

My husband worked with a woman who told him how she had to cook bacon and eggs for her parents as a young child. One day she accidently hit the handle on the frying pan, causing it to flip over and spill hot grease down her chest, burning her badly. She opened the first few buttons of her blouse to show my husband her terrible scars. A few weeks later this same woman was bragging how independent her five-year-old son was for being able to cook his own breakfast.

OBSESSIVE-COMPULSIVE

These uptight adults fear losing control. Subtypes (5): The Self-Controlled Child, The Defiant Child, The Compliant Child, The Slovenly Child, The Sickly (Anorexic) or Secretive (Bulimic) Child

Self-Controlling Child:
Derived from Abandonment

CAUSE

Attachment	Attachment break, which creates fear of loving, trusting or depending on others.
Second Year On	Parents usually admire this child and don't realize his independence is about fear of losing control resulting from attachment issues and fear of trusting.

EFFECT

Infant/ Toddler	Infant/Toddler seems adorably self-sufficient and under control.
	INNER THOUGHTS: Infant or young child decides he can't trust anyone, so he has to maintain control of himself or others. "I'm really on my own here." "I'd better not lose control or I will die." "I don't need to share my feelings to get by."
Child	The child acts **very controlled, organized** and **independent**, as if by doing so, he will be safer. You get a sense that underneath all this competency and order is anxiety. Everything else could be fine and people will just think this is an amazingly independent child. He is now developing a rigid or closed body armor. He does not want to appear vulnerable, especially emotionally.
	INNER THOUGHTS: (This diagnosis is due to attachment breaks and is not a result of second-year-on parenting.)
Adult	ATTACHMENT ISSUES: He has difficulty being vulnerable with his feelings. He has difficulty expressing warmth and intimacy. He has a hard affect. He keeps order. He is **demanding** that things be his way, under his control. He is a "control freak." He has difficulty delegating. He is **rigid** and stubborn.
	SECOND-YEAR-ON ISSUES AND INTERACTION STYLE: Issues could be anything, but broken attachment issue is primary.

OBSESSIVE-COMPULSIVE, cont'd

Defying Child:
Anal Retentive to Rebel against Control

CAUSE

Attachment	Mother is not soft and nurturing. Mother is already **forcing her ways on the child**, including food, schedules, diaper changing rejections and excessive alone time (extended stays in the crib or playpen).
Second Year On	As mom wants to potty train this child, even at a reasonable age, this child withholds pooping in order to defy Mommy. Parenting is intrusive and over-controlling.

EFFECT

Infant/ Toddler	This child has an **angry** cry. INNER THOUGHTS: "I hate the way you treat me."
Child	**Encopresis.** This child is **rebelling** against parental control by refusing to potty train. He will sit for hours on the potty and then poop in his diapers when mommy lets him off. INNER THOUGHTS: She is angry at mommy for having failed to nurture and protect her and for trying to control her all the time. She doesn't want to cooperate. Control of her bowels is the only power she has to rebel and to establish herself as separate from her mother. She **braces** herself against her mother's neglectful and intrusive and over-controlling behavior. "I'll get you. You don't love me, well I won't poop. You want to dominate me? You want me to poop? Well, I refuse to cooperate with you. You'll see, I'll poop when I feel like it." She develops a selfish template: "I'm not giving or sharing with you."
Adult	ATTACHMENT ISSUES: She has difficulty with intimacy. SECOND-YEAR-ON ISSUES AND INTERACTION STYLE: Hoards, skimps, is stingy. Can't throw things out. Is not generous with others. Keeps records of gifts or trades. Doesn't volunteer. She seems selfish. She is rigid and stubborn.

OBSESSIVE-COMPULSIVE, cont'd

Slovenly Child:
Anal Expulsive to Rebel against Control

CAUSE

Attachment	Mother is insensitive to baby's needs. May be suffocating or neglectful. Or baby may be subject to invasive medical procedures.
Second Year On	Parenting is alternately weak and suffocating, domineering and over-controlling. Parent involves child in power struggle over potty training.

EFFECT

Infant/ Toddler	Baby has angry cry. Baby is fretful and frustrated. INNER THOUGHTS: "Damn it! Love me! See me!"
Child	**Encopresis.** This child is also a defiant child. He is angry and refuses to be controlled into pooping on request. He **rebels** against parental authority by pooping and smearing. He harbors contempt for adults, especially because all they want is to control him, not love and protect him. He will poop to express anger, especially if that will bother his parents. He may smear feces on the wall to express his lonely rage and feelings of not being seen and protected. INNER THOUGHTS: "I hate you for treating me this way." "I'll rub your nose in it." "I know you don't see me or get me and **I won't tolerate** the way you're treating me and neglecting me." "**I disregard you** for controlling." "You'll see. **No one will control me.**" "I will be a slob."
Adult	ATTACHMENT ISSUES: Hoards in an infantile way. Builds up useless filthy stockpiles as a sign of self-sufficiency, signifying, however, flagrant refusal to let go or attend to personal self-care. **Lives in junk, saves** everything, refusing to give up anything. Refuses to use deodorant or bathe. May **fart** in theatres and elevators. Angry. SECOND-YEAR-ON ISSUES AND INTERACTION STYLE: Angry. Asocial. Refuses to fall under anyone's authority. Obsessed with autonomy. May be an eccentric hermit.

OBSESSIVE-COMPULSIVE, cont'd

Complying Child:
Anal Retentive to Comply with Potty Training

CAUSE

Attachment	The bonding is not good. The parent **teases or ridicules** the child's pooping or **poop**, even in play. The parent may hold her nose while changing diapers or hold the diaper at arms length dangling off pinched fingers as if it were **disgusting** to her. The parent may even **react to spit-up**. Parent may hand him off every time he poops, saying, "Here, you change him." When the parent even tries to get the child to potty train before he is ready, the results are more serious in an infant under 18 months of age. The younger, the more harmful to the body and to the psyche. Parent seeks to quiet or **control emotions of infant**.
Second Year On	Parent may potty train before 18 months. Parent ridicules poop. Parent "shoulds" the child a lot. Parent **models compulsive tidiness, cleanliness and order**. Parent moves into "No. No. No." "Don't. Don't. Don't." Parent demands obedience and respect from child over personal behaviors. Parent demands that child "CONTROL YOURSELF." Parent **over-controls** the child's behavior. The house has to be kept clean. The child has to stay clean. The child has to put everything back exactly. The child has to eat all her food or the parent controls the child around eating too much or the "wrong" things. The child believes she must **control her feelings** too.

OBSESSIVE-COMPULSIVE, cont'd

Complying Child:
Anal Retentive to Comply with Potty Training

EFFECT

Infant/ Toddler	The child seems somewhat emotionally withdrawn. He may at first laugh at diaper play, but later hates it. Child acts afraid of pooping. Child cries when she poops. This begins when the child gets that there's something wrong with poop. Later, as the child tries to hold back from pooping and develops constipation, the child cries from pain and develops a **fear of pooping** or a retentive, controlled body defense, even though she comes to accept pooping intellectually.
	INNER THOUGHTS: The child thinks that what her body does is disgusting to her mother or caregiver. She doesn't know that her mother and father poop too. She thinks **there's something wrong** with her uniquely and intrinsically that would be fixed if she could stop pooping or control herself better. "If I could control myself I wouldn't be so yucky to mommy."
Child	This child begins to look restricted, lacking spontaneity. The child may stress over homework, even hitting himself when he errs. She may be **excessively clean or orderly**, having a penchant for details, categories, accurateness organization, schedules, lists, definitions, logic, *etc.*, as if maintaining control and **perfection** will redeem her. She is extremely vigilant about morals and ethics. Many adults, even therapists, may admire her.
	INNER THOUGHTS: She wants to be a very obedient and disciplined child, living by the book, in deep hopes she can overcome her flaw: that she poops and she is dirty. This child has a shame-based, self-loathing personality, even though she may be as demanding of others as of herself.
	She thinks, "If I control myself enough, if I try hard enough, if I am good enough, if I protect others from my real secret self and my disgusting ways carefully enough, I might finally be loveable."
Adult	FROM ATTACHMENT ISSUES: He is a **perfectionist**, trying to compensate for his **shame**. He may be prone to colonics.
	FROM SECOND-YEAR-ON ISSUES AND INTERACTION STYLE: He is a workaholic, making little time for play or family. He is rigid and stubborn, a "**should-freak**." He has difficulty delegating. He believes he should be just-so and others should be just-so. He **lacks spontaneity** and is rules-oriented. He needs his rules to live by – **rules comfort him**. He obsesses over dirt. He is extremely neat. He lacks warmth.

OBSESSIVE-COMPULSIVE, cont'd

Sickly (Anorexic) or Secretive (Bulimic) Child: Derived from Need to Control Something

CAUSE

Attachment	Anxious attachment. Insufficient nurturing. Interaction **lacks warmth**.
Second Year On	Mother is unprotective, overcontrolling and perfectionistic. Child is frequently a victim of **sexual abuse**. Mother doesn't see or help. Mother worries about her own weight and her ability to keep a mate. Mother or father may have been critical of daughter's weight or that of other girls and/or women. Father or mother dominates rather than nurtures. Parents/ mother may demand that she eat or ridicule for eating too much.

EFFECT

Infant/ Toddler	Infant may spit up or **reject nursing** or bottle in reaction to mother's nervousness or lack of warmth. INNER THOUGHTS: She believes that if she looks thin enough she'll be lovable or if she looks sickly enough, her mother will finally want to nurture her emotionally or pay attention to her. "I hate having food forced on me your way. It's your love and warmth I want. You make me hate food and I'm so **hungry** for you. I hate you and I love you."
Child	She develops the self-control to refuse food either because it's forced on her in lieu of emotional nurturing and/or in order to attract attention for her starvation to be loved and/or protected. She may hoard and hide food, gorging and, when older, throwing it up. INNER THOUGHTS: This child is desperate to achieve a sense of worth and warmth through self-control and self-determination, controlling one or both of the two things that no one else can control: eating and/or pooping. The child starts to obsess around food and her ability to control her hunger. She is hungry inside. She is reinforced in these beliefs by her mother's disdain for fat and her mother's belief in thinness as the way to get love. She's crying for help and to be seen, perhaps to be rescued from incest or sexual abuse. "If I starve enough I won't look like a woman and he won't continue to rape/molest me." "The one thing I can do to control my worth is practice self-control and not eat. "Everyone will finally see me."
Adult	ATTACHMENT ISSUES: Hunger for food and nurturing. Fear of weight gain to the degree that she thinks she's fat when she's too thin for her health. Hope that if she's thin enough, she will get nurtured and rescued. SECOND-YEAR-ON ISSUES AND INTERACTION STYLE: Belief that being thin enough will establish her worth, autonomy, self-control and perhaps, safety.

OBSESSIVE-COMPULSIVE, cont'd
Anecdotal Application
I once had a student in my parenting class who had a great deal of difficulty with the concept of setting limits. I had recommended to parents that they not go overboard with limits, that three is more than enough. He raised his hand in class to tell me that three limits would be impossible in his home. I told him he would need to correct that. At the next lecture he was excited to tell me he had solved the problem. Of course I was curious. He said, "I only have one limit now. It's the whole house."

Obsessive-Compulsive Personality Disorder as defined in Gerry Grossman Seminars MFT license exam prep materials:
Obsessive-Compulsive Personality Disorder is an inflexible need to strive for perfection which interferes with other activities. Organization, details and order are overly important and there is an insistence that others will comply to these ways. It is difficult making decisions for fear of making a mistake. Being a "workaholic" is common, excluding fun-time and friendships. Often there is little affection or generosity shown to others."

HISTRIONIC

Histrionics are highly provocative in order to re-enact their trauma(s). Subtypes (2): The Shocking Child, The Entertaining Child.

Entertaining Child: Derived from Incest

CAUSE

Attachment	This child may have any level of bonding, from good to neglectful to over-stimulated, with hyper or rough adult playfulness. Occasionally, infants are victims of sexual abuse.
Second Year On	Father, step-father or live-in boyfriend **incests** her. The child doesn't tell her mother because she thinks Mom couldn't handle it or because the perpetrator threatens her or her mother. Maybe the mother refuses to know. In any event, the **mother is in denial** because a tuned-in parent would pick it up. The mother may have been molested as a child, herself and in denial herself. **Mother may be very sexual herself**, believing she has to use her sexuality to keep a man. Mother may be weak. **Father** or father figure **may be macho male**, schizoid (sees child as object), **weak** (feels masculine only with children), **psychopathic** (violent in a multitude of vicious ways) or **sociopathic** (needs to violate norms under your nose while acting appropriate to outsiders). Deep conversation not modeled or encouraged, possibly discouraged.

EFFECT

Infant/ Toddler	Normal. The over-stimulated infant will seem hyperactive.
	INNER THOUGHTS: "See me. See me." Over-stimulated infant: "Don't play so rough. Okay, so play rough."
Child	ADHD. May play the role of **surrogate wife**. Acts sexual with other children. In more extreme cases, she may be caught masturbating at school or frequently at home. May be involved in **compulsive sex play** with other children. Adults will need to keep her away from these children, unless the play is monitored at all times. Learns only way to get attention is to entertain adults.
	INNER THOUGHTS: May have **split off** from incest experiences and recalls them only when the ritual begins. Believes her only worth is her sexuality and her ability to attract men. Infers she need not bother cultivating any depth of education, insight or character. Has **little regard for morals** or virtues. Sees herself in mother's role, taking her mother's place, coming between her father and her mother. Has been convinced by her perpetrator and possibly by her mother's behavior, that mother is a person who needs to be kept ignorant, that she has no one to protect her, that she has to **keep secrets** and can't tell her mother. Feels helpless. Believes she deserves to be treated this way.
Adult	ATTACHMENT ISSUES: May feel empty and unseen. Or may be a hyperactive adult. Neglect may show up as helplessness, futility and emptiness.
	SECOND-YEAR-ON ISSUES AND INTERACTION STYLE: Acts **flirtatious**, yet may fear sex (may not know it). Provocative. Manipulative, feeling herself helpless. Thinks (as she has learned) the only way to get her needs met is through men. **Secretive** and sneaky. May have unconscious drive to come between couples (like mommy and daddy). Acts entertaining and **melodramatic**. Great attention to dress and make-up. May believe because she was treated this way, she is ruined.

HISTRIONIC, cont'd

Shocking Child:
Derived from Lack of Touch in First Year(s)

CAUSE

Attachment	This child has been **deprived of touch** in the first year of life or had only enough touch to crave it.
Second Year On	More of the same **neglect**. May have also experienced sexual abuse, since neglected children have a higher incidence.

EFFECT

Infant/ Toddler	Ambivalent Attachment. Infant seeks touch or affection from anyone. Eyes grab hold of strangers. Head-banging. Rocking. INNER THOUGHTS: "Are you my mommy? How about you? Are *you* my mommy?"
Child	**ADHD. Tricotillomania.** He is continuously seeking proximity to adults and others, finding ways to be seen, to **touch** and be touched. Boy children may begin to play with Barbies or wherever they can find silk. The child can be seen to seek silk or other skin substitute. They seem to have a fantasy life of pretend, involving touching. They may have two dolls lying together just for the touching. Both boys and girls may draw on their skin. They may pull hairs out of their scalp. Other behaviors include scab picking, nail biting, hand flapping, rocking, cutting. They are looking for smooth skin, yet there is no real source in their mother. Girls may want to lay with boys or have sex with boys for the skin. INNER THOUGHTS: This child will do whatever it takes to get skin contact and/or attention. "See-me-and-my-skin, damn you!" "Touch me or I'll hate you." "I'll **decorate** my skin and body so they'll be shocked and then they'll see me." "Be dramatic. **Shock people.**"
Adult	ATTACHMENT ISSUES: He decorates his skin to an extreme. Acts provocatively. Looks radical and seductive. SECOND-YEAR-ON ISSUES AND INTERACTION STYLE: Does outrageous, often sexually provocative things to be seen and to express anger for neglect. Examples: Marilyn Manson, Dennis Rodman, Alice Cooper.

HISTRIONIC, cont'd

Anecdotal Application

I know a histrionic woman who went to a couple's party with her husband. The guys were all drinking beer in the hot tub. She decided to join them in her t-shirt and shorts, which of course soaked through. The wives complained to her. She told me, "I don't know what they mean. I'm not after their husbands." She was a victim of incest.

In past classes on diagnosis, I have wondered aloud to my students about the famous basketball player Dennis Rodman, whose antics have always seemed histrionic. I have speculated that he may have suffered from a lack of touch because of the way he brightened his hair and kept silky fabrics around him. On August 12, 2011, he was inducted into the National Basketball Hall of Fame in Springfield, Massachusetts. One of my former students, Joe Brundige, sent me a write-up on his acceptance: *Known during his basketball career for his outlandish behavior and aggressive play, a sensitive, gentle Rodman gave a tear-filled, heartfelt induction speech. While his self-declared surrogate father Phil Jackson stood by his side, Rodman recounted his rough early beginnings and described how lucky he was to have made it to the NBA. "This game has been very good to me," Rodman said, "I could have been anywhere in the world...I could have been dead, I could have been a drug dealer, I could have been homeless – I was homeless." He went on to describe how difficult it was growing up in the projects without a father and with a mother who worked two jobs and scarcely showed him love. "My mother kicked me out of the house when I was 16. I resented her for a long time...and it's hard for me to even say this...my mother rarely ever hugged me or hugged my siblings. She didn't know how. I'm not like most of you guys who sit there and say 'when I make money in the NBA I'm going to take care of my mother and father.' I was a little selfish because of what she did to me in my life." Despite the lack of love his mother gave, he spoke of trying to heal the relationship and wrapped up his speech by saying to her, "Hopefully in the future...I can love you like I used to when I was born."*

NARCISSISTIC

Subtypes (5): The Demeaning Child, The Fake Positive Child, The Royal Child, The Coveting Child, The Got-It-Handled Child

Royal-Acting Child:
Derived from Superior-Acting Parents

CAUSE

Attachment	Parents may enjoy their **superior baby** or not, but they **don't attune** to her. Parents **lack empathy**.
Second Year On	Parents brag so much that child feels pressure. Parents act superior. Parents train child in appropriateness.

EFFECT

Infant/ Toddler	Avoidant attachment. Indifferent to parents. INNER THOUGHTS: "So, this is how we act."
Child	The child **adopts superiority** similar to mother and/or father out of defense against rejection, a desire to please or belong and imprinting. INNER THOUGHTS: Believes to a great extent, consciously, that he is greater than or superior to others (including adults) and therefore entitled to better treatment and deals. Believes he has the **right to talk down** to others and they shouldn't mind. May be **outraged at negative mirroring**. He handles disagreements by **dismissing** others. Inside, he fears he's only average, which would humiliate and ruin him.
Adult	ATTACHMENT ISSUES: Not very perceptive of others. Lacks empathy. Dismissive. SECOND-YEAR-ON ISSUES AND INTERACTION STYLE: Acts **superior, arrogant**. Acts **entitled**. Looks down nose with **long eyelids**. Holds hands in A-form tent or stretches arms out over sofa back. Talks down to everyone, believing they shouldn't mind. Response to negative mirroring is to "demean, devalue and destroy."

NARCISSISTIC, cont'd

Faking Positive Child (Light Narcissist):
Derived from Insecure Parents

CAUSE

Attachment	**Anxious attachment.** Parent/mother lacks empathy or perception for the infant, displaying superficial affection, expecting the child to engage on a **happy** level. Laughing, lifting, tickling, cheek pulling, blowing, *etc.*
	Mother needs a happy infant. Her own insecurity may be apparent to her baby. She needs the child not to cry. She teaches the baby not to cry by passing her off if she cries, by jiggling her hard and shushing her when she cries, by acting worried and weak or insecure when the baby cries. Mother and father begin the process of projecting onto the infant that they need her to act happy and to hold off crying.
Second Year On	Parents are clear that if you don't have anything nice to say, don't say it.
	They don't want to hear complaining. To get attention the child has to swallow her authentic negative feelings. Mother's intolerance of negative emotions forces the child to develop a false self through **repression of his negative emotions** and feelings. The child has learned to put on a **positive face**. She hears her parents **bragging** about her superiority. She gets that she needs to be better than others. Her mother is concerned about appearances when they go places or people come over. Child has to **reassure** her mother to keep her intact.

NARCISSISTIC, cont'd

Faking Positive Child (Light Narcissist): Derived from Insecure Parents

EFFECT

Infant/ Toddler	Baby **puckers**, trying not to cry. Baby tries to smile when sad, **gasps** when crying to hold in tears. INNER THOUGHTS: "I have to smile to get attention. If I cry, mommy won't love me."
Child	This child **avoids crying**. Will feed herself, **sing songs**, humor herself. She draws and brings mother **pretty pictures** to cheer mother. She draws attention to herself by being entertaining and "happy." She makes superior grades and tries to be perfect for mother. She acts better than the other kids, because it pleases her competitive parents. She tells mother how wonderful or pretty she is. She **reassures mother** not to cry or be sad. (ADHD, ODD) INNER THOUGHTS: The child feels unaccepted for real self. She thinks she has to put up a **false front**. She wears a bright mask. She believes on one level that she IS superior, but on another level she needs and is determined to get proof from others (mirroring) that she is superior. She believes in **inherent superiority** and giftedness and that she must be in that category or she is worthless. To be equal to others would be inferior. She believes in positivity at the expense of authentic expression of negative feelings. She is compulsive about looking at the bright side of things. She imposes that on others and doesn't want to hear their problems. She has a **deep dark secret** that she has negative feelings. That secret haunts her and makes her feel like an imposter. Yet deep down she would be relieved to be exposed for being a normal person with dark feelings if she could be accepted. But she can't risk it.
Adult	ATTACHMENT ISSUES: He feels **empty inside** and desperately needs mirroring that he is wonderful. Is disconnected from feelings, except is always in pursuit of adoration to replace the loss of empathy or loss of self. Requires living in the spotlight. SECOND-YEAR-ON ISSUES AND INTERACTION STYLE: **Inflated sense of self**. Inability to see the world through the eyes of another (**lacks empathy**). Self-important. Has a false self for the world, with an unconscious fear of being discovered to be an **imposter**. When emotionally wounded, he wants to **demean, devalue and destroy**. Often intellectual, analytical and so-called rational. Very **high-functioning** in economic circles. He is difficult to be with in a relationship and often finally ends up alone. He has a dramatic fear of death (without a belief system of afterlife). He is always fending off depression and hidden shame (unconsciously). He is a fanatical positive thinker.

NARCISSISTIC, cont'd

Demeaning Child (Dark Narcissist):
Derived from Weak Parents and Weak Discipline

CAUSE

Attachment	Avoidant Attachment. Mother seems **afraid of infant's emotions** and infant sees she is weak and nervous. Mother fails to offer empathy to infant.
Second Year On	From weak or **inconsistent limit-setting**, the child develops contempt for adult strength (weakness) and escalates negative behavior, daring someone to be strong enough to stop him.

EFFECT

Infant/ Toddler	This may be a **colicky baby**. The baby has learned to steer clear to avoid her weakness. INNER THOUGHTS: "She can't take care of me!"
Child	**ADHD.** Child is arrogant, **defiant** and contemptuous of others while cracking sarcastic, entertaining, judgmental jokes. Child **tests mother**, proving she is weak in limit setting and child develops and shows contempt for her and other adults on discovering that they cannot contain him. Child will probably throw an inordinate amount of **temper tantrums** in a desperate attempt to be contained (have his negative feelings accepted/received) and to get mother to prove her strength. Appears to lack empathy for anyone. INNER THOUGHTS: Harbors **deep anger**. Along with believing rules are not meant for him, he believes there are no grown-ups strong enough to stop him or protect him and that makes him furious. He **dares** them to be strong enough to deal with him and if they don't measure up, they'll be sorry. "Mother is too weak to take care of me."
Adult	ATTACHMENT ISSUES: He **lacks empathy**. SECOND-YEAR-ON ISSUES AND INTERACTION STYLE: He is **contemptuous** of protocol, rules and authority. He is enraged when someone is critical of him and is vicious with words. He can occasionally put someone on a pedestal because they measure up. But when they fail, he will **"demean, devalue, destroy."** Lacks remorse.

NARCISSISTIC, cont'd

Coveting Child:
Derived from Withholding Parents

CAUSE

Attachment	**Ambivalent attachment.** Mother expects infant to attune to her, rather than vice versa.
Second Year On	Mother is emotionally unavailable. Parent favors another child.

EFFECT

Infant/ Toddler	Baby cries a lot, then withdraws. Baby is occasionally **angry at others, but not at mom**.
	INNER THOUGHTS: "Mom's fine. Others are the problem."
Child	**ADHD. ODD. CD.** He has few friends and acts selfishly. Appears very selfish and self-centered. Lacks empathy. May laugh at other people's hardships.
	INNER THOUGHTS: "I have to get mine for myself." "Who wants warmth anyway? I sure don't." "I don't need anybody and I can fend for myself." "It's a dog-eat-dog world and I'll be the best at this game." He is very **jealous** or envious of others.
Adult	ATTACHMENT ISSUES: Lack of empathy. Inability to be intimate.
	SECOND-YEAR-ON ISSUES AND INTERACTION STYLE: Is competitive and jealous of others. Cannot be happy for the success of another. May be judgmental of others. Wants attention from them. May be cold, rejecting, mean-spirited, angry, arrogant or hurtful. May be willing to do anything to get the attention for herself. She may be lonely, but in denial. She seems inauthentic, like she is always acting. She appears to have little going on inside.

NARCISSISTIC, cont'd

Got-It-Handled Child:
Derived from Weak Attachment

CAUSE

Attachment	Broken or tenuous attachment. Child decided in infancy that she was on her own and didn't need anyone.
Second Year On	Child is like a mob boss: he doesn't need anyone, but others need him.

EFFECT

Infant/ Toddler	Baby is unattached and refuses to cuddle, make intimate eye contact up-close and has a demanding cry. INNER THOUGHTS: "I don't need anyone. I can demand what I need."
Child	ADHD. ODD. CD. He has few friends and acts selfishly. Appears controlling and self-centered. Lacks empathy. May laugh at other people's hardships. INNER THOUGHTS: "I don't need anybody and I can fend for myself." "It's a dog-eat-dog world and I'll be the best at this game."
Adult	ATTACHMENT ISSUES: Lack of empathy. Inability to be intimate. SECOND-YEAR-ON ISSUES AND INTERACTION STYLE: **I am the boss. High functioning**. Usually has power.

Anecdotal Application

My son has two uncles: my brother and my husband's brother. Both of them are very self-important, but both are also very helpful and often assume they have something to offer that you had never considered. My husband's brother had to take care of his mother's identity needs and is today a positive thinker by profession as a motivational speaker and hypnotherapist. He knows everything about everything. My brother had the same job and he knows everything too. Both of them became hostages of sorts as their respective mother's favorite, but it's not good when the two of them are together.

My son learned to diagnose people by the age of four. By six, he and I were diagnosing cars. A Cadillac might be a narcissist. By the time he was eight we were diagnosing drivers. Someone who pulled in front of you then drove slowly was probably passive-aggressive. He was very good at this game. Also when he was around eight years old, he, his father and I were invited to a party. There was a guy there who was very judgmental and demeaning. Scott turned to me and said, "Mommy, why are some narcissists light narcissists and others dark narcissists?" And so was born the distinction between those two personality types.

Narcissistic Personality Disorder as defined in Gerry Grossman Seminars MFT license exam prep materials:

Me me me me me. People who exaggerate their own worth, are preoccupied with themselves and have no empathy for others would fit this diagnosis. They cannot take criticism, are envious of others, crave compliments and use others for their own needs. There are fantasies of being beautiful, rich, powerful or famous and an expectation to be treated as such.

BORDERLINE

These children are underbonded and underattached in the first year and unprotected and assaulted in the second year on. Subtypes (5): The Dominated Child, The Unprotected Child, The Head-Tripped Child, The Suffocated Child, The Alienated Child

	Clinging		Clinging/ Distancing	Distancing	
Attachment	insecurely/ anxiously attached	anxiously attached	ambivalently attached, insufficient bonding	avoidantly attached	avoidantly attached
	erratic bonding	erratic bonding	interrupted bonding	smothered	cold mother
	frequent abandonments	frequent abandonments	fear that bonding leads to pain, such as minor abandonments or rejection		abandoned
Second Year On	DOMINATED overpowered criticized ridiculed threatened physically abused sexually abused	UNPROTECTED lack of guidance exposed to risks pedophiliacs substance abuse domestic violence	DOMINATED & UNPROTECTED (head-tripped)	SUFFOCATD over-controlled in the name of love, child can't bond because it's too much	ALIENATED rejected unprotected

BORDERLINE, cont'd

Dominated Child:
Derived from Neglect and Domination

CAUSE

Attachment	Anxious attachment. Infant is probably **undernurtured**. Bonding is probably **erratic**. Parents probably left child to cry for prolonged periods. Parent has erratic moods. Parent bonds and **abandons repeatedly**, leaving child hungry to bond (merge). Child may have suffered rotating caregivers or preschool. Child may have changed caregivers.
Second Year On	Child is not allowed to say no or talk back or even have a different opinion. Parents make a habit of saying **no**. Parent is probably a borderline. Parent is **domineering** in voice and actions. Parent is **overpowering** and **invasive**. Child is always on call to comply. Child is property of parent. Parent can come into child's room, listen on phone calls and invade child's life in any way. Parent presumes to define child's motives and intentions without consulting child. Parent defines and **subjugates** child's attempts to explore. Parent is constantly ordering child around. Parent may practice **verbal abuse**. Parent may practice **physical abuse**. Father may be passive. Father may be **sexually abusive**.

EFFECT

Infant/ Toddler	**Needy** and **clinging**, raging and crying when mother leaves. Rejects mother when she returns. Has a weak identity.
	INNER THOUGHTS: Represses **mistrust**. Fears criticism. **Splits-off** experiences. **Fragments** rudiments of personality. Hates mother for leaving and "could kill her." "I have to try to stop my mommy from leaving me."
Child	Looks oppressed, **hardened, brittle** or **downtrodden**. Looks **defensive**. Face looks worn. May be prone to **hitting** other children. Learns self-consciousness instead of competency. Lacks initiative and personal responsibility. **Blames** others for everything. (Separation Anxiety, ADHD)
	INNER THOUGHTS: "Avoid getting blamed." "Get nurturing however I can get it." "Don't try to take initiative."
Adult	ATTACHMENT ISSUES: As a result of anxious attachment, the adult looks:
	Hungry: Has feelings of **emptiness**, hunger to **merge**, a hunger for things that nurture such as money, food, attention, recognition, understanding, someone's faith in her, help, empathy, sympathy, positive mirroring, sex, skin contact of any kind, jewelry, *etc.* May abuse **substances**. Has tendency to **overspend**, going deep into debt. May have propensity for **kleptomania** or gambling. **Lacking Identity:** Has little sense of self and is thus vulnerable to the opinions and projections of others. Gets identity from others. Struggles against others over negative projections. Worst fears create the projections/opinions of others, including therapists in therapy. Rages **against negative mirrors** or invalidation. Personality depends on moods and projections of others, fragmented. Responds well to straight-forward natural open regardful feedback versus guessing games. Has difficulty with nervous or judgmental people who are prone to lack faith in her. Has difficulty with anyone who criticizes her or defines her negatively or who asserts power over her. **Lacks the power of definition** over herself, the world, reality, others and relationships. In an ongoing struggle to **define herself** or anything and will seek her own categories. May define herself in extremes: communist, socialist, revolutionary, atheist, Satanist, pagan, hippie,...

BORDERLINE, cont'd

Dominated Child:
Derived from Neglect and Domination

EFFECT, cont'd

Adult	...punk-rocker, bisexual, celibate. **Mistrustful:** Mistrustful and rageful, expecting to be abandoned or rejected. Needs to fight for control. Can't handle retentive, non-expressive, secretive, manipulative people who decline to reveal themselves and is a bad candidate for analysis. (Needs to do depth work with a mothering and guiding therapist.) **Suspicious** of and antagonistic towards everyone, especially those who are inauthentic, critical and judgmental. When he meets someone, the **projections** and self-fulfilling prophecies begin. **Fears abandonment:** Tendency to **cling** to others. Her fear of abandonment leads her to **create it**. Could become a victim of **spousal abuse** who would rather be abused than leave. Could be capable of dominating a mate into staying. Could be a **stalker**. Could kill or become involved in a murder-suicide before she would let someone leave her. If someone leaves or betrays her, she will be overrun with a drive for **retaliation** and could use the **children as pawns**.
	SECOND-YEAR-ON ISSUES AND INTERACTION STYLE: **Fragmentation of competency resulting from being dominated and lacking self-determination in early childhood:** Underdeveloped competency and highly underdeveloped automatic pilots. Good capacity to focus on A or B. Difficulty moving from A to B. Good vertical focus, fragmented horizontal movement. Absent-minded. Difficulty getting to places on time. Difficulty coordinating the simplest actions if they require multiple steps. Difficulty managing money and schedules. Expertise in anything should be used for a career. **Believes in luck:** Does not understand her lack of problem-solving limits her success. Wired-in **defense against blame**. Thinks/believes "responsibility" and "blame" mean the same thing, so she cannot take initiative nor does she know how. Professional innocence creates a professional victim. Propensity for gambling and get-rich-quick schemes. Thinks winners are lucky people. Boundary confusion: Tendency to invade another's space. Inadequacy at setting boundaries. Fears of projection are so great that she creates a self-fulfilling prophecy: Rages at lack of faith of others. Can only function in an environment of faith. (The field of psychology considers that her fear of projection is a self-fulfilling prophecy called projective identification. In the borderline's experience, the therapist may actually hold negative beliefs about the abilities of the borderline and compound the projection. See Faith *vs.* Negative Projections, Chapter 6) Rages at abuse of power: Feels and acts persecuted. Has difficulty with persons in power, including parents, therapists, doctors, teachers, lawyers, police, clergy and especially bosses. Probably has to be self-employed. Capable of domestic violence. May become involved in other forms of violent interactions that result from blaming ideation and behavior. Lesbianism may serve as a protection/defense against abusive men. Fears blame and judgment: Can't say no to sexual propositions, pressures or expectations. Often suffers or even creates "date rape" or unfulfilling promiscuity because she thinks she doesn't have choices. Thinks all criticism is because she is misunderstood (and she is), but she is also undereducated about the origin of competency and regard. Rages at criticism or completely despairs: Excessive internal results from feelings of being misunderstood. Creates insomnia. Creates abandonment or threats of abandonment. (Hypersensitivity to others can become an asset when she gives up defensiveness for perception.) Self-mutilating in extreme cases for lack of a better way to communicate and externalize her pain. Imprints: Abusiveness. Violent responses. Struggles for dominance.

BORDERLINE, cont'd

Unprotected Child:
Derived from Failure to Protect

CAUSE

Attachment	**Anxious attachment.** Bonding is **erratic**. Mother is insufficiently available. Parent bonds and abandons repeatedly, leaving baby hungry to merge or bond. Infant suffers short but frequent abandonments. Infant fears future abandonments. May have had different mother figures. The relationship with her mother is insecure. She doesn't feel the mother's investment in her. She is left to cry for prolonged periods. She is **undernurtured**.
Second Year On	Parent is reckless in who she associates with. The child is **unprotected** and **neglected**. Child may be **left unattended** or left with rotating caregivers. The child may be left with abusive caregivers, including pedophiles, substance abusers and physically abusive father, step-father or other father figures like mother's temporary boyfriends.

EFFECT

Infant/ Toddler	The baby is **inconsolable** and sometimes colicky. The toddler cries and **clings** when the mother leaves. Toddler is **needy** and may hoard food or steal. He covets other people's food. He may cling excessively to his transitional object or other toys. May indulge in **head banging** or rocking.
	INNER THOUGHTS: Baby **splits off** from feeling **abandonment and neglect** because it's too excruciating. She needs to be open to mother's infrequent warm moments. Baby develops **fragmented** personality. "This pain is so unbearable, I'd rather hurt myself than feel the pain." "I must be worthless for her to leave me so much." "She seems scary sometimes. I don't want to think about it."
Child	Toddler is anxious and **withdraws or clings** when left. He **fears rejection and abandonment**. He's beginning to act defensively. He's has **self-fulfilling prophecies** of anticipated rejection or abandonment. He has given up being understood. He has **little identity** and is extremely sensitive to name-calling; he develops a chip on his shoulder. He has **difficulty solving problems**, difficulty valuing himself, is prone to injure himself. He is absent-minded and **disorganized**. He is prone to violate other people's **boundaries**. He **lacks social interaction skills**. He acts desperate when little friends leave.
	He has begun to act out specific dramas from home. (Separation Anxiety, ADHD)
	INNER THOUGHTS: "I'm not safe." "I don't matter." **"Don't trust anyone."** "No one is going to protect me. I have to protect myself." **"I'm not to blame."** "I can act like they do. Beat 'em or join 'em."

BORDERLINE, cont'd

Unprotected Child:
Derived from Failure to Protect

EFFECT, cont'd

Adult	ATTACHMENT ISSUES: As a result of anxious attachment, the adult looks: **Hungry:** Has feelings of emptiness, hunger to merge, a hunger for things that nurture, such as money, food, attention, recognition, understanding, someone's faith in her, help, empathy, sympathy, positive mirroring, sex, lesbianism for maternal warmth, skin contact of any kind, jewelry, *etc.* May abuse substances, has tendency to overspend, going deep into debt. May have propensity for kleptomania, gambling or stealing. **Lacking Identity:** Has little sense of self and is thus vulnerable to the opinions and projections of others. **Gets identity from others.** Struggles against others over negative projections. Worst fears create the projections/opinions of others, including therapists in therapy. Rages against negative mirrors or invalidation. Personality depends upon moods and projections of others. Personality is fragmented. Responds well to straight-forward, natural, open, regardful feedback versus guessing games. She has difficulty with nervous or judgmental people who are prone to lack faith in her. She has difficulty with anyone who defines her negatively or who asserts power over her. She lacks the power of definition over herself, the world, reality, others and relationships. She is in an ongoing struggle to define herself or anything and will seek her own categories. May define herself in extremes: communist, socialist, revolutionary, homie, atheist, satanist, pagan, born-again, hippie, punk-rocker, recovering alcoholic, bisexual, celibate. **Mistrustful:** He is mistrustful, expecting to be abandoned or rejected. He needs to fight for control. He can't handle retentive, non-expressive, secretive, manipulative people who decline to reveal themselves and thus is a very bad candidate for analysis. He needs to do depth work with a mothering and guiding therapist. He is suspicious of everyone, especially those who are inauthentic, critical and judgmental. When he meets someone, the **projections** and self-fulfilling prophecies begin. **Fears abandonment:** Her fear of abandonment leads her to create it. She could become a victim of spousal abuse who would rather be abused than leave. She could be capable of dominating a mate into staying. She could be a stalker. She could kill or become involved in a murder-suicide before she would let someone leave her. If someone leaves or betrays her, she will be overrun with a drive for retaliation and could use the children as pawns. SECOND-YEAR-ON ISSUES AND INTERACTION STYLE: **Fragmentation of competency** from lack of guidance into personal habits. He becomes overwhelmed with multiple tasks. Has boundary confusion because boundaries were infrequently honored and he never finished merging. Believes in luck and lacks personal responsibility because his role models lacked personal responsibility and practiced blaming others including him. Puffs up his anger to ensure he is the one in power; that way he's safe. Prone to reckless choices, including reckless driving, drug use, reckless sex, fighting. **Imprints:** Those things she was exposed to, such as domestic violence, blaming, sexual abuse, substance abuse. May be defensive/aggressive. May need to dominate to feel safe.

BORDERLINE, cont'd

Head-Tripped Child:
Derived from Mother's Inconsistency

CAUSE

Attachment	**Ambivalent attachment.** Bonding is insufficient, interrupted and sometimes **unsafe.** The mother is **rejecting** of a clinging child. The mother has **erratic** moods and is sometimes emotionally available to the child and sometimes not.
Second Year On	The parent continues with mixed messages and mixed commitment to the child and is less interested because the child is harder to love now that she's so chronically angry. The parent is ambivalent about the child and the child is ambivalent about the parent. The parent may abuse the child. The parent blames the child.

EFFECT

Infant/ Toddler	The infant is often **inconsolable** and cries for her mother. She is difficult to console or comfort. She wants to be picked up and then wants to be put down. Sometimes she withdraws to protect herself. Disorganized.
	INNER THOUGHTS: Infant is **conflicted** between hope for more bonding and fear of more bonding. The infant fears that if she gets close she will suffer emotional pain, *e.g.*, another minor abandonment, rejection or scary mood of mother. She **hates** or **mistrusts** her mother. She is also **desperate** for her mother's affection. She is attuned to her mother's changing moods and availability and adapts her personality to match. Sometimes she **splits off** from the scary memories to avail herself of mother's good mood. Her personality has begun to **fragment**. She has a love/hate relationship with her mother. "I could bite her for leaving me." "I hate her, but if I get angry, maybe she won't love me." "I must be worthless." "I feel desperately empty and betrayed."
Child	She begins to **rage** and lie. She probably steals and fights and is getting into trouble hanging out with "bad" kids. She's **destructive** and **self-destructive**. This child is explosive and gets into trouble. (ADHD)
	INNER THOUGHTS: "Maybe if I killed mommy she wouldn't leave." "If she knows how I'm feeling I could lose her." "I have to hide my anger and act sweet." "I feel **hopeless and helpless.**" OLDER CHILD'S INNER THOUGHTS: "I hate the world." "I'll hurt anyone before they hurt me."

BORDERLINE, cont'd

Head-Tripped Child:
Derived from Mother's Inconsistency

EFFECT, cont'd

Adult	ATTACHMENT ISSUES: Ambivalent attachment makes the adult look: **Rageful at the threat of abandonment:** He could kill a mate for leaving or seek revenge in a custody dispute. He could stalk a mate he thinks is betraying him or drive a mate away with his anger over anticipated abandonment. He is looking for scapegoats for his rage, especially ones who remind him of his first-year-of-life caregivers. **Mistrustful:** She doesn't trust anyone's love for her and so she is difficult to love. She believes that she is safest with someone who is constantly available to keep or reject. Even this person she mistrusts. **Fearful of abandonment:** He creates self-fulfilling prophecies of rejection and abandonment which become evidence that people will hurt him. He needs people but has a chip on his shoulder. He may try to use force and coercion to keep a mate, even abusing her for lack of sufficient loyalty. **Empty:** She feels empty inside and desperately hungry for love. When she gets close enough for affection, she wants to hurt her love object, maybe biting him. She believes she is owed things that nurture, whether people or material objects. She will sue, gamble, steal, lie or cheat to get. She believes those who have were lucky in life and since she is unlucky, it's fair to turn to crime. She may turn to drugs and food to fill the emptiness. Can cause unbearable and severe depression. Can cause genuine suicide attempts. Can cause suicide threats or ingenuine attempts at suicide to communicate degree of despair, in desperate hope for help and relief. **Lacking Personal Responsibility:** Having no sense of personal power, he sees success as luck and doesn't understand why some people succeed. He lacks problem-solving abilities and perseverance and he doesn't learn from his mistakes. He blames others for his problems and can't get ahead. He feels undiscovered and misperceived and doesn't understand why some people have affinities for some people and not for others. Prone to reckless choices, reckless driving, risky sex, risky drug use. **Lacking Identity:** He lacks identity, any identity. He will settle for a negative identity rather than none. He feels completely unseen like he doesn't exist. **Fragmentation of Personality:** His personality is fragmented into different mood states with different memories, attitudes and beliefs. Sometimes he is sweet and vulnerable or he may reveal a desperate side of himself that is so low and self-deprecating it could be repugnant to others. He may have an arrogant side, a paranoid side and a very sane, wise and healthy side.
	SECOND-YEAR-ON ISSUES AND INTERACTION STYLE: This borderline would not do well to work at a post office or for any authoritarian boss in any rigid environment. This borderline is as **angry** as the dominated borderline. This borderline is the **most capable of murder, suicide, stalking, revenge**. He could commit spousal abuse. He is a full-blown victim and blamer. He feels that the best defense is a good offense. His thinking is disorganized. He doesn't get cause and effect. He doesn't get why some people are loved, why people stay, why people succeed. **Imprints:** Physical abuse. Domestic violence. Child abuse. Sexual abuse. Substance abuse.

BORDERLINE, cont'd

Alienated Child:
Derived from Mother's Detachment

CAUSE

Attachment	**Avoidant attachment.** Mother/parent is emotionally unavailable. May have multiple caregivers. Child may be kept still in playpen or out of the way so that child doesn't get to play and develop competencies and initiative.
Second Year On	Child's opinions are **disregarded**. Child's **emotional needs** for approval and understanding are **rarely met**. Child's **physical needs** may or may not also be **ignored**. Child may be sent away to a boarding school.

EFFECT

Infant/ Toddler	Child withdraws, accepting mother as-is. May accept/give in to multiple caregivers. INNER THOUGHTS: "I don't need much."
Child	Child may have difficulty learning to manage own affairs (*e.g.*, keeping track of things, being on time), especially when overwhelmed. Child looks shut down. INNER THOUGHTS: Child learns self-consciousness instead of competency. Child is subject to **depression**. Child is unaware of own depression and is in **denial**. Child feels **empty** and **worthless** but doesn't really know it. "I don't need much." "I don't need anyone." "I don't trust people." "I can steal or lie or cheat if I have to." "I need food or drugs to be happy."
Adult	ATTACHMENT ISSUES: Forms **relationships at a distance**, *e.g.*, phone sex, internet, videos, long-distance relationships, prostitutes, prisoners. May self-medicate. Doesn't seek to attract high-caliber mates. Senses lack of identity or existence from inadequate mirroring, empathy, understanding, approval and regard. Subject to severe depression, including suicidality. Feels empty with some hunger to merge. SECOND-YEAR-ON ISSUES AND INTERACTION STYLE: (could overlap with dependent personality) Boundary confusion. Gets frightened of feelings awakened when dating or getting intimate. Little or no sense of rights or responsibilities in a relationship. Doesn't trust own abilities to perceive motives of others. Fear of the unknown. Hypersensitive and empathic. Strong victim consciousness and lack of assertive abilities. Feels lack of expertise (resulting from low self-esteem and possible lack of guidance or modeling). Lacks competency in horizontal motion from one event to another. Can be easily overwhelmed. Keeps lifestyle underwhelmed.

BORDERLINE, cont'd

Suffocated Child:
Derived from Smothering Mother

CAUSE

Attachment	Avoidant attachment. Bonding is **invasive**. Infant turns head away. Infant withdraws.
Second Year On	Parent presumes to own child. Mother may spit on child's face to remove dirt or fix a curl. Parent makes all decisions for child. Parent is always watching and commenting on child. Mother dresses child against her choices and will. Mother chooses all child's things. Parent loves child to death, but doesn't know child. Parent considers all child's attempts to separate as a betrayal. Parent uses guilt to control child. Parent becomes judgmental during adolescence. Parent may humiliate child in front of peers. Parent may do child's homework and take credit for child's successes. Parent pushes child to do things parent chooses. Parent doesn't hear the child say no or disagree with parent.

EFFECT

Infant/ Toddler	Infant tries to look away and "change the subject." Infant is resisting mother's approaches and shutting down, going "inward." INNER THOUGHTS: "The only way I can exist is to pull inside."
Child	Child can't say no or disagree with adults and gives up openly disagreeing. Child has to be **secretive** to get own space. Child learns **self-consciousness** instead of competency. INNER THOUGHTS: "I need space." "Avoid getting too close to people." "I feel empty." "No one will protect me." "I have to be sneaky."
Adult	ATTACHMENT ISSUES: Lacks identity of her own and/or has private or secretive identity. Fears criticism, judgment or definitions of others. Despite suffocation, child feels empty. Doesn't get too close to people or speak openly about feelings or thoughts. Fragmentation of personality when she loses distance. Higher functioning than dominated borderline, but harder to treat since she doesn't want to let anyone in. SECOND-YEAR-ON ISSUES AND INTERACTION STYLE: Is protective of own identity, as if her identity is a secret. Needs to distance from others. Avoids intrusive people, especially undernurtured borderlines who want to merge (intrude). May rage against intrusiveness or withdraw. Consolidates personality from too many demands by withdrawal. Has **distancing relationships** with people who are far away, aloof or married. Possible imprinted tendency to invade own child's space. Could be comfortable with children. Hypersensitive to motives of others. **Fragmentation of competency** from too many demands on her at once.

BORDERLINE, cont'd

Anecdotal Application

In Emily's couchwork she re-experienced the chaos and pain of her mother's erratic moods as an infant. "Now she's mad at me, now she's close to me and warm, now she's ignoring me." She realized that the only way to survive was to adapt and dissociate or almost adopt another personality or state of mind in order to tune into the different frequencies of her mother's changing moods and absences. If Emily wanted to protect herself from Mommy when Mommy was mad, then she had to "forget" that a little while ago Mommy was acting loving towards her. So there was one state of mind when Mommy was caring, one state of mind when Mommy was angry and another state of mind when Mommy was gone. As an adult Emily's moods dominated the household.

Borderline Personality Disorder as defined in Gerry Grossman Seminars MFT license exam prep materials:

A disturbance of identity and mood which severely affects relationships. There is also impulsive behavior, including angry outbursts, promiscuity or reckless driving, mood swings and suicidal threats used to manipulate people. People with Borderline Personality Disorder will show an intense need for someone and then reject them and then will fear being abandoned.

AVOIDANT

This personality fears making mistakes and is paralyzed by that fear. Subtypes (2): The Set-Up Child, The No-Mistakes-Allowed Child

Set-Up Child:
Derived from Neglect and Rare Idealization

CAUSE

Attachment	Anxious attachment. Neglect in presence of parent.
Second Year On	Parents do little to praise or even notice the child's competencies, though grown child will have special memories to which he clings. Parenting is probably distant. Parents probably socialize little with child. Parents model little social skills. Parents model little success skills. Child feels hypersensitive. Child is emotionally neglected. Child finds a few safe friends of same sex. **Parents give the child an identity of great expectation, once or twice, telling him that he's special, better than the other kids.**

EFFECT

Infant/ Toddler	Wants to attach despite neglect. INNER THOUGHTS: "I'm ready to love and be loved. It's coming. Maybe next time."
Child	Child seems **anxious** to please and **withdrawn** in anticipation of neglect or disinterest. INNER THOUGHTS: "I don't want to take any chances on getting hurt." "I'm special and superior. They just don't know it." "I don't want to try anything out, because if I fail, people will think I'm not special, that I'm a loser. My father would think he was wrong about me. That would kill me."
Adult	ATTACHMENT ISSUES: Appears highly anxious and withdrawn. Easily hurt by criticism. Has few long-term, also lonely close friends, other than family. Has strong desire for interpersonal relations, but avoids them. Fears expressing feelings or vulnerability in presence of others. SECOND-YEAR-ON ISSUES AND INTERACTION STYLE: Has grandiose idea of himself, which he dare not test out. Limited social and success skills to warrant grandiose identity. Breaking the safe routine is a high risk. Chooses night work and lonely jobs to play it safe. May choose working with non-critical public, such as children, mentally challenged population or animals.

AVOIDANT, cont'd

No-Mistakes-Allowed Child: Derived from Abuse at Every Guess

CAUSE

Attachment	Anxious-avoidant attachment. Parent is probably not attuned. Parents are emotionally unavailable.
Second Year On	Parents are judgmental, critical and possibly abusive when child makes mistakes. Parent may strike child for small error or lack of knowledge. Parent may ridicule a "stupid question."

EFFECT

Infant/ Toddler	Child appears somewhat dull. INNER THOUGHTS: "I'm alone. I'm not any good."
Child	Withdrawn, anxious and depressed. Child stops risking. Stops practicing and **plays it safe**, only doing things he knows how to do well. INNER THOUGHTS: He fears failure. He seems to wish for recognition. He wants to connect. He fears being known. "I'd like to trust somebody."
Adult	ATTACHMENT ISSUES: Wants to merge but fears rejection. SECOND-YEAR-ON ISSUES AND INTERACTION STYLE: Easily hurt by criticism. Has few close friends, other than family (if that). Avoids interpersonal relations. Has strong desire for interpersonal relations. Breaking the safe routine is a high risk. Fears expressing feelings or vulnerability in presence of others. Has strong remorse after revealing self. Appears highly anxious and withdrawn. Limited social and success skills. Often chooses night jobs, lonely work or works with children, handicapped, mentally disabled or animals, where there is little risk of judgment or ridicule for lack of knowing.

Anecdotal Application

I knew one young woman whose stepmother would hit her, often with a ruler to the back of her hand, every time she made a mistake. "How do you spell Mississippi?" her mother would demand. "M. I. S. I." WHACK! "No! That is not the way you spell Mississippi!" Again she demanded, "Now, how do you spell Mississippi?" Every time the child made a mistake, WHACK! Of course she'd be afraid to take a chance.

I had another client whose parents were alcoholics and essentially ignored him, so he developed almost no social skills. Yet one fine day Dad came out of the house and stopped beside his child sitting on the front stoop watching other children play. "See all those kids playing out there [without you]? You are better than them," his father told him. There, upon a vast and barren desert of neglect where no self-worth grew, the rain fell. For one precious moment this worthless child was valuable, even superior. It was to be the memory of a lifetime, the premise of which must never be challenged. If this young man ever made a social mistake or any mistake for that matter, his father would be wrong. The only way to preserve the truth of his dad's priceless words was to never again accept a challenge.

APPROACH-AVOIDANT

This is not a recognized diagnosis by the *DSM-IV-TR or -V*. The nomenclature is borrowed from Developmental Psychology and the Rapprochement stage of individualization where toddlers both want to separate (run away at the mall while looking over his shoulder to see if Mommy is chasing) and fear separating. Three Primary Subtypes: The Custody Child, The Exiled Child, and The Conflicted Child.

Torn Child:
Derived from Oppositional Care

CAUSE

Attachment	Custody Child: **Secure attachment.** Bonding is possibly good. **Ambivalent attachment** if the toddler or infant is sent back and forth and has to break her bond with her mother in order to build a bond with her father.
	Exiled Child: **Ambivalent or avoidant attachment.** Mother lacks attunement for child's needs. Bonding is **aloof**. The mother is **alternately warm and cold** to child, rejecting him when he is too needy.
	Conflicted Child: **Ambivalent attachment.** Mother **suffocates** infant with love and affection and **then disappears** for too long. Infant begins to show signs of turning head away, avoiding unnecessary eye contact (similar to abandoned baby and to suffocated borderline baby). In less severe cases, this stage of life may be normal and mother shows appropriate love and adoring.
Second Year On	Custody Child: The parent with primary custody (mother?) tends to devalue other parent so the child does not get to have an idealized father. The child is often treated to the mother's bitterness and ultimately expected to feel loyal or protective of the mother. The child learns to withhold affection from her father and even carry a grudge against him for her mother's sake. Mother's grudge becomes her grudge. Father may be the alienator.
	Exiled Child: Mother or father locks child out of the house for punishment, sometimes in rain and/or cold, possibly for long duration. The child wants to be indoors, but when he is indoors, he feels so unwanted that he would rather leave (until he feels being cold). Parent is rejecting, judgmental, critical and abusive when child is close. She begins to reject the child with name-calling or **threaten** the child: "If you walk away from me, I'll walk away from you." "If you don't need me, I don't need you." "You do as I say or you'll get nothing from me." Parent is occasionally thoughtful.
	Conflicted Child: Mother does not comprehend the importance of individuation and acts out on her own fears of rejection and abandonment every time her child acts independently of her: "Why did you leave mommy?" "Don't you love mommy?" She gives child mixed messages about maturing. Alternately, mother may take leave of the child for periods of time that create longing but not detachment.

APPROACH-AVOIDANT, cont'd

Torn Child:
Derived from Oppositional Care

EFFECT

Infant/ Toddler	<u>Custody Child</u>: If parents' separation took place after age five, then the attachment may be secure. If the separation took place before age five, then the attachment will not be secure, definitely exasperating the injury.
	INNER THOUGHTS: "Why do I have to go? Why can't my daddy come here and stay?" "My mommy is so upset when I go, but why does she let me go?" "Why is my daddy so mean to take me from my mother?"
	<u>Exiled Child</u>: Infant frets or learns to go inward. Confused, restless, distressed and dissociating. INNER THOUGHTS: "How long is this warmth going to last?" "How long is this rejection going to last?"
	<u>Conflicted child</u>: Child reaches for leaving parent. Child turns head away from up close parent. INNER THOUGHTS: "Where is she?" "Ooh, too close, too much."
Child	<u>Custody Child</u>: Confusion. Sees self as the guilty prize. INNER THOUGHTS: No matter where I go, it's not good. It's wrong here. Dreads being close to dad, because he is betraying mom. Wants to go home, but is afraid to be there and have to take care of her mother's feelings and may secretly miss dad.
	<u>Exiled Child</u>: Appears to want to be close and is afraid to be close. Confusion, seems to be searching, always wanting what's over there until she's there. INNER THOUGHTS: Somewhat disorganized thinking. Child dreads being close for fear of rejection. Child wants to get away to be safe. Child fears being pushed away. Child still suffers from lack of connection and wants it on some level, but the mistrust lingers.
	<u>Conflicted Child</u>: She begins to seem anxious when away from mother and avoidant when with her. INNER THOUGHTS: Child begins to choke at her staying and fear her leaving. "Your love is like bubble-gum on the bottom of my shoe. I feel a tug with every step I take away from you." – Melissa
Adult (all subtypes)	ATTACHMENT ISSUES: Tends to find her loyalty where she is not and has difficulty committing and staying where she is. **Always looking for the right person**, but no one is right for any length of time. Vigorously pursues relationships then when she has them, can't commit or act committed. If she commits, she is driven to continue pursuing others or sabotages the committed relationship. Has difficulty choosing where she wants to be because she always wants to be where she is not. **Can be misperceived as immoral** or lacking conscience for leading people on then rejecting them. Doesn't realize what she does to people or meaningfully remember opposing drives, words and actions. Her drive to be somewhere else is so strong, ethics and previous promises mean nothing to her. She is not ashamed. She has made the other person wrong with narcissism for taking her interest seriously. When she misses them after distancing from them, she becomes dependent and thinks she actually needs them after all. Self-reflection is absent; otherwise she could work through this.
	SECOND-YEAR-ON ISSUES AND INTERACTION STYLE: May be high functioning. Disloyal, hypocritical and fickle. Each side of him seems rational. Each side tends to embarrass, compromise or sabotage the needs of the other side, but so far it appears that each of the two sides of him do not care about the mixed messages. Custody Child as adult may play people against one another and may disrespect anyone who chooses him. Adult always wants to be where he is not. The grass is always greener on the other side of the fence. Adult seems paranoid when rejecting and tentatively dependent when pursuing. This personality is at high risk for having affairs, divorces and custody disputes.

APPROACH-AVOIDANT, cont'd
Anecdotal Application

I met an approach-avoidant mother when I worked for Children's Services. I never had the opportunity to learn about her childhood, but I certainly saw her act out on her sons. "You've got to get my boys back," she would implore me. "I really need to be with my boys and they need their mother." So I pulled strings and wrote reports and got her boys back. "You've got to get them out of here; I can't stand them. Get them away from me," she insisted on the second day her boys were back. So I put them back in the boys home and about two weeks later, she persisted, "Why did you listen to me? I really want my children here." I was persuaded one more time. I brought her sons home again and she rejected them yet another time.

I had another even higher functioning father who was dating another very high functioning woman. He was a mogul in the entertainment industry, and she was an entertainment lawyer. He courted her. She was a beautiful and elegant woman. When she started to give him her love, he began to accuse her of trying to come between him and his children from a previous marriage. They would travel to the opposite end of the state to see the children, where he had a room waiting for him in his former wife's home. When he took his children out for a drive his true love was relegated to the back seat of the car. After a while of being treated like the interloper, she told him she didn't feel wanted. She left him and went on vacation to Europe. He tracked her down. Hundreds of bouquets of roses surrounded her doorway and filled her room. He convinced her to return to him. Afterwards, he began to accuse her of the same thing again. She left him and returned to Europe. He upped the ante and sent her a five-karat yellow diamond ring with a letter of remorse and a request that she marry him. She returned again. When they drove across the state to see his children, he asked her if she would be willing to trade the five-karat ring in for a two-karat ring. She was done.

SCHIZOID

This is not to be confused with schizophrenia, a psychotic thought disorder. All three "schizs" (think "skin") originate from lack of touch, similar to the Histrionic Shocking Child.

Bubble Child:
Derived from Being Treated Like an Object

CAUSE

Attachment	**Avoidant attachment.** Cold mother. Distant or absent father. Lack of skin contact or touch. Child receives care to basic physical needs only. **No bonding** or just enough familiarity to survive (as in not die).
Second Year On	Parents are **detached**. Family life is **mechanical**, **routine** and unchanging. Mechanical and stoical approach to religion may be the family's disengaged escape.

EFFECT

Infant/ Toddler	Infant looks vacant like no one is home. He doesn't look out anymore because there's no one to see him. INNER THOUGHTS: "I give up on people. I like objects like dangling keys."
Child	The child looks **nerdy** and **lacks personality**. The child seems **sterile**. INNER THOUGHTS: "People are too scary. I like machines and statues." "I like silky fabrics and I like to look at skin and pretend I'm feeling it."
Adult	ATTACHMENT ISSUES: Adult may romance a **mannequin** or **blow-up doll**. May join nudist colony. Goes to great lengths to **feel skin** or skin substitute without seeking intimacy. Lacks sentimentality. Schizoid person can't "bond" with another person in adulthood without an exceptional therapeutic experience. Some schizoids may molest a child out of curiosity, not grasping that the child has feelings. SECOND-YEAR-ON ISSUES AND INTERACTION STYLE: Learns to do basics in life. May become a machine operator, mechanic, bus driver, driving instructor, *etc.*

SCHIZOID, cont'd

Anecdotal Application

Schizoid personalities are very mechanical and rather humanoid. Their childhood care was very mechanical and perfunctory. One of my clients – we'll call him Dave - with schizoid personality had a mother who provided the typical-of-the-time toaster and red gingham tablecloth in the kitchen. They had religious statues of Mary posted all around the house. "Everything was there but nobody really knew each other." Parenting was rather a kind of a structure and role-playing. As was typical of the schizoid personality, Dave's work was oriented around machinery as a driving instructor. His employer sent him to therapy because female students complained about him for staring at their bare skin on their legs and arms. I learned that he belonged to a nudist colony so he could see more skin. He also slept with a blow-up doll. He told me he regularly visited a strip club where he would meet one special young lady in the alley after her shift was over and give her $50 to hug him. I told him his diagnosis and we discussed what kind of parenting was behind his stiffness. We discussed his hunger to see skin and be touched. We discussed his lack of emotional interest in others. He understood that he had not been touched and nurtured by his mother. As this insight set in he became more emotional, but he also became more depressed. One day I stepped out of my office into the waiting room and there he was curled up on the couch with his thumb in his mouth. I intuitively did what seemed right and put his heavy leather jacket over him to give him the feeling that someone was holding him or had placed a great big hand on his baby side. Even so, it did not seem heavy enough, so I leaned back in a chair and I put my feet up on his side to put weight on him. I started to sing "Hush Little Baby," a long song that I knew by heart. I sang it for almost an hour. Eventually, he sat up and said, "Wow, now I understand why I have kept long fingernails. I have always fantasized that my mother was right here at my hands." I am happy to report that he formed a long-term relationship with a widow who eventually moved in with him.

I strongly suspect that Jeffery Dahmer was barely touched in his first year of life. He actually reported four significant early childhood memories when forensic evaluator Judith Becker interviewed him for his sanity hearing. One memory was from a time when he was very little and his mother was pregnant with his baby brother; she let him put his ear to her belly. The second was when he was a little bit older; she taught him how to impale butterflies. The third was when his father paid attention to him and taught him how to gut fish. The last time was when he was four years old and admitted into a hospital alone for a hernia surgery. For *some* reason, he believed he was sent there to be castrated. His parents were not with him when he went into surgery nor did they receive him when it was over, so it was many long hours before he learned that he hadn't been castrated. All four of those memories from childhood were about skin, innards and skin contact. He was clearly starving for touch and hungry for skin contact. When he got old enough to date or whatever you want to call picking up guys to take them home, he had such a wonderful experience with the hugging and the holding that he could not bear to see them leave. Some people say that Jeffery Dahmer, like every other killer, killed to exert power. But really, he killed because he couldn't let them leave. He didn't have enough empathy in his body or his experiences to see his victims as human beings. He only experienced his unsatiated drive to be hugged and touched.

Schizoid Personality Disorder as defined in Gerry Grossman Seminars MFT license exam prep materials:

People with this disorder do not desire or enjoy human contact, either emotionally or sexually. They would rather be alone. They do not have strong emotions and appear cold, uncaring and indifferent.

SCHIZOTYPAL

When a child is not held but left to watch and long for the nearby parent, her imagination and sensory deprivation, combined with her parents' mystical ideology, create a personality which de-realizes and seeks the unreal world in lieu of the material one.

Ethereal Child:
Derived from Magical Thinking Parents

CAUSE

Attachment	**Disengaged or disorganized attachment.** Mother does not **touch** the child sufficiently. Mother keeps child close by in an infant seat, car seat, box or playpen where child can watch mother. Mother is not in tune with child's cues. Mother responds at **inappropriate** times, but mother is sometimes loving.
Second Year On	Mother is **erratic** in limit-setting. Mother controls child's behavior with **threats** of what God will do or in more extreme cases mother speaks of evil spirits, voodoo, hell fire or something **intangible**. Mother teaches problem-solving through **appealing to spirits**.

EFFECT

Infant/ Toddler	The child reaches out toward mother and others, usually sitting in company of mother but on her own. INNER THOUGHTS: Child visualizes/**imagines mother's touch**.
Child	Child seems airy. INNER THOUGHTS: "I don't feel real (touched). I must be spirit." "The less I see what's real, the better chance I have of seeing what's unreal. I need to see what's spirit (unreal) to increase my safety." Child fathoms continuous threats and control from the invisible.
Adult	ATTACHMENT ISSUES: Adult doesn't feel real and relates best to the **unreal**. This adult may not be able to manifest a long-term relationship. She may instead be prey to exploitive men or passers-in-the-night. SECOND-YEAR-ON ISSUES AND INTERACTION STYLE: She is **sweet**, **innocent** and almost of another world. She is almost out of touch with reality. She is **impractical**, low-functioning, possibly even a homeless person. She may be saint-like or martyr-like in pure innocence.

SCHIZOTYPAL, cont'd

Anecdotal Application

I know a woman who was raised in a cult. Her parents divorced and she was allowed to visit her father by plane. When her mother would take her to the airport to see her off, she would get down on her knees at kid-level and say to her, "See that man over there? He has an orange aura. See that woman right here? She has a purple aura. The woman over there has a yellow aura. If you are ever going to get on a plane and just one person doesn't have an aura, don't get on." Later on, her mother told her that her guru said that the world was coming to an end, but all who were in their cult would be saved. She was allowed to visit her dad to say goodbye without telling him that he would be dying and it was their final farewell. Fortunately, this woman had fairly good bonding in her first years, so she was able to fend off what would otherwise have become a Schizotypal Personality. Schziotypals believe the forces for all development are in the invisible and what is knowable is just about irrelevant.

I knew another close call. The child was being raised to believe in the *The Secret* from the book by the same name. Her mother brought her daughter in to see me because she was developing Obsessive Compulsive Disorder, not to be confused with Obsessive Compulsive Personality. (OCD is an anxiety disorder, not a personality disorder. It includes a variety of superstitious ways of fending off potential danger, such as checking the stove, doors and windows numerous times every night or kissing paper towels before throwing them away.) The child's symptoms included avoiding stepping on cracks and watching what she was saying. I asked her what she believed in and she said, "Money, lots of money." She then pulled out of her pocket a dollar bill and kissed it. "I am going to be rich," she said. "How are you going to do that?" I asked. She seemed shocked that I didn't know the answer. "I just have to believe it *completely*," she said with emphasis. I will be rich if I believe it hard enough. Whatever I think will come true, so I have to be careful what I think." "Oh boy!" I said. "Then somebody needs to tell you that thinking something does *not* make it so. Yes, if you take your thoughts seriously, they will direct your actions correctly or incorrectly. However, it will be your actions that will make you rich or not. You need to learn about cause and effect. You need to understand which actions cause which results. Stepping on a crack will not break your mother's back and carrying around a dollar bill to kiss will not make you rich." She looked at me like I was the devil, then finally spoke. "My mother would not approve of what you are telling me." "Do you want me to speak with her?" "No. Just my dad," she said, possibly trying to protect me for telling her the truth. "You will need to make a plan for your life to become rich and then follow that plan with good self-discipline. You need to work hard in school. While you're at it, you might also want to decide what else you will value in your life besides money, including how you want to live and treat people. Sometimes those choices affect your wealth and mental health too."

Schizotypal Personality Disorder as defined in Gerry Grossman Seminars MFT license exam prep materials:

Having peculiar ideas, behavior and appearance. There may be social anxiety, eccentric behavior, bizarre speech (vague and abstract), illusions and a tendency towards superstitiousness or magical thinking. This is similar to schizophrenia, but does not have a psychotic phase.

SCHIZOPHRENIC

Due to sensory deprivation from lack of touch, a bombardment of parental projections and a lack of quality personal interaction and communication around the child's feelings and truth, the subconscious becomes more vivid and hallucinations begin to superimpose over reality when there is no real, material support. Traumatic experiences are definitive.

Mind-Raped Child:
Derived from Crazy Treatment and Intrusive Projections

CAUSE

Attachment	Disengaged/disorganized/avoidant attachment. Bonding lacks touch, leaving infant with a tenuous sense of self. Mother tends to **project** onto infant rather than perceive infant. Mother responds inappropriately to infant, *e.g.* picking him up when he's sleeping, feeding him when he's full, rocking him when he just woke up.
Second Year On	The parent responds **inappropriately** to the child's needs. The parent sends **mixed messages** and "double binds" (*e.g.*, parent tells child "We value the truth." Parent asks child how she feels about something she doesn't like. Child tells truth. Parent scolds child for thinking/feeling something true.) The parent requires child to perceive, believe and act on what is not. The parent **projects** motives onto child which are not the child's, requiring the child to repress his authentic self and live in the parent's projections. Parents may institutionalize older child who refuses projections in order to express his own truth and feelings. Dialogues with child about reality and problem-solving are rare.

EFFECT

Infant/ Toddler	**Dazed** or boggled. INNER THOUGHTS: "I don't get it. Why won't she touch me. What's she doing now?" This child has a weak sense of his own existence due to lack of touch. The child doesn't have a strong enough sense of self to fend off the mother's and father's projections. "I don't know where I end and others begin."
Child	This child looks **confused** about what's real. He may have already developed an interest in the surreal or a vocabulary which takes him out of reality. INNER THOUGHTS: "I have to find safe thoughts and safe things to think or talk about." "I need new words or codes to **stay safe.**"
Adult	ATTACHMENT ISSUES: Adult has a tenuous sense of himself. He thinks he's **reading people's minds** and they are reading his. He feels **too mentally weak to fend off projections**. He has **no sense of physical existence or skin**. (Adhesive Identification) SECOND-YEAR-ON ISSUES AND INTERACTION STYLE: He **doesn't trust** words or people's construct of reality. He is starving for dialogue with someone about his internal experience. When he has to live on his own without material help, his buried issues start talking to him and showing themselves.

SCHIZOPHRENIC, cont'd
Anecdotal Application

I saw one young man whose mother was a very religious woman. She went to church for three hours in the morning every day like clockwork. While she was at church, Daddy regularly took him to bed and molested him. Once he tried to tell his mother and she was appalled. "How dare you say something like that about your father!" she accused him. The abuse continued until about five years before we met, when he turned 18 and his mother divorced his father for other reasons. After we worked together for about two months and he seemed to trust me I approached the idea of inviting his mother and siblings to a family session. I believed that a supportive response would help him find comfort in reality. They all came, including the sister who had referred him to me. She would soon be marrying one of my husband's co-workers. Two younger brothers who still lived at home also came with their mother. As my client told his story again, everyone sat very still. When he finished telling what happened nearly every day of his life behind closed doors, no one moved or said anything. I asked questions to provoke dialogue. "Mom, do you remember him telling this to you once before? Did either of you boys ever suspect that anything like this could be happening in your home? Is this something everyone wants to pretend is not true? Do you believe him? Can you see how this might explain his difficulty understanding reality, when his mother is very religious and his father is very dangerous? Has anyone else in your family been molested by him? Does he have access to the boys?" No one said a word until finally the sister spoke. "I didn't know that by treating our brother, you would be asking our family such prying questions." Finally, his mother got up and walked out, followed by her daughter and three sons. My client did not return. My husband and I were invited to the wedding like nothing had ever happened and the father walked his daughter down the aisle.

I treated another client who had been in day care since he was an infant, where there were six other infants. When he was around two, Mom had an affair with Dad's best friend in the family home. Dad made Mom leave and he began to take the baby with him to work because he was self-employed. The child was sent to see his mother two weekends a month. Dad ended up falling in love with a woman who loved the boy and he began to call her "Mommy." Then, one day when he was visiting his biological mother, he slipped and referred to his step-mother as "Mommy." His mother turned red-faced and skewed up her mouth. "*She* is not your mother," she yelled with her face in his little three-year-old face. "*I* am your mother." After that, the child withdrew from his relationship with the loving and available woman. He waited to see his mother twice a month on the weekends. Unfortunately, she cancelled most of the appointments. She admitted to me that she didn't really like visiting the child because he acted so weird. And besides, he was too needy.

DYSTHYMIC OR CYCLOTHYMIC DISORDER

Derived from having all needs met and no guidance into independent problem-solving. Child lacks experience with deferred gratification or consequences for not trying. Life is rather provided for. This is not a personality disorder, but is a mood disorder that involves some cycling (cyclothymic) highs and lows or a rather flat, uninspired (dysthymic) person. There may be other causes.

Bored Child:
Derived from Having All Needs Met

CAUSE

Attachment	Secure, perhaps.
Second Year On	Mother and/or parents are indulgent and meet all their child's needs. The child doesn't have much to work toward and has little feelings of accomplishment. The parents don't realize they are supposed to be coaching their child for independence, problem-solving and accomplishment.

EFFECT

Infant/ Toddler	The baby is satisfied and accepts dependence. INNER THOUGHTS: "I'm not supposed to have problems or bad feelings."
Child	Looks normal. The parent assumes they are supposed to meet all their child's needs and head off any problems, and the child assumes her parents are supposed to meet all her needs. She doesn't really get that she is supposed to be learning how to achieve and developing her self-esteem by hard work and a job well-done. She may be entitled and she is starting to shown signs of ennui, boredom or dissatisfaction with her life. INNER THOUGHTS: "Is this all there is?" She has no idea what could be wrong with her life and why everything feels so pointless. She seems like a shallow person, lacking curiosity or commitment. She is prone to making everything about her.
Adult	ATTACHMENT ISSUES: She has a strong but meaningless sense of herself. SECOND-YEAR-ON ISSUES AND INTERACTION STYLE: The clients I have known like this have seemed chronically dissatisfied, as if they are waiting for someone to make it better.

BIPOLAR

Derived from expectations without guidance. This is not a personality disorder, but it is treated like one so often that it's included in this list. This child is expected to become great, but is given barely any guidance.

Wishing-It Child: Derived from Traumatic Neglect and High Intellectual Expectations

CAUSE

Attachment	Ambivalent attachment. The myth is that the bonding is good.
Second Year On	Parents may be highly successful and too busy to parent or they may put high expectations on child without guiding him. In neglect or abandonment, child experiences trauma and dissociates. The dissociation is a shelter and perhaps is held with religious overtones that seem to parent and guide her. The Repression ethic is in play.

EFFECT

Infant/ Toddler	The baby is compliant, seeking more attention, but lost. INNER THOUGHTS: "But, who am I?"
Child	Looks normal, but perhaps has some false self developing to cope. INNER THOUGHTS: "But how?" Wears the identity that she is supposed to be special, but doesn't know how to get there unless thinking makes it so.
Adult	ATTACHMENT ISSUES: She has a tenuous sense of inner self. SECOND-YEAR-ON ISSUES AND INTERACTION STYLE: Can't handle the pressures of adulthood because she doesn't know how to cope on her own and flounders. She has some religious experiences of dissociation in which she finally experiences her inner self as divine. She takes these experiences to the bank and concludes she is special and thinking makes it so. Acting "as if" also makes it so. Seems arrogant in her grandiosity. Proceeds to act as such, spends money, makes expansive decisions that ultimately backfire, then she crashes into depression. As she languishes she eventually burns the depression up, has another "religious" or "enlightened" experience and rises again. The experiences are valid in large part, but the desperate interpretations that inflate the ego are not valid. We are all divine, but she thinks she is more divine. She needs to work on her problem-solving skills, earn her way into significance and learn relationship skills of give and take. Has an aversion to the hard part of therapy because she wants to believe she is special and can do it on her own. She doesn't want to go into the pain. She prefers dissociation.

Bipolar Disorder as defined in Gerry Grossman Seminars MFT license exam prep materials:

This person has experienced some religious experiences akin to enlightenment experiences, but has not developed the character and personal discipline to apply the experiences in any enlightened way. Rather, the mind-body gave him the experiences to protect him from excessive suffering, self-deprecation and isolation. He then goes about invalidating his insights with his flamboyant actions that lack the humility that normally accompany enlightenment. He is resistant to the hard work of therapy that would give him substance.

DISSOCIATIVE IDENTITY DISORDER (MULTIPLE PERSONALITY DISORDER)

This disorder results from a human capacity to dissociate during terror, creating separate "personalities" which are stuck in different states of repressed trauma, serve different purposes and express different experiences.

Terrorized Child:
Derived from Both Normal and Horribly Abusive Treatment

CAUSE

Attachment	Good or not. Infants can dissociate too. The younger they experience dissociation, the more it becomes hard-wired as a coping skill and they can learn to split and split again and split again.
Second Year On	Child enjoys some wonderfully **normal** experiences. Child also begins experiencing some **horrific** torture at a very young age.

EFFECT

Infant/ Toddler	Healthy or normal. INNER THOUGHTS: Could be normal.
Child	Child seems mostly normal, but may appear to zone out. She will have outbursts of terror and cowering or fighting. INNER THOUGHTS: Adaptive thoughts develop out of awareness, borrowing from other models around her.
Adult	ATTACHMENT ISSUES: A healthy first year could give her a solid core personality. SECOND-YEAR-ON ISSUES AND INTERACTION STYLE: Her abuse at a very young age causes her personality to dissociate into multiple states, each with different memories and attitudes. The essential standard personalities are: **Core, Aggressor-Protector, Child-Victim** and the **pathological re-enactor of the trauma**. Other personalities develop according to need.

Anecdotal Application

I saw one man who suffered from DID. He couldn't hold a job because his personalities kept switching, so I told him he really needed to get disability pay. I wrote a letter for him and filled out the forms. We got him on disability. Unfortunately, one of his personalities was "the preacher" who went down and cancelled it because "collecting disability pay was unethical."

PARANOID

When extremely cruel punishments or scapegoating take place against this child out of the blue, the only way she has to protect herself is through continuous hypervigilance. Subtypes (2): The Tricked Child, The Double-Crossed Child

Tricked Child:
Derived from Physical Abuse Out of the Blue

CAUSE

Attachment	**Anxious and/or avoidant attachment.** Bonding may or may not be good. Bonding is **erratic**, possibly **threatening.** Baby never learns to trust once abandoned. Baby may already be a scapegoat figure.
Second Year On	Father or parents harass the child and provoke him. Parents **entrap** and punish the child **unpredictably.** Punishments are physically and psychologically **traumatic.** Parents humiliate and require unqualified subservience and obedience. Most punishments have no rhyme or reason so child cannot prepare for anything except by watching for moods. The **Repression Ethic** is full blown.

EFFECT

Infant/ Toddler	The baby is shut down. INNER THOUGHTS: "Don't trust anyone. Pull inside."
Child	Child is jumpy, suspicious, **guarded**, jaded, street-wise and aggressive. INNER THOUGHTS: Child finally comes to identify with parent's idea of him. "Scan the surroundings. Look for threats and evidence of deception or insincerity." "Don't trust anyone."
Adult	ATTACHMENT ISSUES: She may lack trust from first-year attachment breaks or even abuse. SECOND-YEAR-ON ISSUES AND INTERACTION STYLE: She often appears extremely intelligent and astute. She tends to **scan** her environment for negatives, either threats or evidences of weakness in others. She has a great memory for detail in a room. She seeks **dominance** and control as quickly as possible. This is necessary and for this reason she is unlikely to enter into therapy. She is prone to committing child and spousal abuse. The world is a put-down contest. It's her or you. She usually wins. She is extremely critical, but cannot handle any criticism at all. She carries **grudges** and keeps lists. She measures and memorizes people's flaws to use against them. She anticipates the kind of betrayals from others which she would do. She has a family and they keep to themselves.

PARANOID, cont'd

Double-Crossed Child:
Derived from Landmines in Parental Intimacy

CAUSE

Attachment	**Anxious attachment.** Attachment may have started normally. Infancy may not have been secure.
Second Year On	Parents **harass** the child and provoke him. Parents compliment the child and then ridicule her if she believes it. Parents give child information and deride her for believing it. Punishments have a psychologically **humiliating** angle to them. Humiliation, subservience and unqualified obedience are aims of parenting. The Repression Ethic is full blown.

EFFECT

Infant/ Toddler	Anxious. INNER THOUGHTS: "Is it safe?"
Child	Defensive. Guarded. INNER THOUGHTS: Child finally comes to identify with parent's idea of him. "If I act soft, I will be hurt."
Adult	ATTACHMENT ISSUES: Fear of intimacy. Failure to trust. SECOND-YEAR-ON ISSUES AND INTERACTION STYLE: The grown child often appears **leery** of your motives. Compliments and motives are scrutinized. They seek to maintain control or steer clear. They are unlikely to enter into therapy and surrender to the work. They cannot handle criticism. They keep mental lists of grudges or failures. They are unforgiving. They seem **fragile** and frightened. They **isolate**. They make strong mental notes of your weaknesses and failures which they may use against you. They don't trust and they are not trustworthy.

PARANOID, cont'd

Anecdotal Application

I had a paranoid client see me because his wife accused him of domestic violence. He scanned everything about my office. He knew what my car looked like, even informing me my tags were going to expire next month, and he told me my undergraduate degree was more valuable than my graduate degree. When he was little he had to live with his father and his grandmother. He never knew when his father would come after him and his grandmother was under strict instructions not to rescue him. As a child, he hid under the bed when his father came home. His father would take a broom and begin jabbing and poking at him until he came out. His grandmother once hid him in spite of her strict instructions. When Dad found out Grandma protected his child from him, he became livid and locked her in her bedroom for three months. When Dad found out that the child was trying to help Grandma, he locked the boy in a closet for a week.

I knew a woman who didn't trust me, including any kind thing I had to say. She believed that behind every compliment was a hidden sword. She was the least favorite child in her family. She had two sisters that her dad openly preferred. She was the odd-man-out, so-to-speak. Perhaps there was a family secret that she wasn't his biological child. In any event, one evening she sat alone with her father in the living room for probably the first time that she could recall. He looked up from his newspaper, made eye contact with her and smiled. He patted his lap in a gesture for her to come over. She perked up and went to him, a moment she could barely believe was happening. He took her onto his lap, carefully placing her arm around behind his neck and then he tenderly said to her, "You know I love you, don't you?" "Oh, yes, Daddy," she said in this, her sweet moment of belonging. "But not as much as your sisters."

Paranoid Personality Disorder as defined in Gerry Grossman Seminars MFT license exam prep materials:

People with this disorder generally feel suspicious and mistrustful of others. They may be easily hurt and defensive (*e.g.*, if married, they may feel unsure of the fidelity of their spouse). There are no delusions as in Delusional Disorder and no hallucinations as in Paranoid Schizophrenia.

ANTISOCIAL
Severe abuse and neglect in a self-destructive environment of poverty and dangerous choices create this personality who is damned as a child and damned as an adult.

Violated Child:
Derived from Neglect and Extreme Abuse

CAUSE

Attachment	Early onset: Ambivalent attachment. Infant is neglected a lot and overhears fighting. Mother is angry, crying or absent a lot. Late onset: Normal attachment, maybe even secure attachment.
Second Year On	Neglect. Parent(s) use child as a scapegoat. Child suffers and imprints parental cruelty and mean treatment from others. "Family" is of **lower socioeconomic status**. Child is raising himself with parent's friends indiscriminately coming to stay, any of who could molest or abuse. Parents are often involved in domestic violence, drug usage, promiscuity and crime. Education, honesty, integrity and working to get ahead are often **not family values**. The family is usually poor and self-defeating, lacking impulse control. Teachers and others will begin to treat a hateful, rageful child as if he is truly intrinsically bad instead of a victim of parental neglect, cruelty and meanness.

EFFECT

Infant/ Toddler	Early onset: Infant seems withdrawn. Infant refuses to make eye contact up close. Infant has an angry cry. Infant is somewhat unresponsive. Face looks hard for a baby. Late onset: Infant may look normal. INNER THOUGHTS: She hopes for love. "I am unsafe. I may not live."
Child	**Separation Anxiety, RAD, ADHD, CD. May be a bed wetter.** This **rageful, impulsive** child still has **some heart** and some conscience, but lacks remorse because she feels so betrayed. Rejects domination and even guidance of others. Expresses rage in a variety of ways, including **pyromania** or **cruelty to animals**. Lies, steals, hits, fights. Finds no other source of relief besides **getting even**. (Will test kindness relentlessly and can only be saved if a kind person endures and passes the test. This person/program is still rare.) Very protective of her parent(s). Finds relief in dominance and abuse of others. Has no experience with or feeling for the values of society. Thinks social values are pure hypocrisy. Has contempt for truth, fairness, justice and other humane values. Lives in fear of abuse. Bullied and injured repeatedly. When she finally fights back, she gains self-esteem for the first time in her life and now has respect. She'll never go back. INNER THOUGHTS: Believes that she can **depend on no one**. Becomes **mistrustful** and independent of parents. She feels **unbearable pain** and **uncontrollable rage** and/or absence of feeling. She believes she is **bad** and her hatred is part of her identity. She tries to repress her feelings and claims "this is just the way I am."
Adult	Low socioeconomic status. Probably abuses substances. Has a violent approach to life. Often involved in physical fights and may be a child or spouse abuser. Could join a hate group. Will probably spend most of his adult life in prison as the result of imprinting an uncontrollable drive to "get even".

ANTISOCIAL, cont'd

Anecdotal Application

During the 1992 Los Angeles riots, four guys beat up a white truck driver, Reginald Denny, to scapegoat him for what happened to Rodney King. These men would be classified as Antisocial. Antisocial personalities often use and deal drugs and run in gangs. They often get into fights. They walk around violent and angry with a chip on their shoulder. They wear their rage on their skin and on their clothes. They scapegoat innocent people.

I knew a sweet young man who was very hard on the outside. His father was the man of his mother's dreams but their relationship didn't last. After the father left, he never missed a day of child support. The mother eventually settled for another man who was jealous of the child's father and because of that he hated the child and beat him regularly and violently. He also beat the child's mother. She never protected her son from his step-father, but he was expected to protect her by not complaining. By the time he was a young teen he was in trouble with the law on a regular basis. His father finally found the woman he could love for a lifetime and his new wife began to ask about the boy. When the boy's mother could no longer manage the child, she sent him to live with his father. The step-mother moved heaven and earth to keep him out of jail, yet when they tried to set limits on his behavior the teen keyed his step-mother's car and killed one of her cats. She had become the one he could love to hate for coming between him and his father. He began using drugs and joined a gang. What he wanted more than anything in the world was unconditional acceptance and respect, which he got from his gang.

I was in a gas station mart looking for a treat one night. Another customer was checking out a few items when a couple of men stopped by, looking quite dangerous. A scary guy restlessly hung by the doorway while his companion approached the cashier asking for directions in a tone that had no curiosity to it whatsoever. The cashier began to shake and the other customer left with his items still on the counter. It looked to me like the man inside had his hand in his pocket holding a gun. I realized that neither of the men saw me, but I thought the clerk might be in danger. I reflexively stepped forward to offer directions. I made warm eye contact, smiling and speaking with the kindest, most respectful delivery of information I imagine anyone had ever offered him before that moment. He looked at me first with surprise and then as if he was not the slightest bit interested in my directions. Instead, he appeared thrown by my kindness. I watched his demeanor soften as I spoke to his soul and he left with the other man without speaking another word.

Antisocial Personality Disorder as defined in Gerry Grossman Seminars MFT license exam prep materials:

People with this disorder display irresponsible, dangerous and aggressive behavior since the age of 15. Before age 15, they must have had a Conduct Disorder. They may harass others, destroy property, fight with others, have no clear goals, lie, steal, have trouble keeping a job and have no long-term relationships. As parents, they are either severely neglectful or abusive. There is no sense of guilt for harming others.

SOCIOPATH

This diagnosis is not in the *DSM-IV* because it is not considered a mental illness, just a bad seed, because they are capable of presenting so normally and the field is still dominated by the medical model. I find there are two types of sociopaths: light sociopath and dark sociopath. One likes to steal from others under their noses and the second likes to torture weak people under the noses of others. Both *can* lead to murder, but murder is not a given.

Cold Charming Child (Light Sociopath): Derived from RAD

CAUSE

Attachment	Avoidant attachment. Major, major attachment break or total lack of bonding and empathy altogether. May or may not have suffered severe physical abuse and other traumas. Parent may tease infant because it's funny. Background usually is high socioeconomic status and imprinted.
Second Year On	Parents model strict façade of **appropriateness** in an upper class context. Parents model **deception** and lying. Parents commit crimes and violations **behind closed doors**. Parents threaten children for revealing anything about the family. Parents are mentally and physically **abusive. The Repression Ethic is full-blown.**

EFFECT

Infant/ Toddler	Infant refuses eye contact up close and arches back to pull away.
	INNER THOUGHTS: "I'm never going to trust or give my heart away to anyone ever again." "It's every man for himself." "I don't respect anyone."
Child	Learns to survive by pure **deception and cunning**. Develops a lifestyle of **charming authorities while deceiving them**. Builds skills to achieve power. Pyromania, cruelty to animals. Child's soul or spirit dies, probably irreversibly. He lacks empathy, remorse and a conscience.
	INNER THOUGHTS: "The more I can fool people and take advantage of them, the more valuable I become."
Adult	**He affects a superficial charm and sophisticated insight into social appropriateness.** He is acquisitive and makes a good superficial show of material success. He is deceitful, lying easily and **may pass "yes/no" lie detector tests**. He likes to "put one over" on people, to manipulate, to line up a power base and to beat the other fellow to the punch. He loves the intellectual skill of manipulating people, especially of staying one jump ahead. He has **contempt for authority** and is particularly **thrilled when he can manipulate those in power**. He is **bold and daring** and hungers for thrills and excitement. He has a compulsive and impulsive propensity for **sexual deviancy**, especially in the realm of the **forbidden**. He enjoys **derogating and humiliating others** and has a propensity for violating the rights of others. He has a **guiltless insensitivity** which is undaunted by danger and punishments and rather, seeks to provoke and attract them. He has an **inability to love**, a **lack of empathy** and a lack of conscience. **He is a sore loser.** He enjoys **vindictive** retribution, often in ways that are not socially disreputable, irresponsible or even illegal.

SOCIOPATH, cont'd

Diabolical Child (Dark Sociopath): Derived from RAD Plus Abuse

CAUSE

Attachment	Avoidant attachment. Major, major attachment break or total lack of bonding and empathy altogether. May or may not have suffered severe physical abuse and other traumas. Parent may tease infant because it's funny. Background usually is high socioeconomic status and imprinted.
Second Year On	Parents model strict façade of **appropriateness** in an upper class context. Parents model **deception** and lying. Parents commit crimes and violations **behind closed doors**. Parents threaten children for revealing anything about the family. Parents are mentally and physically **abusive. The Repression Ethic is full-blown.**

EFFECT

Infant/ Toddler	Infant refuses eye contact up close and arches back to pull away. INNER THOUGHTS: "I'm never going to trust or give my heart away to anyone ever again." "It's every man for himself." "I don't respect anyone."
Child	Learns to survive by pure **deception and cunning**. Develops a lifestyle of **charming authorities while deceiving them**. Builds skills to achieve power. Pyromania, cruelty to animals. Child's soul or spirit dies, probably irreversibly. He lacks empathy, remorse and a conscience. INNER THOUGHTS: "The more I can fool people and take advantage of them, the more valuable I become." "I hate everyone except my parents but they won't know because I can use and hurt them."
Adult	He affects a superficial charm and sophisticated insight into social appropriateness. He is acquisitive and makes a good superficial show of material success. He is deceitful, lying easily and **may pass "yes/no" lie detector tests**. He likes to "put one over" on people, to manipulate, to line up a power base and to beat the other fellow to the punch. He loves the intellectual skill of manipulating people, especially of staying one jump ahead. He has **contempt for authority** and is particularly **thrilled when he can manipulate those in power**. He is **bold and daring** and hungers for thrills and excitement. He has a compulsive and impulsive propensity for **sexual deviancy, sadism and torture, especially under the nose of others.** He enjoys **derogating, humiliating and abusing others** and may even request a thank you. He has a **guiltless insensitivity** which is undaunted by danger and punishments. He has a drive to see how much he can get away with and who he can fool. He has an **inability to love**, a **lack of empathy** and a lack of conscience. **He is a sore loser.** He enjoys **vindictive** retribution, often in ways that are not socially disruptable, irresponsible or even illegal.

SOCIOPATH, cont'd

Anecdotal Application

Sociopaths are neglected and tortured children who gave up on adults and authority at a very young age. They tend to be from a higher socioeconomic status and learn to act like the adults around them. They may train themselves in appropriateness or they may be carefully taught how to act. A sociopath might be living right next door to you. You might even be married to one. Sociopaths are charming and very appropriate, but they lack empathy and a conscience, which is what the book, *People of the Lie* (Peck, 1983), is about. Sociopaths become judges, gynecologists, psychologists and psychiatrists, presidents of the PTA, scout masters and clergy. They make it their strategic goal to achieve power and prestige, and their greatest thrill is to violate ethics and social norms right under our collective nose. Sociopaths have been severely neglected or tortured, but trained to act appropriately. They have no spark, but like all pathological personalities, they protect their parents. Some are light sociopaths and others are dark sociopaths.

Bernie Madoff was a light sociopath. He was a former non-executive chairman of the NASDAQ stock market and perpetrated perhaps the largest Ponzi scheme in history, defrauding investors of almost $65 billion. His wife, Ruth, and two grown sons allegedly didn't know of his illegal activities. Of course there is speculation about how much they knew, but after seeing Ruth and one son interviewed on *60 Minutes* (October 26, 2011), I believe they didn't know. The second son committed suicide because his mother refused to reject her husband. After his suicide, Ruth walked away from the marriage, but by then her husband was already in prison. It appeared that Madoff and his wife lived in their insulated roles. Even after she learned of his activity, she did not have the ethics to leave him.

Scott Peterson was a dark sociopath who killed his unsuspecting pregnant wife, Laci, in order to maintain an affair with another woman. He was raised to maintain appearances at all costs. Scott was abandoned only once, at birth, for medical reasons, but he never really attached to his mother. She was unable to extend empathy and understanding or to parent him with values. Nor was his father able to have an authentic relationship with him. Both parents acted out roles in a play as if they were scripted and expected their son to do the same. It took a while to find one another, their nearly precise counterparts. When Scott Peterson's mother, Jackie, was two years old, her father was murdered by an employee and her mother gave her up to be raised in a Roman Catholic orphanage, where she learned to play a role to survive. It was a place where children were regularly raped and beaten. It was there she learned to pretend that everything was fine and emotions were unnecessary. When Jackie was 18, she began her search for love in all the wrong places. She became pregnant three times, each time abandoned by the father of her child. Twice she gave up her children. The third time her physician told her she couldn't keep doing this, so she kept her third child but never liked him. She finally gave him up when he wrecked the family car as a teen. Scott's father, Lee, was raised in utter poverty and had to travel with his mother wherever she found work. When he was old enough to work, he managed to buy a home and expensive cars for appearances, despite his difficulty paying bills. He even took on a pseudonym once to avoid creditors. He didn't like being a father because children were too active, and probably too real. When Jackie met Lee Peterson, he had already left his first wife and was relieved not to have the children around anymore. He accepted Jackie and her son though, and when Scott was born, Lee was pleased because he never seemed to cry. Despite Scott's life-threatening illness at birth, Lee said Scott was born beautiful and "shiny." Jackie told people that the blended family was like the Brady Bunch. What did they know about normal? Peterson was a child whose only role models were emotionless play actors. Scott understood the drill and always gave his parents what they wanted. He copied their ways. When his father wanted him to play golf, he learned to play golf and love it. He didn't complain. He didn't have emotional meltdowns. He became proficient at smiling big and charming adults. For this they called him their "golden child." He was perfect and expected to stay that way. He never discovered his own voice, his own feelings or his own thoughts. Peterson was raised in a family where there was no apparent authenticity or intimacy, no apparent ethics and no apparent consequences (Albow, 2005). It seems that his core self shriveled without acknowledgement. Any sexual conquest would prove to him that he existed. What is often left over by the time the role-playing child grows up is a strong sexual drive that satisfies two needs: feelings and mirroring. Living a real life had become out of the question and all that mattered were appearances. Thus those who are trained to *act* rather than to *be* are at the greatest risk for sociopathic choices.

Jose Menendez must have been a diabolical child who became a dark sociopath as an adult and married Kitty, an apparent light sociopath. He was an appropriate, high functioning executive in the record industry and once told a colleague that he would rather be feared than loved. He molested both his sons, but focused on Erik, the younger child. He dominated him, pushing him hard on the tennis court while escalating the sexual abuse at home. Jose threatened to kill Erik if he ever told anyone. Jose stuck pins in his son's penis while asking him, "What will I do if you tell?" Eric was to answer repeatedly, "Kill me, father." He told him that he would not kill him at first but that he would act like everything was fine and then would kill Erik when he least suspected it. This became a setup for enormous paranoia once Erik told brother Lyle and Lyle confronted his father. The two young men came to act as if they were living through a horror movie. I watched the entire trial on Court TV and found that Lyle and Eric's adult behavior and testimony were completely congruent with their story. I noticed that the public could not believe that these parents would have tortured their sons so horribly, or that children would kill their own parents if they were terrified. Kitty spied on the children for their father, but otherwise committed few crimes against them. However, she, like Ruth Madoff, held her husband to no standard at all. To a large extent, she enabled his choices. It was Kitty Menendez who put alcohol on Erik's penis after his father stuck it with pins, gaining some pleasure herself from inflicting pain on her adolescent son in the name of caring for him (Court TV, Dec. 11-15, 1995).

PSYCHOPATH

Psychosis resulting from bizarre and cruel parenting leads to violence, which this personality thinks is logical and justified even though he may or may not know the difference between right and wrong. Not in the *DSM-IV-TR*.

Tormented Child:
Derived from Early Emotional and Physical Abuse

CAUSE

Attachment	Infant loves and hates mother. RAD.
Second Year On	Parent exposes child to chronic and severe multiple types of torment, usually with a mental twist. Mother or father torture child while other participates or fails to protect. Torture probably includes sexual abuse. Child is tortured further for acknowledging the truth of his torment. Child may be abused by siblings while parents watch and egg them on. Child learns to maintain nothing is wrong at home. The Repression Ethic is full-blown.

EFFECT

Infant/ Toddler	Infant doesn't smile or engage in eye contact and arches back when held. INNER THOUGHTS: Infant loves and hates mother. "No one is safe. I want my mother. I hate my mother."
Child	**RAD. CD. Enuresis.** Wets bed late into childhood. Thinking and logic is disorganized, lacking cause and effect reasoning. Moves in and out of "normal." When abnormal, she is extremely violent. She is hard to understand. She is clearly disturbed. She lies. Pyromania, cruelty to animals, fascination with gore. INNER THOUGHTS: "I'll show you." "You're making me do this."
Adult	ATTACHMENT ISSUES: He makes **abnormal attempts to merge**. He rages at rejections. He uses force and manipulations, having never learned social skills at home. He lacks empathy or remorse. SECOND-YEAR-ON ISSUES AND INTERACTION STYLE: He scapegoats to get even, while maintaining his childhood was fine. **Scapegoating is a violent re-enactment of his early childhood treatment** although magnified due to the additional rage brought on by an unsafe attachment figure. Uncontrollable drive to re-enact and scapegoat a rendition of how he was treated with a rationale that victims deserve it. Psychotic confusion (due to his own history) over right and wrong and cause and effect.

PSYCHOPATH, cont'd

Anecdotal Application

Jared Lee Loughner is the psychopathic mass murderer who shot and seriously wounded Arizona Congresswoman Gabrielle Giffords and nineteen others, killing six of them, including a child. Loughner demonstrates the kind of disorganized thinking found in paranoid schizophrenia, but his violent actions transport him to the level of psychopathy. Disorganized thinking results from a disorganized attachment where the infant craves his mother/caregiver for survival yet fears her for the same reasons. "I know who's listening: Government Officials, and the People," Loughner wrote, "Nearly all the people who don't know this accurate information of a new currency aren't aware of mind control and brainwash methods. If I have my civil rights, then this message wouldn't have happen (sic)" (*New York Times*, Jan. 8, 2011). According to Pima County Sheriff Clarence Dupnik, "He has a troubled past, I can tell you that" (*The Guardian*, Jan. 9, 2011). In the article on Wikipedia, two sources offer information affording some reasonable speculation regarding what makes Loughner tick. One source said he was angry at Giffords because he believed women should not be in power. Another source in the same article said that he started changing radically when his "girlfriend" broke up with him. As a forensic evaluator I would form the following working theory and modify it as new information came to me: A breakup with a girlfriend of whatever magnitude that fostered a regression in his personality would have indicated early abandonment trauma. Additionally, we have reason to believe he suffered a disorganized attachment since his actions and speech are clearly disorganized. The trauma of such an attachment, where he fears his mother or caregiver as much as he needs her, can be exacerbated by a taboo against expressing his fears, as opposed to having a mother who comforts him. That he was enraged at Congresswoman Giffords because she functioned in a position of power – and women should not be in power – suggests a temporary hypothesis that he believes women should be home taking care of their babies. This would become logical thinking if he spent the first few years of his life in unsafe day care, an infant's first experience with government.

RAPIST

This misogynist has a burning hatred against women because his mother hated men and boys.

Emasculated Child:
Derived from a Mother Who Scapegoats Her Son's Masculinity

CAUSE

Attachment	**Ambivalent attachment.** Mother tortures and/or rejects infant.
Second Year On	Sample possibilities: Mother turns child over to abuser, complaining about what child did to her. Mother abuses and sexually tortures child.
	Mother ridicules child's masculinity. Mother repeatedly abandons child with pedophile.

EFFECT

Infant/ Toddler	Inward.
	INNER THOUGHTS: "Oh, no, here she is again!"
Child	Child hates women. Child begins to obtain sexual materials and use them to act out anger.
	INNER THOUGHTS: "Women are bitches, whores and sluts (and worse)."
Adult	ATTACHMENT ISSUES: Hates women. Mistrusts Women.
	SECOND-YEAR-ON ISSUES AND INTERACTION STYLE: He has a drive to find a woman he can dominate and hurt. **He seeks the type of woman that corresponds with his own abuse.** For example, if mother was a prostitute, he'll pick prostitutes. If mother sent him to live under an abusive nun, he'll pick nuns. If mother says, "No woman would ever want you," he'll pick peers.

Anecdotal Application

Everyone knows what a rapist does to be a rapist, but we don't all know why. We don't all know that there are different types of rapists. While sexual abuse may be part of a rapist's childhood, there is more evidence that violence is the abuse they suffer the most (Simons, D.A., *et al.* 2008). Whatever the injury, it includes toxic, hurtful and neglectful experiences with mothers. These hurtful experiences are not allowed expression by the child. He cannot tell someone in order to be understood. The child is left with no social skills to achieve a successful relationship with a woman and even hates women for the love that was withheld from him. In some cases the mom is emasculating, demeaning or abusive. Sometimes mom turns the child over to an extremely violent father for "discipline."

There are several types of rape and rapists, defined by their mode of operation. Date rapes constitute the largest number of rapes, but are not considered in the following statistics: Power assertive rapists, 44%, claim to have a weapon but prefer not to use it. They sometimes feel remorse and are sometimes referred to as gentlemen rapists. Anger retaliation rapists, 30%, are out to hurt women. Power reassurance or opportunity rapists are the type that will commit rape during a robbery, kidnapping or military conquest. Anger excitement rapists or sadistic rapists, 5%, are the most dangerous type of rapist; most of them torture and kill their victims. Juvenile sex offender rapists, on the rise, are the type that have problems at school or with authority and take it out on women. Female offenders or accomplices are another category, but they are relatively rare, usually offending on children.

MASS MURDERER

He is usually and primarily a father's creation, exploding under pressure when male bosses or authority figures punish him or fire him for inadequacy.

Postal Child:
Derived from a Domineering and Abusive Father

CAUSE

Attachment	Insecure-anxious or ambivalent attachment. Passive mother.
Second Year On	Authoritarian father is violently abusive, often using fists, whips, belts or other objects. Father bosses child around incessantly. Father rages at and ridicules his son. Son is almost never good enough. Father may be fanatically religious and judgmental of his son. The Repression Ethic is full blown.

EFFECT

Infant/ Toddler	May fear abandonment or may refuse intimacy. INNER THOUGHTS: "Don't go!" or "Back away!" or "Don't go. Back away!"
Child	**Enuresis. OD.** He is a pressure-cooker. He is stifled, sitting on rage. He explodes from time to time. He sets fires. INNER THOUGHTS: "I hate being bossed around." "I'll never be good enough for my him (my father)." "I'm worthless."
Adult	ATTACHMENT ISSUES: He has difficulty with intimacy and women because his mother didn't protect him. He's angry and capable of domestic violence. SECOND-YEAR-ON ISSUES AND INTERACTION STYLE: He is a **hair-trigger** that could avoid the catalyst which would set him off – **authoritarian environments** (the post office, the electric company, McDonald's). He will sabotage his job with questionable behavior. He could kill anyone for firing or criticizing him. He could kill any abusive boss. If no cruel incident takes place at work, he may never be a mass murderer.

Anecdotal Application

Most mass murders are sons of dictatorial, rejecting and abusive fathers. They are usually triggered by a rejecting boss in an authoritarian, paramilitary type workplace where they return for revenge and "go postal." Probably the best example of a mass murderer is Adolph Hitler, whose childhood you read about in Chapter 1: Creating a Personality.

There is no criminal gene, and neither is there a gene for a Michelangelo.
– Bruce Perry, MD, Researcher, Clinician, Neuropsychiatrist

SERIAL KILLER

He is usually and primarily a mother's creation, waiting to unleash. He has an odd capacity to sustain a normal persona between killings while he daydreams about the next release. This trait might make one think that he could control his behavior, but the daydreaming and the final acts cannot be forestalled indefinitely.

The Double-Damned Child:
Derived from Extreme Maternal Rejection and Abuse

CAUSE

Attachment	**Ambivalent attachment.** Mother **deprives** infant of nurturing and **abandons** infant. Mother enfolds and rejects infant. Mother **tortures** infant or fails to protect from torture.
Second Year On	Mother tortures infant or fails to protect from violence and torture. As opposed to repeated whipping by father, child suffers more **bizarre and ritualistic abuse** including **emotional and sexual abuse.** Mother may be the perpetrator or facilitator. Parents require secrecy. They start talking about how he's got the devil in him. Repression Ethic is full blown. Usually says he loves his mother.

EFFECT

Infant/ Toddler	Child may look somewhat normal, though a little inward.
	INNER THOUGHTS: "See me. See me. See me."
Child	**Enuresis. ADHD. CD.** Fire starter. Tortures animals. Likes gore. Sometimes seems arrogant and angry, other times friendly. Dominant behavior.
	INNER THOUGHTS: "Someday. You'll see." "Someday people will fear me."
Adult	ATTACHMENT ISSUES: Buried rage over betrayal.
	SECOND-YEAR-ON ISSUES AND INTERACTION STYLE: Stalks, kills for release of internal pressure and saves souvenirs (evidence). Rarely married with children to abuse. Represses truth about abuse and neglect. Declares parents were good people. Is totally numbed out over childhood feelings. Believes his evil feelings are because he IS evil. Has obsessive thoughts and uncontrollable drives to act out specific fantasies. After he acts them out, he gets relief for awhile until they build back up. (Would never surrender control to do therapy.)

The Double-Damned. Many children who have been abused in childhood are rescued slowly, if at all. They act badly and we really don't like them. They are not cute anymore, so it's hard to care, and besides, as a society we don't believe in blaming parents, so we blame them. They act out and are not loveable anymore because they are not very compliant. There is a war within them. This is because it is not easy to break a child from believing that they shouldn't be mistreated. They are in the process of trying to swallow their pain as if they deserve it, buying that they *should* be abused and rejected because surely there is nothing wrong with their parents. We look at the child and we look at the parent and we feel for the parent. He doesn't have a chance, really, as long as we look at a symptomatic child and think the problem is in him, not in the way he is being treated. This child is double-damned, for when he is grown and faces the punishment he is heir to, he will be righteously despised for how he had to turn out. Damned in childhood and damned in adulthood, he is double-damned.

SERIAL KILLER, cont'd
Anecdotal Application

Ted Kaczynski was the Unibomber. He mailed packages to sites that pioneered in technology. Ted's mother adored him and he was a sweet, happy baby, in love with her until he developed a bad rash all over his body at nine months old. At doctors' recommendations, she placed him in isolation for three weeks. In those days parents could only visit their child for a few hours every other day. He lived inside a see-through oxygen tent, monitored by pumps, dials, lights and equipment surrounding him instead of his mommy. After two days she was allowed to hold him for a few hours, but when she handed him back to the nurse, he screamed and screamed in terror. He cried for her, but finally gave up wanting her. He never wanted her again and he had developed a hatred for technology, which the infant in him saw as coming between him and his mother. Ted's mother said when she got her son back that he had changed and he was never the same again. He had withdrawn and he didn't trust her anymore. He didn't go limp in her arms and conform to the shape of her body. He didn't like to cuddle. As he got older he appeared to be introverted and private, although he had outbursts of anger. When his little brother asked why Ted was so strange, their mom explained that he came back from isolation this way. She told her younger son, "We just have to accept him now."

The Ice Man, Richard Kuklinski, was born to Anna, who had been raised in a brutal Roman Catholic orphanage where she was raped and regularly beaten. She was not capable of nurturing because she had never been nurtured. However she was capable of marrying Stanley, an alcoholic, and she prayed for help when he beat her and her children. Not only didn't she protect them, she beat them too. On their wedding night, Stanley discovered Anna was not a virgin, thus she must be a whore. Anna was too afraid to tell him the truth so she took to praying harder and harder for her safety. Stanley concluded that his first son, Florian, was not biologically his and beat him regularly for the slightest indiscretions such as wetting his bed or crying. Richard was their second child. Florian took to protecting his little brother from their father's rage by holding him through scary times. They became each other's source of comfort. The more children Stanley and Anna had, the higher the bills, the more Anna had to work, the more Stanley would drink, the more he would beat the kids and her followed by sex at his sole desire, the more Anna would beat her children and the more her children went to school looking like waifs. When Richard turned five, Stanley hit Florian so hard on the back of his head that he killed him. Anna told Richard to tell people that he died falling down stairs, which devastated Richard. Neighborhood boys took to making fun of Richard and two boys in particular tormented him. One Saturday he escaped them and ran home for safety, where his father took off his belt and beat him for running from a fight. Richard learned to kill or be killed. When he earned enough "respect" to be safe on the streets he organized his own gang. It was not long before he was a cold-blooded killer-for-hire.

The Ethics of Personality Types

Every personality structure or disorder has a lack of ethics at its root. Each personality type has different ethical shortcomings and beliefs. If you could change the beliefs and ethics, I wonder if you could heal the disorder.

Personality Type	Unhealthy Ethic (except for Healthy Personality)
Healthy	I will treat others as if they were me. I will take responsibility for the quality of my life and do what is in front of me to do, no matter how difficult.
Passive-Aggressive	I don't need to keep commitments.
Dependent	I shouldn't have to take care of myself.
Obsessive-Compulsive	People should do things my way.
Histrionic	I can have an affair if I want to.
Narcissistic	I matter more than others.
Borderline	I'm innocent. It's not my fault. It's your fault. Loyalty is everything and don't trust anyone.
Avoidant	I don't want to do anything that is scary, especially anything that will make me look foolish.
Approach-Avoidant	It doesn't matter what I said yesterday.
Schizoid	You are just an object to me.
Schizotypal	God matters more than people.
Schizophrenic	Reality is what I make it.
Bipolar	If I think it, I am. I don't have to earn it.
Dissociative Disorder (Multiple Personality)	I don't want to know what I know.
Paranoid	I'll get you before you get me.
Antisocial	I will dominate and abuse whoever I have to in order to be safe and respected.
Sociopath	I love to get you without you knowing it.
Psychopath	I will believe what I have to believe to do what I have to do.
Rapist	Women owe me.
Mass Murderer	I need to retaliate as big as I can to survive these humiliating feelings.
Serial Killer	Someone will pay for what happened to me (but not my parents).

Positive Traits of Personalities

Passive-Aggressive. They appear the healthiest, though their pathology sneaks up on you. They have a natural manner, even a peaceful or spiritual countenance.

Dependent. They are compulsive caretakers, subconsciously hoping they will earn someone caring for them. They make good nurses or teachers. They're the ones who bring refreshments to a gathering.

Obsessive-Compulsive. They are great organizers or economizers. They make great accountants or bargainers. They are good business people, engineers, programmers and mathematicians.

Histrionic. Many people enjoy their seductive qualities. They can be very entertaining.

Narcissistic. They are high functioning and perform well in the professional world. They enjoy performing on stage. They make good lecturers, high profile personalities, doctors, lawyers and entrepreneurs.

Borderline. Once healing has begun and projections have been identified and clarification skills learned, they can be extremely perceptive. They have a powerful focusing ability. They make good political protestors when injustice is at hand.

Avoidant. Loyal to friends. Good night guards.

Approach-Avoidant. Often very high functioning.

Bipolar. Bipolar personalities are very difficult to heal. I have found that they only want to work during a crisis and they drop out when they get corrective mirroring or when things are good. If I ever meet a Bipolar who makes the choice to work consistently and honestly, they will be halfway there.

Schizoid. Mechanical aptitude. Can work in non-human environment with only machines and equipment. Do not appear emotionally needy.

Schizotypal. Great clairvoyants for those who seek them.

Schizophrenic. Great capacity to see through inauthenticity and even into real danger when others don't see or suspect it.

Dissociative Identity Disorder (Multiple Personality Disorder). These are basically healthy people at their core, perhaps healthier than most. (Their extra personalities have the personality disorders.)

Paranoid. They make good detectives.

Antisocial. They are a good barometer of family pathology from a sociological point of view.

Sociopathic. They are the karmic results of failure to bond and abandonment. Socially, when we fail to perceive them and heal them, we will be rewarded with a reminder that empathy is critical in the human drama and without it we suffer inhumanity. Hopefully, we can read and heed our reminders.

Rapists. Rapists are the results of men injuring their daughters who then injure their sons. These children remind us that we need to deal with sexual abuse earlier rather than later in order to protect ourselves.

Killers. Serial killers and mass murderers are the natural results of our very worst parenting and our most grievous social neglect. When they were children we failed to intervene on their behalf and now they provide us with someone we can love to hate and a stark reminder that all our children are our responsibility, sooner or later.

CHAPTER 3

Healing

"Your being here, your being alive makes worthiness your birthright.
You alone are enough."
-- Oprah

Heal Thyself

I know that how much you hate your pain is a measure of how bad it is.
But do not hate or despise your pain because that only makes it worse.
Then you become the source of your suffering.
Do not fight your pain because you injure yourself more.
Do not deny your pain because you will compound it.
Do not fear more pain because that will magnify it.
Do not dramatize your pain because then you cannot be heard.
Don't hate yourself for having pain because you injure yourself more.
Don't act like you don't want help when you do and
Own that you don't need as much help as you want.
Do not waste excessive dialogue on how bad it was or how bad it is
Because no one can make it better except you.
Commiseration about your pain is harmful. Do not waste your witness.
The more angry or distraught you are for having pain, the more you postpone healing.
Your pain is a priceless message that something is wrong. Find it.
Accept your pain.
Go into the feeling so it can be heard and perhaps be released.
Take your witness.
This is how you heal.
Be brave enough to go quietly into the pain
And loudly out, if need be.
Do this to heal thyself.

-- F. S.

Children will turn themselves into pretzels for us in order to meet our needs. They are born to please, and they are born seeking our love and approval until we inspire them to rebel. *From* us they get their identity and *for* us they will do anything unless we destroy their hope of being able to please us. Nevertheless, we must resist the temptation to seek children who satisfy us. We need to remember we are the grown-ups and they get to be the children who look to us for protection and counsel. We must not ask them to put our feelings before theirs, lie for us, swallow the truth as they have experienced it, take care of us or cover for us. In order to do this job of parenting well, we have to work on ourselves, face our own truth, history and character, as well as that of our own parents. We cannot raise a healthy child without becoming conscious of our roots and theirs in their life with us, including the automatic impulses parenting unleashes, born of our past, for good or bad.

For this reason, as you journey through this book, keep your own childhood in mind along with that of your child. Parenting can be a process of discovering yourself while you witness the unfolding of your child. This book, like parenting, is designed to be a journey into self-awareness, as you were once a child too, and you are the product of your own childhood. Keep your eyes wide open.

Responses to Injury

The normal response to an assault or threat is a reflex reaction in the form of fight or flight. However, for any variety of reasons a child may be unable to fight or flee, so an injury is sustained and the child cannot release it.

Healthy Response to Injury

The healthy response is to process feelings immediately. No matter how severe, injuries that are processed immediately will prevent long-term emotional effects. The healthy outcome of an injury is catharsis through crying, screaming, raging, talking, being witnessed and acknowledging the truth of the event.

Another essential factor in a healthy response is the freedom and right to acknowledge the injury and all its components. This includes identifying the role of a parent who seemed vengeful or selfish. For example, if someone on the street hits us because they were insulted, we can accuse them of assault and battery. If someone out there rapes us, we can charge them with rape and attend the trial. In the healthy response, we get to momentarily blame the offender and move on. In best-case scenarios, the injured party is seen and understood and justice prevails. The injured party gets to have and express her feelings openly with dignity, responding to her offender.

In the case of the child with a parent who acts out his own childhood injuries on the child, the child may be told she deserved the beating or she invited the incest. She may be told to stop crying or the parent will hit her again. She may be told, "If you tell anyone, I'll prove you're a liar." Or very often, the child may be cheated out of maternal affection by a favored sibling and told to stop crying because it hurts mommy's feelings. He may be told that by raging, he becomes a "bad boy." If mommy drops him off at day care, he is expected to be happy to see her when she returns. He thinks if he isn't, if he shows his hurt or anger, she may drop him off even more.

Unhealthy Response to Injury

When fight or flight is not possible and an injury is sustained and not processed, a "freeze" response takes place (Levine, 1997), beginning with repression. Injuries that are repressed will fester in our bodies until a process of healing old wounds is undertaken.

The unhealthy response to injury is repression, resistance and denial, leading to symptoms and acting out.

Repression. Repression results from the child accepting the parent's point of view over his own. The parent is offended when the child mirrors the parent without unconditional regard. This "enlisted" child learns to come on board with the ethic that the parent is always right. This commitment lasts a lifetime and makes the best soldiers in pro-parent theory. This child protects the parents' feelings and identifies with them at the expense of his own feelings, healing and identity.

Repression takes place when:
- parents need, expect or require it.
- parents seem too weak to accept the child's feelings.
- parents repress their own feelings; it's the family way.
- parents don't seem interested.
- child has already detached and "doesn't need" anyone's help.

Repression occurs when an emotion resulting from trauma is not allowed. When we swallow a feeling, the body stores it, then creates a multitude of symptoms to get the mind to finally pay attention to and release the embedded suffering. Emotions are restless. They get "louder," attempting to create a crisis so the intolerable contradiction within can be released. They speak to us through:

- psychological/mental disorders or symptoms like anxiety, phobias, depression
- scapegoating via acting out imprints
- physical illness
- projections
- projective identification (attributing motives to others that have been internalized from the parent and acting on these projections, thus creating an impulse in the other to make them come true, like a self-fulfilling prophecy)
- pretense to omnipotence
- obsessive searches for and attempts to create power
- fantasy, delusions, hallucinations

> Once we have learned to live with our feelings and not to fight against them, we see in the manifestation of our bodies not a danger but helpful indications about our own personal history.
> – Alice Miller, M.D., Psychohistorian

Denial. Denial is a form of resistance and is the mental act of defending against the truth in order to protect a parent, a belief, or a fragile idea of one's self. Denial may begin as an attempt to shake off an assault on our worth or protect the perpetrator. It may present in the form of a rationalization. It could be a reaction to a trauma that we believed was unbearable even though we survived it. Childhood traumas often seem unbearable to children. Children cannot handle what adults can handle, yet we often ask more of the child than we ask of ourselves.

As grown children, however, we can handle the memories and buried feelings, especially since the worst has already happened. It exists only as a memory to recall rather than an actual threat. The offensive behavior of the primary caregiver or parent was taken personally and must be faced and discredited for us to heal. Any negative conclusions drawn then about our worth are not true and must be recognized as false messages.

Children blame themselves and make excuses for parents upon whom they depend. As adults, they defend themselves and blame others and/or conditions. Sometimes people:
- deny what happened or that anything happened at all.
- deny that it was, in fact, an injury.
- deny that they didn't deserve it.
- avoid by taking drugs or alcohol, eating, sleeping, overworking, socializing to distraction, etc.
- explain things away or rationalize them.
- ridicule the process of retrieval for healing, including the work others have done to heal, because to honor it would threaten the self's own tenuous denial. In order to recognize symptoms of denial, you must undergo extensive prideless self-reflection and self-observation.

> The price of such strategies, aimed at the total denial of pain, are the depressions and other symptoms suffered by not only the founding fathers of such schools of thought, but also by legions of their patients.
> – Alice Miller, M.D., Author

Resistance. Resistance to empathy for ourselves or feelings for what happened is the psycho-physical armor we construct to protect the world from knowing our injury. It requires us to become inauthentic and lie to ourselves. Ultimately, our resistance, not the injury itself, is the pathology. The injury could be healed in a moment or several hours at the most with empathy. It is the lack of access to the injury at all costs that is so toxic to the original self. Dissolving resistance is what takes the longest time in therapy. How quickly someone heals depends on how well they drop their resistance, including their fear of revisiting buried suffering. Much of therapy is spent on this process, helping the client get in touch with their original feelings, their defenses, and their truth.

Examples of resistance lies created by parents:
- You're ugly when you cry.
- Boys don't cry.
- If you cry, you'll make mama feel bad.
- If you don't cry, the feeling will go away.
- If you cry, you're being self-indulgent.

Examples of resistance lies we create for ourselves:
- If I revisit the pain, it will destroy me.
- If I revisit the pain, I'll fall apart permanently.
- If I revisit the pain, it will be more than I can bear and I'll humiliate myself.
- If I revisit the pain, I'll be a baby.

> Resistance is the fortress of lies that surrounds an injury.
> Eliminate the lies and the injury will heal naturally. – F.S.

Forgiveness

It's common to be told we need to get on with forgiving our parents, yet there is a risk to forgiving before we gain the insight we need to self-reflect, heal, transcend and reverse trends. As previously stated, children are predisposed to swallow themselves for their parents, so as adults we are hardwired for that task. Owning the truth of our childhood is usually the harder work. There is concern that we will contribute unwittingly in **parental immunity**, where parents inherit a lighter code of personal responsibility than the rest of the world. Of course, that's hypocrisy and it's not fair. Children are in need of ethical protection more than adults.

We are not here to blame parents because parents were children too, yet the best parents would want us to do whatever it takes to heal from any of their inadvertent mistakes. Lesser parents can still learn to heal from their childhood and to put the needs of their child above themselves. The first step is to change the ethic into a new value. Just as blaming could be a chain reaction from generation to generation, so too could healing.

I am afraid we may forgive parents and become insensitive to the plight of suffering children, or fail to compassionately see the results of major abuse in grown children. Many of my students have asked their parents to learn healthier ways to relate before they continue their interaction. The results have usually been fantastic. I have watched so many parents get on board to be the best parents they can be for their adult children. They want to turn the legacy around too.

Alice Miller tells of a man who was asked by his therapist when he was going to get over it and move on. He went home and shot himself in the head (1984). Asking someone to deal, get on with it and move on is harmful if they have not finished exploring, witnessing and processing their past. We cannot move on without insight and usually we require empathy. Positive thinking, on top of our behaviors without insight, doesn't work for long and then we are predisposed to pass along the injuries that we suffered. More importantly, self-awareness is our life's mission. It's our very own adventure. When we attain self-awareness, forgiving happens naturally and with certainty.

Commit to Healing

It is never too late. Sometimes healing can happen quickly, even in one session, whereas other times it may take months or years. Older people and children take longer, generally speaking. That's where persistence and patience come in. Keep in mind that in the long run, it will be far more difficult to give up and get the results of giving up than it will be to keep trying and get the results of persistence. When you tire, think of it as a test. Rest, and then just keep doing the right thing. When you see behaviors you don't like or accept anymore in yourself or your child, you simply continue the process of requiring new choices. It is never too late. The most important way to look at this journey is as if you are steering a ship and when you see you are off course, you correct it. No one ever steers perfectly on course. There is no perfect self or perfect parent. The best we can be is corrective and when we see clearly enough, reality gives us the feedback we need. The work only begins as we see clearly and know how to respond accordingly.

Good parenting is a joy. When you realize that you are in a miracle, it becomes so much fun, probably more fun than you have ever had. Loving the truth and taking a long hard look at your assumptions will be the hardest part, but the truth isn't that hard once you make the choice to pursue it. You can do it for your child, the one in you, as well as the one in front of you.

Healthy vs. Unhealthy Responses to Injury

Healthy	Unhealthy
INJURY ↓ Accept the injury ↓ Cry Express feelings Express memories ↓ ♦ HEAL ♦	INJURY ↓ Reject the injury ↓ Repress emotions ↓ Resist with metaphorical armor, preserve original threats, admonitions, self-repression, maintain a fear of vulnerability ↓ Deny your truth and feelings, maintain denial with self-deception and inauthenticity. ↓ EFFECTS: imprinting, scapegoating, self-destruction, personality disorders, depression, shadows, anxiety, phobias, nightmares, acting out, projections, physical illnesses, psychoses, self-fulfilling prophecies, loss of intellect

Process of Healing Old Wounds

Love the Truth

↓

Surrender defenses

↓

Pass through resistance

↓

Revisit original injury

↓

Cry
(or Rage or Scream)

↓

♦ HEAL ♦

↓

Enter
STATE OF GRACE:
relief, lightness,
reconstituting world view,
epiphanies, insights, wisdom,
enlightenment

Four Traits Necessary for Healing

The four necessary traits for healing (which are the same traits that lead to greatness and wisdom) are: courage, love of truth, self-observation without judgment and surrender of ego. You will need to cultivate all of these traits to heal your shadow. If one is avoided or omitted, you won't heal.

Courage
It takes courage to:
- Go into the shadow of painful feelings and beliefs.
- Surrender your ego and pride.
- Give up your resistance (defenses that protect you from emotional pain and vulnerability).
- Give up your denial (protection of your parents).
- Face the truth of what has happened to you in your childhood.

Love of Truth
The love of truth must be:
- equal to your love of your God.
- greater than your love of yourself or your parents.
- held above your existing beliefs. It is better to *see* right than to *be* right.
- able to help you break through the real illness – resistance – which is held together by one or more lies, keeping you opposing yourself, blinding you to words or actions your parents committed against you deliberately or inadvertently, blinding you to the truth of your own role in the results of your actions.

> The key to healing your anxiety is making the choice to face your fears and become a warrior rather than a worrier. -- Daren Lawe, LMFT

Self-Observation without Judgment

Self-observation. Self-observation is the capacity to observe yourself while you are thinking and speaking. Examples of self-observation:
- As long as I let myself eat more than I need, I'm going to feel bad about myself.
- When I don't prioritize my day, I have difficulties getting ahead.
- I seem to scapegoat people when I'm tired.
- I try to seduce married men. Why?
- I can't stand to be alone. What am I afraid of?
- I act like I'm afraid to face the truth. What do I think I'll find?
- I act more interested in what people think of me than who they are.
- I lose things when I hurry.

The difference between self-observation and self-consciousness is judgment. The former uses the Third Eye to witness; the latter uses the Third Eye to judge, and then turns on the self (Snyder, 1982).

Judgment. People who judge others often judge themselves. Living in judgment and self-judgment is self-imposed suffering. When you are self-judging, you cannot heal. You can't even self-correct. In order to heal or self-correct, you have to remove judgment from your life.

Judgment is labeling the essence or core of a person rather than mirroring their behavior. It shames a person. It is sometimes thought to be a tool to bully someone into being better. It is a "12 o'clock high" for the judge, a power trip that makes the judge feel good or better. It damns the judged person and has no constructive value whatsoever. It is retributive for having been judged as a child. It is scapegoating a present-day party for an injury caused in childhood, probably by parents. It has been seeking or waiting unconsciously for a scapegoat to get even.

Harms of judging:
- Judgment interrupts healing.
- Judgment creates a resistance to or retards growth.
- Judgment is for the judge, not the judged.
- Judgment is scapegoating and imprint energy.
- Judgment exacts retribution.
- People despair or rebel under judgment.
- It may create a temporary compliance without insight, but it will ultimately lead to the oppression or the deterioration of another.

Examples of judgment:
- Eye-rolling.
- "There's no excuse for that."
- "You stupid asshole."
- "You're worthless."
- "I don't like her. She's a liar." (vs. "She tells lies compulsively.")
- "I don't trust her." (vs. "Until I can talk to her about it, I'm not going to trust her.")
- "She'll never change."
- "He's been like that since birth."
- "He's just like his father."
- "They're not as good as us."

Assessment. Assessment is useful and replaces judgment. Assessment assumes that a person can heal and correct actions that have been backfiring on them. Examples of assessment:
- "I cannot be in a relationship with him if he continues to judge me."
- "Until my mother stops drinking, I won't take the kids to her house to visit."
- "Since he doesn't appear to give honest feedback, I can't tell where I stand."
- "I'm not going to date anyone who doesn't honor my healing process."
- "I don't want to be around her because she smokes."
- "She seems to blame a lot. If I stick around long enough someday she will blame me."

Surrender of Ego
- Surrender of ego is the same as surrender to your god.
- You cannot heal if you are defending your identity in any way.
- All healing takes place at 6 o'clock or in a humble state (further explored in Chapter 5: Imprinting).
- You need to have complete faith in the divine design of your mind/body/spirit so you can let go.

Ego is the enemy of healing and this program teaches students not only how to heal going into the pain, but what the necessary traits are for self-correction and ultimately wisdom and insight, including spirituality. Everyone has these traits and they can employ them if they choose, although these are the kind of traits that test our character and some of us have let them atrophy. The good news is that healing requires us to improve the traits of character first.

It is also important to replace bad habits of interaction with healthy ones. In order to achieve this transformation, a student does well to accept the role of a Zen student, whereby ego and identity become irrelevant. This model is the fastest way to work things through. Meeting with potential clients to explain this theory and technique is not feasible in one session, so the course is an opportunity for students to grasp the nature of this approach and to decide whether this is what they really want to do. More is asked of our students so they can have deeper results in a shorter period of time. Students know what Causal Therapists offer and require after they have taken the class. I am continually amazed that most people prefer to do The Work so they can get in and get out.

Yet I have had new students who changed their mind once they got into the requirements of the theory. If they have not fully chosen me or another causal therapist as their teacher, I may stop the process and ask them if they have chosen me to be their teacher, because the therapist cannot be more invested or work harder than the student. It's not a process that is worth it to me nor is it good for the student. Of course, this is also a re-enactment of a parent-child dynamic and I am game as long as the student surrenders once they have argued all their yes-buts. This Theory works exquisitely, but it works when the student surrenders. The greater the surrender, the greater the results. Students best prepare for boot camp if they choose to do this work. It is not for everyone.

I have heard students in the relationship skills workshop complain that the leader is at 12 o'clock (in power) because they misunderstand the roles of teacher *vs.* student. I believe that healing is an evolutionary process. It belongs to those who are willing to do what it takes. True transformation is not a process for people who would rather find the softer more painless route. True transformation to a healthy personality requires courage when one is afraid. It necessitates a profound love for the truth and, ultimately, a willingness to live life openly. True transcendence can only be earned by a diligent commitment to observe oneself and others without judgment. Lastly, in order to heal or to become a wise person, one must discover the virtue of selflessness. I do not believe that therapy can transpire at this depth or pace without these values in place. If they are not in place, they are the first goal of treatment.

> **Nobody but you is responsible for your life. ...You are responsible for the energy that you create for yourself, and you're responsible for the energy that you bring to others.**
> **– Oprah**

Steps for Healing

Pick Your Therapist

This book contains all the concepts you need to heal yourself and your child. However, most of us have blind spots when it comes to self-reflection and we need feedback to see around them. Further, having a consultant is helpful when parenting a child out of his injuries. Now that you are more informed, you can shop skillfully for a good therapist and guide. Search for a therapist with the best possible theoretical orientation for addressing your issues. Ideally, you'd want a trained Causal Therapist. If one is not available, the next in line would be a therapist who is familiar with Causal Theory or one who is willing to bone up on it to facilitate your work within that framework. There are many good therapists who do not use this theory and who will not budge because they are good at what they do, their way. This is something you will have to weigh. A skilled therapist who is good at what they do is probably better than a therapist who is trying on a great theory for the first time. It's your choice.

First, review the chart on War of the Researchers and Theoreticians Grid at the end of Chapter 1, and read "Types of Therapy by Philosophy." Translating the chart, seek a combination of Cognitive or Behavioral Theory with Attachment and Trauma Theory, if possible. If you know you suffered trauma, including attachment trauma, maybe you should focus on that first.

Ideally your therapist will understand the impact of attachment in the first few years of life, appreciate the harm of repressing feelings for our parents' sakes, have techniques for dealing with trauma and understand how important relationship skills are. She'll be open to dialogue with you about what she thinks about you and what she sees when relating to you. She'd never presume anything about you is genetic. Here are some questions you might ask:

- What impact would you say the first few years of life has on personality?
- Do you advocate the use of medication?
- Do you think it's all right to put a two-year-old in day care?
- What do you think causes ADHD?
- Do you believe behavior is a result of a person's genes?
- To what degree do you think genes cause the symptoms of schizophrenia or the creation of serial killers?
- Are you familiar with The Causal Theory?
- Are you willing to familiarize yourself with Causal Theory to help me?

Choose Your Teacher

I don't mean to confuse you. Your therapist is your teacher, but I want you to be careful whom you choose as well as what theory you seek. I am suggesting that you investigate for authenticity. Seek a teacher/therapist who has done the work and lives authentically as much as possible. Finally, once you've chosen, treat your therapist like a Zen Master. Surrender if you want your work to be deep and swift. Don't worry about giving up your power because you can always get it back, and do take it back and question if you witness a lack of ethics.

In my field, you don't have to employ any of the above traits to go to therapy. You just show up. However, I recommend you approach Causal Therapy differently. Gurus, masters and therapists must be vigilantly scrutinized for their openness (Love of Truth), integrity (Self-Reflection) and Courage. If these three are in place, I promise you that the teacher in question will seem authentic and will have honed the practice of profound humility (Surrender of Ego, the fourth trait. Once these four traits that create authenticity can be observed and the student chooses this teacher, it's time for you to surrender. Now the once humble teacher must assume the authoritative role to move things along at a deep yet swift pace. This, by the way, is why Causal Therapists have to do the work themselves before they can lead anyone else.

The founder of The Self-Realization Fellowship, Paramhansa Yogananda, repeated the words of his own teacher, Swami Sriyukteswar Giri:

"If you do not like my words, you are at liberty to leave at any time. I want nothing from you but your own improvement. Stay only if you feel benefitted."

For every humbling blow he dealt at my vanity, for every tooth in my metaphorical jaw he knocked loose with stunning aim, I am grateful beyond any facility of expression. The hard core of the human egoism is hardly to be dislodged except rudely. With its departure the Divine finds at last an unobstructed channel. In vain It seeks to percolate through flinty hearts of selfishness...

"I am hard on those who come for my training. That is my way. Take it or leave it. I will never compromise. I try to purify only in the fires of severity searing beyond the average toleration. The gentle approach of love is also transfiguring. The inflexible and yielding methods are both effective if applied with wisdom..."

Students came and went. Those who craved a path of oily sympathy and comfortable recognitions did not find it in the hermitage... The departing preferred life's countless humiliations before any humility. Master's blazing rays, the open penetrating sunshine of his wisdom were too powerful for their spiritual sickness. They sought some lesser teacher who, shading them with flattery, permitted the fitful sleep of ignorance (Yogananda, 1998, p. 391).

I went though my own therapy with the heart of a Zen student. I took instructions. I dropped my ego. I preferred to "learn right rather than be right" (Zen Napkins, Snyder). It's the most efficient way to go. Assume there is nothing wrong with you at your core (because it's true), but you have been taught wrong things and wrong practices. Now you need a new mother/father, in the form of a teacher, your teacher. Assess your teacher/therapist. Choose your teacher/therapist. Then clarify, but don't argue. Allow yourself to be taught.

Face Your Shadow

A shadow is a dark buried feeling (anger, shame, sadness, hurt, guilt, *etc.*) which sometimes or even frequently pushes us around. It has a belief and a drive (to act out or act in) that work together. How a shadow shows itself:
- scapegoating with imprint energy (wanting to hurt someone or talk down to them)
- acting out
- re-enactments of childhood traumas or relationships (maybe we don't take care of ourselves because our parents didn't take care of us)
- aversions and phobias
- substance abuse
- other compulsive behaviors (cleaning, talking on the phone, surfing the web endlessly, reading instead of living)
- acting-in behavior
- depression, anxiety, suicidal ideation
- psychosis, hallucinations
- neurosis
- lowered intelligence, reality testing and reasoning abilities
- fear of betraying parents (the ultimate taboo), going into or through emotional pain, emotionality, revisiting emotional pain from childhood, fear, falling apart, losing control

A Shadow Always Lies.
- "I'm no good."
- "I ruined my mother's life."
- "I made my father abuse me."
- "I'm tainted."
- "Life is too hard."
- "Nothing I do is any good."

Acknowledge the force your shadow has had upon your worldview. Know that it is composed of at least one lie from childhood, thus it misinforms you and instructs your actions incorrectly. Then, listen to your inner dialogue. Listen to what your shadow says. Self-observe. When you're in a shadow, you think, talk and act differently than when you're not in a shadow. You can create negative consequences for yourself later by buying into your shadow or allowing it to drive you. You can think and act without self-awareness or you can turn your shadow into a wealth of information.

Go into the Shadow. The shadow is what some people call depression. Some people know it as the source of underlying rage. For others it is a state of fear that takes them over. Most people try to find ways around the shadow (*e.g.*, addictions, compulsions, obsessions, positive thinking), so they never heal and the shadow ends up chasing them their whole lives. Commonly, people say out loud or to themselves that the pain is too awful to explore, or they may say, "I hate this feeling" or "I want to get this over with" or "How much longer do I have to feel this way?" All of these manners of impatience only prolong healing or therapy. To heal the shadow, do the following:
- Get to know the contents of your shadow and become an expert on it.
- Write about your shadow, if you can. Write the thoughts you have again and again. Find the lies in your shadow.

Healing

How much do you really believe them? Why? What would you lose if you had to give up believing them? What would you gain?

- When your shadow is kicking you around, stop and "wear" it. Pull off the road. Take a bathroom break. Go sit still somewhere. Feel and see what's going on in you. Become a detective. Go into your shadow with a flashlight and identify the creepy-crawlies. See what they are. Get in touch with what they remind you of. They are familiar. What are they about? Trace them back in time.
- Discover your projections. Discover your projective identifications or self-fulfilling prophecies on others. See how you inadvertently make "bad" things come true.
- "*Seeing* is change." (Michael Lilienfeld, MA, my former therapist) Change happens automatically when we observe ourselves, as long as we remain nondefensive.
- Express your shadow to someone who is nonjudgmental and interested in listening. Recruit someone to help you call up, relive, and fully process the old experiences as they come up. It will be like peeling layers off an onion. This may take the form of doing breath work or couchwork. It may take the form of honest and open disclosure. In the ideal world, parents make the best healers of their own children. You may need to hire a professional guide.
- Love truth like a lifeline. Truth makes sense of everything.
- Move into a state of surrender in a safe environment with a guide, nurturer or therapist, where the process is understood and valued.
- Going into the center of your shadow is a great opportunity, no matter how scary or painful.
- Feel it and re-live it. Let yourself fall apart. Stay in the memory or familiarity as long as it will have you. Cry, scream, or rage, *if that is what your body feels like doing*. If you have a *choice* not to hold back, don't. The more expressive your cry (or scream or rage), the more you heal and never have to come back.
- See your part, if any, in the memory, or see your response to your pure victimization.
- If you finish processing that shadow, you will feel relief. Follow or enjoy the feeling (a state of grace) as long as it lasts. (See below.)
- If you don't finish, don't shove the feelings back down. Live in the depression or shadow until your next opportunity to "go in." Observe it. Wear it. Enjoy it. It won't hurt you.

Processing *vs.* **Loitering**. Know the difference between processing your shadow and loitering. Sometimes people will say that they cry and cry and cry, but never heal. Some say they even get worse. We do get "worse" before we get better. But often people are loitering rather than doing the work. Loitering involves making any one of the following mistakes:

- You buy the lie rather than expose it.
- You repeat the lie again and again, re-injuring yourself repeatedly.
- You cry because you feel the way you feel (pain or fear) rather than allowing yourself to feel the original feeling and cry. The former would be a fear of fear itself or a fear of pain. The latter would be crying and releasing your original feelings as you let yourself finally feel them.
- You focus on things in the present tense (scapegoat crying) rather than know that the present issues are residual from the past, and thus should be used to trace back the feeling to an earlier familiar time. Almost anything that may happen to you in the present to make you very upset probably touches on something unhealed from your past.
- You process your injury from power rather than from surrender and rage

against someone in your present life (scapegoating).

> **The state of your life is nothing more than a reflection of your state of mind. – Dr. Wayne W. Dyer**

State of Grace. Following catharsis, one can expect lightness of being, insights, learning of unlearned lessons, revelations, spiritual experiences, and religious experiences (*a la* William James, *Varieties of Religious Experience*). Such an experience may include clear seeing or loss of our superficial projections and illusions about reality.

There is often a change in the state of mind, as well as a physical regeneration. It is a highly spiritual, vulnerable, and suggestible state, which is absent pride, defensiveness or false self. After catharsis, it is not a good time for practical endeavors, but rather reverie, reflection, introspection, and recollection. It's a time for a walk in the park, a frozen yogurt, people-watching, a sunset, daydreaming, *etc.* Relax. Be quiet. Be. Don't cling to the state of grace or it will leave instantly. (Therapists should be mindful of this time and encourage clients not to return directly to responsibilities after such sessions. Their brain benefits with some time to reconstitute.)

Ethics and Changed Attitudes. Begin to assume responsibility for all of your adult experiences. The more ethical you live your life, the healthier you will be.
- Never blame.
- Cease self-criticism; begin self-observation.
- Cease judgment; begin observation of others.
- Begin to live life heroically and courageously. Do what is in front of you to do.
- Discover new creativity and "follow your bliss." (Joseph Campbell)

- Remember that fear begets more fear (and illness). Face your fears and your fear of fear.
- Become interested in the world OR yourself (in the direction ignored).
- Become a problem-solver. See the results of all your actions as your greatest teacher. This is the real meaning of karma.

Express the Content of Your Shadow. When you're in a shadow in the presence of someone close, you can express your shadow if they can be nonjudgmental and interested in listening. You may want to protect them by "framing it." In this way, you and your listener know together that what you're about to say is temporary, born of the past, and it's understood that you don't completely mean it. It's only a part of you, the unhealed part, which is talking. In talking about it with overview, you are investing in healing it, and you have invited your listener to be your sounding board. Once you frame what you are about to say, you have created an understanding that you need to get something out, no matter how angry or scary-sounding. In this way, you can listen to yourself think outloud and get useful feedback. Perhaps the lie that encapsulates your shadow will pour out for you to see. Listen to what your shadow says. Self-observe.

Examples of ways to frame your shadow for talking:
- "I am in the shadow, and I'm dying to say..."
- "I don't know how to say this without hurting anyone, but I've got to get this off my chest, so here goes. I'll try to do damage control afterwards. May I?"
- "I don't know how to say this right, but I don't think I should hold it in. So, this is what I'm feeling and thinking..."
- "Let me frame this: ..."
- Draw a frame in the air [ ] with two hands (for someone familiar with "framing" or what you mean by this).

- "I'm going to say this out of skill, and then you can tell me how I could have said it better."

Conversely, someone may say to you, "That's your shadow talking," or "Is that your shadow talking?" when you say things without framing, like:
- "I'm no good."
- "I'm a loser."
- "I want to die."
- "I don't see the point in trying; it never works."

- "You don't really love me."
- "I hate you."
- "You never tell me the truth."

Do Not Take Someone's Shadow to the Bank. Shadows express temporary feelings and thoughts rooted in past injuries and traumas. Most people don't always live in their shadows and it's not who they will be or what they may want to say again once they express their shadow talk, so you may not want to over-react.

The CTT Modality

Causal Therapy & Treatment is a somewhat different process than more traditional therapies. It involves a three-pronged approach. First you take the theory class so you can understand the assumptions and agreements in the work before you invest time or money in private therapy. It's also an opportunity to see which of the teachers you feel most comfortable with. Second is the private meetings, which usually include couchwork so that you can visit your childhood experiences that negatively affect you now, including trauma. When you revisit these experiences, you get to heal and transcend them. Lastly, because healing does not solve the problem of dysfunctional coping skills, how you interact with others needs to be replaced or enhanced with healthy interaction skills and healthy ethics.

1: Theory

The first element is the parenting class, which is more than a parenting class. It is a class in self-awareness. The class explains thoroughly what a healthy childhood would have been like, the origins of pathology and what has to take place for one to heal. This class is a resistance buster. When clients have taken this class, they are so much easier to work with. They can then take a proactive and consulting role in their own case. They diagnose themselves after verifying historical data from childhood and the negative coping mechanisms they utilize in adulthood. From the beginning of therapy, they present their own history and identify formative issues. Clients are more willing to do "The Work" since they understand why we're doing what we're doing; consequently, we waste little or no time with resistance or pulling teeth. We probably cut one to two years off therapy by having clients take the parenting class first, even though it may seem like a hurdle or detour. Sometimes therapy only takes six months to one year. How long therapy takes is entirely about how much resistance is in the client.

2: Treating Trauma

Talk Therapy. The second element is the private session, composed of half 'talk therapy' and half couchwork, usually totaling one-and-one-half hour.

The client understands that defensiveness will cost time, money and lessons. Talking is to assess the thought processes that backfire. The dialogue is often direct; you can ask any question you like and you will get an honest answer. It may seem confronting when you are told how you seem (without judgment), what the healthy living rules are or asked what might be the reasoning or experience behind a given action or statement.

When one is fortunate enough to see how thoughts and beliefs sabotage life, it's a good idea to reflect on the effects of the old thought process and entertain possible results of a proposed new perspective. Rather than hoping thought processes will not be exposed for their dysfunction, the client needs to aspire to discover and uncover as much as he can digest. He is paying to discover this critical and useful information. Ego and defenses slow down the work and cost money in the long run. Of course, the client needs to be sure that his therapist is his advocate. Ideally, the client comes in to talk like a curious and open student, bringing up the most obvious problems of his life.

> Your task is not to seek for love, but merely to seek and find all the barriers within yourself that you have built against it.
> – Rumi

Couchwork. Couchwork appears to be a natural, built-in healing process. Most of my clients are amazed it is not well known. I am amazed myself. Trauma researcher and expert Bessel van der Kolk, himself a clinician, has been searching for an efficient way to treat PTSD. "His growing sense that the body, as much as the mind, might hold the key to recovering from trauma ran up against the sacrosanct tradition of the talking cure as the alpha and omega of all psychotherapy. It was about this virtual monopoly of mainstream therapy by institutionalized talk that van der Kolk was becoming increasingly skeptical (Wiley, p. 35)." Although talk is essential, too, van der Kolk adds, "[F]undamentally, words can't integrate the disorganized sensations and action patterns that form the core imprint of the trauma (p. 35)."

I believe that couchwork is what van der Kolk is looking for. It is simple, natural and built into our design. The client lies on the couch, breathes deeply for an extended period of time (15 minutes to one-half hour). It's work, but it doesn't hurt. I think of it as the price of healing trauma or uncovering deeply held beliefs and patterns of thought that repeatedly injure us.

- **Learning How.** People seem to do couchwork the way they do life. A passive aggressive client may do very shallow breathing and create a battle with the therapist when she pushes the client to breathe harder and deeper. Someone who is prone to dissociation will dissociate and have to learn how to come back to being in his body. Someone who is defended will not relax and will have to learn to relax. Someone who is unaware of their body will learn to look inside. Someone who is proactive in life will do couchwork with commitment, while someone who is a perfectionist will worry whether they are doing it right. These are the most important lessons in couchwork. Learning *how* to do it and to see how one does life clearly is invaluable and tends to dissipate unconscious instructions for life.

> When people get close to re-experiencing their trauma, they get so upset that they can no longer speak…It seemed to me that then we needed to find some way to access their trauma but help them stay physiologically quiet enough to tolerate it, so they didn't freak out or shut down in treatment. It was pretty obvious that as long as people just sat and moved their tongues around, there wasn't enough real change.
> – Bessel van der Kolk, MD

- **Witnessing the Self.** The client breathes with conviction and descends into a slightly altered state that is useful for self-awareness and helps her witness her own "program." She witnesses herself with a deeper awareness, learning to meditate on her inner being and focusing on her body. She learns how to relax and surrender from the inside out. She pays attention to her feelings and armor, which for a brief time have primacy over thoughts. In doing so, she self-observes and learns how she holds herself together, how she sees herself, how she presents herself and how she copes.

Van der Kolk believes patients really need their "therapist's attuned attention to the moods, physical sensations and physical impulses within. The therapist must be the patient's servant, helping him or her to explore, befriend and trust their inner felt experience (Wylie, 2004, p. 36)." I think this is what he was getting at. Couchwork is such a tool for self-awareness that the therapist need only sit as an enlightened witness. When the client finishes his experience he will describe for his therapist what he saw of himself. From sharing, he will experience the empathy and understanding he never received in the past.

A former client of mine noticed he'd been going through life asking, "Is this all there is?" and realized his expectations had caused him to miss out on his life. Another recalled "long waits" for his mother to pick him up after school or get off the telephone, which explained his chronic thought, "How long will this last?" He, too, realized his impatience had been causing him to overlook his present moments. Another saw how she had been holding back her feelings almost all her life because she recalled her mother telling her, "You're ugly when you cry." In any event, the cognitive theme of your couchwork is a dominant yet invisible theme in your life. Observing these unconscious instructions we once took in or gave ourselves allows us to let them go. Even though students may return to the same issue or insight repeatedly for chronic childhood experiences no two couchworks are alike. Such a return to a pervasive theme means the student suffered a chronic injury or recurring maltreatment that may take quite a bit of self-observation to dissolve.

- **Resolving Trauma.** Techniques other than couchwork do exist, but couchwork, in my opinion, is the most productive technique for healing buried trauma. Some students make the assumption that "nothing is happening" because they are looking for something more dramatic like their last couchwork. Every couchwork is profound without exception. I tell my students, "Sometimes the message is that you look past what is in front of you. Never underestimate your couchwork, because it's an important clue or message to you from your child-self."

I often advise my students, "Buy yourself a special journal and write in it after every couchwork what you think could have been your lesson. Maybe it was that you were too guarded to go in. If you were too guarded, what does that tell you?" After we learn how to do couchwork with an awareness of our own make up, we may go deeper. Clients may then discover traumatic or formative moments. Perhaps they see that they suffered a chronic type of trauma that was relived on a daily basis. For example, one client may face his feelings of being unloved by his parent because she gave him approximately ten beatings, while another client may revisit the experience of feeling negligible, non-existent, unimportant, unseen, and unloved almost every day of his childhood. The latter client may have to revisit the same condition again and again and again to burn it up, while the client who had a physical trauma once or ten times may be able to process these more specific events in less time.

When the client has sufficiently breathed and surrendered to self-observe, she may notice that she is experiencing physical changes. One woman felt a sting on her left cheek. She ended up reliving or remembering being slapped across her face while her mother told her, "If you cry, I'll slap you again." This time, she let herself cry and she broke down a piece of the wall between herself and her feelings. Some people have more shocking experiences in their body, feeling paralyzed in some way. Again, the sensation is only temporary. The places where you experience paralysis are blocks of forbidden feeling that are dammed up inside. If the client focuses on the strongest sensation, something will be relived or remembered. When they remember, unconscious material becomes conscious. When they relive and allow the emotions to flow, they heal. They would have healed when the original injury took place, but for some reason that they will observe, expression of their feelings or acknowledgment of their situation was taboo at the time. Seeing how or why the expression of feelings was disallowed may be even more important than processing the injury itself. Sometimes a person remembers in one session and processes the emotions in the next session. In such a case, they may feel depressed between sessions while the emotions hang close to their skin. The louder or harder they allow themselves to cry or scream or roar, the more completely they heal.

On the other hand, it does not work to try to think of something to remember or to *try* to cry. The more intrusive the left brain's will, the less the process works. This built-in healing design works with surrender and allowing very old messages buried within to surface. It is essential to let go of control over our thoughts. I believe that the more blank we make ourselves, the more we are able to let these body memories return to us. It is not *vice-versa*. Finding memories will not take us to buried feelings. <u>Only following feelings takes us to buried memories. If one tries to will or direct this process, the subconscious mind cannot get through.</u> The client's job is to channel or allow himself to "receive," which is most possible when he is paying attention to how he feels. He learns to let himself feel. When this is done, the rest will take care of itself. Learning to "channel" is as profound as performing the couchwork itself.

It goes without saying that the therapist is not to make suggestions to the client about what those feelings indicate. Even if the therapist has a suspicion, the most they should do is ask clarifying questions. If the client seems stuck, I may ask, "Do you feel older than ten or younger?" If the client says younger, I ask, "Do you feel older than five or younger?" "Does it feel like you are indoors or outdoors?" "Does it feel like you are alone or with someone?" Sometimes with these simple questions, the client is "there" reliving something they had forgotten or something they had never forgotten but they're now remembering it in vivid detail. With such questions, they may see more clearly what really happened or this time, they may cry and release.

In some situations a client will dissociate, have a memory out of awareness, then experience a jolt back to consciousness. He might sit up or attempt to run and fall off the couch without remembering why. Another might relive an experience and his lips will move, his hands will gesture, his face will make dramatic expressions, but he'll remember nothing. When clients dissociate, couchworks may take three to ten sessions or more to recover one deeply buried memory. These couch-works resulting from dissociation need to be pursued. Sometimes it helps to talk about how safe the client feels and how it might help to understand what has already happened. This can relax the subconscious guard. The childhood experience may be so traumatic that the subconscious mind thinks it has to reveal the event to conscious awareness very slowly. However, the more willing the person is to remember, the more the subconscious mind has the faith to allow conscious recall. Sometimes the memories come in flashbacks or quick snapshots. Sometimes they come in clues like smells or wallpaper patterns into which the child disappeared during the trauma.

I have told my clients that some people have great difficulty surrendering. As you do the work to dissolve your defenses and resistance, you prepare to receive and heal the buried pain of your childhood, which because it is unprocessed, has been pushing you around, causing you to act out or against yourself. Sooner or later, the deep breathing will cause you to have some strong sensations in your body. Some students have 'freaked out' over the sensations thus missing the point. These sensations are messages or body memories stored by your child self. Focus on the sensations until you receive the message or relive the memory. Often the message turns into an experience that you've forgotten, or maybe you hadn't forgotten but your body wants you to relive the experience, only this time to cry in response.

- **Rage Work.** Some people need to perform rage work, which is especially critical for those who are driven to blame, threaten, shame, judge or otherwise scapegoat others. It is useful for people who have a short fuse, chronic impatience or frustration. These are people who were blamed or abused by parents and then asked or were expected to repress their feelings for their parents' sake. As adults they walk around righteously taking it out on others and getting even with the wrong people. Rage work helps reduce or rid the drive to rage or retaliate on others, no matter how appropriate that retaliation seems to them. The fundamental concept for rage work is to focus on the original injury. I tell my clients, "When doing rage work, you must focus on your parents (in an empty chair) on behalf of the young child you once were. You retrieve the memory of the original injury. You give the child you once were a voice and speak as if you were that age to your parent(s) in the chair. This is not about blaming your parent. It's about giving back your anger for having been hurt. It's something people do in relationships. It's something people do in courts as well. Your parents are not here. To protect them now betrays your own right to heal. They would want you to be your healthiest self." Sometimes it is very difficult to get an angry person to give their feelings back to the one who hurt them so deeply. In my opinion, the more they cannot do this, the more injured and dangerous they may be. It's this stored anger that, up to this point, may have caused them to subconsciously choose relationships that re-enact original patterns or insults so they could "get even" or continue to scapegoat. Scapegoating is exacting retribution on the wrong person (repeatedly), pretending it's the right person, while insisting there is no issue with their parents since their parents "did the best they could." The best they could would be to support their child in releasing buried pain and anger.

3: Relationship Skills

Although the Relationship Skills Workshop ("Shop") has also affectionately been called "Group," it is not conventional group therapy. It is a class and no issue presented would be considered a therapeutic one. One issue is not prioritized over another due to content. In fact, content becomes irrelevant and the predominant matter is the process by which a person handles his issue. The group forum only deals with interactive skills. If an issue arises that the facilitator deems more appropriate for private therapy, she'll recommend it. The facilitator is teaching relationship skills. A person's therapist may also recommend this workshop as an anger management workshop or an assertiveness training workshop. In any event, the relationship skills workshop does not dive into childhood pain or sharing for empathy or support. It is not a support group.

When one does couchwork and clears out their self-destructive and destructive drives, they are not left automatically knowing how healthy people think and behave. In fact, they are left with coping mechanisms that worked once in their family context, but now remain as bad habits that are no longer adaptive. These coping mechanisms are actually personality structures or disorders. The workshop environment helps teach the needed replacement skills. Even though this is not group therapy and is a workshop instead, it is profoundly effective in helping students transcend personality structures and disorders. Everything that is needed to make the change is here. The final determinant is the client's willingness to surrender to the instructions. Some completely make it. Others change significantly, which is enough. Calling the process a workshop makes it available to more people and gifted coaches can teach it.

Everyone brings their bad habits from childhood. Since all childhoods were unique, no two people are working to shed the same bad habits. However, bad habits often overlap with other workshop members', so students can see themselves in others, and by observing their examples, see more objectively how their coping skills backfire. They can more easily self-reflect and understand why others respond to them the way they do. Fellow workshop members are also unlearning bad habits, so they all become skilled in identifying the origins of others' coping mechanisms. Everyone discovers the coping mechanisms they must shed and what healthy new skills will replace them. Students use 'mirroring' to facilitate the process and everyone learns the same rules of interaction. All learn how to have a clean fight.

In workshop, students learn how to represent themselves to people who think differently than they do. They learn to see what they all have in common. They learn to shed their own dysfunctional skills with the mirroring provided by Workshop members and from the corrective guidance offered by the facilitator. All leave behind different bad habits and learn together to practice the same healthy new habits.

Workshop members do not judge. When someone is being judged by another member, the facilitator will become a cop and have to step in and "make an arrest." This is a moment when they will be stopped from speaking. The other affected party will be protected from judgment. Once the person stops judging, the facilitator checks to see if they are alright, hears their feelings, explains again that no one is judged and if the facilitator had been there in his childhood she would have protected him too. Then the facilitator teaches the judger another way to say what they need to say. The facilitator may teach how to mirror or express feelings. Feelings are valued. Communication is always more effective when offered from a 6 o'clock, vulnerable position *vs.* the 12 o'clock, superior position. More information on relationship skills is in the last chapter of this book.

There is another time for an "arrest." When a student takes a dominant position with the teacher, the facilitator may arrest the student. "Stop." "No." "If you do not allow me to teach, I do not want to be your teacher." No teacher is required to put up with a student who is driven to challenge authority from 12 o'clock. It becomes a war of power. It is too much work, which is why most teachers will either "arrest" or fire a student who does not take the 6 o'clock position. This does not mean the student cannot ask questions. It simply means that trying to dominate the teacher in the name of questions is unacceptable. Student and teacher are not equal and not a match, not in this context anyway.

Everyone in the Workshop has taken the parenting class or read *The Manual*, so all are aware that any dysfunctional interaction habit is learned in childhood as a survival tactic. Bad habits are perceived with insight, understanding, acceptance and empathy so that mirroring becomes an uncharged tool that can be used to create new behaviors that better meet our needs. Students learn how to be less defensive when they learn how to give and receive feedback. Witnessing someone accept correction with humility is a powerful teacher because we can see how much respect it brings them.

These groups are not uniformly composed of couples, though many couples participate. It is not uncommon for a grown sister and brother to attend together to learn to communicate. Older parents and their adult children attend to learn to communicate better. Sometimes divorced parents agree to learn these skills together for the sake of the children. Friends come to work on their skills together. Sometimes employers and employees attend workshop together. Often people come alone to learn to develop their interaction skills with others in the Workshop.

Beginning students or individuals attending alone often bring up problematic situations from the outside world. These students get help with implementing the new skills in situations that can only be described to the group.

Often, pairs bring disputes to the workshop and try to communicate for the group to witness. Other times individuals in the workshop have issues with each other. This advanced work we call Stage Two. If a Stage One issue (from outside in the bigger world) ever precipitates a here and now issue in the room (Stage Two), we will always give the immediate Stage Two priority because we never sit on an issue (even if it changes the subject). Also, Stage Two work (in the presence of other members of the workshop) is always far more productive. It invites immediate and accurate feedback about the person's actual relationship skills in the presence of the entire group. Further, when students resolve issues and correct skills on the spot, then these new skills get wired in more profoundly. Most importantly, unresolved issues in a room contaminate everything else, so in order to be current in a relationship, all issues must be resolved sooner than later.

Stage Two work is a goal for each person. In the workshop, interacting with others in correct skills is critical. We encourage students to practice communication skills throughout the Workshop with one another. When our students interact with the rest of the group in ways that reveal their bad habits, they get opportunities to learn quickly. When they interact on a regular basis in a healthy way, they are ready to terminate.

Students who deal with a conflict by quitting have not finished their work because how one leaves characterizes and even defines their health or lack of it. The last skill that students refine is their ability to end relationships and to say good-bye cleanly.

Relationship Skills Workshop is further explored in Chapter 8: Relationship Skills.

Becoming a Healer

> *The little boy wasn't even in kindergarten yet when the sweet old lady next door died. The old couple used to sit in their rocking chairs together on the porch; now the old man rocked alone. The little boy began to take leave every morning to sit in the empty chair next door. The odd couple sat together for what seemed like hours every day. After awhile the old man began to weep. "What do you talk about?" the little boy's mother asked. "Nothing. I just help him be sad."*

You need to have done the work yourself to guide another. You must be clear that others must go through their own pain. You calmly represent that you cannot take the place of the person suffering or relieve them from their pain. However, you can witness them process their pain. You may offer empathy, but not too much empathy.

You represent correct choices following catharsis. People who have been injured in childhood have bad habits. You need to represent ethics and courage yourself. You need to understand that the credit for the healing goes to the child or patient, not to the healer.

Couchwork

- Client lies down on the couch straight, unencumbered, head only slightly up (to remain vulnerable). Put a cushion under the knees of tall people, so they don't get scrunched up.
- Client may request dimming of lights or eye-cover, though at some point the self-consciousness may be important to address by doing the work without aids.
- Client starts breathing deep and hard. Breathing continues for a long time, though sometimes results take place in a few minutes. Sometimes it takes even 45 minutes if clients are "locked down" with physical armor, mental dissociation, misplaced loyalty to their parents or resistance to losing control.
- Pockets of sensation show up. When sensations are strong, stop breathing and focus on them. Let the feelings get strong, so they will last long enough for the client to focus and go into the feelings. Clients need to stop breathing before the sensations become physically painful, because the physical pain will detract from body memories. The pockets of feeling are "body memories" of repressed trauma and are held in literal or metaphorical storage. Examples: A client feels a red hot stinging on her cheek and sees her angry mothers face, telling her, "Cry and I'll slap you again." Another client has a pain in his face around his mouth. He focuses on the pain and hears his mother say, "If you don't have anything nice to say, don't say it," realizing he has been denying and censoring his feelings since then. Another client feels a paralysis in her hands. She realizes she feels helpless. She hears her mother say, "Don't touch." She realizes she grew up holding herself in from exploring and discovering. The body memory comes first. Then either a clarifying thought or insight and/or buried emotions will come up. If the client goes into the feelings, healing takes place.
- Sometimes clients have become so concrete in their thinking, they cannot read their own body. They need to learn to recognize emotions in their body and armor, before they can meditate on a feeling to get a memory.
- Therapists must not make suggestions to the client of what the feeling might indicate if the client seems stuck. A few times in my career I would have bet that I could guess what the body memory was about when the client hadn't quite

registered the memory. I never offered my suspicion because that would invalidate the experience. It interests me though how wrong I have been on occasion. I was surprised that the memory turned out to be something unexpected.

One client kept reaching for her crotch but couldn't say what it was. This is somewhat common. It may seem obvious to the therapist what is being recalled, but we need to keep these suspicions to ourselves. It turned out that the client recalled having suffered horribly as an infant from diaper rash. Her memory was of having to pee, fearing she would pee and feel the burning acid. This became a somewhat common theme, as well as people remembering being unbearably swaddled or over-clothed in hot weather as infants.

Another client (who came to me because he feared women and bragged he'd had a stay-at-home mother) appeared to have suffered from sexual abuse because he kept holding his bottom during a few couchworks. I wondered if he'd been molested or given an enema or had a chronic dirty diaper. It turned out that his mother had burned him with a cigarette on his bottom as a punishment. He was a doctor. His dad was a doctor and his son was a doctor. I asked him to see a dermatologist. He asked her if his scars were moles (unconsciously trying to lead her off the track). She said they appeared to be scar tissue, perhaps very old burns or puncture wounds.

Clients do not need suggestions from the therapist, but ironically, because these are body memories, a therapist probably could not make a suggestion anyway that does not fit. I have discovered over the years that clients resist suggestion. On a few occasions I mis- understood what they were telling me and was corrected with certainty or told what I said didn't fit with what they were experiencing. The client apparently knows when a suggestion is off because the body memory is vivid and dominant. Nevertheless, we don't make suggestions.

- Results of couchwork:
  - Learning how to do life and to live inside oneself, *i.e.,* dealing with feelings of impatience, laziness, entitlement, fear, *etc.*
  - Learning how to go into and be in one's own feelings, especially when prone to dissociation.
  - Learning courage and how to face pain without fearing it.
  - Learning how to be in the here and now.
  - Learning to surrender.
  - Learning self-observation.
  - Seeing old trauma.
  - Seeing the moment when a life's philosophy or personality choice was made.
  - Healing trauma by crying it out to an enlightened witness.
  - Healing trauma by seeing the truth.
  - Healing trauma by encapsulating it, giving it a story with a beginning, middle and an end (Solomon, 2003a).
  - Developing major self-awareness.
  - Becoming clear about the truth.
  - Becoming more perceptive.

> ... [T]he ability to perceive and understand someone else's suffering depends more than anything else on the degree to which one has experienced the suffering of one's own childhood.
> – Alice Miller, M.D., Psychiatrist

Learning to Look Inward

Sometimes I feel trapped inside my body. In such moments I feel an atomic bomb suspended inside my chest. I hear the click-clack of the ticking clock counting down the seconds until it blows. My ears start to ring. A thousand needles poke my skin and engulf my arms, shoulders and back. Then a strong sense of curiosity washes over me. I wonder what is sitting beneath the bomb. I shiver a bit at this thought, but I know what I must do. I start observing my way around my body from my ringing ears to my parched tongue slowly passing by the click-clack of the ticking clock. Holding my own little-girl hand, I walk my mind toward the bottom of my chest knowing a mystery is awaiting my recognition. The thought of it overwhelms my heart with heat and I feel my skin and hair cells standing like dominos. One foot in front of the other, I approach a tall wooden door. A paraplegic god opens and welcomes me inside. A vast dark and empty space surrounds me. Fear wobbles in with a cigarette in her hands and takes a seat. I can hear flying geese in the far distance. I turn back to locate the scatter plot that is my consciousness. Dots stick to me like mud and direct me to dive in. I take my first breath and fall down a dark hole. Any minute now I am expecting an orgasmic relief at the expense of the atomic bomb sitting on top of my lungs because I have been to the center of myself before. At the end of the dark hole, my breath catches god's breath. I bloom into flying little pieces of spring and the geese invite me to join their migration. – Neda

Healing the Child

Often the parent is better than a therapist to do the healing work with their own child, especially if the child has suffered neglect, separation anxiety or abandonment trauma from that parent. The therapist would do better to coach the parent into better parenting specific to that child's needs. A therapist who bonds with a child who has suffered separation trauma may inadvertently reinjure the child when therapy ends. If the parent abused the child the parent can make amends by receiving the child's pain under the therapist's guidance. Of course, this would be inappropriate if the parent is predisposed to injure the child again. The parent is the one who should do the work with the child whenever the parent is able. The therapist should act as a guide, consultant, resource and even supervisor to the parent.

The most important thing a parent needs to know to heal their child is what heals and what injures. Children and people are resilient. We can surmount almost anything if we are allowed our feelings. This is not to say we should be emotional about everything, but expressing emotions purifies the body of trauma. These distinctions need to be digested.

The parent reads and interprets the acting out, inquiring and dialoguing with the child about where it comes from. Wonder aloud if "I don't know" is really true. We at least know need to know what we think and feel. Children need to develop the capacity to have these kinds of self-reflecting dialogues. Have the child tell you all about it in detail without becoming more upset than they do. Invite the child to give you their feelings.

If it's a physical injury, a "little hurt", ask about how it happened, how it feels, and offer to kiss it. If it's an emotional injury, ask how it happened (always inquiring what the child did first), then how they feel. Offer empathy and then ask what they think they will do differently next time. If the child doesn't think of everything that would help her, ask if you could make a suggestion. Then gently offer the suggestion, and ask the child if she thinks that would help.

For deeper traumas or "big hurts," learn how to contain the child who is evidencing trauma. Learn how to do couchwork for yourself and learn how to facilitate couchwork for the child.

> Parents who freely acknowledge the harm they have done can experience enormous moral relief and rediscover their potential to positively influence the lives of their offspring.
> – Peter Breggin, MD

Containing

Containing, also known as Holding Therapy or Rage Reduction, has been around for a long time, perhaps since humanity began, because it appears to be a built-in natural remedy. Martha Welch suggests the process as a staple to raising a normal, healthy loving child (1988).

PaRC's term "containing" comes from the analytic terminology, which refers to the therapeutic "holding environment" where the therapist "contains" the feelings of the patient unconditionally. The therapist, or preferably the parent, simply contains these released feelings.

Holding Therapy and Rage Reduction have been used by professionals for children who have more serious trauma and behavioral problems, many of whom were on their way to becoming killers, rapists, or other types of criminals. It is a valid therapeutic intervention for dangerous and domineering children too.

Containing also helps remedy a child's trends toward a personality disorder. For example, a child who has been allowed to become rude and superior-acting by the age of three or four (in the belief that her parents are weak and unable to stop her) may need to be contained as a way of showing her that her parents are strong now. A child who has been left in day care may need to be contained to get all her abandonment rage out and have an opportunity to re-bond with her parent, assuming there will be no more day care. I refer to it as containing to differentiate it from the other systems that include abuse or abandonment and because we use it for both mild and severe issues.

Some theorists have added abuses to the treatment (elbowing, pinching, nose holding, blindfolding) for the sake of expediency, so the work can be done on schedule in the therapist's office or to get these children to give up defiance/independence and cling instead to the grown-up for protection. It is a valid therapeutic goal for dangerous and domineering children to learn to cling to adults for protection. However, PaRC is highly critical of abusing them to get them to react. There is no need to do this to instigate the process. It creates further injury and if one wants to instigate the work, all a parent needs do is whisper "I love you" in the child's ear or stroke their cheek, presuming intimacy when the child feels betrayed or angry. That will set off an explosion of feeling and emotional release.

Function of Containing
- The traumatized child gets his feelings up and out, and heals.
- The repressed child breaks out and becomes authentic.
- The under-bonded child breaks through anger about trust and re-bonds.
- The unprotected child proves to herself that her weak parents are strong after all.
- Appropriate response to a tantrum when the parent intuits that the tantrum is from feeling overwhelmed by an emotion or experience (such as injustice, sibling rivalry).

The process is very intimate. When the child ultimately surrenders in the end from exhaustion of her feelings, she bonds, or rather re-bonds, in the final stage of containing or holding. I believe it is inappropriate for a child to bond with the therapist who will then send her off with her parent or foster parent, thereby abandoning her, especially if one of the child's previous traumas was abandonment. Some facilities think all they need do is teach the child to attach, without realizing they set the child up for another abandonment. Thus, in an ideal world, the parent would be trained to heal his own child. PaRC has a goal to create a residential facility where parents can come with their child to live while the child is corrective coached into re-bonding and the parent into re-parenting.

Process of Containing
- Parent holds child in loose fence.
- Child tests parent, possibly to an extreme.
- Child fights parent in a rage, but not completely with all her might, because she secretly wants parent to win.
- Child fights and rages to exhaustion (ten minutes to three hours).
- Child finally says the things she's been wanting to say: "I hate you for leaving me", "You can't take care of me" or, "My babysitter hurts me."
- After child reaches exhaustion, child enters state of grace.
- Parent pets the child, strokes him.
  - "I love you. You're mommy's baby boy."
  - "Daddy's here now."
  - "Mommy's got you."
  - "Mommy hears you. Mommy's going to stay home now."
  - "Daddy knows."
  - "Daddy's not going to hurt you again."
  - "Mommy's sorry."
  - "Mommy's strong now."
  - "Mommy's back."

Three Primary Positions for Containing
- Child sits on parent's lap facing in (younger child).
- Child sits on parent's lap facing out (safer for parent).
- Parent sits on the sofa, child's head in his lap, legs outstretched (older child).

Rules about Containing
- Never contain in anger or use it as a punishment or discipline.
- Contain a child who is already exhibiting major stress (flipping out, wigging out).
- Contain a child who won't let parents get close (who is suffering from a broken attachment). WARNING: Only repair a broken attachment if you don't intend to re-injure the child again in the same way. For example, if you left for a week and will be leaving again, do not set the child up to trust you again if you plan to break that trust again.
- Always finish. If you stop prematurely, you may create more damage, especially if the child sees you as too weak to set limits or to protect him.
- Be prepared. See "Preparation Checklist for Containing."

Re-bonding
- Introduce a security blanket with rocking chair.
- Stroke and pet the child's face and skin.
- Find a soft silk-like brush to slide over her skin.
- Offer a sweet treat (symbolic of mother's milk, like ice cream or yogurt).
- Refuel with eye contact, special words and personal communication.
- Consider containing your child again soon if the above endeavors do not repair the bond.

Preparation Checklist for Containing

- Get a letter from your child's therapist to keep with you or photocopy these pages. You can also send a registered letter to yourself to prove forethought.
- Tell neighbors if necessary. Some parents even inform the police that they are doing a healing process, not abusing their child. Know that Containing looks like abuse to outsiders. Explain the process to whoever is relevant. Someone intervening can be very detrimental.
- Make sure your mate is supportive and will not come home and demand an end to the process.
- Remind yourself that you are not abusing your child; you are healing her. Those of us who have been conditioned to avoid expressing feelings will have the most difficulty doing containing, but it will be good for us too.
- Have a coach available by phone, so keep the phone within reach.
- Understand that children who are being contained may try to fake you out or manipulate you by telling you that you are hurting them (be careful and clear that you are not), that they have to go to the bathroom when they just went; that they need a drink of water when they just had some, *etc.* Do not abuse your child by denying them their needs, but don't let them down by becoming their fool.
- Ideally, you need to let your child go to the bathroom shortly before you begin. If your child says he needs to go to the bathroom, you may let him go once or at reasonable intervals. Some children won't tell you they need to go and will save up urine so they can pee on you. It's a test; don't over react. You may want to choose the kitchen floor or put a rubber sheet under you.
- She may say she needs water. Have some ready beside you.
- He may bite you. If your child was severely injured, you may want him to get as much anger out as possible, in which case you can wear long thick sleeves. Or you can make a no-biting rule or a no hair-pulling rule, although don't make too many rules. Hitting, kicking, screaming, name-calling and swearing must be absolutely acceptable.
- Do not turn this into a philosophy that a child can tantrum to get contained. This is a special time for healing, not an interaction technique.

Healing Your RAD Child

The most injured of all children have Reactive Attachment Disorder (RAD). They have the most ominous futures as well. They have never had a safe attachment or if they did, it was broken. There are numerous controversies surrounding treating RAD kids. One that made the newspapers was the re-birthing scandal that involved a non-therapist having a child navigate a pretend birth canal. On that occasion the child suffocated and died, but not before trying to tell the adults that she couldn't breathe. Other controversies, previously mentioned, include techniques of therapists to get the process started within a therapeutic hour by pinching or elbowing the child. Another controversy includes having "therapeutic parents" bond with the child, develop trust, then abandon them again by turning them over to a parent who was not part of the therapeutic process. None of these techniques are acceptable. The treatment of children who are prone to violence or a lack of empathy or conscience, never having successfully attached, is serious business.

The most successful treatments are in some disrepute because Holding Therapy has been misapplied. Even so, holding is a powerful tool that seems to come with evolution as a natural therapy. Those who don't work with these high risk children often don't understand the high stakes and the need for these seemingly radical interventions.

The learning process is not over yet and the dialogue continues as to what are the most efficient ways to treat RAD kids. There are no bad guys here, only heroes. I don't even think the birth canal idea was such a bad idea, but it was implemented recklessly. I say this because I knew a child who wanted to be born to his step-mother, at least symbolically.

We are all learning from each other's mistakes and I love everyone involved in these controversies because we are pioneers sharing insight into the dangers of attachment breaks and failed attachments. It's a lonely world out there, even amongst psychologists. We are treating those children who others consider bad seeds. We all care about these kids and get more than anyone the extent of their injuries.

The latest controversy is this: One camp says give the child natural consequences for abusive and illicit behavior (Cline & Helding, 1999). The other camp says give the child empathy, understanding and guidance when he commits a crime because he only commits the crime out of anxiety or terror (Forbes & Post, 2006). Both camps teach about the terror a RAD child feels, along with his fear of vulnerability. A child cannot re-attach without becoming vulnerable. He is designed to learn in a vulnerable, open and receptive state during the learning years. Both camps notice that the child resorts to aggressive behavior in states of anxiety by acting like a little Mafioso.

Here's how I see it: There are two types of aggressive behavior: offensive and defensive. Offensive aggression I call "12 o'clock high." Defensive aggression I call "12 o'clock fright." I am crystal clear about the power clock and its actual existence in human thought and behavior. All of us have drives to treat others the way we were treated, and we all experience the intoxication of power. We all have to deal with our drives to do to others as we were treated, just like RAD kids, only on a lesser level. Our drives and theirs were imprinted. There is a comfort to be the one in power. We want to be the one who is one up, while the other is one down. To discipline without awareness of the 12 o'clock high or the terror behind 12 o'clock fright is to discipline with blinders on about cause and effect.

There are moments when a RAD kid or any one of us at some time in our lives crosses the line and abuses power by demeaning. A RAD child may be embarrassed because her teacher exposed her ignorance. She may experience a rush of humiliation and in that state she may reflexively ascend to 12 o'clock in fright and become uncooperative and defiant as a cover for her feelings of shame. On the other hand, that same child may lure a younger child into a secret space and molest the child, swearing the child to secrecy. That would be a 12 o'clock high. It is a re-enactment of what the child suffered, only from the other end of the dynamic. Yes, there is suffering behind all the bad behavior, but when the behavior is diabolical, we have to make an arrest and stop the child. We need to ensure that the child returns to 6 o'clock.

We all have to face the desire to enjoy the relief and even pleasure of becoming the perpetrator rather than the victim when it comes to imprinting and imprinted drives. Sometimes it is as invisible as becoming the person who employs the housekeeper as subservient, treating her more like an object than a person because that's how we were treated when we did housework for our parents or others. All of us have to face the work when we are at 12 o'clock abusing power, give up the stance of dominance and descend into the original pain we are re-enacting. We need to remember what it was like to be the victim.

We need to go to that vulnerable place to cry and heal. If a child has perpetrated on another child, this is a time for a sixty-second scolding, *a la* Foster Cline and Cathy Helding (1999). The short, intense scolding is powerful because children do get their values from a need to please their parents. After that, the child will need your empathy for what originally happened to him and often this is the most efficient route into original injuries so healing may take place.

Our job is to identify the difference between the 12 o'clock fright, which is designed to cover shame or fear, and the 12 o'clock high, which is imprinted abusiveness born of victimization. In the latter, the child becomes the perpetrator and either feels relief or enjoys it at the same time he knows he is doing something bad and wrong, racking up a negative identity and convincing himself that he is actually evil. He may even look to see if you notice and if you are appalled.

In the first situation, the child needs help coming down from 12 o'clock. He needs empathy, safety and coaching. He needs understanding and guidance in techniques to self-sooth and modulate his own stress. Think of ways to cajole him to safety, even offering him some chocolate cake and milk.

In the latter case of entering into the state of the perpetrator, the child needs the parent to briefly shame his abusive behavior, expressing disappointment in his choice, which conflicts with the imprinted message of entitlement by his own abuser. This will put him in high conflict, but it is a conflict he has anticipated and needs to process. He received one message that it was okay for him to be abused and now he's receiving an opposite message by his therapeutic parent, a role model who was not there to protect him in the original injury. Yet he has deeply disappointed his parent, something he is loathe to do.

If he is RAD because of another parent or parents (adopted) or you (whether you were misinformed, perhaps putting your infant in day care, ill, depressed, emotionally injured yourself, involved in a contentious custody dispute or took an unconscious vacation), you must offer complete empathy with no defending. Modify the dialogue. Tell it your way. Tell it from the heart. Tell it 100 times or 1000 times. Keep it on the table figuratively or literally. She will be all ears even if she acts like she's not listening. This is the dialogue she longs for to make sense of everything, but it is the worst thing that could ever happen too because it will make her want to love you for helping her. She will be as conflicted as anyone could ever be. It is the dialogue that makes her wish it was safe to open her heart again and she is sure if she does, she will be hurt so bad it will kill her. Adapt the monologue below to the child's age. Let it turn into a dialogue where she begins to ask you questions, challenge you and dare you to keep your word. She will test you to see if you will abandon her again. She will do worse things because of what you are saying to see if you will change your mind. If you ever saw *The Exorcist*, this is a measure of the work ahead of you to save your child's soul. In my opinion, you have no choice. See also Disciplining Your RAD Child in Chapter 7: Discipline.

The following text box contains an excerpt of the message you give your RAD child; the full text can be found online at drfayesnyder.com.

> ### Excerpt: Message to Heal Your RAD Child
>
> *My furious child, I love you with all my heart and I know at this moment that you doubt me. I am also imagining you think the world is unsafe. I know you are not about to love me or give your heart away to me because you believe if you do, I will break your heart again and you couldn't bear that another time. Do you remember when it happened before? I want you to know that I don't need you to love me. I am strong enough to love you without you loving me back, but nothing in the whole world would ever make me happier.*
>
> *Do you think something is wrong with you? I suspect that you think I think you are bad or not good enough. I am an expert on you, or at least on how good you are. I know that all babies are born miracles and so were you. You were a little angel when you were born and you were perfect. Everything was in you to become a great person who could be creative and loved by everyone who ever met you. You were as holy as you or anyone could be. That very same little angel is inside of you now. The only thing wrong with you today is that bad things happened to you and you began to think those bad things defined you and that they would keep happening. They also seemed to define everybody else in the world for you at such a tender little age. Because of the few sick people closest to you, you came to think that the whole world was dangerous. [Change all relevant words to make this your own.]*
>
> *There are words for a child who had such bad things happen to him so young. It is Reactive Attachment Disorder. If you use the initials, it's RAD. For now, until you heal, you are a RAD kid.*
>
> *I know what happened to you, so I want to tell you a story about the beginning of your life... [Tell her the whole story. She knows it anyway deep down inside and the truth feels real and validating. The things that happened have nothing to do with who she is and who she was born to be. You may also decide to take this text and adapt it to your child's story, put her name in the title, add color photos and turn it into her very own book with hard copy. You can read it together again and again. Give her a copy for herself and keep one on the coffee table. Maybe give a copy to all her significant relatives if it helps them understand her and what you are doing for the next one or two decades.]*

Healing Your Grown Child

As human beings, we are not perfect, nor do we parent perfectly. Our children are resilient for the most part and can recover, especially if they're allowed to tell us how they feel or tell someone else who can act as an enlightened witness. Our expression of feelings heals us; the sooner we say 'ouch', the sooner we heal. If we deny emotional pain and trauma for years, the feelings get stuck inside and eat away at us, demanding that we acknowledge them. They may come out sideways or we might develop symptoms or act out in ways that make no sense. These feelings may turn into self-destructive urges or may fuel blaming and scapegoating of others. Perhaps they manifest as low self-esteem, anxiety or depression. It's only when we give our feelings back to our 'offender' that we heal. If it's impossible to do that directly with the person who hurt us, it can be accomplished with a therapist.

You might have failed to help your children heal when they were injured. Things could have happened to them that you didn't realize caused them pain, or when they happened, you overlooked the lasting effects they could have. Perhaps you believed, as many do, that what doesn't get expressed disappears. "Ignore it and it will go away."

Perhaps in teaching your children not to backtalk or be disrespectful, you inadvertently took away their voice altogether. Maybe you didn't know how healing works and you were just practicing what you learned from your parents. You could have been holding in feelings to protect your own parents too. Maybe you lost your temper and caused harm and you are too proud to apologize.

When we have young children and they experience real pain or trauma, we need to listen to their feelings so they can heal and move on. When they get to express themselves and heal, we get to be guilt free. Our part is done. It can be over immediately when we allow them to tell us their feelings.

This is not to say that feelings reign over moral choices or a parent should raise children to think their feelings are generally so important that there is something wrong if they don't get their way. When the role of feelings is over valued it creates spoiled attitudes in kids who believe they can do what they want and say whatever comes to mind. On a lesser scale, we all need our voices, but our voices don't need to flood other people or make choices for us. We need to listen to our voices, but they shouldn't guide our moral choices. Often in life, we need to do the right thing despite how we feel.

If you made mistakes in parenting, which is guaranteed, it may have been all you knew to do. Or, truth be told, you may have simply felt that your feelings and needs mattered more than your child, the way your parents mattered more than you.

You can still help your child heal. This is the point where a grown child can get clear as to whether you deliberately or accidentally shut them down. Many patients wonder whether their parents truly loved them because they were required to swallow their feelings to take care of their parents' feelings, needs or wishes. They wonder whether that was because their parents considered their own feelings, ego or identity more important than their child's injured feelings or identity.

Parents who maintain their right as parents to be spared their children's feelings or complaints we call "false parents." Even if they would run into a burning building for their child, they may not be willing to hear their child out, even if they know it would heal them. This choice not to hear their adult child out is the great clarifier because the grown child gets to finally see clearly their parents' motives and priorities. If the parent says, "I did the best I could," but doesn't want to hear their child out, it becomes clear that their parent is not now and never was willing to do the best they could for their child. These parents have such fragile egos that they cannot hear their own child's pain or mirror, perhaps because they were treated just as selfishly by their own parents.

Sometimes parents are willing to do it just one time. Then if that is not enough, it's too bad. Fortunately, once is often enough, but if not, a "true parent" will listen until their child is done processing her feelings. Some grown children have more to process than others.

The parent who made endless mistakes, committed abuse and neglect in large measure, but is remorseful and willing to hear their child's feelings, is considered a true parent nevertheless. This is because all parents make mistakes. What ultimately matters most is whether we are willing to put our child's feelings above our own to heal them, which really is all we need to do.

This approach has so many other benefits. Grown children can then learn from your model how to make amends with their own children. It is a way to end a legacy of transmitting injury from generation to generation.

In addition, if you are willing to hear your grown child's feelings now, you can rid yourself of guilt. All you have to do is hear your child's point of view without defending yourself. We all want to defend by saying we did the best we could. But we can actually prove we're up for doing the best we can by being available to hear our children without defending ourselves.

Please remember your child believes you did the best you could, which is why she has been holding in her feelings her whole life, so defending yourself is not moving forward. It has been for your sake, not hers, that she has been holding in her feelings all these years. But if you do not hear her out now, she will no longer be able to convince herself that you did the best you could. She will finally be free from idealizing you. It hurts, but it has its own reward. The truth sets us free to feel and acknowledge the truth of our feelings and our past.

Your grown child needs to represent his point of view now, despite yours. So we as parents need to listen, offer sympathy or empathy, without cutting them off or making excuses. We need to apologize sincerely for our part in causing their suffering. We might also want to apologize for not understanding sooner so they could heal sooner. Apologizing sincerely is key after he told you what it was like for him and how he felt.

Seeking Forgiveness. When you express remorse, you are a true parent. You have proven that you never wanted to hurt your child and you truly did do the best you could. In this way you can make amends and heal your own child significantly, if not completely. Then you will be absolved and free of guilt and may, in the process, put an end to a legacy of family pain. You have helped heal your child.

You don't want to ever ask your grown child for forgiveness when expressing remorse. People can't really forgive before they've healed; true healing creates forgiveness. Forgiving before one gets their feelings expressed leaves buried feelings in the body that can putrefy and make us sicker. It can be a head-trip to agree to forgive when the anger and hurt are still in the body. Feelings must be owned and processed first.

Healing the Adult Parent-Child Relationship. Sometimes after the grown child has expressed her pain, sadness and anger to the parent, the parent thinks she is still unsatisfied because she requests more respect or wants freedom to express her point of view safely now. I have seen parents get really confused when the grown child tries to build upon this new foundation by asking the parent to honor certain precepts now. For example, maybe the grown child was angry that the parent bossed her around too much as a child. The parent hears her and apologizes. Then a week later, the parent bosses the adult child, who reacts by saying, "I really need you to stop bossing me now." I have seen many parents interpret this new system as an ongoing failure of their grown child to forgive and get over it. The parent begins to complain that the therapeutic process is unending because she's still complaining. But this is no longer a complaint about the past; it's a new healthy standard for the present. Your grown child has the right to establish healthy interaction systems in her life now, so you may want to do some adapting to these new healthy systems, allowing everyone to grow.

There are two components to healing your relationship with your grown child. The first was hearing and allowing your grown child to express her buried feelings, however long that took. You did it as a true parent. You did it because it was your amends. You did it because it was the right thing to do.

The second component in healing your relationship with your grown child is learning how to relate to them in a healthy way. If your ways of interacting and disagreeing are still unhealthy, your grown child will still need to distance from you for their sake, their mate's sake and the sake of their own children because if the way you relate continues to injure them, they will transfer that injury to their own family, perhaps scapegoating and acting out in their own home.

Rather than be offended that you have been asked to change the way you relate, you can turn to Chapter 8 and study. Allow your grown child to react, mirror you and speak up until you learn a new system together. The new system protects everyone, including you.

Healing Personalities

Common Issues

All people with personality disorders share common problems. They all become inhibited from an emotional release and cognitive ownership of their traumatic experiences, most often because they had to protect their parents. They will all need to revisit old pain and vent. The traits needed to process these corrections remain (1) surrender with faith in the process and/or your design, (2) self-observation, (3) love of truth and (4) courage. Everyone will still observe their shadows for the lies and release old festering feelings. Everyone will still need to learn relationship skills to replace dysfunctional and obsolete coping mechanisms.

Unique Issues

In large part the diagnostic goals for each personality are diverse because each personality type suffered different types of injuries and developed different types of coping mechanisms.

Passive-Aggressive. When he knows it's the right thing to do, he needs to act before everything is perfectly known or ready and stop waiting until it feels good. He needs to take a leap to commit and confront. He needs to learn to value his own feelings and speak on behalf of what he feels. He needs to give up his sarcastic or judgmental view of himself and others. He needs to risk telling the truth. He needs to find his passion and commit to it. He needs to practice assertiveness skills. He needs to not give his word unless he is willing to make himself keep it or at least openly declare that he changed his mind.

Dependent. The "Princess Baby" (or "Baby Prince") must own how she was cheated out of childhood lessons and not privileged or protected as she once thought. She must learn to face fears and challenges courageously and philosophically. She must do catch-up to develop basic skills in independence. She must avoid enablers/rescuers. This goes for the Baby Prince as well.

The "Baby Mom" (or "Little Man") must mourn her lost childhood. She must be invested in and willing to process her hidden rage at her mother for her selfishness and at her father for allowing the sacrifice of his child to his wife. Cognitively, she has to realize no one can "make it better" for her. She has to become her own source of power and accept complete responsibility for the quality of her life and give up living through others. She needs to stop rescuing others, especially her parents (and especially if that rescuing is causing her to neglect her children). She must invest in herself. Or she needs to stop leaning on others and accept that she creates her own fate. She needs to learn that helping others at her own expense is draining and re-injures her, while she heals by nurturing herself. She needs to cut needy or demanding people out of her life (except her employer or her children of course). If she has agreed to a traditional marriage, she only needs to ensure it is equitable. Finally, she needs to expect others, including her parents, to take responsibility for themselves.

Obsessive-Compulsive. An obsessive-compulsive who has lost touch with his spontaneity and feelings needs to give up trying to figure out life and begin instead to perceive it in a right-brain way. He needs to work on understanding those things throughout reality that defy category or logic. It would be helpful to study dreams or Zen (Reps, 1957). He needs to discover the things and processes to which words and symbols only refer. The overly controlled OC needs to learn to tolerate loss of control. He needs to learn to communicate in "I" messages rather than "you" messages, and to rediscover his feelings. ("I feel hurt when you criticize me.")

An obsessive-compulsive has to give up control. He doesn't get to control what others do and must be willing to watch them fail. If they don't ask for advice or help, it probably isn't welcome. He needs to work on his own ability to give up the illusion of control. We can manage our own life, but we will never control it. The best we can do is to steer our life to the best of our ability, remembering that sometimes we need to let go of the helm.

Histrionic. If she is touch-deprived, she may need to invest in regular massage, join a relationship skills workshop for feedback and mourn her lack of mothering. If she has to process remembered sexual abuse, she may want to attend an incest survivors group or read *Courage to Heal* (by Bass and Davis), while she does couchwork or other trauma work. Her mate may need to agree to an indefinite period of abstinence if necessary. She will need to learn to meet her own needs and to give up previous manipulative techniques born of learned helplessness. She may need to learn to tell the truth of what happened to her openly and freely when she is safe and discreetly when she is not safe.

Narcissistic. The light narcissist needs to face the source of his deep, hidden depression that he was not truly accepted for who he was. He needs to give up hiding behind his positive thinking ethic. He will need to begin observing the false self with a goal of living in the authentic self. He will have to discover that his authentic self is better than the imposter he has created.

The dark narcissist needs to see that his selfishness and arrogance is an illness born of cold or weak parenting and needs to terminate ongoing demands from living parents. He will have to mourn his lost childhood and/or trace his rageful feelings from present to past. He will need to know that arrogance is repugnant and unless it is transcended, he may die alone, for his arrogance benefits no one.

Borderline. The most important thing a Borderline needs to know is that she is responsible for everything that happens to her and then learn from her mistakes. She needs to learn that ultimately, no one is to blame, but everyone is responsible for their own experience and how they process it. She is responsible for her choice of relationships. She needs to give up investments in blame and revenge. She needs to learn her rights and responsibilities in a relationship. She needs to abandon victim-like behavior and realize that no one is in this world to rescue her. Her childhood is over. There is no parent/mate solution to her pain, and it is time to mourn her barren infancy.

She needs to find the courage to go into the heart of her pain with a loyal witness. She needs to enter her original pain and rage against her parental losses and betrayals once and for all.

She needs to distinguish between perception and projection. She may be helped by studying Zen in order to see more clearly. Perhaps she will see how she comes across and why people respond to her the way they do. Perhaps she will discover that no one is to blame and that all relationships are lineages and systems of interaction, not one "good guy" and one "bad guy." Maybe she will realize that she is completely responsible for the quality of her life.

She may need to be self-employed and develop an expertise so no one has defining power over her. She needs to be brave, courageous, self-reflecting, self-observing and self-correcting. She needs to unwaveringly face mistakes and learn from them until her sense of accomplishment begins to fill the emptiness within.

She needs to represent her own boundaries and honor other people's boundaries. She needs to realize that she doesn't get to be domineering and intrusive of other people, that other people get to learn from their own mistakes. She cannot make or persuade another person to meet her needs or do what she thinks should be done. She cannot finish healing until she fully realizes that no one is to blame, that judgment is not allowed and that the rage she feels is born of childhood pain and injustice. She needs to learn that clinging creates abandonment. She probably cannot self-correct her self-destructive behavior and beliefs until she opens up to corrective criticism which will require giving up defensiveness and professional innocence. She needs to give up defending her ego because there is nothing to defend and no one to blame (except her parents while she is doing regressions in order to heal).

Avoidant. This person is in serious defensiveness and can only heal when the defensiveness is dropped. He needs to courageously face his childhood betrayal without protecting his parent(s). He needs to stop recanting any rage or healing work he accomplishes and stop feeling remorse for being vulnerable or accusing his parents (in private). He needs to spend time in his fear of fear to burn it up, staying there no matter how bad it feels. It is just a feeling from the past.

He needs to have the courage to risk social blunders and to practice relationship skills. Perhaps he should start with those who are less skillful or popular than he is.

He needs to learn the principles of a healthy relationship including that he is responsible for his life.

He needs to be humble enough to learn from his mistakes and take criticism and correction. He will be heir to more than most. He has been playing it safe and is coming from behind due to prideful fear of criticism. The more he practices accepting criticism the more he catches up. Everyone needs to be able to take criticism, but no one needs to develop this skill more than the Avoidant Personality.

He needs to work from the premise that he is mediocre in his abilities because he has refused to try things without being able to do them perfectly the first time. Before he will ever begin to accomplish anything well he must practice. He needs to give up how he looks when he fails and the most efficient way to do that is to practice looking mediocre while practicing life. A Zen nun was once told she could not do the work because she was too beautiful. She put acid on her face. He needs to metaphorically put acid on his face. I asked one avoidant person to make ten mistakes every day on purpose, but I gave him credit for practicing something that would require many mistakes to get up to speed.

So, to get started practicing, be prepared to look like a beginner. Accept mediocre achievement for a while. It's okay. The more he can accept looking like a beginner, the more he will make up for lost time and skills. He needs to have an ultimate goal of excellence in his career so he knows he is accomplished in life at one special thing. These endeavors will be most therapeutic.

Approach-Avoidant. In order to transcend the Approach-Avoidant personality, she must acknowledge it to herself and others. She must begin to say things like, "I know yesterday I said such-and-such, and it must make you feel crazy for me to change my mind so much. I can understand why you might not want to believe anything I say until I become more consistent in my representations of myself."

When she has approached her limit (her fear of being too close), she must sit in her drive to leave and observe all the make-wrong thoughts she generates to get away. She needs to assess what commitments she can live with from each side of herself and then live with these commitments. If she chooses a place to live, she needs to choose well and stay in order to burn up the drive to leave. If she creates a relationship, she needs to stick it out as long as she can, assuming the other person is willing and able. She needs to work in therapy on the drive to leave (fear of staying and the illusion that something is always better over there), including staying with her therapist who pushes her to stay in her feelings rather than "make wrong" so she can leave.

Meditation would be excellent since it deals with internal dialogues and helps a person to be in the moment or, as Ram Dass would say, "Be here now."

Schizoid. He would do well to learn all the diagnoses because the more he understands the mechanics of personality, the more he discovers himself. He could try Zen, people watching, painting and music. He might want to join a club (and I don't mean a nudist colony). He could practice actions of sentimentality year in and year out until he finally enjoys the effect. He needs to do therapy with someone who is open to bonding with him. He might want to have a massage every week. Mostly he needs to grieve the loss of his infancy and that he never had a nurturing and cuddling mother.

Schizotypal. She needs to be willing to consider that what she believes in was taught to her to the exclusion of learning about reality. She needs to make it a priority to learn about the way of reality over the way of spirits. Maybe she will consider that energy and spirits never exist separate from matter. If she considers that and can recognize that development takes place from the inside out, not the outside in, she can catapult her growth. This is a big "if". She also needs experiences that could enhance her sense of physical existence: mirrors, massage, letters to herself, physical creativity such as singing, recording or pottery. If she could do something physical with nature like grow a garden, that would be even better.

Schizophrenic. He needs touch and massage. He needs to talk to a safe person about his life and get feedback about how the mind-raping he suffered sounds to someone else. He needs such reality checks to begin to believe in his senses and intuition. He needs mirroring to give him a stronger sense of existence. He needs to become an expert on the difference between projection and perception and the way to tell the difference: ask questions. He will really need support regarding the pressure his family will put on him to keep him schizophrenic. His parents are likely to be opposed to any emotional expression or release and may shame him if he blows. They may still be into making his memories, thoughts and beliefs wrong and insisting that he needs to stay on his medication, in part because he was born this way. If the therapist can enlist the parents to prepare for the explosions to come and be accepting and even apologetic, then this patient has a 1000% better chance of healing.

Bipolar. They have to give up the notion that they are special, a notion which once saved them from trauma, probably abandonment trauma as infants, when they thought they would die. They developed the ability to dissociate to a better place, which has become a bad habit now. They experienced some true insights, but in taking these insights as evidence that they are deserving of special recognition, they have misinterpreted the experience. People with Bipolar personality have to accept that they are like all of us. We are all special and divine as long as our egos are disabled. A truly spiritual person is humble, not self-important and doesn't have to be superior to feel good.

Bipolar personalities have to accept that believing in themselves as the way to heal is irrelevant. Rather, it's an exercise in their pathology. The way to a stable foundation of mental health is pouring cement, not dreams. Bipolars need to earn their way up the ladder without skipping a single step or borrowing from tomorrow. When we build our foundation on real skills, earning our way, we are less likely to collapse and be forced to face our inadequacies, which creates depression. When depressed, Bipolars see that their expansive self-image was made of hot air, which then makes them feel hopeless.

The key to healing Bipolar is to commit to humility, accepting a mirror every time they get expansive, arrogant or adopt magical thinking. They need to come up with a realistic plan for their career. Coming up with a viable plan may be the most important part. They need to persist in earning their way up the ladder of their plan. When they are depressed, they need to know that everything that they hate about how they feel and think about themselves will be remedied as they earn their way. No free lunches and skipping steps (by practicing believing in themselves). By the way, Bipolar personalities deserve sympathy and empathy for their neglect. They need to be reminded that it's not in their genes. Lastly, they need support and protection from a family system that is probably committed to believing in genes as the origin of their personality, which is very undermining.

Dissociative Identity Disorder (Multiple Personality Disorder). She needs to face her fear of fear. When the terror comes, sit in the feeling. Knowing the truth will set her free and the past cannot hurt her now. It's just old pain to let out. She is safe now. If she sits in the fear, other personalities are not necessary (and they are all her). When "the change" starts, don't split off. Stay present and cry, scream or rage out the very thing she wants to escape. Be her enlightened witness, hearing her and understanding her. She has to burn it up and wear herself going over her trauma, expressing her feelings until the grace comes.

Paranoid. He needs to consider the same things that a borderline needs to learn. Additionally, he needs to know that he is paranoid and that *paranoia is a self-fulfilling prophecy.* He would need to do autopsies on how his projections have brought out the worst in others. In this way, he can gain insight into how other people's perceptions bring them better results. Even though he is extremely observant and perceptive, sometimes he is just plain wrong. He needs to ask questions and be humble.

He needs to learn who to trust rather than how to trust. Trusting only those who declare loyalty is a set-up. No one is in the world to care more about someone else than themselves, but a trustworthy person will hear out anyone who says they have been hurt and self-reflect. Those who are trustworthy consider their past when an issue is presented to them. He needs to become one of these people so he can qualify to find relationships with people who self-reflect.

Trustworthy people are not those who have your back no matter what. They are the ones who have high values and ethics. He needs to become trustworthy by consistently owning his part in an issue. He needs to practice relationship skills. He also needs to weed out judgment and revenge when he has been hurt or angry. He should perfect his ability to go to 6 o'clock and express an injury. He owes others the same forgiveness that follows when they self-reflect.

He cannot heal until he learns to trust his therapist. He also needs to know that the mistrusting of his therapist and others close to him will probably create a self-fulfilling prophecy. He needs to take charge of creating safety in his life by choosing who will self-reflect in an issue. He must lose control, break down and relive his original pain with an enlightened witness.

Antisocial Personalities, Sociopaths, Rapists and Murderers. If there is any hope for these people to live without extreme acting out behavior, they would have to do such deep rage work at their parents, whom they have learned out of survival to protect at all costs. This reversal would be equivalent to facing the pain and surrender of hanging on the cross. Whoever is willing to do such work will heal enough to cease his threat to society. He would also need to accomplish all the material that borderlines and paranoid personalities must accomplish.

Rather than trying to heal them, I would prefer we invest in understanding them and letting them know they were not born this way. Finally, I believe we need to be perceptive of high-risk children to right our wrong. By identifying and rescuing these children, we can make amends to those despised children who we failed to protect and who had to grow up anyway.

Sex Abuse

If you learn that your child has been molested, do not react except to allow empathy to be seen in your face somewhat briefly. This is one of the most important times for you to be the grown-up. If you overreact, you may shut your child down and he will begin to tailor his words to relieve you or your suffering. Listen to your child and when he is complete, tell him you want him to know that what he has told you is very important. Tell him you are proud of him for telling you. Tell him you are very sorry he had to go through that. You want to take care of him no matter what. Tell him not to be afraid because now you are here to help. Put him in your lap if he is small enough. Cuddle him and love him up. Tell him you want him to tell a few more people. You need to call a therapist, who will videotape the disclosure to preserve the initial disclosure and reduce the number of times your child has to tell strangers about it. If they are not prepared to do that, find another therapist. (The younger the child, the incrementally less detailed the story will become each time it's told because the words may take over for the memory.) The therapist will call Children's Services directly if the abuse took place in your home or someone else's home where there are other children. If not, the therapist will contact the police. If you resist this step of reporting, you will lack ethics.

Recovered Memories *vs.* False Memories

Smack in the middle of the debate about whether trauma is remembered or whether it creates long-term symptoms is the 20-year-old proposition that recovered memories are false memories. I have had many clients doubt their couchwork because they have heard that there is no such thing as recovered memories. I have had a few parents criticize their grown child's couchwork, claiming that their memories must be false and that I have something to do with it. Fortunately, all the conditions of remembering have been safe the way I work. I make no suggestions. My clients know that. Everyone knows that. Many of them have confirmatory memories and documentation that fit right in with the recovered memories. Finally, most of the recovered memories have been about physical abuse or attachment trauma. It appears important to address this debate at this point, as it is another battle in the War of the Researchers.

I believe it is possible that therapists have persuaded clients to remember events that never happened, mostly because I know people who have done regressions and come back claiming to remember who they were in another life. I feel certain that I have also met very young children who were brainwashed to accuse their other parent of sexual abuse in custody disputes. However, I think it is rare that a therapist influences a patient to believe she has been molested when she hasn't. It would require a very driven and persuasive therapist.

Beginning in the early 1990s, a scare swept over the mental health community as accused pedophiles began to blame their victims' therapists for brainwashing the accuser into having false memories. They held that there was no such thing and that these so-called recovered memories had been implanted. Such a preposterous premise is the fantasy of scientist Martin Orne who actually participated in research to develop brainwashing techniques for the military. These procedures were quite involved and were motivated by military funding and objectives.

We have some very neurotic therapists among us, but I would conservatively guess that for every therapist who influences a patient to believe he was molested, more than one hundred molested patients are afraid to reveal their abuse, have been convinced by relatives to recant or have not been supported by their therapist.

Witnessing the results of my own techniques for depth work causes me to believe it is possible to recover memories in couchwork without any suggestion. Almost every week I witness clients recover memories that they had completely forgotten. When a client of mine recovers such a memory I believe him. To disbelieve him would be to harm him further.

The False Memory Syndrome Foundation (FMSF) was founded in 1992 by two couples, Peter & Pamela Freyd and Ralph Underwager & Hollida Wakefield. Peter Freyd was a professor of mathematics at the University of Pennsylvania and a graduate of Princeton. He had also worked for the US Office of Naval Research where he met Martin Orne, who was involved in the brainwashing research upon which the film "The Manchurian Candidate" was based. The four founders were able to recruit Orne and other influential espionage scientists and psychiatrists in order to argue that brainwashing was not just feasible but probable in cases of recovered memories. Orne had performed experiments allegedly proving that hypnosis could be used to plant memories, create multiple personalities and possibly even commit murder without recollection.

The Freyds had a transparent motive for founding the FMSF as they were seeking an offensive position against their daughter Jennifer, who sought to privately discuss her memories of childhood sexual abuse with them in 1990. They apparently wanted to head off any formal accusations even though their daughter never had any such intentions. They took measures to discredit her by reporting to her employer that she was unstable. Then they founded the FMSF, collecting as many sympathetic therapists, researchers and experts as possible to criticize other therapists and to defend accused pedophiles, beginning with themselves.

Jennifer Freyd was a psychologist, professor at the University of Oregon and eventual author of Betrayal Trauma: The Logic of Forgetting Childhood Abuse. She responded to her parents' offensive tactics by going public with her story, revealing that she had a diary from her childhood that verified memories she'd never forgotten. Nevertheless, it was in therapy that she gathered her resolve to confront her parents, albeit never with the intentions to charge or sue them.

Ralph Underwager was a psychologist and minister who came to the FMSF from the Institute of Psychological Therapies in Minnesota. As an alleged forensic expert, Underwager defended a cult of pedophiles and lost credibility in court. In the presence of his wife, he admitted affably to a Scandinavian publication that he was a pedophile and there was evidence that molestation was even good for children. When the journal article was translated into English, he became a liability and was forced to resign the FMSF even though his wife, Hollida, remained on the board.

The FMSF exploded into the domains of Psychology and Law with funding and public relations help from their silent partner, the US military, which around the same time was trying to deny soldiers' claims of Post Traumatic Stress Disorder. Researcher Elizabeth Loftus joined the FMSF as its leading forensic expert, along with America's most prominent behaviorist, Aaron Beck, and other pro-parent researchers.

Interestingly, in 1976, before coming on board, Loftus developed and provided research affirming that repressed memories could later be recovered. However, in 1990 she flipped sides and joined the defense in the McMartin preschool trial as an advisor.

The FMSF was highly involved in marketing their new premise, finding researchers, therapists and theorists who supported their position. They were on the offense with what appeared to be significant resources and remarkable planning. They used the mistakes of the McMartin Preschool trial interviewers, who asked leading questions of the children, to promote the idea that children who reported sexual abuse had been coached by therapists. They also advanced the ethic that therapists should research and confirm an accusation before reporting it to the Department of Children and Family Services (DCFS), which was contrary to the law and therapist training. Suddenly therapists and lawyers were being retrained in continuing education courses to doubt their clients' memories. Lawyers everywhere seemed to be assuming that therapists should investigate even though it was not legal, ethical or standard of care. Hypnosis was now quickly discredited as a tool for recovering memories.

From the pro-child research, Loftus was recruited to co-author a book in 1994 that might have already been substantially written by Katherine Ketcham by the time she got there. Loftus and Ketcham's book, *The Myth of Repressed Memories*, was extremely aggressive and accusatory. It was not only popular amongst pedophiles and their defenders but it was popular amongst pro-parent researchers who wanted to prove the innocence of parents. Loftus gained fame rapidly. She consistently blamed the therapists for planting these memories and she earned exceptionally high fees in the process (1994).

Once when Loftus was deposed, she admitted under oath that she was a victim of childhood molestation who can remember the event but not the offender. From an analytic point of view, what we block out is the most unbearable information. When the "who" is more untenable than the "what," it will be the "who" that gets repressed. It's as if Loftus is acting out through her professional endeavors: "If I don't remember, you shouldn't either."

Loftus received most of the referrals from the FMSF and she testified consistently and without exception on behalf of the accused, against the therapist.

Highly credible pro-child researchers began to organize and take on Loftus in court. In Shahzade v. Gregory, the prosecutor revealed that although Loftus had testified in 113 criminal trials, she had not once testified for the prosecution. (Brown, Scheflin & Corydon, 1998)

One court, having heard all the arguments on recovered memory and normal memory, held that recovered memories were as credible as any other memory. Major research projects challenged her work effectively and Kenneth Pope, psychology's ethicist, severely criticized her claims and affiliations. She left the American Psychology Association, reportedly because she was dissatisfied with its tendency to focus on childhood issues. Interestingly enough, she is still hailed as an expert on false memory and is invited annually to address students at California

State University, Northridge, where I was taught.

If one looks up False Memory Syndrome online, they can find it even though it is not in the Diagnostic and Statistical Manual. The last time I looked online, most of the articles supported the notion that recovered memories were false memories, and many of the websites were established by the late Ralph Underwager. The worst part is, if you take a licensing exam to become a psychologist, you still have to agree that recovered memories are suspect in order to get that answer right. Hopefully, when this book is five years old, that will no longer be true.

A Note about Identity

I am not very interested in building identity, although I am highly aware that negative identities are toxic and even deadly. If someone has a negative identity, the solution is not to give them a positive one. All the compliments, self-hypnosis or affirmations are not going to solve the problem of a negative identity or a lack of identity.

You were born a perfect baby. You were born Good. Put another way, you were born Divine. You were adorable and deserved to be cherished and protected. You made mistakes and you were open to guidance. If you don't believe now that you are Divine at your core or worse, you think you're a fraud or a failure or unlovable, or whatever is eating at you, then you are buying the lie of your shadow. You are reinjuring yourself repeatedly with this lie inside of you. These beliefs are not true, nor are you more holy inside than anyone else. You can continue to reinjure yourself with your lie or you can decide to uncover where it came from.

Take out your flashlight and shine it on the lie. Follow it back in time and see who taught you this lie and why you believed it. Expose the lie every time. When you are done exposing the lie, allow yourself to be without an identity. You don't need some special thing to think about yourself. An identity is a waste of your resources. You have to advocate it to yourself and to others. You have to believe it, forward it, market it and defend it – all that for just an idea. You are not your idea of yourself. You are independent of your idea of yourself. You are an ever-changing, adapting organism. There is no defining you. If you get lost in the search for identity, you will miss the miracle of your life and everything surrounding you.

Moving forward, you earn your identity. You build your life and skills from the bottom up. You work on yourself. You work on your ethics and relationship skills. You get your career going and work your way up from the bottom. That will be fulfilling. When you work hard, you get recognition. There's no free lunch and there's no substitution for earning your way, like trying to just *believe* in yourself. Don't waste time believing in yourself. Just do and learn from your mistakes. Be humble. There's nothing to believe other than you are Divine when you are without ego. When your ego is on the line, the divinity is gone and you become a fraud, marketing yourself without merit. Drop the ego; it isn't on your side. It slows your growth. Your most fun life moments will occur when you just live your best and do your best. Don't waste time looking for feedback and mirrors unless you want them to help you self-correct. No one defines you. You are here to witness, enjoy and engage with this geography before you, this sample of the Universe during this tiny slice of time. Don't miss it. Enjoy it. Oh, and leave the world a better place than you found it. It's a privilege to be here.

Recommended Reading for Healing

Theories
Assault on Truth, Jeffrey Masson
Uncommon Therapy: The Psychiatric Techniques of Milton Erickson, MD, Haley

Attachment
Holding Time, Martha Welch
Touching, Ashley Montague
Born for Love, Bruce Perry & Maia Szalavitz
The Interpersonal World of the Infant, Stern
The Psychological Birth of the Human Infant, Mahler, Pine & Bergman
The Secret Life of the Unborn Child, Verney & Kelly

Reactive Attachment Disorder (RAD)
Can This Child Be Saved, Cline/Helding
When Love is Not Enough, N. Thomas
Rebuilding the Broken Bonds, N. Thomas
Holding Time, Martha Welch
Disorders of Attachment, Zeanah, et al.

Trauma
Sibling Abuse, John and Alison Calfaro
Broken Brains or Wounded Hearts: What Causes Mental Illness?, Ty Colbert
Guilty by Reason of Insanity, D. Lewis
For Your Own Good, Alice Miller
Treating Attachment Abuse: A Compassionate Approach, Steven Stosny
The Trauma Model, Colin Ross

Ethics/Consciousness of Mental Health
People of the Lie, M. Scott Peck
The Road Less Traveled, M. Scott Peck
The Passionate Mind, Joel Kramer
Zen Flesh, Zen Bones, Paul Reps

Family Systems
On the Family, John Bradshaw
Healing the Shame that Binds You, Bradshaw
An "Incurable" Schizophrenic, B.P. Karon

Denial
Thou Shalt Not Be Aware, Alice Miller
Banished Knowledge, A. Miller

Parental Arrogance
Narcissism and Intimacy: Love and Marriage in an Age of Confusion, Solomon
Children of the Self-Absorbed, Brown
Why Is It Always about You? Saving Yourself from the Narcissists in Your Life, Sandy Hotchkiss

Identity
Lost in the Mirror, Richard Moskovitz

Repression/Expression
The Body Never Lies, Alice Miller
Breaking Down the Wall of Silence, Miller

Emotional Clearing
Releasing Negative Feelings and Wakening Unconditional Happiness, John Ruskan
The Body Remembers, Babette Rothschild

Repressed Memory
Sexual Abuse Recalled: Treating Trauma in the Era of the Recovered Memory Debate, Judith L. Alpert (ed.).
Memory and Abuse: Remembering and Healing the Effects of Trauma, C. Whitfield"
Betrayal Trauma: The Logic of Forgetting Childhood Abuse, Jennifer Freyd
The Body Never Lies, Alice Miller

Pharmaceuticals
Toxic Psychiatry, Peter Breggin
Talking Back to Prozac, Breggin
Medication Madness, Breggin
Reclaiming Our Children, Breggin
The Anti-Depressant Fact Book, Breggin
Your Drug May Be Your Problem, Breggin & Cohen
Rape of the Soul: How the Chemical Imbalance Model of Modern Psychiatry Has Failed its Patients, Ty Colbert
Ritalin Nation, Richard DeGrandpre

Genetic Deceptions
Broken Brains or Wounded Hearts, Colbert
"Childhood Experience and the Expression of Genetic Potential: What Childhood Neglect Tells Us About Nature and Nurture" (Brain and Mind 3: 79-100, 2002), Bruce Perry
Biology as Ideology: The Doctrine of DNA, previously The Dream of the Human Genome, Richard Lewontin
Not in Our Genes, Lewontin
Pseudoscience in Biological Psychiatry, Ross & Pam
Blaming the Brain, Valenstein
The Missing Gene, Jay Joseph
The Gene Illusion, Joseph
Exploding the Gene Myth, Hubbard & Wald

CHAPTER 4

Stages & Ages of Development

> Jeffrey Dahmer's favorite song lyric:
> See me.
> Feel me.
> Touch me.
> Heal me.
> -- From the rock opera *Tommy* by Peter Townshend
> Performed by The Who

Feminism and Children

More recent human history has been dominated by patriarchal systems that have deprived women of their full potential. Women's wages were not comparable to men's. Women have been subject to domination and exploitation. Our roles as mothers relegated us to second-class status. Girls were raised to sacrifice and abate their own aspirations while boys were generally treated as the important offspring. Men were often arrogant, abusive and quite deprived of the opportunity to develop their whole selves, including sensitive and intuitive awareness, if they did not want to risk ridicule. They went off to earn the bread and came home to the family as guests, instead of as fathers who enjoyed close relationships with their children.

The Women's Movement got off with a bang as they identified dominant, exploitative and disparaging men as chauvinistic and sexist. Many honorable men began to accept the ideologies of feminism and spent more time with their children, helping around the house even after a full day's work. Women began to get jobs to establish their worth in the market place and achieve some financial independence.

Dating became complicated. Men didn't know if they should open doors or pick up the tab anymore. Women began to express more anger and even dominance in some relationships. Women were allowed to taunt and even emasculate their husbands, yet striking back was not an option. Some parents switched roles so the mother could bring home the bread and butter and the father could stay home with the children. Day care became a viable option and strangers began to raise our children. Some parents gave their sons dolls and their daughters trucks. Pink became an ugly color for some women. The family system was up for grabs. Parenting in the Age of Women became confusing as more and more parents disciplined out of guilt or with no discipline at all because they knew their children suffered in day care. Yet other women began to abuse their boy babies more than ever. Serial killers became a regular phenomenon. Some men became bitter and disenfranchised, not clear what had just happened. What evolution had refined was eschewed in less than two decades.

Lessons from Feminism

- Girls are not inherently inferior or born for subordination and boys are not inherently abusive. Parents raise them to be so.
- Girls should be encouraged to become the best they can be with no ceilings on their aspirations.
- Women should be free from sexual harassment in the work place.
- Women should receive equal pay for equal work.
- There need to be new ethics for dating, marriage and child rearing, to include men and women negotiating up-front how equal they want their roles to be.
- When dating, if the man makes more money, he should pick up the tab. If they make the same, he should pick up the tab and she should contribute in other ways, unless they agree up front to take turns picking up the tab. If she makes more money, she may want to slip him a credit card for dating purposes or pay some of his primary dating expenses in other ways, like buying him a nice shirt. If both parties are amenable to androgynous roles, then it still needs to be determined who would stay home with children if they fell in love. If the woman wants to be a stay-at-home mom, when she finds the right man for her, she needs to establish her preference for a traditional role in the beginning. She should add that when the youngest child becomes kindergarten age, she may not want to stay home and remain in the childbearing role, or he may add that he would want her to go to work after the youngest child becomes five.
- Women should be protected from abusive husbands even if it means another party presses charges on behalf of the woman.
- Abusive and neglectful mothers should be held accountable. Boy children must be safe from scapegoating by their mothers.
- Neither mothers nor fathers should be allowed to spank or whip their children.
- It may be possible for mothers and fathers to share parenting and work, establishing a shared primary relationship.
- Boys should be allowed to develop softness along with strength, but they should not be raised to be feminine any more than girls should be raised to be masculine. On the other hand, girls should be free to aspire to whatever they choose to be in life.
- Fathers need to be active in the home with the children and even help out some with the chores.
- Fathers have a responsibility to stay clued in about the welfare of the children.
- Mothers need to honor the role of the provider if they are blessed to stay at home and they should give what they can to show that appreciation, enabling

fathers to spend more time with the children during non-work hours.
- In traditional families, both parents are equal in so-called "rank" while enjoying different roles if they like.
- The primary caregiver should be the primary disciplinarian. The other should discipline only when the issue is his issue (for example, if the child was rude to him).
- The role of the stay-at-home parent needs to be elevated to the most important job in the world.
- Day care should be the last resort and it should be realized that day care stunts, if not handicaps, the development and personality of the child.
- Society needs to understand that it's often the mothers who raise their sons to be misogynists, often castrating them with demeaning discipline and words or by turning their sons over to abusive fathers or by giving them power as children.
- When women choose to be wooed and treated as feminine, they should not have to sacrifice their equality and worth in the relationship.
- Men still do well to establish themselves as the protectors and women still contribute most to the family when they are soft and nurturing. They can be strong and decisive at work.
- Biologically, women fulfill the mother role better than men. If incomes are equivalent and the mother is at least as nurturing as the father, the woman should plan to spend the first five years home with her youngest child. The couple should plan to live as humbly as necessary to make this possible.
- Fathers will still need to plan to carry the financial burden to provide for a stay-at-home mother and children. In other words, while the youngest child is below the age of five, traditional roles are best.
- Sometimes men make better mothers, so-to-speak, than women do. When this is the case, the father should take the role of the mother and be the stay-at-home dad if financially feasible. When a father embodies the mother role, a child's emotional requirements do not change. He needs to offer soft (not scratchy) skin for cuddling. He needs to speak in a high-pitched (and maybe playful) voice during moments of approval. He needs to offer warmth and understanding as well as values and consistency. Another manual is not necessary for fathers who become the primary parent. He can simply adapt this book to meet his children's needs. Where good mothering is described, he needs to think, "That's my job."

Single Parents

Generally, children of single parents do not thrive as well as children of two-parent households when the single parent is not able to stay home with her children in the first years of their lives. This is one of the reasons why it is important to offer and seek child support.

I would recommend that a single parent couple up with another single parent and see if they can cover for each, especially working different hours, if possible.

A single mom may need to discover ways to involve her child in all of the chores so the child feels included and cherished, but not exploited. She may need to lower her bar for housekeeping so the child gets sufficient attention.

Single parents would do well to specialize in trades that allow for them to be home with their children the most, even if that trade is not their final career. Many trades indirectly lead to future careers. For example, a working mother may want to spend her pregnancy becoming licensed as a beautician, bartender or massage therapist so she can put herself through college once the youngest child is in kindergarten. The virtue of such trades is that they can be more easily adapted to your schedule.

Gay Parenting

To Straight Parents. First things first. Researchers Stacey and Biblarz reviewed more than 80 studies over a two-decade span on the subject of children being raised by gay parents or exposed to gay adults. No evidence has been found to prove that gay children result from homosexual parents over straight parents. As a matter of fact, it appears to me that more gay children have straight parents, especially with father figures who are coldly macho men aloof from their sons and mothers who are emotionally unavailable to their daughters.

There is no evidence that there are more gays than straights who perpetrate incest on their children. There is evidence in some children with no same-sex role model of feeling more challenged to invent or figure out how to express their respective masculinity or femininity in imperceptible ways, something any gay couple can solve by having a same-sex role model regularly in the child's life.

There is evidence that children of gays in the United States are ridiculed twice as much as children in the Netherlands by straight children and adults. There is evidence that children from foster care and from one-parent households are not as emotionally healthy as children who are raised by a gay couple, regardless of the couple's gender (Stacey & Biblarz , 2001). There is no evidence that exposure to gay couples or gay teachers will influence children to become gay or confused, unless their parents do not know how to clarify things for their children. For example, in one anti-gay ad, a child says, "Mommy, my teacher is gay and married to another woman. Do I have to marry a woman too?" If any child drew such a ridiculous conclusion, assuming her mother is married to her father, then the mother could simply say, "Of course not, honey. You marry who you choose to marry." Frankly, it sounds like parents making up dialogue for children. It is not Child Speak. It is Parent Speak.

Gays should be allowed to marry and adopt or raise children, especially when children are in orphanages or group homes waiting to be chosen.

There is no such thing as separate but equal domestic unions for gays. If we want the state to only permit marriage to straights for religious reasons, it's a basic violation of church and state. If the people of any state finally become educated enough to rise above bias in appreciation of science and open-mindedness, then laws may change in favor of fair play. The status quo may be dragged kicking and screaming defending tradition and even the Bible because for them, gay marriage is not only against their religion, it is counter-intuitive on a gut level. Through their upbringings, their sensibilities have become hardwired with norms that include a revulsion against and disdain for homosexuality. In the process we can expect history to repeat itself while the long-oppressed gradually become visibly outraged at those who judge and diminish them. Some commentators may see this outrage as equal to the bad behaviors of the bigoted "defenders of marriage" who are actually speaking to oppress the rights of others (Dr. Phil, Nov. 27, 2011). The oppressed should be civil, holds Dr. Phil, trying to mediate the issue and apparently taking on new territory. Personally, when I am judged so harshly that it threatens to deprive me of my inalienable rights, I can become pretty nasty. Whether or not Gandhi's path is more effective, I wonder. I suspect it is.

The solution for gay marriage is not alternative terminology such as "civil unions." If we seek to use other terms for marriage, the betrothed will further be deprived of all the accompanying special words, as well as rites of passage. Will we accept the word "fiancé?" Marriage includes proposals; engagements, announcements and showers; relatives and friends arriving from out of town; wedding rings; nuptials or wedding ceremonies; wedding dresses and tuxedos for those who want them; ring bearers and flower girls; maids of honor and groomsmen; and honeymoons. Marriage must not be a luxury or reward for being straight. We cannot take all those experiences and words away from two people who are in love, want to commit to each other and be known by their family and friends as a couple for a lifetime.

Love makes us sweeter and healthier. If we ban these words from their precious rite of passage we may be actually depriving our own child of such joys someday. Further, the children of gay unions will also be deprived of the terminology, having to refer to their parents' partnerships as civil unions, despite possibly having been married by willing clergy. If there is any religion or cleric willing to perform a marriage ceremony, how does one religion seek to trump another by denying the legitimacy of that ceremony in the eyes of the state?

No one has an ethical right to impose their religious beliefs and definitions upon others who are unwilling to accept such definitions. No one gets to say that it is wrong for another person or couple to have the same rights we enjoy. It's like refusing to share. It's mean. It is not religious or Godly. Rather, it's arrogant. It's diminishing and demeaning. It's enraging and inflammatory. It's a variation on a caste system.

Further, there is absolutely no truth or mental health in proposing that the recognition of one person or couple diminishes another person or couple. Your happiness does not diminish me. I have no right to say that if someone else gets recognized the same way I have been recognized, that my recognition is diminished (unless I am in a contest with a limited number of winners). It is a remarkably unhealthy argument that by definition, I lose something when someone else is blessed. It's a sin to covet and such behavior does covet marriage jealously for its own keeping. "It's mine and I am not going to share." It is greedy, selfish and ugly. It makes religious motives and their representation of God very unappealing. It is mean-spirited, not spiritual. It is not generous. When straights covet marriage, they demean, devalue and destroy. Then when gays try to defend themselves and fight for their rights to the same dignity and respect, it is even more absurd to complain that they offended us after we offended them. You cannot provoke another, depriving them of their liberties and dignity, then point at them for expressing their outrage or for even wanting to fight for their rights. Anyone who wants to judge a gay relationship is a tyrant, in my opinion, diminishing the life of another. Stop it.

I say take care. Make your life the best it can be. If you want to defend marriage, choose your partner well. Live ethically. Don't judge, should or blame. Teach your children how to understand and accept others. Straights have too many problems with domestic violence and divorce, so marriage is a fragile heterosexual institution. Discrimination won't make it stronger.

To Gay Parents. When parenting, gays need to ensure that each child has a dedicated role model in their lives of their same sex who can also model how they should treat and be treated by the opposite sex (this also applies to single parents). To adopt practices from this book, gay parents will have to interpret and assign their own mutual roles, such as who does the mothering (most or both) and who does the fathering (most or both), who is the primary caregiver, who is the supporter, protector and provider and who will be invited to represent the style and ethics of the opposite sex in the child's life on a consistent basis. In the absence of such a role model, these values can still be taught (see also Chapter 5: Imprinting and Chapter 7: Discipline).

The First Year: Bonding and Attachment

There are essentially two stages in the formation of personality. Stage one, the first year, establishes the child's capacity for intimacy while forming a sense of self, as well as the sense of self in the world. Stage two, the second year forward, establishes the child's autonomy in the world, responses to the world, coping mechanisms and the personality structure or disorder which will form according to how the child is treated in the process of trying to become an individual.

The first year, formation of the core self through quality of attachment begins with bonding: falling in love at the beginning of the baby's life just out of the womb.

All of us are born with the same drives to attach. How well we are able to do that affects what follows. The way you love your child creates the kind of attaching your child will manifest for the rest of his life and the core personality he will have, including how secure and worthwhile he feels. Be clear that the drive to attach in the First Stage of the First Year naturally begins to extinguish if the need to attach is not met. If it is not met, he will begin to withdraw. His neurons, previously expecting to connect, will begin to prune and he will become cold, hard or indifferent to people. The older he gets, the harder it will be to turn this around.

We all have the same genetic instruction to attach, but our different experiences and our reactions to them are what make us unique. Every single one of us has different experiences, especially how we are coached, disciplined and taught to be self-disciplining as we move to individuate.

Practical Advice: Dos and Don'ts

- Do treat your baby like you're Mary or Joseph taking care of Jesus or an old soul.
- Do cradle her when she cries and look into her eyes ever so gently and sincerely, as if you are talking to The Buddha. Tell her you see her and reassure her that you're there.
- Do play him classical music often.
- Do rock your baby every night, perhaps before bed. Rocking an infant creates a mellower personality for the long haul.
- Do take plenty of photos and video. Maintain photo albums and frames for her to see how you value her.
- Don't carry your baby in a bucket/infant seat, especially with your knees banging into it as you walk.
- Don't face your baby away from you in the stroller where she can't see you before one year of age.
- Don't carry him facing out. Let him mold himself to your body.
- Don't cover her face in the stroller (reducing stimulation). She needs to see out to see what's happening, especially to see you.
- Don't wrap your baby too tightly after two weeks of age, even though "they" say you should.
- Don't wrap your baby too warmly in warm weather or too sparsely in cold weather. They need what you need.
- Don't pass your baby around for many people to hold him.
- Don't let him sit in a wet or soiled diaper. Change the diaper as soon as possible and ideally, rinse her bottom with lukewarm water (putting your hand in the water first) so that you NEVER put her body under water that is too hot or cold. Pat dry. Diaper rash is traumatic.
- Don't bond by dangling toys for the baby to see. Talk. Make eye contact. If you don't know what to say, pretend you're talking to God.

- Don't walk your baby to sleep. When he's too heavy to carry you'll be sorry.

The First 15 Minutes

The baby actually starts organizing his personality before birth, during birth and in the first 15 minutes or so. That is, his temperament is forming over the tiniest events to us, but they are very big events to him. These events and how we ameliorate them affect his personality more than any genetic predisposition ever could.

She is, or can be, ready to make eye contact in the first 15 minutes. She comes out curious to see who you are, unless she has heard too much screaming, you seem depressed or something has happened in the birth process that makes her more concerned with what's going to happen to her next. Whatever the first experiences, the baby expects more of the same and even at that tender age, an infant can create a self-fulfilling prophecy in her parents, especially if they believe in genes as the origin of her personality. So if, for example, she cries because she thinks her parents don't care, her parents may become agitated and distancing because they think they can't console her. When more of the same happens, she begins to adapt her personality to the patterns that can make her optimistic, desperate or inward to hide and shut down. On the other hand, perhaps she anticipates being held, loved and enjoyed. As she discovers gazing and nursing, she begins to see normal as being treated well because it's through those interactions that she quickly learned that she is loveable and the world is good.

Negative events need not be permanent conditions. Just because a baby was squeezed, pressed and pressured into a tight spot, unable to move for hours and hours and, when he was barely out, he had his nose sucked out, his foot pricked and was thrown under a light in a plastic see-through box away from human contact, doesn't mean that he's given up hope. If the beginning was rough and Mommy and Daddy know it and they go out of their way to become his rescuers and welcomers, he'll shift his expectations to a capacity for things to be rough then smooth. This is the first step toward resilience. Convincing him to keep the faith is up to you.

The First 48 Hours

The first 48 hours are an extension of the first 15 minutes. This is bonding time. Your baby is still longing to be welcomed. If she doesn't get welcomed, she will draw further conclusions. Of course these deep conclusions can be overturned with new experiences that create resiliency, as already mentioned. However, when the parent doesn't understand that his baby's "temperament" is related to what she's experiencing, then the parent won't tune in as well. At some point the baby's moods may become prolonged and adaptive when conditions are not modified, so an adaptation may be thought to be her "natural personality" to which the parents begin to anticipate. One baby is said to be mellow. Another baby is said to be more difficult to soothe. One sleeps through the night. Another wakes up a lot. One mother sleeps with the baby and another puts her behind a closed door so she can get some rest. These moods-turned-traits are not inherent. They come from first experiences and can still be changed toward the positive or negative according to future experiences. Further, some babies have not finished physically forming by birth, so they may be in some physical discomfort in the first days or weeks of life.

Forming Temperament and Personality

Some parents treat a baby like a cute, helpless object that needs attending and will someday reveal the personality it already has. When they believe that personality is inborn, they think that its appearance is just a matter of time. They believe that intelligence is inborn too. Development is thought to be a waiting game of discovery. This is not the case.

Some parents treat a baby like a thing, and they will raise a child who is autistic or who has Asperger's Syndrome or an adult who is schizoid, because there is no clear interest in the child's feelings or experience in the earliest months or years. These mothers may leave their baby alone in the crib all day with only perfunctory interaction. The mother may have almost no dialogue with the child, and perhaps she barely touches him. He begins to become a thing, rather than a warm-hearted person. Another mother might get such a kick out of the first gaze that she can't hold back. I have seen mothers who have to keep that gaze going so much that they don't let the baby take a break. They may hold the baby's head so she can't look away, so the baby learns to see but tune out. I know a mother who held her baby's lids open when the baby tried to close his eyes to get a break. This type of child grows up to think everyone is watching him and is preoccupied with his every move. I know someone who acts like people in cars are paying attention to him if he stops to tie his shoe. "Get over it," his companion said. "The world is not interested in you." But he can't get past his belief that he is being watched all the time. He keeps the curtains closed so people can't look in (as if they would want to).

I tell you those two stories even though they are extreme because I want you to understand that little things build personality in a child. The more attuned you can be to your child when he is young, the healthier he will be later. Little compulsive gestures or patterns can create a termperament or personality, so watch for clues as to what you are creating. I know one child who became rigid because his mother had a rigid schedule for him; another had a hard time mentally organizing and anticipating his life because his mother had no schedule. He came to act more helpless and dependent than most toddlers his age. I know adults who can't sleep at night unless everything is really quiet because their mother "shushed" everyone when the baby was napping (probably because she didn't want the baby to wake up and take her free time away). I know someone else who can sleep through every thing, but likes the television on when he sleeps.

Good bonding includes a joy to see the child. It includes willingness to look away so the child can look longer to study you and love your gaze. If the child looks away, the mom does too. It's a dance that an attuned mother honors.

Calling the Baby Out. Rather than just waiting for the personality to appear, another approach would be more exciting and would yield a brighter baby/adult. I call this approach "calling the baby out." Calling the baby out requires that the parent realize that this baby is waiting to be called out. Ideally, the parent sees the soul of the child, becomes delighted with looking in, and is sensitive to when it's time to give her a rest and look away. The parent smiles, engaging in eye contact, trying little tricks of interaction. She speaks with tender and loving tones and big smiles. Dad can stick out his tongue and watch the baby stick his tongue out too, creating an interactive dance. The parent alternates between soft, deep, intimate tones of love and tones of playful joy. The parent offers tones of sympathy when the baby cries. The parent chooses some basic words for interacting that are used again and again, such as the baby's name, Mama, Daddy, nurse or bottle, hungry, crying, diaper, *etc.* Using the same simple words again and again when talking with the baby gives her a chance to develop awareness of symbolic representation and a vocabulary long before she ever has the capacity to speak. The parent talks to the infant with respect, as if she's an old soul with a fully formed right brain, knowing she understands intentions, emotions, and attitude from birth.

Pre-Symbiosis. Some psychologists believe that the first three months are the pre-symbiotic stage when the baby is still not smart enough to bond yet. The concept was introduced by Margaret Mahler based on her observations of mothers and infants. The information is no longer credible. Still, Mahler is one of my heroes. She was an advocate for the needs of infants and contributed significantly to Attachment Theory.

I believe the reason babies haven't bonded in the first days, weeks and months is that the parents haven't called the baby out. They have not interacted sufficiently to create bonding. If parents begin this dance of interaction from the first moments of their infant's life, then there will be no pre-symbiotic stage, I promise you, and when your baby smiles, it won't be gas. It will be a genuine smile.

Bonding Becomes Attachment

When bonding is established, attachment begins. <u>Bonding is falling in love. Attachment is staying in love.</u> The early stages of attachment include symbiosis, where the baby and mother are as one.

The Need for Quality Attachment

A newborn baby will follow and favor her father's voice but seek her mother's breast. She will seek the gaze of both. Her vision is very nearsighted. She can see exactly the distance of breast to eyes. Thus she is designed to watch her mother's eyes while she nurses or seek her father's gaze while he is holding her. <u>She is drinking in her identity while she drinks in her food.</u> She is getting a physical sense of herself from her mother's skin on her skin. So if a parent strokes her baby's skin and makes loving eye contact, then the most important part of nursing is happening, whether the baby is on a bottle or the breast, though there are many good reasons to favor the breast. A father or adoptive parent can do without nursing. Do not nurse or bottle-feed without the gaze and the loving touch.

If the parent calls the baby out, the baby will go straight to symbiosis. Babies seek to merge, to trust, to maintain proximity to mother and to feel safe, protected and understood by her. They assume this safety as long as there is no experience to the contrary. A safe child is a mellow happy child. As soon as the mothering parent lets her child down, his assumption of safety is gone forever. The once mellow child is no more. Now the possibility of "safe" or "not safe" has come to mind for the infant. With measures to repair, the breech may be forgotten and an assumption of safety may return tentatively.

In theory, during symbiosis, the secure baby thinks mommy and he are one mutual organism. There is truth in this. When he cries, mommy's milk "lets down" (beginning to drip from her breast) even if she's in another room listening to the lyrics of a song and thinking about something else. When she's out of the room, he may think she's disappeared and it causes him anxiety until she returns.

Quality of attachment is almost invisible to most people and it is very difficult to explain. A quality attachment is one in which mother or father is tuned in to the child so well that they can tell almost what she is thinking, feeling and needing. Then, as a result of that attunement, they are able to rock and soothe her when she needs to be soothed, feed her when she cries to be fed and put her down for a nap when she is tired.

Further, a quality attachment is one in which parents have begun to dialogue with the infant in order to give her words for her feelings, their interaction and for things. These parents relate in a way that is intelligence enhancing. Their regard for her emotions, including appropriate responses, is the very interaction that creates the foundation for mental health, resilience and intelligence. She feels understood and validated.

If parents are not attuned, the child will not be able to form a secure attachment. That insecurity will become a part of the core personality and without deep corrective work, it will stay within him the rest of his life. Onlookers may assess that this apparent insecurity or restlessness is temperament. <u>Adults interact in a way that reenacts the quality of their original attachment.</u> For this reason, it is important to assess your own attachment style. You may do so with the help of a quiz later in the chapter, the results of which will help you see your own child's risk of an insecure attachment.

> There is no such thing as a baby.
> There is a baby and someone.
> – Donald Winnicott, M.D.

The Need for Continuous Attachment

Many people believe babies don't notice when their parents aren't there or that their absence doesn't send them into deep suffering. Proximity of the primary caregiver is critical, yet this belief that babies don't mind being shuffled among various caregivers is a pervasive blind spot for parents and psychotherapists alike. Parents and psychotherapists who assume babies won't mind are thinking as their parents did and may have a blind spot because they were shuffled around as babies or not seen clearly enough by their parents.

It seems that no one wants to presume what babies observe, feel and think, so they presume babies don't think. Many people believe that a baby's only needs are having their diapers changed and their bellies fed, as if babies are organisms that don't have feelings or awareness of how they are being ignored, handed off, treated like a cute little thing or taken for granted (Schore, 2001). Many people believe it doesn't matter who changes their diapers or feeds them. Worse, some people believe it doesn't matter if parents go to work and come home or leave for the weekend. Babies notice if their primary parent leaves the room. They suffer until she returns. Some babies suffer so much they bang their heads to relieve their emotional pain. When mom leaves them for work every day, this chronic abandonment causes them to define themselves as insignificant in an indifferent world. These definitions can last a lifetime. Babies need continuous attachment. If this does not happen and their heart is broken as a result, they will become insecure or less interested in humanity.

Touch. Touch is critical for a baby. If they are not touched sufficiently in infancy, they do not have a sense of where they end and others begin. It's as if they have no container to hold themselves. Some children who suffer a lack of touch develop "skin issues." They may seek ways to decorate their skin and some say getting a tattoo is as fulfilling for them as having the tattoo. See the histrionic personality and the schizoid personality. Some teens actually become "vampires," seeking to bite and suck the blood of one another, almost as if they were nursing. Others join nudist camps or bring home mannequins or life size blow up dolls. All are prone to schizophrenia and would develop symptoms if they were treated to additional injuries such as abuse, intrusive treatment and mind-warping experiences such as teaching a child to distrust his own perceptions and feelings of self-preservation. Babies need touch and if they don't get it, they develop skin fixations and deep hungers for experiences of the flesh.

Insufficiently touched children may

grow up with a craving for touch or a fixation on skin that manifests either as a schizoid personality or a histrionic personality. The former may add "skin" to their wardrobe, favoring leather and hides. The Trench Coat Mafia of Columbine High School may have been wearing a uniform of skin. Schizoids may fixate on skin, touch, silk, women's undergarments and cross-dressing or blowup dolls and mannequins. Some may later focus on provocative dress to draw attention to their skin or hair, such as tattoos or piercings or extreme hair. (Fashion has moved more in the direction of these choices of late, as more and more children are raising themselves in the early years. On the other hand, more and more pierced and tattooed young adults may do so only for fashion and not necessarily because they suffered insufficient touch.)

Rocking. Babies need to be rocked. There is a critical time for rocking and if they get it during that critical time, they are more likely to be mellow and far less likely to become violent later in life. While researchers have not identified exactly when that critical time may be, I would recommend that you rock your baby every night for the first year. If you can, add a lullaby.

Hatching. Hatching – when a child contemplates exploring away from mommy – normally takes place at around seven to nine months in a secure infant. Hatching is the process of discovering "I am a person separate from Mommy." The baby will feel Mommy's face and nose and even explore what she'll do if she squeezes Mommy's cheek, grabs her glasses off her face, pulls on her hair or bite's Mommy's breast. She is more interested in her impact on Mommy and the world.

A poorly bonded infant might need to nurse longer, need the family bed because both parents work and may have withdrawn months earlier.

The baby listens to words that distinguish her from mommy like "Mommy," "Daddy," "Baby," and the baby's name. She is a little more sensitive to the loss of her mother, yet willing to crawl away from her in a spurt of independent zeal when she's feeling secure.

Healthy hatching has two fun developmental signs. One is the infant's first joke; the other is taking bows. It's also during the hatching phase that a well-attached baby will begin self-weaning.

Self-Weaning. If a baby is well-attached, during the time of hatching, he begins to show some indifference to the breast maybe just one time in one moment, showing curiosity about other foods. If mother is fully tuned in, she'll notice his indifference and follow it. If mother respects her securely attached son's cues, she'll let him exercise that autonomy sometime around seven to nine months and not pull him back to the breast. This is a fragile first expression of independence. It's a new template for the personality. Will mother honor the first expression of independence or will she discourage him for her own benefit or because she is not tuned in? How that goes affects future personality and initiative.

La Leche League provides an invaluable service encouraging mothers to breastfeed. We love what they do. Unfortunately, we run into a disagreement at around eight or nine months. Some infants need to extend breastfeeding, especially if Mommy works, but a truly secure infant may be done and it would be nice if Mommy could read the cues and allow her child to assert her autonomy. Missing the cues could create dependency of personality that might be remedied fairly easily if caught soon enough. How much impact this might have on personality might be proportional to how long breastfeeding continues. It could just be a minimal parental mistake and may even just be a matter of taste in what kind of person you want to raise. If you believe in La Leche theory, please don't throw the baby out with the bathwater just because we say healthy babies like to begin separation and hatching at around eight months. I hope you will stay with us for the rest of what we teach.

Some argue that many cultures nurse for extended periods of time. The anthropological evidence on this matter suggests that this preference made more sense when cultures were mobile or food supplies were limited. In some cultures there were even pre-adolescent ceremonies where young children were completely taken from their mothers, sometimes at five years old, so they wouldn't end up too dependent or weak. Where children nursed until they were five years old, there were often quite ruthless puberty rites to correct signs of overdependence.

Baby's First Joke. There are occasions when an adult may actually be physically lower than a baby. The baby could be in his father's arms following his mother down a staircase. Mom could be lying on the floor beneath his crib waiting for him to see her after he wakes up. She could be sitting on the floor while he sits in daddy's lap on the couch. All of these are occasions for baby's first joke. This situation is hysterical to a bright infant. He perceives the above position as a state of power. He thinks it is uproarious for a grownup, especially his parent, to be below him. The laughter of this child is something you don't want to miss.

Another joke has surfaced online in which two different babies respond to their daddies tearing pieces of paper in two, while the infant holds one half of the paper. These babies absolutely crack up with infectious laughter. Both fathers appear to have discovered this joke by accident. I suspect parents of all infants could try this out to see their child's delight. The baby holds half the paper, as if to have half the control or ownership, and watches the other half ripped away. What do you suppose it is about tearing the piece of paper in two that causes an infant such delight?

Taking Bows. Taking Bows is another phenomenon related to power. This one is related to competency. Usually only nursing babies take bows. While lying in her mother's lap, nursing, aware that another person is in the room, she will suddenly break away from the nipple and throw her top arm high into the air, swinging it all the way back so her body follows, waiting until she catches the approving gaze of her audience who is situated somewhere behind her and toward her feet (rather than above her head). They smile, even nod and perhaps chuckle at the grandiosity and cockiness of the child. When she has absorbed the recognition she was sure to receive, she suddenly lunges back to the breast. She's clearly showing off and feeling good about herself and the world. She's showing off her competency. Neurolinguistically, she is looking down to her audience, as if standing on a stage above them. She is in her area of expertise, feeling cocky and worthy of admiration. She knows what she's doing; this is her domain.

Dad's Checklist

Dad's Adventure is a wonderful organization that guides new fathers. Visit the website (dadsadventure.com) for even more information like their advice provided below.

Get a list together of the items you want to bring on delivery day and keep it with your bag to double-check before you leave. Get ideas from the hospital staff and through birthing classes. Talk to other expecting couples or someone who recently delivered. Many pregnancy books will offer suggestions on what to bring. Here's a "starter list" of items to bring; edit as you see fit.

- Everything your partner needs.
- Everything the baby will need, such as an outfit and blanket for the trip home.
- A few copies of your birth plan (whether intending natural childbirth, father cutting cord, intentions to keep the baby close, dad goes for the initial assessment and bath, dad intends to sleep in the same room, *etc.*)
- Change of clothes, toothbrush and shaving kit for you.
- Comfortable shoes as you may do a lot of walking.
- Something to read to her that she would love.
- Bathing suit for you, to help mom take a shower or bath to ease labor pains.
- Something to eat and drink; power bars and juice are suggested.
- Champagne (put your name on it and ask the nurse to chill it).
- Camera.
- Cash.
- Have a folder ready with important documents: insurance cards, pre-admission forms and any other documents.
- MP3 player with her favorite music.
- Tylenol or some other headache medication.
- Any pain-easing tools recommended at your birthing classes: balls to squeeze, hot or cold packs, massagers, *etc.*
- Address book/list of phone numbers to announce birth.
- Calling card (you may not be able to use a cell phone inside your room).

Fathers

The quality of the first year is established by the father for the most part. He sets the tone. He needs to help the mom set up a baby room and prepare for the baby's arrival. He creates the environmental attitude for mom as to whether the coming of this baby is a miracle or whether she can expect to parent alone. She learns whether she is in good company if the couple celebrates the baby's conception and prepares for the impending birth with excitement. The father will indicate that he is in and committed to making it possible for mom to bond and remain attached with the baby.

I believe that fathers can reduce or incite postpartum depression, which is a significant psychological danger to the baby's well-being. When fathers show enthusiasm and offer protection for mommy and baby, the baby's psychological life is much more likely to be safe and healthy.

After birth, fathers need to stay involved and interested. They need to keep a watchful eye to make sure that mom is not in postpartum depression. The father's initial role for a secure infant is support. After the first few years, dads need to become more involved in order to provide a role model for a boy or to establish a healthy standard of interaction for his daughter.

As I have already indicated, it is alright for parents to reverse roles as long as they are consistent. If the dad is more nurturing, he may become Mom; and the mother, if her earning potential is better, may choose to become Dad. For purpose of discussion, it is less complicated to refer to the traditional terminology with Mom as the nurturer and Dad as the supporter, protector and provider. Parents who reverse roles can revise the terminology themselves.

I knew a couple who switched roles when the baby was two months old and she decided to return to work leaving dad as the primary caregiver. I asked if they planned this and they said that they did. I would have advised them then that dad should be the primary caregiver from birth. He told me he wanted his wife to enjoy at least the first two months of motherhood before returning to work. My thoughts: That was for the mom, not the baby. I saw a radical change in the baby's personality at about two and one-half months, the next time I saw the child. Interestingly enough, the parents didn't see it until I pointed it out. We tend to see what we want to see.

The baby comes out knowing the mother's body, heartbeat and smell but knowing the father's voice. The mother's voice has been distorted through her body as the sound travels from her vocal cords to her womb. The father's voice has come through a few layers of skin pretty clearly.

After the birth, if the baby is whisked away from the mother, the father should follow, talking to her and comforting her with the sound of his familiar voice. The baby will know that her father is there and is not the one doing these things to him. She will know she is not alone, "Daddy knows," you say softly, with empathy.

Babies need skin contact, and they prefer soft skin without stubble. I believe fathers who hug and kiss their babies may need to be careful and thoughtful or shave first. Also, when talking to their baby it is best if the father can use a high falsetto voice sometimes, especially if they are going to be the primary caregiver. Hopefully this can be assessed before the baby is born. If mom truly wants to go back to work, then dad needs to take the maternal role as soon as possible and let mom look over his shoulder.

Postpartum Depression

Postpartum depression is a common complication in bonding following childbirth. There could likely be a re-enactment of the mother's own birth or infancy, complicated by immediate issues. A history of the mother may reveal an abandonment of some sort during infancy (unconsciously recalled). Perhaps she feels overwhelmed or abandoned and unsupported by the child's father.

The case of Andrea Yates, who drowned her five children in the bathtub, is not very clear since I don't know her history, but it appears to me that she was never allowed to have her own point of view as a child because if she had, she'd not have acted so mindless and voiceless. She was drowning in her husband's wishes to have more and more children. She apparently wasn't consulted by her husband or seen by her community. That is, while she was suffering silently, there was no perceptive person from her hyper-religious environment to notice her distress. She was completely tapped out, probably even before she had her first child, and she was expected to nurture and care for more and more children. She was developing problems with her sanity, given what she never got and interpreting ongoing expectations to give more. Further, my understanding is that she was on psychotropic medications which can put a person over the edge (Breggin, 1999).

In the case of one client of mine, the mother was told sharply as a toddler not to touch her infant sister. "Don't touch the baby!" she heard time and again. If her mother had been nurturing and perceptive, she would have realized how hurtful the delivery of that message was. Further, such a sharp message compounds the experience of feeling unloved, especially when one has not finished being a baby herself. When the child grew up to become a mom, she was afraid to touch her own infant daughter. It was some time before she dared to pick her up. This mother was a fragile adult when I met her many years later, living on psychotropic medications, something her husband insisted on because he couldn't handle her pleas for help and understanding. I assume she must not have been very nurtured to begin with since she never experienced internal stability.

In the case of another client, her own mother had not nurtured her sufficiently. When it was time to deliver her first born, there was a complication with the anesthesia and she nearly died. She knew what was happening because she couldn't breathe for awhile. The experience was highly traumatic since no one seemed aware or concerned. Her husband seemed unaffected, although it had come out that she wasn't breathing. The doctor and staff didn't speak to her about it until after the procedure, when she was admonished not to complain since her own father was a doctor. Other than the admonition, no one acknowledged her situation after childbirth. She felt so insignificant that she slept all day while her husband was at work. Actually, she saw him off to work, put the infant in his crib and closed the door on him. When the time came for her husband to return home, she would go pick up the infant and the two of them would meet him at the door. She handed her baby boy over to his dad, went back to her bedroom and closed the door. I learned of this history when I was asked to treat the son who had developed Aspergers and RAD. It was not until I expressed empathy for the mother's neglect during childbirth that she confessed the whole story of how she had neglected her son.

It is better to get to the cause of postpartum depression than to simply medicate the mother. The sooner she is understood, the sooner the cause can be addressed and the sooner the mother can nurture her own child. The infant is painfully waiting and growing through critical stages. When fathers are nurturing to their wives in the early months after childbirth, they can mitigate any predisposition from mother's childhood to postpartum depression. This is extremely important because when a mother has this depression, the baby suffers while taking in all the wrong messages and the personality becomes inadequate.

If moms have good reason to know or anticipate that the father will be thoughtless and uninvolved, then they need to let go of any expectation and get professional help. When we expect help and we don't get it, it is far more painful than if we never expected help at all.

Multiples

Twins or multiples are more at risk for insufficient parenting because there may not be enough of mom and dad to go around. Twins can fare well when they have very intuitive and attuned mothers and fathers. It takes this because each twin, like everyone else, needs bonding and a continuous attachment. They too need the experience of feeling seen, of feeling cherished and having a strong parent who can protect them and stop them from behaving badly. The mother of twins will have to be twice as good and of triplets, three times as attuned and nurturing.

Twins sometimes cope with the lack of an attuned, strong and consistently available mother by turning to one another. They become symbiotic with each other and begin to grow themselves as a unit. They give each other the experience of feeling seen, cherished and consistently attached.

Twins sometimes cope with the lack of attuned maternal care by polarizing. Both want mother's love and symbiosis, but there isn't enough to go around. The most primitive response is to fight for this love or attention. Yet this is a probable course for them because a struggle for dominance often begins in the womb, possibly won by whoever was on top. Sometimes whichever twin is the strongest is dominant and conversely whichever twin is the weakest is submissive. Sometimes dominance turns out to pay off and sometimes submissiveness pays off, especially if it is safer to give in. Further, submissiveness can be reaffirmed by protective attention from mom while a different mom might look at the stronger child as the one who will achieve greatness. So in some cases, the stronger child wears the crown depending on the mother's orientation.

To reiterate, sometimes twins become a unit; sometimes they polarize. When the parents are nurturing, there is a higher probability that the twins can each become unique from one another as well as healthy individuals who are also great team players.

When twins discover that they can turn to each another for affection and understanding, parents often become more disposed to see and treat them as a unit, especially if the parents believe their personalities are genetic and essentially the same. They may become referred to as "the twins." They may be dressed similarly. They are tended to together, at the same time. When this takes place, the twins are not experiencing the precious one-on-one experience of being seen individually. They are treated as if they are alike and expected to be alike.

Parents of children who have elected to become a unit by the end of the first year are encouraged to see each child as special and nurture each child's voice and accept each child's point of view. Offer them recognition of their uniqueness without holding them to any particular identity. Twins, like any child, get to evolve, allowing some choices and preferences to die away while taking on new choices and preferences.

Most parents of twins who polarize look at the dance between them and begin to characterize one twin as the submissive one and one child as the dominant one, especially in the case of fraternal twins where parents are thinking genetic temperaments and personalities are inborn. When this happens, the parents compound the process by projecting identities onto the twins, further feeding into the children's ideas of themselves, confirming the dynamic into actual personalities. They begin to look at the dominant twin as the strong, bad or great one and the submissive twin as the weak, innocent or good one. So the twins believe these projections are accurate rather than the result of a probable competition for a scarce but essential source: mother love.

I knew one mom of fraternal twins who favored the daughter and thought the son could take care of himself. Her son became a jealous, violent and angry monster and the mother came to despise her own son. The daughter became an entitled princess who must have been riddled with guilt for being the favored child.

Born to be as good as any child, they unfold into roles they cannot transcend as long as their parents neither expect nor require anything better or different. The more parents affirm this dynamic, the more the children develop opposite environments. One child has a tough sibling for a primary relationship or formative experience, while the other twin has a weak sibling for a primary relationship or a formative experience. Thus, their environments are opposite and even more influential in the formation of these diametrically opposed personalities. I have seen the dominant twin become the one who gets into trouble, spiraling downward, while the passive twin becomes the intuitive and sensitive one, earning her way into acceptance. On the other hand, the dominant twin may become the successful one and in some cases, the submissive one can even develop schizophrenia.

Correcting the Bully Twin. The more frequently parents mediate these differentiating processes by encouraging, sharing and offering separate and reasonably equal affection, the more the children thrive. The more parents discipline mean behavior consistently, the more the children can transcend these polarizing identities.

An attuned parent would recognize this dynamic very early and begin to mediate and compensate for it. They might want to separate the children as often as possible so each can enjoy individual attention. They might take a stand with the dominant child, tolerating no meanness under any circumstances, doing whatever it takes to ensure that this be true. Mom or dad could also encourage the weaker twin to become stronger and take a stand against bullying behavior.

This is tricky because when the parent does encourage the weaker twin, this can make the dominant twin more jealous of the attention and protection that the weaker twin is receiving. Then the dominant twin may become more abusive out of sight because what he seeks is tender adoration, like any child, and he can hate the weaker twin for winning the protection, nurturing and favor he craves. I would consider a nanny-cam in your home, so you can watch their interaction when they think you are not around.

Unfortunately, babies, toddlers and young children may reach a point in their young lives when they decide they are tough and will never ever be weak again. When a child adopts a dominant identity at a young age, that child is in trouble. A twin can actually develop RAD without being officially abandoned because it is the actual adaptation of refusing to ever be vulnerable or trust again that creates the RAD personality, not the actual abandonment itself.

A RAD child needs to be subject to experiences that are designed to break the unnatural will of the dominant child and recreate an attachment so he can be a vulnerable, sweet child again. As soon as the will is broken, the child needs to be cherished and adored. An example might be of a dominant twin who yanks the weaker twin away from mom or steals a toy. Mom would then take the dominant twin to a chair to sit and watch while the other twin gets to continue to play with the toy or even sit in mom's lap. When the dominant twin says "I'm sorry," or gives the toy to the sibling, mom will then let the dominant twin sit in her lap. Or perhaps the dominant twin can sit in mom's lap later when there is no correlation between taking and sitting in mom's lap. Just know that this is a symptom of deprivation and maladaptation to a need for more attention.

Sometimes the first attempt to "break" the child's pathology may be a war of wills for the mother or father. The parents cannot give in even if it takes hours. If the child won't stay on the chair, the parent has to keep putting him there until his will or resolve weakens and he apologizes. The apology and the choice to become soft must be immediately rewarded with affection and attention. (See Chapter 7: Discipline.)

A parent who has a weaker will than her own child will be in for the most difficult of parenting experiences as the child gets older, but it will be the child who pays the real price for the parents' weakness.

The younger this correction process takes place, the better, because the older the child gets, the more difficult it is to create surrender. An unsurrendered or invulnerable child can't learn as well and will develop an adult personality that is also tough, having trouble with intimacy and in extreme cases becoming more prone to criminal behavior, while his sibling may develop some victim consciousness, possibly even marrying an abusive spouse.

It is also tough on a mother to discipline a baby or toddler, but unless this is done, the child begins to believe he is expected to dominate because that's who he is. Of course disciplining a baby is calculated and stern, but not mean. (See Chapter 7: Discipline.)

At the other end of the spectrum, the

vulnerable twin could develop schizophrenia if mother love is too illusive and her protection is too rare; she could learn helplessness, becoming convinced that there is no one to protect her. The dynamic of tough versus weak is even further complicated by the introduction of third or fourth caregivers, helper nannies, who sometimes or often get replaced, contributing further to an insecure attachment.

When parents need help, hire cooks and housekeepers, not nannies.

Parenting Triplets or More. If there are three, four or five babies all at once, the issue remains the same. Each child requires the experience of being the apple of mommy's eye. The most important factor is the mother's capacity to love, to attune, to divide her attention and to discipline fairly and consistently. The children will need to feel both part of something big and wonderful for who they really are as individuals.

The ideal situation would be two perceptive parents, a housekeeper or two (who take care of the house and the parents) with each parent being mommy. I have seen some cases where it was better for each parent to take a child and then enjoy liberal "visitation" with the other child(ren). On the other hand, the best cases I have seen were cases in which mom successfully managed to spread herself around, as did dad who was also highly involved. That seems like more of a juggling act, as ideal as it is. If parents feel challenged, I would recommend that they each take a child (or two) to "mother". If there are too many children, they may need to arrange for another primary caregiver, that is another fulltime, permanent (un-fire-able) mom who doesn't take vacations until the child is older and perhaps brings the child on the vacations.

See if there is a way dad can be home full time as much as possible. Mortgage the house, work from home at night with an employee who takes direction, move in with the mother-in-law, or everyone lives in a studio apartment for a minimum of three years to make it happen. After the first three years in which a secure attachment has been established, dad can go back to work and mom can take over. She can go back to work when the children enter preschool or kindergarten, the latter of which is always better whenever attachment issues threaten the foundation of children or when parents are going for greatness in their children. Of course, all of this is easier said than done. The most important thing is to be aware of how lack of maternal attunement and contact can deeply hurt a child who comes to feel left out.

Adult Attachment Issues

A filmed experiment of mothers and infants by Dr. Mary Ainsworth, "The Strange Situation," (1978) led to categorizing and typing different attachment styles. Mothers with toddlers were situated in a waiting room. The toddlers were invited to make themselves comfortable on the floor with some toys. A stranger entered the room and the researcher recorded the infant's response. The mother was asked to leave the room for a short period. Researchers observed and recorded whether the stranger was able to reassure or comfort the child. However, the high point of the experiment was how well the mother was able to reassure her baby upon return and it was upon this ability to comfort that the type of attachment was identified. Securely attached infants were identified as consolable.

From the experiment, two primary categories of insecure attachment were found: avoidant and ambivalent. Later, another category was recognized by Mary Main in which some toddlers were classified as having disorganized attachments. A corresponding adult profile was drawn from the Adult Attachment Interview also developed by Mary Main (Sonkin, 2005).

Researcher Main demonstrated that an infant's style of attachment is predictive of adult romantic attachment styles as well as the probable attachment style this grown child will have with her own child.

Adult Attachment Styles

From Secure Child to Secure Adult

Secure Infant. The toddler explores the room and toys with interest, tolerating a five-minute separation. He misses his parent, crying upon a second separation. The baby prefers his parent's comfort over that of a stranger. He greets his parent actively upon return, initiating physical contact. He may cling somewhat after a second separation and then finally settle and return to play again.

Secure/Autonomous Adult. As an adult, he values attachment, but seems objective regarding any particular event or relationship. He participates in a coherent dialogue about himself, specifically his childhood and his adult relationships.

From Avoidant Infant to Dismissing Adult

Avoidant Infant. The avoidant infant fails to cry upon separation from her parent, often continuing to play even when entirely left alone. She actively avoids and ignores her parent on reunion by moving away, turning away, "changing the subject" or leaning out of her arms when picked up. She won't make eye contact with her mother while in her arms. She shows little distress and displays no anger about being left. Her responses to her mother are unemotional, focusing instead on the toys.

Dismissing Adult. Dialogue with this adult about his childhood is not considered coherent. He has a tendency to dismiss attachment-related experiences and relationships, normalizing them with overly brief generalizations not supported by history. For example, childhood was "excellent, very normal mother."

From Ambivalent or Resistant Infant to Preoccupied or Entangled Adult

Resistant Infant. This child may be wary or distressed even prior to separation with little exploration. He may be preoccupied with his parent, scanning for what she is doing now and going to do next. He may seem angry or needy during reunions. Following a reunion, he fails to settle and take comfort in his parent's presence, usually continuing to focus on the parent and crying. He won't return to exploration.

Preoccupied Adult. This grown child's recounting of childhood is also not coherent. He seems preoccupied with or by past attachment relationships, appearing sometimes angry, needy or fearful. Sentences are often long, grammatically entangled or filled with vague usage ('yada yada yada,' 'and that').

From Disorganized Infant to Disorganized Adult

Disorganized/Disoriented Infant. The infant appears at a loss and displays disorganized and/or disoriented behaviors in the parent's presence after the mother returns. The infant may freeze with a trancelike statement, hands in the air; may rise at parent's entrance, then fall prone and huddle on the floor; turn in circles; bang his head; or cling while crying hard and leaning away with gaze averted. The infant is damned if she does and damned if she doesn't. She is afraid of her mother and afraid to be on her own. She may otherwise seem to fit in the above categories.

Unresolved/Disorganized Adult. During discussions of loss or abuse, this individual has a striking inability to reason or dialogue coherently. For example, she may speak as if a dead person is still alive, as if thoughts could kill, as if feelings are dangerous, or become suddenly silent for an extended period of time if a probative question is asked the truthful answer of which may have once been threatening. At other times she may seem to fit into any of the above categories

Adult Attachment Assessment

While the Adult Attachment Interview (AAI) developed by Mary Main is actually quite complicated to administer, here is a quick measure of your own attachment style that I designed for easy scoring. The use value of this quiz is to see how your attachment as an infant and toddler affects you now in your adult relationships and is predictive of how you will be inclined to relate to your own child. With some self-awareness, perhaps you can stay awake and work through inclinations and reflexive reactions.

Instructions: Rate the following statements in terms of how you generally feel about intimate relationships whether you are in one now or not. Think of "Disagree Strongly" for something that has no (0) truth for you. If it seems completely true, give the statement a 5. If it seems in between, rate the item according to how strongly you feel.

Disagree Strongly		Neutral/Mixed		Agree Strongly	
0	1	2	3	4	5

_____ 1. I enjoy being vulnerable with someone I trust.
_____ 2. I don't want people, even my mate, to know how I think and feel.
_____ 3. I feel uncomfortable when my mate is gone too long.
_____ 4. I love knowing the truth of how someone thinks even if I could feel hurt.
_____ 5. I don't like depending upon my mate.
_____ 6. Sometimes I feel out of control when my mate acts like s/he doesn't need me.
_____ 7. I like to talk about personal issues and problems with my mate.
_____ 8. I don't like to be vulnerable with anyone, not even my mate.
_____ 9. I don't like to be alone.
_____ 10. I don't feel like I need a relationship to be ok.
_____ 11. I don't really want to hear from my significant other all about his/her day.
_____ 12. Sometimes I feel like I cannot get close enough to my mate.
_____ 13. I like doing things by myself and with someone close.
_____ 14. When my mate gets too close, I tend to pull away.
_____ 15. I don't take rejection well.
_____ 16. I enjoy physical and emotional intimacy.
_____ 17. When my mate gets too close, I feel suffocated.
_____ 18. I merge so quickly with a new partner that I can scare them away.
_____ 19. I can talk about almost anything with someone I trust.
_____ 20. Even when I don't have anything to hide, I'd rather keep my view private.
_____ 21. I worry that I care more about my mate than s/he cares about me.
_____ 22. I readily accept comforting from my partner.
_____ 23. I prefer a conversation about shared interests rather than about each other.
_____ 24. I sometimes try to get my mate to tell me things that make me feel wanted.

There will be three scores, each estimating the security of your attachment as a child and in turn, its impact on your ability to have an authentic intimate relationship with your mate as well as how you will relate to your own children and how they will be inclined to relate to their significant others and children some day.

☐ The first score is for Secure Infant/Secure or Autonomous Adult. These statements are every third item, beginning with the first response (1, 4, 7, 10, 13, 16, 19 and 22). Total your scores for these items. A perfect score of 40 represents a wonderfully and securely attached person. A good score is 30-35. If your score is lower than 30, consider accelerated self-awareness (this course will help). If lower than 25, consider relationship skills training, if not therapy.

☐ The second score is Avoidant Infant/Dismissing Adult. This is the attachment style that refuses to get too vulnerable. If you scored high in this category, you decided a long time ago, before your memories, that you didn't really need anyone. Your ability to converse or relate is very superficial and stuck in roles and expectations. The items to be tallied for this score are 2, 5, 8, 11, 14, 17, 20 and 23. The perfect score for Avoidant is zero, the lowest possible score. The highest and most pathological score is 40. You could be happy with a score of 10. Above 20 suggests a need for deep work in therapy unless you prefer to live as someone somewhat superficial and shallow.

☐ The third score is for Resistant Infant/Preoccupied Adult. This child probably clung a great deal but exhibited anger at mom for leaving so often and for her emotional inconsistency and unreliability or for possibly suffocating or dominating her. As an adult she is extremely disturbed by a lack of demonstrated commitment and may even be very combative in her insecurity, perhaps creating self-fulfilling prophecies of abandonment. The items to tally for this score are 3, 6, 9, 12, 15, 18, 21 and 24. The best possible score is 0. The worst score would be 40. Concern begins with a score above 20; even a score of 15 warrants some attention. A person with a score of 25 or higher should benefit greatly from therapy.

Hunger to Merge

Those of us who did not develop a secure attachment or separated prematurely are at risk for a hunger to merge. It's as if the brain will take another opportunity to merge as an adult. Unfortunately, as teens or adults we will choose someone else who had an insecure attachment. They too will have a hunger to merge.

This is not a conscious process. It actually seems magical and out of our control. Yet this lover becomes both the high point and low point of our lives. We merge like a heroine addict seeking another fix. We become obsessed. We fall in love beyond normal variations of "in love" like we are cast in a spell.

Almost always the two lovers completely lack relationship skills and are prone to fears of abandonment and even stalking. They each take things personally and are likely to blame and judge instead of processing disagreements constructively. Altercations often show up in the form of scapegoating (from childhood issues) and may eventually manifest as control issues that end in violence. These love/hate relationships usually end in disaster and often take years to recover from. As far as I can tell there is only one such love of our life. After that, no one will ever make us feel that way again. Even though these obsessive relationships end badly, our hunger to merge has been significantly "healed" or met. We may be healthier as a result and no longer need to be in such an intense relationship.

Some people make the mistake of failing to grieve and instead chase after the person or the feeling for a lifetime. The healthier choice is to grieve the loss of our earth-shaking romance, find our gratitude for what we had and appreciate that now it is done. Now we can seek a more mature relationship with a "good enough" lover who isn't unpredictable or dangerous. Maybe we can truly assess the partner that we will come to admire and favor for their values, company and conversation.

The truth is, we were not in love with our merging partner. We were in love with our idea of them. We never really knew them. We didn't love them for their ethics or character. We loved them for the warm, fuzzy mirror they gave us in the beginning, the familiarity we experience and the way we had to earn their affections, the way we felt when we were with them, the way they craved us and ate us up and the way we wanted to devour them right back.

As far as I can tell, healthy people do not go through this. They fall in love, but their head is screwed on correctly. They get to know a person before falling in love. If she turned out to be someone they were wrong about, they can turn it off or grieve within a normal period of time and move on.

Your Crying Baby

Your child's core identity and personality lay in how you respond to his needs as an infant. I've known many mothers, adults, babysitters and older siblings who tried various abusive techniques to stop their babies from crying. I know of mothers who suffocated their infant with a pillow to stop the crying, then lifted it away when they were quiet. One mother I know put her hand over the child's mouth, pinched his nose until he passed out and said, "If he doesn't stop crying, then I stop him myself." Another mother choked the child to stop him from crying, but let him live after he passed out. Another mother teased the infant's genitals to distract him. One shook the baby to stop him from crying. Still others raged in their child's face. They swaddled their child and left him alone in a room with the television blaring and the door closed. The variations are endless.

The most common response I see is a parent passing their child off to the other parent because he has started to cry or he won't stop crying. One woman told me that her worst fear was that she would have a colicky baby, "So of course I had a colicky baby." Yes, of course she did. The more we fear our baby crying, the more our baby will cry. Our baby can read our body language. He knows how we feel and he can intuit our opinions of him and his body.

Suffocated babies may die from Sudden Infant Death Syndrome (SIDS) or grow up with claustrophobia, asthma, or intolerance to necklaces and shirts that button at the collar. Some children suffer blindness, brain damage or death from having been shaken so hard. Others learn to masturbate and/or develop sexual addictions whenever they feel upset. Some become afraid of anger or have little affect or emotional expression. Still others develop Aspergers or even autism. Some become paranoid, but all of them develop a fear of expressing their authentic feelings because their parents couldn't handle crying. They are the most difficult to treat because they can't cry in order to heal.

I can imagine no greater terror for an infant than to realize that his own mother cannot stand his feelings. It seems like such a mind-warping realization that the one who is supposed to nurture and protect you gets mad at you or rejects you if you express pain or fear. With this lesson learned in the first year of life at the very core of the child's personality comes a fracture, a fear of his own authentic self and his own feelings. This child learns that in order to be safe, he has to fear himself and the enemy within: his emotions. Nothing could make him want to cry more. Nothing could make him fear himself more. When you reject your baby's feelings, you become a danger to your child. Then the child who was born to idolize and depend upon you has to agree with you and pretend that you are right in thinking his emotions are bad.

The more you react, the more frightened and upset your child gets until he develops neurotic coping mechanisms. I know one young man who withdrew from his mother as a small child and talked to himself in private by cupping one hand to his ear, the other hand to his mouth and then tried to connect them so he could hear his voice directly. Another young man learned to fall between the wall and his bed so he could feel the illusion of being held and comforted. Another young man learned to think that if he loathed himself, his mother would like him for agreeing with her. The adaptions are many; the issue is the same.

The first thing you need to do is assess your baby. Is she crying because she is wet, hungry, too hot, too cold or too confined? If you have fed her, changed her diaper and ensured that she is comfortable, then you need to find out if the suffering behind her crying comes from within. Does she have gas? Does she have a bowel obstruction? Does she feel pain? Study and learn the Dunstan Baby Language and study your child. Listen to the sounds she makes to learn if she is crying because she is hungry, tired or suffering. If she is suffering, figure out if she needs to burp or poop or pass gas.

Once you have developed a hypothesis, you will be able to decide if what he needs is your reassurance and understanding. As you do your inventory, maintain a soft and empathic voice so he knows you are present and investigating. Even if he feels pain, from your soft and reassuring voice, he will know his mother is taking care of him.

To have that soft and reassuring voice, you have to forget yourself. You have to let your soul connect with his soul. You have to want to reach into his little heart and tell him that you care and that you know he hurts and that you will take care of him. Then you can sit in the rocking chair and hold him in a way that will help him release gas (vertical) or lie her down so you can feed him (horizontal) or hold him over your heart so you can soothe him, rock him, sing to him and look into his eyes (vertical or horizontal). The more you commit to calming your baby as if he were yourself, the calmer and easier to soothe he will become.

Dunstan Baby Language

Perhaps the most attuned mother of our time is Priscilla Dunstan. She discovered what her baby was saying by learning his cries. She came to realize that his cries were universal. All babies "spoke" the same words to communicate the same needs. As an older child, Dunstan's son introduced his mother on her CDs and DVD. Although he was a child, he spoke like a professional. He sounded like a Miracle Child: healthy, resilient, confident, authentic and very much alive. Buy her DVD to witness his voice, even if you don't have a baby. It also makes a great baby shower gift. Your infant's five Dunstan words are:

Neh.	(Think **need** to eat.)	Hungry.
Owh.	(Think night **owl**.)	Sleepy or tired.
Eh.	(Think "Excuse me.")	Upper wind, needing to burp.
Eairh.	(Think **air**.)	Lower wind.
Heh.	(Think "**Help**!")	Uncomfortable.

The Second Year On: Freedom & Discipline

Separation and individuation truly take place on a backdrop of secure attachment and mutuality. Essentially, the more secure the first years, the stronger the sense of self and the more independent a child or adult can be when facing adversity. To be clear, healthy human beings never outgrow the need for intimacy and are excellent at achieving it.

Separation-Individuation is a process that evolves for the rest of our lives. Every effort toward becoming an independent person and establishing ourselves worthy of regard is in the direction of further individuality. Successful individuation takes us toward achievement and greatness.

In an ideal and secure childhood where parents are creating a Miracle Child, the child will separate and individuate in the way discussed more thoroughly in Chapter 6: Faith Parenting.

You Choose Your Child's Potential

It's up to you who your child gets to be when she grows up, or at least it's up to you how prepared for greatness your child will be. Every time you compromise your child in the first three to five years of his life, for your own interests, you lower your bar as to what kind of person he gets to be in this one life of his. You make the difference between a saint or a sinner, a president or a criminal, a professor or a teacher, a CEO or an employee, a record-breaker or a cheater, or anything along the Continuum of Potential (COP). Perhaps the only difference will be whether or not she has a happy marriage or multiple divorces, a successful career or a lack of achievement, or a feeling of worth versus a feeling of emptiness.

You gamble that this little choice you make today won't hurt tomorrow, but the hurts add up based on your priorities. When you make the day care decision, you have lowered your bar tragically. The Continuum of Potential mostly applies to the security of your child's attachment, including how warm, attuned and involved you were versus how many rotating caregivers he had, how much bouncing back and forth he suffered and at what age. The continuum weighs whether he had to endure early separations such as vacations, adoption or illnesses, whether his own or his parents'. The security of the attachment determines how resilient he is to traumatic events in later years of childhood.

In the second stage of life, individuation, you determine how safe your child feels as she gradually grows away from you. When exploring and pioneering, you praise her sense of curiosity and adventure or you scold her for leaving the box. Perhaps you endeavor to teach her ethics and values or maybe you believe that a whoopin' was good enough for you so it's good enough for her. Another way to lower the bar for what kind of person your child gets to become is to be her jailer or a weak parent rather than a coach when she begins to investigate the rest of the world. By inhibiting her sense of measured adventure, you also lower the bar on how wonderful your child gets to be.

In the second stage, imprinting is the predominant force in the formation of personality (see the following chapter on Imprinting) and nothing is imprinted so significantly as our own self-discipline and the ways we respond when our child endeavors to separate, test, rebel and experiment. There is almost no factor so impactful on our children's personality as how we act, as well as how we discipline our children or even how we don't discipline them. Essentially, how we discipline tends to determine the type of personality our children adopt and imprint from us.

Continuum of Potential

10 Highly regarded. Happy in personal and social life. Creative and groundbreaking. Courageous yet capable of vulnerability. Honorable. Empathic. Humble yet resilient and goal-oriented. Charismatic. Strong and enlightened sense of self and others. Someone everyone loves to love. Promotes good parenting, concern for the earth and other socio-ethical standards. Accepts personal responsibility for everything. Can take a strong and authoritative stand for an ethical issue without flinching.

9 High achiever. Respected. Good communication skills and capable of empathy. Some blind spots, perhaps as a parent or mate or regarding conventional wisdom. Could be satisfied with being a great parent and/or a meaningful career. Can handle major problems effectively.

8 Good person. Respected. Sometimes makes impulsive choices that can have a high cost to self and others, but problem-solves and self-corrects. May have some personal unresolved issues that get in the way of social *and* professional satisfaction. Probably succeeds at one more than the other. OR may be relatively successful in career and marriage, with perhaps some occasional distancing or clinging to cope. May have secrets.

7 Likeable. Has personal pain, but most people don't know it. Gets along in life without making a splash one way or the other, accepting less. If she makes a splash, there are ongoing complications. Loves and holds grudges. May have had a hard time choosing a good mate and being a good mate. Tries to be a good parent, but blind spots lead to problems for the children. May have secrets.

6 Tries to be a good person and wants to be liked, but feels so empty she keeps sabotaging her opportunities. May blend in. May be defensive, asserting nothing is wrong. Problems with judgment and blame. Problems with authenticity.

5 Can't maintain a relationship. He has as a mediocre job. Perhaps smokes and drinks. Has terrible relationship skills and is an average to poor parent. May have problems managing money or difficulties in vulnerability and trust.

4 Is not often successful in her endeavors. She is so empty and needy that she is a poor mother or worker, or she is so cold she can't be intimate with anyone. May abuse substances. Probably abuses children in the name of discipline. Makes unethical choices and defends them as a victim with excuses or blame. Cannot keep a job or rise up the ladder.

3 Tries bitterly to taste the good life, but doesn't know how to get there. Has to cheat to get by. Adopts loyalty ethics.

2 Bitter person in a lot of trouble most of his life, in and out of jail. Has experienced unrequited love and is abusive or pitiful in relationships.

1 Violent criminal, psychotic, hospitalized or seriously unsocialized person everyone loves to pity or hate.

Separation

STAY HOME FOR YOUR CHILD'S FIRST THREE YEARS, at least. Ideally, stay home until she goes to kindergarten, the extra two years can make the difference between fairly healthy and very healthy, unless your child's preschool teacher is more attuned to him than you are. Total your actual costs to work (transportation, childcare, *etc.*). Your net income may not be that much greater than not working at all or working from home. If it is, consider that the long-term emotional rewards of raising a Miracle Child may far outweigh the long-term financial rewards of working outside the home and raising a dysfunctional child whose costs and troubles (bail, boarding school or Wilderness Therapy, school loans *vs.* financial aid, ongoing therapy, to list a few) may actually end up draining your savings. By staying home, you may instead enjoy the child with a healthy, moral, optimistic personality who's unbelievably fun to love. Further, financially speaking, the healthy child is more likely to obtain scholarships and achieve goals creatively.

Ideally, you begin separating when your child begins kindergarten at about five years of age. Of course, gradually, you prepare him for separation when you take him to Gymboree, leave him for a few hours with a babysitter on Friday nights and leave him with Grandma every Thursday afternoon. Maybe by the time he is four you take him to a pre-school for the mornings or afternoons. If you absolutely must return to work, do not do so before your child turns at least three.

- Don't bond with your baby and then go back to work. Go back to work before three months or after three years. Four years is better, and better still is five years. If you must go back to work at all, you will be the secondary caregiver. Establish her primary caregiver at birth.
- The person who will be the primary caregiver needs to do the bonding. If you must hire a caregiver, try to choose someone who will stay. Screen these caregivers for warmth and longevity. Consider putting in a secret television monitor because it's common for people to treat your infant better in front of you than when you are gone.
- Avoid hiring new caregivers when the baby is between three months and three years.
- If caregivers have to be replaced, try to transition gradually. Remember, however, that any caregiver who has taken off two days weekly or for a vacation may no longer be bonded to your infant or toddler anyway. Observe the child's reaction.
- If you have had multiple caregivers, you will be the primary parent by default. The child is primarily bonded to you, but the attachment is insecure. Take measure to rebond as much as possible.

Three Separation Schedules

Ensuring a secure attachment and a secure human being requires special dedication. It yields the ultimate reward of a low maintenance, delightful child you wouldn't even want to leave because the child is so amazing to you and everyone he encounters. Perhaps these schedules are conservative, but it's better to take no chances. Even using conservative schedules, the child will suffer, whether or not he internalizes long-term damage. Often we hear someone say, "My mother went to work when I was two and I turned out fine," while we observe that she is overweight, socially awkward and overly disposed to please or to complain. What is the gauge for turning out "fine"? (See the Continuum of Potential on the prior page.)

For years parents have asked me how much separation a child could endure on a daily basis and at what age. Other parents asked me how long they could leave their child if they had to go away. Of course the primary consideration was the age of the child in question. The former question was about the sort of chronic abandonment children suffer when they go to day care. The latter was about the acute abandonment children suffer when their parents go away on vacation or mom gets sick and has to go into the hospital, or worse, the child is sick and has to go into the hospital.

I intuited good answers but looked for scientific studies as well. I could not find any recommendations even by pro-child researchers to answer the questions, while pro-parent researchers failed to address the consequences of leaving a young child. Nevertheless, I added my recommendations to *The Manual* anyway.

I had been observing children and their situations for years, but I had also been asking every single adult client about their early childhood experiences with abandonment, day care or loss. I took note of the impact of these experiences on my adult clients and how their symptoms fit.

I also was invited to visit a classroom where many of the children were disruptive and even violent. I did an informal research study of my own. After observing the children for two days, I wrote little notes on each child. I rated how much attachment trauma they had suffered and how much violence they had known on a scale of 1-10. Then the teacher told me each child's history. I had two witnesses. I was remarkably accurate.

I was also able to intuit an answer and produce two formulas for two situations that have been useful to parents, probably because they are a bit conservative. When parents follow a formula, their children's attachment is not threatened. See the Abandonment Schedule and the Continuity-of-Care Schedule.

Recently I discovered an out-of-print book, *Day Care Decision*, that revealed a very similar formula for how much abandonment a child could endure, chronic or acute. The book was written by a very empathic couple who had operated a day care but closed it down. They discovered how much the children suffered and that no matter how hard they tried, they could not compensate these children for their loss. Due to popular demand, or lack thereof, the book was never reprinted (Dreskin, 1983).

The Snyder Child Custody Schedule (SCCS) arose from multiple requests by parents, lawyers and judges involved in child custody cases seeking estimates of how much shared custody a child could endure, sometimes when the child knew the other parent and sometimes when introducing a father into the child's life. Some parents have wanted exact measures for every detail, but our general preference is for the parents to use their intuition, perception and conscience rather than rely on strict formulas. A formula for every permutation cannot be provided, so you will need to use your very best judgment, and hopefully my schedules will aid you. Fortunately similar schedules to this one are becoming more popular.

Abandonment Schedule. This schedule protects against major disruptions in the relationship that destroy trust in a young child and create fears of separation and abandonment. The intensity of those fears depends on how severe the attachment breaks are. If one break was already worse than what is allowed below, modify the schedule to be more conservative or the parent will re-injure the child. In other words, if the parent left the child with a relative for five days at one year, she cannot put the child in day care for two hours twice weekly at age two. Each injury is cumulative and drives the scars deeper.

The following schedule is for a one-time-only event in early childhood. Perhaps a child can handle one such abandonment per year if everything else is going very well, but personally I wouldn't risk it. If you share primary care with your mate, neither of you can abandon your child without injuring her deeply. However, shared primary care does allow each of you to leave for short periods of time more often than a single primary caregiver can. If it happens on a predictable schedule, that helps too.

- A one-month-old can handle one hour away from mother.
- A two-month-old can handle two hours away from the primary caregiver without developing a permanent lack of trust.
- A three-month-old can handle up to three hours away from the primary caregiver without developing a chronic fear of abandonment.
- A six-month-old can handle six hours away from mother.
- A one-year-old can handle only one day (twelve waking hours) away from mother without losing his ability to trust, but it will be painful.
- A two-year-old can handle two days.
- A three-year-old can handle three days.

- A four-year-old can handle four days.
- A five-year-old can handle five days.
- A six-year-old can handle a week.
- A seven-year-old can handle two weeks.
- An eight-year-old may be able to handle a month.
- A nine-year-old may be able to handle a summer.
- A ten-year-old may be able to handle nine months in boarding school.
- An eleven-year-old may be able to handle a year away, perhaps longer, not that you would want them to.
- A twelve-year-old may be able to handle a permanent loss without core damage to his personality, even though the sadness and depression would be deep and pervasive.

Continuity-of-Care Schedule. This schedule applies after the first year, *assuming no major attachment breaks have already occurred* and that all other solutions have been researched before settling on third party childcare. If you are the primary caregiver and wish to remain so without injuring your child, please follow the schedule below. If you share primary care equally with your mate, also equally share the following schedule.

These separations should be developed. On the first day, visit the babysitter or the day care facility with the child. Then you leave for five minutes and return. Do this again until the child develops certainty that you always return. The next day, leave for ten minutes and return. The following day at the school, leave for fifteen minutes and return. The next day, 20 minutes, then 30 minutes, then 45 minutes, then an hour and a half, *etc.*, depending on the age of the child. In other words, build trust that you always return before you leave. It is possible you can double up and have two visits to the school per day and cut the process time in half (*i.e.*, the first day leave for five minutes and return. A little later, leave for ten minutes and return).

- A one-year-old can handle one hour away from Mom once per week without developing an anxiety that she cannot be taken for granted.
- A two-year-old can possibly handle two hours twice weekly.
- A three-year-old can possibly handle three hours three days per week.
- A four-year-old can handle four hours four days per week.
- A five-year-old can handle five hours five days per week - the length of kindergarten.
- A six-year-old can handle the length of a full school day five days a week.

The person who takes care of the infant during the day is "Mom." If there is a regular nanny, the nanny is Mom. If grandma offers care while mom works, grandma is Mom. The main problem with this arrangement is that nannies leave for weekends and vacations. Grandmothers relinquish the child for weekends and vacations too. Children who don't have stay-at-home mothers will have a more fragile core personality and difficulty trusting. It could show up as ADHD, a recent epidemic of our time. Another recent epidemic is Pediatric Bipolar, which results in large part from putting infants into day care (Carmichael, 2008; Kaplan, 2011).

Infants and small children cannot handle rotating caregivers. Any caregiver who leaves is not bonded to the infant. A bond is with someone who stays continuously. If a day care facility takes care of the infant during the day with rotating caregivers, then the facility itself is Mom at the same time no one is Mom. If the infant is raised for a year or more in and out of hospitals with rotating doctors or nurses, the hospital is Mom, and no one is Mom. The infant is not bonded or attached to people. The infant won't trust people and she will likely be out for revenge against the medical establishment. As a related example, Ted Kaczynski (The Unabomber) was someone at war with technology for having been taken from his mom and put into an oxygen tent in his first year of life.

Snyder Child Custody Schedule (SCCS). Follow the Snyder Child Custody Schedule, or Success Schedule, in cases of parents living separately with shared custody of a child. For the sake of the child, one parent must be designated as primary caregiver and the other as secondary, with whom regular visits increase as the child gets older. Even when followed conservatively, the SCCS is a risky schedule; please follow the child's lead. If the child clings to Mom before leaving to visit Dad, receive the cue and alter the schedule accordingly. Dads, please don't lie about how well your child handled her leaving mom because it will cost you and her later. Don't forget you are her protector, not her kidnapper.

This schedule may incur criticism by anyone who has seen children handle much worse without appearing damaged for it. Note that this schedule is not suggested for raising just an average child, but for raising a Miracle Child. How high is your bar? (See the Continuum of Potential.) Further, how perceptive is the person who says the child "handled it without appearing damaged"? Many therapists, child custody evaluators and even master parents at PaRC can miss the cues.

The SCCS is premised upon an otherwise secure history of attachment, and I may be pushing the child's developmental readiness for the sake of the courts and parents whose affinity for adult justice calls for shared custody sooner than later.

If the child acts indifferent to parents coming and going there is already a severe attachment break with the child and someone needs to do the work to re-bond as soon as possible. This means visitation needs to be put on hold.

Children who bounce back and forth come home grouchy, even when they love both parents. That's a bi-product of living in two homes. In other words, it's hard on the child to have two homes even though they have successfully bonded with both parents.

The SCSS or Success Schedule is also premised upon cooperating parents. In some cases the acrimony is so strong that it is not possible for a new father to visit the infant or toddler in the mother's home. In this case fathers must adapt. Take the child out and sit on the porch for short periods in the beginning or until she wants to go back in. You might have to bring a toy for the two of you to play together. Gradually walk down the sidewalk and return and increase the time together. Take your time. Your goal is to get up to speed in the schedule without alarming the child. The dad who plays it slow and easy will have the best long-term bond.

> **If any mother knew how deeply her child suffers when she leaves, she wouldn't consider substitute care. Children are designed to be closest to their mother in the first five years of life. The lessons learned last a lifetime.**
> **-- Mary Jane Julius, PsyD, postpartum, infant and attachment expert**

Snyder Child Custody Schedule (SCCS)

Age	Early Introduction Example	Late Introduction Example
1 wk	1 hr daily or longer in Mom's home and Mom's presence. Rocking. May have to feed baby or leave when Mom does.	
2 wks - 4 mos	1 hr, as many days as feasible in Mom's home. Rocking.	
4 mos	1½ hr four times weekly in Mom's home. Rocking & talking. (6 hrs)	
8 mos	2 hrs four times per week in Mom's home. Rocking, talking and changing diapers. (8 hrs)	
1 yr	1½ hrs in Mom's home and 15 minutes out twice to four times weekly, to 1½ hour with Mom and ½ hour out, 1 hour with Mom and 1 hour out, ½ hour in Mom's home and 1½ hrs out, to 2 hrs out twice to four times weekly by 10 months to 1 year. (4-8 hrs)	1 hr visits four times a week beginning with Mom present. Mom starts leaving the room for just a few minutes, increasing to longer exits until she can achieve 2 hrs out of the room without the child crying. This could take a year. (4 hrs)
2 yrs	3 hrs out two to four times weekly. (6-12 hrs)	Three visits weekly. Dad starts taking child out in the yard for a few minutes, increasing until he can take the child to get a yogurt and then to dinner and home before child starts crying. (If child never frets when Dad pushes the limit, child may have avoidant attachment with Mom. If child only frets on leaving Dad, he has the stronger attachment.) (3-6 hrs)
3 yrs	Two 3 hr meals out and one short overnight weekly beginning after dinner, ultimately increasing to before dinner. (16-20 hrs)	Increase visits to 3 hrs, then turn one visit to short overnight, meaning 7pm to breakfast and eventually 5pm for dinner and returning child after lunch. (9-20 hrs)
3½ yrs	Two 3 hr meals twice weekly and one overnight for 24 hrs. (30 hrs)	Same.
4 yrs	Two 3 hr meals and one short weekend from Saturday noon to 5pm Sunday before dinner. (35 hrs)	Same.
4½ yrs	One meal out Weds and Fri. night to Sun. 5pm.	Same.
5 yrs	One meal out Weds and Fri. end of school day to Mon. start of school day, twice monthly. One meal out (Tu?) and one overnight (Th?) on alternate weeks. (69 hrs, then 22 hrs, then 69, then 22)	Same.
9 yrs	Consider switching, especially if child is a boy.	Same.

Divorce Issues

The above SCSS reflects all the information to follow on the topic of divorce and child custody. If you are an attorney, judge or child custody evaluator, you may be put in a position of determining the custodial arrangement that is best for a child. In order to make this determination in the best interest of the child, I recommend that you consider how much separation from his or her primary caregiver a child can endure without causing the child undue harm. I recommend that you balance the child's need to have frequent and continuing contact with both parents with the child's need to form and maintain a *secure and continuous* attachment with a primary caregiver.

Well-intentioned attorneys, judges and evaluators often err with orders on introducing an estranged parent or supporting parent into the child's life too much, too soon and too young in hopes that this "early intervention" will strengthen the bond with the newer parent. They do not understand that by doing this, they are forcing an attachment break between the child and his primary caregiver at a crucial stage in the child's development. Such an attachment break will forever diminish her ability to trust and have healthy attachments with either parent, as well as with partners as an adult.

The result of early attachment breaks is abandonment trauma, which is the predecessor to serious, long-term personality injuries, adaptations and disorders in the adult years. A child who suffers an attachment break in the early developmental years may, as an adult, engage in behaviors such as stalking or staying with an abusive mate. He may develop personality adaptations such as coldness, bossiness or controlling behavior, if not explosiveness or intrusiveness.

In less severe circumstances when the child is a little older and at least able to understand that it is not her mother's choice to give her up, but that of "the big world," as one child described it to me, she will only suffer injuries that would look more like neediness, generalized anxiety, major depression, fickle behavior, or most likely, always wanting to be where he is not.

All who are involved in recommending or making custody orders need to understand this: You cannot break a child's bond with one parent in order to create a bond with the other parent. Once the bond is broken with the primary caregiver, the child will have difficulty trusting and forming a secure bond with anyone. What fathers need to know is that the more they respect those first three years, allowing the attachment to be unbroken, the more the child will enjoy trust and attaching to him. A securely attached child is warm, loving and affectionate. An insecurely attached child will act neurotic at best.

> **You cannot break a bond to make a bond.**

What the other parent actually would want the most if he knew how children develop would be for the child to complete the formation of a secure attachment so she can securely attach with him, and others in her later life. Because the resulting personality damage may not be evident to most if not all adults for years, most attorneys, judges and evaluators do not witness it and mistakenly believe that the children they ordered to leave their primary caregiver did so without adverse effect. Because the resulting personality damage does not appear to immediately follow the attachment break, most people do not make the causal connection between attachment break and new insecure behaviors; instead they may blame the child's genes.

The Child Custody field is newly developing dynamic theory. While they claim to be "child-centered," the primary voices continue to protect the rights of the parents and the desire to make everyone happy by splitting the baby in two, which causes life-long disturbance for the child.

Court psychologists teach us that children are resilient, that they can survive a broken home, two one-parent families, being thrown into a blended family, new step-parents, new step-siblings, switching houses and rooms every week or even every couple days, enduring long drives to see the other parent, being tested and evaluated during the custody process by a grown-up stronger than their parents, parents vying for them by not enforcing consequences, having one parent alienate them from the other, being asked to spy, keep secrets from or lie to the other parent, having parents sit on opposite sides of the room when they have a school or extra-curricular function, parents arguing over which extra-curricular functions they can attend, parents undermining each other's discipline, not having holidays, birthdays or graduations with both parents together, alternating holidays between parents or having to eat an afternoon holiday dinner with Dad and an evening holiday dinner with Mom, parents putting them in the middle by passing messages to the other parent through them because they do not want to talk to that parent, parents fighting over each little thing they do, guilt trips for loving their other parent, parents blaming each other for the high cost of the divorce and custody case, parents accusing the other of lying about income and payments for the child, having a mom jealous of the step-mom and demanding he not call her "Mama," listening to parents constantly disparage each other, and on and on and on...

Perhaps children can survive all of this, if survival means that they continue to live and breathe. But certainly everyone must agree that these custody arrangements cannot be without long-term cost to the child, even if it means that they too will someday make babies in impulsive circumstances only to repeat the pattern again. Certainly these are not the perfect nurturing childhood environments that most parents would desire for a child they love.

Courts are asked to treat parents like two three-year-olds fighting over a toy, keeping the parents happy by dividing time with the child. The small child has no voice, so I am presuming to speak for all small children. Even though the court intends to make child-centered orders and often assigns a guardian ad litem or minor's counsel for the child who has no knowledge of attachment needs, the innocent child is still left out of the consideration and is the one who suffers most. I do not believe anyone who does not have a background in the needs of small children can represent a child.

It is not the child's fault that the parents couldn't work it out. If the orders were really "child-centered," they would award the child the family residence and let the parents move in and out every other day until the child is old enough to have the parents alternate every other week. This could be two apartments and one house or three apartments. In some cases parents live back to back and the children can come and go through the fence or parents can have separate apartments in the same building so the child can easily go back and forth. As the child gets older, Dad may want to live around the block or a few blocks away so the children can walk to Dad's house when they want to see him, given a co-operation between the parents. The child always has to have permission, leave a note and/or leave word or be available by cell phone (I can't believe I said that). Some parents actually do some of this for their children.

An alternative is to allow the child to have a primary residence with liberal visitation increasing for the supporting parent as the child grows old enough to handle dual residences. Additionally, it is more ideal when the father lives within walking distance for the child so daddy can walk her home and she can internalize an awareness that both parents are close at hand.

The feminist movement called for greater equality between the sexes and was instrumental in making our laws gender-neutral. Because of this, the law now treats mothers and fathers equally with equal rights to children, and in many cases, even newborn infants.

The law is also gender-neutral when it comes to payment of child support. This combination of equality and neutrality has led to one scenario of dad being awarded custody and mom paying child support. My beloved women's movement has turned out to be harmful for children in custody issues as well as popularizing early day care.

Teamwork between Two Parents. As a child custody evaluator, I would tend to favor a parent who is willing to honor his child's attachment needs over his parental rights. I would be disinclined to report kindly about any perceived revenge by one parent against the other using the child as a weapon. Further, when I detect that one parent blames and judges the other parent without self-reflection, I would begin to become concerned about the blaming parent. Healthy parents take responsibility for their choices and self-reflect about their own shortcomings while unhealthy parents do not.

Mom and Dad need to work out a schedule in the *spirit* of a healthy attachment and stick to it while being as reasonably flexible with one another as possible.

You don't want to be a parent who telegraphs to their child that they should be afraid to leave you or who withholds their child unnecessarily from the other parent unless there is a damn good reason. If the child is symptomatic about leaving mom too soon, then the other parent needs to be of a generous heart for the child's sake, not the mother's. The father needs to visit more, perhaps in the same home, even with the mom peeking in and leaving now and then. Gradually the child will handle more time away from her primary caregiver.

Remember an unattached child will go to a stranger and "dis" mom. That means it is not okay for this child to have a normal separation schedule. An astute observer should determine who can best create an empathic and continuous attachment for healing the abandonment trauma. To not do so will add to the child's pathology.

Ironically, many mothers actually complain that the weekend parent gets the better deal because they are the fun parent and have more play time with the child, while Mom becomes the disciplinarian, tutor, cook, chauffeur, *etc.* I believe this is a fair schedule for both parents.

If one parent is significantly a better parent, they should have more time, including some weekend time. Further, children may visit the father on weekends, but they need at least one, if not two weekends in their primary neighborhood so they can develop friendships locally. A child who has no local friendships becomes socially estranged.

Parents must never undermine one another's discipline because a child can learn to pit two parents against one another once he internalizes that they're enemies, and he can just walk out the back door to the other rescuing parent. Undermining the other parent's authority may leave your child with a major personality disturbance, unless that parent is flagrantly unethical. Be careful. It doesn't matter if Dad doesn't do laundry the same as Mom, give a bath at the same time or orders meals in. Her dad is her dad. You chose him to be her dad when you had sex with him. Don't nitpick now. He will figure things out and his relationship with the child is more important developmentally than his parenting habits or experience.

Sometimes Divorce Is Best. While divorce is harmful to children, clearly it's a reality of life and sometimes necessary. Sometimes parents stay in bad relationships when they should leave. There are times when staying is more harmful to the child than leaving, especially with domestic violence or when the child is being mistreated by one of the parents.

In these cases, divorce should be considered if the non-violent, non-abusive parent has a reasonable belief that the other parent is harmful and she can obtain protection for the child away from him with an order for primary or sole custody. She needs to seek official support such as a shelter. She also needs to document her issues with the other parent because too many mothers have been unable to protect their children when the courts did not see how serious the threat was. Some courts don't see the true picture, often because one attorney is highly priced and highly skilled while the other attorney is inexperienced. Too often, children's social workers, child custody evaluators and judges do make wrong calls.

Also, there are parents who are not good parents in a contained environment, but as weekly visitors taking the child out for fun can be perfectly safe parents. Usually these parents are open to not having joint custody, but would like ongoing contact in smaller doses. Interestingly enough, often the child experiences better quality time with these parents because of the divorce.

I have recommended divorce to parents who lived in such an unhappy environment that it seemed feasible to set everyone free, as long as they negotiated a solution that would be easiest on the child. In these cases the father would hopefully agree to two or three weekends a month with his child and one or two weekly dinners. As I have said the quality of the relationship may improve with these appointed times for contact.

Sometimes an agreement to obtain primary physical custody is easier to achieve when there is an understanding that the father will gain primary custody of the child when he turns nine, thereby reversing the agreement. Sometimes, in the case of an infant, this offer may be necessary to save a male infant from a father who doesn't appreciate attachment issues.

In another case, I recommended a divorce where the custody agreement actually provided more time scheduled by the father with his son, as the father was doing everything he could to stay away from his wife. In yet another case, I asked a mother to stop trying to have her cake and eat it too. She wanted almost exclusive custody and child-support too. I understand that it's customary to give child support to the parent who cares for the child, but some mothers have successfully achieved full custody of an infant by agreeing to relinquish the child support or most of it. Of course, such a mother would need to be financially independent. I find such an offer is a great clarifier if nothing else. Some fathers fold quickly when offered possible relief of the financial burden and others do not.

Primary Caregiver. With the graces of nature, we humans have evolved over hundreds of thousands of years to present day as products of one primary caregiver in the attachment stage of development with one provider/supporter. When a child became old enough, the provider became more involved. He was a role model for separation and individuation since he was usually playful and modeled courage and honor. Unfortunately this model often failed to manifest a healthy marriage and ultimately took advantage of women, who were locked into a role that lacked social and economic worth. As a result there was a backlash, so today mothers are in the workplace and children are floundering. Children were not evolved or "designed" to be raised in day care by rotating caregivers.

I shared the role of primary caregiver with my husband. I would be hard pressed to guess who was the most primary between us. If one of us had to work, the other one cared for our son. He occasionally visited his grandmother for a few hours weekly during my graduate school years, knowing his father would pick him up shortly after I dropped him off. Fortunately, the three of us shared many hours. The majority of our time was together as a family unit.

As I have indicated, it's possible for an infant to bond with two people as the primary caregiver. If both parents are together significantly with the infant or toddler and then substitute for one another, we can consider the two parents as one. In this case, a long departure by either parent would be discouraged and would once and for all eliminate the accurate representation of two primary caregivers. Whoever leaves on a trip can no longer be primary caregiver.

In such cases divorced parents often live nearby and one bathes the child, puts her to bed, gets her up in the morning, gives her breakfast and takes her to school. The other parent picks her up at school every day, brings her home, helps her with homework, feeds her dinner and takes her to the other parent for bedtime.

I would like to see all parents who parent in a similar way share custody when possible, whether living together or apart. If they divorced, however, it would not be healthy to create time together as a family unit because that would tease the child into hoping and fantasizing that his parents could reunite. It would also be hard on the child to have two homes, time away from each parent lasting too long and no primary residence.

But the skeleton of this idea can be preserved with both parents trading childcare between them with minimal third party interruption. If there is acrimony between the parents, perhaps there is still a way that they can take turns stepping out and in without even seeing one another, especially if the child has the primary residence and there is a back door and a front door.

To be clear, if the father works, he is not the primary caregiver and his absence on a business trip may create sadness and anger but will not create damage to the child's core self. Conversely, if the mother works and the father is the primary caregiver, she can go on a trip without harming the child's internal capacity for resilience, but the father could not leave.

If both parents work, then hopefully they alternate shifts. One parent's stronger opposition to day care over the other would indicate a primary parent consciousness. To be clear, a parent who intends to put her child in day care should not be thought to be a primary caregiver except by default (because the supporting parent cannot provide at least a meager living for the primary parent and the child, and neither is he able himself to afford to stay home with her). If a primary parent puts her child in day care, the other parent should have the right of first refusal to take the child instead and I would think that the other parent should have an opportunity to appeal to the court for joint, if not primary, physical custody.

If both parents need a backup person, I suggest that they share the same backup system such as a healthy grandmother or nurturing aunt.

I have known fathers who didn't care or believe attachment was a critical concern. Rather, they treated it like some rigmarole intended to keep them away from their child. I would say such a parent is lacking the most important of parental traits, selflessness, and he is not showing up to be parenting material. I have also known mothers who wanted primary custody and as soon as they got it, they put the child in day care. I suspect in both cases the prize was retribution or related to child support payments.

When a father requests equal custody and parenting with a mother who is also working, it is important to ascertain whether these were always the roles. Is the father suddenly requesting more time with than previously requested with the child? Will he ask someone else to care for the child so he can go to work or do other things? Is it his way of creating consequences for having been left by the mother? Is the mother suddenly working because she is otherwise unable to support herself and her child? Does the mother have the appearance of instability because she has a history of taking temporary residences with different relatives in order to care for her child without relinquishing her to someone else? Was the father withholding a minimal income that would allow her to provide a roof, food and shelter for the child until there is a ruling from the court? For whatever reason, if the father is seeking more prominence in the child's life than he had before, were I a custody evaluator or a judge in the case of a young child, I'd be hard-pressed to grant joint physical custody if it would cause an attachment break with the primary caregiver.

Is the father someone who was not married to the mother or never cherished the mother, but now wants partial custody? One of the assessments of the father's capacity to parent in the best interest of the child is how he helped the mother prepare for birth. Did he buy the child a crib? Did he help pay for hospitalization? If the father did not participate in this level of supporting the mother before birth, he needs to be patient until the child has achieved a secure attachment before seeking overnight visits.

If Dad is clearly the better parent and has the primary attachment because Mom lacks attunement or works full time, then as I have said, Dad should be the primary caregiver. Of course this may take an evaluator since most people cannot assess their own capacities well. Unfortunately child custody evaluators are expensive and often they do not appreciate the full importance of attachment issues or ulterior motives. I would refuse any child custody evaluator who is a behaviorist unless they have studied this book.

In cases of shared custody, parents need to not tear their child in two. The parent who loves the child selflessly will not pull her apart and will follow something akin to the Success Schedule for joint custody. Once again, children need a primary and continuous attachment and a residence in a primary neighborhood with primary friendships in that neighborhood.

If the father chooses to exercise his right to take the child at age nine and mom chooses to pursue her career again, I would still suggest a mini-evaluation of girls before proceeding with this arrangement. Daughters definitely need to have a healthy male model against whom to measure future suitors, as much as a son needs a good role model to become a good man. But in some cases it remains more important for the girl child to continue to live with her mother during adolescence.

The Virtue of Patience. If the secondary parent is patient during the first three to four years, he will have a child who is eager to bond with him because she has not been injured by betrayal and because she wants a daddy like any other child. The tricky part for judges and evaluators is to identify how much the primary parent is already involved in order to preclude creating an attachment break while attempting to facilitate another attachment with the father. In other words, sending a one-year-old on a two-day visit with a father who is not already a primary caregiver too will create an attachment break that will be proven afterwards by a refusal of the small child to make eye contact with the mother *or father* while being held. The worst-case scenario would be breaking a bond with mother for a child to "bond" with his father, especially if that father comes and goes.

The right of the other parent to take the child rather than putting her into day care or leaving her with a stepparent for extended periods should be foremost. A child should not have to attend day care, especially if another parent wants the child.

It is important to note that when a divorced father sees his child two weekends per month and two additional overnights, he is possibly paying more attention to his child than he did before the divorce. If he is truly engaged with the child during this time period, the child is blessed. There is no need for 50/50 physical custody unless a parent is trying to avoid child support, which would be shameful.

Child Support. When there is a young child, a primary parent must be able to afford to stay home, hence child support. In my opinion, child support does not need to be paid to a mother who puts her child in day care or who chooses to work (unless they literally cannot legally live on the child support allotted). I do not quite understand the necessity of the win-win/lose-lose scenario wherein one parent gets primary custody *and* receives child support when the child is old enough to be in school.

The parents might not fight as much over the child and there may not be as much acrimony in the divorce if there is more equity in the custody arrangement and the child support. Inequity can be the cause of seeking custody and can disguise real motives in both parents. I believe child support should be a major issue until the child begins kindergarten if the father can afford it. After the age of five, the mother can work and child support could supplement her income, meaning she would not need as much.

If the child support issue was not so taxing on the father of a school-aged child, he might be more comfortable with weekly dinners or overnights between two long weekends per month where pick-up and drop-off would always be at the school. This would leave room for the child to make friends in her mother's neighborhood and it gives the child a sense of a primary residence. I also believe if the father lives near the mother, the father could have more time with the child, taking him to extra curricular activities and can even take the child home more often for three-hour dinners with homework. Arrangements should include a rhythm to which the child can adapt and depend.

Move-Aways. I believe if the primary caregiver moves away from the other parent, they should have to do the bulk of the driving. They should have to pay the plane fare if it's that sort of distance.

Sometimes I hear the mother has to move away to be near her support network. Unless the father is harmful to the child or fails to pay the most minimal child support, I think the father's proximity is more important, especially if he is willing to exercise a right of first refusal and provide childcare instead of relatives. If too much childcare or extended family is needed, then the mother is not the primary caregiver. Perhaps the father should have primary custody and the mother can visit weekends.

Sometimes I hear the father has to leave for a better job, in which case he needs to forfeit any claim to joint custody. He should plan on renting a small unit near the child's primary residence for visiting with the child.

During longer holidays an older child can visit his residence out of state, alternating those holidays with the primary parent. It is important to remember that children like the weekends to play with their friends in the neighborhood. When they have to go visit a parent on the weekend and forfeit time to develop friendships, resentment may understandably develop.

Move-aways should provide for a temporary residence for the visiting parent and the child should not be asked to fly as a rule. When it is time for longer visits to the other parent's residence, the parent who moved away should pay for the plane fare.

When a mother leaves the state with the child due to financial necessity and accommodations have not been made to afford visits by the father, the father may want to take this opportunity to put aside money for the child's college so one day he can explain that even though it was too difficult to visit, he saved money for his child to go to college.

When there Is More than One Child. I have predominantly written about custody for one child, not two or more children. I do not believe the needs of siblings to be together trump the needs of children to be with their parents except in the unusual case where both parents have been insufficient and the primary attachment is between siblings. When I hear a mother argue that she should have primary custody because the child at issue is more bonded with her sibling or step-sibling than her parent, I am suspicious.

Also, since I believe custody arrangements need to be age appropriate, I believe arrangements need to be made more on a case-by-case basis than for all children together. Of course, the agreement should be as uncomplicated as possible no matter how many kids are involved.

Each child, whether a subject of a custody dispute or living in an intact home, should have significant quality one-on-one alone time with each parent.

Step-Parents. I strongly recommend if you are parenting according to this theory, you insist your intended spouse learn Causal Theory. Hopefully both parents and their new mates can all be on the same page.

There are essentially two roles from which a step-parent can choose. After the child has had a chance to know you, you can check with them to see what they prefer. You can be the child's coach and teacher, letting yourself be someone to whom they turn for help and advice, in which case they may choose to call you by your first name with your blessing. This role will create the least friction for both of you. However, this role includes the right to establish your own bar in this relationship. The child must practice relationship skills with you and vice versa. If you have an issue with the child, the child needs to work it out with you, not run to the parent. If and when the child turns to the parent to avoid working things out with you, the parent needs to back you up and send him back. If the parent disagrees with you, that disagreement needs to take place at another time away from the child, assuming you are not acting in an abusive manner.

If your mate has a low bar set for the child's ethics, you may have to watch them reap the consequences of an entitled child. You can politely warn them once every six months, but other than that you have no power or influence. Can you live with that? If you are already married, you may want to see a therapist to mediate this disagreement. I have experienced step-parents coming to me to seek help to reason with the other parent about their child. One latency age child strolled into my office with a t-shirt that read, "Lady's Man." I mediated and agreed with the father, and they never returned.

If all parents are on the same page, you can even give the child a consequence for disrespecting you or for breaking rules of ethics. For example, if she needs a ride to school and doesn't ask nicely, you can decline. If she lies to you about her homework being done, you can tell her that you are disappointed in her. If you make a cake, you can refuse to give her a piece until her books and belongings are put away. You may choose to talk to the child briefly about feelings and choices when he rebels or rejects your authority. Remember this is a grieving child and it is not appropriate for you to be jealous of him or the other biological parent. If those feelings come up, get yourself into therapy now. Only if you don't practice relationship skills with the child should the parent step in to mediate until you learn the skills.

The other role for a step-parent is that of a parent. I recommend this only when there is no actual parent filling this role or when the child seeks affection from that parent. For example, if Dad moved away or is in prison, it is appropriate for the step-parent to move into the role of a father with a different word (like "Pa") than the one the child has for his biological father (Dad). In this case it is imperative that the step-parent be in the correct theory and that there be more affection and attention than discipline. When the step-parent takes this role with the negotiated blessings of the present biological parents, then that parent must not intervene during a disciplining moment.

Another time for the step-parent to be in the role of the full parent is when the child has very disruptive behavior for lack of a strong parent or from attachment breaks. Either way, the child needs a strong fence and somebody's got to do it. You need to represent love, strength, consistency and justice with an even temperament.

Needed Research. I would like to see research of children from divorcing parents in custody disputes that would be evaluated by some simple criteria, including the conclusions of the evaluators as compared to other children of cooperative divorce, before shared custody begins. I would like to see these same children as young adults in a follow-up study wherein they would be interviewed at age eighteen, twenty-five and perhaps thirty-five. They would be invited to register their thoughts and feelings, offer their experiences for the record and allow themselves to be evaluated for their adult traits as compared to a control group. The results of these interviews would hopefully help mitigate the experiences of children to follow. I would like to know if they were as aware and candid at all ages or whether their opinions became clearer and stronger or more vague and weaker as time progressed. We could compare different custody arrangements of different types of circumstances and their effects as compared to grown children of intact families. It would be also interesting to see how well the children were originally understood and what factors were the most influential, both positive and negative.

Rules of Shared Custody. Parental Alienation is a dangerous outgrowth of shared custody and revenge ethics. (Experience has shown that in most cases, but not all, Mom is the primary caregiver and Dad is secondary. As such, again in this section we use the general terms Mom and Dad for ease of reference, acknowledging that actual roles may be reversed in your personal scenario.) In order to avoid the long-term harm to children of parental alienation, I offer the following guidelines, many of which have already been stated elsewhere but bear repeating in this context.

- DO establish and maintain a primary caregiver for young children. In the first few years of life, a primary custody parent is essential for a healthy child. In the grammar school years, children need a relationship with both parents. If you think you can convince the court that you should be the primary parent and the child should be given over to you, know that they have heard it all and it will not look good for you unless you have legitimate, damaging evidence against the other parent.
- DO defend the stay-at-home mom role, whether it is you or your child's other parent. When possible, a custody arrangement involving a young child should provide for a stay-at-home Mom in the early years.
- DON'T complain that the other parent has the better schedule if you are using the SCSS Schedule. The SCCS is fair. Many Moms actually complain that Dad, oftentimes "the weekend parent", has the better deal because the he gets to share more fun play time with the child while Mom is the disciplinarian, tutor, cook, chauffeur, *etc.* Arguing against it

is not productive and need not be true. It's up to you to enjoy your role.

- DO put the child's well-being first. If the child is symptomatic, Dad needs to have a generous heart for the child's sake. He needs to visit, perhaps in Mom's home and perhaps with Mom peeking in and leaving. Gradually the child will handle more. Mom should be as supportive as possible of the child's relationship with the father while representing the child's need to maintain a continuous attachment. Remember that an unattached child will go to a stranger and disregard Mom. That doesn't mean it is okay to follow a normal separation schedule, which would add to the child's pathology. Mom and Dad need to work out a schedule in the spirit of a healthy attachment and stick to it while being as reasonably flexible with one another as possible. If the child shows evidence of stress over the visits, cut back until she no longer stresses to accommodate known or unknown factors.
- DON'T break a bond to make a bond. Do not break a child's attachment with Mom in order to create an attachment with Dad. Such a move will backfire because a broken attachment creates a fear of intimacy forever, in addition to a fear of abandonment. All children need fathers and will want more and more contact with them naturally. Without fathers in their lives, they will feel abnormal and if they can't idealize their fathers, they will feel cheated.
- DO be patient. A child with a secure attachment to one parent will have secure attachments in general, especially toward their fathers. Wait for your baby to mature securely. Don't be guilty of tearing your child apart unless you know for sure that you are the stronger parent, the one with whom the baby is more attached and that the other parent is truly putting your child in jeopardy.
- DO have representation of both sexes in the child's life. Children need models of both sexes. They need someone of the opposite sex to model how to be treated by the opposite sex and they need someone of the same sex to model how to behave as their own sex. When there is no such model available in the form of a parent, find someone such as a grandfather or aunt who would love the job and can be trusted to be continually involved in the child's life. Introduce role models as early as possible.
- DON'T put the kids in the middle. A common mistake of separated parents is putting children in the middle of their dispute. Children absorb the energy like sponges and are deeply injured by it whether or not you can see it.
- DO offer some stability in an otherwise unstable situation. To offer the child some stability in an otherwise unstable situation, perhaps Mom and Dad could alternate their locations rather than making the child move back-and-forth, as previously discussed, or set up an agreement and rhythm that has the lowest possible stress on the child.
- DON'T undermine the other parent's discipline; if possible, support the other parent's discipline. A child will learn to play two parents against each other once he internalizes that his parents are enemies or that all he has to do to disobey is walk out the back door to the other rescuing parent. This torn child is going to have a major personality disturbance, very possibly the one I call Approach-Avoidant. Be careful. (See Chapter 2: Preventive Diagnosis.)
- We know that the child who has weak attachments from bouncing around without a primary caregiver does not attach well to anyone, including Dad. If a child is well-attached to Mom, she will also attach well to Dad within a few years as she develops. If Mom has the primary relationship (rarely is there a 50/50 attachment prior to a split) and Dad is also a good parent and is given increased time spent with the child, by

the time she is four or five, Dad has an almost equal attachment. He can feel secure relinquishing 50/50 time so the child can have her necessary primary residence.

- DON'T convey to the child that she should miss you. As a worried mother you could be telegraphing to your daughter that she should miss you, a message she will begin to carry. You don't really get to tell your child that she can contact you whenever she wants, whoever she's with (especially Dad). Such messages create anxiety in her that she *should* be staying in touch with you. Soon, she will wear your abandonment and begin to feel responsible for your pain. That is a heavy load that will backfire some day. Symptoms may include bedwetting beyond five years of age, possibly indicating a child who had to grow up too soon and who feels too responsible too young.

- DON'T be played. Some parents get it into their heads that if they really love their child, they will fight for her to the end, even if it means both parties go broke doing it. That is not good parenting, unless you are fighting to protect your child from a parent-predator *for real*. Frankly, one of the worst consequences of shared custody is when the child learns to play the parents against one another. You begin looking for the parenting flaws of the other parent to the detriment of your child, who needs to idealize each parent. Your child will begin to lose respect for the grownups, both of you. The older child will play each parent and become a master manipulator who is never happy where she is, always wanting to be somewhere else. She may develop the art of telling people what they want to hear and become a gossip. She may be prone to affairs and infidelity because she has not learned the virtue of fidelity, since to be loyal to one parent is to betray the other. Lastly, she may later resent you as an adult for depriving her of a secure relationship with the other parent.

- DON'T sweat the small stuff. As you have seen from this book, what matters is that the child has a secure attachment, healthy separation, positive role models, positive mirroring, consistent limits and a home free from abuse. Beyond that, their sleeping schedule, the size of the apartment or the bed, what they eat (within reason), whether the parent swears and so forth, are not reasons to intervene in how the other parent parents. You chose him and made a baby with him. It doesn't matter if he is bad at potty training or other details of care. Your child will survive. It is more damaging to your child's psyche to bicker and nitpick over details of his life than to protect him from his father's ineptness.

- DO take interest in the child's life when away from you too. When your child is with his other parent, that person is the parent. Accept it. He is in his other life away from you. Your best tactic is to be interested in his entire life. Encourage him to be open about his experiences and to express his feelings to a sympathetic ear when things are hard. If you turn to rescuing, your child will shut down and tell you less and less.

- DON'T compete for affection. Your child wants and needs to adore you. If you are insecure, get therapy. If the other parent plays unscrupulously like buying all the best toys, just be consistent. Your child will see through it sooner or later. If you have integrity you will look good. If you act petty she will suffer your lack of ethics and faith. She will remember it in the long run and you can count on hearing about it later in her life. Some grown children distance from the parent that caused them to look suspiciously at the other parent, feeling they were tricked and cheated.

- DO live in dignity. Don't act like a victim. Take responsibility for the quality

of your life and become a heroic role model for your child.
- DON'T parent the other parent's parenting whether you are living together or apart.

Sharing Holidays. Divorced parents need to share holidays with their children. They usually set something up where they alternate each year. Sometimes one parent will regularly ask for Christmas Eve while the other will ask for Christmas morning.

When it comes to sharing holidays with the grandparents, it seems to get overcomplicated. Some come from a distance; some live nearby. Those who come from a distance still need to alternate with grandparents who live nearby unless a contract can be created whereby the one who travels and comes less often can have more time when they are in town. Otherwise, I recommend alternating every year. Perhaps the child's father's parents come for Christmas one year and the child's mother's parents come for Christmas the next year. Sharing holidays works well if one parent has Jewish parents and the other parent has Christian parents. I make the following recommendations in accord with American culture.

- Go to grandparents' house for Thanksgiving with the children and enjoy a day and the meal there. You may have to alternate your visits every year. Grandparents should not have to come to you for Thanksgiving.
- Grandparents go to the home of their grandchildren for Christmas. They should arrive in the early afternoon on Christmas day. Christian children or children whose parents celebrate Christmas need to wake up in their own beds to see what Santa brought. Additionally, their parents get to be alone with their children Christmas morning.
- Children of Jewish dissent can alternate years or days of Hanukkah. These holidays may best be spent at the grandparents' house, since it's a holiday of ancestors, for the first and/or last days of Hanukkah. Some evenings should be designated for the core family at home.
- The entire Mother's Day is a day of privilege for mom, and it belongs to the mother with the youngest children. I don't think it is appropriate for her to have to make the rounds to see her mom, her mother-in-law or any stepparents on her special day. If there are too many "mothers," let the one with the youngest children stay home and receive guests. Dad, send your own mother flowers and a card and/or invite her to come by for pie (that you buy and serve), but stay home with your wife most of the day. Bring her flowers and cook for her or take her out. And be sure you take the children out the day before to buy her a card and gift (if they didn't already make one). Grandpa, celebrate Mother's Day with your wife. Grandma, celebrate Father's Day with your husband. The same guidelines apply to Father's Day.
- Spend children's birthdays at home. Invite grandparents to the celebration, provided they get along. If one grandparent is particularly contentious, that grandparent should be invited to the end of the party or for another day, if they are invited at all.

How to Separate

One could arbitrarily say that the process of separation begins at about eight months or one year, although babies actually begin to separate when they begin to act on their own behalf. You might say that separation takes off when they learn to walk. In a way, they are separating while they are attaching. If they are not threatened with the loss of you, their separation is a gradual process that peaks at about four years of age, leaving the child excited about the prospect of exploring the world, just in time to go to school.

Parents facilitate separation gradually

from about eight months by supporting acts of autonomy.
- Introduce a transitional object during symbiosis at about 3-9 months.
- Begin separations gradually. Allow the child to leave you.
- Ensure the child has his transitional object when he leaves.
- Tell him how much you love him and how much you will miss him. Come up with a special phrase from you to him, like "Go have an adventure," or "Learn something new."
- Ensure when the child leaves you that he does not develop the thought that if he leaves you he loses you.
- Use your Childcare Checklist.
- Have caretakers attend good parenting classes if possible.

Use Transitional Objects. Transitional objects facilitate separation and reduce shock on an infant or small child. If the transitional object reminds the child of the parent, it could be a great help in reducing the impact of premature separations. Use objects that have satin or silk because they feel like skin. Use objects that are easily replaceable in case they get lost. (Sears has a line of satin-edged baby blankets they've sold for 30+ years.)

Introduce the transitional object during symbiosis in such a way that the object reminds the infant of you. For example, when you nurse, you put the satin edge near the infant's hands or sometimes you carry the object around on you for the infant to see. You give it to the infant or toddler at naptime with the implication that you believe it will be comforting. When you go in the car make a big deal, "Where's your blue blanket?"

First Briefcase. Along with the security blanket, introduce your child's first briefcase. When he just begins toddling you always remember to bring his briefcase. It can be a cute little lightweight child-size carryall that has a few important items in it.

Teach the child to keep track of this "briefcase." Wherever he goes for the rest of his childhood and adult life, he will always have something to bring with him so he will have the habit of organizing what that is and becoming mindful of his own transitions.

WARNING: Monitor this endeavor so your child does not develop back problems at a young age. Keep it very light. Let your toddler carry his (lightweight) briefcase and help him make sure it's always with him with special belongings inside. Make a point of remembering it aloud, just as you make a point of remembering his blanket or security object. The goal here is to hardwire his capacity to remember his things.

Never ever scold him for failing to remember. You are responsible for helping him remember. With enough attention, the intention to remember it will come naturally. You can also teach him the trick of whenever you leave a room, turn around to see if you left anything behind or left a trace (for others to clean up).

Checklist for Finding a Pre-School
- Are there any complaints from the Better Business Bureau or any online customer satisfaction web pages?
- Are you free to leave and return again and again over a period of many days to gradually extend your time leaving your child?
- Even though they are a day care or a pre-school, do they appreciate attachment issues?
- Are you free to visit the school as long as you like without notifying the school in advance?
- Does the school accept any special accommodations?
- How long has each teacher worked there?
- Are the teachers paid well?
- How do they handle a meltdown?
- How do they handle an issue between children?

- If your child cannot sleep during a nap, what would they do?
- Can your child bring a transitional object?

Going to Pre-School
- Visit the pre-school, leave for five minutes and return. If this is the school you choose, begin increasing your time away slowly. You are acclimating your child to your absence and proving to him that you will return. Then take ten, then fifteen, then twenty minutes, then one-half hour, then forty-five minutes, then one hour, to one and one-half hour, to two hours, three hours, four hours and then, whatever you *have* to do.
- Before arriving at the school in the morning, talk to the child about what kind of day he might like to have. Does he think he can make it happen?
- When dropping the child off, walk him to the door.
- Get down on your knees and hug and kiss goodbye.
- Maybe you can say, "I love you. I don't want to go. But you have fun and learn something new to tell me about."
- Incorporate rituals in parting. Say something like, "Go have an adventure," or "Have fun learning," or "Learn something to tell me about."
- Make sure the pre-school honors his security blanket.
- See if the teacher can help him leave you. Say, "Okay, now *you* leave Mommy. Let me see you find a friend." (The last admonition may be asking too much; you decide.)

Troubleshooting: The child doesn't cooperate in the morning.
- Is the child too young for this?
- Has the child had sufficient bonding or time with the parent?
- Has the child had attachment breaks in the past?
- Has the child already suffered premature separation?
- Has the child had enough of you lately?
- Did you prepare his clothes and supplies the night before?
- Did he get enough sleep?
- Did you get yourself ready before getting the child up?
- Did you allow enough time so as not to rush the child?
- Do you have a fun morning ritual?
- Are you in a good mood in the morning?
- Do you boss your child around in the morning?
- Do you offer the child choices?
- Do you help him get ready?
- Do you offer the child enough security and limits?
- Has there been a recent and/or sudden upset or change in the family structure or process?
- Is there a problem with the school?
- What kinds of fears does he have? What doesn't he like about going to this school? (Talk to the child on the way to school about the upcoming separation.)
- Are there problems in the school you don't know about?
- What is the child telling you he or she needs?
  - Is she saying she needs to finish being a baby? (*e.g.*, there is a new baby in the house)
  - Is she saying she needs more empathy? ("The teacher doesn't like me.")
  - Is he saying he feels empty without you? (*i.e.*, hasn't internalized enough positive sense of self from you? A bonding issue?) "Don't make me go."

Troubleshooting: The child doesn't want to go to bed.
- Has the child had sufficient time with the parent?
- Is bedtime appropriate to the child's age and needs, or is it possibly too early?
- Does he have a nightlight?
- Does he have a transitional object?
- Is a bedtime ritual in place?

Separation Rituals

Incorporate rituals in parting. Do the same things in the same order every time you're preparing to separate. Examples follow.

Daytime Separation Ritual
- parent gets ready first
- five minute wake-up conversation ("How did you sleep?", "What did you dream?", discuss the day's plans)
- breakfast
- wash face and brush teeth
- get dressed
- get blanket or other transitional object
- leave for school
- discuss landmarks on the way
- talk about positives and negatives of school
- talk about how you feel during your day since you can't be with your child

Nighttime Separation Ritual I
- family dinner
- bath
- pajamas
- choose morning clothes
- bedtime snack
- brush teeth
- bedtime story
- goodnight ritual (kiss/hug, last words, transitional object, nightlight on, lights off)

Nighttime Separation Ritual II
- dinner
- dishes to sink
- brush teeth
- do homework
- place homework by front door
- television, games or free time
- prepare clothes for next day
- read
- parent checks in with the child (sits for a while)
- child sets alarm
- lights out

Insecure Attachments

Children with insecure attachments are similar to children with broken attachments: they don't trust. One child might have never attached (and may never suffer abandonment), even though she had a stay-at-home mother. Another child may have had a loving and attuned parent but was nevertheless abandoned. As much as the child who was loved and abandoned is deeply injured in her core self, she did assimilate some intellectual sharpness and neural connections before the betrayal. The child who never knew bonding and attachment, especially by a safe, attuned parent, will likely have compromised intelligence, a bitter cold heart or an empty sense of self. The abandoned child will feel a continuous fear of loss, with a sore spot that can be triggered by any future relationship, in anticipation of loss. A parent may be a stay-at-home mom, but if she doesn't engage with her child on a regular basis, she may do more harm than a mother who alternately works and engages with her child. In a sense, one child may grow up with a perennial broken heart while another may seem to have no heart at all. One child may just learn to tune out while the other never turned in. All the while a child of day care, who is insecurely attached, but attached nevertheless, may be bouncing off the walls with heartbreak due to so many tenuous attachments.

The unattached child will never be as fully human or humane as he could have been, something he may be judged and blamed for later in life.

The secure child who is abandoned once may never trust again. If an incident upsets the assumption of trust when his parent "disappears," it will leave a lasting impact for a few reasons:
- He has learned that he is not secure after all. Mommy could leave again at any time out of the blue. He can take nothing for granted. He has no idea when

she'll be back or why she left. Nothing can be assumed anymore.
- He has learned that he cannot trust her love for him anymore. The love of his life, his mother, is perfectly willing to leave him. Even if she leaves him and comes back on a regular basis, she is willing to leave him with someone else.
- He feels betrayed, helpless and hopeless about his future. He can't count on her anymore, but he is afraid to let her know because then she might permanently leave him. He knows he needs her to survive, at least for now. He has learned that she does not know how much pain she causes him by her leaving. Or, maybe she does. In his eyes, she does not consider him important enough to stop leaving. She does not value him enough to stay.
- He has learned that she does not understand his emotional needs. She does not realize that her leaving breaks his heart and changes his view of himself and the world. Or worse, maybe she does know. This small child doesn't have the communication skills or experience to understand that she'll be back or that her leaving is not a betrayal.

The younger the infant, the less separation she can handle without creating an attachment break. The older the child, the more separation she can handle if her bonding has been secure up to that point. If her bonding has been rocky all along, every additional separation further alters her personality structure and a major commitment is now required to heal her. The healing commitment is much more demanding than the original task of getting her through the first few years of life looking healthy, happy and secure.

In order to understand how she feels, we need to remember how an adult feels when she finds out her husband is having an affair, only the feeling is many times stronger and more harmful because an adult is more inoculated to betrayal and an infant is delicate and still forming. For a baby, the pain is excruciating. Some bang their fragile heads against a wall or the floor to distract themselves from the pain. Does that tell you how bad it hurts?

Premature Separations

Infants take everything for granted. Their current course of events is what they believe will always be their course of events. If the infant is treated well, he develops a positive attitude about life, that life is good and he is good.

Premature separations change everything, almost as if the secure attachment never existed. Signs of premature separations are the same as signs of insecure attachments. They include:
- failure to thrive or crib death
- clinging behavior
- anaclytic depression, including self-rocking and head-banging
- "changing the subject" (pointing away when the focus is too intimate)
- arching of the back and pushing away when being held
- rigid body while being held or carried
- self-soothing (*i.e.,* thumb sucking, hair twirling, fiddling, bouncing, or pulling out own hair or picking at skin)
- withdrawal
- nightmares
- crying and raging so hard the infant throws up
- withdrawing due to severe neglect, perhaps looking dull in the eyes and retarded (and can even lead to retardation)
- refusal to make eye contact when held up close
- bossy personality
- insecure personality

Broken Attachments. The first few years of life are the most detrimental time for mother/primary caregiver and child to be separated. The less a child can count on her mother to be there when she cries, the less attached and secure she becomes. She's fallen in love once and if she learns she can't count on her mother to be true to her, to stay with her, she'll withdraw her love. She'll decide she can't love anyone or count on anyone because they will abandon her too. She's on her own. Her little personality is forming around an island consciousness:

- "I don't need anyone."
- "I'm strong and I will take a position of power and stay there."
- "I'm not weak."
- "No one will see me weak, ever."
- "I'm not giving my heart away again to anyone."
- "I'll manipulate them to meet my needs."
- "I'll tell them what they want to hear."

A child of a broken attachment, an unattached child or an underattached child will "change the subject" if you get too close. He will avoid eye contact in his parents' arms by looking all around the room, pointing to anything to avoid paying intimate attention to his parents. Often the parents will exclaim, "Oh! He's so curious about the world!" Later, this same child will change the subject in school when too much focus is expected, especially if he feels vulnerable or on the spot. He will become distractible, especially if the topic is too personal, or he feels exposed for not knowing. He may use this same tactic with an intimate partner if they get too close.

He is someone who has lost the ability to trust, had too many disappointments, now fears vulnerability and is already turning himself into a pretzel to adapt.

The two best tests of a child's ability to bond and trust are in his eye contact with his parent while being held and in his ability to melt into his parent's arms, molding her body to the parent carrying her while being held. A healthy baby will make comfortable eye contact with the parents while up close in their arms. A child who is threatened by intimacy will arch his back and push away if his mother holds him too closely. Ironically, he may ultimately appear to be affectionate with anyone but his mother, including a total stranger. If he wants something, he will assume dominance, give a kiss or make close eye contact to ask for something he wants. He will establish affection on his terms.

Separation Issues

Babies who never fully bonded or who had broken or damaged attachments are weaker at creating individuation. They move toward individuation with trepidation or with inauthentic strength.

Childhood Disorders of Insufficient or Insecure Bonding

- Separation Anxiety Disorder. Child suffers distress upon separation from major attachment figure or upon leaving home. Child fears something will happen to self or caregiver by way of an accident, getting lost, kidnapping, *etc.* Child resists separation including going to school. Child fears being alone without a significant other. Child fears going to sleep alone or away from home and has repeated nightmares involving separation. Child develops physical symptoms when threats of separation occur.
- Attention Deficit/Hyperactivity Disorder (ADHD), whether Predominantly Inattentive or Hyperactive Impulsive Type. These hyperactive children are bouncing off the walls because they feel an ongoing state of major separation anxiety. Their bodies have an overabundance of the stress hormone cortisol (Brandtjen & Verny, 2001). There are other reasons for ADHD, specifically having parents who are not tuned in, or having feelings no one wants to hear about. This causes a barrage of unprocessed thoughts and experiences, and children don't know what to do with this growing internal dialogue. When parents aren't dialoguing empathetically with their children

about their experiences, they are at high risk for ADHD. They don't know how to process their experiences by themselves.
- Attention Deficit Disorder (ADD). These children are distractible without being hyperactive. They are lost in thought. Many of them are depressed. Some are just out of body and not present to their lives. Depression can result from loss, especially feelings of abandonment brought on by day care on top of previous abandonments. This can only happen if the child enjoyed a loving attachment preceding their loss. Those who are out of body, so to speak, have suffered a trauma that they have never been allowed or helped to process. They may not even realize their issue anymore because they have learned to deny and override their thoughts and feelings. If you ask them why they did something, they may not able to tell you without some practice.
- Reactive Attachment Disorder (RAD). RAD kids are often misdiagnosed as having ADHD because their behavior is out of control. They have suffered a failure to attach created by an unresponsive parent or they have suffered one or more major abandonments. In other words the infant was betrayed and has decided she will never trust again so she withholds love and vulnerability from her parent. She will look around the room, "changing the subject" when she's in mother's arms rather than make eye contact. There are actually two types of RAD.
  - Disinhibited Type. "Indiscriminant sociability or a lack of selectivity in the choice of attachment figures." This child appears to bond with anyone or everyone except his own parents and/or the bond with the parent is feigned to some degree while the child keeps up his protective shield. This child learns to con and charm adults while never trusting them. He may be an adorable cute little man, but he is actually presuming power over adults. He is extroverted, bossy, generally unlikable, refusing to acknowledge authority, as he can't trust grown-ups and has no regard for rules. He may become diagnosed with Oppositional Defiant Disorder or worse, Conduct Disorder. As an adult, he may be one day labeled as narcissistic or borderline, or further out the continuum, he may one day become diagnosed with an Antisocial Personality Disorder.
  - Inhibited Type. "Persistent failure to initiate and respond to most social interactions in a developmentally appropriate way" [Diagnostic and Statistic Manual for psychotherapists (*DSM-IV-TR*)]. The severity of the break and the capacity of the parent to repair the break determine the severity of the adult symptoms. This child is very introverted, like a wounded bird. He's so shy he seems chronically injured. He too has suffered major abandonment after having enjoyed a brief attachment. He may become an extremely dependent, avoidant or paranoid personality or even schizophrenic depending upon how things go as he becomes disciplined.
- Aspergers Syndrome or Autism. Aspergers is less severe than autism. Children with Aspergers seem rather stiff or mechanical, but they function in the world with some inhibited social skills. Children with autism have a great deal of difficulty connecting with other human beings and often their academic abilities are impaired too. They are Thing Children, not People Children. They stimulate themselves with repetitive actions as a form of self-soothing.

There are no identified genes for autism even though it is on the increase like an epidemic that results from foreign causes. Some children may have become autistic for biological but not genetic reasons (such as vaccinations that were too potent or some other invasive toxin before or after birth). Other children may have suffered a medical procedure or physical illness that was excruciating beyond their ability to cope. In a painful, bitter moment, they concluded that adults couldn't help and replaced their craving for nurturing with a conviction that there is no such thing and no such safety. After that, only self-soothing and tangible objects could comfort them.

Parents can create autism by severe neglect of their infant. Some mothers who had postpartum depression may be holding the world's best kept secret: that she left her child in the crib all day, picked him up and met Dad at the door saying, "OK, now it's your turn." Even dad didn't know about the lack of contact. I have known three such mothers who broke down and told me similar stories, often infused with their own bitterness. Maybe the mother was barely nurtured herself as an infant.

Mothers who return to work right after birth may have autistic children, depending on how much they are neglected by the unattached caregiver. They may become diagnosed with pediatric bipolar disorder or develop other severe symptoms of personality.

All these children suffered such events that disabled their ability to bond. Some organizations are available for parents who have children diagnosed with Autism. Then the doctor, friends, relatives and father commiserate about how sad it is, without any inquiry into the isolation of the child. Some members join with their secrets intact, agreeing with one another in a silent or unconscious conspiracy that their children's problems must be genetic or biological, that it couldn't possibly be be a parenting issue. I recall one group called Mother Warriors regularly compares notes on what they have tried in order to heal their children, also comparing notes on what works. These mothers are having some significant success, probably because they are giving their children focused attention.

To a lesser degree, dismissing parents (once avoidant children themselves) may create avoidant children who become dismissing adults. These parents may have dangled keys and objects before their child to entertain her or to keep her from crying because they didn't know how to socially engage with the child. Such parents are not good at relating to adults either because their parents didn't relate sufficiently to them. They would be incapable of assessing or implementing a healthy attachment without coaching. They would score high in avoidance on the Adult Attachment Assessment herein.

Adult Disorders from Early Failed Attachments
- Generalized Anxiety Disorder. Separation anxiety may lead to Generalized Anxiety Disorder. Abandonment issues, fears of leaving or being left may be so strong that the grown child may be willing to suffer spousal abuse, commit spousal abuse (as a means of preventing a mate from leaving as well as scapegoating his rage against his mother), be driven to stalk and perform checking-up behaviors, have panic attacks, suffer from agoraphobia and be diagnosable as Dependent Personality.
- Depression. Children who have been abandoned may slump into a depression that never lifts, even as adults.
- Borderline Personality Disorder. Children of erratic bonding and those who have been repeatedly abandoned and revisited are at high risk for BPD, especially if the abandonments were followed by rough discipline or abuse.

These children are so injured by attachment trauma, they often behave in ways that invite mean forms of discipline. Further, they often invite sexual abuse by telegraphing their desperate neediness and (feelings of) worthlessness to those who would prey on weakness and isolation.

- Adult Sociopathic or Dark Narcissistic Traits. The adult RAD child (Disinhibited Type) will also have contempt for authority and is always in power. Vulnerability is his worst enemy; he would rather die than be vulnerable. Underneath his tough guy routine is terror of ever being vulnerable to anyone again. As an adult, he is capable of power games and committing high crimes under one's nose. He may be a violating gynecologist, sinister judge or jaded politician. He may commit incest with his own children (consider Jose Menendez who would "rather be feared than loved") or he may develop Antisocial Personality Disorder.
- Adult Psychotic or Psychopathic Disorders (not the clinical diagnoses). These grown children have an inability to relate to other adults without paranoia, mistrust, self-consciousness, rage, delusions, psychotic projections, *etc.* They could easily become rapists or killers, depending on other childhood experiences. Usually these children also experience extreme abuse and humiliation. Ted Kaczynski (the Unabomber) experienced abandonment in his first year of life from medical isolation at a hospital for ten days. Eric Harris and Dylan Klebold (committed the Columbine High School massacre) suffered from chronic emotional neglect by role-playing parents who appeared to live normal lives. Additionally, Harris was on psychotropic medications that could have put him over the edge (Breggin, 1999).
- Schizophrenia. As children, schizophrenics suffer four injuries: 1) insufficient bonding that includes sensory deprivation and a profound lack of touch. They feel invisible, transparent and porous, as if they don't have a container in which to exist; 2) intrusive parents who presume to read the child's mind with invasive messages like, "I know what you are really thinking," "I know you don't mean what you said," "No one would believe you;" 3) a major mind-blowing, terror producing experience where no one says, "Wow, that was terrible!" or, "Wow, that was wrong!"; and 4) the child is not allowed his own point of view or perspective and cannot safely tell anyone how his life is going.

Repairing Insecure Attachments
- Reread prior section on bonding to grasp the importance of the concept.
- Introduce a security blanket with the rocking chair.
- Learn a good lullaby.
- Refuel with eye contact, special words and personal communication. If child won't make eye contact, you can give her an M & M every time she does, or pat her or stroke her hair gently.
- Consider a bottle again for a little while in a "frame," a special appointed time for re-bonding.
- Consider containing your child if the above endeavors do not repair the bond. (See Containing in Chapter 3: Healing)
- Seek an attachment therapist. Read up on healing broken attachments.

Jeopardy in Day Care

Please don't shoot the messenger. NO ONE CAN TAKE YOUR PLACE. If you let someone attempt to be your substitute, your child will not be as amazing as he was born to be.

Major research studies by both the National Institute of Child and Human Development (Belsky, 2006) and the University of Minnesota (Brandtjen & Verny,

2006) were definitive. In the largest long-term study in the United States on day care, NICHD found that the more time children spent in childcare, the more likely they were to be aggressive. They found that some factors such as a mother's sensitivity could partially offset the aggressiveness but not completely (Belsky, 2006). The UM study (Brandjten & Verny, 2006) found that children in day care had higher levels of cortisol, a stress hormone, on the days they were in childcare centers than on days at home. The levels were even higher in shy children. Another study, which consolidated seven other studies, found that the younger children went to day care the higher their cortisol levels in day care, especially children under the age of three (Vermeer and van IJzedoorn, 2006).

This and other ongoing research provides information supporting what we at PaRC Foundation have been saying for years, but industry journals have failed to report the results of these studies in full. Professional journals have often found commentators who interpret the findings for publication by claiming they still believe higher quality day care centers would not create these problems. The journal, *Child Development* (University of Michigan), published data with nine commentaries from nine reputed childhood experts, most of whom advised parents on ways they might mitigate the results of day care (*vs.* bluntly stating day care causes damage and parents should avoid it). As usual, research that makes parents uncomfortable has been presented timidly, almost apologetically. Professionals are afraid of worrying the public. Most of them want us to feel good about leaving our children in day care. They put a pro-parent spin on our children's unmet needs for the sake of the grown-ups, at the expense of small children.

Most of the so-called childhood experts miss the point when they talk about quality day care. Children don't need better day care. They need their mothers. They don't need nice things in the early years that can only be afforded by a two-parent income, or placement in day care so parents can get a head start on saving for their child's college tuition. They need their mothers.

Some want us to feel good about day care because they need us in the work force. Some want this because they truly believe our choices won't affect our children negatively or that parenting doesn't make that big a difference, but that education does. Some want this because they profit from pharmaceuticals like Ritalin. Some want this because they profit from day care. Some just don't want to hurt our feelings. Probably all have a pro-parent philosophy on parenting stemming from their own childhood.

Recently, a pregnant client of mine walked into my office and presented a brochure about how mothers can learn to deal with the guilt of leaving their baby. This brochure was published by a local parenting magazine, *LA Parent*.

Our socioeconomic system has become highly invested in and dependent upon day care. Parents seek reassurance that day care is a good idea. Research is funded to prove that day care is safe for children, even necessary, and that we cannot raise our children better than a professional (Robertson, 2003). Nevertheless, the studies continue to show that children in day care are more aggressive, less stable and less secure than those reared at home. Actually, children who attend day care are more frequently diagnosed in grammar school with Attention Deficit Disorder (ADD). More children who attend day care are eventually put on medication.

A Gallup poll of schoolteachers reported in 1940 that their two greatest complaints were of students chewing gum and cutting in line (DeGrandpre, 1999). Now only seventy years later, we have serious problems with bullies and weapons. We have occasional mass murders in our schools and the common presence of drugs and alcohol. In Los Angeles County the "illegitimacy" rate was 74.69% (National Center for Health Statistics, 2003). Children are not what they used to be. Neither are adults.

The pharmaceutical industry wants you to believe that our dependency on legal drugs does not influence our children's dependency on illegal drugs, but it does. They want us to believe that the epidemics of Attention Deficit/Hyperactivity Disorder (ADHD) and autism are genetic. No genes have been isolated to show cause of ADHD or autism. The problem with that myth is that gene mutations evolve slowly and create improvements, and epidemics are produced by medically and consistently identifiable causes. No viruses have been identified to cause an epidemic of ADHD, but day care was introduced simultaneously with the Women's Movement, when children began to change. Even the pharmaceutical industry knows this, which is why they have changed their public relations campaign to state that ADHD has always been a problem, but we just haven't been able to recognize it. ChADD, Children and Adults with Attention Deficit/Hyperactivity Disorder, puts out a pamphlet to that effect. ChADD appears to be a group of pro-parent thinkers who receive millions in funding from the pharmaceutical industry (Breggin, 1998; DeGrandpre, 1999).

The feminist movement wants you to believe that equal opportunities for women include equal freedom from the responsibilities of child rearing even when children are involved. It's not a coincidence that the timing of the ADHD epidemic correlates strongly with the second wave of feminism when mothers began leaving the home and dropping their children off at day care in order to enter the workplace.

Children are designed to thrive on interacting with us and they shrivel without us. No one can take our place, not even Mother Teresa. Attachment Theory has proven again and again that children require secure attachments with adoring parents who don't shrink from setting values. However, secure means that they don't have to fear abandonment from these strong, loving parents. Once children learn to assume you may leave them again, they develop fears of abandonment and their capacity to trust is lost. They begin to suffer anxiety, if not rage, as a core personality trait.

Your child needs you to stay home with him whether or not experts have been invited to interpret the data in a way that will not disturb you. It would be a great challenge to find any child who entered childcare in the first year of life who is not seriously symptomatic. Find a child who entered day care in the second year of life who does not evidence symptoms like separation anxiety, depression or extreme shyness. These symptoms foretell long-term ingredients in the child's personality. Even children who enter day care full-time in the third year of life are unlikely to be secure adults as they may otherwise have been. These children are arguably normal or average because most parents put their children in day care these days.

To reiterate: Happy children who become inspired and productive adults are raised in the home by one or two adoring and reliable parents in the first few years of life, with occasional visits to Grandma or others for babysitting where the frequency and duration of those visits increases gradually over time according to the Continuity-of-Care Schedule.

To be fair, some parents are so unhealthy that their children are better off being raised by a professional, in which case the professional will take on the mother role and should be kept in the child's life for as long as possible to avoid abandonment trauma. Unfortunately, when different professionals (nannies or babysitters) are hired to be with the children, they still suffer abandonment trauma on weekends and vacations when the nannies leave.

The experiences of infants and toddlers run on a continuum of healthy attachments to unhealthy attachments and the resulting personalities also range on a continuum from wonderfully healthy to seriously unhealthy. Pretending the dye is genetically cast at birth is a costly form of denial, and our children end up sacrificed. The most important time for our children to matter more than ourselves is the first few years of life. Parents who step up to the challenge enjoy wonderful children who become amazing students and remarkable adults.

I would live under a bridge before I put my child in day care. Further, childcare is expensive. I know I could find a way to stay home, including work from my home, pair up with another mother and trade shifts; trade shifts with my husband; turn my car in for a clunker and walk everywhere and/or scale down the size of my residence.

I would like to see an agency or private business established to offer brainstorming. If the economy is such that this type of service would be seen as a luxury, then perhaps there are retirees who would volunteer to brainstorm. I would be happy to train them. Every family I've met that thought both parents had to work to survive was able to find and recognize solutions with creative thinking. Perhaps social workers with economic savvy could help a mother structure her expenses such that she could ameliorate the cost of staying home. Perhaps the same agency could subsidize her staying home if there were any costs that could not be mitigated. Mothers could begin to repay their debt over time after the child reached three years, like a student loan. Perhaps they would get a bonus from the government for raising a healthy, resilient child since these children are identifiable and likely to make a great contribution to society.

ADD/ADHD

Attention Deficit Disorder (ADD) with and without Hyperactivity (ADHD) has become a popular diagnosis of the classroom, which the field of psychiatry represents as a genetically-based chemical imbalance previously undetected and under-diagnosed, even though children are not what they used to be. Consequently, 20% of our children are now drugged with Ritalin with a 700% rise since 1990. More Ritalin is dispensed in the United States than in all other countries combined.

The organization formed to "educate" the public about ADD and ADHD is Children and Adults with Attention Deficit/Hyperactivity Disorder (ChADD). ChADD maintains that these very real childhood symptoms are "nobody's fault" since the problem is genetic. ChADD receives millions of dollars from Novartis Pharmaceuticals, the makers of Ritalin. ChADD invests millions in propaganda about ADHD and lobbies the Drug Enforcement Agency to "loosen its regulation of Ritalin by moving the drug to a less oppressive Schedule II Class, which includes mild painkillers like Tylenol with codeine and headache remedies with low-dose barbiturates."

Psychiatrist Peter Breggin uncovered the relationship between ChADD and Novartis, upon which the Drug Enforcement Agency looked dimly, calling it an "unhealthy commingling of medical and commercial interests (1998, p. 10)."

If children repressing emotional pain have a chemical imbalance, it is due to emotional suffering, even though these emotions may vary throughout the day. Medications can dampen or disguise their symptoms, often at a cost to the child. Medications do not heal their symptoms when changes in parenting could.

Children with ADD or ADHD don't feel truly seen or understood. Parents who are not around for most of their children's childhoods are not tuned in. These children are under-bonded, even though everything may look good to outsiders. The earlier the separations (day care) began, the more severe the symptoms generally appear. Of course, there are "mitigators" and "compounders" of the child's painful experiences.

One parent needs to stay home for the first five years and parents need to be taught deep, accepting and understanding interaction. Upon hearing this, many parents have told me, or bet their child's soul, that they and their child are the exception and that their love will be enough. These parents in denial begin with the misconception that love is equal to bonding. They deeply love their child. Therefore they assume the bonding is good. They argue quality not quantity or even that stimulation by a professional is best!

These parents may need to have their empathic failures gently pointed out to them on the spot even if it offends their egos. After all, it is not to the parent's ego we need to protect if it is at the expense of the child; it is the child's formation of personality we need to tend. This is the test of the True Parent.

Some children are repressing a secret such as physical or sexual abuse, or they are repressing their feelings because they have been taught to do so. I recommend that some time when you are in a situation out of your control that seems unjust, notice how distracted you are, how unclearly you think and how agitated you act. Now, imagine how well you would perform on a test in this moment or how easily you could be taught material that is irrelevant to the stresses of your life. How well would you focus? Often children with ADHD live in a distracting internal dialogue that they are unable to identify or represent without help.

The Causal Theory suggests we read symptoms as early as possible so we can identify conditions at home and make recommendations that can put children on the mend sooner than later. We propose that parents and clinicians forget genetic explanations so these clues can be recognized, identified and heeded. Historically, we have avoided identifying symptoms and diagnosing children other than to label them for what we believed to be genetic disorders that can be treated with chemicals. We need to stop blaming the child's genes and start placing a higher priority on parent education because educating parents is responsible, truthful and loving. Parents need to know how critically important they are to their child. And really, wouldn't any healthy parent rather learn about causes behind their child's problem that they can reverse than learn their child has a genetic condition that will require long-term reliance on medication? The answer to this question defines a true parent or a false parent.

Tantrums

There are a number of reasons why a child throws a tantrum. The most common are neglect, injustice or arbitrary power and weak limit-setting. A fourth cause may be a child's refusal to surrender to authority.

Neglect. Sometimes a child will throw a tantrum to get attention. We are accustomed to thinking of that as a bad thing. Perhaps the child knows he is entitled to attention. If Mommy or Daddy has been sick, busy or away, the child feels uncontained and is experiencing a loss of his sense of self, which happens when he goes too long without attention.

Some say a child who tantrums as a tool to get attention should be ignored. We propose that, usually, a child who tantrums is in dire need of attention from you; give him that attention unless the child is used to so much attention that he has become narcissistic. It's up to you to determine whether you've been overly or insufficiently attentive.

Containing the child and his anger may help the child come back into his own skin because it definitely provides attention and gives the child an emotional outlet. "Mommy knows. I have not been giving you the attention you need and deserve. Mommy is here now."

Arbitrary Power. Another reason children tantrum is a strong objection to what appears to be an arbitrary use or misuse of power in the eyes of the child. If our power seems unfair, they don't feel safe. Even if you are making reasonable choices, your unexplained actions may appear unfair and self-serving to the child. For example, you are walking down the aisle of a supermarket putting everything you want into the basket. So when the child imprints and wants to put something that he likes into the basket and you say, "No." To him that's arbitrary. It's an abuse of power. He's right; it's unfair.

If funds are limited enough that you cannot let him chose an item, or for another reason you have decided he's not entitled to a treat, take the child to the car and return for your basket later. You may want to contain him or hold him with a loose fence and say something like, "Daddy knows, Daddy understands. It's not fair. It's not fair. But I love you."

Perhaps next time when you go to the market, you can give your child advanced notice of the conditions. If funds are limited, perhaps you can explain something like, "Today, we have just a little bit of money and Mommy has to buy the things we really need. I wanted to get some berries for my cereal, but I can't afford them today. If I had money for berries, I would let you have a little treat (or a toy or a ride on the horse) first. Then I would get berries. Maybe next time you can have your treat and I can have my berries."

Let the child know that three out of four times, he can have something little. On the fourth time, explain first that this is the day we have to save our money. Soon you can introduce an allowance and she will learn money management.

Children have an acute sense of injustice. If you seem to favor one child over another or if they are told they did something wrong when they didn't, they will feel outrage. If you tell them they can't swear and you punish them for swearing while you still swear, it's arbitrary, inconsistent and it ignores imprinting. Children sometimes rage over the injustices of our arbitrary use of power. If we acknowledge to them what we think they are right about, that may enable them to tolerate the injustice. Sometimes someone simply acknowledging something inconsistent makes us feel sane again, especially when we are offered a reason.

Weak Limits. Yet another reason for a tantrum is that you have been weak in limit-setting and/or your consequences have been erratic. The child thinks you're too week to manage him. He is daring you to be strong enough. When you are weak in following through with consequences, he is threatened. I cannot count the number of times children of all ages have told me how angry they are that their parents are not strong enough to parent them, meaning setting standards and consequences and following through. When the child is daring the parent to be strong, containing can once again be a healing experience, given you can prove you are strong and you don't quit early because you got tired or had something else to do.

There are children who are not seeking attention per se, but are seeking to get their way at the expense of others. Some children have had parents who never set limits. Actually there are a significant number of parents out there who believe if you give your child what he's demanding, he will leave you alone and in peace. These children become little monsters who will get louder and louder and try to embarrass the parents because they have discovered that the parent will eventually cave. This tantrum is not a real tantrum. It is a discipline problem that is best solved by not giving in and not responding with any attention at all until the child behaves. Depending on how long the child has been indulged, the parent will have to hold the line even longer. If not, the cost rises. The good news is that the child will love the parent for actually being strong to the end and will feel relief. If the parent never gets strong, the child becomes an arrogant, hostile adult who has contempt for others and authority.

Refusal to Surrender Power. When a child has suffered a failed attachment, he may tantrum at any suggestion that he surrender power to an authority, whether a parent or a teacher. This is a RAD child who will not want to surrender power to anyone. He has it in his head that there is no one to trust and he can never surrender again. He cannot afford to be vulnerable again, nor will he allow anyone else to be the boss of him. The RAD child will try to be his own boss. He will perfect his skills as a master manipulator who knows how to seduce adults into meeting his needs.

RAD children and narcissists-in-the-making do not learn well in school because they do not want anyone to realize they don't know everything already. They develop what educational psychologists come to call learning disorders. They miss out on important lessons and having failed to wire in these lessons, the evaluators think they have cognitive deficiencies. They do, but in my clinical opinion these deficiencies can be filled in with missing information. Education is a series of building blocks and sometimes children have to go back to pick up what they missed.

The child who tantrums out of refusal to surrender power needs to be contained until he can be a child again. This may take many containments. (See Containment and Healing Your RAD Child in Chapter 3: Healing).

Potty Training

Do not attempt to potty train before 18 months! Some parents were potty trained too young themselves. Some of us have phobias about dirt and poop. I have seen parents squeeze their own noses while sitting over their baby's bare bottom, going "Pee-ewh." Even in humor they are shaming their baby, making him think there is something wrong with his body or what his body does. The child may conclude that his parents don't have this problem stinking, that only he does. It is perhaps the first time the child feels ridiculed by his parent, who is just making a dirty joke with a mixed message. I have seen a father hand the child over to mom as soon as he poops, "He's yours now." Other parents get uncomfortable about cleaning their child and many infants have terrible rashes on their bottoms and live in fear of peeing because that makes the rash burn even worse.

Some really terrible abuse has been done to children over potty training issues. It is an area that presents major abuse, shaming and control issues. Parents make demands on their children beyond their ability, which sets them up for early failure.

Diaper changing skills. Parents need to have good diapering skills:
- As soon as the child poops or pees, make the change so she doesn't develop diaper rash or get used to the feeling of a wet or soiled diaper.
- If you are capable of being very conscious, the best thing you can do after your child pees or poops is walk to the bathroom, run the water until you have a lukewarm temperature and rinse him off. Be sure your hand is in the water the entire time so you can catch any sudden change of temperature. NEVER allow the water to get too hot or cold. Ignore phone calls or conversation that would distract you. If you can ensure that your child is safe under this running water in your hands, this is the most natural way to clean her, without chemicals. You may also want to place some sort of padding in the porcelain sink.
- If your bathroom sink does not allow for this or if your hands are not that steady, you may need to use diaper cream if you see any rashes develop.

Stages & Ages of Development

- When she is clean and her new diaper is on, you might kiss her belly to let her know how sweet she is.

Potty training warnings. Potty training early or incorrectly can have dire consequences. Parents need to know:
- The child is physiologically unable to potty train before 18 months.
- The child will fear disapproval and losing control of his or her own body, later developing rigid armor and fear of his or her own emotions, as if they were equivalents of losing any physical control. This can manifest as a personality disorder (most often obsessive-compulsive).
- The obsessive-compulsive personality has an impaired ability to be spontaneous, expressive, empathic and communicative. They fear the functioning of their own body as if they are out of control.
- The grown-up will likely be obsessed with rules, "shoulds" and "shouldn'ts".
- He or she may be unable to be giving and sentimental.
- The grown child will probably be restricted in affect with a dry, cutting voice.
- The older grown child will have illnesses related to early potty training: constipation, hemorrhoids, spastic colon, bowel cancer or loss of bowel control when relaxed, fatigued, aging, after drinking alcohol, or ill.

How to Potty Train
- Allow the child to visit mommy and daddy on the potty once or twice. Tell her you're pooping (or whatever language you prefer).
- When the child is visibly having a bowel movement, give her words ("Are you pooping?")
- Once or twice only, allow the child to play naked in the back yard so he can see what comes out of him when he goes pee-pee (or poop). Tell him, "Oh I see you had a little poop." Take the "little poop" to the toilet with the child and let him flush it away.
- Ask the child if he wants to learn to use the toilet or if he wants his own potty. If he says he wants to use the toilet, you can say, "Well, let's try it out and see how you fit." Hold him carefully until he learns secure seating. If it's too scary or he slips, ask if he changed his mind and would rather have his very own potty. There are also child seats that fit over the toilet seat.
- Give the child a potty wrapped in a big bow or wrapping paper. Make a ceremony of the gift and make it a rite of passage. Maybe you and daddy clap with him when he opens it.
- Place the apparatus near or on the toilet. Invite the child to sit on it without underpants like mommy and daddy. Say something like, "This is for pooping. Amy's a big girl now."
- Introduce her to the children's books, *Prudence and the Potty* and *Everyone Poops*.
- Perhaps you can invite an older child to visit who goes on the potty or on the toilet. It is especially good for boys to see another little boy standing at the toilet like his daddy does.
- Be patient. Be accepting of however it goes. Have faith that the child will know when it's time. Don't let others pressure you to potty train. *You* are the professional parent.
- As long as you don't push the child, you can comment now and then about trying out the potty, what it's for, that big people don't wear diapers, *etc.*
- NEVER humiliate, embarrass or ridicule a child in diapers or a child who wets her pants.

Potty Training an Older Toddler
- If your child is three and refusing to potty train, you can say, "Okay, Mommy's going to stop changing diapers next week. Do you want me to

teach you how to change your own diapers (or use pull-ups)?"
- Has wiping the child become the most personal attention he gets all day? Consider whether you are creating a desire in your child to continue in diapers. Some children get the best attention of the day when their parent tends to them and they will potty train when the parent pays more attention to them over other things.
- Have you taught him how to wipe himself? Maybe you should buy damp toilet wipes for him to use at the toilet. Warning: some are not flushable.
- Have you pressured the child too hard to potty train or to be too grown up in other ways?
- Do you have another younger child in diapers who gets more attention than this child?
- Have *you* shown a lack of interest in the subject?

Symptoms of a Child Potty-Trained too Early
- Child fears germs.
- Child has constipation.
- Child is unusually private at bathroom time.
- Child may have accidents at school.
- Child tells bathroom jokes with too much enthusiasm.
- Child develops controlling behavior.

Adult Traits of a Child Potty-Trained too Early
- Problems with colon

- Body armor (musculature for the purpose of maintaining emotional control)
- Fear of germs and dirt
- Does not like messes or clutters
- Obsesses over details
- Physical/medical problems

As a clinician I have had a number of older clients come in with their baby books, bragging or complaining about how young they were when they were finally potty trained. There was a race back then between parents; so-called good parents had their babies potty trained earlier than others. Most of these clients were potty trained before their bodies were ready – before 18 months – and now as adults they are rigid and obsessive-compulsive.

The practice of infant potty training has resurfaced. However, I am fairly certain it will lead to some sort of neurosis or preoccupation, probably in the area of anal retention or anal expulsion in the personality. Proponents say that parents become more attentive to their child. I say cleaning your baby is an important parent/child ritual. It seems to me that their focus on catching the child in time could become neurosis inducing. I would rather see care of the infant followed by intimacy and dialogue about how to do this or that and what words are for which thing or experience and how the child is feeling.

Parents may be racing other parents or afraid of germs, which puts pressure on the child at far too young an age. Don't risk it.

Latency (Grammar School Years)

The habits you want your child to develop for a lifetime need to be established during latency (ages six to twelve). The building blocks to for those habits can be found through learning good grammar, study habits and personal discipline.

Good Grammar

Your child will be learning to write well during these years. He will write what he hears, which means his parents need to practice good grammar in the home. If he has difficulty writing, it may be because his parents are using bad grammar with a poor vocabulary. Perhaps the parents can hire a tutor for themselves for a couple of meetings to assess their grammar and teach them what they need to know.

Parents often get their pronouns wrong as soon as they add another person to the mix. For example, most parents will say, "I went to the store," but when they add another person, they say it wrong. The sentence should make sense with or without the addition. Examples follow.
- Incorrect: "Dad and me went to the store." Correct: "Dad and I went to the store."
- Incorrect: "Dad is bringing dinner home for you and I." Correct: "Dad is bringing dinner home for you and me."
- Incorrect: "Her and I went to the store." Correct: "She and I went to the store."

There are vocabulary books and audiobooks you can purchase or borrow from the library. Learn and model correct grammar for the benefit of your children. Use a rich vocabulary too. You will be glad you did.

Good Study Habits

Homework. Your child must develop good executive systems and habits. He needs to be someone who brings his assignments home, does them and remembers to turn them in. If he cannot do this, he is in trouble in school and perhaps in other areas for the rest of his life. He may need an orderly room to keep his mind orderly. He may need to not play music or have a television on while he is studying. He may need no other chores than keeping his room straight and his homework current. Parents need to ensure as early as possible that these habits are enforced and consistent.
- The child needs to practice bringing home all the necessary materials for completing homework, including written details of assignments, the necessary books, handouts or whatever is required that evening. Remind her. Help her think it through out loud when you pick her up. Check with the teacher before leaving for at least a year or as long as necessary. Praise her for remembering accurately without your help. Start in kindergarten or first grade. Hopefully the teacher will send home a simple written assignment from the beginning to get good habits started. If not, explain your goal to the teacher and tell her that you need a daily list of what the child needed to bring home and return.
- From the beginning, your child should not be banished while doing homework. Sit beside her for the first few years doing your own bill paying, reading or letter writing. Let her imprint it from you. Actually, I loved that time with my son and I extended it as long as I could. I can imagine a mother, father and five children all sitting together quietly in the living room doing homework together. Anyone disruptive has to finish in her room. When each child is done they get to go outside.
- Teach him deferred gratification, that is, to come home from school and do homework before playing.
- After it's done, she needs to put her homework in a special place in the backpack. The backpack should always be kept in the same place so it's easy to remember and find, preferably beside the front door.
- Forgetfulness is the enemy of successful children. Teach him to turn around and look behind him every time he leaves a room. Make sure he has a place to keep each and all his belongings ("leave no trace"). Habits like these help him keep agreements, stay conscious and develop good ethics.
- Your child needs to learn to take the homework out and turn it in before sitting down at his desk at school or to put it in a conspicuous place where it is out of the backpack and ready to be turned

in if the teacher doesn't like papers turned in immediately. He needs to identify his cue to turn it in. Find out from the teacher what that cue is. If the teacher asks for homework at different times on different days, ask if she can allow your child to turn his homework in before he sits down for the day. If that is not acceptable, ask her for a ritual.

- It might be a good idea to put the homework in the clear plastic window in the front of his binder. (You have to make sure you get those types of binders.) Teach him that inside-pockets should be for the special categories most needed, such as 'homework I need help with' and 'homework I can do on my own'. Buy as many pockets as necessary. Help him organize often.
- Don't allow your child to procrastinate projects. Procrastinated projects need a significant penalty. Projects finished early should be especially rewarded.
- Place a high premium on deferred gratification without demoralizing your child.

Grades. Do not reward your child with money or praise for reading because that may diminish her joy of reading. However, you may reward good work, which includes good grades. Celebrate good grades. Make a big deal over them. If you are trying to turn around bad grades, you may reward good grades with payments (for example, $10 for an A, $5 for a B). Or depending on your child's currency, a different bribe may be better.

The point is a good worker is rewarded financially in the real world. It is appropriate to reward your child financially for schoolwork done well if you need to. How she does in school is very important.

Attend Parent's Night and all the events to which you are invited at her school, with rare exception. Show an ongoing interest in school from beginning to end.

Learning Disabilities. So far, I have found that learning disabilities are nothing more than a wobbly foundation of knowledge, Without learning the building blocks of academics including reading, writing, addition, subtraction and our multiplication tables, we cannot retain newer knowledge. We won't understand it. We won't know where to connect it. This happens when one's lessons got skipped. In other words, if your child had the mumps when his class was learning all the special rules of reading and spelling, like "i before e except after c", and, "The e is a policeman at the end of a word that makes the vowel say its name," then he might have difficulty reading, especially aloud. Self-consciousness may set in, followed by the child thinking there is something wrong with him. Instruction moves forward and the child is feeling behind the other students, so he starts to think he is not as smart and develops ways to cover up that he doesn't know what he knows he should know. He starts judging himself and then can't learn as well. He gets further and further behind, developing bad concentration habits and a nagging and distracting internal dialogue. Perhaps the child becomes reckless, guessing and shotgunning responses. Any answer seems better than looking completely dumb or admitting he doesn't know what is happening anymore.

Sometimes narcissistic children develop "learning disorders" because they go to elementary school with arrogance and a know-it-all attitude. They don't pay attention and before they know it, they feel secretly dumb, and the insecurity that underlies all narcissism shows up as a learning disorder.

I have taught numerous so-called learning-disabled students with complete success after only two to eight sessions. Their parents update me on how their child became an "A" student or student-of-the-month or that she is no longer in Special Ed. We simply sought to identify what they couldn't do or didn't learn amongst the building blocks of their education and then filled it in. I asked some parents to get flash cards. I asked others to get lined paper. Yet others, I asked to get books to practice reading together.

Some have one child re-do all work until it looks good. Give him a pep talk on catching up. With new self-esteem or hope, they catch up. The summer is a wonderful time for this work and I recommend starting the next year having prepared ahead, which will dismantle an old, self-defeating self-concept.

Personal Discipline

Have your child make her bed every day. Make it simple with just a pillow to plump and a quilt or spread to throw in place with a few smoothing gestures. It doesn't have to be hotel perfect. But she needs order and her things should be kept where they belong. She needs to tidy her things every night and set her things out for the next day (even if she showers in the morning). Friends aren't allowed to visit if her belongings are strewn about the house or her room is messy. If friends have to wait outside until she tidies her room and picks up her belongs in the living room, maybe she will begin to leave her room tidy in the morning before leaving for school.

Don't burden your child with other chores unless you have a big family or both parents work. The only reason a child should do additional chores is to free her parents up for quality time with the children. Otherwise, your child's jobs are to pick up after herself wherever she goes, make good grades, keep her environment attractive, tidy and organized and have healthy friendships. Don't depress or overwhelm her with too much responsibility.

Deferred Gratification

Deferred gratification is best introduced gently in earlier stages of individuation, but in the mildest forms. For example, you might say, "Anyone who wants dessert now can have one scoop of ice cream. Anyone who will wait an hour can have two," or, "If you finish your homework before the weekend starts, we can all go to Sea World together."

My son pointed out to me a father standing at the pastry counter of Jerry's Deli with his three children admiring the pastries and talking about how good they looked. The children chimed in proposing which ones looked best. At first I thought it was cruel and teasing. Then as I watched closer, I came to realize the children were not suffering. The baker behind the counter overheard us and said they come in every week for dinner and every weekend they come in to buy pastries.

By latency, children should be learning to work hard for big rewards in the end. Children who go on to financial greatness have learned deferred gratification. Those who develop discipline and skills which lead to major achievements must learn deferred gratification. Good parenting must include careful construction of this trait.

An important practice of deferred gratification is finding at least one skill that your child likes developing. Practicing is an excellent development of deferred gratification, like practicing ballet before the recital or going to baseball practice before the game. The same model should be used for homework and other goals of achievement, including buying special purchases after saving.

Perhaps a kindergartener can save for two weeks to buy a hair band she loves. A first grader can save for one month to buy a sparkly barrette; a second grader can save for two months to buy a special mitt; a third grader can save for three months to buy a video game; a fourth grader can save for four months to take her friend to Disneyland; a fifth grader can save for five months to buy a bicycle; a sixth grader can save for six months to take a friend to Magic Mountain; a seventh grader can save for seven months to buy makeup; an eighth grader may save for eight months to buy the latest digital device. A ninth grader may begin saving for a car and you can look at ideas together monthly because he will be saving for about two years.

I recommend paying children for work as long as you don't burden your child. I recommend three savings accounts, one on his dresser and two at the bank. Let one be for short-term goals like a video game, cell phone or a computer and one for long-term goals like a car. Daydream about goals with him. "How would you like to earn a cell phone?"

Maybe at first, divide payments into a half, a quarter and a quarter. Then as the child gets into it, break it into thirds with his permission.

Again, don't overload your child or withhold thoughtlessly. Don't break your commitments. If your child earned a reward, make sure you give it to him. One way to kill incentive is to have children do work with little or no reward, or worse, give away their things. I knew one child who was bar mitzvahed and his father had him donate all his presents to charity, as if that was some sort of lesson for the child in generosity, when in fact, it was just cruel.

Extra-Curriculars

It's important to find a balance between giving children growth and social experiences without depriving them of quality time at home with you and the family. Some theorize that too many extra-curricular activities make a child dependent on outside stimulation and they have difficulty establishing a calm and centered core that contemplates, imagines and creates. Others notice that these children often feel overwhelmed with too much responsibility.

On the other hand, children need experience and expertise. Some parents make sure their children are good in sports, giving them lots of exposure to these activities. Others take them to dance and theatre classes. Still others take them to the desert to learn to ride motorbikes. Still others take them to learn martial arts and other children learn to play chess. In any event expertise gives them an experience of competency in the world and a sense of identity. Ideally, we need to consider that what activities a child is offered may become the course of his life. Do you really want him to be a professional dirt bike racer?

Parents need to stay awake as to whether the child is getting his social needs met and is keeping up on his schoolwork. Lastly, he needs to love and enjoy this endeavor. Don't risk living through your kid so much that you can't see that he is doing it for you, not him.

All children need social skills. I am not just speaking of relationship skills for children, where they learn how to process an issue with their parents and each other. I mean the kind of social skills where children learn to relate to each other so that by the time they hit adolescence they are comfortable with socializing. We need to make it a goal, if reasonably possible, that they enjoy high school as the heyday of their young lives rather than the time they suffered for lack of belonging. When your children are approaching grammar school, see if you can make an adult friendship with someone who also has a child in your kid's age range. If that doesn't work, try Brownies/Girl Scouts. If that doesn't work, move to a neighborhood where children play.

Your child will need to grow up with friends. If he is the subject of a custody dispute, the worst part may be that he can't develop after-school friends in his neighborhood. Because each parent wants his time, sadly, the child may not develop social skills.

Masturbation and Sex

Younger Child. A parent can cause harm

when they create a fear in the child of masturbation. As a matter of fact, if we shame a child for masturbating, I would consider it another form of sexual abuse. Yet we want to be aware as parents so we do not miss the clues to sexual abuse. If I had a child who seemed to regularly masturbate or recruit other children more than once or twice to participate in sex play under the age of eight or nine, I would become hyper-aware while seeming very blasé. This can be a sign of sexual abuse because, while children that young are curious, they tend to satisfy their curiosities about their bodies and move on rather quickly. Look for other signs of sexual abuse such as sudden changes in personality ranging from withdrawal to hyperactivity to exhibitionism. Renewed bedwetting is another symptom indicating possible sexual abuse. These are signs, but do not guarantee that sexual abuse has taken place. Be careful in your assessment; to believe sexual abuse has happened to a child when it didn't can be harmful too.

I would ask a young child under nine open-ended questions in the most casual way if she has discovered how her body feels in her privates. If she says she likes the feeling, make her feel safe. Smile. Nod. You might ask her if she remembers how she discovered that feeling or where she learned those words or does she know anyone else who plays that game? If you are uncomfortable asking questions, unfortunately you may telegraph to her that something is wrong, which may or may not be true.

If she acts afraid to talk, ask her if you have made her afraid to talk to you about grown-up things. "If I have, sweetheart, I am so sorry." If she still seems to want to change the subject, biting her lip or looking away, tell her that no grown-up or child ever gets to ask her to keep a secret from her mother or father. Ever. Then say, "Has a grownup asked you to keep something a secret?" Tell her you cannot protect her if she keeps secrets from you.

If she tells you a grown-up taught her, stay calm. Ask a few more open-ended questions in a soft voice, including, "Who was that?" An open-ended question is a question that does not have the answer in the question. For example, a leading question would be, "Did you and your brother play sex games?" An open-ended question would be, "Do you remember where you learned to play that game?" Notice that I asked, "Do you remember..." rather than, "Where did you...?" Soften your questions so they don't sound accusatory. You may want to rehearse the questions you want to ask before you talk with your child.

If you learn that your child was molested, you must first ensure that she knows you believe her. Second, you must stay calm and safe for her and tell her how sorry you are that you didn't protect her. Third, you must ensure that this person is never with her again, not even in a monitored way, even if you have to leave home and live under a bridge. Fourth, you need to tell the authorities because this person will probably offend again. Fifth, if you have verbal contact with the offender, tell them they need to get into therapy now.

Older Child. If your son is eight or older, it is time to have a talk. Prepare him for wet dreams if his father hasn't already. Tell him they are normal and natural. Tell him that he is of the age that a boy may want to masturbate. It's nothing a parent ever recommends to a child, but it's his body. Tell him if he chooses to masturbate you would like him to keep tissues by the bed to flush in the morning because it is a private matter and you would rather not know about it since you prefer that he never grow up. (Smile.)

If your child is a girl, you can tell her, "Girls masturbate too, you know. I want you to enjoy your own body, but remember it is a sanctuary. Choose very carefully who you share your body with. Take your time and don't grow up too soon. You can never be a child again."

There are two kinds of sexual abuse. One is committed by offending. The other is committed by instilling fear and shame in the child. Negative messages leave scars and create repression or deviancy, if not a kind of sneaky or sleazy orientation to sex. Try not to give your child any of your sexual issues.

Talking about the Birds and Bees. If a four-year-old asks where babies come from, you can say that mommies and daddies get very close, so close that they make a baby. Just leave it at that. They really don't want to know more.

At about six you can say that babies come from a seed that grows inside Mommy's tummy. If she asks, "How does the seed get there?" you can explain that mommies have seeds already in them. You can say when mommies and daddies get naked together in bed and hug and love, sometimes it makes the seed grow.

At about eight, you can say that mommies and daddies like to put their private areas together to make a baby. When she says, "Yuck," You can say, "Well, it's something that is only special to people who really love each other and I really love your daddy. That's how we made you."

At about ten, a patient father can talk to a boy or a patient mother can talk to a girl about how babies are made. Men are able to create an erection when they become excited about a woman and women have vaginas that are just the right size and shape to receive a penis if they really, really love the man and he is very gentle and caring. This is why intercourse is best when two people are married.

When your child is in the early teens, you want to say, "Whoever has sex needs to be prepared to raise a child or prevent a child from being conceived. This is why having sex is something that smart children wait to do until they are mature enough to choose the right mate carefully. They have to be old enough to take care of someone else who will need a lot of love, attention and sacrifice or they need to choose someone who will participate in making arrangements with a doctor for protection, which doesn't always work and doesn't protect us from AIDS and other venereal diseases. These are diseases that can ruin lives, so it is important to finish childhood safely." Take questions after that. Look up together what you can't answer simply and accurately. You can find diagrams, drawing and photos to help you out. Tell your child there may be more to talk about when he gets older, and you will always be here to answer questions and talk.

Adolescence

Responsibility

Upon adolescence, the parents' days of lecturing are over and hopefully we didn't over-lecture in the first place. Parents now become listeners and offer advice upon request.

If your adolescent acts irresponsibly, a privilege of the same magnitude must be withheld, absent lecture. For example, if she gets a speeding ticket, take away the car keys for a month or two while she earns the money to pay the ticket. In some cases, you may have to inform her that you will now spy on her to make sure she is not shooting herself in the foot with irresponsible choices.

If she is caught lying, say something like, "I am disappointed. It is so important to me that you become an honest woman. I trust you will learn from this." If she continues to lie, the time must come when she tells the truth and you say, "Because you have lied in the past, I cannot believe you now. If you tell me the truth in the future, I will learn to believe you again."

Be careful not to load the adolescent down with too much responsibility or agreements so much that he may fail. Some teenagers who have jobs do poorly in school. They cannot balance a social life, important for their development, with work and good grades. To facilitate a social life, you may need to give your child money for good grades and perhaps create debits for bad grades or bad acts. This can become complicated when you are trying to teach him to save money as a goal to get things because you may lose that lesson when you take his savings as a penalty or consequence for having cost another person. Try to figure out a way to encourage saving while holding him financially responsible for expensive wrong acts. Maybe he will have to work over Winter Break. If you have to choose, go for the ethics over saving.

Sometimes an older child will still wet the bed, yet the doctor sees no physiological reason. One major psychological reason for bedwetting is the feeling that they have been forced into maturity too soon. This can mean too much actual responsibility or too much psychological responsibility. In the case of psychological responsibility, the child could possibly be keeping a secret, including sexual abuse. He could be taking care of the parent's ego, acting as a confidante to their parent, having too much responsibility or worrying that the family is falling apart.

A teenager is responsible for good grades, earning his spending money, keeping his room tidy, picking up after himself wherever he goes, keeping track of his things and treating people with respect.

Love

Above personal responsibility, another major job of the adolescent is to love and be loved. This is not to say that we should push our teenagers into early romance; we mustn't. However, we should not stand in their way, and we should help them with courting skills if they need them or want our help. If we are on the fence about a girl he says he loves, we need to help make the most of the relationship rather than forbid it or frustrate it. Forbidden romances need to be limited to criminal behavior such as drug use, truancy, falling grades, lying and other serious and recent infractions.

Hopefully by now, you will have given your child good values and good modeling to choose his first romantic pursuit and to be successful in love for awhile. Even though young love is usually temporary, it creates important memories and identity.

I knew some parents who told their child to choose a "practice date" on a couple of occasions. They decided to start several years too early because they didn't want the child embarrassed. They double dated without calling it that. After a few good experiences over a few years, the lessons germinated and he turned into quite a gentleman.

He was asked to choose a girl at school who he would like to invite to go out with them. He was then taught how to ask for her (parents') phone number. These parents had already called the girl's parents and asked if they would be up for allowing their daughter to learn dating etiquette with their son under their tutelage. They explained clearly that they wanted their son to practice courting by bringing a small gift, meeting her at her door, introducing himself to them, opening doors, having her walk ahead at the restaurant and behind at the movie and ordering first. They doubled-dated and it was such a good idea that the other parents wanted in. They too took the kids out on a double date. When the date was over they talked about different moments and how he handled himself. I trust they gave him lots of praise.

Where you have not been a good role model, apologize and share your mistakes. Tell him what you would do differently if given the opportunity to do it all over again. Ask him what he would do in your past situations. Tell him you want him to be good at picking girls and you want him to be worthy of winning and keeping a quality young lady. You may need to teach how to date in a healthy way, if only by dialogue and coaching.

Boys to Men. If your child is a young man, tell him to exhibit good phone etiquette, introduce himself to her parents, find out when her curfew is and keep it. Teach him to bring her flowers and to open the door for her. Teach him to take her to dinner after the movie, pay for it and ask her what she thought about the movie.

This is not a sexist role. The romantic role of the female is biologically a submissive one and girls and women need courtship to feel safe. They are the ones who have to go through childbirth for good or bad. Courtship skills do not mean he can't respect a woman in the work force as his superior or equal. Teach him not to push her sexually unless they are both willing to give up their goals if they become parents. If she is younger than him, it is even more important that he not push her sexually. To do so would make him a manipulator or a bully.

Adolescent girls do not have the emotional strength to say no and adult women often regret giving up their innocence too young. Talk to him about male peer pressure and being more proud of himself *vs.* having to show off to others. All other things being equal, treating young ladies this way may make him quite popular. There is always a time for good manners, regardless of what year it is.

He should know that some girls will be known for being 'easy' and these girls have likely been molested, neglected or both. Taking advantage of an 'easy' girl would be beneath him. He should know to treat a young lady who has low self-esteem with extra respect. He should also know how to treat someone who favors him when the feeling is not reciprocal. He needs to let her down kindly, gentlemanly.

Proper Condom Use

- Leave ¾ inch space at the tip for ejaculate. Putting the condom on too far can lead to failure.
- Wear the right size condom. If it's too loose, a leak could occur.
- Avoid inverting or spilling a condom once worn, regardless of whether or not it contains semen.
- Only use condoms made of latex or polyurethane to ensure protection against HIV.
- Avoid using oil-based lubricants with latex condoms; oil disintegrates the latex.
- Limit use of flavored condoms to oral sex only. If used for penetration, the sugar in the flavoring can lead to yeast infections.

Oversight of the guidelines above perpetuates the common misconception that condoms are not designed properly. (sexually transmitted disease [n.d.]. Retrieved April 8, 2010 from http://en.wikipedia.org/wiki/Sexually_transmitted_disease)

Girls to Women. If she is a young lady, teach her to respect herself and to only date young men who are respectful of her. Avoid young men who are controlling or expecting sex. Tell her not to make love with a young man unless he would be willing to support a child if contraception fails or to accompany her to get an abortion. Teach her how to assess a good prospect in a boyfriend and how to learn from her own failures as a girlfriend. Ask her to expect him to be respectful of her parents. Tell her that controlling guys can ultimately be dangerous. The best way to assess a good guy is by how he treats her, how he broke up with the last girlfriend, how he disagrees with her, how he treats her parents and how he treats a server.

Talk to her about abortion, sexually-transmitted diseases and abstinence. Tell her you prefer she wait to have sex until she is engaged or she has a commitment. Many young women have had to give up their dreams because they were weak or impulsive. While petting is safe, it often leads to further unplanned passion. Tell her once innocence is lost, childhood is over. Encourage her gently to wait as long as she can wait. She'll be a woman soon enough, and she'll never be a child again.

Tell her that many women often regret they had sex too young and later report they felt pressured, although they often didn't realize it at the time. Many women say they wished their parents had set limits and rules for them so they wouldn't have had to deal with pressure before they were strong enough.

Teens are often relieved when their parents play the role of the over-protective mom or dad. Talk to her about how strong she feels in setting limits, and ask her what kind of help she'd like. Ask her how she'd set limits. Ask her if there is a code the two of you could create when you could become the tough guy so she doesn't have to deal with peer pressure herself. "Daddy, I want to stay out later. I am with the coolest friends. Jack's wearing... Can I come home later?" When she says, "wearing," dad knows to say, "Absolutely not. You come home now. Where are you? I'm coming to get you." She can then say, with greatest disappointment, "OK, Dad. I'll come home on time."

Let her know that you encourage her to set limits for herself as soon as she is ready while you will do it for her until then.

Tell her if she decides to go against your wishes and have a sexual relationship to let you know and you will go with her to get birth control and to inquire about inoculations for Sexually Transmitted Diseases (STDs). Prevention is key, but if any symptoms develop, he or she needs to see a doctor immediately.

Tell your daughter you would like her to discuss attitudes about sex with anyone she dates and to let him know that if the relationship does get serious, she would want the two of them to be tested for STDs before they sleep together.

STDs

Signs and symptoms of Sexually Transmitted Diseases (STDs) may appear a few days to three months after exposure, depending on the organism. They may resolve in a few weeks, even without treatment, but progression with later complications, or recurrence, sometimes occurs. (MayoClinic.com) STDs have a wide range of signs and symptoms:
- Sores or bumps on the genitals, or in the oral area or rectal area.
- Painful and/or burning urination.
- Penile discharge.
- Vaginal discharge.
- Unusual vaginal bleeding.
- Sore, swollen lymph nodes, particularly in the groin but sometimes more widespread.

Talk to her about how the kind of guy she picks will be a reflection on her. Tell her you would love to trust her and she has your blessings to fall in love. Tell her love often brings joy and pain and you will be there to listen to her painful lessons in love and self-worth. Tell her that whatever happens you will always be there for her and she doesn't need to keep secrets. You would rather be a resource for her than a judge. Thus, you set the bar high and let go.

Try to head off a Courtship Disorder, but if she develops one, help her work it through.

Overcoming a Courtship Disorder. Someone with a Courtship Disorder is unable to assess a good mate, has an unrealistic expectation of too much too soon and lacks social skills. This disorder (not in the *DSM-IV-TR*) shows up in histrionic personalities, stalkers and rapists. It also shows up in people who have weak boundaries and merge too soon. They may be people who enter into relationships to get their own wants and childhood needs met or who settle for the first person who shows interest in them. They may not know how to have an open or vulnerable conversation about preferences and values. They may not know how to have a healthy disagreement. They might not practice respectful dating etiquette or maybe they suffer gravely from lack of trust. Perhaps they believe love is the warm (temporary) feeling they have, not the action of "investing in the growth of the other," as M. Scott Peck suggested (Peck, 1971). Perhaps they seek a person who flatters them or makes them look good by association.

For those who have a Courtship Disorder, love is about getting, not giving. They will ultimately complain about how they're not getting their needs met. A Courtship Disorder involves dishonesty and lack of fair play. Parents need to ensure that our children have the capability of assessing future dates and mates. They need to know how to proceed in the process of courting.

Drugs

Be sure to talk to your child when she is pre-adolescent about drugs and how drugs ruin lives and dreams. If you find out that your teen is using drugs or is associating with teens who do, then you may have to take away her friends. Frankly, I'd move if I had to. If she violates this restriction, you may then take away her private phone, her Nintendo, her television or something valuable that you have given to her for being responsible. You may tell her that you now have the right to spy on her because she has made choices that violate your trust. Have a level-headed conversation about values, goals and worries, never missing an opportunity to tell her how much you love her, that you want the best for her and that drugs can ruin her life.

The following scale is provided for you to share with your teen. This is an age of substance use and abuse. There are drugs that are more dangerous to the body. There are drugs that are more harmful to the soul. There are drugs that kill ambition and ruin potential. None of these drugs are good for children, but some are worse than others, generally speaking.

Substance Use Harm Scale

	Body	Spirit	Ambition
mild harm	coffee	marijuana	coffee
	marijuana	coffee	cigarettes
⇕	cigarettes	cigarettes	heroin
	heroin (pure/measured)	alcohol/heroin	amphetamines
significant harm	alcohol/sedatives	amphetamines	alcohol/sedatives
	amphetamines/meth		marijuana

Of course, some of these substances would not be harmful in moderation. Some people have a glass of wine now and then and others think they are only having a nightly glass of wine, which for their body is simply too often to not develop some sort of tolerance or dependence. It's not far from there to two glasses now and then and so on. The same could be said for an occasional joint of marijuana. The problem is the moderation part. Most people don't know when they cross the line. When someone says they need to cut back but can't, they have crossed the line and probably can't ever use in moderation. They need to abstain. They have become addicted.

Alcohol is a far uglier drug than marijuana, so it seems ironic, if not unjust, that alcohol is legal and marijuana is not. Alcohol kills on the road. It often inflames domestic violence and crime (Dutton, 1998). It harms the body. It is the drug of arrogance while those who use it to medicate their self-consciousness think it sets them free to be themselves. One way to get an alcoholic to stop drinking is to videotape them so they can see themselves the next day. They will not like how they seem. By all rights, alcohol should make someone self-conscious rather than disinhibited.

In contrast to alcohol, marijuana creates contemplation, unfortunately so much so that it destroys action, and magnificent thoughts are often forgotten long before the next day. Talented people waste away from pot. When teens use marijuana more than experimentally or occasionally, their grades begin to plummet. Their future falls to the floor. In the hands of teens, marijuana can ruin a life. Excellence and persistence, not luck or daydreaming, is rewarded in life. When you fall behind in achievement, you give others the edge and you handicap yourself. Marriage, success and parenthood hardly have a chance where marijuana has any frequency at all.

Teens think they are invincible, so they think they can abuse substances and get addicted without painting themselves into a corner they will regret later. Amphetamines, especially meth, are seductive but emotionally and psychologically difficult to quit and they make ugly people. The prognosis for someone addicted to methamphetamines is very poor even though it is out of their system in 48 hours. Speed freaks think it makes them inspired, effective and thin; instead it makes them nervous, agitated, contentious, paranoid and even violent. It ruins their judgment and yes, they may lose weight for a while, but it is a boomerang that will return to haunt them because they will gain the weight back, plus some, if they ever get clean. Meth will ruin their health, especially their nostrils, teeth, skin and face. It will ruin their life in so many other ways too, especially anything to do with relationships (jobs, parenting and marriages).

Kids have access to all drugs at school. They can get downers and pain killers too. They usually get it from grownups, often via somebody's parents. These addictive drugs promise to take your child down. Some will end up dead, others homeless or in jail. Some will lose years, perhaps decades and cost their parents great sums of money before a treatment program finally works.

Parents, talk about drugs to pre-teens. Tell them all about them. Read these pages to them multiple times. Give them photocopies. Make them experts; don't shelter them. Let them be forewarned. Role-play with them when they are young teens, so that they are prepared to resist peer pressure. And parents, if you have injured your child, know that he will be more prone to try and abuse drugs to medicate his pain. If you abuse substances and still manage to function, don't think for a second that you are not setting your child up to fail.

I know a father who didn't believe his daughter was using drugs. Then he didn't believe she was buying them. Then he didn't think she was selling them. Finally, he didn't believe she was using and driving. Then he didn't believe she was sexting (texting sexual photos and messages via mobile phone). All the while he was smoking marijuana. Everytime she was busted, she would say to her father, "Why do you get to smoke pot?" He never believed that if he stopped smoking marijuana she might stop trying to rebel against the father's blindness, self-absorption and neglect. Actually, I know many such cases in which the parent used and then the child used. To be fair, in each of these situations, there were other problems in the family too, but I notice that in each case the parent seems to prefer denial so they can continue using.

I have also seen families in which there was moderate use of marijuana or alcohol, healthy interaction with the child(ren) and the child turned out fine. Parents who seek to employ moderate use of marijuana or alcohol need to heed the cues of their children. Children should not be using drugs. Period. They stunt emotional growth.

Heal your children sooner than later. Parents, don't be naive or liberal about drugs. Stay awake and take a stand. If your teen is using substances, become an expert. Spy and drug test if you need to. Don't let the problem grow before you take action.

Signs of Drug Use

- Cigarettes stink. Watch out for extra doses of cologne and mouthwash.
- Pot causes red eyes, stupid monologue and dumb laughter or giggles so they will avoid you and sequester themselves in their rooms. If your teen is hiding out, it's time to snoop.
- Alcohol leads teens to become AWOL. They stay out late, oversleep, are truant and their grades suffer. You know the smell on their breath. If your child is abusing alcohol, this is on you. Get the alcohol out of your house now.
- Downers are taken and retaken by very disturbed teens. Sometimes they mix with alcohol and you can have a very dangerous situation, including overdose and death. Teens on downers slur their speech. Their pupils are contracted. They lie flagrantly.
- Pupils dilate on amphetamines or meth. The teen can't sit still, is agitated and may become verbally abusive or violent. Yet in the beginning, you may think she is finally taking care of business. If your teen is not on meth, then she may be having a psychotic or manic episode. In any event, if your child is suddenly extremely talkative, hyperactive and even hyper-vigilant or paranoid, you need to get a hair sample immediately.
- Steroids show up in boys as sudden bulk. Muscles and necks get thicker almost overnight. They experience premature skeletal maturation and accelerated changes of puberty. They suddenly look like stocky men. Boys should know that steroids tend to reduce the size of their testicles and sperm count, lead to baldness and development of breasts. For women, steroids lead to development of facial hair, a deeper voice and the possible cessation of their menstrual cycle. Users may suffer from paranoia, extreme jealousy or a combination of paranoid jealousy, as well as extreme irritability. Users often demonstrate impaired judgment and delusions due to feelings of invincibility. They compound childhood pathology. A teen prone to jealousy or anger who is on steroids could be a dangerous mate for anyone's daughter. These boys don't know their own strength or understand their own hormones and emotions.

Review of Developmental Symptoms

Complete Attachment Break: Early Symptoms
- "changing the subject," arching back, pushing away
- no transitional object
- refusal to make eye contact while being held
- withdrawal
- a vacant look, like "nobody is home"

Attachment Break: Later Symptoms
- Reactive Attachment Disorder (RAD)
- Conduct Disorder, arrogance and over-independence
- lacking sentimentality, empathy and conscience
- cold: no crying, non-emotional
- hostile affect
- alternating complete lack of trust for anyone and a loyalty ethic

Failure to Attach
- asperger's
- autism

Separation Anxiety or Fear of Abandonment
- anxiety
- clinging behavior
- terror of being left
- sleeping problems
- fear of being kidnapped or parent dying

Separation Anxiety Manifesting in Adult
- Generalized Anxiety Disorder
- fear of fear
- fear of abandonment
- stalking
- staying with abusive mate
- intimate partner violence

Early Potty Training: Symptoms in Child
- fears germs
- constipation
- unusually private at bathroom time
- may have accidents at school
- tells too many bathroom jokes

Early Potty Training: Adult Symptoms
- problems with colon
- body armor (musculature for the purpose of maintaining emotional control)
- fear of germs and dirt
- compulsive neatness; no mess or clutter
- obsession with details
- rigid personality

Symptoms of Latency Issues
- problems with reading or math
- problems with homework
- problems with grades

Symptoms of Adolescent Issues
- problems making and keeping friends
- problems attracting romantic partner or attracting too many romantic partners
- courtship disorder
- lack of personal responsibility
- lack of values and ethics
- disrespect for authority
- criminal behavior
- problem of too much responsibility

CHAPTER 5

Imprinting

> For what I want to do, I don't do.
> But what I hate, I do.
> And if I do what I do not want to do,
> I agree that the law is good.
> -- Romans 7:15-16
> (Jeffrey Dahmer's favorite Biblical quote)

The key to being a good parent is learning to truly see your children, read their behavior and accept their authentic feelings (not fake manipulative ones; know the difference). As long as you believe what you see is inborn, you cannot read all the messages they are sending you. These messages guide you, indicating how you are doing as a parent and how they're doing in your care. These messages are essential for you to heed so you can correct the course of your child's path. Likewise, you need to pay attention to yourself and your internal messages.

Love, Then Discipline, the Dominant Imprint

Unique personalities are not genetic, as the only behaviors that genes instruct are universal. All of us are born with the same drives to attach. How well we are able to do that affects what follows. The way you love your child creates the kind of attaching your child will manifest for the rest of his life and the core personality he will have, including how secure and worthwhile he feels. As we have discussed the drive to attach in the First Stage of the First Year naturally begins to extinguish if the need to attach is not met. He will begin to withdraw. His neurons, previously expecting to connect, will begin to prune, and he will become cold, hard or indifferent to people. The older he gets, the harder it will be to turn this around.

While we all have the same genetic instruction to attach, <u>the experiences that follow attachment, or lack thereof, are what make us unique</u>. Every single one of us has different experiences, especially how we are disciplined, coached and taught to discipline ourselves. Our different experiences and how we react to them based on previous experiences are what make us one of a kind.

If our drive to attach is sufficiently satisfied, a subsequent drive to separate and individuate in healthy ways will follow. As we have already seen, this latter drive is determined by the developmental stages of life through which we all pass successfully or unsuccessfully. The nurturing functions that compliment these drives will determine how well we bond to our parents and how securely we pass through this stage (including whether we are left hanging or injured) and how willing we are to separate from them, yet remain connected.

In the second stage of personality formation, children learn how to behave, having formed their core selves, which now may or may not feel like behaving depending on the quality of their attachment. Some children are very securely loved and attached, so their parents can safely coach them into self-sufficiency, good manners, ethics and problem-solving. Other children are insufficiently attached, insecure and perhaps abused, and then to add insult to injury, lack healthy guidance through the developmental stages. Ironically, some children have had secure attachments and then had terrible discipline. They could bear the terrible discipline better when the attachment was good.

To reiterate, the first stage forms the core and the second stage forms the personality adaptations primarily through discipline. In the second stage, we ultimately need to learn self-discipline, which we may learn successfully or unsuccessfully by the way we are disciplined.

In the second stage, parents model how they treat each other and us. The child internalizes the way we treat him as the way to be. Since 1988, I have been calling this drive imprinting.

How parents model behavior, demonstrate self-discipline and/or manage their child's actions become what she imprints. Their discipline methods not only modify the child's behavior, but they also teach her how to relate to others and determine her future coping style. There are ways to discipline that lead to self-discipline, self-reflection and self-correction. There are many ways to discipline that lead to abusive behaviors, guilt-trips, sarcasm, neglect, persecution, revenge ethics, defensiveness and/or inoculations to feedback and boundaries.

The less you repress your child, the more self-aware she may be, enabling her to revise and rewrite her imprinted script.

Imprints Become and Determine Drives

What goes in must come out. What doesn't go in can't come out. What I don't get to do, I don't want you to do. What was denied me I will deny others. What was given to me, I can give to others.
- No two people imprint the same things.
- No two people contend with the same drives because no two people have the same experiences.
- Almost all of us have imprints that drive behaviors that we may likely fail to control despite our best intentions.

It is the job of mirror neurons to store experiences with a drive to replicate them. That is to say that people are genetically driven to imitate what they experience (Rizzolatti, 2006). Everyone imprints, though each person imprints different and unique experiences. Imprinting is a function of both nature and nurture, but what we imprint from our parents is the nurture function. No two people, including siblings, imprint the same experiences. Essentially, personality is the result of attachment plus imprinting.

Perhaps most of our experiences are positive ones so we enjoy positive imprints. Yet all of us have negative imprints, and some of us have imprinted such negative experiences that we're doomed to harm others or ourselves until we become conscious of them and choose to override them.

To escape their imprinted ideas of themselves, some people (mostly women) withdraw and go inward, abusing themselves, driving themselves to self-harm. Some people become insane or suffer degrees of mental illness, anxiety and/or depression that can lead to suicide. Most, however, are driven to re-enact or act out what we imprint. The most common acting-out behavior is imprinted behavior.

Examples of Imprinting

- If we are bossy, our children will be bossy.
- If we are controlling, our children will be controlling.
- If we are rude, our children will be rude.
- If we are respectful, our children will be respectful.
- If we are rejecting, our children will be rejecting.
- If we are critical, our children will be critical.
- Dominated children will become attracted to war, cops & robbers, good guys & bad guys. They will need to act out on others. They will have a drive to punish or seek revenge.
- Controlled children will need to control others. They may become behavioral psychologists or religious leaders.

We Imprint while Out of Power

Imprinting experiences (*vs.* genes) simply, yet profoundly, explain the origins of personality. How we treat others comes from what happened to us, especially if we repressed our feelings. Within us, we carry a drive to scapegoat others from those hurtful behaviors we received that we refuse to acknowledge. If we are injured and bury the urge to give our injury back to the source (our parents), the next time we are in power, we are left with the urge to pass it on to the first weaker person or symbol of us over whom we have power. Then we can enjoy the role of the perpetrator and identify with our aggressor. It feels great. I call it the "12 o'clock high."

The Power Clock

The Causal Theory includes the concept of imprinting along with an essential awareness of the role that power plays in all our lives. To illustrate how power works in the context of imprinting theory, I use metaphorical terminology relating to a clock. *Out of power* is the same as "6 o'clock". Children are usually at 6 o'clock. *In power* is the same as "12 o'clock."

In domestic abuse cycles, the people *in power* often drop into remorse and *out of power*. They eventually return to *power*, round and round. Many relationship issues are power issues. 6 o'clock vs. 12 o'clock dynamics play out visibly once we awaken to these attitudes of dominance and submission.

In Power
Imprint Out

Imprint In
Out of Power

6 o' clock: Out of Power. When we are out of power, we are more able to learn, especially if we are at a "healthy 6 o'clock." 6 o'clock is an ideal state for learning. It is in this state of powerlessness and openness that we take in and digest new behaviors and attitudes as our own. We internalize the unique circumstances of our lives and these imprints mix with attachment strengths and weaknesses from the first year of our lives. Healthy people who are not attached to their idea of themselves don't have much ego and can easily go to 6 o'clock in order to learn quickly and deeply, self-reflect and express remorse with ease. It's a healthy way to "be here now."

Sometimes we are at an unhealthy 6 o'clock because we have been shamed or belittled into it. Sometimes 6 o'clock is a self-conscious state in which it is difficult to think. We may feel judged or be judging ourselves as we were so often judged. In this state of victimization we do not learn well, but we internalize or imprint behaviors we will probably later unleash as a perpetrator.

12 o' clock: In Power. 12 o'clock is an attitude of power or superiority. When we are at 12 o'clock for unhealthy reasons it looks like arrogance or dominance. When we are at 12 o'clock for healthy reasons, we look confident, comfortable and helpful.

We are often unconscious about our attitudes of power. For most people, perhaps it feels better to be in power. It certainly feels safer and there is some sort of presumed regard that goes with power. For that reason, power is attractive.

For people who like to learn and grow, powerlessness is attractive, but usually it is a conscious choice unless you are a child. Healthy children are in a state of openness and powerlessness. This is because they feel safe. A child who does not feel safe cannot enjoy 6 o'clock.

Even a helpful person gains ego identity from being at 12 o'clock, especially if they really feel qualified to be there. People often unconsciously seek power at the expense of other people because it feels good. A know-it-all gains ego identity at the expense of others by taking the 12 o'clock position. Thus 12 o'clock can be healthy or unhealthy. It should be appropriate and invited and not presumed. When we are at 12 o'clock – in power – we are most likely to deliver injuries to others via stored up imprint energy that we acquired from the way we were once treated. At 12 o'clock is when we are inclined to reenact attitudes, behaviors, drives, philosophies and dramas that happened to us, either as a perpetrator or hero.

In Power *vs.* Out of Power

Both states of power have healthy and unhealthy versions.

	Out of Power	In Power
Healthy	A great time to learn	A time to teach and lead
Unhealthy	When a person feels shamed, unsafe, abused, disrespected and is too self-conscious to learn	When a person is driven to revenge, scapegoating and getting even for his childhood abuse

Unloading Imprints In Power

What comes out of us may surprise us. We may have even promised ourselves that we would never do this or that to our child. Then, one day when our guard is down and we're tired or stressed, our child, employee or dog will suddenly become, for us, the child we once were. We become the perpetrator and the roles are reversed. It's as if we are spring loaded, awaiting our first weak moment and real opportunity to reverse roles and achieve relief and retribution on a safe and relatively innocent scapegoat. We become the offender from many years earlier when we were injured. But it wasn't the injury itself that caused us to build up this explosion-waiting-to-happen; rather, it was the subsequent repression and denial. It was our failure or inhibition from returning the favor on the spot. A person can only handle the pressure of withholding an imprint for so long before he eventually explodes and often an innocent, out of power victim is the recipient of the withheld imprint or, in some cases, the repressed rage.

When it unleashes, we like to think it has nothing to do with the past. The more unconscious and shut down we are, the more we can't see the connection between what we've just done to another and what happened to us as a child.

What comes out may not only be reminiscent of the original injury from the opposite side of our childhood experience, but it also includes the attitude and beliefs our parents held when they injured us, even if they were never verbalized. What is imprinted is a complete package of consciousness, including parental immunity and the ethic that the child should not cry or complain. The child needs to swallow her authentic self to satisfy the parent's identity needs or ego to force a dishonest and vindicating mirror.

Sometimes people say, "I don't do this with anyone but my wife; surely it's because of the way she is," or, "My son is the only person I treat this way; he just knows how to push my buttons." What's really going on is that some people fit better than others into the template or atmosphere of the old injury, which evokes our imprints. Sometimes the people who are those closest to us fit the bill, allowing us to treat them as we were treated. Sometimes it's an age or gender catalyst of the comfort of being with someone who is as weak as we were then. The fact of the matter is, if our response is disproportionate to the offense, then we are unleashing our pent-up past (hysterical = historical) onto a person whose actions may have been genuinely irritating to anyone, but we found their actions deserving of very old retribution. If we think the person deserved it and others think we're over-reacting, then we're probably in our past. (Beware of friends who tell you what you want to hear.)

Something interesting about this is that the more injured a client the more certain they are that the person they scapegoated was asking for it while they are sure that what their parents did to them was OK, and even proper. Perhaps taking on the role of the perpetrator is another way of vindicating parents. On the other hand, the more injured and repressed a person is, the more difficult they find "rage work." I ask them to imagine their offending parent in an empty chair and express their feelings on behalf of the child they once were. I find a distinct correlation between those who are the most abusive of others and the least able to express anger at their parents, even when the parents are not really here.

For example, serial killer Aileen Wuornos, depicted in the film "Monster," told her interviewer on Court TV on August 25, 1999 that she killed the guys that refused to take no for an answer, but she didn't think that had anything to do with the incest she suffered throughout her childhood by her grandfather (who, at the time, she thought was her father) because it wasn't that bad.

These are the "enlisted" children. They

have completely internalized their oath to hold their parents harmless for the rest of their lives. No matter what their profession or position, they will protect not only their parents but they'll protect all parents everywhere. It doesn't matter whether they are sitting on a jury, assuming the role of a forensic expert defending perpetrators of incest or reporting bogus genetic explanations for behavior. They are enlisted for life. They seem blind, but if pushed on the subject they become irritable or worse. It's both automatic and highly personal. Without the enlistment and the repression, scapegoating others would not happen.

Imprinting Issues

Before "reading" imprinting issues, rule out developmental stage issues mentioned above, which often overlap. For example, we may have a fairly healthy mother who seemed like she would have made all the right moves, but then we discover that she was hospitalized during the child's infancy. On the other hand, we may have a parent who was a stay at home mom, but she learned in her childhood not to show her feelings and her child imprinted it from her. Pure imprinting issues are not stage related and seem more like re-enactments.
- A child who was hit in the face hits her doll's face.
- A child violates other people's boundaries because her boundaries were violated.
- A father yells at his son; grown son yells at his son.

Some acting out behavior is the result of first-year-of-life attachment issues. Some behavior results from second-year-on imprinting issues. Some behaviors result from both. Our job is to interpret behavior as clearly as possible. For example, if a child fails to groom herself, it may be because she is a victim of neglect even from the first year of life or it may be that her mother does not groom herself and she is imprinting poor hygiene from her mother. Or it could be both. In many cases the child may have directly experienced neglect and further imprinted her mother neglecting herself. In this case we would speak of first generation neglect (the child neglected by the mom) and second-generation neglect, when the child imprints her mother's self-neglect as well. Truthfully, most imprinting is both first and second generation. That is, the child had the direct and the indirect experience.

To further illustrate identifying what is an attachment issue and what is an imprinting issue, consider obsessive-compulsive behaviors and drives. A child who was potty trained before 18 months of age will likely be prone to fastidious choices, even if the mother is not. However, if the mother is fastidious having also been potty trained too early or having herself imprinted exacting and perfectionistic behaviors from her own mother, the child may have learned the behavior either experientially or from imprinting or both. An example of strictly imprinted behavior could be a child who becomes histrionic for having been a victim of incest despite being raised by a matronly and dependent mother. On the other hand a child could appear histrionic for simply having imprinted it from her mother's histrionic behaviors even though she never experienced incest herself.

Four Types of Imprint Energy (Acting-Out Imprints)

Generational. This form of imprinting extends from one generation to the next through a repression ethic. It is the prototype for this theory, taking place between two people, typically parent and child. In this case, a child may someday become the parent who injures her own child in the same way her mother injured her, passing the injury on to even more than one child, who may themselves each have more than

one child.
- Father hits son. Son grows up to hit his daughter
- Mother is an alcoholic. Daughter grows up to be an alcoholic.
- Father molests son. Son molests his son and maybe even his son's friends.
- Mother is passive. Daughter is passive.
- Mother treats her child with respect and her child treats others with respect.

Scapegoating. This form of imprint energy extends from the grown child to others outside of our families, such as strangers, employees, patients and subordinates. When we repress our imprints we often unload them on unsuspecting scapegoats.
- Abused child hits schoolmates (bullying).
- Neglected child becomes a nurse who neglects patients.
- Abused child becomes abusive cop.
- Abandoned and abused child becomes a spousal abuser who batters a wife for threatening to leave.

Instant Imprinting. This form of imprinting extends immediately from one person to another like instant karma. It often takes place as a cyclical escalation of positive or negative behavior. Instant imprinting can take place between two people, adults or children. In this rotating dialectic, we can observe two people imprinting off each other in an escalating argument or love fest.
- Two people fighting and the fighting escalates, getting worse and worse.

- You are nice to customers and they are nice to you.
- You are nice to the bank teller and the bank teller is nice to you.
- A well-loved person is nice to everyone.

Transcendent Children may be free to give their imprint right back to their parent(s) safely. In seeing ourselves in the other, especially our child, we can patiently allow our child to give us back what we gave out. We can earn some spiritual-like experiences of self-awareness and interrupt the chain reaction into future generations.

Groups, Societies, Nations. This form of imprinting takes place from one group to another. It is fascinating to watch how whole societies imprint experiences and pass them on, or to watch them backlash, albeit to lesser or greater degrees.
- Germany was beaten up in WWI, so Germany wants to beat up countries in WWII.
- American racism creates black nationalist separatists, such as Stokeley Carmichael, Joseph Waller, Elijah Muhammad, Malcolm X, Reverend Louis Farrakhan and the Black Muslims.
- Great Britain treated American colonies badly, then American colonists conquered Native America, Mexico, Puerto Rico, Guam and the Philippines.
- Upper class whites treat poor whites badly, then poor whites treat blacks badly. OJ Simpson's jury eventually gets even on a smaller scale by finding him innocent.

Reading Acting-Out Behavior

Not all behaviors are imprinting. Some behaviors result from stage-related interruptions that can create fixations, self-fulfilling prophecies, anxiety or depression.

Stage Issues

Stage Fixation
- Fears germs, dirt, letting go. Because of parents' reaction against poop, spit-up and dirt, child is stuck in potty-training stage (Obsessive-Compulsive). This would actually result in first and second-generation anxiety over dirt, germs and poop.
- Has a need to talk about himself and his accomplishments to hear back how wonderful he is, since he spent his infancy giving mirroring instead of receiving mirroring (narcissism). This is first generation since we don't know if mother talked about herself too. She could have done so, or she could have required a lot of reassurance from the child to keep going or both.
- Seeks merging to complete attachment needs (first-generation borderline). However, mother could have suffered insecure attachment herself (which could create second generation imprinting) or she could have died, been arrested, become hospitalized, gone on a vacation or back to work when the child was small (first generation injury to the child), which creates a stage fixation rather than behavior imprinted from the way the mother acted. Both could be true. For example, if the mother was raised in day care and then put her daughter in day care, it would be both first- and second-generation injury constituting a stage fixation *and* imprinting.
- Hoards food or gorges to meet need for nurturing (*i.e.*, Dependent Personality). This could be imprinted or first generation. It could be both.
- Blow-up doll is just fine since he completely gave up on bonding as an infant (Schizoid). Probably first generation since few schizoid personalities have sexual contact and make babies. He would have suffered a significant lack of touch in the first year for some reason.

Stage Fearing
- Creates abandonment by fears of separation and individuation (borderline). This fear becomes a self-fulfilling prophecy because clinging behavior drives people away. This would probably be first generation only resulting from incomplete fulfillment of a stage because if the mother clung to her child, she would suffocate her and probably drive her away, making her afraid of intimacy rather than seeking it or craving it.
- Fears of intimacy will sabotage relationships with anyone who needs to get too close (distancing borderline, narcissist, sociopath) by pushing them away. This could be a first generation fear only because the mother was scary when she got close. Otherwise a child will not likely imprint a fear of intimacy because the human drive to bond is so strong.

Imprinting Cousins

Re-enactments. As opposed to acting out on another that which was done to her, the child or victim finds a way to tell what happened, which she could do by injuring herself or drawing pictures.
- Little Jenny draws three equal people in her family portrait (narcissism because the child sees herself as an equal in her family).

- Jenny hoards cupcakes for her parents at a school function they didn't attend (dependent). This child was *really* taking care of her parents.
- Family therapist who comes between couples because she learned this role when she was incested by her father (histrionic). If she imprinted this experience and acted it out, she would have molested a child instead, possibly her own.
- Parent pressured child to potty-train, so child pressures herself to be in control (obsessive-compulsive). Still, someday the child may do the same to her own child.
- Mary projects her doctor will blame her for her illness (borderline) like her mother regularly did, so she avoids going to the doctor when she has serious symptoms.

Self-fulfilling Prophecy. A person lives the identity of the assault victim. An incest victim may become a prostitute. Or a despised child might begin cutting herself and attracting people who will treat her badly. Perhaps a little poor boy will grow up to become a beggar or thief.
- Father tells Jenny she's better than other children are. She acts superior in order to meet her father's projection (narcissism).
- Creates abandonment by clinging (borderline). Creates mistrust by mistrusting (borderline).

Rebellion. This is a healthier reaction to oppression. This child or adult may go to the other extreme in trying to throw off these experiences, perhaps rebelling against other authority figures as well.
- Refuses to self-control and is, instead, anal expulsive (obsessive-compulsive).
- Refusing food even when she's starving for nurturing (anorexic).
- Serial killer Aileen Wuornos picked up hitchhiking men and killed the ones who refused to take no for an answer (borderline).

Repression. Repression leads to acting out. It shows up in the form of smiles when one is unhappy, eating junk food or consuming alcohol or drugs to drown the pain. Repression may show up in the form of positive thinking, compulsive behavior, denial or major body armor. Examples of repression:
- Positive-thinking beliefs born of cheering mom on (narcissist).
- New Age thinking, reincarnation and positive affirmations designed to mask old trauma or hold child responsible (narcissist).
- Christian Science, AA, hypnotherapy designed to override acting out from trauma (Narcissist).
- Internal Drive Theory designed to save reputation of Freud by denying patients' actual abuse and "blaming" patient's inherent character (narcissist).
- Behavioral therapists would rather manage behavior than understand it (narcissist or obsessive-compulsive).
- Prosecuting attorneys would rather punish behavior than understand it (obsessive-compulsive, narcissist, paranoid and borderline).
- Accountants and computer programmers would rather focus on details than feelings (obsessive-compulsive).

Examples of Unloading Imprint Energy

- Robert Alton Harris was executed in California on April 21, 1992. He had killed two teenage boys by shooting them in the back. The reason he was sentenced to death instead of life imprisonment was because, after he shot the boys, he sat down and ate their cheeseburgers. As a child, Harris' father didn't believe Harris was his son. He hated the baby before he was born. He kicked his mother in the belly numerous times while she was pregnant with him. In order to avoid injury, she ignored the infant, later her child, so as not to anger her husband. When Harris was a boy, his father took him to the desert with a gun, told him to start running and began shooting toward him, just missing him again and again. What went in had to come out. What didn't go in (empathy) couldn't come out. He'd never had empathy. Why not sit down and eat the cheeseburgers? Maybe he simply had the thought, "I'm hungry," when he saw the burgers.

- Friends complained to a mother about how she did something and she'd respond in a sing-song way, "Sor-ry." The mother didn't realize how insincere this sounded until she heard her son respond to her the same way.
- Greg was a victim of sexual abuse and when he grew up, he was promiscuous, even after he was married. Though he was a great father to his daughter, he fell in love with a teenage girl. When she flirted with him, he acted on his feelings.
- Mario was raped by his uncle many times as a child. Mario molested his brother and other boys in the neighborhood.
- When Nancy had surgery, the nurses were on strike. When her friend Mary arrived at the hospital, another friend was there already, looking as lost as Nancy, who was just coming out of her anesthesia. As Nancy started to throw up from the anesthesia, Mary went to get a basin and some wet washcloths. As Mary wiped Nancy's face, the lost friend backed into the corner whimpering, "No one ever did that for me. I was here for the same surgery six months ago and no one ever did that for me." It's likely no one did it for her as a child either. She was actually saying, "I can't do this for Nancy because it's not in me."
- When I was foolish and impressionable, my mother talked me into marrying my roommate in order to spare her family embarrassment. We agreed to marry. Arrangements were made for us in a town we'd never been to before or since with about six guests at the ceremony, all relatives. After that I couldn't bear to attend anyone else's wedding because I'd never worn a bridal gown or been a celebrated bride. It wasn't until I married my current husband, Ron, many years later in a lovely wedding where my dress even had a little train, that I finally felt comfortable attending other people's weddings.
- Susan's mother used to whip her bare legs with a switch and tell her to dance while she laughed at her. Later as an adult, Susan's mother confided in her that as a child her own mother, Susan's grandmother, had whipped her daughter's legs, that is Susan's mother's legs, with a switch while telling her to dance. Where'd that come from?

Attribution Theory

> Attribution Theory = Hypocrisy
> If I stumble over the hole,
> it's not my fault.
> If you stumble over the hole,
> it's your fault.

If I stumble over a hole in the concrete, it is because of the hole in the concrete. Someone will get sued someday if no one does anything about it. If you stumble over the same hole, I may think you weren't paying attention, that you're unconscious or even that you might not be that bright. This is Attribution Theory. This self-serving bias runs deeply throughout our lives because those of us who are not filled up see ourselves in competition with others and compare ourselves with others to see if we're ok. If we come out better we feel good enough for the moment. We blame others for things we do and we forgive ourselves for things for which we would not forgive others. We seem rather ruthless with one another, which goes to the core of many relationship issues.

Fortunately, if we are full, we may demonstrate more empathy and less competition. If we are not full, we need to at least be aware that we are operating on a double standard until we make a choice not to do it. It is the Golden Rule: "Do unto others as you would have them do unto you." Until we see this we are hypocritical. To have a double standard that has a lower bar for ourselves and a higher bar for others is a form of scapegoating. The reverse is also true; when we tolerate others' blunders or bad choices but are exceptionally hard on ourselves, we're failing to set a uniform bar. Ethics involves holding ourselves to the same standard we set for everyone else and holding others to the same standard without becoming a "should"-er. In other words, if someone is teasing a child, we intervene. If we hit a car in the parking lot, we leave a note.

Often in life we meet people who instruct us how to relate to them; they sort of establish their conditions. In turn, we tell them how to relate to us. I might say, "I can't be your friend if you continue to talk down to people," or I might just say, "It makes me uncomfortable when you talk down to people." I will not say, "Don't talk down to people," because that is not in skills *a la* Chapter 8: Relationship Skills. We need to set the standard we hold for ourselves and others with each of us choosing to be responsible for living up to it.

If we disagree on the standard then we have to assess whether we'd be lowering or raising our bar to be with them and then decide whether or not we're willing to proceed. Yet raising the bar is really the only choice. How does a husband who won't give up alcohol ask his wife to give up drugs? How does a woman get to yell at her husband when she admonishes him, "Don't raise your voice at me?" How does someone who is uninterested in "doing the work" themselves bring a relative, child or mate to therapy? The healthier option is to say, "I'll work on me. Will you work on you?"

> Is it not a coherent hypothesis that this evolution of parent-child relations is the sole cause of changing adult personalities, which is then the cause of all socio-technological change?
> -- Lloyd deMause, psychohistorian

Experts on Acting Out Imprinted Trauma

The late Alice Miller wrote: "Every crime contains a concealed story which can be deciphered from the way the misdeed is enacted and from its specific details...Someone who was not allowed to be aware of what was being done has no way of telling about it except by re-enacting or acting out" (1984, p. 177).

John Bradshaw was remarkably clear about the imprinting process, without naming it: "Whenever we are confronted with a new experience that is in anyway similar to the original unresolved stress, we feel compulsively forced to reenact the old experience...When a child is being violated, his normal reaction is to cry out in anger and pain. The anger is forbidden because it would bring more punishment. The expression of pain is also forbidden. The child represses these feelings, identifies with the aggressor and represses the memory of the trauma. Later, disconnected from the original cause and the original feelings of anger, helplessness, confusion and pain, he acts out these powerful feelings against others in criminal behavior or against himself..." (*On the Family*, 1988, p. 82).

Center for Recovering Families states in its brochure: "You either pass it back or you pass it on."

Domestic Violence

The names of the five categories of domestic violence continually evolve as experts ferret out the different types of domestic violence (Holtzworth-Munroe & Stuart, et al., 1994; Jacobson & Gottman, 1988; Johnson & Ferraro, 2000). All of the versions of domestic violence betray the truth of the perpetrator's childhood and often the victim's as well.

Intimate Terrorism Violence. An abusing male partner has suffered a severe insecure attachment where he experienced just enough intimacy with his mother or parental figure to crave more. He also very likely imprinted physical abuse as a child and possibly witnessed his own mother's abuse. He believes he has to control all events to be safe and he lives in fear of being left or abandoned again, something he would never acknowledge, even to himself. Instead, he formulates an opinion that anyone who leaves him betrays him. Further, if he has imprinted abuse he likely has a drive to abuse when he feels wronged. Since he received little empathy as a child, he has little or none to give, but he knows how to feign enough caring to court a woman. He wants a relationship but he believes the only way he can ensure it will work is with an iron fist, intimidation and even brutality (Dutton, 1995). The probability is high that his behavior will escalate over time. The woman in this relationship is ultimately at risk of her life.

The profile of the woman who stays with such an abusive man is likely to include emptiness, abandonment trauma, physical abuse, helplessness, low self-worth and the belief (often religious) that she should stay. The combination of her hunger to merge and those intoxicating symbiotic moments leads her to believe she's in love. She lives for those highs of mutuality, believing that who he is in those moments is her real husband and his other ways are her fault for setting him off. Or, perhaps, she lives for the moments of intimacy that he offers, especially when they make up, if ever. Her bar is low. While she attempts to be perfect to please him, her childhood provided her no real values by which to measure him. He may not be that different from her dad or maybe he offers her a lifestyle she wouldn't otherwise have. Maybe she doesn't know how she'll care for her young children if she leaves. She may have learned helplessness from her childhood. Maybe she's afraid he will kill her if she leaves. She often thinks she has no choice because she has no skills to take care of herself or get away, and she fears for herself and her children if she tries to go.

Mutual Violent Control. Both parties in the couple are contentious and possibly borderline. The violence is instigated about as often by women as by men, however women suffer greater injuries overall. Both parties probably suffered child abuse and ridicule as a form of discipline. They blame, judge and inflame one another, and were probably blamed and judged as kids. The method of discipline in which they were raised, blaming and shaming, was believed to be the way to force a person to correct. Consequently, blaming is the dispute resolution skill these two practice and just as it never worked when they were children, it leads to escalation now. Even so, both parties devoutly believe that if they hold their offense, the other party will see the light and perhaps say, "Oh gee, gosh, you're right; why didn't I see that? You are innocent and misunderstood and I am wrong." If that were the response, the conflict would end there, but since neither thinks they are at fault, the response of each is quite the opposite and the scenario escalates.

If there are children, punishments are probably physically and emotionally abusive, and these children will find their way into adult relationships to continue the pattern.

Dysphoric Borderline Violence. A borderline personality experiences extreme emotional dependence and neediness and becomes demanding, blaming and complaining, resulting in self-fulfilling prophecies of abandonment and rejection. She becomes further enraged and driven to attack her partner. The majority of these offenders are women in dire need of therapy, revised coping mechanisms and better relationship skills.

Common Couple Violence. The abuser is someone who probably would not abuse if not for his circumstances. The violence may be a one-time event. The couple probably does not have the skills to have a clean fight. The victims of this type of violence are almost as many men as women, although women usually suffer greater injuries. Fueled by childhood experiences, they have negative projections on each other that create self-fulfilling prophecies.

What fascinates me about this type of violence is that often but not always, the victim is the provocateur and once she has finally been struck, she seeks validation everywhere, from the police, his and her therapist, parents and even the children. She wants to prove that he is dangerous. She wants him to pay while she wants to prove her own innocence.

Violent Resistance. This type of violence is similar to Common Couple Violence because it is a response to a perceived threat and often is considered self-defense. It is often a one-time offense.

I was in a continuing education class at the courthouse for child custody evaluators. We watched footage of a very contentious couple. He had put his hands around her neck, threatened her and thrown her up against the wall. Nevertheless, the woman was extremely demeaning and provocative. I spoke up, saying something to that effect and discovered once again that it is politically incorrect to show empathy for the man and hold a woman responsible for how she is being treated.

However, any woman I have ever treated I have taught two things: First, you are responsible for protecting yourself and problem-solving. I will help you. Second, you must not provoke a dangerous person. He cannot handle hearing negative things about himself. Blaming him will not make him better. If you choose to stay with him, stop poking at him and learn relationship skills.

I have told men I have treated who were abusive, whether physically or mentally, that they were not fit to be in a relationship. They needed to step away until they had discharged most of their childhood abuse (in rage work), learned other ways to express their feelings and learned ways to calm down or step away from a provocative situation. Further, perhaps they need to become better at assessing a life partner.

> Substance abuse, especially alcohol, seems to be a common ingredient of domestic violence. Women whose partners abused alcohol were 3.6 times more likely to suffer an assault by their partner. Nearly half a million children are abused by parents under the influence of alcohol. 40% of convicted sexual offenders say they were drinking at the time they committed their crime(s).
> (http://www.marininstitute.org/alcohol_policy/violence.htm)

More on the Double-Damned

No one is immune to imprinting, the source of the most powerful internal drive known to humankind. From how we are treated we develop undeniable drives to respond in kind. Tenderness begets tenderness, empathy creates empathy and the abandoned will abandon. Cruelty leaves us with a drive to be cruel. Empathy and conscience are qualities we never experienced and yet we will be judged for not having them.

When the cruel person is our parent and we are warned not to fight back or even to complain, we enter into a dilemma of the highest magnitude. The way we were treated includes a mandate to hold harmless our provider-perpetrator. Our authentic self dies inside. We lose our ability to perceive and reason. We kill off parts of our inner guidance system, reason and intuition. We have to change our brain to make their mean behavior right. We have to enlist in our parent's defense against us. By protecting the person who hurt us because we love them and so want their approval, we must dumb down and go a little bit crazy.

Most importantly, we will now defend our parents to the death. We will defend what we have learned to think and believe against any threat to think otherwise. To survive, we believe it's right to protect our parents from any assessment that what they have done to us is wrong. It's a door we won't open and anyone who opens that door or their own door is a threat to us.

We develop a reactive defense mechanism and an "ethical" system that prioritizes the nobility of revering our parents and their deeds above all else. It's as if we have found honor and goodness. The next noblest quality is blind loyalty.

We swallow the pill just like in Alice in Wonderland and once this distorted world view is in place where up is down, in is out, right is wrong and wrong is right, we activate our automatic defenses and our automatic pilot. We have enlisted. We are free to reflexively judge others ruthlessly while we grant our parents absolutely immunity. We are blind and do not see. We will not be guilty of thinking independently. We can never become self-reflective, questioning or intelligent, lest we risk our self-deception. We cannot open the black box, nor should anyone. We become enraged at any suggestion that any parent is to blame or simply responsible for abusing a child. Personal responsibility is for criminals, not parents. A ruthless, judgmental god and the threat of hell forever as a penalty for failing to be sufficiently loyal may make sense to us.

> **Defending parents creates blindness and scapegoating. – F.S.**

We now belong to a special Agreement Club where we all collectively idealize our parents. Badly behaved children will never be considered a reflection on their parents.

Some of us join them and others of us become intolerant of these badly behaved children because they did not sufficiently survive to tow the line. They are seen as bad because they do not agree yet with the pervasive assumption, have not been saved, were born under the wrong sign, were bad in a previous life or have a chemical imbalance and bad or weak genes (the latter explanations being the most popular).

We are hypocrites, speaking of our parents like they were saints, believing every word we say, still hoping for their approval. We create an internal division within ourselves, whereby we immunize our parents no matter how badly they behaved and we judge others without patience or mercy.

If we can't give back our hurt feelings because we must be loyal to our provider-perpetrator at all costs, we develop an unconscious yet irresistible drive to treat someone else the way we have been treated. When we can't admit that what happened to us was wrong because the perpetrator was our sacred parent, we need to treat someone else the way we were treated. We are driven from within to do so. It will make us feel better to dump it out and relieve us of the nagging, driving and angry feeling of injustice that's eating us up from the inside.

Now we are prone to scapegoat innocent people. From this backward way of thinking, we develop a desire to blame-lest-we-be-blamed and judge-lest-we-be-judged. Whether we must kill or advocate the death penalty, we will find our homeostasis.

When the deed is done, we won't have to consider the harmfulness of our parents anymore because by harming someone else we made our parents right. When we scapegoat someone, it's as if our parents become vindicated and we feel more sane. What they did to us was okay now because we do it too. We have established normal. The drive for self-defense that we had to turn upside-down and inside-out has been revised. Justice prevails. Wrong is right and right is wrong. What a relief!

A new division unfolds before us. We see those children who pulled off the appearance of normal, like ourselves, as living evidence that abuse doesn't matter. Perhaps we are one of them. We get to judge those who had more abuse than they could bear or even than we could bear. They, the most abused of all, will be our scapegoats. It will be them we love to judge and hate.

I am not advocating that the double damned be set free, only that we be conscious from whence they came. Let us gain clarity that none of us could have done any better in their circumstances.

> ...[N]othing reflects the humaneness and ethics of a society as much as how it treats its children. That view can be taken a step further: Nothing reflects a society's moral attitudes toward children as much as how it treats its difficult children.
> – Peter Breggin, MD

Evil: When Trauma Is Denied

The victim must identify with evil (the inner drive to hurt back) to protect his parents, rather than to face what they have done to him.

One day I asked Richard Ramirez, convicted Night Stalker, "How are you doing?" He said, "Pissed. Really pissed. Some days I wake up angry, so angry I know I'm going to regret what I say. I know I'm going to get into trouble here and I can't stop myself." In another conversation, he disagreed with me that everyone is born pure and innocent and good. "Some men have no morals, no honor, no scruples," he said. In another conversation, when I asked him to talk about some of his childhood trauma, he said, "I know enough about psychoanalysis to know what you want of me. Right now I'm strong. You want me to remember things with you, but the mind is like a jigsaw puzzle: you take one piece out and the rest will fall apart. And where will you be then? You won't be here to pick up the pieces."

Richard was very protective of his parents, which caused me to realize that no one honors thy father and mother like a serial killer. I have been checking that hypothesis since then and it almost always proves true. They endure and repress more trauma than anyone else. From this insight, I deduced that no killer or violent criminal can be said to be rehabilitated if they are still protecting their parents.

An Operative Definition and Description of Evil

Evil is the choice to sacrifice another for one's own comfort or pleasure and then assume, expect or demand that he, the victim, has no voice. If the victim didn't have to keep the secret, it would not meet my definition of evil. It is the secret-keeping that sets up the chain reaction of scapegoating, leaving the victim without an opportunity to heal. If the perpetrator gains pleasure from the victim's pain or puts his comfort over that of the victim and the victim has no voice, it is evil. If an eyewitness to cruelty puts their comfort over telling the truth or taking a stand, that is evil.

Evil is planted and unleashed when one injures another and then requires the injured person to stuff their feelings. **This evil is at its worst when an adult injures and represses a child, especially his own child.** This evil is transported like the vampire's bite when the child represses his anguish for his own sake or the perpetrator's sake. The poison will lie within and wait until it finds an opportunity to release its venom on the next generation of victims. The younger the victim, the more toxic the eventual results will be. Therefore, in accommodating the identity and feelings of our oppressor (usually a parent) we suffer a quadruple whammy.

First, we are **betrayed** by the very person upon whom we depended for love and protection; second, we have been denied the opportunity to heal since we must **hold our feelings in**; third, since we must **swallow the truth** to survive, our repressed emotions will putrefy and eat away at us until they can be expressed; and fourth, **we must pretend** that the behavior of our offender was acceptable to us, thereby losing our authenticity and sacrificing our ability to reason.

In digesting this quadruple whammy, we internalize feelings that will eventually lead to scapegoating. We may injure ourselves, or more likely, we may injure others. Thus we will be driven to injure an innocent person like the child we once were, rather than face the painful truth and turn our anger on our offender, which would not be safe. As we imprint this selfish model, we learn to make the easy choices to sacrifice others and we can't wait until we're finally in power, when we can seek the relief of retribution.

Ultimately, evil is scapegoating an innocent party for what another (usually a parent) has done to us, protecting the guilty out of loyalty and scapegoating others instead. Evil is failing to step up to the plate when evil is being done to another, allowing someone to be sacrificed for the release or pleasure of another. Evil manifests in doing the wrong thing because it's easier than doing the right thing, especially when we'd rather scapegoat than get therapy and face our original pain. Evil is also avoiding doing the right thing on behalf of the truth because there's something we would rather do for our own comfort that will sacrifice another. Evil is failing to understand the origins of evil because that would mean we'd have to take responsibility for the drives within us and look at the actions of those we're protecting. Evil multiplies itself and interferes with truthfulness and healing.

> The cornerstone of evil is the mandate to protect and regard parents no matter how badly they treat us. It is this immunity that creates and propagates evil. When the deed is accomplished the child has been enlisted, usually for life. – F.S.

The origins of character and behavior are in childhood, yet there is some sort of glossing over of the origins of evil because it would put responsibility on parents. Children are always held responsible for how they turn out while their offenders are granted parental immunity. In holding the child responsible for rising above the whims and fancies of the parents' selfish indulgences, the child learns a set of values that get transferred to the next generation.

The child carries within him the material that his design cannot tolerate. To heal and reverse this legacy, the child will need to say what is true, express his feelings and do what is right, while society continually advocates that he should honor and forgive his parents. As a bully society, we will pressure the victim to honor his parents.

Then we do evil as we encourage this child to repress his feelings and truth, for one day he will victimize another, perhaps his own children, his mate, a student, a stranger or his employee.

To fight evil, we have to begin to hold the parents responsible at the source. It's already a given that we spend fewer social and economic resources on the first three years of life than on any other time in the life cycle, yet it's in these three, if not five, years that most of our character develops. The smartest move for a nation is to invest in the welfare – simultaneous prevention and greatness – of children in the first three to five years, especially since pathology becomes increasingly expensive as people get older.

Holding parents responsible doesn't mean we stop respecting them and start blaming them. It means we identify the source of the problem, invest in healing the parents through catharsis and correct it with conviction. As the parents heal, we help them become healers for their own children. We develop an ethic that protects children and encourages parents to get help and in some cases requires they get help.

To eliminate evil, we have to educate the public (parents) and protect and relieve children. Further, if parents hurt children, they need to know that it is critical that the children get to cry, be angry and express their righteous indignation. Crying and raging is not blaming parents; it is simply relieving one's body of the injury. If a criminal accosts an adult, the adult is allowed his right self-defense and complaint. A child's body deserves the same rights. We need to let go of this evil-producing ethic that silences child-victims and grants parental immunity.

At the Santa Monica Zen Center, it is held that when we learn to forgive our parents, we have broken through. We are supposed to get off it and grasp that we took on an act or a "racket" (EST/Landmark Forum lingo employed by the SMZC) and we can simply let that act go and become The Buddha we were born to be. This is done by seeing that the past is the past. Perhaps it's also done by working through the childhood material to the other side. Perhaps, it's done by simply appreciating that our parents, at least, gave us life. There's something valid to all of this, but there's something missing too. This philosophy has blind spots. It looks as if everyone is held accountable except parents. It ignores the necessary process of owning and untangling the repressions subsumed for our parents' sake.

> **Evil is the action or choice that diminishes the aliveness of another.**
> **– Zen Master Bill Yoshin Jordan Roshi**

Zen has turned the endeavor of reversing one's childhood into a pilgrimage that ends in enlightenment: seeing and embracing one's Original Nature. Unfortunately, this theory works in Zen and gives Zen Buddhists the impression that it's a valid theory for all. The reason it works for Zen Buddhists is that Zen generally attracts relatively healthy people initially and weeds out those who can't make it. Zen practice at the Zen Center attracts and demands the crème de la crème, ironically leaving little understanding or compassion for the less fortunate or double-damned, even though it is called "the religion of compassion". Many Zen Buddhists don't fathom how impossible and useless their philosophy is for highly traumatized people and therefore develop an impatience that can injure further. During one of my visits to the Zen Center, a schizophrenic woman, perhaps homeless, joined us for comfort. The woman attended the introduction and then attempted to participate in the service with the rest of the sangha (congregation). In accordance with protocol, her coach stayed beside her for the service to whisper instructions to help her keep up. In this case, the sangha sat, walked and chanted, and finally at the end of the ritual, hit the floor for Three Bows again and again, but the woman received no guidance from her coach. She decompensated in confusion and isolation, while her coach remained stoically beside her. When I asked the coach why she didn't guide her, she said, "I didn't want her to want to come back. She was a psychopath." In reply, I said, "She's psychotic, not a psychopath. She's in pain. She wouldn't end up staying even if you were kind and helpful, but now she has been injured by us." We let her feel worse than when she joined us.

The Cycle of Evil

- The victim is injured.
- The victim is expected to repress the injury.
- The victim holds the injury within until he grows into power.
- The victim refuses to revisit the truth because he is protecting his parents.
- The victim *fears* revisiting the truth because he fears vulnerability and the old feelings.
- The victim needs to explode.
- The victim chooses to scapegoat another rather than face the truth of his injury (and betray his perpetrator), so the injury is transmitted to another.
- The cycle begins again. He will then become the perpetrator of others and the effect is multiplied.

Anecdotes of Evil

Once upon a time, there were two parenting course graduates who were friends with a couple. This couple was throwing a big birthday party for one of the graduates before the couple left on their two-week Caribbean vacation. The plan was that after the party, the couple would fly their four children to San Francisco where each child would stay with four different relatives for four days at a time rotating until their return 16 days later. One child was ten months old, another child was two years old, a third child was four years old and the fourth child was ten years old. **These children were sacrificed for their parents' pleasure and they had no voice.**

When the graduates mentioned to the couple the effect their abandonment would have on the kids, the couple informed them that they had no intention of changing their plans. When the graduates told me how the couple responded, I told the graduates that if they went to the birthday party, they would be dancing with the devil. I said I would not have accepted a birthday party on my behalf at the expense of the souls of little children who would never, ever be the same again, and I would not give anyone who treated their children like that the comfort of my friendship. **If the graduates accepted the gift of the party for their own pleasure, they committed evil.**

Once upon a time, the students at Columbine High School stood by and watched other students ridicule Dylan Klebold and Eric Harris. As the most unpopular students in the school (who are usually neglected at home), they had no voice. When we stand by and witness an act of cruelty (including judgment or blame) without speaking up, we are a party to evil.

Once upon a time, a small child was abandoned, neglected and abused. He complained that nobody liked him, especially at school. To cope, he took charge of his life, willing himself to never give away his heart or become vulnerable again. He became a little tyrant who bossed others, including adults, and scapegoated smaller children for his pain, the same way he'd been scapegoated for his mother's pain. And of course, his mother had been scapegoated for her mother's pain. And so on.

This small child was asked to do couchwork for which he was paid a penny a breath. Yet as he approached his body memories, he struggled to become more and more defensive, bracing himself, clenching his fists and becoming quite rigid. I said, "Jay, if you want to heal your pain, you must surrender and become sweet weak." He rose up off the couch protesting violently with a roar, "No! I will never be weak, ever, ever, ever!" To this I responded calmly, "Well, Jay, you have a choice. You can go into your pain and heal, or you can protect yourself from the pain, even though you will continue to hurt other people and make them not like you. Which path do you want to take?" Jay declared, "**I would rather hurt people than feel my hurt.**" **This was a choice for evil. He was choosing to keep his victimization repressed and silent even though he would someday scapegoat others.**

This was the exact moment of choosing, when one makes the choice between evil and virtue, between hurting others to comfort our own pain or entering our own pain to face our sacred parents and heal. From that choice, we will either injure the innocent or heal. Fortunately, Jay ultimately made the brave and noble choice to heal himself instead.

Once upon a time, I asked a client's parents to come into therapy to support their son. They had provided him a good home in a nice neighborhood with good schools. He was chronically depressed, struggled with heroin addiction and his hunger to merge. All his numerous wives had left him. It had become clear to me that his mother did not nurture him as an infant; maybe she didn't know how. She said he was a happy baby, that he would approach everyone, even strangers. She didn't realize that a toddler's willingness to bond with anyone was a sign of an unattached infant. I explained this to her, but as they left, she turned to me and said, "He's not my problem anymore; he's your problem now."

Once upon a time, I learned that my client had a brother who lived in a long-term psychiatric facility. Apparently when he was about 20 years old, he flipped out and started raging on his mother and father about how they never loved him. They took him to the mental hospital, where he was drugged and has been there ever since. I met the brother during one of his furloughs. He brought a tape of himself playing the saxophone to our meeting. He was very good, but very mathematical and unemotional. He also spoke in a very measured way as a result of the pharmaceuticals. When asked if he ever wanted to leave the facility, he said with alarm, "Oh no, I couldn't do that! I'm too explosive; it wouldn't be safe." What happened to Tom was evil. Had his parents listened and really received the feedback in what their son was yelling to them when he "flipped out," he could be living vibrantly and productively now. We only have one life to live.

Once upon a time, I was invited to speak to my son's class about self-esteem. Since my belief is that it is our parents who give us self-esteem, I respectfully declined, but offered to teach responses to hurt feelings instead. (Now, I would teach that achievement gives us self-esteem.) While I was presenting to the class how to heal hurt feelings and find a secret place to cry, one second-grader spoke up, "I don't need to cry; I just need to wait." I asked, "What are you waiting for?" "When I grow up, I can beat my own kids. I can get even on my kids, and I just can't wait!" he said in relished anticipation.

Once upon a time, a mother said to her child, "Cry, and I'll slap you again," and the child sucked it up so as not to be hit again. This mother had a mother who hit her too, and used the same words when she did it. When I asked the mother why her mother hit her, she said, "Because I deserved it." When I asked her why she told her daughter not to cry, she said, "Because I don't want to see it. It makes me look mean and I'm not mean. She can hold it in; I did." This woman's sacrifice of her child for herself and her mother creates evil. Rather than acknowledge her mother was wrong to hit her and tell her to hold it in so she couldn't heal, she protected her mother and hit her small child. Without healing, her child will likely grow up to do the same thing, or worse, thereby continuing the pattern of evil.

Once upon a time, a mother opted not to believe her fiancé, Jake, when he told her that her son, little Cody, did not do his homework. Jake and little Cody had a deal that Jake wouldn't tell little Cody's mom he didn't do his homework if he promised to do it the next day. The next day when little Cody still didn't do his homework, he said to Jake, "I tricked you." Jake said he'd tell little Cody's mom, at which point little Cody hit Jake. When Jake told the mother what had happened and that little Cody had hit him, Cody denied it and the mother believed Cody. She didn't see his behavior clearly and didn't love the truth as much as she loved the idea of a good son. In so doing, she perpetuated her own evil and also created it in her son: bury the truth, avoid the discomfort of right action and feel free to sacrifice another person to do it.

> We are blinded by the assumption that parents can never do something *that* bad. – F.S.

Degrees of Evil

	1st Degree Evil	2nd Degree Evil
Inflicting Pain	Hurting others for pleasure: Requiring the victim not cry, complain or tell (perpetrator/parental immunity)	Hurting others for relief: Requiring the victim not cry, complain or tell (perpetrator/parental immunity)
Repression	Enjoying the injury of another: Making the victim wrong, which creates contagious behavior	Passively witnessing the injury of another: Keeping the secret, covering up, denial, creating contagious behavior

Bullying

The Bullying Child

When your child is small you teach her not to bully. Throughout her life, you let her know that you will not tolerate bullying behavior. Talk to her at length about it. If she has already developed major abusive behaviors, you must self reflect first. Then swiftly begin to take control with some of the suggestions provided herein. Giving up is not an option, ever. If parents take no action to stop their child from bullying, especially if they've been notified by the school, they could lose custody to juvenile court, be accused of criminal complicity and/or be subject to lawsuits.

> ## Your Child is a Bully
>
> - Did someone bully your child? Was it you? Was it a sibling you failed to control?
> - Is it because you gave up disciplining him or her?
> - Have you been a poor role model?

Bullies are becoming increasingly exposed in society. It's becoming public knowledge that bullying behavior is evidence of a person who feels weak inside, which creates a drive to pick on those who are weaker, younger, smaller, alone or unsupported. It's a clear case of scapegoating and if it continues, it will transition completely into evil. Someone bullied him until it hurt, so he grew callous and mean. He has a drive to get even and/or ensure it will never happen again. He is carrying pain inside that makes him feel "less-than" and bullying makes him feel "more-than."

If your child's school informs you that he is bullying someone, it's imperative that you have a serious philosophical discussion with him about treating people how he wants to be treated: with dignity. In this conversation, you must be soft, caring and a good listener, alternating with being a stern voice of authority.

If you bullied him, you must apologize, show affection and be caring. If you did not bully him but also didn't protect him, apologize, but also gather information. Let him know that it's common for bullies to have been bullied by their peers or someone else. Ask if he has been bullied. Express empathy. Ask why he didn't tell you. Ask what he needs to feel safe because if he could feel safe at a school where no one bullied him or others, it'd help him stop.

Tell him he must stop bullying; it's non-negotiable and we have to fix it. If not, there are serious consequences (take away the car; cancel the trip to the capitol; take away the cell phone; forbid his fraternizing with friends who are bad influences, *etc.*). If you say these things, you may reach him with this one history-making conversation. Ask him what he needs from you to become someone you could be proud of again. "Do we need to change your friends?" "Do we need to change your school?" "Do we need to attend family therapy?" "What do you need?"

So-called "mean girls" exist. They are the children whose parents didn't discipline them when they were little, so they've turned into monsters. They may need to be expelled. If I were a school principal and parents were seeking to register a girl who was expelled from another school for bullying, I'd require her to enter family therapy and/or, if parents have the funds, send her (or him) to Wilderness Therapy.

Predator-types leading to criminal behavior also exist; they are those children who are trying to ensure their own safety with thoughtless and mean behavior. These children need to be arrested. Perhaps they can agree to intensive private therapy, family therapy and peer group therapy in lieu of juvenile detention. If this isn't possible, hopefully your community has or will develop a juvenile hall with state-of-the-art education and treatment.

The Bullied Child

The bullied child is often an outsider. He is often shy or small and likely suffers from low self-esteem and neglect in the home. He could be gay or perceived as gay. If so, you need to double-down and let him know how much you value him. Get him into an activity that helps develop his expertise. If you are biased against your boy for being effeminate or your girl for being masculine, release your parental rights and emancipate him or her.

Ask your child if he has ever been bullied. Ask him if he has ever bullied another child. Both have probably occurred.

More than anything, the bullied child needs protection. Do whatever it takes to protect him. Don't follow him and make him seem like a mama's boy or a sissy, which would be like putting a V for victim on his chest. Anonymously hire someone to be hall monitor. If the school won't allow for a hall monitor, address the school board and ask for protection for your child. If that fails, file a lawsuit. A number of lawyers would take the case on contingency if you can't afford to pay. It may be an up-and-coming field of practice.

Pay lots of attention to your child. Make sure he doesn't have to walk between school and home. If you can't be there and can't afford a taxi, go to the local taxi business and ask for a volunteer, preferably a woman, to help you by escorting your child. Be sure to get all their information, discretely if possible. Give them what you can give. Show gratitude. Ask your child to show gratitude. You can also ask the school bus authorities to help. The public is becoming increasingly aware of the seriousness of the problem.

Help beef up your child. Get him stronger. Pump iron with him. Feed him healthy foods. Get him into martial arts. If you can't afford it, make the circuit to every local martial arts center and tell them you are a single mom or your husband is unemployed and you can't afford them, but your child is being bullied and you need help. Perhaps take him to an acting class where he can develop some social skills. Some children who are knowingly odd-looking can joke their way out of danger by making fun of themselves before the bully can. Seek out a relationship skills workshop. Seek family therapy so the child feels his whole family's support.

Ask the school to keep a record of all the bullied students, who need to stick together. They should have a chance to meet every week, at least, to listen to each other's bad experiences (with parents sitting outside the circle and listening), and they should be able to give each other empathy and encouragement. No child is going to commit suicide if he feels valuable and supported. The school should ask the student body for volunteers to stay with them during lunch and recess. The volunteers can do it together or they can take shifts by day. Maybe your child can be a volunteer for younger children and an older child who was once bullied can be a volunteer for your child. Brainstorm. Problem-solve. Every situation is unique and every situation has more than one solution.

Bystanders

This is where I recommend that children with cell phones record abusers abusing. Give the videos to the principal or police or both. Do it anonymously if that's more comfortable. Braver children can agree to step between the bully and his victim, especially of one of their friends agrees to record them. Some children are strong and brave and would be happy to be the anti-bully. Other children are not suited for this kind of heroism and should never be asked to do it if they think they'd be at risk, in which case, they could just go get help. Being a silent witness is not an option. Tell your child you expect her to be on the side of the group that won't condone bullying. Tell her to speak up. Tell her never to simply walk away. If children are afraid to do something vocal, tell them to write an anonymous letter to the principal. The more letters, the safer the school.

If bullying is bad in your school, dads should volunteer to monitor the halls and schoolyard. If dads are working and can't be there, they can develop a fund to pay someone who can make their presence known in the school. Even dads of kids who aren't bullies or bullied can pitch in to make the schools safer.

How to Break the Cycle of Abuse

- Go into the pain and let out old feelings.
- Do unto others as you would have them do unto you, especially when you want to hit back.
- Turn the other cheek. The greatest spiritual growth comes from being the first one to swallow his drive for revenge in order to de-escalate an encounter. Whoever is at 12 o'clock can give in.
- Don't engage. Find a way to say, "Is that so?" (Reps, 1957, p. 7).
- Be a lion tamer. "I can tell that what you are saying to hurt me is what someone said to hurt you. I am so sorry you were treated this way. It makes me sad, but I hope you can remember how it feels for my sake now."

  Richard Ramirez, who always referred to himself in the third person as The Night Stalker, told me one of his victims asked him, "My God, who did this to you?" He sat down with her for 20 minutes and they talked, then he left without harming her. (Nevertheless, she called the police and testified against him in court.)
- See your mirrors. Child's play reveals imprints, offering us insight into how we're doing and a window into their future. If we read the mirror, we can modify our behavior and our legacy.
- Be self-aware. Self-awareness results when we see clearly into how we treat others, and from where and whence it came. Transcending imprinting is an opportunity for a spiritual or enlightening experience. When my husband and I were first married and had to share a double bed, there were times when he would grab the covers and roll away from me in his sleep, taking the covers with him. In my deep sleep I imagined him as an adversary, the one I fought against for warmth. In return, I would grab the covers and roll in the opposite direction so I could be warm. In a more awake state one morning when I rolled away from him, I realized we were the same. He was both the thief and survivor. I was both the thief and survivor. Any difference between us was an illusion. Seeing ourselves in others creates self-awareness.

> **You do not kiss your children so that they kiss you back. You kiss them so that they will kiss their children and their children's children.**
> **– Unknown**

Confronting Bad Seed Theory and Research

Warning

The following material is critical of the medical model and genetic theory upon which prescriptions for psychotropic drugs and other pharmaceuticals are based. If you are currently on medication, you must not quit these medications unless you are supervised by a psychiatrist who will help you develop a plan to gradually titrate off your medication after having assessed the quality of the therapy you are doing. Your psychiatrist will help you assess how prepared you are to reduce your medications and whether you have sufficiently competent therapeutic support to help you heal the injuries leading to your personal struggles.

Misrepresentation by the So-Called Experts

There is an ongoing debate as to whether personality stems from 'nature vs. nurture.' We have good reason to believe there are no genes for personality, both from experience and scientific research. Alan Zametkin asked whether there is a gene linked to ADHD in his 1995 JAMA article, "Attention Deficit Disorder: Born to Be Hyperactive?" In his article in 2000, Jonathan Leo answered, "To even seriously consider that ADHD is due to a single gene goes against everything that science knows about genes and behavior." Leo pointed out that Cal Tech geneticist Seymour Benzer has shown that even in fruit flies, a behavior as simple as moving toward a light involves hundreds of genes.

Any genetic predisposition for temperament is just as unlikely. I cannot assume it like many of my colleagues. Temperament appears to be the result of an unconscious process between parent and child. Temperament is simply an extended and unmitigated mood that ultimately creates a parent's projected expectation of that mood. It becomes a self-fulfilling prophecy and finally some harder wiring results as the child experiences the same treatment again and again.

The bodies we are born into are of pure nature. Of course how well we are fed and cared for will make a difference. Our bodies have genetic coding for height, coloring and perhaps tastes (*i.e.,* preference for spearmint gum over peppermint). Our features may influence our choices or activities one way or another. The country, class and era into which a child is born is nature's choice; these will bring inevitable lessons from the environment that nurture the creation of a personality.

Bruce Perry, neurophysiologist, made an argument (1997) that all criminal behavior is born of neglect, abuse and repression. Where there is neglect, neurons die away. Mirror neurons record that treatment and then instruct us how to treat others according to those instructions. So where there is abuse, connections are made, specifically and especially with mirror neurons. Where there is neglect, available neural connections die away in a process called "pruning" from lack of use. Likewise, all gifted behavior is born of nurturing, including exposure to relevant dialogue and problem-solving. This creates an abundance of neural connections that enhance personality, mental health and intelligence.

To be fair, some parents have become convinced that their infant is a genius, so they stimulate the child as such and the intelligence does not go to waste. Then when the child is four or six, they say the child has always been exceptionally bright, are certain it's genetic and prove it with testing. In this example, the parents have created their child's intelligence by projecting it and stimulating it. Our foundation maintains that all children could be geniuses with the same attention, sans the superiority that accompanies the projection.

This section on Misrepresentation of the Experts has been included because so many of our students, the general public and even honest scientists have been led to believe that their genetic makeup has a determining role in their mental health, their pathology or their ability to heal. This section briefly shows you reasons to question what you have been hearing regarding the validity of genetic influence on personality traits.

For my entire career as a psychotherapist, clients who come to heal want to know how much of their problems are genetic, asking, "How can you argue the research?" Here is my response: There are two opposing camps of research and only the one with the funds reaches you. Follow their motives. Question the research you hear about and find the other research that's not publicized.

The research that promotes the notion that pathology originates in our genes is predominately generated by the pharmaceutical industry, which uses its false results to convince the public that psychological symptoms of all degrees are genetic and thereby treatable with drugs rather than healable with guided work. Some give lip service to parenting, but in the final analysis, we are led to believe that the symptoms we treat are genetic.

A section of Breggin's book, *Toxic Psychiatry*, is entitled, "Toxic Parents Join Toxic Psychiatry," wherein he identifies a growing population of parents who advocate for psychiatry and medicating children. "The National Alliance for the Mentally Ill (NAMI) lobby on behalf of the pharmaceutical industry. They work hand-in-glove with NAMI. They lobby Congress together and meet the press together (1991, p. 363)..." Taking this stand on behalf of pharmaceuticals is critical to the position that their children's symptoms are none of their making. They are far more invested in their own parental immunity than in learning ways to actually help their child become normal.

The War of the Researchers

I have been observing a war of the researchers over the causes of pathology. Anyone who looks closely into the issue of nature *vs.* nurture will see this battle. Some of the contenders are misinformed yet sincere. Others are very proper yet dishonest. Others are so angry they sling mud as if they are defending their own parents to the end. All of them appear to represent the voice of authority. It is our job to identify researchers' agendas as they oppose one another and to identify which research is credible, not which research gets the most press.

The clinical field is represented by multiple theories designed to either protect the parent at the expense of the child (pro-parent) or protect the child at the possible cost of the parent's ego (pro-child). While a pro-parent theory may explain behavior in terms of the child's responsibility by blaming his genes, another pro-child theory will explain the very same behavior in terms of the parenting.

Researchers may approach this primary issue using the terms "nature *vs.* nurture." Ultimately, the compromise of the open-minded seems to be a combination of both. However, in practice, the nature-and-nurture-together theory ends up simply pro-nature. I say this because it seems that under this model we assume whatever we don't understand in behavior must be inborn, and we choose to understand so little. In effect, espousing nature *and* nurture is essentially espousing nature. If it leads us to assume the parents were not essentially the cause, the assumption is nature. I assume nurture because parents must be ultimately responsible for whatever happened. I have clients who reveal a trauma they have been keeping secret for their entire lives in order to protect their parents. Even in this case, I hold the parents responsible for not teaching their children that they can handle the truth and to always bring their problems to them.

Behind every theory there are motives and ramifications. This field, as I have said, has been divided between pro-parent thinking and pro-child thinking since Freud. Research has been produced to prove that genes cause traits, and research has been produced to prove that parenting causes traits. Both findings cannot be true. It cannot be true that genes create personality and pathology if parenting creates it. It's as if one child is saying, "She did it," and the other child is saying, "He did it." Who's telling the truth? How do you figure out which one is lying?

My field, from the bottom to the very top, has accepted that both sides are telling the truth and it is not the job of our leadership to get to the bottom of the conflicting information, even though deception is unethical, something a clinician would lose her license for, and so much is at stake. Inaccuracy leads to unnecessary suffering. The scientists and their sponsors are expected to be self-regulating but they aren't.

One side has been consistently more truthful and more rigorous in their research. The other side has a history of rigging results. My field sees no evil, hears no evil and speaks no evil. They don't look at the two children blaming one another with any parental responsibility for getting to the truth. This, in my opinion, is malpractice at the top.

Pro-parent research has to falsify the truth in order to contend. It is my intention to clarify what tricks geneticists usually use. I want my students to know what questions to ask of studies to see if the "evidence" they've been presented measures up. Unfortunately, more and more recently the studies are written in such code that even other scientists cannot follow a study well enough to question it. I would like my field to call for transparency in research. I would like us to insist that any study that cannot be scrutinized should be discarded and that our field will take no study seriously until it has been replicated.

Even pro-child researchers get timid under the pressure to "believe in genes." They sneak their theories and observations past the pro-parent gatekeepers by agreeing with the premise that human personalities are made of nature and nurture. Then when you read what constitutes nature and what constitutes nurture, they actually represent that personality adaptations come from experience. The genes provide for the body-self and experiences provide the personality adaptations. By nurture they do mean experience and only experience. By nature, they mean the genetic instructions given to all humans across the board and not uniquely variable from person to person, so as to constitute personality or temperament.

None of us are born speaking Chinese. Only those of us exposed to Chinese speak Chinese. Yet all of us are designed to learn to understand and ultimately speak to one another in shared verbal symbols that convey information regarding the interactions of matter and energy. A linguist would say that Chinese is learned, but could say that speaking Chinese by a Chinese-born person is genetic and environmental. We must assume that the actual specific Chinese version of language rather than any other language is the environmental part.

However, when it comes to personality, a great leap is regularly taken in assuming that the personality of any given person could possibly be genetic. In the most serious cases, we assume that the Psychopath, Sociopath or Antisocial personality is the result of bad genes, at least in large part. If we assumed all the behaviors of serial killers were created by their parents, then we would be seeking interviews with these parents and we would want to hear the hard questions and the hard answers. Brutal parents might begin to fear the repercussions of their parenting and get help if enough of these parents were interviewed.

Even one of my all-time favorite skeptics, neurobiologist Sam Harris, makes the tragic assumption that, "The men and women on death row have some combination of bad genes, bad parents, bad ideas, and bad luck—which of these qualities, exactly were they responsible for (p. 109)?" In another reveal of the genetic orthodoxy of this thinking, he writes, "While it may be difficult to accept, the research strongly suggests that some people cannot learn to care about others (p. 99)." It's hard to imagine someone as skeptical as Harris being so blind, or perhaps sheltered, to evidence to the contrary. I wish he would become as skeptical of the myth of genes as the origin of personality as he is of religion. The truth is, if an infant is not protected and shown empathy, he cannot give it later on. Good science would rule out the acute neglect during infancy and/or the terrible abuse that happens to all violent predators during their youngest years before assuming any of their traits are due to their genes. Just find one predator who wasn't violently abused or severely unattached or both, and then we can discuss genes as the origin of personality (Lewis, 1998).

The problem is that where Harris works and studies, everyone assumes the source is genes. He may even be a bit of a renegade for factoring in parenting as much as he does. The rigorous studies that account for all pathological behavior by environment or parenting are strategically ignored in his environment, just as evolution is ignored by the very religious. Children will continue to turn out violent as long as they are treated in the cruelest of ways. As long as we make allowances that these symptoms may be the result of bad genes, suffering children will continue to slip through the widely woven net of science and we will be pawns of deception on the moral landscape.

If pro-child scientists were braver or more suspicious of the pro-parent research results, they would report unequivocally that genes provide the blueprint for the body while experience creates the individual personality. They would clearly educate us that there is not yet any scientific evidence that nature designs personality or even temperament. None. Those who believe otherwise are operating on faith and mutually reinforced assumptions (Ross & Pam, 1995; Valenstein, 1998; Leo, 2000; Lewontin, 2000; Whitaker, 2002; Galves, 2002; Joseph, 2004; Scott, 2006; Wilbur, 2008).

Business of Science

The Human Genome Project was a highly funded research experiment and biogeneticists were wild with anticipation that they would find the genes for all behaviors. Finally the proper genetic experiments in the engineering of behavior could begin. It was proposed that this would lead to a Utopia. Originators of the project, Robert Sinsheimer and Charles DeLisi proposed, "For the first time in all time, a living creature understands its origins and can undertake to design its future (Kelves & Hood, 1992, p. 18)." For that to happen, one would have to study this manual.

Biological geneticist Robert Plomin wrote about the Human Genome Project, "Just five years ago the idea of genetic influence on complex human behavior was anathema to many behavioral scientists. Now, however, the role of inheritance in behavior has become widely accepted even for sensitive domains as IQ (Kelves & Hood, 1992, p. 283)."

Biodeterminist Koshland advised that some of us will not be able to tell which influences caused which behaviors. That will be the purview of scientists and pharmacology: "We are dealing with a very complex problem in which the structure of society and chemical therapy will both play roles. Better schools, a better environment, better counseling and better rehabilitation will help some individuals but not all. Better drugs and genetic engineering will help others but not all. It is not going to be easy for those without scientific training to cope with these complicated relationships even when all the factors are well understood."

Robert Weinberg, a prominent molecular biologists from MIT, predicts: "Over the next decade one may begin to stumble across genes that are surprisingly strong determinants of cognition affect and other aspects of human function and appearance. [To deny this would be] hiding one's head in the sand."

The business of genetics is broad and lucrative. Geneticists have tried tirelessly to apply genes to personality, which could then be treated with "chemical therapy," a euphemism for pharmaceuticals. The presumption is that behavior or at least some behavior is genetic, *a la* the medical model. So it should be possible to isolate the broken genes of personality disorders like we isolate the genes responsible for physical maladies such as Huntington's disease (affects muscle coordination) or Turner syndrome (absence of a sex chromosome).

It's difficult to trace the logic of the qualitative leap from using genetics to explain physical traits and maladies, to using genetics to explain psychological traits. Nevertheless, throughout every fiber of the society people willingly and almost automatically make the leap without looking.

Research Fraud

Many credible researchers and scientists have reviewed the pro-parent research and found it completely lacking and filled with tricks. A partial list of these researchers and scientists follows: John Bowlby, Peter Breggin, Ty Colbert, Richard DeGrandpre, Albert Galves, Jay Joseph, Richard Lewontin, Bruce Lipton, Jonathan Leo, Bruce Perry, Jonathan Pincus, James Prescott, Colin Ross, Allan Schore, Elliot Valenstein, Donald Dutton and Robert Whitaker. With their help I have been able to identify the common errors that support the research we hear so much about. Below is a summary of techniques many dishonest researchers practice in order to misrepresent a genetic link to personality and pathology. I hope you make use of it when you hear about research allegedly proving genes cause any behaviors.

Standard Practices
- Researchers infer gene association from pathology amongst relatives. It is assumed that if relatives have similar symptoms, it must be genetic. Yet there is abundant research demonstrating that behaviors are learned and imprinted amongst families. (See Chapter 5: Imprinting.)
- Researchers don't rule out environment. They don't even collect information on parenting, attachment and trauma history.
- In answer to the criticisms of genetic researchers that symptoms that run in families could be learned, they develop adoption studies and twin studies to prove environment isn't a factor.

Adoption Studies
- Adoptions are often represented to have taken place at birth when they actually take place anywhere between birth and four years old, or in some cases up to ten, or even fifteen, years old.
- Children placed at an older age are averaged with newborns so the average age of the index groups is often about four to six months at adoption, or placement matches closely to the average age of the control group, which has no older children.
- The "meaningful statistics" can then come from including older children who were removed from troubled households (even though these breakdowns are not ruled out or available).
- Further, scientists have dramatically lowered the bar for what would prove genetic influence. It used to be that 100% concordance (when two blue-eyed parents produce one blue-eyed child), or 50% concordance (when one brown-eyed parent with a recessive gene for blue eyes and one blue-eyed parent have a 50% chance of producing a blue-eyed child or a brown-eyed child), or 25% concordance (when two brown-eyed parents each with recessive genes for blue eyes have a 25% chance of having a blue-eyed child) to so-called evidence of genetic inheritance at only 8%. It isn't even said to be a concordance, but to be of "statistical significance." Concordance is used to represent real, identifiable, predictable genetic ratios between parent and child or siblings. For example, identical twins would be 100% concordance in nearly all their genetic features.

- The term "statistical significance" was taken from other forms of research that use samplings to predict probabilities. These lowered standards that show significance in an experiment are now used to imply evidence of genetic influence, when in fact the true reading of the research suggests environment is everything. Research into genetic studies lowers the bar so that numbers that would ordinarily prove no genetic concordance now show "significance." "Statistical significance" would now be reasonably claimed when a teaching technique caused an 8% improvement in learning. However, to say there is evidence of genetic causality for schizophrenia because there was an 8% statistical significance in the number of schizophrenic parents who had schizophrenic children is a way of obscuring language to make it appear that results were achieved. The term "statistical significance" should not appear in genetic studies. Whenever that term is used in genetic studies it means nothing was proven about genetic cause in personality or behavior. In this 8% hypothetical, we would have to conclude that environmental factors are supported by a 92% probability and the causes behind the 8% significance are unknown.

Identical Twins Separated at Birth
- The concept of identical twins separated at birth having schizophrenia is a myth. The average age in one study for separation was ten, the youngest five and the oldest fifteen. These were called Separated Twin Studies. The twins were considered separated after five years of separation, even if they were separated at fifteen and evaluated at twenty, yet studies were written so the reader might assume they were separated at birth.
- There have only been about ten known pair of adopted identical twins from schizophrenic parents who both turned out to be schizophrenic. In all known cases they were adopted after infancy, usually around three to four years of age. In each case the core damage had been done. Further, these twins were also adopted into similar circumstances such as separate orphanages or by grown siblings of the mother, if not the mother's mother. Thus many of these twins have cause to see each other again as they may live nearby or attend the same church, like looking into a mirror, sometimes extensively. Such reunions can trigger schizophrenic breakdown when the twins start comparing notes about who got to live which life. Triggers for schizophrenia always include mind-bending experiences.
- Research actually proves that schizophrenia is not genetic, so they bolster their statistics by "age correcting," meaning anyone who is expected to become schizophrenic before the age of 45 gets counted as half-schizophrenic, even if they are not yet symptomatic. "Age correcting" is not "blind" (meaning that scientists have the opportunity to influence results). If scientists age corrected for all twins whose sibling became symptomatic, the results would dramatically exceed 100%, thereby invalidating the statistics, so scientists have to limit the amount of age-correcting they do so that the results don't invite scrutiny.

All in the Family
- When scientists speak of schizophrenia in the family they actually have redefined who is schizophrenic so they can increase their statistics into the realm of "significance." They now have broadened definitions and have invented the "schizophrenic spectrum of disorders," covering people who were never diagnosed as schizophrenic, including categories of which clinicians have not heard: "borderline states," "inadequate personality," "uncertain schizophrenia" and "uncertain borderline state." The meanings and qualifications for these definitions are unclear and have no clinical significance.
- Even though schizophrenia is supposedly a different gene than bipolar, they often include bipolar in order to boost the statistics. Lately they are saying schizophrenics and bipolar personalities are genetically related so they can overcome criticisms of this tactic. Thus, contrary

to implied results, most schizophrenia studies have few, one or no actual schizophrenics in their purportedly meaningful results. Rarely does a real schizophrenic subject come from schizophrenic birth parents or grandparents.
- When biogenetic researchers document pathology in the grown children born of "schizophrenics" and reared by "normal" adoptive parents, scientists fail to acknowledge that the grown children who were most symptomatic in their study were also the ones adopted many years later, having been through the attachment stage with the "schizophrenic" parents before being adopted out. The reasons for being adopted out at a later age suggest trauma from leaving the mother to whom the child was attached or trauma leading to the adoption out, such as child abuse or traumatic loss of a parent due to hospitalization or death.
- Scientists have been known in major studies to switch first-degree relatives with second-degree relatives to achieve results. This destroys the validity of the genetic research (because we are no longer talking about genes which were directly inherited), but it pumps up the statistics.

Statistical Problems

- Two major researchers, Cyril Burt and Franz Kallman, were exposed for having fabricated/padded their statistics, yet almost all subsequent research employs similar, misleading techniques.
- Geneticists are utilizing meta-analysis (averaging) to boost their validity. The problem with this method is that they utilize flawed and outdated studies. In essence there is no quality control. They generalize in order to support their claims and agendas.
- Researchers funded by pharmaceutical companies have no problem misleading the public. When their studies are found to be flawed or not replicable, their retractions go unheralded and scientists, whether involved in the studies or not, actually write, speak and continue to represent the studies as if they were sound.

Chemistry and DNA

- Researchers infer gene association from chemical imbalance, assuming that only genes can create a chemical imbalance, while major research is available to demonstrate that environment, especially trauma, changes chemistry (Valenstein, 1988). It's pertinent to point out that the medications that many subjects are taking also change chemistry.
- On the other hand, most of the studies that allegedly detect chemical imbalances cannot be replicated. Often our chemistry changes from moment to moment, hour to hour and day to day, depending upon environment.
- Researchers assume that if a medication works there was a pre-existing chemical shortage. By that logic, if aspirin works, we could infer there was a shortage of aspirin in the brain.
- Scientists study large families and if they find a gene in common for another family trait, say visibly larger upper bodies, the same gene is theorized to be the cause of the family psychopathology, even when the gene appears to be for some physical condition. Later, the correlation cannot be replicated elsewhere. However, the family members who are symptomatic can be shown to have an unusual gene in common, then officials, editors, journals, APA Presidents and scientists hold press conferences and announce that a common gene has been located.
- Behavioral scientists have turned the scientific rule inside out that says a discovery is only valid when it can be replicated. The new procedure is that when the study can't be replicated they declare the lack of ability to replicate as evidence that there is more than one gene. In my business, that's called reframing. The number of genes that create schizophrenia is growing and it is not clear whether they supposedly combine or trade off since there are no consistent results in this regard.

- More and more markers are "identified" to cause schizophrenia. The pattern seems to be when each discovery cannot be replicated, new discoveries are said to have been made that again cannot be replicated. Then newer discoveries cannot be replicated but show that there are more and more elements to the genetic cause of schizophrenia. Each discovery warrants a press conference. Each failure to replicate is reframed as another great discovery into the complexity of schizophrenia.
- The more causes it takes to produce a phenomenon, the rarer it will be. For example, if I have to inherit five different markers on my genes in order to become schizophrenic, I am far less likely to inherit all these factors than to inherit either a dominant or recessive gene. Yet it is claimed that different combinations of markers may produce the same or similar results since schizophrenia takes so many shapes.
- No gene has been isolated and replicated to account for any mental illness.

Interpretation of the Data

- Gregory Mendel's model of genetics is nowhere to be found in genetic research for personality. This is explained as "incomplete penetrance." Incomplete penetrance is a hypothesis that is not proven. It is a circular argument used to explain research failures to achieve significance. Incomplete penetrance implies that scientists failed to completely penetrate the genetic code that presumably existed because it was simply not completely penetrated. By its use it is assumed to be valid. Even biogeneticists say this concept is over-used. It's an explanation or rationalization that is thought to offer proof where there is lack of proof.
- If parents, the pharmaceutical industry, the American Medical Association, the American Psychiatric Association and genetic researchers didn't have so much invested in psychopathology being a medical problem, their research techniques and "results" would be either deemed clearly bogus, fraudulent or comical.
- The more biologists have difficulty isolating "the gene," the more they modify their tune like a shell game. They introduce new concepts like the Diathesis-Stress Model. This model has no evidence behind it other than that it is an explanation for failure to achieve evidence of genetic causation. Evidence produced for environmental causes by pro-child scientists continues to be ignored by geneticists. So the Diathesis-Stress Model proposes that some people have stronger genetic constitutions and others have weaker constitutions, thus some are more susceptible to injury than others. Of course, this hangs out to dry the children whose parents need education and correction. This allegedly humanitarian model fails to consider very early attachment trauma as a cause for fragility; rather, it explains pathology in terms of genetic weakness. Most people introduced to the model appear to believe it is actual science. It is not; it is an unproven theory. The Causal Theory states that early childhood trauma, especially failure to attach or premature separation, accounts for "fragility," and likewise, early healthy childhoods account for resilience.
- Another new shell-game theory of terminology is the epigenetic model in which it is proposed that genes may be modified by the environment. Epigenes modify the genetic expression without changing the nucleotide sequence (DNA). However there are no epigenes, *per se*. Once you wade through the double talk you find out that the environment simply remains the determinant. Nevertheless, the geneticists try to interpret the data to mean that if genes are not the determinants, then at least the epigenes are, only they are called epigenetic factors. Epigenetic factors are not part of our makeup. They are introduced from the outside into the organism. Even mother love has now been said to be an epigenetic factor. Epigenetic factors are environment. The only value in reframing environment in terminology using the root word "gene" is that the reader or listener assumes genes are involved in causation that is nothing else but environment. That's the general and intended idea.

- While there are mounds of evidence which have been replicated ad nauseum for environmental causes of behavior, there has been no such evidence for genetic causes. Yet the environmental research is essentially ignored.

Chemical Imbalance and Brain Abnormalities
- Chemical "imbalances" such as surges of cortisol or adrenalin and other chemical reactions to stress, loss or trauma, are reported by biogeneticists to be evidence of chemical imbalances presumed to result from genetic inheritance.
- Many times subjects are reported to have chemical imbalances or show up as having brain abnormalities in brain scans, MRIs and other such tests, but other researchers have demonstrated that these abnormalities result from neglect or trauma. What is proven to be a result is said to be a cause.
- Many times the actual chemical imbalance is caused by long-term or recent use of medication, which is not ruled out in the research design. Again, what is proven to be a result is said to be a cause.

Politics
- It is a known practice for many scientists to be under contract with pharmaceutical research grants that require pro-genetic outcomes. If the scientists do not produce the desired outcome, they do not get paid, they do not receive their bonus or they are obligated by confidentiality agreements to keep the results quiet.
- Scientists and publicists are paid to write scientific reports that put a positive spin on negative results. Pro-child researchers are not under pressure to produce specific results, so there is no incentive to slant data. There is no public relations agenda influencing the results.
- One researcher's study explored whether people are more likely to seek treatment (with pharmaceuticals) if they believe their mental illness is genetic.

CHAPTER 6

Faith Parenting

> "Treat people as if they were what they ought to be
> and you help them to become what they are capable of being."
> -- Johann Wolfgang von Goethe

Faith parenting is a thoughtful, non-controlling awareness of a child's actions so we can protect him when it's necessary. <u>Faith Parenting is allowing your child to learn naturally.</u> It helps avoid many glitches in personality, including fragmentation, and is a way to strive for greatness.

Children are designed to learn naturally from their own mistakes. Physically, toddlers have less chance than adults of being injured from small natural accidents because of their design.

- Children are built low to the ground.
- They have soft bones.
- They have a reflex to relax when they fall or are thrown.
- They are in their peak of learning. Neurologically, early childhood is a critical wiring period.
- Young children are naturally curious and naturally sponge-like.
- Children learn through exploration and experiential knowledge.
- Geniuses gain experiential knowledge, developing their right brain's ability to picture reality before the left brain learns the nomenclature for their experiences (*i.e.,* words, symbols, categories and compartments for sorting and storing information).
- Children learn naturally from their own mistakes if they aren't embarrassed out of the lesson.
- They are naturally self-invested, self-representing and self-correcting if not embarrassed or shamed out of this proclivity.
- They do not learn in a state of defensiveness, self-consciousness or shame.
- They do not learn through obedience (except to be obedient and to require obedience as an adult).
- Controlled children are guaranteed harm because control harms the body and psyche, so parents who overprotect or over-direct their children harm them in the process.

Over-Control

Children cannot learn well when they are made to feel self-conscious or ashamed. Children don't need you to control everything they do. They don't need you to suffocate them with discipline and advice. This is because they learn naturally from the consequences of their actions. If you say, "See, you ran too fast so you fell down," your child will probably not wire in the lesson as well as if you had not introduced self-consciousness into the experience.

On the other hand, this is a profound time for us to dialogue with them about what they are experiencing, thereby giving them words and teaching them to represent their experiences and communicate thoughts and feelings.

Fragmentation of Competency

Both domineering parenting and neglect can create a fragmentation of competency. Fragmentation of competency is a kind of absent-mindedness that results from a person's failure to create their own organizing schema in their very own brain and thought processes.

It is unnatural for one body to follow another's mind. If a child grows up following orders, he does not develop his own advanced ability to conceptualize and solve problems himself.

Fragmentation of Competency:
- Results from following orders during a critical wiring period (between ages 1 and 5) instead of following initiative and learning by experience.
- Is very difficult to reverse because it occurred during this critical wiring period.
- Creates an absent-minded adult who has to concentrate during transitions from A to B so as not to fall off-track.
- Is remedied by staying underwhelmed and under-extended with pre-planned, self-designed organizational systems (especially checklists) to live by.

False Parental Beliefs
- You have to make a child good or they will be bad.
- If I don't control my child, she will never learn appropriateness or how to act.
- If I don't make them good, they won't be good.
- If I don't control them, I'm neglecting them.
- If I don't control them, they'll get hurt.
- If they don't obey me, there's something wrong with them.
- If I don't control them, they'll never learn self-control.
- It's for his own good.
- Honor thy father and mother.
- What was good enough for me is good enough for my children.
- It's the only way I could have learned to behave.

Control Ethics
- Child-as-Property Ethic: I am responsible for everything my child does (a climate for abuse since this is impossible).
- Obedience Ethic: Children owe their parents absolute obedience (and taken too far, they will lose their curiosity and not learn initiative, creativity or leadership, only authoritarianism).
- Born-Bad Ethic (projecting evil into the child's identity): Good parents shame children into good behavior.
- Worry Ethic (instilling fear): Good parents worry.
- Father/Mother Knows Best Ethic (smothering): "You don't want to do this; you want to do that."

- Control Ethic (learn to stifle and regiment yourself): "Don't get dirty. Be still. Don't cry."
- Domineering Ethic (spare the rod, spoil the child): "If you make a mistake or hurt yourself, I'll have to punish you so you'll learn." "The harsher the punishment, the better you'll learn." "It's for your own good." "This hurts me more than it hurts you."

Faith Parenting Defined

> The greatest honor in my life is witnessing the truth come from a child's heart.
> – Stacy Moya, children's relationship skills expert

When my son, Scott, was in kindergarten he told me one night that he was very unhappy about a new teacher's aide because she wouldn't let the children talk to each other at lunchtime. "When it's recess we need to play hard so we can sit still. When it's lunch, it's the only time we really get to talk to each other." He intently waited for my reply. "Wow!" I said. "You really do have a problem." He looked at me perplexed, realizing I wasn't going to intervene for him.

"Do you think I should talk to Miss Brenda (the principal)?" he asked, genuinely wondering.

"That sounds like a wonderful idea," I encouraged him. The next day I got a phone call from Miss Brenda. "When Scott got here this morning he asked if he could make an appointment with me, a 'first' for me. I told him I was too busy until lunch, but at lunch he could come on by. Honestly, I forgot all about it. So at lunch he knocked at my office door and I invited him in. He climbed into the chair beside my desk with his little legs dangling and said, 'We have a problem.'"

"We do?" I asked.

"Yes, when it's recess the children need to play hard so we can sit still in class. When it's lunch, it's the only time we have to talk to each other and the new teacher's aide won't let us talk. Can you help us?"

"It was really remarkable," she said. "You should have seen him. He was so cute and smart. I just had to call and tell you what an amazing child you have."

When Scott came home, I asked him how it went. He said in an understated way, "Miss Brenda said she would talk to the aide and now we get to talk at lunch. It all worked out."

The Faith Parenting Way

- It allows children to learn to how to multi-task (which means they won't have a problem later with absent-mindedness).
- It is a basis for learning cause and effect.
- It is a basis for karmic discipline or discipline by natural consequences.
- It is a foundation for insight and self-awareness *vs.* self-consciousness.
- It is a foundation for initiative.
- It fosters curiosity.
- It provides a climate for creativity.

Faith Parenting is used by parents who strive for greatness. The Kennedys were faith parented. When JFK was in the White House, he let Caroline talk to J. Edgar Hoover, much to Hoover's dismay, I imagine. Picture it: "Daddy, who are you talking to?" asked Caroline. "J. Edgar, honey." "Can I talk to him?" "Sure." Then JFK put Caroline on the phone.

Scott's first speech was when he was three. I put him up on the table in front of me. I said, "These people have come to learn to be better parents. Do you have any ideas about what a child wants parents to be like?" "Yes," said Scott. "OK, please tell them what you think children want," I requested. "Love your children. Never spank them. And give them plenty of cookies."

If you are a drummer, put your son on your lap when you play.

If you are an artist, give your child paints and place an easel beside you.

If you are a public speaker, bring your child and introduce her and let her speak on every possible occasion.

Traits of Faith Parented Children

- calm
- conscientious
- strong sense of self
- a sparkle to their personality
- indignant when treated disrespectfully
- have sort of a sense of rights and right-and-wrong, even a higher standard for how adults should act
- healthy and quick to heal
- adept
- able to confront in a constructive way
- hard to repress
- hard to swear into secrecy (by a potential abuser), hard to abuse (especially sexually) and hard to abduct

One day we were in Tower Records and I realized my outgoing child was hugging my leg. I asked him why and he said, "That man over there has scary eyes."

Another time I was with my business partner and her toddler, who was sitting on the counter at Kinko's. A man came up to her and said, "You're such a pretty little girl, I bet you like me." She shrank back and grabbed hold of her mother. She intuitively knew that this man was unsafe for her. Her instincts were in good shape. At that age, I know my instincts would not have been reliable, for I'd already been taught to honor all adults, whatever they expected. I have memories of feeling threatened by certain adults and believing I had to sit in the fear without being rude.

On another occasion, when Scott was about four, my husband and I took Scott to the drive-in movie theater. We had a spot up close to the playground area and Scott made friends with a young child there. After it was time to come back to the car and watch the movie, the child followed Scott and got into our back seat. Scott asked him sweetly, "Aren't you supposed to go to your car?" After the child left, he asked us if he was right about that. Of course, we said, "Yes".

Examples of Faith Parenting

When parenting with faith, you might allow:

...climbing on furniture. Scott started climbing to get out of his crib. Next he wanted to climb into his high chair. After that he pushed his high chair up to the kitchen counter so he could get on the counter to get some cookies stored on top of the refrigerator.

When he was a little older he got up on our big wooden coffee table and used it for a stage to sing and dance for us. It was quite providential. Play is practicing for adulthood.

Once when Ron, Scott (10) and I went hiking in the mountains, we took a trail that was pretty difficult for me. Scott scaled the embankment to the right and ran across over the top to meet me in front where, walking mostly backwards, he coaxed me to keep going. "You can make it, Mom. You can make it." Then, he'd run backwards over the embankment to get behind me and push me gently and firmly from behind. It was hard to be tired as I watched my agile and tireless son bounce in front of me and behind me, scaling sharp rocks and cliffs as if they were nothing. He affirmed Faith Parenting was good.

...jumping on beds. When Scott was old enough to walk and jump, I knew it was time for my husband and me to buy a serious mattress. I went to Macy's and bought a king-size mattress that would be good for jumping. I had it placed on the floor with no bedframe. When friends visited, Scott invited them to jump on our bed. They had a few pillow fights too. When our mattress needed replacing, it was not because children had jumped on our bed; it was because it was old and there were two trenches where Ron and I had lain.

...standing in the stroller. When Scott was about nine months old he had become good at standing on the stroller with one foot on each stroller arm, holding the handle and rocking. I thought it looked like a fun thing to do and wished I could do it. At the department store one day, surrounded by mattresses and carpeted floors, Scott climbed up on both arms of the stroller and began to rock. I was less than arms reach away, but an alarmed woman came over shrieking, "He's gonna fall! He's gonna fall!" I calmly looked at her and said, "He may." (Of course I would have broken his fall had he fallen.)

...playing in and tasting dirt. Playing in the dirt is an important experience for children. Hopefully they will make roads, meet critters and eventually plant some plants. All children have to taste dirt at least once. Don't worry. Once will be enough and she will spit it out.

...dropping food from the high chair. Babies love to drop food from the high chair just to see it fall. Then they get to see someone pick it up again and again. Don't get mad. They are discovering The Way of the Universe. After ten times, you can sternly tell her, "No more. Daddy doesn't want to pick it up anymore."

...playing in the toilet. Every American child has to discover a toilet and how amazing it is. It's part of demystifying it and getting ready for potty training. It's a good idea to schedule a time for this discovery, scour it out, put in a few drops of bleach and let your child have at it.

...unrolling the toilet paper all the way. All children need to unroll the toilet paper all the way. Sometimes they need to do it a number of times. It's a wonderful experience. Try it yourself. You can always put the unrolled paper in a little basket in the bathroom and still use it.

One little girl had a brilliant idea. This little scientist figured out she could put the toilet paper in the toilet, flush the toilet and the toilet paper would rapidly unroll and stream down the toilet with the flush. What a brilliant, thrilling discovery that was...until she was punished!

...climbing up a slide. It's a child's duty to climb up the downside of a slide at least once. She needs to find out what it's like to climb up a slide and prove that she can. Of course, children need to pick a time so that they're not interfering with another child's play. Watch out for adults who want to tell a child that it's against the rules, even when no one's waiting to go down. It will be up to you to speak up for your child and say, "Since no one is trying to slide down, I thought it would be a cool experience for him to have."

...learning the audio-video player. It's a great idea for your toddler to learn how to operate a video player as young as he is ready. Videos are much better for children than television because you can pick them for content. Your child can load them and play them repeatedly; it will give him a sense of independence and competency. He listens to the words, the diction, the accents, the logic and the attitudes again and again, digesting them for himself. Also, operating safe electrical and mechanical equipment like a DVD player is a great learning experience. They're not too expensive to replace these days if they break. If you have an expensive one, get your child a cheap one or used one of his own.

...flipping power switches. I had a partner once whose toddler was turning the stereo on and off again and again. She began to get anxious about it and asked me how long I thought it would go on. I asked her, "What are you worried about?" She said, "What if she wears out a switch?" Since I knew she was an audiophile and knew a bit about audio equipment, I asked her how many times she thought that switch could be turned on and off before it wore out. "Oh, probably more than 100,000 times," she sheepishly replied, getting it.

Stages & Ages of Faith Parenting

Faith Parenting from Birth

Children usually know what they need. They cry for attention, to be held, to be fed, to get a diaper change, to be seen, to engage in dialogue and to feel involved.

It's good to let a child decide when to end a stage. A nudge can be OK, but do not pressure. They give clues that they could stop nursing around eight months, when everything is going very well or they could be open to potty training at 20 to 36 months. They will relinquish a bottle for a cup when it's time.

- Toddler-proof the house at about seven months.
- Get rid of all sharp furniture such as coffee tables with sharp edges.
- Put away valuable and fragile objects.
- Lock up poisons or store them way out of reach.
- Cover sockets.
- Faith Parenting may feel threatening without limits, but the most important limits need to be about ethics: how to treat other people.
- Set absolute consequences for meanness, rudeness and bossiness.

Starting to Faith Parent a Child New to Faith Parenting

Gradual
- Explanation speech: Mom and Dad are learning new ways. Responsibility begets freedom.
- Set limits with natural consequences.
- Give freedom as child earns it.

Abrupt
- Preparation speech: Mom and Dad are learning new ways. More freedom includes responsibility and good choices. I/We expect a period of over-doing. Your consequences will be more natural. Explain.
- Create a rite of passage to start Faith Parenting.
- After that, begin to set limits with natural consequences. (See Chapter 7: Discipline.)
  - Cold dinner if late for dinner.
  - Cancel Disneyland trip if bad report card.
  - No friends over if room is a mess.
- Parents should expect their children will not know what to do with so much freedom, so they'll overdo at first.
- Prepare natural consequences before warning so you can act swiftly without buying time to think. However, if necessary you can always say, "Get away

from that pool while Mommy thinks of your consequence."
- No warnings or one warning only. No changing your mind.

Scott had been faith parented since he was a baby, so as he got older we upped the ante. When he was about three, he had his own TV/VCR and video game console. He also knew how to have a grown-up announce my name and where to find him over the loud speaker in a store. I made sure we practiced that experience a few times. (No one knew we were practicing but me.) He rather enjoyed it, so he disappeared about six more times to have our names announced.

When he was about six we gave him his own phone with business cards. He found it too pretentious and hasn't used them since. When he was about eight we gave him voicemail so he could learn to check messages. At about age eight, he knew how to order a pizza (which is actually a pretty complicated process, relatively). When he asked his cousin if he wanted to do it, his cousin panicked.

Set Limits: 10-Time Rule or 3-Time Rule

Some things can only be experienced once. Before you show or allow the child to discover the thing, you say, "OK! One time. Just one time. You only touch the bird one time," holding up one finger. Now you have set a limit. Do not break your word.

Some things you can only let your child experience three times. Before it begins, you say, "OK! Three times. Just three times. You can only play in the toilet three times. Then no more. Today is one time... (holding up three fingers) Time's up." Be sure you give a fair amount of time, perhaps half an hour. Then tomorrow, you may say, "Do you want to play in the toilet today or another day? You have two more times (holding up two fingers)."

Some things a child can only do ten times and that's all the time you can give to it. "OK, you can sit in daddy's lap and play with the steering wheel ten times (after the car is parked in the driveway, of course). Today is one time. After ten times, no more."

Faith Parenting Is No Excuse for Neglect

- Do not let your child stand up in a stroller over a marble or concrete floor.
- Do not let him run around a swimming pool.
- Do not let him go naked on the front lawn or when company is visiting.
- Your children are well-groomed before you leave the house. They may pick their own clothes, which you've helped them choose in the store. Even if they wear mismatched items, their hair and teeth are brushed and their skin is clean because after we get dirty, we wash up.
- Your children don't go to another person's house with bare feet.
- Your children are not allowed to put their feet on another person's furniture while wearing shoes.
- Your children must obey adults immediately when necessary (in case there is an emergency), especially in another person's house.

Dealing with Danger

- Cars: Say in a big voice, "Car BIG! Car *hurt* baby! No street!"
- Sharp: Allow your child to lightly touch the point of a sharp object. Say, "Sharp!" Say "Sharp!" to several sharp items, followed by "Hurt baby! Sharp hurts baby."
- Hot: Tell your child a toaster is hot when it's hot. If he reaches to touch it, he will experience hot. Or use a hot cup of coffee. If he touches it and pulls his hand back with tears in his eyes say, "Hot! Hot!" Then walk over to the stove and say, "Stove hot! Stove can

hurt baby. Hot!" Of course we don't want to say this when the stove is cool. The child needs to believe our warnings.

Special Faith Parenting Situations

- **Discovering the water cooler.** If you have a water cooler, this will be an issue sooner or later. You can let your child imitate you three or ten times while you stand with her. You may even have a stool for her. You may have paper cups near by. The rule going forward is: "You drink what you fill." If the child is too young for that rule, after you let her experiment with the water cooler (and a towel or cup is underneath), then you say firmly, "No more!" This becomes another limit until she is old enough to try it again.
- **Koi ponds.** We have a koi pond in our garden. When Scott was a toddler, we took him to the edge of the pond and showed him how he could lie down on his belly and touch the water, but he could not walk in the pond or walk close to it. Scott never questioned us once he knew what he could do and had tested limits in other arenas. That said, it does not mean that we ever let our guard down.
- **Mommy's busy.** A Master Parent told me this story. Her darling little daughter was hanging all around her while she needed to get chores done. She wanted to get through her chores so she would have time to spend with Taylor. She kept telling Taylor to move over there and stay "this far" away from mommy while mommy swings this hoe and shovels dirt. Taylor was having a hard time watching and not imprinting. So Taylor finally solved the problem and found a toy shovel and started working alongside mommy. This Master Parent realized that she and Taylor could do things like this side by side all day and have qualitative time together.

Faith Parenting in Someone Else's Home

- **When in Rome...** Young children find it confusing if parents change rules. Children learn to be sensitive about the ways of others when they set their own rules. Teach them Romans are in charge of Rome. Different people have different rules and we always follow the rules of the home or store we are in.
- Explain to host (*i.e.,* Grandma) about Faith Parenting, that the child gets to set his own limits in his own home, but Grandma gets to have her own rules. Tell Grandma that Romans get to announce their limits and speak up for themselves. Romans may have their own consequences (*e.g.*, if you walk on my sofa, I will turn off the TV).
- Your options if you don't like their rules when visiting are:
  - Accept them anyway.
  - Leave (and do not return until child is older).
  - Invite them to your house the next time.
  - (in extreme cases) Require they take this class before visiting again.

Other Parenting Hints

- Pick appropriate restaurants – family restaurants – and leave big tips.
- Never leave dirty diapers behind in someone's home or store, including in their trash.
- Always recruit your children to pick up their mess before you leave or before putting them to bed ("leave no trace").

Faith vs. Negative Projections

Faith parenting addresses another mistake parents could make; it replaces potential negative projections with positive ones. When you worry, you send a negative projection. When you don't trust, you send a negative projection. When you judge or label (as opposed to assess for the purpose of correction), you can entrap your child or your client in an invisible prison of damnation that he might not escape unless he breaks off his visits with you.

Therapists hold negative projections too. A therapist is sort of a person's second shot at having a parent or a guide who believes in them. Some therapists forget that. When I attended California Graduate Institute, I took a course in Freudian Analytic Theory. I studied under two professors, a man and a woman, who co-taught. He was a psychiatrist; she was a licensed clinical social worker. She taught the class while he sat in the corner listening with authority and occasional approval, even though he rarely looked at us or at her. A student once asked if they were married. I looked up to catch their reactions. I was stunned because I never saw them interact in any way. The professor's response was a question of course: "Why do you ask?" Wow. Analysis appeared to have an adverse impact on the behavior of the practitioners I thought.

These two were living their roles, not only aloof from us, but their relationship was so private they couldn't even acknowledge their marriage in front of their students. To me, it seemed like an occupational hazard that they lived such stuffy lives; I didn't think it could be healthy. I had the thought that maybe they enjoyed that role of separateness and superiority dictated by analytic practice, yet another indicator of a lack of mental health practices. I digress. To give them the benefit of the doubt, perhaps they were modeling how to act like a blank slate. (By the way, I've never seen an analyst succeed at this even though they assume they do. In my experience they give away their judgments, but are just unapproachable about it.)

One day the woman taught the Internal Drive Theory and I smelled projections and genetic inferences since it is held that our behavioral drives are inborn. I asked if she or they thought that killers were born, not made. She affirmed with the tone of an expert that they were born that way. I spoke back in disagreement, sharing with the instructors and the class that I had a video of a mother pinching her baby's nose and slapping his face back and forth, and it seemed to me when I watched the tape that the mother was making a killer. Dr. Professor Man spoke out of the distant corner simply to say, "That's extreme." Another student supported me, "Exactly. Isn't that the point? Extreme parenting creates extreme results."

That night I reviewed my syllabus to see what lay ahead for the next lecture. I saw that we would be covering projective identification and the following one was on interpreting dreams. I read ahead and discovered that projective identification was a concept intended to identify an assumption by a patient that becomes a projection onto the analyst (an authority figure, as a result of how the patient was treated by her parents). It may be experienced by the analyst as an invisible pull from the client onto the analyst, causing the analyst to feel certain feelings toward the patient in countertransference (therapist's redirection of feelings toward a client), maybe even causing the analyst to respond with strong feelings. For example, if the patient mistrusted the analyst, the analyst might begin to feel contempt for the patient for mistrusting him. Then the analyst would take that feeling as information about how the patient goes through life making people feel. I saw, to at least some degree, the analyst was the innocent party of the client's strong thoughts and assumptions.

At the same time, I wondered whether it was possible the analyst could actually feel that pull without having judgmental thoughts of his own. I concluded the answer was yes and I was sure it worked the other way too. It seemed important to me that the instructors advise future analysts and therapists that they can erroneously project onto their patients, causing potentially harmful responses to the projections and creating self-fulfilling prophecies. I suspected that they were capable of committing this sin since they believed in internal or inborn drives and genes as the origin of personality. I hoped they would be aware of how their negative views of the patients could dangerously affect and define them. We hold the stronger projection since we have the power of definition, not unlike a parent. It is when our client doesn't trust us that we must show them that we trust them. How we see our clients, how we hold them in our thoughts and speak to them affects their identities and reactions to us. Admittedly, expectations and projections travel in both directions, but we as the adult figures hold responsibility for defining someone dependent upon us for our opinions. Perhaps if the patients struggle against our projections, we might find it disturbing, but I would hope we could tell them what we are feeling and what words or action seems to give us that feeling (like mirroring, addressed in Chapter 8: Relationship Skills). I would hope we would contemplate their experiences, benevolently offering some sort of attempt to self-reflect and disavow them of any fears about what we think, thereby helping heal them from paranoia and perhaps previous negative projections.

As scheduled, the lecture on projective identification began and when it was done, I asked if analysts ever have projective identifications on the patient. The answer was an emphatic "No," moving the discussion on to dream analysis. I interjected that I had a dream I thought would make a perfect segue into the next lecture and I wanted to share it. I knew I was pushing the envelope, but I soldiered on. "Last night I dreamt I was with a little girl in a two-story courtyard in a Mexican villa. I sensed danger and took her to the balcony. Suddenly, two desperados, one male and one female, burst through the double doors, each carrying big guns with ribbons of ammunition hanging from the shafts as they aimed at us. I stood in front of the little girl to protect her as they began to shoot at us."

The professors were silent. "No one likes my dream," I thought. Maybe I had become a nuisance. It was clear in that moment how the silence of an analyst was not blank. On the contrary, the analyst's silence can be a real message of disapproval. Still, it was represented both in training and to the patient that reading the silence negatively was a projection belonging to the patient. I found it to be an inauthentic mind game where we hold all the cards.

After the lecture on dreams was over and class was dismissed, I leaned down to get my books from the floor and when I sat back up, Dr. Professor Man was standing over me. He said to me in a harsh whisper, "If I am on your committee when it comes time to evaluate your dissertation, I promise you now I will vote against you and you will not pass." Clutching my hand to my chest, I looked at him and said, "Bang! You got me."

All I ever wanted to hear from him was that he could handle the feelings of the patient and that we need to be aware of our capacity to abuse our power as analysts. Truth-be-told, I wished he would revise his beliefs in genes as the origin of personality because they can be harmful projections onto patients. Instead I found myself on the receiving end of his abuse of power, which turned out to be my proof and my own self-fulfilling prophecy, obviously created by my projective identification in accordance with his inability to hold the neutral position he is supposed to maintain.

As therapists, we take responsibility for the reactions we create in our clients, even if it is only to discredit a projection, so the client can see they are projecting, assimilate the information and enjoy the relief. As parents, let us not abuse our power to define our children by assumption. Let us watch out for our beliefs that our children are born the way they are. Let us have faith in our children instead, while holding our bar high, so they can see how we believe in them.

> I officially broke away from the Swiss as well as the International Psychoanalytical Association. I was forced to take this step when I realized that psychoanalytical theory and practice obscure (*i.e.*, render unrecognizable) the causes and consequences of child abuse, by (among other things) labeling facts as fantasies, and furthermore that such treatments can be dangerous, as in my own case, because they cement the confusion deriving from childhood instead of resolving it. -- Alice Miller, psychiatrist and psychohistorian

CHAPTER 7

Discipline

"To be nobody but yourself in a world which is doing its best,
night and day, to make you everybody else
Means to fight the hardest battle, which any human being can fight;
and never stop fighting."
-- E.E. Cummings

Parenting only by disciplining can't work. Parents may be able to create obedience by intimidation, but they do not create character, especially healthy character. Children must be cherished and protected by whoever disciplines them. In this way the child welcomes their lessons. They internalize behaviors and insights for life. Discipline only works well when there is love and when the child feels valued and protected by their disciplining parent.

The parent who truly engages with their child as a coach is the parent who doesn't have to use harsh discipline *ever*. Children want to please their parent, especially if it is a parent with whom the child has a positive relationship.

A child who appears to need harsh discipline has been emotionally neglected. Some parents may see what needs to be disciplined, but not their child's emotional needs or the causes behind bad behavior.

Children need to feel seen and understood. They need to be able to safely share their mistakes, dilemmas and problems with their parents in order to receive guidance. They don't necessarily need to be rescued, but maybe they need to know you care and can share some hints on how to cope. Maybe they need a dialogue about how to deal with friends, teachers or other adults. They need to hear your philosophy of life and how your ethics inform you. They need to see how you process your feelings, self-reflect, have a disagreement with their other parent and how you keep your word. They will incorporate your way of treating others into their own ethics.

Children need to dialogue about their experiences. They need to know that you sit in the front seat of their life's vehicle and look with them through the same windshield. You see much of what they see and you have good ideas about how to best proceed. Sometimes you instruct. Sometimes you ask good questions. You seem patient. Always allow them the space to make mistakes and learn from life's lessons. You are able to be their witness, not their boss (unless you have an arrogant child).

If you discipline your child, you must also show approval for at least twice as many choices as the ones that you discipline. When you discipline, it must be swift and brief. A child must know that they will not be labeled for their wrong choice and they can change quickly.

Limits and Clarity

A toddler who has been faith parented (as well as any child, actually) will reach for the pretty flower and crush it to discover the properties of a flower. A little older, the toddler will reach for the pretty flower, crush it and look to see your reaction. This is a test. This is your moment to clarify, it's your essential moment to offer discipline if you haven't already begun. Do not fail in this moment. The longer you wait, the more difficult it will be to turn around bad behavior, which can become a personality disorder with a gradual loss of empathy and ethics. This is behavior that eventually becomes selfish, mean-spirited and repellant to healthy people even if the child is well-bonded and faith-parented.

If your child can make the world his oyster but treat others well, he will be a low-maintenance child. That doesn't mean you are done, but it does mean your work will be seasoned with joy, pride and wonder. Parenting your child will be far easier for you than for most parents. Yours will be an enchanted, ethical child while other parents struggle with children who are shut down, hyper, mean or arrogant.

All Miracle Children (those parented according to this theory, or very similarly) go through these three stages successfully:
- They are well-bonded, adored and secure infants and toddlers.
- They are "faith" parented and their curiosity and drive to discover is nurtured and valued.
- They reach a point where they assume they are superior and without limits and then must be confronted by their parents at the first signs of arrogance. The parents may need to contain the child until the child agrees to be obedient and sweet. This creates clarity for the child, when the child becomes clear that the world is his oyster if he treats it well.

Alison Gopnick writes in *Philosophical Baby* (2010) that babies are ethical. I agree. I also believe they are seeking limits. When your baby first bites your nipple or pinches your cheek, she is checking to see if it really hurts you or if you will stop her. She wants to see what you will do if she hurts you. She is finding out about you, her limits and the world. She knows what she is doing.

Some mothers maintain that their infants don't realize what they are doing. That is the beginning of proving to your child that you don't see her. It is a distressful moment for an infant. The child will test more and more, hoping that you will finally see and stop her. I have seen a toddler pinch a baby and watch for mommy's reaction. When I told mommy what I saw, she replied that her toddler didn't realize what she was doing. Yes, she did. When you make that assumption, it's like assuming your daughter is an airhead; it's insulting. Pinching and biting are obvious gestures of aggression to an infant. As we have discussed in Chapter 1: Creating a Personality, babies' right brains are born sufficiently developed to recognize emotions, positive and negative, and are able to store holograms of whatever they experience.

"No bite!" you say and you put her down. Let her cry if she must. Do not recant your decision to represent yourself. The next time you nurse, she will respect your breast and feel safer for it, for her burning question has been answered and satisfied.

She pulls your hair or pinches your cheek. "No pinch!" Put her down swiftly. "No hurt mommy!" you say with a frown.

I used to cringe at the idea of disciplining my child because of the way I was disciplined; it made me feel small and worthless. Then one day on a ride home from two wonderful days at Disneyland, just my son and me, my four-year old sat beside me in his car seat (which was legal then), speaking to me in his wise voice. It had been a long time since I had disciplined him for anything. I was having too much fun being his mom and taking care of him, discovering the world through his eyes.

"Mommy, if I ever do the wrong thing, you can stop me," he said.

"Oh, I see," I responded, realizing he would feel better if I disciplined him.

"Yeah. You could take away my Nintendo...(long pause) or just threaten to take it away."

Not long after this conversation, he dared me to discipline him, so I sent him to his room. We lived in a humble cottage and his room had no door. I watched him enter into exile and turn around, put his hands on his hips and step just one foot out to defy me, "You call yourself a therapist! You're a child abuser." Then he jumped back behind the line. I could tell he thought he had been brave. I could also tell he respected the line. I didn't deal with his name calling at that moment because I was taken by the respect he showed for the invisible line.

There had been other times when he tested me, but sometimes I thought by trusting him I was passing the test. Other times, I knew better. I remember once when he brought me drawings. I fell all over myself in genuine praise, but then he returned to present me with a shabby drawing. I told him I didn't think it was so good. He looked relieved now that he knew I had standards.

The Foundation seems to attract blind and weak parents who were either disciplined so harshly they don't want to discipline their own children or parents who are just too weak, guilty or selfish to enforce good behavior. Some seem to be afraid that their children won't love them if they discipline them. Some need to love unconditionally. Some think their children's arrogance is evidence of true superiority. At the risk of seeming to support abusive parents, I need to say that I have been appalled by the failure to discipline by many of our graduates.

We have had graduation ceremonies where we provided entertainment and parents brought their children. Despite having attended the whole lecture series, we've seen parents allow their children to run around squealing and shrieking at the graduation ceremony. They heard the faith parenting part, but appeared to overlook the discipline part. They seemed afraid to make a scene.

I have seen children of PaRC Foundation graduates show up at other people's homes without having brushed their hair or put on shoes, as if they were faith parenting. I have seen PaRC children manipulate their parents with transparent lies. In other words, I have seen our children turn into narcissists because the parents loved them unconditionally. At one graduation concert where Scott was performing and children were running around, he put down his guitar, looked at me from the stage and said, "It appears you have failed them, Mom." I saw and I agreed.

After that I called a meeting of the teachers and told them under no uncertain terms can we fail to be clear about the critical importance of setting bars and consistent limits and with follow-through. Parents need to look at their children's behavior now and see what they will look like as adults without intervention. They need to read that behavior. I told them we cannot let parents leave this course without being clear how important it is to set the bar and hold it. Since then, students have been told that when they bring their children, if they fail to discipline them, the teachers will step in. At least the parents can see what they should have done.

Why We Discipline

Why Bad Behavior?

All children are born G∞d. Most bad behavior is an expression of weak parenting or something stuck in the body: a trauma, a bad experience, lack of nurturing, an imprint or a projection. Before you discipline, you need to see what you're disciplining as your own mirror or guidance system. Read the mirror before you smash it. Your child's behavior is feedback about how you are parenting.

- What have you done to (or not done for) your child that is causing her to act this way?
- What do we need to realize before we discipline?
- What information is this behavior providing you?
- How does bad behavior tell us what our children need?

Possible causes for bad behavior are:
- discipline issues: neglect, weak limits, inconsistent limits
- imprinting: abuse, shaming and violent punishments
- imprinting (learned behaviors): abuse, neglect, powerlessness, self-fulfilling prophecies
- sarcasm
- bonding and attachment issues: hunger for attention, lacking empathy or conscience
- repression
- projections
- feelings of worthlessness

Unhealthy Reasons to Discipline

- Protect an image
- Force obedience
- Break the mirror that your child is acting like you
- Keep from losing control (in itself a loss of control).
- Toughen up the child
- Create obedience for its own sake

Guidance

We discipline to give guidance, hence the root word for discipline: disciple. Your child is your disciple, ready to learn from you directly and by your modeling. He will learn from you how to ultimately discipline himself. From you he will get his values and ethics.

One time Scott came home from school highly distraught. Children had called him names that day. I was fascinated by how sensitive our little egos are; names seem to really hurt like stones. So Ron and I sat with Scott on the patio that warm afternoon and called each other names. Ron first called me a name and I saw Scott's head whip around to see my reaction from the corner of my eye. I picked it up and I called Ron a name. He called me another name and I called him another name. Then Ron called Scott a name and Scott, having caught on, called his daddy a name (a once in a lifetime opportunity). After we exhausted ourselves with as much creativity as possible in the field of name-calling, he never suffered again from insults. Had we not dealt with this quickly and philosophically, it's likely he would have begun name-calling other kids. I share this story to underscore the premise that discipline is guidance. You are your child's life coach and you help him through life, offering him attitudes and alternatives with which to get by. How would you have responded?

On another later day, Scott was on the phone with a friend who wanted to schedule a play date. It was the third such offer and his friend had cancelled former invitations at the last minute. I watched to see how this would go down because Scott did not seem to remark to his friend about the two previous experiences of disappointment he had endured. They made the date. I consented to take Scott. And sure enough, just before it was time to leave, Benny changed his mind. I told him, "Next time make no agreements. Tell him you can't make plans with him because you can't trust him to keep his word, but you will consider spontaneous invitations in the moment, if you are available."

Thus, discipline is mostly guidance and the better your guidance, the more children will respect your word. If all we have to say to our children is "Stop!" and "Don't," we are poor disciplinarians.

Obedience

A healthy child who has passed through the three necessary steps of clarity for a resilient personality (good bonding, faith parenting and the clarity exercise outlined in the beginning of this chapter where the child tests you and you pass the test by disapproving) will be respectful of you and others whether they are above or below in the power structures of their lives. They will also be creative, problem-solving and resilient.

Most of the time, you will make your demands of a child after first saying please. You do not want a child you have beaten down to obey for the sake of obedience. It is not good parenting and it takes the extra special stuff of life out of their reserve and repertoire. As mean as my mother could be, she would always say to me, "Yes, ma'am," or to my brother, "Please, sir." She was born and raised in Selma, Alabama, and I was born in Charleston, South Carolina. I put some time in Florida and lived a bit in Atlanta. Down South, ma'am and sir were required. It became a sweet habit my son uses today.

You do want a child who will follow instructions instantly upon request. If there is an emergency and they must move in order to be safe, you want a child who will "Get off the stairs now!" when the piano is coming down.

More abusive parents believe in ordering their child all day every day. They may think they are toughening their children for a challenging life ahead, but what they don't realize is the more we prepare a child for that tough life, the more he will lack resilience, attract bad relationships and have poor coping mechanisms. He will have that tough life.

Finally, you do want a child who is both obedient and free to express herself. You don't want a child who is willfully disobedient. Such a child, as we will see later, has been neglected or has had weak parenting. This is a child who is out of control. You will have to control him to teach him self-control. This child, who wasn't disciplined from the first moments of testing, will need to learn to believe in you again. We recommend a technique very similar to Super Nanny's. As a matter of fact, I recommend you and whomever you co-parent with, watch her television show religiously until you are clear how to effectively discipline. I recommend that you don't debate what you see, since you have already had your chance to try it your way. If you are prone to debate the contents, I will bet you have taught your children to debate you.

Dr. Phil's Technique

Dr. Phil's Commando Parenting suggests stripping the defiant child's room of everything but the bed and bedclothes. Then he must earn back all non-essentials with good behavior, one act at a time (McGraw, 2004).

Super Nanny's Technique

Super Nanny recommends the following steps to discipline a child who has learned to be willfully defiant:
- After making your request for cooperation give the child an opportunity to comply by hanging back or walking away.
- If she disregards your request (such as to stop hitting, pick up her mess, come to the dinner table, get back in the house), tell her calmly with strength, "Now you are going sit on the Naughty Chair."
- Lead her to the chair. If she resists, pick her up and place her on the Naughty Chair or Time-out Bench (or whatever you want to name it).
- Stoop down to her eye level. Try to make eye contact so she can see the intention in your face. In a stern, low-pitched voice, tell her she must stay on the Naughty Chair for ____ minutes (one minute for each year of age) because she did not _____ (fill in the blank; be specific).
- Walk away. Do not dialogue with the child. The consequence includes the loss of your attention, but also gives her a moment alone to choose to obey or not. Choosing to obey is important learning and long-term "wiring" in self-discipline. You may walk back into the room to make sure she is sitting there, but you must act like you are there for another reason. Do not look at her. Pass by her to check something.
- Your goal is for the child to be successful at staying on the chair for the full length of time. Every time she gets up and leaves the chair, you pick her up, put her back and restart the time without talking. You may want to buy yourself a timer that you can put in her view. The first time you restart the timer, you can say, "starting over." If you start over more than one time, she knows what is happening and you must not talk to her. Eventually, she will stay the full time.
- When she has stayed on the Naughty Chair for her ascribed time, go to her, briefly say again why she had to sit there and ask her to apologize.
- After the apology, you can say, "Good girl!" in a pleased voice or ask for a hug and kiss and then move on with the rest of the day. Moving on creates resilience.
- When she tests your limit again, repeat the process.

Remember, the reason you are going through this ordeal is because you have been weak and inconsistent. You must be strong and consistent as long as it takes. Be prepared for the process to last multiple hours. Do whatever it takes to right your own wrong. Do not fail or it will get worse as she ages, which will be far more difficult for you. It will eventually work if you are consistent and do not falter. Stay strong.

Basic Discipline Guidelines

Set and Maintain Personal Boundaries

Parents need loose boundaries for very young children. Children need to have the freedom and right to climb on their parents' laps at will, unless the parent truly can't handle it and will hurt the child. When they are very young, children need access to their parents even when parents are in the bathroom. Boundaries (personal limits) mostly belong to the child. This includes learning the lesson in front of them and acting accordingly.

Children may tell a parent not to tickle them, throw them up or tease them. We must honor these requests. Needless to say, it is not okay to ever violate a child's body by molesting or hitting him or her. It is not okay to devalue children, name-call or label them, nor is it okay for children to name-call or label others. Parents need to set some boundaries for self-preservation (*e.g.*, bedtime, quiet time) and model the concept of setting boundaries for others. Children may not hit their parents or anyone unless they are being contained or engaging in approved play. Such play needs to have rules, limits and must be constructive (such as creating masculine affection when dad doesn't know how to engage affectionately or to teach martial arts).

Set and Enforce Limits

- Set limits with natural consequences unless natural consequences aren't available.
- Set limits without guilt.
- Give one or no warning, preferably no warning.
- Display cool implementation of consequences in a low-volume, close-up manner, or with indignation and outrage, depending on the seriousness of the offense.
- Give explanations only when necessary.
  - Unnecessary explanations to a three-year-old, like, "We don't hit" imply you don't recognize your child's own ability to perceive or figure things out. Instead, "You hit? You leave the game NOW!"
  - Unnecessary explanations imply you don't see your child and realize that she already knew what she was doing was wrong and was daring you to stop her.
  - Unnecessary explanations cause children to eventually tune you out.
  - Children learn best from experience and natural consequences.
  - Arrange to be available to discuss the issue afterwards in a calm way *without lecturing*.
- Allow your child to mourn the limit. If you set a reasonable limit, let your child flip out until he has internalized it. Do not, under any circumstances, give in or you will create more difficulties accepting limits and eventually, you'll have created a monster.

Discipline Rationally

Do Not Abuse Your Child. If you have abused your child, you did it because you were abused and possibly neglected by your parents. You may have even learned from them that a child has to be frightened or even traumatized into good behavior to learn it once and for all. Perhaps you even think you deserved it. Perhaps you think it was the right way because it was good enough for your parents. The truth is, your parents didn't know better. They didn't have good interaction skills with children and perhaps not even with adults. Good parents don't resort to violence. Violence becomes an imprinted model for behavior. You need to get in touch with the truth of what happened to you, how it felt, how you are taking it out on your child and how you are injuring your child rather than teaching her to be a better person.

A child who is in fear cannot learn. Children who have been disciplined with threats (rather than consequences) live as adults in a chronic state of anxiety. They have cortical steroids running through their body in a low-grade state of on-going fear. They mistrust. They cannot think or reason as clearly as they could have or as compared to other children. Instead they learn defensive acts and hypervigilance, honing their expertise around paranoid ideation.

They become experts at perceiving danger or what could be danger. They develop clandestine ways. They fail to enjoy the process of learning. They seek opportunities to get even and gain power so they can abuse instead of being abused. Their growth is stunted. At the very least, they learn to cope by inflicting pain on others.

Discipline with Disappointment, Not Anger. Show disappointment or even disgust, but not anger, when she does something abusive to another person. The best discipline in that moment is for her to see the major disapproval on your face and to hear it in your voice. This is to say if your child ridicules another child, you need to say with disdain, "I am so disgusted to hear you treat another human being that way." However, this expression of disapproval is measured and under control.

If you erroneously rage at your child or discipline in anger, be careful not to retract what you have enforced or even to apologize. Apologizing is appropriate once in awhile, but if you keep apologizing, you will convince your child you are not in charge of yourself or him. This is a little bit worse than having a parent who rages.

Do Not Brainwash Your Child.
- Some parents teach their children to prefer them above the other parent (especially in divorce cases).
- Some parents teach their children to lie to protect them, especially abused children.
- Some parents teach children to suck up their feelings and their truth.
- Some parents teach their children to fight their parents' battles and their own battles, but don't really protect them.
- Some parents reinforce behaviors of kissing up or of giving rote, artificial responses. This works in the beginning, in the learning stage, but if you detect after awhile the child is just appeasing you and is without remorse, you have a

problem. You need more heart-to-heart conversations about ethics.

Do Not Guilt-Trip Your Child. Some parents actually think it is a good technique to guilt trip their child to get them to modify their behavior, but in fact, it sends a message to your child that you are weak and the only reason to behave is to take care of your feelings. It makes them sick inside to think you are so weak. Don't use your neediness to discipline your child.

Avoid Lecturing. If you are a parent who lectures, your child will eventually tune you out. They learn from natural consequences more than from lectures. However, you can discuss their process with them. You can ask poignant questions and teach them to self-reflect. You can talk to them about the feelings behind their bad choices and you can give them empathy for their feelings when appropriate. Discuss what they could have done with those feelings instead.

Teach that we need to make the hard decision if it is in front of us to do, even though it may not be what we want to do or what feels good in the moment, and in the long run, we will feel better about ourselves. Maybe you can tell them about an ethical decision you had to make that was difficult for you and how you are proud of yourself now. Let them experience you as someone with whom they can discuss their problems.

Avoid Inoculations. Do not start with weak discipline and gradually increase the intensity of your responses as offenses worsen. You'll be inoculating your child to your feedback forever without results. Establish your power initially by having fewer, more memorable moments. If you are too lenient, your child will continue to test you. If you are too harsh, you may damage his resilience, trust and enthusiasm for life. Walk the middle ground, intuiting when to lighten up and when to toughen up. Pick your battles judiciously, but do not inoculate.

I knew a mother who had a narcissistic child, even though I had been coaching her since birth. When the baby bit the breast, the mother laughed because she was so cute. I warned her. As her child got older, she still tolerated her child's bad behavior and failed test after test. The child became even more narcissistic. Then one day, shortly before Christmas, the child choked a playmate. The mom asked me what to do. I said, "Cancel Christmas." Her response was, "Then I would have to punish myself!" It was clear the mother would rather take care of herself than her child's bad behavior. It gets damned inconvenient sometimes, but that's the price we pay to save our child's soul.

Keep a United Front. Be on the same page with your spouse if you can. Don't disagree with the other parent in front of the child *unless the child is in danger*. Work out your disagreements later in private. Every time you intervene on your child's behalf in disagreement with your spouse, you drive a wedge between your spouse and your child, damaging their bond. It cannot be worth it, unless the child is at risk of violence or emotional injury and needs to see you stand up for him.

All children need to idealize *both* their parents. Only if the other parent is clearly living an unethical life, such that he ends up in prison, becomes a drug addict or has an open affair, can we make an exception to this rule. Even then, we want to say, "Daddy loves you very much, but he doesn't know how to live his own life or to be a good husband because he did not learn it yet."

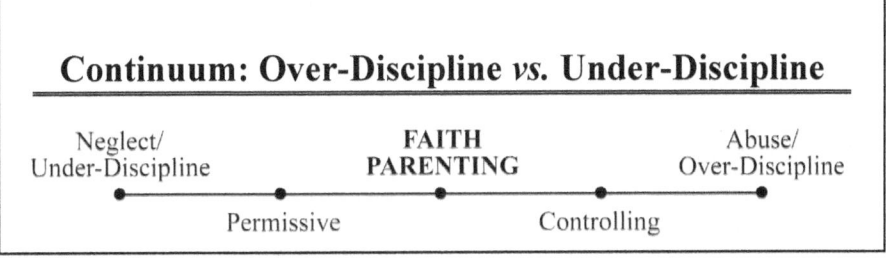

Continuum: Over-Discipline *vs.* Under-Discipline

Major Failures from Over-Discipline/Abuse

Pro-Parent Discipline

I have met a number of children who seemed like robots without souls. It is really hard to be with these children. It's as if nobody is home inside. They lack curiosity. They sit for hours without complaint. They have nothing negative to say about their parents. They are preoccupied with a clean image, but when their parents are away, they cackle with evil glee, stick a twig in another child's side, use fake gang jargon to be hip or otherwise look for superficial ways to get attention. They appear to have no curiosity or depth of thought. They memorize things to say. These children who are designed to make their parents look good are flat and uninspired. They cannot possibly develop an IQ any higher than 100. Perhaps they will even do some things well in school, but it won't be around creative thinking or asking good questions. They are role-players in life.

They are already frauds and they got this way by dutifully following instructions from their parents on how to act. As a matter of fact some of the worst cases I have witnessed have practically been under our collective noses here at PaRC. Parents have admitted later that before they arrived for classes, they ordered their children not to embarrass them; they better look good. We helped train these children along with their parents on how to act, focusing as much as possible on what the child was thinking and feeling and whether they were acting for their parent's sake. It's not hard to detect. The child looks to the parent for instruction every time they are asked a question that they don't have programming to handle.

Ironically, they also seem to lack self-awareness. Once the child is hardwired for this personality, I recommend that the child learn something with great expertise in an arena where parents do not reign, wherein they will find all life's problems and lessons to explore and solve authentically. We continue watching them and teaching parents how to have deep dialogues with their children about their points of view, the antithesis of pro-parent discipline.

Don'ts for Over-Disciplinarians

- Don't discipline in anger.
- Don't discipline without self-reflection.
- Don't hit your child. It teaches hitting as a solution to conflict and stunts intellectual growth.
- Don't use violence or violent words.
- Don't discipline sadistically.
- Don't humiliate your child (*e.g.*, wash child's mouth out with soap).
- Never laugh at your child when she's in a consequence.
- Never call your child names.
- Don't shame the child.
- Don't discipline for your own convenience.
- Don't discipline to get even (for something that happened in your childhood).
- Don't rage or lose control. You'll actually look weak.
- Don't discipline out of fear unless someone is in danger.
- Don't hold a grudge. This is a key to resiliency *vs.* hopelessness.
- Don't give illogical punishments (*e.g.*, taking away baseball when he doesn't practice piano or assigning mowing the lawn for hitting another child. Make punishments related to the offense.)
- Don't use a double standard by disciplining the child for something you do too. (*i.e.,* don't hit him for hitting.) Change your behavior first.

Primitive Parenting

Most of the abusive parents I have known were abusive because that's how they were parented. They imprinted abuse. It came naturally or so they thought. Sometimes they admitted they couldn't help themselves. But mostly, what they had imprinted was their sole repertoire. They actually thought that terrifying their child was what they had to do to control and stop the bad behavior. It's as if they thought there was a demon in their child with whom they had to compete. They had to scare the badness out of them. Make them fear the consequences of bad behavior. These parents think that if they scare their child into good behavior maybe they won't do the same thing again. If you don't have any better ideas, that's what your parents did and you don't want to complain about how you were parented, it seems right. Most parents abuse because they love their children (and their parents more). They are practicing primitive parenting in the name of love.

Repressive Parenting

These parents have secrets or live in extreme privacy. Frankly they cannot be trusted. I am still looking forward to meeting someone who is big on privacy and is still healthy, honest and authentic. They also don't want their children to give them feedback for how they are doing. These parents live inauthentic lives and want their children to be frauds as well. Many times these parents think they are teaching their children appropriateness. Unfortunately these children cannot heal life's injuries that accumulate because they will learn to fear expressing the truth they know and their own emotions.

If they are molested, they will know not to tell. If there is a custody dispute and they are taught by one parent to lie about the other, they will do so without compunction. They have not learned ethics. They have not learned to love the truth. They have learned instead how to act to look good. Someday their own children may hate them for that. A sociopath develops in this context when this style of parenting is taken too far.

I knew a child who used to debate with his mother about what happened. It was quite an enthusiastic contest and it happened over so many things. They argued over what time she woke him for school. They argued over what she said or didn't say to him that upset him. They argued over whether she hit him or didn't hit him or whether she accidentally did this or that or did it on purpose. I wasn't their therapist so I didn't have an opportunity to truly get to the bottom of this debate, but it seemed like both of them were so credible, yet one of them was lying. I wanted to see video footage. I actually recommended it to the dad. I have since heard that the boy has developed symptoms of paranoia. I am now sure who was lying (the mom).

Barbaric Parenting

Some parents are so injured from their own childhood that they look at their children as objects to dominate, as they were treated themselves. These parents are capable of mean-spirited teasing, tickling and even torturing their children because it's fun to see them react and it's fun to be the one who's finally superior. These parents have a drive to hurt their children and they create children who are so unlovable they are easy for others to hurt, as there is no constructive goal in any punishment. The vicious cycles of abuse in these homes lead to perverse, paranoid, antisocial, sociopathic and otherwise deranged behavior.

In my twenties, I sat in a Manhattan diner at around 2:00 am and witnessed a mother, her man and her two-year-old interact. The adults sat on one side of the booth, the somber little boy on the other. They indulged in two plates of food for themselves while ignoring him. He sat eye level to the table and attempted to reach all the way across the divide to try to secure a French fry. The mother whacked him on his head so hard his head sank between his shoulder blades, but he did not cry. Several minutes later he tried again and she pounded him another time with a loud hard blow. Still, he did not cry. I studied this tiny child and thought someday I would hear of him on the news. (If it had happened within the last thirty years of my life, I would have submitted a police report.) This was barbaric parenting.

With this kind of parenting, at best, the first year of life creates a disorganized attachment, if there is any attachment at all. In the second year on, the child begins internalizing and imprinting violence, degradation, rejection and scapegoating.

How to Make a Killer

Criminologist Lonnie Athens offers the most detailed description of the childhood experiences that lead to creating violent criminals. He breaks down the necessary ingredients into three main stages in which the drive to kill is ultimately established (1992).

The first stage, **Brutalization**, involves subjugation, or being controlled. The child is treated violently. If that dominance is challenged, the perpetrator beats the child into submission. Once the child pleads for mercy, the beating stops. However, there is another level of subjugation in which the brutality is out of control and surrender does not stop the beating. This beating is a retaliatory beating resulting in a bitter, buried drive for revenge. The child resigns to the ongoing beating, but fantasizes ways to stop the attacker by killing him. When the child is treated to <u>horrification,</u> he helplessly witnesses the abuse of a loved one such as a sibling or a mother. The child thinks of rescuing his mother or sibling by attempting to attack and even kill the abuser, but instead develops feelings of helplessness and guilt for not being able to do anything about it. He has to listen or watch, knowing that if he intervenes the attacker will turn on him. His helplessness and guilt turns in to excruciating self-loathing and fantasies of killing, possibly in order to rescue.

Additionally, if he <u>lives in a violent neighborhood</u> he is not safe to leave the house. The other children in the neighborhood have turned into bullies from similar abuse. It is not only dangerous at home, but it is dangerous to even go to school. The child has begun suffering the social experience of being picked on and ridiculed by his peers. His persona becomes identified as a subject only worthy of ridicule, rejection and abuse.

In the second stage, **Besiegement**, he is pressured into becoming violent with <u>violent coaching</u>, which consists of ridicule and coercion. He is harangued with relentless taunting to fight. "If you don't beat that kid up, you stupid wimp, I'll give you a beating you'll never forget." At around the same time he is introduced to <u>vainglorification,</u> where someone established in the neighborhood takes an interest in him and shows him how wonderful it is to be feared.

The third stage in creating a violent person is the **Belligerency** stage. The child becomes older and bigger and begins <u>reflecting</u> about the world and its seemingly contradictory values. He has heard of law and order and seen or heard of some members of society who enjoy the good life while the child's life has been riddled with nothing but fear and jeopardy. He wonders why his parents hate him and he thinks about the hypocrisy in the world, that he is not protected and the world is not the place some present it to be. He tries to make sense of the contradiction between his experiences and the way society represents things. He sees he is under siege, not only by his own parent(s), but he is also in jeopardy in the world at large. It's "me vs. them," he thinks. The child faces the dilemma of whether or not he can bear any more abuse and what he has to do to stop it. He decides in one downtrodden moment that he will do whatever it takes to fight back to win, even kill, to protect himself or his loved one. The day comes as he gets older and his body gets bigger when someone attempts to hurt him and he actually <u>retaliates</u>. Usually this is in the form of a violent personal revolt on behalf of a family member or himself. It may be to protect himself from a bully. It's a dangerous crossroad. Once he decides he will kill to protect himself or another, he faces whether or not he can. It is a kill-or-be-killed choice. He cannot afford to lose and there are no draws or ties. He contemplates weapons. He has to reign or he is in greater jeopardy than ever.

<u>He wins.</u> Once the older child becomes successful in defending himself, he discovers there was a greater reward awaiting him than simply avoiding further abuse. Much to his bewilderment and delightful surprise, he has merited a sudden change in his reputation. Now he is someone who is highly regarded. He has a new identity. Now people in his life speak of him differently and treat him with deference. He becomes intoxicated with power and enjoys an identity for the first time in his life that is positive, not negative. He has a new role and perspective on life. He decides that no one will ever hurt him again. He devel-

ops a chip on his shoulder and he begins to interpret the slightest disagreement as disrespect, which he will put down. He begins the transition into becoming a predator because it is such a relief and feels so good. Now no one can ever convince him that he should give up violence.

Stages of Creating a Violent Criminal

- **Brutalization Stage**
  Subjugation
    Brutal domination by someone in child's life.
    Pleas for mercy to stop the beating. Pleas for mercy don't stop the beating.
    Child fantasizes murdering his perpetrator.
  Horrification
    Child witness brutalization of someone he loves.
    Child wants to rescue, but shrinks back knowing the attacker will turn on him.
    Child suffers guilt and helplessness.
    Child experiences deeper self-loathing.
    Child fantasizes vividly about killing and rescuing.
  Living in a Violent Neighborhood
    Regular interaction and terrorizing by bullies.
    Worthless identity, good only for others to bully and abuse.
- **Besiegement Stage**
  Violent Coaching
    Ridicule: Family members and peers ridicule child for weakness.
    Coercion: Significant others try to coerce the child into violent activity.
    Haranguing: Taunting to fight is relentless.
  Vainglorification
    Someone takes child under his wing.
    Child admires person who boasts of violent accomplishments.
    Person enjoys respect from others. Oh to be like him, safe and respected.
- **Belligerency Stage**
  Child gets bigger and older.
  Reflection about his circumstances and his dilemma and the double standard: Good values will kill him. Bad values may save him.
  Moment of retaliation brought on by real threat: If child loses, child may die. If child wins, child may live. He thinks about weapons.
  Child wins! Child is praised and newly regarded, something he didn't even anticipate. Child swears he'll never return to old identity.

Major Failures from Under-Discipline/Neglect

Blind Spots of an Under-Disciplinarian
- Guilt leading to inadequate discipline
- Mistaking the child's arrogance for self-esteem
- Thinking bad behavior is cute
- Excusing bad behavior

- Failing to set limits and/or setting limits then failing to enforce them
- Changing limits erratically or setting limits sporadically
- Thinking they will grow out of it
- Overreacting then backing down
- Allowing the child to be boss
- Seeming weak to the child

- Faith Parenting without values, limits, consistent discipline or standards for the child

Day Care Parenting

Working parents are led by conventional wisdom to believe they can have their cake and eat it too. They can pursue their careers without consequence to their child. They believe in the Tulip Theory, where everything the child needs is already within the child (like the tulip bulb) and can just sit back and wait. They don't even need to add water. They believe that their child just needs someone who knows how to treat a child to take care of her. It could be anyone as long as they are professional. It doesn't have to be a parent. Yet children in day care are alone and lost.

As I have discussed in Chapter 4: Stages & Ages of Development, the more recent research reveals that children who are put into day care at an early age have more difficulty in relationships, especially with jealousy and competitiveness, and they are more prone to violent and disruptive behavior. They have more cortisol (a fear hormone) in their blood chemistry. The earlier in life the child is put into day care and the longer the hours per week, the more symptomatic the child will become, guaranteed. Children at this age cannot learn well in distress. They are preoccupied with their abandonment and what it must mean, taking it personally. They are designed to favor one or two adults. This means that day care providers will be the primary parent and every day you bring your child home with you from day care, you are taking your child away from her primary parent. Or, if you are actually the primary parent your child won't want to go. He just doesn't want to leave you, and learning will be difficult at day care. If you want to know who is the primary, you can tell by who the child most passionately does not want to leave.

The Director of the Parenting and Relationship Counseling Foundation had a weak moment and put an ad in the paper for childcare in her home so she could stay home with her own young children. A father brought his infant and explained that the baby would be in day care from 8:00 am to 6:00 pm, so they just needed someone to watch her from 6:00 pm to 9:00 pm.

"Wow!" Stacy remarked, "That's a long day for your baby!"

"Not nearly as long as it is for her parents," the father retorted. This father had no idea how much his infant was suffering. He had no empathy for his baby. He had no idea what a monster his child will be because she will be completely unattached and untrusting of any adult.

Not all day care parents are so thoughtless. Some feel guilty and will let their child behave badly because they don't want to ruin time together by disciplining.

We know of a professional couple who paid a lot of money for a surrogate baby because they wanted to be parents. The baby was not even two weeks old when the mother returned to work and hired a part-time nanny. When we met this couple the baby had no particular primary caregiver and cried a lot.

Neglectful Parenting

Neglectful parents have been known to be a combination of day care parents and stay-at-home preoccupied parents. They have found a way to parent by the Tulip Theory with a sort of hands-off approach and the children grow up feeling unwanted.

I know of one mother who was extremely neglectful and yet very overprotective. She managed to keep her children home as if that somehow compensating for her lack of nurturing. She did not let them do anything as small children or even as older children and left them most of the time with babysitters or alone with each other. Her daughter will have nothing to do with her now and has even changed her identity so she cannot be found. Her son believes he is inherently defective and suffers abandonment trauma when he dares to love. He has an internal dialogue that haunts him, although he is beginning to get a handle on it and starting to dissolve it. Before he began treatment he was in recovery for heroin addiction. He could not maintain an intimate relationship and he was frequently preoccupied with cutting himself.

Abandoning Parenting

Duchess of York "Fergie" was encouraged to take an extended vacation when her baby was a newborn. A famous television psychologist advised parents of a newborn to take a long-awaited honeymoon to restore their marriage while another famous psychologist looked on without objection.

Many professionals are wrongly informed about children's needs and many advise parents to take breaks from their children and so many children are abandoned early in life, resulting in children who are much more difficult to deal with later and parents who want to take breaks all the time.

Sometimes mothers simply die. Some are sent overseas to combat. It could be that an ignorant judge ordered parents to share custody of an infant with each parent having one week on and one week off. It could be parents took two weeks of vacation and left their baby boy with grandma thinking nothing would be wrong with that, but the child would never be the same.

Ted Kaczynski, the Unabomber, was hospitalized in isolation at five months of age for several weeks to protect him from an allergic reaction or possible infection. His mother said that as a result of this intervention, her cuddly baby boy was never the same. Psychologically, in those early months of his life, he developed a deep hatred for the dials, tubes and technology that surrounded his crib, keeping him from his mother. One can imagine how he perceived the cold, sterile environment as having stolen his mother from him, an abandonment from which he never recovered that left a deep drive for revenge against technology.

Weak Parenting

Let me not mince words. Weak parents are either bloodsuckers or self-indulgent. Either way, they make monsters. I recently received an email from a mother whose daughter is burning out from helping people because she was raised helping her mother, hoping someday that her mother would help her. In the process she became visibly angry with her mother, her daughter's grandmother, for being so weak. When I told the mom she had to stop leaning on her daughter, her response was, "What about me? What if my daughter is mean to me?"

I heard from another mother that she considered herself a good mother, but her daughter was cold. I learned from her daughter that she stopped loving her mother years ago because her mother was "too much work."

Another mother confided to me shortly before her death in her 90s that her daughter had been too much trouble as a toddler because, between ages three and four, she had had to wear casts to straighten her legs and was always "crying, whining and complaining." The daughter, now grown into late middle age, confided in me that even though she had allowed her mother to live with her during her entire adult life, she didn't feel like crying at her mother's funeral. That would have been alright, but I witnessed that she had become dependent upon her eldest son and had little left to give her younger son.

Weak parents also create monsters. Children look to their parents to see where the bar is set. If their parents have no bar, children will dare them to set one. If they refuse to set one, children come to disrespect their parents and they'll grow to not believe in limits and instead will test them at every opportunity.

I knew a mother who confided in me that she didn't want to discipline her daughter because she was afraid her daughter wouldn't love her if she did. What she didn't see until it was too late was that her daughter was respecting her less and less over time and eventually she wanted nothing to do with her. This mother essentially became a parent who was willing to throw her own child under the bus because she, the mother, wanted to be loved. This parent chose to put her own needs over the needs of the child to be taught right from wrong.

Confused Parenting

Some parents don't know what to do, so they don't do anything. Their childhood was so disturbed they have no internal working model for how to raise their children. They do their best, but when it comes time for discipline and setting a bar, they are at a loss. Sometimes they discipline things that require no discipline and then let things go that should be absolutely addressed. After good bonding, healthy separation, individuation and ethical guidance must follow.

A mother told me that her daughter had a new friend at school, Classy, who didn't want her to play with Virtue, her other friend because Virtue had tattled on Classy for cheating off her test paper. "So, what did you say to your daughter?" I asked.

"I didn't know what to say," she reported. "I told her that whatever was her decision, I would support her."

I told her I would have said this: "Sweetheart, you have to pick your friends by how they treat people. You don't want a friend who treats other people badly, do you? I would say to your new friend that you will be friends with her only if she is sorry for cheating and if she is all right with you being friends with both of them. Otherwise, I think you should stay with your old friend because you like her values better. Classy may not want to change her mind and she may be mad at you too now. Can you handle that?"

Enabling Parenting

Pathological behavior could not persist without other enabling adults to advise, cover up and make the parent's choices seem normal. A weak parent and an enabling parent are much the same and can create the same pathology in the long run.

I know the parents of an adult child who has been abusing substances for years. I've heard she's been in and out of treatment facilities more than five times. The other day I learned she walked into their house with a chip of methamphetamine on her shoulder and the dog began to growl at her. Someone in the family warned her that the dog was growling. She barked back, "I don't give shit if the dog growls," she scowled, putting her face in the dog's face. "Go ahead, bite me," and the dog snapped at her. She then began to beat the dog mercilessly about the face and jaw, and kicked it in the stomach. One relative was yelling for the girl's mother to stop her.

The mother said, "I don't think there is anything I can do. Besides, she's a human and the dog is just a dog."

When I heard the story I understood why all the treatment facilities were not working because they had not taught the mother that she was an enabler. Until people take a stand in this grown child's life for ethics and refuse to relate with her unless she gets a long stretch of sobriety under her belt, she will not heal.

I heard that the daughter was at another rehabilitation facility still trying to get sober. I also heard that she got angry at her mother for telling the counselor she was in a romantic relationship (prohibited or discouraged at this stage of treatment). Mom was supposed to lie for her daughter and was beside herself with remorse.

Entitlement Parenting

Some parents think they are superior to other people and they think their children are superior to other children so they don't discipline bad behavior. When their children behave badly, they think it's just a phase or it's cute, or they take them into the other room so they don't embarrass them during discipline. Sometimes they think arrogance in a child is a sign of self-esteem.

I had two neighborhood children playing at my house. One of them was telling the other that she couldn't come to her house anymore because she wasn't good enough to be her friend. The second little girl began to cry. I picked the first little girl up like a football under my arm and delivered her to her mother's house to hear her mother ask, "What's going on?"

"Oh nothing, except that your daughter has just told another child that she's not good enough to come to your house so I want her to know she's not good enough today to be in my house. Now I'm going home to serve cookies to my other guest."

Mom didn't tag-team with me because her bratty-acting child showed up at my door again taunting the other child through the screen, so I had to close the door in her face after she saw me serve cookies and milk. Before I shut the door, I said to her, "I wish I could be giving cookies to you too. I cannot give cookies to a child who says mean things to other children. You are not better than other children and if you think you are, it makes you less. Putting people down makes you ugly. You can come back tomorrow if you want to try again."

Over-Protective Parenting

I know a mother who likes to fathom that I am a mean therapist because I have taken her child to task for abusive behavior to another child. She likes to imagine that she is the noble, patient one and I am the intolerant one. In the meantime, I watch her child become more and more abusive. I watch her remain blind and unmoved from her position as her son's behavior escalates. This mother is so stuck in her identity as a noble parent that she is arrogant and unable to self-reflect. The cause of her son's behavior cannot possibly be her because she is obviously such a loving mother to protect her son from my feedback. Her identity as a loving mother is more important than her ability to recognize that her child is becoming a criminal before her eyes. One day soon, the jig will be up and reality will smack her in the face. Unfortunately it may be too late.

Feuding and Alienating Parenting

You cannot feud over your child and if you warn your child about his other parent, you may do grave harm to your child if that parent is in your child's life. If one parent corrects the parenting of the other they tend to break the bond between that parent and child, which is probably not worth it. When parents argue about parenting in the same household, they teach the child to divide and conquer. The child may develop an Approach-Avoidant personality and learn to manipulate too. He may never achieve a mature relationship. He will probably re-enact his childhood with two-faced commitment and a drive to betray the other.

If the parents are divorcing or divorced the worst scenario is when parents begin to use the child as a pawn for revenge. Some fathers will seek custody to establish power over the mother even though they left the parenting up to her in the past. Others want to seek joint custody to get even or so they don't have to pay child support. They feel so jilted they want revenge.

I have seen a working father achieve joint custody and put his daughter in day care rather than allow the three-year-old to be with her mother. Joint custody provisions should give the other parent the right of first refusal over childcare.

Some mothers can never get over the betrayal and move on. The children of these parents bear an ugly legacy and deep scars. They cannot enjoy either parent without feeling guilty, so they end up hating the other parent and eventually both their parents for having to feel torn between them, which is almost like having no parent at all.

If both parents move on, the child is relieved of course, but if one parent continues to carry a grudge and wallow in the victim role, the child is held as an emotional hostage. He thinks he has to take care of his mother's feelings because she leads him to think so, or she certainly does not try to convince him otherwise.

He thinks he has to hate his father for her sake, even though she may sometimes dutifully instruct him to respect his father. He is not blind and he sees that she takes every rebellion against his father as a validating and comforting gift, which she uses as evidence in her war against her child's father. She seeks every opportunity to make him wrong. She also seeks to prove that she is the most cherished parent so when dad disciplines, she undermines him. She may even have a belief, as her deepest fear, that if she disciplines the child, he will love his father more.

The child learns to play the parents against one another and may even become diabolical in the process because it is a lot easier playing the parents against each other than suffering between them and it's a sort of sweet (unconscious) revenge. Sometimes he wishes she would get married or move away and leave him with his dad so he wouldn't be torn or burdened anymore. But as he gets older, he becomes more and more self-destructive and conniving under the weight of her parental alienating behaviors.

I have witnessed parental alienation that I predict will end in disaster. The father left the mother over ten years ago because she was too controlling and demeaning. When the child was a young teen, her dad heard her whisper to her mom, "Don't worry, Mom, I will testify against Dad in court for you." When she came for visits with Dad, she was rude, rejecting and miserable. When Dad tried to talk to Mom about this behavior, Mom would say, "She's angry because you left her." Dad would insist that he didn't leave his daughter, only her mom. For years, out of guilt, he tried to treat Mom as nicely as possible, even after he married, until it became a strain on the new marriage. When Dad had financial difficulties, Mom would tell her daughter that he was giving all his money to the other family since he remarried. When Dad couldn't drop everything and pick her up at school, Mom would tell her that he loved the other children or his work more.

The daughter became a bitter child who could fake nice to get what she wanted and learned to play the parents against each other. She has said that she hated that her mother needed her so much, yet her mother denied depending upon her daughter at all. "No one is there for Christmas except me," the daughter told her dad. "I have to buy all her Christmas presents, so I can hardly buy anything for you, Dad, or for anyone else."

As a teen she has begun to abuse numerous substances, has driven drunk numerous times, has been kicked out of a number of schools, has wrecked the car, has sent naked photos of herself via text and has been promiscuous online. When Dad tries to take a stand by taking away her phone, Mom buys another one. When he takes away the car, Mom buys another one. Every time Dad tries to do something to save his daughter, Mom predicts she has gotten better and will not support him. Ironically, when circumstances become most dire, Mom switches horses and maintains that she is "so far gone that there is nothing else I can do for her. I have done all I can do and even if she dies, I will have no guilt because if you hadn't left none of this would have happened."

Ethics

Ethics are how a child's character is established. If we discipline nothing else, be sure to focus on ethics. Ethics include making correct choices, even when they involve sacrifice. Ethics include respect for others and their property as well as the ability to share and play fairly. It requires honesty, openness and compassion. Ethical people develop good personal habits, picking up after themselves and taking responsibility for the results of their actions.

When a child does something unethical or immoral such as tease another child, move swiftly with a 30-second scolding. Keep it short and "in your face." Make it stern and abrasive and let your child know you are appalled and disgusted. Then let it be over. Return to your role as guide and witness. If the child hit another child, banish the child from social contact for awhile. If it happens again, combine the banishment with a 30-second scolding and another cause and effect response. Once I told my son sharply, "I won't have a bad child."

Model Personal Responsibility

It is important that we look at our own ethics. We are models for our children; they notice and remember. You are not ethical if you hold a low bar for others while holding yourself to a high bar. Likewise, you are not ethical if you hold a high bar for others while holding yourself to a low bar. Ethics are an agreement we make with the world to treat others as we wish to be treated so that everyone can be safe.

- Monitor your ego. Do not indulge it as your ego is your ball and chain. Don't act entitled. Don't practice a double standard.
- Be a problem-solver.
- You may enjoy what you have, but you don't *deserve* anything you have not earned. If you want a good partner, be a good partner. If you want a good career, set the goal, plot the course and do the work. Earning creates self-esteem.
- Cherish your precious life. Study, learn and make the most of this opportunity to become a person of substance.
- Do what is in front of you to do. If it seems too hard, do it anyway. It is not too hard. Learn the lesson that presents itself and act accordingly.
- Be truthful, even if it means looking bad.
- Don't play victim. The suffering of the world before you is far worse.
- You are responsible for your own mistakes and your own self-correction. Self-reflect to see how you created your circumstances.
- You are responsible for how your children turn out.
- Don't blame, judge or shame others. You may correct facts in error, but seek the lesson in someone's accusation against you.
- Do your best to understand others' points of view. Don't bully.
- Don't look down on others. Treat others as you want to be treated.
- Respect the path of others. Don't *should* them.
- Assess others for their ethics. Guide your children's ethics. Avoid people who seek retribution.
- Take a stand against bad ethics and scapegoating. Do not scapegoat someone in order to avoid facing your own childhood.
- If you treat another badly, apologize, correct yourself and make amends.
- Understand the forces of history in terms of motives and ramifications.
- Question.

- Live with gratitude.
- Never sacrifice your child for your parents by putting your parents' feelings or needs over your child's. Speak up when your parent is hurtful towards your child.
- Leave no trace. Keep your own areas organized and inviting; leave community spaces how you find them or better. Handle your own messes.
- Do your job.
- Make your word your bond.

Observe Zero Tolerance for Some Things
- scapegoating
- cruelty to children or animals
- meanness
- selfishness, unless it's a baby
- arrogance
- rudeness
- accepting bad behavior in others
- dishonesty, stealing, cheating
- name-calling, ridiculing others or judging them (assessing is okay)

Ethics for Others

Someone...	You may...	You may not...
...makes a mistake that affects only them.	...say nothing. ...acknowledge their experience (ask, "Are you alright?").	...tell them what they should have done differently, especially if the mistake could have taught them what they needed to learn. Exception: If they ask, explain a social or natural rule they may not already know.
...repeatedly makes a mistake that affects only them.	...ask them if they want help or advice. If not, back off and/or tell them they can contact you any time.	...offer unsolicited advice.
...does something wrong that affects only them.	...mirror, saying, "You do not seem inspired."	...offer unsolicited advice. If the person seeks your agreement or opinion, say, "If you keep sleeping in, you set yourself up for failure."
...makes a choice you don't agree with, but it hurts no one.	...say nothing. ...say, "I am not comfortable with marijuana. I think I should leave." ...say, "I don't smoke pot, but I would vote for your right to do so."	...judge or shame them or make an attempt to take that choice from them. To do so is immoral and unethical, no matter what your religion says.
...makes a choice you don't agree with and it hurts them.	...make another choice. "If you keep drinking so much, I can't be around you because it hurts me to watch you self-destruct." "You are too young to smoke pot because it will ruin your drive to succeed," so give it to me now.	...nag or judge. Take a stand. ...give comfort by remaining friends as if nothing is wrong. It is not cool to give comfort to destructive choices. Make them choose between hurting themselves and others so that continuing to self-destruct has a higher price.
...makes a choice that you don't agree with and it hurts someone else.	...say, "Please don't do that. I can't give you the support and comfort of my friendship if you don't stop drinking. I will have to leave." ...say "If you don't tell her the truth that you are not faithful, I will tell her."	...stay friends just because you want to be liked. For God's sake, don't join in.
...gets relief by hurting someone else.	...say, "Please stop now!" ...say, "This isn't going to make you feel better any more than a minute or a day. You need therapy for what happened to you." ...say, "I cannot be your friend." ...when you can, tell the victim it was not their fault, they should get help, you will report to authorities and they should report also.	...look the other way. ...keep this a secret.
...gets pleasure by hurting someone else.	...say, "Who enjoyed hurting you?" ...say, "I can't stay around to watch." You must speak up to the victim and authorities as soon as you are safe to do so.	...look the other way. ...keep this secret.
...gets relief/pleasure from hurting someone else who doesn't have a voice or who is warned not to tell.	...tell the victim you see what happened and you are sorry. They didn't deserve it. The offender is sick. Offer help. Report the offender.	...look the other way. ...keep this secret.

Consequences

Some children are bitter and simply wait to be seen and understood. These children are acting out to express themselves and get your attention. Before you start dropping bombs on bad behavior have some serious heart to heart and soul to soul talks. I am not talking about lectures. I am talking about getting in the front seat of your child's life and looking through her windshield to see what she sees. Do your best to understand her and tell her what you understand, so that she can hear it and even correct whatever you misunderstand. Let her know you and what is important to you, without lecturing. Tell her why it matters to you so much. You must be as authentic as possible. If you cannot get out of a role and be your real self, then you may want to skip this part for awhile and go to therapy. Your child needs the real you to relate to the real him.

Having said that, you need to let your child know that there are some things that your family values highly and cannot be tolerated in your family. The sooner you give this speech the better. You then list the things that are not acceptable in your family. You talk about them and how you would respond to them. These rules and consequences represent the most important of all ethics, they must be required in your family and you need to model these values. When you see these values in your child, be sure to praise him. Tell him how proud you are.

Consequences for bad behavior should be something to remember, but they should be relative to the sensitivity of the child. If your child is typically sensitive and thoughtful, then consequences should be softer. If your child already practices a repertoire of thoughtless behavior, then consequences will need to be stronger. They should be delivered in such a way that when the child imprints from you, you will feel proud to see it in him later. In other words, if you are correcting violence, don't be violent. If you are correcting meanness, don't be mean unless it is a mean or violent child you seek to raise.

The consequence for a Zero Tolerance Violation may need to be very creative. For example, if your child scapegoats another child and you have scapegoated your husband, you may need to apologize to the child for scapegoating in her presence, then tell her you realized how ugly it was when you saw her doing it, and you are both going to give up scapegoating innocent people. Further, you might tell your child that she has to write a letter of apology (and maybe you would do so also).

If your child is cruel to animals, you may need to get your child to say what he is really angry about. Maybe you already know. You can set up a soft chair that he can pretend is the original source of his anger and give him permission to wail away and say whatever he wants to that person who hurt him so bad, even if it's you. Then you tell him he can do this anytime, but he may not ever injure another animal. If he has pets, you begin giving them away every time he hurts another animal. If he tortures an animal, then you give all the pets away.

If your child was mean to another child, he may have to apologize and lose some social privileges, like the birthday party he looked forward to attending. The same would be true for name-calling, ridiculing or judging others. If he did it in the presence of other children, then he would need to apologize in the presence of those children and do something to make amends, such as giving that child something he prizes, or serve him for a week.

If your child is arrogant, you may need to exile him for his arrogance or tell him he can return to the family when he can apologize and act humble again.

If she was rude, you may require that she go to her room, write a letter of apology and list ten healthy ways she could have spoken differently.

If your child accepts the bad behavior of a friend without speaking up, then your child may not be able to visit with that friend for the rest of the month or until he asks his friend to stop so their friendship can continue.

If your child is dishonest by lying, then you may tell him you cannot trust anyone who lies to you. If he continues to lie to you, then you will lie to him one time so he can see what it is like. One day you may offer to go to Disneyland or go to dinner and when he plans on the event, you can say, "Oh, I guess I need to tell you, I was lying." After that, you explain for one paragraph that when a person lies to another, there is no real foundation left to support their relationship. It becomes guesswork.

If your child cheats, then there should be consequences that are responsive to cheating. For example, if he got a bicycle for good grades, then he loses the bicycle. If he stole from another child, then he will have to give the item back to the child, or give its equivalent plus something he loves. If that doesn't work, perhaps he will have to serve that child for a week or replace that item plus labor to earn the cost of replacement.

Impose Karma

Nature provides us with karma or karmic discipline throughout our adulthood. These are the universe's natural consequences for our behaviors. A natural consequence is something that logically happens as a result of our actions or choices. For example:
- If we drive above the speed limit, we may get a speeding ticket. If we get too many tickets, our automobile insurance premium goes up.
- If we commit domestic violence, we may get arrested, go to jail, establish a record, be ordered to attend domestic violence class and we may lose our relationship.
- If we don't become an expert at something through diligence, we will not be paid well or we will have to work very hard to make a decent living.
- If we don't show up for work, we won't get a paycheck.
- If we do a good job, we may get recognition and a raise in pay and perhaps in title and position.

Children need the same sort of natural consequences or life lessons.
- If they come too late for dinner, they eat a cold meal.
- If they leave dirty dishes against your request, they will eat off of dirty dishes from their own cupboard, and they will have to wash them to use them.
- If they don't put away their toys at the end of the day upon your request, hide them for a week.
- If they don't brush their teeth before bed, you brush their teeth for them.
- If they don't make good grades, they don't get their allowance.
- If they make bad grades, charge them and they can't go play until you see their work.
- If they lie quite a bit, tell them that at some point, you will lie to them so they can see how it feels. Then choose a time for one good lie.
- If they refuse to share their toys, make them keep toys in their room in a toybox that they can't bring out around other children unless they are willing to share.
- If they are rude to their guests, have them publicly apologize and send them to their room (exile).

Escalate but Don't Inoculate

A more detailed look at escalating cost to a child for wrong behavior, *i.e.*, Too Late for Dinner:

- If they come home late for dinner, Mom has a heart to heart and explains why the family would appreciate it if she came home for dinner on time. Maybe they discuss the obstacles for compliance.
- If they *still* come too late for dinner, they only get to have bread and milk, or they have to fix their own food. (Now you decide whether to force this further. Pick your battles.)
- If they *still* come home too late for dinner, no dinner and no more visits to that friend until he learns to comply.
- If they *still* come home late for dinner, talk to the parent where he has been visiting and tell them that there will be no dinner here, unless he leaves by such-and-such a time (the embarrassment measure), or perhaps the child is not allowed at the friend's house until he learns to come home on time.

Late for dinner is just an example. Different parents have different important issues. This example is to show you how you can try different related things for one type of issue until you make your point. Let the attitude of the child determine the degree of consequence.

It is also important not to inoculate, so it might have been an even better strategy to jump to the phone and call to the other parent. However, pick your battles thoughtfully. I would have loved my child to make friends, while he would have loved coming home for dinner. I might have encouraged him to stay if it was truly acceptable with the other parent and of course, we would have had to invite the child to our house for dinner too. Different issues need different corrections for different children and different families.

Discipline through Loss of Privileges

- She doesn't practice the piano. Cease piano lessons.
- He spends too much time on the Internet. Take that time away or cut it back.
- He doesn't finish his homework because he was watching TV. Take TV away for a week.
- He lied about his homework. Go to school during class to find out what his homework is (the embarrassment measure).
- He doesn't bring the car home by the agreed time. He can't use the car.

Think Ahead

- Know what you'll do instantly if a child misbehaves.
- Don't lose your temper.
- Always give the impression that you are fully in charge.
- Be sure your child feels that she can learn the lesson and move on, that she can rebound. This teaches a child resiliency and forgiveness.
- Do not nag. A nagging parent eventually gets tuned out.
- Pick your battles. Discipline consistently, but choose your battles carefully. Parents who over-discipline create a monkey on their back because too much discipline causes bad behavior. Worse, they stop having fun with their child. The child becomes defiant and the parent will have to discipline more and more to keep up with the defiance.
- Do not give more consequences than praise.
- Give rewards that will hurt to be taken away.

Don't Set a Consequence You Can't or Won't Enforce

If you set a consequence in anger, you may be sorry. For example, you may tell your child she is not allowed company for four months. Then you see her begin to shut down or realize she is dallying after school or rebelling by sneaking out. Maybe you feel sorry for her or can't enforce the limit for logistical reasons. Now you're stuck. Change the consequence next time, but this time stick to your word unless like one father, you told your child he would never eat in a restaurant again. In that case, Dad needed to find a way out. He decided to charge his son for "parole" by dropping the penalty in some low-cost way. I like the idea of "making" him do something intimate with you. I would tell him you will not reinforce that consequence beyond four months (keeping it stiff) if he will go to a baseball game with you (something that would create a loving memory) and punctuate an end to the consequence, rather than just letting go.

Know Your Child's Currency

When a child is undaunted by a natural consequence, you must resort to your child's "currency", as Dr. Phil would say, the objects or privileges your child values most.
- The child wants to wear pajamas all day. Take away her pajamas one at a time (each occurrence) until she decides to get dressed for the day without a struggle. Notice that this is also a natural consequence.
- The child sneaks more than his allotted time with videogames. Remove the door to his room so he can't sneak.
- The child is continuously trying to get presents or money, but doesn't care about school. You could pay the child for good grades because an employer will pay her some day for the quality of her work. Maybe he'll become a great businessman.

Build Up More than You Tear Down

Never discipline more than you praise. If you are dealing with a child who has almost nothing to praise, find something to praise. If all you can praise is how nicely he breathes, start with that. If you find nothing, then I just have to say, you are not the mom or dad for the job. You must love this child. You must be able to see the miracle inside of him. Start by reinforcing the miracle before you critique. Always discipline from a place where you see so much good inside and you just want to help make sure that he doesn't shoot himself in the foot.

Likewise, never correct an employee more than you praise. Don't critique a book or a movie without saying what is good about it. If you have nothing to critique, you have a low bar. You need to set higher standards for your child. The bar you set is likely the highest to which he will aspire. If you have nothing to praise, you are too judgmental.

Be sure you are someone whose approval they seek. Be sure you use that desire for approval to push them to strive for a high bar. Use it to encourage and make sure you reward with praise. Finally, good feedback also includes a theory of how to make your child's behavior better, not just point out what is wrong. Treat your child the way you would have wanted your parent to treat you.

Don't Be Afraid to Create "Bad" Feelings

I have ruefully watched many children become narcissists right before my eyes. I warned the parents repeatedly, they responded as if they understood but continued as if they didn't. For me, teaching this concept is sometimes like single-handedly trying to stop a freight train. These parents love their children but somehow believe that disciplining them is cruel. They don't want them to feel bad. Perhaps they also fear their child won't love them anymore.

It is not kind to spare your child his negative feelings. It is harmful. He will learn to fear his own emotions and think he is not supposed to have or acknowledge bad feelings. From there comes entitlement and a lack of authenticity.

I know a dear woman who has refused to housetrain her dogs since they were puppies. She has to replace her carpet every year. She doesn't want to hurt their feelings. This same woman has a friend who stole large amounts of money from her checking account, but she doesn't want him arrested because it "won't help him get better." He even wrote her a letter blaming her for making him steal her money. She tolerates an infinite amount of bad behavior and I believe it makes her sickly.

Unfortunately, parents who are being so careful not to react to bad behavior with disgust, disappointment, surprise or shock often develop resentment that leaks out all over the child. It can become a confusing message. The child would prefer the consequence over the resentments.

As good as you are, if you tolerate bad behavior, you are unethical too. You are also an enabler. You have a low bar. People who hurt other people or do wrong things are not entitled to feel good or okay about it. Children may need to have their feelings hurt when they do bad things. It is a natural consequence. It teaches us. Do not fear your child feeling bad in order to learn a lesson. Don't think that his feelings or yours are to be spared. Feelings are only feelings. Anyone can handle them unless someone made them taboo. Sparing consequences now creates a shock when they are grown. Consequences then can be life-altering.

I have had many conversations with young narcissistic children who complain that their parents are too weak. They wish they had a parent strong enough to discipline them. It would make them feel more seen, more protected and more loved. They also say they would respect their parents more. The thought that our children won't love us if we discipline them is rubbish. The strongest drive to break is the one we have to seek our parents' approval.

Further, when I am teaching parents to discipline some of these children, a child may get stubborn, take a stand against their parent and refuse to budge. Sometimes they will take that stand for hours. Sometimes they will cry and cry, trying to get the parent to change her mind. I have watched the suffering on these parents' faces and it perplexes me. They act like they are torturing their child. But the child has the choice. As soon as the child chooses to do the right thing, the issue is over. I believe it is wrong to have compassion for someone who is acting badly. When they stop, we can have compassion, but not while they are in the act.

When I talk about the harm of repressing a child's feelings, I am talking about trauma done to an innocent child who is also made or encouraged to repress those feelings and deny the truth of what was done to him. I am not talking about a child who calls his parents "mean" for requiring him to do his homework after school. Discipline is not abuse. Consequences are not abusive. They are necessary to build character. If you want to raise a man of honor, you have to set your bar high. Set standards. Hold values. If your child behaves badly, impose consequences. If that makes him cry, think, "If you don't want to feel this way, do the right thing." If your child can manipulate you with feelings, your child is in trouble.

The good news is that when your child expresses a strong feeling resulting from deep hurt (*e.g.*, "I hate you, Daddy," "I want a new mommy."), that feeling fades.

The more your child expresses feelings of deep injury, the more healed he is, the more resilient he becomes and the more wonderful will be your child.

If you focus on making sure your child never hurts your feelings, you may save your fragile ego, but your child's identity will pay. You want an authentic child who feels safe to express feelings without using them as a weapon. You want to be a strong parent who can take your child's feelings as the result of your consequences.

Let Yourself Have Your Feelings

I don't teach "Make Nice;" I teach "Make Real." I find that once I give parents permission to have their feelings, they become more real, and their children become more authentic. When we stop pretending with each other, we are more effective and actually make better role models. My authentic parents have a longer fuse because they don't bottle up their feelings. They have more honest dialogues with their children. They have better results.

As long as you are a fairly healthy parent, your emotions are very useful. Don't bury them. Don't bite your tongue. Use your disgust, disappointment or disbelief when you feel it. I would not, however, lay a guilt trip on a child, like, "You're hurting Mommy's feelings." Don't be weak. Be strong and dignified. I would, nevertheless, tell a lying child that what he is telling me is bull. "I won't tolerate being lied to." I might say to a bossy child, "You are not the boss of me. I am the boss of you," in a very dominant voice because children need to be humble at six o'clock to develop normally. If a child was rude to me, I might say, "Are you kidding? You are actually going to talk to me like that? Here's your consequence..."

And yes, I do swear. I actually believe there is a time and a place for swear words. It helps us get the venom out of our bodies and to call a spade a spade. Sometimes I swear with children who like to think they are tougher than me.

My child was allowed to swear at home. I tell all the children I work with that it's OK to swear at home and at therapy, but never at school. It works. Scott never swore at school until most of the other kids were swearing. I think that was in middle school. I have had children try to correct me for swearing. I tell them, "Do not correct grown-ups. Your parents don't like swearing, but I do. That's my choice."

One parent came to see me with her problem child when he was only 15 months old. I asked her to take the parenting class, but she and her husband left because they concluded they were much better parents than the other parents since the class addressed physical abuse and neglect. She continued to favor another child over the 15-month-old. She blamed his genes for his behavior. She found psychiatrists to prescribe drugs that didn't work. She never learned how to discipline him, but had no problem blaming him.

Six years later she returned with a child who stole, lied and committed frequent acts of violence against his sister, her favorite child. I invited her child and her to come to my RAD class in order for her to observe that the children were healing. It was the holiday season and one mother brought festive cookies. I saw the new woman refuse to allow her son to eat one cookie even though other children got to eat them. I saw him reach for one of her corn chips and she said, "No, that's mine."

When I asked her how the RAD class seemed, she focused on my use of swear words with the children. She wanted to protect her child from sweets and swearing. She had interesting priorities. I proposed to her that she had a difficult choice. Behind door number one was a woman who could finally teach her how to heal her child who swears sometimes. Behind door number two was the continued search for someone to fix her child.

The narcissistic mother responded very well. She liked the way I saw her. By the way, I did see the injured child inside her as well as the woman who really wanted to be a good mom. She did become a good mom once she learned what really mattered.

So, there are times when I discipline with my tone of voice even when speaking to adults, or with my attitude in a child's face. Children are very sensitive to the attitudes of adults, especially if the adult is onto them and sees them. Interestingly, most children whom I challenge love me. I see them and they believe I can help them. I use my feelings, my values and my authenticity. I relate to children soul-to-soul through the sweet and the sour.

Beware of Blind Spots

Every parent reading this chapter for advice on discipline needs to be clear what their blind spots are. Identify and study the part of this chapter that seems most foreign to you. I say this because as thorough as I try to be, I find that many of my students continue in their blindspots. It is not as if it is something I have not already addressed. It's just that there are some things that are so foreign they don't register until they hear it several times. Since I can't be there with you, I am suggesting that you seriously consider that you do have blind spots and start looking for them. Prepare for them. See through them.

Age-Related Discipline Issues

Too many NOs in a child's life shut down his natural curiosity and undermine your authority and credibility. But sometimes you need to say no, mean it and enforce it. The following are a few age appropriate discipline issue guidelines.

Toddlers
- Remove dangerous items from reach to limit NOs.
- If something can't be removed, say NO and place a gentle fence between the child and the object. Stay aware to testing.
- If the fence doesn't work, say NO firmly and remove the child.
- Provide replacement and/or distraction.
- Children deserve an explanation of what is going on and why in strange and unusual situations. Otherwise, children already see what is going on.
- If removal of the child doesn't work, swoop in, abruptly lifting the child away when you catch him and scare him a little. A little crying would be appropriate.
- Dialogue afterwards: "You're a good boy, but you're doing a bad thing. I'm going to help you stay a good boy. I will not let you become a brat." (Child feels comforted.)
- Return to normal after discipline; otherwise you create hopelessness.

Three Years and Older
- Consider the parents' lesson (what you see is what you created).
- What, if any, is a constructive karmic lesson for the child?
- If a karmic lesson is not possible, try communication.
- If karma and communication don't work, try enforced self-reflection (time out).
- Give as few warnings as possible.
- Be consistent.
- Know the child's currency and remove what he loves or add what he dislikes.
- Try removal of a privilege.
- Let consequences be extreme or sudden enough to create an aversive response and to avoid possible inoculation.

- When you don't know what to say or can't think of a consequence on the spot, say something like, "Go to your room while I think of how I want to handle this."

Latency (6-12)

Latency is actually the age for most discipline. It is the most important time to dialogue, philosophize, guide and share family time. I love the games Loaded Questions and Scruples; they present your child with plenty of hypothetical ethical dilemmas. Ask your child what seems like the best family system, the best economic system and perhaps what she would do about certain things if she were God or the president or the principal or the parent.

It was during latency that Scott and I started taking baskets to homeless people the day before Christmas Eve. Also at this age, Scott started borrowing drawings from his friends to see if I could interpret them. He started writing more provocative assignments for school. This is a really good time to stretch the mind. If you guide your child well and their first five years were good, this should be a fun time. If not, you need to repair as quickly as possible.

Allowance. An allowance may be a good idea for children because it teaches how the world works, how to budget and it teaches deferred gratification. You can even set it up so a small but regular part of their allowance goes into savings to collect interest. On occasion, tap into savings so they are reminded that saving is a wonderful thing. It can be used to buy something they really want. However, it should not replace generous gifts from you at winter holidays, birthdays, graduations and 'just because I love you'.

An allowance can also be used to deduct for failures to comply or bad grades. Bonuses may be given for exceptionally good grades. If you give an allowance, don't make your children beg to get it. Keep up your side of the commitment and pay on time.

Some parents believe children should contribute to the family and an allowance is contingent upon this contribution. It's not abuse or neglect or a bad system, it's just not endorsed by the PaRC because it could make a child feel that she's not good enough just as she is. I believe children don't need to work to be a valuable part of a family. In struggling or larger families, however, this is necessary.

In my opinion, the only jobs required of a child are to keep his room tidy for visitors and a clear mind to study, leave no trace in the common areas and make good grades. When he makes good grades, be thrilled for him and give him an allowance for his job well-done. If he wants additional income, come up with additional responsibilities (if he is already making good grades) and pay him what you would pay an adult to do the same thing. Do not exploit child labor.

It would be a wonderful addition to your family legacy, however, to hold regular collective workdays. This could be a memorable opportunity to teach children how to do laundry, load the dishwasher, pull weeds, take out trash, wash floors and tile, *etc.*, given that everyone in the family is doing it together for a reasonable period of time in good spirits. (If someone has a bad work attitude, then they might just have to wait in their room until it's over and miss out on the fun and the reward at the end.) I would include music while you work followed by a trip to get frozen yogurts at the end, or go to a movie the next day. This would teach your child how to "kick it into gear," work as a team, learn basic survival and self-maintenance skills and good work attitude and ethics.

Sibling Rivalry and Sibling Abuse. Sibling rivalry is normal in milder forms. It is not normal in more extreme forms. It may be that the older child wasn't finished being a baby before the younger child came along. The older child may have suffered insufficient bonding and nurturing. It could also be that the older child is too close in age to the younger child and doesn't want to share the nurturing. The older child resents the next child for stealing her time with mom.

Also, sibling rivalry may be a re-enactment of hostilities between parents. Sometimes the most abused parent takes it out on a child, who then takes it out on a younger or weaker child. Thus, sibling rivalry may be hostilities modeled from the parents.

In any event, parents need to protect a child from an abusive sibling. Sibling abuse is traumatic, especially when there is no justice in the home. It also creates a mind-warping situation for the abused child. It's one thing for a parent to discipline or even abuse a child. It's another thing for a sibling to do it without consequences or protection. That means there is no justice in your home.

In the all-too-common scenario where older brother Bobby hits younger sister Sally, follow the below-listed steps:
- Send Bobby to his room with a time-out to self-reflect. "You can come out when you can tell me/show me you know what you did was wrong and apologize sincerely to Sally."
- Give sympathy to Sally.
- Talk with Bobby later: "I know you're angry. I know it wasn't fair Mommy and Daddy had a baby after you. It's not Sally's fault. Mommy and Daddy enjoyed having you so much we wanted to have another child. Now it seems like we don't pay as much attention to you. We will try harder. We're sorry. You can tell me how you feel for as much or as long as you want. I understand. I will never allow anyone to hurt you, but I will not allow you to hurt Sally either. If you do, I will spend time away from you."
- "You're a good boy, but you're doing a bad thing. I'm going to help you stay a good boy. I will not let you become a brat." (Child feels comforted.)
- Return to a normal attitude after discipline; otherwise you create hopelessness.
- Know when to enfold (give comfort) and when not to enfold. Enfolding too quickly creates an association of love with pain, especially if that is the most attention the child gets.
- Be careful not to create additional hidden resentment in the older child that could come out when you are not there. This may be a time for hidden video cameras. Also, you need to be sure that the younger child is not provoking the older child with arrogance or taunting.

Some parents just let the children work it out. This is the source of sibling abuse. Other parents use this as a form of discipline. When sibling abuse is out of control, the child does not simply experience brutality from his sibling, he gets the message that his parents don't cherish him or want to protect him from injustice. This is such a mind fuck to the child that it may create schizophrenia or another major thought disorder. Protect your children from each other. Take a moral and ethical stand about unethical behavior. Lastly, if this is happening, who is the role model for this abusive behavior? Fix it.

Narcissistic Children. Tough love is for children who don't believe their limits. (Tough love is NOT for RAD children, whose special discipline is highlighted later in this chapter.)

If narcissistic children see you as weak, perhaps hypocritical and disinvested in their character, their tantrums and testing will be huge. Prove yourself in extreme ways. Stay consistent and level. Offer fun adventures and take them away as consequences until the child behaves through the experiences. Set up the same reward-and-consequence contingency at home.

Examples:
- Go out to a family-friendly restaurant the child likes, knowing you won't be staying, and leave when bad behavior starts.
- Plan a trip to Disneyland knowing you won't be staying, and leave when bad behavior starts (or turn the car around and go home if the bad behavior starts in the car).
- If you send the child to his room and he won't stay, lock the doors and windows. If he breaks the door or window, go out instantly and buy five more doors to replace them, each time telling him what he now has to do to earn or work it off.
- Take away the valuable gifts you have given him one at a time until he folds.

Heart to Heart About Safety. When your child is school age and you haven't already done so, it is time to begin dialogues about safety, self-discipline, ethics and self-representation. Actually, these dialogues would best begin at birth and gradually unfold.
- No Bad Touches. Talk about loving touches and icky touches. Icky feels like you want to say, "Uh oh." If it feels icky he needs to say no, move away quickly and go tell. Tell your child *not* to announce he is going to tell, to just leave and find you. Repeat several times, "No. Go. Tell." Even though it is an old video, Henry Winkler narrated an excellent message for children (Strong Kids, Safe Kids, 1984).

   No one has the right to ever ask him to keep a secret from you. Warn him that secrets are ways people use to avoid taking responsibility for their actions.

   If your child is discovered in experimental play, do not traumatize or shame her. She could actually learn from you to fear her own sexuality, which is another form of sexual abuse.
- The Birds and the Bees. Always respect your child's body. Don't pinch it, manhandle it or slap it. If you respect her body, you can easily tell her that her body belongs to her. No one has the right to her body except her.

   Tell her that when she is older, she may feel deeply loving feelings for someone and she may choose to share her body with them before they even ask. Tell her to think twice because no one should share her body unless they are willing to raise a baby with her. If they ask before she has given it thought, she needs to feel comfortable saying no.

Teenagers

Whatever you didn't take care of before your child reached adolescence will come back to haunt you in his teens. If you lectured and nagged, he may turn a deaf ear now. If you used physical punishment, he may have begun turning to violence in his other relationships to defend his point. If you didn't require the truth, he will be lying to you now. If you used substances, he might be using them too, possibly to a greater degree or he may even be dealing. If you had a number of boyfriends over to the house, he could be trying to bed all his girlfriends, or she will be easy for the boys. If you were too busy for her or put her in day care as an infant, she will probably disrespect your authority because no one deserves to be the boss of her. Perhaps you can take away the car keys, withhold an allowance or use whatever leverage you have left, but nagging, judging, blaming and complaining are out.

Drugs and Alcohol
- Eliminate substances, including alcohol, from your house. You need to abstain.
- Confront your child on what you know (and know as much as you can before you confront her).
- Tell her that you are going to help her end this problem. It is over. That means:
  - You will spend more time together working things through and solving problems.

- Your child will begin a program (Ala-teen? Inpatient detox? Wilderness Therapy?).
- The whole family will enter therapy together so he can lodge his own complaints.
- If you find more substances in his possession, such-and-such will happen (choose that consequence before you take the stand).
- You will be spying on him until you can trust him again.

Letting Go of Tough Teens. If your teen uses drugs, doesn't do homework and cuts school, you can't kick her out of the house until she is 18 or has graduated. You can always have her arrested and put her in a detox center. But if she is only smoking pot and angry at you for having neglected her so much all her life, then you may have to apologize deeply, see if you can make it up now and let go if need be, providing her a home and becoming available for advice if she seeks it. But don't rescue bad behavior. You can always use a need to be rescued out of consequences as an opportunity for leverage, such as a detox center or therapy.

For example, your seventeen-and-a-half-year-old is self-destructing from over-control. Back off. Make yourself available as a non-judgmental guide and witness. "I would...in your shoes." (when asked) "You seem lonely (lost/angry/hurt/ etc.)."

If your child is self-destructive or badly behaved, you may need to consider the last resort: Wilderness Therapy. It works miracles. It costs about $40,000 per month, but payments may run as low as $400 per month. This is your karma. If you want to live with yourself, take care of this. Get out of denial now. You are damn near out of time.

Disciplining an Abused or Betrayed Child

Before you begin to discipline an abused or betrayed child, you need to make amends, which may require some creativity. First, the alienated child needs to become verbal about his feelings, for which you will not defend and will instead offer remorse. Then he needs to help you determine what will compensate him for the betrayal. When you contract to make amends, explain that at the end of the amends he will be expected to become a normal child who does the right thing when it is in front of him to do. In extreme cases, the child will need therapy, perhaps intensive therapy for an extended period of time, in addition to these same amends.

Disciplining RAD Kids

If you abandoned a child, whether innocently by illness, thoughtlessly by vacationing, or just plain recklessly, or if you adopted a child a few weeks of age or older, you may have to be on him continuously for a period of time until you gain control. Children who have experienced a broken attachment need to be parented in a very special way, which can be taught by experts. These are often children who don't trust adults so they act like adults themselves, even at one year old. These children have Reactive Attachment Disorder (RAD). They need a parent who can take power back from them so they can become children again, learn as a child and, at the same time, totally earn their trust and rebond with them.

Before you discipline a RAD kid you need to be crystal clear that your child is not behaving badly out of arrogance. This defiance of authority results from an early childhood moment when he realized there was no adult in his life who could protect him or who wanted to take care of him. In that moment, he decided he didn't need anyone anyway, that he was on his own and entitled to do whatever he needed to do to survive. The injury behind this choice was so deep that it followed a moment or moments when the child thought he would die and it preceded the burying of a great deal of betrayal and rage.

Further, the moment of making this choice is no longer recalled. The child has come to believe over time that this is just the way he is, someone with a hard heart who decides he will never be vulnerable and open to the dangers of love. He has become someone who cannot be convinced ever that anyone is worth trusting. He not only doesn't trust anyone, he holds contempt for everyone, especially adults. A RAD child often acts like a little Mafioso (Disinhibited Type) or an ever-frightened child (Inhibited Type).

The Inhibited Child is easier to discipline and harder to calm and reassure. The Disinhibited Child can seem very arrogant and composed or insanely defiant. They use the skills they have to survive, which include lying, stealing and cheating. They cope with their rage by abusing others and sometimes even setting fires. They are attracted to other RAD kids who they can admire and often enjoy taking a younger child under their wing and possibly corrupting them, perhaps creating something in common. In a funny sort of way, they see themselves as doing a good deed, rather nurturing this other, younger child to become safe as a badass. The RAD child could actually seem protective while corrupting.

They have discovered the power differential and they live at 12 o'clock, imitating adult-like behavior. There is no desire whatsoever to ever be at 6 o'clock. RAD kids believe vulnerability equals suicide and there is nothing left for them to learn. Unfortunately, a child needs to live at 6 o'clock. Otherwise he won't learn what he needs to learn to be a healthy adult.

After the slate is clean, you can ask him what he thinks is a fair punishment for the specific wrong behavior. Note that most abused children suggest very harsh punishments, something they probably couldn't endure. If he does, you can tell him it's harsh. Help him compose something corrective, ideally a natural consequence that's not demoralizing. Write it up. Have him sign it.

Therapeutic Parenting Guidelines for RAD Kids

Disciplining a RAD child focuses more on healing the child. This means that several issues need to be on the table.

- Read *When Love Is Not Enough* by Nancy Thomas, *Love and Logic* by Foster Cline and *Beyond Consequences, Logic and Control* by Heather Forbes. Also purchase the DVDs, "Captive in the Classroom" by Nancy Thomas and the book *Holding Time* by Martha Welch.
- Do not see a therapist to treat a RAD child who is not specialized in treating RAD. Such a therapist will never treat the child alone without the therapeutic parent because the child must not bond with the therapist and have another broken attachment. A RAD therapist understands the child needs to be with you and bond with you; their job is to facilitate that endeavor. If the therapist makes an appointment to see the child alone, despite information that she is RAD, you have already learned that the therapist is not an expert in RAD. Cancel the appointment unless there is no other therapist available. If you must, educate your therapist. You will still need someone with whom to brainstorm.
- The therapeutic parent is the one to treat the RAD 24/7. Plan on being with your child full time, or as much as is feasible, to repair her and catch her up to speed with other children's social skills and self-esteem. No one else should be bonding with your child unless you have no bond and someone else is more willing to do the therapeutic work. In that case, you may want to consider relinquishing parental rights for your child's sake.
- Everyone else, especially teachers, must have a respectful and educated relationship with the child. Give all her teachers copies of Thomas' DVD, "Captive in the Classroom."

- Educate your child about RAD. Tell her, "You were *not* born this way. You learned to be this way because you were deeply injured..." (Tell the child about the injury, offering empathy and understanding through her story. Then talk to her soul-to-soul about how to climb out of the hole.)
- Teach your child what RAD kids do to cope and how they become like Pinocchio (that the choices are unattractive) and establish that your goal is for him to become a real boy (or real girl), which means he will not need to be fake, deceptive or arrogant anymore to survive. For younger children, Pinocchio is a good book to read or video to watch that can be used as a springboard for discussion. If possible, take him to a RAD class where he can meet other RAD children and they can talk about what it's like to be RAD.
- The most important first discipline step is to reward the child for choosing 6 o'clock every time he does and offer less rewards or interaction when he is at 12 o'clock. Some RAD kids don't know how to be at 6 o'clock, so it may take time to get there, like learning to wiggle your ears. Develop the skill for dropping from 12 to 6. You may even want to give big rewards for developing this critical skill. Practice it yourself. Maybe you could say, "If you can drop to 6 o'clock in one hour, we will go to Disneyland (or some amusement park near you)." If you give a child a major incentive, she will learn once and for all that it's a real choice. Talk about it. Talk about what is threatening her and why she is acting so proud and arrogant. Ask her what she thinks is the first thing she would lose when she goes to 6 o'clock. Does she think others will no longer respect her? Does she believe 12 o'clock looks good and gives her self-esteem? Does she think people will mess with her less if she looks tough? Would she lose an opportunity for revenge (on an innocent party)? Teach her to self-reflect. Is she covering up feelings of (imagined or imposed) shame? Did someone hurt her feelings?
- Define a child at 12 o'clock as weak (not tough) and the child at 6 o'clock as strong (not weak). Every time she acts like a child and makes an effort to be open and receptive, go over the top with recognition.
- Prepare for 50 to 500 times that she will challenge you to see if you are really there for her. She may do something deliberate in order to see how you will cope. You may want to put a little tablet in your pocket. Every time she challenges you, you pull it out and record another line. This way you can remind yourself that she has only challenged you 207 times and she has 293 more to go. It will help you maintain your patience. If you get to 500, reflect on how far you have come, then start over.
- Never forget you are modeling for her how she should cope when someone provokes her at school or out in the world by the way you respond to her provoking behaviors.
- Plan to bond (adoptive parents) or re-bond (corrected parents) with your child to repair the attachment breaks. If you were the offending parent and you healed enough to be the therapeutic parent, you need to apologize deeply for the injury and know it's your karma to heal your child without complaint. Read *Holding Time* by Welch. Be informed before attempting holding. Review the process in this book in Chapter 3: Healing. Do not abuse your child by provoking him in order to initiate holding. If you need to get the holding started, stroke and kiss his cheek, tell him tenderly that you love him. He will fight this assault for all he's worth with a secret wish to surrender while he is terrified of the injury he will suffer if he does. If he surrenders, he will be looking for the betrayal at every turn. You need to be very sensitive to his expectation of your forthcoming abandonment or rejection. Prove him wrong.
- Now you must earn his trust. You must prove to be a parent who is strong, loving, consistent and ethical. You need to be a parent who doesn't blow your stack or act like a victim of your child. Stay level headed. You may need to have your own therapist.
- Begin teaching the child another thing about RAD kids. They do things to provoke people, sometimes on purpose and sometimes by accident or ignorance, but then when the person re-

acts, they truly forget what they did to create the reaction against them. In other words, RAD kids provoke and then see themselves as the victim of others. It's their blind spot. They will blame and not take responsibility. Sometimes they lie about their part so you won't abandon them. You have to convince your child that you love the truth. Let her know it is critical to have a dialogue about cause and effect. The more she learns how she creates the way people treat her, the safer she will become. Ask her if she understands the concept. Does she know why she becomes safer when she learns how people react to different types of treatment? You will have to teach this cause and effect concept again and again and again. It seems to be a very hard concept for a RAD child to learn, but it is essential and critical. If they don't learn it, they cannot heal. If they learn it, they may not be RAD anymore.

- When your child provokes someone to hurt her, have her apologize for provoking the child unless she does not have the self-worth to apologize, in which case, maybe you can help her write a simple letter of apology. Do not believe the child when he tells you the other child started it unless there is a witness to support this claim. Tell him when he has a track record for telling the truth and taking responsibility you will believe what he says. If your child is at the sinister state of RAD, it is more harmful to believe him (and he thinks now he can fool you and you are dumb) than to tell him you cannot afford to believe him because of his track record/reputation/karma (something he will eventually consider).
- Hold the position, "While I don't believe you, I believe in you. You will get this," so that when you don't believe him, it's not an injury, just a temporary fact.
- You may need to teach him that people who don't trust are often not trusted. The way he treats people affects how people treat him. When he bullies other children, especially girls or smaller children, teach him the Vietnamese haiku, "Boys kill frogs in play, but frogs do not die in play, they die in earnest."
- RAD kids don't have empathy because they didn't get empathy. You will be giving it (so he can get it, even though it will take longer at a later age to internalize). When your child is out of control, you give empathy by showing you understand what he is thinking and feeling to do such a thing, but the consequences will be such-and-such anyway. Put more emphasis on understanding his feelings and thoughts and less on the consequences, which should be as natural as possible. Unless someone has been injured and you have to employ the 30-second scolding with disgust, stay cool headed with a cool voice.
- Always try to give more praise than consequences.
- If he lies, you can tell him you see he is feeling too unsafe to tell the truth or too weak to accept consequences, so he has to do something-or-other to make him strong enough to tell the truth. If you can't think of anything, have him do some push-ups to get stronger. If he steals, tell him ways to make money, but make sure he pays for what he took by working it off to get his privileges back. If he cheats, have him do three times the work, *etc.* For example, if he rushes through his homework and does a sloppy job, have him re-do the homework, maybe even twice. Next time sit with him. He is not ready to do homework on his own. Where there are missing basic skills (from when he was too proud to learn), teach them until he knows them. Go back, catch up and learn basic skills. If he missed out on how to make proper written letters, go back and learn it. If he missed out on "i before e except after c," go back and learn it. Get flash cards. Help him become an A student at school. That will really boost his self-esteem.
- Do not punish a humble child even after he committed the crime. I would say, "I wanted to take away your computer games, but since I see you so soft and humble, I think you get it and we don't need a consequence." Talk about ways he can cope better and represent himself so he doesn't have to make such wrong choices. Discipline the child's arrogance. Take away some privileges until he is back to 6 o'clock.

- RAD kids may appear to have learning disabilities because they are often too defensive to learn and later too proud to show they don't understand a concept. Make sure he learns all the material he has missed. When he is being disciplined for Mafioso-type behavior, you may want to have him work on concepts he doesn't know well, such as better printing, reading, writing, or addition, *etc.*
- Learn the difference between when your child is acting out because he perceives forces outside of him as threatening versus practicing the sinister behaviors of a perpetrator; you will be responding differently to each.
- If she is in 12 o'clock fright, try to calm her down. Visibly become her ally in trying to turn this around. Maybe a dish of ice cream will break the ice. Try to talk in ways that seem like you are hanging out together. Adopt casual poses, not power poses.
- If she is at a sinister 12 o'clock, give a strong mirror and then remind her of what it was like when it happened to her. If she doesn't crack and remains at 12 o'clock, send her to jail (ideally a room that is not her room) or have her stay with you at all times until she goes to 6 o'clock and is ready to speak about what happened in a self-reflective way. She is in jail only until she comes down to 6, not as a punishment for bad behavior.
- When she behaves badly, rescue her from her feelings of fright, scold her for not using another response you have taught her and always require amends for the behavior.
- If your child is so injured it appears he simply can't go to 6 o'clock, you can propose to him that he become the anti-bully. He can become a hero who watches out for children who have been bullied. Enroll him in karate so he can play out that role in his lifetime and learn the form of self-discipline he needs. Let him become a self-disciplined Samurai.

Therapeutic Responses for RAD Kids

12 o'Clock Fright (when the child is defending his fragile identity by bluster, arrogance and toughness)	Rescue the child. Help him calm down. Maybe even introduce a ritual that calms him now and for life. Offer understanding first. Then offer guidance with coping techniques. Repair any damage he did as a natural consequence. If he broke a window, he can work to pay for it or give up such-and-such. Try to make the work of making amends and coming to 6 o'clock more attractive than the alternative of becoming a public enemy. Maybe you will even work along side him to help write the amends letter.
12 o'Clock High (when the child chooses to be the perpetrator)	Administer a 30-second scolding in her face, showing your disgust or profound disappointment in a big way. You must be bigger than her. Then it's over. No more disgust or disappointment *at all*, otherwise she will not become resilient. Then remind her softly of what happened to her and how it felt. Describe the experience so vividly that you get her to cry for herself, if possible. Maybe you can get her to do rage work for what happened to her so she can get her anger out at the perpetrator (the only valid object of rage work). She must make amends unless she wants to give up something meaningful to her (an alternative that is far less attractive). No going forward until the child is back to 6 o'clock or a cooperative state. This is jail, whether she is joined to your hip with no freedom or must wait in jail (her bedroom?) until she agrees to become soft again. You have to decide which because in creating attachment, you don't want to break it with discipline. Some children are attached enough that they will go to 6 to come out of jail. The food must be very plain in jail where there is also no freedom. You may even want to give her a port-a-potty in her bedroom, especially at night. This is not abuse because it is her choice to surrender. Once she surrenders, she may come out and join the family for something fun or richly rewarding.

Sample Discipline Scenarios for RAD Kids

- Your child has just attempted to strangle another child at school and then told you that he deserved it.
  Find out how it happened. Was he attacked by an insult and upset? Was this more like a 12 o'clock fright reaction? If so, talk him down. If not, give your child a 30-second scolding and then ask him softly if he remembers anything like that happening to him. If you can't get him to go soft, tell your child he needs to go to jail, where he doesn't get any privileges until he gives up his 12 o'clock stance. After he goes soft, help him write a letter of apology or apologize in person.

- Your child has started stealing lunch from other children, telling them if they don't give up their candy bars or potato chips, she will tell the teacher they cheated on their math test. Your child looks visibly ashamed because she was caught.
  If she seems at 6 o'clock, tell her you are proud of her for going to 6 o'clock and that you are proud to see that she knows the difference between right and wrong. Tell your child she has a choice to apologize to the children and earn the money to buy them lunch for each occasion or she will not get the privilege that you know she loves (unless that privilege is a character-building privilege, in which case think of another loss that she loves).

- Your eight-year-old child molested a four-year-old child.
  Call the parents of the child and tell them what your child has done and tell them that the same thing happened to your child. Once you know you can work with these parents, take the child to their home and have him tell the parents what he has done. Have him tell the child what he did was wrong and have him apologize to the child, telling the child he knows what it was like. Have him commit to do something for the child to make amends. Maybe the other child's parents have a good idea of what would help the victim feel repaired. Have him write the child a letter of remorse and apology, including how he felt when the same thing happened to him. Then offer to pay for the molested child's therapy because you were responsible for your child's actions and should have kept him home until he was healthy enough to be with other children. If you cannot afford therapy, find a local intern or clinic that will help you. Talk with your child about his behavior, thought processes, drives and memories in his own therapy and at home. You should contain or hold him to get these feelings out.

- You find your child is hiding knives under her pillow.
  Put a lock on her door at night until you believe she is safe. Leave a portable potty in her room. Talk to her about her drives to hurt you and who she really wants to hurt. Get her to express her rage at whoever abandoned and/or injured her, perhaps at a pillow or an easy chair while you stand behind it and listen as her witness.

- Your son broke a window when you told him he couldn't come out of his room until he self-reflected on beating up another child.
  Put a bar on the window that can be removed when he comes down to 6 o'clock. Help him write a letter expressing remorse and have him talk or write about the trigger, what happened to him when someone beat him up and what he could have done instead of break the window. Did he break the window because he could not bare being locked up? Did he consider going to 6 o'clock instead? Did he break the window because he refused to go to 6 o'clock? Stay in the room with him part of the time and then leave. If he doesn't drop to 6 o'clock within a

couple of hours, tell him you are all planning on going to a local amusement park, but you won't leave him. When he gets humble, you can all go. Ask him to see if he can find a soft spot in his heart as you talk. As soon as he gets vulnerable, praise him and ask if he can stay there for awhile. Then, go to an amusement park and have fun.

- Your daughter refuses to do her homework neatly. She rushed through it so she can go out and play.
  Tell her she can go out to play when her homework is neat.

- Your child assaulted another child who ridiculed him for having to go to "Resource" (where children get special attention for deficiencies in academic skills).
  Get the teacher to have the offending child write a letter of apology to your child (the world is fair) and tell the child's parents that a reciprocal letter is on the way. Before giving him the letter of apology, have him write his letter apologizing for hitting the child and expressing how it felt to be ridiculed. Then discuss how your child has to accept that apology.

The trauma your child has already experienced still resonates, but that does not mean she is too fragile for instruction or correction, neither of which are traumatic or reinjuring if handled well. You can tell your child she needs to eat with her mouth closed, that her homework needs to be waiting for her in the morning by the front door and that if she forgets her homework she has to do twice as much the next day. You can set requirements for a RAD child and still love and nurture them through their days, especially through their reactivity.

Gang vs. Anti-Enabling Theory

When healing an older RAD child or deciding how to respond to a family member or friend who is on a self-destruct mission, you need to discuss and educate about the two opposing lifestyles. Your goal is to get him from the Unhealthy Path to the Healthy Path. Unhealthy values lead to prison, death or self-destruction, any of which pave a much harder road than earning one's way. Healthy values are difficult in the beginning, but he will have support if he does his best and in the end, he will feel proud of himself and have nice things and wonderful opportunities and experiences.

Gang Think	
Unhealthy Path	**Healthy Path**
Enabling wrong choices	Rewarding good choices, withholding for wrong choices
Loyalty at any cost	Loyalty to ethics
Enjoying respect and escaping rules	Earning and enjoying respect
Blaming others	Taking responsibility
Entitlement (for having been screwed over)	Humility, teachability
No vulnerability (thinking it makes him stronger)	Vulnerability
Lying, cheating and stealing	Honest living, working and earning
Rebelling	Exercising self-discipline
Scapegoating	Respecting others
Secrecy	Being open
Destructiveness	Constructiveness, problem-solving

To be clear, one who follows the unhealthy path will enable bad behavior in others and want to be enabled by someone who is loyal to him no matter what. He will seek opportunities to show off for approval by exhibiting shocking and nihilistic behaviors. He will seek to escape responsibility, enjoy and hang with his homies where for moments in his life he is respected and valued unconditionally. This is powerfully attractive to a child who has suffered an abusive or neglectful life. It is also a powerful force for drug addicts or grown children who have never learned to earn their way. When he does something to get himself criticized, he will see himself as the innocent party and the other person is to blame. He is entitled to good things in life without having to earn them because he has already been neglected, abused or betrayed. He will seriously consider easy, fast income. He will not choose to become vulnerable with anyone because it is not safe, even if vulnerability will lead him to healing and intimacy. He believes he has a right to lie and cheat anyone who is in authority or who has a better life. He is quick to rebel anytime someone tries to hold him responsible for failing to earn his way. He will pick victims to scapegoat so he can feel power and unload the abuse he took from someone else. Finally, he will keep secrets as a lifestyle because he has so much to hide.

The Healthy Path will allow a person to help another who is working to have a better life, but they will not help someone who doesn't do the work. They will reward healthy choices and withhold support for unhealthy choices. They have good ethics, earn nice rewards and have healthy, happy relationships. People respect them because they have worked hard to earn expertise in their career and trustworthiness in relationships. They take responsibility for their mistakes with humility and they don't assume anyone owes them anything. They have no problem being vulnerable and enjoy healthy moments of intimacy with their mate and friends. People respect them for the path they have taken and their integrity in making honorable choices. They have the strength to stand up for victims of injustice. They do the work on their childhood injuries so they won't want to scapegoat others. They prefer an open life to one of secrecy.

When parents are investing in a child or anyone, they need to adhere to the Healthy Path and never enable the Unhealthy Path. However, there is no benefit to being impatient or judgmental about all the backslides a RAD child will make. When they make an unhealthy choice there is a consequence, even if it is simply the face of disappointment, and when they make a healthy choice there is a reward. It's as simple as that. When they return to the Unhealthy Path, disengage and step away. There are some exceptions, such as pulling the plug on a hard-won accomplishment, when the sin is understandable. This is not a theory of intolerance because rejection will lose the child forever. When they return to the Healthy Path, step up and praise. You can dance this dance for years and years. There is no need to set a limit on how long you will respond positively for attempting to do better. Remember these children have some strong self-defeating messages in their brains. They are double-damned, so we can be patient. We have nothing to lose.

> An unexamined life is a life not worth living. – Socrates

Consciousness Ladder

Vantage Point	Attitude/Consciousness	Ethics	Motives	Ramifications	Work to do
No self. Clear seeing. Connected to Everything.	Comfortable and accepting. Life is a video game. Expect the unexpected.	Other is Me.	Do not waste a second in regret. Mentor. Enjoy. Never shrink from right action.	Clear seeing. Channeling. Good guidance. Self-aware. Expects respect from the student for the sake of student.	Empower others who will do the work. Build. Counter bad works.
Transcendent. Re-birth. Joy.	Gratitude. Enchantment.	Give back.	See clearly. Act correctly.	Thinking and speaking clearly. Useful insights. Service.	Practice humility. Be present. Live in integrity. Keep your word. Do the hard/right thing when it's in front of you to do.
Healthy curiosity.	Cheer. Empathy. Openness. Honesty. Curiosity. Problem-solving.	Listen, learn, understand.	Learn. Grow. Achieve.	Contributes to society and/or children. Finds solutions.	Practice humility. Be present. Meditate.
Questioning. Confusion.	Courage in the face of the unknown.	Do the right thing when it's in front of you to do.	Surrender of identity. Faith. Courage. Love of truth.	Healing. New insights.	Redesign life values and goals. Communicate with purpose. Be present. Meditate.
Seeking. Openness.	Anything to heal, grow, transcend.	Sacrifice to grow.	Give up assumptions. Unlearn to relearn.	Questioning old beliefs and expectations. Revising outlook.	Investigate your history. Meditate.
Successes.	Do your best.	Obey most rules.	Compete and achieve.	Satisfaction in endeavors, but emptiness around things ignored.	Become curious about yourself and others.
Neutral.	Lack of judgment. Lack of assessment.	Be positive. Enjoy.	Comfort. Ease. Fun.	Openness to see other's perspectives.	Face what's really going on. Question everything. Meditate.
Normal. Self-conscious.	Don't make waves. Conform. Be appropriate. Focus on others.	Mind your own business.	Seek esteem. Seek agreement. Make contracts. Enforce contracts.	Resent agreements. Maintain status quo. Boredom. Reluctance. Obligation. Forcing agreements. Disappointment. Shallowness. Blindness.	Question assumptions. Learn relationship skills, ethics, and clean fighting. Become invested in your reputation. Recognize your *real* choices.
Insecure, but trying to be good enough.	I'm not good enough. I need others to validate me and agree with me. Hide my inadequacy.	Look good.	Find the positive mirror. Hide inadequacies. Choose loyalty over ethics.	Dependency/insecurity turns people off. Denial of personal truths leads to acting out.	Contemplate your life without approval or help. Act independently. Take unpopular stands.

Consciousness Ladder, cont'd

Vantage Point	Attitude/ Consciousness	Ethics	Motives	Ramifications	Work to do
Expectation vs. loneliness.	Someone should love me (no matter how I act).	I have a right to be loved. I deserve to have. I can take, if necessary.	Fill emptiness from childhood with food or drugs. Force an intimate relationship with persistence. EXPECT BETTER with no knowledge of how to earn it.	Backfires. Self-fulfilling prophecies.	Face abandonments of childhood. Get a therapist/coach to see regularly until you begin to fill up. Meditate on your pain. Become the one you want to find.
Absent insight into what creates true winning. Contest/conquest vs. hopeless, helpless, needy victim.	Arrogance. Hostility. Defiance. Judgment. Lack of sympathy, self-pity, fixation on injustice instead of karma.	Me versus them. The way to be good enough is to be better than…	Be the best or else. Demean, devalue, destroy. Judge and suppress others. Make ambition a virtue at all costs. Establish myths and lies to control others. Seek power vs. blame, whine, complain.	Maintain power. Abuse power. Unholy alignments. Politics. Cheating. The end justifies the means. No empathy. Lack of authenticity vs. self-fulfilling prophecy, raging, abusing substances, self-destruction.	Can you compete without greed? What is the cost of winning? Are you leaving a wake of destruction? Is it worth it? Make a healthy plan and force yourself to earn your way. Take responsibility for everything. Discipline your ego. See your own part.
Defensive. Aggressive.	Unteachable. Requires positive mirroring. Devalues those who criticize.	If you don't admire me, you are against me.	Establish superiority. Build identity through the way others see you. Get that mirror.	Jealousy. Driving people away with a false self and arrogance.	See how you are driving people away. You do not deserve anyone until you can be the results you seek.
Paranoia. Hidden resentment. Veiled hostility.	Humiliation. Suspicion. Blame. Use paranoia of others.	I'll get you before you get me.	Suspect everything, but don't disclose anything. Sneak. Leave before they leave you. Use others first.	Mistrust. Self-fulfilling prophecy.	Realize your self-fulfilling prophecy. The world isn't your parents.
Perpetration.	Malice. Self-contempt. Contempt for others. No empathy.	Don't trust anyone. Oppress rather than be oppressed.	Get even. Get what you want, whether it hurts anyone or not. No one will ever hurt you again. You will be the one who hurts others. Dog-eat-dog. Repress weaker parties.	Violent crime. Chain reactions of more violence. Suffering. Death.	Get into intense therapy. Rage at your parents. Learn new coping skills.

See Vern Black's Integrity Tone Scale, Erhardt Seminars Training, 1970, 1974, 1980, 1982

CHAPTER 8

Relationship Skills

"Love is investing in the growth of another."
-- M. Scott Peck

You cannot have emotional health or be a good parent if you do not have good relationship skills and good ethics. Everyone needs to know what healthy people know: how to chose people for healthy relationships, how to be one of those people who should be chosen, how to model healthy relationships for your child, how to have a clean fight, how to make ethical choices, how to take responsibility for social choices made and how not to be a victim. With this knowledge, one can relinquish a personality disorder or structure by implementing healthy interactive skills and real ethics. The best way I know to break your old habits and employ new ones is to join a relationship skills workshop, wherein bad habits are dissolved and replaced with new, healthy skills. Since these workshops are difficult to find, following is a detailed description of the skills you need to have to be healthy. Maybe you can find a few people with whom you can practice.

How to Choose a Friend, Mate & Partner

Relationships Recapitulate Childhood

Adult romantic relationships tend to become re-enactments of the first year or two of life. We gravitate to the familiar. We seek mates who fit with the family system from which we grew. We also seek mates who we think will compensate us for our childhood, offering us what we missed. In any event, we seek and get what we always wanted along with what we can't stand. All these reasons will wear off soon enough and backfire at the end of the honeymoon stage if we don't stay conscious.

Adult Stages Re-Enact Childhood Stages

Stage	How the Stage Manifests in Childhood	How the Stage Manifests in Adulthood
Co-Dependent	Bonding, merging, symbiosis	Merging, symbiosis, honeymoon stage
Counter-Dependent	"Terrible twos" of separation-individuation with little opportunity as a toddler to work it out with parent who defines everything	Symptomatic acting out of family system from childhood with partner who is acting out family system from childhood, each rebelling against the other
Independent	Transition from adolescence to adulthood, where doing things your way matters more than anything	Reactive process entails rejection, disengaging and abandonment. The corrective process includes living side-by-side, independently in a truce, while rebuilding new skills and standards for relating over issues
Interdependent	Healthy child matures and becomes adult, capable of autonomy, problem-solving and compromise. From there intimacy is a long-term option.	When the healing couple has had an opportunity to learn correct interaction skills, they have an opportunity to fall in love all over again.

Healthy people manage to assess their mates before giving their body and soul away. Unhealthy people have no such skill. If we have an unhealthy relationship, in order to get to healthy we may pass through the stages of childhood from symbiosis to the "terrible twos" of fighting back, to making demands that things go our way, to daring to disagree, to disagreeing in an unhealthy way, to independence, to learning to disagree in a healthy way, and finally to merging in a healthy way without neediness or demands. We may merge and then rebel. When we choose a mate we think we are choosing our ideal partner, but she may morph into our nightmare. This disappointment may result partly because of our immature expectations or partly because we had no assessment skills. When we sleepwalk through the dating process we may gravitate to friends, partners or mates for all the wrong reasons. Usually, they seem to compensate us for the deficits in our childhood nurturing and treatment.

Many things can shock us out of the symbiotic/honeymoon stage (when everything seems happy and stable and the main focus is on each other, often to the exclusion of friends, family and individual routines) other than the end of the courtship. The main reason it ends is that our fantasies and idealizations of our significant other fade as our unconscious assumptions, needs, expectations and emptiness begin to surface. We may have come to want more than we give. Men and women often wake up to realize they have made a baby with someone who is not committed to working things through or maybe we had sex with someone we don't know, may not respect or with whom we may disagree profoundly.

Just as there is bankruptcy court, there is divorce court. Divorce is extremely expensive and it is usually mean spirited. Often kids are stuck in the middle. Perhaps we have been making choices out of loyalty. Maybe we have been seeking people who tell us what we want to hear and back us up even when we're wrong. We might choose a friend or mate because she makes us feel good instead of choosing her for traits we respect. Maybe we choose people who offer us a warm, fuzzy mirror or a flattering one. We may have chosen because the other is a positive reflection on us or will serve us well. Some people think that the most important thing is to find someone to love them. Some think it is all right to drop ethical standards in order to maintain a relationship. Others think it is important to prove how attractive they are to as many people as possible. Then again, some think that this person who shows an interest in them is the last person who will ever be interested, while some actually think that if someone shows an interest in them there is something wrong with them.

One of the biggest mistakes is to choose someone just because they can merge with us emotionally, an addictive feeling similar to heroin, especially for those who were not sufficiently bonded or adored in infancy. Those of us who experience this intoxicating, heroin-like, warm, symbiotic merging with another person are likely involved in a very unhealthy, if not dangerous relationship. Usually two people who merge for this feeling have never been intimate with anyone else, including their mother. If you have such an experience you may lack the good values needed to pilot a relationship. The likelihood exists that the relationship will blow up on you, involve abuse at some point or end in a major rejection and abandonment experience. Even though moving on is a monumental endeavor, some day you can look back and know that you did experience real symbiosis or merging. It's an experience of a lifetime. You won't likely find it twice.

If we choose our relationships poorly, we are in for a rough ride and the children who are by-products of such a choice may suffer more than us. Before you marry someone, you may want to read their divorce file if they have been married before. It's a matter of public record and you can see what a previous mate blamed them for and see if it matches what they told you their previous mate said. Of course, your suitor could be a victim of false accusations. That's why you ask them how they chose this person. If you have just lost your marriage to divorce, you might do well to take off a year to contemplate your mistakes so you will be wiser in your future choices. Don't waste time blaming.

I am a trained child custody evaluator. Disputing parents often claim that they had no idea that the other parent was so bad when they met and married. My response, whether I say it aloud or not, is, "It was up to you to assess him and you picked him. You slept with him and made a baby with him. Before you sleep with anyone, you need to understand that he could become the father of your child. No one person is to blame here."

The people we choose are usually rather equal to us in their abilities to assess and relate, which implicates our own abilities to relate. Most of us can't choose or don't attract or even deserve a more evolved person than we are. Most of us wouldn't recognize someone healthier than ourselves because we can only identify qualities familiar to us, not ones we have yet to discover and employ. Having knowledge of relationship skills can get us healthier partners and longer-lasting relationships.

People also tend to choose mates who are similar in mental health, even if opposites in many other ways. For example, someone who marries an alcoholic may be an enabler of the same magnitude. Someone who is domineering may marry someone who is equally submissive. Someone who gets his value in rescuing waifs may marry a victim of equal and opposite dysfunction. Someone who is a blamer may marry someone who is accustomed to criticism.

If you had healthy standards and could perceive well or assess well, you would have been able to recognize a person's strengths and weaknesses in a date or two. Actually, a perceptive person can tell a lot in five minutes or even thirty seconds. One way to tell what kind of behaviors someone will resort to after the courtship stage ends would be to observe how they treat a server in a restaurant.

Some people have courtship disorders and they do not know how to date or assess. Some people have lower standards for other people because they suffered so much of their life and are desperate to find someone. Some people think it is uncool to set standards.

We need to assess the character of a person above their attraction to us or ours to them and we need to be worthy of a person with character. To have a wonderful home and family some day, we also need to become a worthy mate, friend and/or partner while we learn to pick well. The best way to choose someone worthy of love and regard is to respect them for their character, the way they live their life, how they choose and how they commit. Unfortunately, or rather impractically, the best way to really understand and assess a person is by how clean they fight and how they end relationships. I always say you never know a person until you have an argument with them. Moreover, you really see who they are when you see how they leave you.

If you are dating and have children, don't introduce your child to anyone you know you would not marry. Ideally, you introduce the children when you are close to engagement. Many children become attached to their parent's new mate. When you break up with him, it's heartbreaking and may reopen any old wounds of abandonment. It's a decision that can be devastating to your child. If your child has too many losses, he may have difficulty with commitments. On the other hand, you want to model shopping then commitment to your children.

Before you date someone, be sure they are divorced or single. If there is a custody arrangement, be sure it's something you can live with. If their child has problems, be sure you can handle them. Find out how intrusive the other parent of the child will be in your life. If your date is in a custody dispute, you should steer clear, especially until it's over.

> Love does not consist in gazing at each other but in looking outward together in the same direction.
> – Antoine de St. Exupery

Character Assessment of a Future Mate (and Yourself)
- Do they have a chosen profession?
- Do they believe a mother should stay home with the child in the first years of life?
- How do they treat a waitress/server?
- How do they treat children?
- Have they had long-term relationships in the past?
- Why did these relationships end?
- How did these relationships end?
- How do they have a disagreement? Do they fight clean?
- Are they blamers? Do they take responsibility for their part? What was their part?
- Do they drive your part home after you already apologized?
- Do they bring up their issues by blaming or by "I messages"? ("When you...I feel....")
- Do they judge, "should," advise or blame as a lifestyle?
- Do they accept responsibility for their choices and how their life is going?
- Would they take a parenting class with you?
- Would they learn relationship skills with you?

- Are they hostile to therapy? Why?
- Do they need to make you wrong in a discussion to survive critical feedback?
- Do they overkill with feelings or feedback?
- Do they merge too quickly?
- How do they feel about commitment?
- Do they want sex without commitment?
- Can they date for a while without having sex?
- How do they take responsibility for birth control and communicable diseases?
- Would they be willing to test for communicable diseases with you?
- How do they feel about birth control?
- How do they feel about abortion?
- Would they want to keep a fetus which is deformed? Would you?
- Do they avoid intimate conversations of content?
- Are they truthful?
- Are they normally self-reflecting?
- Do they use feedback to grow?
- Would they make a good growing partner?
- Do they want you to know them? Do they want to know you?
- Are they clear about their limits?
- Do they tell you their issues with you in a timely manner?
- Do they say, "Would you...?" or "Could you...?" or "Please..."?
- How do they feel about responsibility?
- How do they feel about pain?
- Are they able to express their feelings?
- Do they express their feelings too much?
- Do their feelings guide their choices over ethics?
- Would you want to change them if you were to live with them?
- Do they face the truth in their own pain?
- How long do they think you should know someone before sleeping with them? Before becoming engaged? Before getting married?
- How do they feel about your religion?
- How do you feel about their religion?
- Are your important beliefs compatible with their important beliefs?
- Do they do the right thing when it's difficult to do?
- Do they do the right thing when it's in front of them to do?
- What's their thinking about why serial killers kill?
- Are they big on punishment?
- What's their opinion of spanking?
- Are they big on enabling destructive or self-destructive behavior?
- Are they capable of meeting their financial obligations?
- Are they over-controlling?
- Are they both faithful and trusting?
- What are their parents like?
- How do they feel about their parents?
- How do they feel about how their parents feel about you?
- Do they smoke?
- Do they use recreational drugs? If so, what drugs? How often?

Relationship Guidelines for Dating

These guidelines are not rigid. They can vary depending on age and could even be modified for gay couples. The original intent was to provide a gauge for our youth to follow, whether they already know each other or not, but the concept applies to any generation. I suggest you adapt these guidelines to your personal circumstances. Don't get caught up in the exact rules; just follow the spirit of the guidelines. They are intended to facilitate knowledge of each other, create emotional intimacy and ensure regard before becoming deeply involved and committed, all of which should precede sexual intimacy. Daters should not jump into bed with one another and expect to find someone who will come to love, regard and commit to them. Likewise, anyone who treats dating as a sport or conquest should be avoided as toxic, shallow, unhealed and possibly dangerous to our physical and mental health. The guidelines will help you assess this and other types on your own.

- Pre-1st date: The man gives the woman his phone number instead of asking for her number. This makes the woman feel safer and still lets the woman know that the man would like to go on a date with her. Women, if you think he is interested in you because he's showing extended eye contact and you would like to know him better, you can give him your phone number. Ensure the first date is lunch.
- 1st date: This should be a lunch date. Each person should drive his or her own car, arriving and leaving separately. This is an opportunity to see if you like each other. There is no touching on this date.
- 2nd date: This should be a dinner date. It's a good opportunity to ask some of the assessment questions. If you want, you could also go to the museum, a movie or do something else after dinner. When the date is over the man might kiss the woman's hand while maintaining good eye contact. This shows the woman that the man respects her. There is no touching otherwise.
- 3rd date: This date should be an extended daytime date, ideally about eight hours long. Go to Disneyland, skiing or some other activity. The man can put his arm around her, link arms while walking or holding hands in line. He can also put his smiling face close to the woman's face, almost touching foreheads. This presumes closeness but is not continuous. At the end of the date he can kiss the woman on her cheek. He should get her home on the early side, around 7:00pm.
- 4th date: This is another date when you might go to dinner and a movie, then something else like coffee or dessert. The man can hold hands with the woman during the movie; if this is well-received then he can kiss her on the mouth at the end of the date.
- 5th date: During this date the man and woman should talk about how they feel about each other and if they want to date exclusively. If you both decide to date exclusively and are willing to take responsibility for any actions resulting from sexual intimacy, then you may start to move slowly towards sexual intimacy. Prior to sexual intimacy, agree on how you'd proceed if the woman becomes pregnant.
- If you decide to move toward sexual intimacy then make a date of getting tested for STDs, including HIV/AIDS. By this time you will have asked many of the dating questions of each other.

Principles of a Healthy Relationship

- Each of us is entitled to their own feelings and history, whatever they are.
- Each of us is responsible for what they do with what has happened to us.
- Each of us is "in our own experience" and just may not be aware of "yours."
- Each of us is responsible for how we treat other people.
- Each of us is responsible for how others treat us.
- We do not take personally the words, actions or choices of others.
- Other people are not objects to manipulate, defend against or validate us. We don't "*should*" on people.
- Each of us is responsible for telling the truth as best we know it.
- Each of us is responsible for living our life with courage and doing the right thing when it is in front of us to do, even and especially when it is difficult.
- People we love deserve to know what we are thinking. We can learn constructive ways to tell them.
- Live authentically; express your true self.
- We do not power-trip other people.
- We support others in following their hearts to be the best they can be and make the most of their lives.
- We realize that life is a journey or series of problems to be solved.
- We understand that each of us has to do our own life and trust the process of the other.
- We will honor the spirit of the other in all our relationships unless they are actively oppressing someone.
- We will leave an unhealthy situation after giving enough feedback and warnings.
- We will learn from our losses and mistakes as if they were a dress rehearsal for this moment on.
- We cannot spare another person their pain, nor should we want to.
- We do not expect another person to own their own bullshit if we don't own ours.
- We speak in terms of vulnerable feelings instead of criticizing the other person with blame.
- To earn understanding, we will give understanding.
- We let the results of our actions be our guide. (*i.e.*, If we keep losing friends, we will search our souls for what we are doing to lose them and why we chose them in the first place.)
- We seek mirroring to see how we are coming across.
- We are not be afraid to express strong emotions if they are authentic.
- We do not wear our egos like they matter. They don't.

John Bradshaw's Change Model

PERCEPTION	"When I (see, hear) you..."
FEELINGS	"...I feel (mad, sad, glad, scared)."
INTERPRETATION	"My fantasy is..." or "I imagine/worry that..." or "I wonder if you're thinking..." or "I suspect that your motives are..."
NEEDS	"What I'd like from you is..." or "I wish that..." or I hope that..." or "I would like it better if..." or I would deeply appreciate..."
CONTRACT	"If we could agree to..."

Adopted from The Communication Model by marriage and family therapy communication theorists.

The Side-by-Side Model

(You live your life; I live mine.)

You are only responsible for making your own choices and managing the subsequent results. Trying to change others is not your right, nor are their actions and behaviors any of your business until you are hurt by them, at which point you owe them clean feedback about your hurt feelings only. You can tell someone when their actions hurt you. Then they are free to care about your feelings and self-correct defenselessly if they so choose. But continuously focusing on correcting someone else's weaknesses pushes them further into those weaknesses and in the end, you appear as the obnoxious one. Everyone has a right to discover life's lessons themselves; it is their adventure.

Where children are concerned, consider living with your poor choices because putting them through the loss of a parent (causing abandonment issues) may be a selfish action that could necessitate therapy. Try to work things out. If you can't, or if there is abuse, adultery, addiction or abandonment in the house, staying with the offender is more detrimental than leaving, especially since the abuser, adulterer or addicted person has already abandoned the children emotionally. If you are in a custody dispute, read about custody issues in Chapter 4: Stages & Ages of Development.

The Side-by-Side Model illustrates that you have no right to teach, scold, judge, blame or otherwise control anyone else. People are repelled by scolding, so this alternative model is necessary. If people responded positively to scolding, this model would not exist.

Your Action	My Response in Feelings
You hurt my feelings. (ex. by forgetting a birthday, not returning a call, not helping clean when company is coming)	"Ouch" or "My feelings were hurt when..." or "I feel..." (without judgment, nagging, "should-ing," blaming, complaining)
You harm my life. (ex. by judging, blaming, standing me up, putting me at risk)	From John Bradshaw's Change Model (from above) plant the seed. "I hate it when you treat me this way. I don't know how long I can endure this." "It hurts so bad when you demean me. I can't bear it." Don't expect or wait for an answer you like.
You hurt me again.	Repeat Change Model language (minimum 3 times, up to hundreds).
You fail or refuse to change.	I choose to live with it or leave (while maybe or maybe not continuing to say "Ouch").
With children involved, you commit one of Dr. Laura's* three As: Abuse, Adultery, Addiction or Abandonment**.	I leave and immediately file for divorce and custody.
With children involved, after I'm gone, you fail to change, or you seek to correct yourself.	I may or may not choose to reunite after Dr. Laura's* Three Rs are achieved: Remorse (apologize), Responsibility (get treatment and work hard), Repair (make amends). In the meantime, there is no begging, stalking or threatening. How humbly you work on yourself without agendas may determine the future of the relationship.

* Dr. Laura Schlessinger is a well-known radio personality and licensed marriage and family therapist.
** Added by Dr. Faye.

Resolving Incompatible Sex Drives

Theory of the Existential Dilemma

I have been told my dating guidelines are sexist. Nevertheless, I believe that there is an emotional bio-sexual component to sexual intimacy. There are many patterns that lead to loss of emotional-sexual intimacy, but one seems to be quite predominant. It presents an existential dilemma based on biology.

Women lie down. Men lie on top. Women's bodies are more vulnerable and designed to receive and experience penetration. Men's bodies are stronger and they typically assume power and practice sexual dominance. Before a woman (or gay man) is ready to open her legs to a man, she must be pursued, wooed and made safe. Courting rituals are designed to end in commitment, if not marriage and children. In an age of communicable diseases, assessment and commitment are even more important.

After the honeymoon stage is over, what is left is the "existential dilemma." Most relationships are designed to evolve into a mature stage where self-awareness, consciousness and problem-solving replace role playing and courtship. When adults first enter this stage, men often begin to expect sexual encounters.

In this climate many women respond to the change in sexual assumptions by withdrawing or becoming less sexually interested. The less bonded their childhoods, the more women respond this way. Men respond to this withdrawal as if it's a personal rejection. The less bonded he was, the more he will feel this way. Thus the man is hurt and he may begin to claim or imagine that he has been tricked out of his marital "right."

When a man begins to assume, expect or promote his "right," he has mentally moved off the romantic end of the continuum of physical intimacy in the direction of the other end of the continuum: entitlement and even rape in extreme circumstances. When this attitude occurs, the woman retreats and withholds even more. The man becomes even more offended and puts more pressure on the woman, at which point she continues to lose interest in any sex at all.

Sometimes it is difficult to tell which occurs first, the man's sense of entitlement or the woman's loss of libido, but the two shifts are often predictable, hence the "existential dilemma", a vicious cycle which takes two to reverse. It may be the most difficult endeavor in a lifetime for either party, yet both need to participate.

I know one woman who had a dream she was terribly embarrassed to tell me, but it was a brilliant dream. She had a small son, but in the dream, she had two boys. One of the children she had to masturbate and she did it dutifully, without any pleasure. Sheepishly, she promised me she had no interest in molesting children. It was clear to me that she experienced having sex with her husband as taking care of his childish needs for reassurance. Men need to know that neediness is not attractive to women and this dynamic will often drive women away.

In order to transcend this existential dilemma, both partners have to rise above their present consciousness. They may both need to revisit childhood issues of deprivation or injury. It is a fragile endeavor because men appear to hold a great deal of their core identity in their penises, while women seem to hold their identities in their sense of worth. Ultimately, the way out of this conundrum appears to be generosity and gratitude.

The woman has to identify with her mate to see his feelings of personal rejection as she becomes less and less sexually interested. She will need to work on finding her capacity to give, perhaps reminding herself again and again what he was like when she met him. Likewise, the man needs to find in himself the capacity to understand that he may never take the woman for granted. He may need to court his woman for the rest of their marriage. He needs to discover what she needs from him for her to want to lie down.

One of the most important things many or most woman need from a man is a sort of autonomy or indifference. This is the lesson of "reverse effect". Women don't want another child. They want to make love with men who protect them. As men act more mature, independent and self-composed – that is, less needy or less demanding – they become more attractive. They become someone with whom women can flirt and seduce again. In order to get there, men have to be a bit unavailable, which may be the very last thing they want to do. This is not game playing, by the way. It is a search for higher consciousness, which must be sought and discovered. At this point some men would rather stray than do the work.

On the other hand, many women are highly attracted to men who have the capacity for vulnerability. It makes them feel safe. When vulnerability allows for revealing buried truths and deep feelings, these men appear to have higher consciousness, greater self-awareness and wisdom. Thus for many women, what may be considered weakness by some men appears to most women as strength. The ideal man, most women say, is both vulnerable and aloof. I know, that's a tough one. It's why I call it the Existential Dilemma. In order to work this through, you both have to work to find your higher selves.

Sensate Focus

There is a process called Sensate Focus developed at Masters and Johnson that helps with this "separation of interests."

Both parties agree to return to zero. They agree to date regularly, perhaps dinner and a movie and then begin their rounds of approximately sixteen meetings. Some meet three times weekly in bed for ten or fifteen minutes and others once a week after a nice date for a longer thirty minutes. In any event, they are re-wiring their relationship since a lot of bad habits and memories have flowed under their bridge. This process takes them back to innocence. The first or second night they may tell or write to one another about what was wrong or missing for them in their sexual intimacy. Each has to listen without comment unless it's absolutely impossible, in which case maybe one comment is allowed as long as it is clarifying, not defensive or aggressive. If you can't handle this feedback, get yourself into therapy.

The next night, they may ask and answer questions of clarification as long as there is no defending. This is only an information gathering process. They eventually advance to massage without any sexual expectation. Couples may want to tailor this to fit their needs, but once it is designed and agreed upon, it is a contract that may not be broken under any circumstances. Here is a modified Sensate Focus to help with the existential dilemma:

Stage One
- Week 1: Dinner and a movie and coffee afterwards to talk about the movie and ask one another's favorite color, size, food or something similar (something you never bothered to find out before and something that may inform your gift-giving) and to find out if your mate has developed any new goals or fears of late.
- Week 2: Dinner and a movie and coffee afterwards to talk about the movie. Then present one another with a few written disappointments (in terms of feelings, not criticisms) from your past sexual encounters together. For example, "I feel unimportant to you when

you jump my bones without holding me and kissing me and I feel rejected when you roll over and go to sleep after you have an orgasm." No comments afterwards. You may want to set a therapy appointment for the next day to discuss your feelings and thoughts.
- Week 3: Dinner and a movie and coffee afterwards to talk about the movie. Then ask and answer clarifying questions about the previous feedback, if needed. If you completely get it, say you do.
- Week 4: Dinner and a movie and coffee afterwards to talk about the movie, philosophy, feelings, memories and read to one another written descriptions of what you loved or liked about lovemaking in the past. You can each keep your written descriptions as mementos.

Stage Two
- Week 5: Dinner and a movie and coffee afterwards. Return home and continue the conversation. Talk about your week, if nothing else. It must be a continuation of the "getting to know you" conversation. Set up low lighting or candles in the bedroom. Meet in bed for Sensate Focus, partially undressed in the beginning dates and then undressed as time progresses for not-just-a-massage. One partner starts by touching hair, face, hands and feet of the other who is lying face up, for fifteen minutes. The partner being touched then lies face down for fifteen minutes while the partner focuses on the back, legs, arms and hair. Breasts and genitals are *off limits*. No talking unless there is a need to point out a discomfort. The focus is on how it feels to touch more than to be touched and the toucher is allowed to explore. The toucher is relieved of responsibility for making their partner feel good. Trade roles, letting the toucher become the touchee. If sexual arousal occurs, no progression to intercourse is allowed. No discussions afterward of what it was like until your date next week.
- Week 6: Dinner and a movie. Sensate Focus as above.
- Week 7: Same as above. Add full body without genitals, adding buttocks, stomach, legs and back.
- Week 8: Same as above.
- Week 9: Same as above, with oil.
- Week 10: Same as above.

Stage Three
- Week 11: Same as above, touching the entire body (with or without oil) and gradually, very gradually, moving to genitals using oil. Intercourse is prohibited. "Hand riding" is allowed in order to give partner non-verbal cues about what is not wanted or wanted more, but hand riding is not allowed to become controlling. Stop before orgasm. Intercourse remains banned. If you cannot respect the bans, get to a therapist.
- Week 12: Same as above.
- Week 13: Same as above, touching mutually.
- Week 14: During dinner talk about how it's going. Does it feel safe and intimate? What internal thoughts still get in the way, if any, or is it getting better and better? Decide whether you are both ready to move on or need to go back. If this dialogue goes well and progression is something you *both* want, then move on to Sensate Focus, Stage Four. If the dialogue leads to an indication that it would help to stay at this level in order to talk through some remaining injuries and negative associations, do so or you will regress. Talk about whether you could do this for the health of the relationship for another month, two months or a year. Both partners must agree to go to the next level. If one of you is tired of waiting, maybe you want to discuss the pros and cons of divorce with a marriage counselor. While it is too hard for some people to wait until the partner is

ready, it is unhealthy for the partner to feel pressure or impatience.

Stage Four
- Week 15: Mutual touching slowly leading to intercourse, ideally with the woman on top (by her choice) exercising control over entry, unless that is not her desire.
- Week 16. Same. May progress to other forms of interaction, as long as both parties seem to be in accord.

Relationship Skills Workshop (RSW)

There is one main bottom line to this Causal Theory that especially tests us in relationships. If you embrace this theory, you embrace this bottom line: No one is inherently bad; we are all "born divine." In this theory, everyone is safe. Once they get the deal here, everyone gets a chance to redeem themselves. Everyone gets an opportunity to self-correct. They are entitled to hear a complaint about them at least three times before we quit them. For my part, there is no three-time limit because as long as a person is in the struggle to self-correct, I hang in there. No one gets labeled as the irredeemable bad guy in this theory. Everyone gets mirroring and an opportunity to change. Change is possible. The biggest obstacle to change is pride or ego.

We don't quit anyone without giving adequate notice. No one deserves to be rejected without warning. We don't get to assume someone cannot change with feedback or that they are essentially stuck this way. We don't get to say we are afraid to confront them because we are too weak or fearful (unless there is a history of violence). We don't get to say that the way they are now excuses us from our responsibility to give feedback to see if they change. Only when we do our part can we show or prove our prediction that they won't change. To be clear, anyone who quits anyone without three times addressing the issue is committing the gravest sin of The Causal Theory. If you love this theory, you give people the same chance they give you.

We never quit a relationship in the middle of an issue. It is not okay in this theory for someone to decide they just don't like someone and choose to not deal with them. We stick an issue out until it is resolved or proves irresolvable.

Predicting how someone will act if we give notice or feedback is never an acceptable reason for not communicating or giving them their chance to take feedback and change. We must act with integrity and if they don't digest the feedback or information even though they are being taught on the spot what to do, then and only then do we prove our point that they can't be reached. Only when the other person is given a chance and they refuse to take the cue have we created our supporting evidence. It is by acting in skills that we get support for leaving. It is by acting in skills that we demonstrate we have done our part and still the other person refuses to change or look at their part. That is the only way to prove you are the "good guy". Never can we say we don't want to try because we already know what they will do and never can we say we tried if it wasn't in skills (especially if there was judgment, blame or condescension in your delivery).

However, after presenting an issue at least three times in a respectful way, one may disengage knowing they have done their part to state their case. When we do our part and they don't correct their skills, then we can quit and give up. Later in their life, they may get it and correct themselves if they so choose. So before you leave, plant seeds so you are invested in the growth of the other.

It is my ethical duty to leave any person I reject with the information they need to self-correct. It is unconscionable to reject someone without giving a reason or being crystal clear. I have experienced a number of rejections that, had I been told the reason for the rejection, I would have self-corrected so many years earlier. We can all change with feedback.

To deny a person feedback because we are afraid of confrontation is cowardly. Buck up and do the right thing. If you are afraid of how the other person will respond, that is wimpy. Let them have their feelings. They will get over the hurt feelings and remember what you said. It is more important to give someone the truth than to spare their feelings (for your sake, not theirs). So, if they tell you that you hurt their feelings, you can say, "I did you a service by telling you the truth and I believe you can handle it and self-correct if you want to, when you are ready. It was my gift to you. Besides, don't you want to know how you seem to people? Would you really rather pretend they think something they don't? You can change anything you want to change. You are not being judged for who you are. You are getting feedback for how you seem, even though that is not who you are."

Of course there are exceptions to this concept. If you are dating someone too short, you may or may not tell them. If you don't like how their eyes are set too close together, don't tell them. If their teeth are too yellow, tell them. If they have wax in their ears, tell them. If they chew with their mouth open, tell them. If they seem shallow, tell them. If they are too exhibitionistic, tell them. If they don't have a good enough job, tell them. If they are too serious, maybe don't tell them. This is a matter of taste and telling them may make them more serious. If they are too self-conscious, don't tell them because it creates more self-consciousness.

> ...[E]very single person you will ever meet shares that common desire. They want to know: Do you see me? Do you hear me? Does what I say mean anything to you?...
> Try it with your children, your husband, your wife, your boss, your friends. Validate them: "I see you. I hear you. And what you say matters to me." – Oprah

Goals and Guidelines

How you process an issue with someone reveals how healthy or unhealthy you are. It's important to be able to handle yourself in the heated moments of life more than the easy times when those who like you surround you and don't challenge you. In relationship skills, we follow the Side-By-Side Model and practice the Principles of a Healthy Relationship.

Often I hear from clients that the problem is definitely the other person. She knows because she doesn't have this problem with anyone else. Often the other person is her child or mate. Maybe she's even had other mates, but he's the only one that pushes her buttons so strongly. My answer to that is this is the person that triggers her childhood issues the most. Honestly, if she were a captive of a serial killer, she would still need to practice her best relationship skills. These skills are most important in the most difficult situations. There is no situation wherein we can righteously give up on relationship skills because we think the other person doesn't deserve relationship skills or worse, deserves our untamed judgment or wrath. If we don't use skills, we deserve what we get.

You do not need to be in a romantic relationship to learn relationship skills. You can work on these lessons with a friend or a relative. They should apply to your entire life. You have relationships with everyone you know: family, friends, neighbors, clerks and even other drivers on the road.

This workshop prepares you for those interpersonal moments in life you haven't lived yet so you'll handle them without regret, loss or harm.

No matter how much you heal your childhood traumas and drives, the bad habits you learned from your family system will remain. You need to replace bad relationship skills habits with healthy ones if you want to be healed. Otherwise you will go back into the world creating the same types of experiences.

Further, no matter how much you meditate, practice affirmations and go to church, if you do not see your part in an issue, then you are missing the boat and you are not enlightened, self-aware, spiritual or religious—yet.

If you discover a pervasive pattern of issues in yourself, it may be a good idea to deal with them in private therapy so you can get honest yet compassionate feedback. Sometimes these patterns will not go away until you address their origins. The more you understand the childhood sources of your adult issues, the easier it is for you to replace them. Understanding the origins of knee-jerk responses does not justify them, but once we are conscious of them, it mandates us to correct them. Also, understanding your own relationship skills issues will give you patience in others who need to replace bad skills with good ones. They just don't know it yet.

If you can find someone with whom you can partner to practice new skills, you will more quickly change your ways for the better. Taking feedback and making changes is like baptism by fire. As much as you can study and absorb this guide, you will still make your mistakes because they are hardwired in you. The fastest way to make deep change is when you can be corrected on the spot while making one of your common mistakes.

We are all designed to learn the hard way. We all go through it. Each of us is no more foolish than the next. It's just that we adopted different mistakes to survive and have different blind spots.

We can leave mistakes behind as quickly as we can learn from them. We all need to become good at recognizing when people do new healthy things and give them kudos for changing.

You will experience what it is like to have someone not recognize your effort and treat you like you are the same. You will also experience feeling discouraged when you are trying to change and someone holds up an "old mirror" to you, treating you like you have not improved. We may want to say, "That's an old mirror. I have changed quite a bit. Haven't you noticed?" By the same token, we don't want to be someone who holds up an old mirror. The truth is that each of us can change on a dime if we understand what we are doing wrong and what we can do instead. At that point, change just takes seeing and practice.

My readers who will never have the opportunity to attend a Relationship Skills Workshop are on their own. This chapter is to help them. In a Relationship Skills Workshop students get mirroring for how they seem. It helps them see how they seem so they become clear about what is wrong with their old skill and how it backfires on them, then they become motivated to change. When they change, their mirrors change, helping them hardwire in their new skills.

How do you come across? On your own, you can create the same insight if you tell yourself the truth. You have been receiving feedback your whole life on how you seem in an argument. What is it that you do to cope? How did your parents cope? Do you do what they do? Has anyone ever told you how you were treating them? Have you been accused of being over-controlling? Have you been told you were arrogant, selfish, blaming, abusive, evasive or something else? You need to determine what you do that isn't good relationship skills. Then as you read forward think about what good skills could replace those bad habits.

You might want to ask people you love if they would tell you your five worst traits in a relationship. What are your five worst traits in a disagreement? Get to know yourself. Most people never get honest feedback in a lifetime, but if you really want it, you can get it.

I knew a woman who was about 5'5" and 300 pounds. I was working for a dating service and she had spent more than $1,000 on the program. It seemed unscrupulous for my company to have sold her a membership. I couldn't find her a date. I bit the bullet and decided to see if I could persuade her to lose weight. I called her and said, "You have many wonderful traits that most men would enjoy, but there is one huge problem that we need to face together." I paused, waiting for her to volunteer her awareness.

"What's that?" she asked me. I was a bit incredulous. I took a breath.

"Your weight," I stated, trying to break the ice.

"What's wrong with my weight?" she asked, placing herself in a universe different than mine. I took a deep breath.

"You are about 100 pounds overweight and we don't have any men looking for someone your size," I said, not quite believing I had to explain myself.

"There is nothing wrong with my size," she said. It was a conversation I will never forget.

"Would you do me a favor and interview 20 people tomorrow and ask them? I would like you to ask ten family members and ten strangers on the street or at the grocery store what they think." With some relief, she took my challenge and the following day, we spoke again.

"How did your man-on-the street interviewing go?" I asked.

"Great," she said. "Everyone told me there was nothing wrong with my weight. I interviewed ten relatives and ten strangers in front of the grocery store. They all agreed with me, not you."

I have thus seen how we can at once ask people questions and telegraph to them our desired responses. We can live in a closed circle of enablers. It's how the earliest contestants on American Idol, one of my favorite shows, were so remarkably deluded about how they seemed.

Using Feedback. When we ask people in our life for feedback about how we seem and what communication traits we would do well to change, we very well could telegraph our sincere desire for honest feedback. When it comes to self-correction, the only shame is having too much pride.

When you get the honest feedback you seek, tell your mirror that when they see you change, you would love it if they would give you a new "mirror." By the same token, when you see someone grow, you will offer a new mirror to them too. Our most immediate goal is to become self-correcting and someone who recognizes growth in others.

When meeting someone who could be a potential mate, if you try to come across already perfect, you'll quickly learn it's a wasted effort. The ideal person in a relationship is the same as in life: one who wants to be in the truth and will take any correction to get there. This is a person who comes from a reasonably humble or unassuming demeanor, without defending his idea of himself or his persona. He appears absent expectation and hidden agendas. He exudes courage and integrity. He gives uncharged and clean feedback. This kind of person becomes a natural leader with an easy ability to inspire others to risk and invest. These people may seem rare, but the higher you climb in life, the more of them you will meet. In the meantime, you can work on yourself. When you choose to be as natural as possible, you will know more about who other people really are and they will know more about who you really are. This is how you will attract healthier people into your life.

Growing partners are treasures when we can recruit them; we may want to set this as a criterion for new relationships. When dating, we may ask potential suitors if they would be willing to learn to practice relationship skills with us.

Egos. Growth is least painful and most swift for those who leave their egos at the door. Giving up our pride or our idea of ourselves is a great lesson because we can then discover that we have nothing to defend. Hold as your highest priority the attainment of the lowest degree of false pride possible. This goal will enable you to come closer to the original you, before you adopted false fronts, self-consciousness and defenses. The better you can get at giving up your pride, ego or defensiveness, the faster and deeper you will grow, and the more natural and authentic you will become.

If we're not defensive, we grow faster. Look for the truth in the feedback you get and give yourself a chance to see if the feedback reveals a pattern which is likely real. Everyone gets feedback, but each person gets different feedback because each has different issues. For the most part, defending doesn't work because it shows you are too proud or defensive to self-reflect and it invalidates the experience of the other. Then you will get feedback that you are too proud or defensive. Even if you win the argument by overpowering another person, it doesn't mean you actually changed their mind.

I love to watch reality shows for this reason. You can see how a person's ability to gracefully receive feedback tends to put them at the highest level of functioning, whether you are watching Idol, Chopped or Celebrity Apprentice. The most injured and unhealthy people are the ones with a chip on their shoulder. Study these reality shows to see what I mean if you don't already know. Make it your goal to be one of those people who can put her pride aside to hear constructive feedback.

> **EGO = Edging God Out.**
> **– Alcoholics Anonymous**

Process, Not Content. It is important for you to know that in a disagreement, it is never the content that is truly at issue. It is how you argue your content. You can get yourself an arbiter this time, but what about all the other issues in your future? You can't take a mediator with you everywhere. Not only that, but a once-neutral party may be ultimately influenced by how argumentative and contentious you seem. In order to have good skills, we need to be able to have an issue in a healthy way. The issue will not be about content. It will be about process. You will be learning *how* to argue, not *what* to argue.

The world does not want to find fault with you. They want to find heroes and reasonable people with whom to ally. When you develop healthy skills, you will be able to give and receive feedback in a constructive way that will create a profound foundation for relationships. Problems will be dealt with in a healthy way and resolutions of content are often a by-product of the process.

Traveling to a RSW. Students who attend our Relationship Skills Workshops enter into a sort of boot camp. They change quickly and deeply if they can find their humility. Can you do this for yourself by yourself if there are none near you? Perhaps you may want to attend an extended seminar to get started and practice. We do not consider our RSW to be therapy, but we do know that the effect is extremely therapeutic. It is an effective way to break down personality disorders and to replace the coping mechanisms of these disorders or structures with healthy interaction skills. Until RSWs are in your neighborhood, we offer intensives to travelers.

To therapists in the field, I imagine our workshops may be similar to those held for borderlines by Marsha Linehan through

Dialectical Therapists. Our workshops address the skills and ethics of all personality structures and disorders and we hold that these disorders are no more than coping mechanisms children adopt in order to adapt to the circumstances of their childhoods. This system of feedback and coaching enables students to transcend personality disorders and structures and learn how to relate with the skills that healthy people enjoy. *The Handbook* that contains the guidelines for running or participating in a workshop is available online at drfayesnyder.com. We train therapists in how to run these workshops. As you can see, before we start training we emphasize how important it is to drop egos and defenses. It is the first skill.

The workshop leader is a teacher and students have paid and agreed to attend to learn. It is not an appropriate place to debate or rebel because you would end up wasting the group's time. You may ask theoretical questions, however. You may even ask critical questions. But if you decide to take on the leader in class, you will be most likely acting out. The leader is supposed to be at 12 o'clock and that is not arrogance. You are supposed to be at 6 o'clock and that is not inferiority. This is the design of any educational process, but especially this one. When you attend, you come to be taught cognitive restructuring, to include new ways to relate and new ethics for higher functioning. If you fight the process, you are resisting. If you resist too much, too long, you may do well to find another path by which to grow.

Breaking Bad Habits. All of us accidentally, subconsciously or habitually practice our childhood coping mechanisms in adult daily life. These habits served us very well once, when they were appropriate. Now they are no longer appropriate and have become deficits or disorders because we use them as if we still need them. Onto others we project assumptions from our childhood. Rather than perceiving clearly and responding appropriately, our reactions may be dysfunctional, reflexive, reactive, inappropriate and against our own good.

The process of *mirroring* helps wake us up as others let us know how we're coming across. We *un*learn *un*healthy interaction responses and replace them with healthy relationship skills.

> Wherever you are, be there.
> – Alcoholics Anonymous

The Rules

Bring the necessary traits for healing. Anyone who does this work has to want to heal. This work requires the traits discussed in Chapter 3: Healing: surrender, courage, self-observation and love of truth. These qualities must be so important to you that you are willing to learn to develop them if you have not already acquired them.

- You need the courage to bring up issues, be vulnerable with others, receive feedback and accept and own your feelings.
- You need to love the truth so much that you are willing to own your part in any misunderstanding.
- You need to be humble and surrender your ego or your idea of yourself.
- You need to be self-observing and self-reflecting so you can observe yourself from within, whether or not you have help from without.

This work will help you develop these traits as well as other valuable relationship skills. If you do not value these traits deeply or seek to develop them or if you think you may be too fragile for this type of work, seek another type of therapy where you may be allowed to set the pace for yourself.

Own and share air time. Everyone's *air time* is valuable. When you are in a dialogue with someone, be sure that you share the time. Do not make it all about you and do not listen more than your share because you need to be open too. Relationships are about give and take.

Be authentic in trying. Students often rebel against new skills in the beginning, saying "I can't say that; it's not me," or, "If I talk that nicely, I'll sound fake and obnoxious." When you say and believe these statements, you're implying that your personality disorder is your real self when, in fact, your personality disorder is just a bad habit, the way you've been coping since childhood. You're identifying your real self with the way you cope. Your coping mechanisms are not your real self.

Personality Disorder = Coping Mechanisms ≠ Real Self

The more you push yourself to try these skills, the closer you will get to the real, forgotten you. It feels inauthentic at first, but you are on the way to becoming more authentic than ever. As you drop your ego and replace your defenses with skills, you will get lighter and lighter. The transition will be difficult at first. Hang in there; it's worth it.

Do not judge or blame. Simply stated, healthy people do not judge, blame, shame and/or condemn. People who do these things often believe they are righteous and perhaps that others may support them. Perhaps they will seek support. Sometimes people who judge or blame have an unconscious drive for revenge, especially toward a significant other. The drive to condemn and/or seek retribution in order to resolve issues can be ineffective, inflammatory and even dangerous and is clearly a result of the condemning party's childhood trauma or parental modeling.

In my practice no one is allowed to blame anyone. If they don't stop after I ask them to stop, I "arrest" them. It is an abrupt interruption of the blaming. My rule that there will be no blaming is non-negotiable. Anyone who comes into my sphere of influence will be safe from blame. On the other hand, I teach my students how to take responsibility for their actions and if someone has been injured, I teach them the skills they need to express that injury without blaming, so the injuring party can listen, understand and probably find remorse.

If you have difficulty letting go of judging, blaming or punishing, then you would need to explore your childhood treatment and relive some of the memories where you were over-controlled, judged, blamed or punished. You may need to cry or rage to exhaustion against the original injury and the parents or persons involved. You would do this in private therapy.

Depending on the amount of trauma you are processing, you should be able to greatly reduce the drive to scapegoat others in a relatively small time through catharsis. This is not about extended self-pity or blaming your parents. It is about doing the work to reduce the drives to attack by facing and discharging the repressed emotions of old trauma. Cathartic work is very efficient when it is directed against the person responsible for the original injury and to whom you were not then allowed to respond or react. In fact, there is no other viable target for cathartic work. Any other target is scapegoating.

> If it's hysterical, it's historical.
> -- Alcoholics Anonymous

No advice giving and no "shoulding." In life, do not offer advice unless you are asked. If you are crawling out of your skin watching a disaster about to happen, you could offer to listen which might eventually generate a request for advice. If you must, you could ask, "Would you like to know what I would do?" After you have offered your opinion, do not expect it to be followed.

A person who is shoulding may believe he's being helpful, but if someone has not asked for help, the advice is oppressive. It puts the advisor in a "one-up," 12 o'clock, superior position that may satisfy his need to feel useful, but the recipient just feels like he's being parented, something most of us don't ever what to revisit. Most people do not appreciate unsolicited advice and will often say yes to someone's offer for advice when they really mean no because they'd rather endure the temporary advice than hurt the advisor's feelings. People need to live their own lives and adventures; when they are ready, they will seek advice and teachers.

Often it is necessary to teach one's child things they should do, especially in the realm of morals and values. Parents can and should advise their children. Just don't go overboard. There is a point where advice-giving gets tuned out, especially in adolescence. Watch for symptoms of tuning out.

If someone has paid you for your advice, you're obligated to give it. Graduate students of psychology are often taught never to give advice, which protects them from responsibility for their clients' choices. If a therapist doesn't give advice, she can't be blamed. Unfortunately, one does not have to be healthy to be a therapist and I have heard of some terrible advice coming from therapists. The real issue is that we need to have good theory before we give requested advice.

On the other hand, when one has never had a helpful parent, he or she deserves advice and guidance, which could be one of the best reasons for coming to therapy. It is certainly one of the reasons my therapy took so long. Clients come to us to get caught up and to find out what they didn't learn in childhood. To expect them to figure things out takes too much time and creates an uneven playing field. Most kids got to learn from parental guidance before they finished high school. Our clients should not have to spend years and large amounts of money trying to figure it out with only a few well-positioned questions here and there. This is one of my biggest issues with the field. I am also concerned that this field does not have a set of values upon which we can offer good advice.

Sometimes withholding such advice is plain wrong. Other times, offering it is wrong. Therapists need to make the distinction between when it would be withholding and when it would be oppressive. I have found that one way to make the distinction is, "Do I feel certain about this advice? Is this something a child should get to learn? Am I afraid of being sued for giving it? Am I healed enough to give this advice?"

If you are a person who gives really good advice, who lives by your own advice knowing it works, you can offer a person a template for a lifetime. So give it. For example, "Do unto others as you would have them do unto you," is really good advice. This manual is intended to be a composite of good advice. I sat with a woman recently who wanted to know whether she should date one guy or another guy from the Internet service to which she subscribed. Instead, I told her what criteria I would use to choose. I offered my advice on how to choose since I had given it a great deal of thought.

Lastly, sometimes I hear my students talking to one another, even veterans to new-bees, saying "You should ask your mom...whoops, I'm so sorry. That was a 'should.'" I have heard, "You shouldn't date a married man. Oh, I'm so sorry, that was a 'should.'" Yet when we are privy to a lack of ethics, we should take a stand.

Or, I have heard parents say, "You should do your homework. Whoops. I'm sorry I was giving advice." Parents are responsible for giving advice.

Parents, therapists and teachers need to give advice. When it comes to good theory, skills and ethics, I think advice is fine if not necessary. However, if you are not yet qualified to give advice, don't.

Would You...? Could You...? Please...

Have a humble consciousness when you ask anything of anyone. No one, especially your mate, is in this world to receive your orders, with the possible exception of a subordinate in the military.

Expecting things from people without a humble request is inflammatory. If you receive anger in response to your tone toward your mate, the issue is more likely with you, or both of you, than solely with your mate.

Start your requests with "Would you...?" or "Could you...?" or "Please..." and/or touch his hand gently or use eye contact and you're more likely to get exactly what you desire. Proceed with the knowledge that anything anyone does for you is not owed to you; it's a favor.

The Four Skills of Interaction (based on The Change Model)

- **Express how you feel subjectively.** FIRST, we communicate our feelings by saying some variation of "Ouch!" or "When you..., I feel... (hurt, manipulated, angry, sad, guilty, lonely, betrayed, threatened, unsafe, *etc.*)." Feedback in terms of feelings is easy to hear because it is vulnerable. This is subjective communication because we are expressing feelings instead of opinions or judgments.

- **Objectively express what you see (mirroring).** SECOND, we communicate our uncharged observations.
    - "When you..., I see... (helplessness, neediness, joy, withholding, health, sadness, confusion, armor, fearlessness, fake behavior, *etc.*)."
    - "Right now, you look... (arrogant, confused, controlling, contemplative, insincere, worried, threatening, defensive, unavailable, *etc.*)."
    - "When you..., I hear... (aggression, blaming, whining, a monotone, *etc.*)."
    - "You seem... (confident, unfocused, uninvested, disinterested, selfish, hypervigilant, loving, nurturing, dependent, *etc.*)."
    - "You seem... (out of skills, tired, ready to hurt someone, disconnected from your feelings)."

This kind of communication is objective and impartial. It's designed to be used by the recipient as a painless tool for self-awareness. The idea is to give an impartial mirror and have it received like the mirror in a bathroom; it's nothing personal. It doesn't matter if the mirror is right. What matters is how others experience you. For example, if you get a lot of feedback that you seem manipulative, that's what counts; whether or not you mean to manipulate is less pertinent. Pay attention to what you're doing or saying that is making someone feel manipulated. Odds are that later, you'll own that you were manipulating. Often body language is a match for consciousness. It's just that consciousness is often born of a wrong or outdated lesson.

- **Express what you think/suspect/ assess/wonder.** THIRD, we delicately explore possible motives using careful phrasing and a humble tone. Speculating on someone else's motives can be very presumptuous and offensive, although everyone does it. Even if we're right, speculating out loud without any sense of fallibility is wrong, intrusive and rude, especially if we impugn someone's character in the process. We cannot speak as though we know a person's motives. However, we can report on where our mind goes when speculating why a person acts a certain way. We address our own projections about a person's motives and intentions by airing them for confirmation, correction or communication. Explore them using spacer words like "fantasized," "imagined," "speculated" and "wondered."
    - BAD "When you... didn't answer my calls, I knew you... were avoiding me."

- BAD "You wanted to... exclude me from the party (injure me, leave me, lie about me)."
- BAD "I think you... had no intention of ever paying me back (are a liar, lack integrity, intend to drop out, can't be trusted, lack dedication)."
- BAD "Do you think you were trying to get attention?"
- BAD "Did you feel guilty? Is that why you said that?"
- GOOD "When you didn't return my calls, I *imagined* that you were... avoiding me (lying, giving up on me, colluding against me). Can you help me with what you were really thinking?"
- GOOD "My mind goes to a place where I wonder if you intend to... disregard me (betray me, cheat me, harm her, trick him, give up, run away). Please tell me if I am wrong."

- **Give and receive feedback with grace.** FOURTH, we release our defenses and aggression, accept feedback with grace and apologize where appropriate. Learn to appreciate feedback for the direct and indirect information it provides. If someone's feedback is too harsh, you might learn how to get her to be more kind. Ask her, "Is this for you or me?" If she says her feedback is for you, you can tell her it's so harsh that it's hard to hear, learn and grow and that you're feeling too defensive to listen. In the case where she eventually owns this, or you decide to speculate that the feedback is for her destructive pleasure, then you can inform her that you are not obliged to listen.

In the beginning of an issue you may want to bombard people with metaphorical flowers and feathers during feedback. Some people are sensitive and adjust to feedback quickly while others are very hardened and require harsher words to really receive it. Perhaps you have a regular meeting, dominated by an arrogant person who doesn't want to listen to anyone else. Maybe you escalate to mild outrage after having dropped feathers and pebbles, so you begin to drop rocks. If he responds with indignation, "You don't have to be so rude," you can mirror that you tried many softer ways that he couldn't hear. (It's likely that this follows his life outside workshop as well.) Start with feathers and progress to pebbles, rocks, boulders, etc., only if necessary.

The Four Skills of Interaction

There are four skills needed to communicate well through any confrontation in any relationship, romantic or otherwise.
- Express how you feel subjectively. "When you..., I feel..."
- Objectively express what you see (mirroring). "When you..., I see..." or "You seem..."
- Express what you think/suspect/assess/wonder. "When you..., I imagined that you intended to..."
- Give and receive feedback/mirroring with grace.

How to Have an Issue

Stage One and Stage Two. The only terms at PaRC that are obscure, exclusive to workshop or off-putting are these Stage One and Stage Two. They just evolved and stuck. These terms represent two different types of issues.

In the RSW, we call the first a Stage One, which is an issue presented about an outside relationship for the purpose of creating clarification. It is the opposite of gossiping or venting. For example, you may want to tell your mother you are having trouble with your boss, but you are afraid she will jump to conclusions that make you feel crazy, so you want to plan in workshop how to explain to her what's going on at work. You want to be able to think out loud to come up with a plan. If someone is dumping on me, I like to make sure we are brainstorming so they will take it to the source as constructively as possible. We could also call Stage One "Practicing" or "Sorting" in a safe place with people we trust.

A Stage Two at the RSW is a "Live Issue." It is an opportunity to identify and correct communication problems on the spot. Within reason, the more explosive the situation, the more valuable it is.

A live issue should always take priority over all else. It should be dealt with immediately and not avoided. When we avoid a live issue, it contaminates the room and everyone is affected, whether they consciously know it or not. If it is just you and someone else, you cannot authentically go forward without cleaning up this issue. Some people live with thousands of buried issues and they do not think clearly or respond cleanly. They do not perceive clearly either. They are so back-logged that they cannot be present with anyone. You can actually feel this kind of build up once you discover what it is like to be "current."

When someone is avoiding an issue, so many other unspoken factors are in every interaction with this person that you don't really know what you are dealing with. It's quite off-putting and confusing. Live issues affect the quality of relationships and become toxic if not addressed as soon as possible. They often explode on unsuspecting people and they still might not get what's going on because even in the explosion, the truth might not be told.

In my workshop I employ The Change Model. Instead of saying, "You bad person, you did this to me and you should be stopped, blamed and punished," I teach students to say, "When you do this thing it hurts me and I feel such and such and I want to this-and-that. In my mind I imagine that you are judging me and want to harm me on purpose." That is, we start with "When you...," followed by "I feel," and finish with, if necessary, "My fantasy or internal image of what your motives are about looks like..." In more conventional language, "When you ignore me in most of our family gatherings, I feel unwanted and I imagine that you are not happy to have me there." It could come out another way, "When you ignore me in most of our family gatherings, I imagine that you are not happy to have me there, so I feel unwanted."

Framing. In the early days of practicing relationship skills with someone on the same page, you may want to say something you don't know how to say. We have a way for you to get going and say it anyway. You don't have to have the perfect words in the beginning. Especially in a charged issue, you may want to say something that you fear you'll say incorrectly, but sitting on it until you can say it right will not benefit anyone. Perhaps you're really angry and you feel inclined to judge or blame and don't know another way to represent yourself yet. Maybe you're thinking you could hurt someone if you get it wrong. That's OK. Just frame it. When you "frame it," you can say almost anything. Say, "I want to frame what I'm about to say." Or, draw a square in the air with two hands and begin. At least the listener knows that you are aware that you're probably saying things incorrectly and without skills. The listener won't want to correct you before you finish. They'll feel free to listen, knowing you know and are sensitive that what you're saying is possibly incorrect and even hurtful and you are self-observing as you say it. They will be patient with you until you finish. Once you are on the same page, you can both discuss how you could have said it.

If speaking to someone who never heard of framing, you can say, "I need to share a thought which really concerns me and I'm sure there might be something wrong with the thought or the way I might say it, but I'd like permission to put it out there so we can deal with it together."

The Eye of the Needle. The right to legitimately represent and protect ourselves is inherent, whereas the drive for revenge is imprinted from childhood injury. It is exceptionally sinister when it is not returned to the imprinting parent, but instead delivered to another in a state of vitriolic rage, otherwise known as the "12 o'clock high." Coming from powerlessness (as a child), it is cathartic to rise up, unload on and scapegoat an unassuming person who offends us. But scapegoating only provides temporary relief; it does not heal us. Our drive to fight for ourselves was repressed by our parents and is now misdirected toward an innocent victim, redefining us as the perpetrator.

Revenge thinking reveals pathology, no matter how horrible the complaint. Revenge seekers often unconsciously choose mates with whom they can exercise a revenge dynamic. A child custody evaluator or mental health professional might think or even ask a person who is trying to paint a picture of themselves as the innocent and wronged party, "Why did you pick this person? Do you have problems seeing red flags (warnings that a person is 'trouble' or unhealthy)? Have you committed your own hurtful actions or are you in denial about your part? If this person is that bad, why did you make a baby, or multiple babies, with him? Are you a professional victim?" Healthy people do not find themselves in such a relationship and if they did, they would self-reflect about how they got into this situation. They would be grateful to see clearly and would be looking for the quickest, smoothest way to distance from such horrible behavior without inciting it further or seeking to blame or complain.

The more charged the revenge drive, the more profound is the opportunity to heal the pain. In the middle of a rage, transitioning from a reared-up, retaliatory stance of aggression to a vulnerable expression of pain, absent of ego, is as difficult as passing through the eye of a needle. It may be the hardest thing you have ever done while it's also the easiest thing you have ever done. Like learning to wiggle your ears, when you find it, you will slip right into the place your body wants to go. Just let your ego drop or fall. It's an instantaneous occurrence that offers the fastest, single-most profound opportunity for a rage- or blame-driven person to heal. In one moment of surrender, she can rewire her entire defense mechanism and personality disorder. All it takes is dropping her ego. She might do it by seeing herself as vicious as her original victimizer. Maybe she finally really sees the pain on her victim/beloved's face. Or she really does want to save her marriage and decides to be her own hero. She may have mentally prepared herself for the opportunity and simply waited for it to avail itself. When she is ready to surrender the power and instead take a vulnerable stance, she breaks the cycle of trading injuries.

One can "fall" to 6 o'clock and feel suddenly vulnerable. Ideally, you will let yourself feel the original injury and begin to cry. You may actually remember what it felt like to be on the victim side of revenge. When very old pain is finally released, defenseless crystal tears will clean and heal your deep, old wound.

Mirroring. Mirroring is objective feedback about how we're coming across in order to self-reflect and correct. It is especially useful when we are sure we don't seem a certain way, but ten people tell us otherwise. We learn to mirror safely and impartially, like our bathroom mirrors that simply reflect the truth without judgment.

As a matter of habit, one person might be prone to dominate and control. Another might tend toward rebelling, while another may be arrogant. Still others in similar circumstances might seem passive or helpless. Some might appear histrionic or reactive. All these ways of coping are simply bad habits. Through impartial, nonjudgmental, uncharged mirroring they may wake up. Perhaps you may pick up on a person's inability to sincerely express her feelings. Or maybe you can see someone failing to take responsibility for their actions and natural consequences. You may choose to develop skillful ways to offer a hint of a mirror or clear and nonjudgmental feedback. Do not become the hall monitor though. Work on yourself twice as much as you mirror others. For example, perhaps there is someone in your life who seems to have a lot of emergencies and need a lot of help. Maybe the next time she asks you for help, you might say, "Sure, but I was wondering if you have any thoughts about why you seem to need so much help." If they are offended by this mirroring, you might say, "I always thought that when people ask for help, they are inviting feedback as well."

One of the most common forms of denial is the refusal of feedback by holding that, "I'm not that way with anyone else so it must be about you," or, "I'm only this way with my mother and my husband so you're mistaken to see me that way," or, "My friends and employees don't see me this way." However, if there is someone with whom we can't get along or have difficulty interacting, this is where we need to focus because it is with them we are re-enacting childhood issues. A healthy person doesn't get hooked in with someone who gets their goat so badly.

How we handle disagreements defines our character and degree or severity of personality disorder(s). You don't really know a person until you've worked through a fight together. Learning to have a clean fight can heal any personality structure or disorder; let it be a primary goal to hone this skill.

A product of mirroring, though not necessarily a goal, is that we refine our persona, that part of our exterior that affects the way others relate to us. This may include acknowledging a false self we didn't realize we had or thought no one else saw, or refining rough and coarse mannerisms. We learn to adjust our demeanor, reactivity, guards, defenses and/or armor such that we refashion our personality structures and disorders into authentic, responsive and productive people. We even learn to give up caring how we are perceived and focus on whether or not we are acting with integrity and authenticity. While learning to hold up useful and safe mirrors for others, we learn to accept those mirrors from others, even if they are not presented skillfully or diplomatically. The information is still useful.

Another product of mirroring is learning to read people better. We might get to see the link between the childhood experiences and the coping mechanism right before our eyes, as well as watch it dissipate. We learn how to understand people better as we grasp what's behind hurt feelings and misunderstandings. As a matter of fact, we come to understand that every issue or disagreement is ultimately born of a misunderstanding.

Mirrors are neutral forms of witnessing. All mirrors are different and have differnt impacts. However, I've seen people use mirrors to the point of annoyance. "You seem angry," to which the other responds,

"Duh. Of course I'm angry." Save your mirroring for times when the person has no idea how they seem.

Ethics/Issues that Arise in Workshop

Enabling. While we develop empathy, we also need to refrain from rescuing. We learn that people need to have the natural consequences from their experiences. As a matter of fact, allowing a person the natural consequences or honest feedback is what almost magically comes to replace nagging and blaming. Karma is a far better teacher than nagging and rescuing a person from karma. Rescuing will cause them to atrophy or miss out on the opportunity for growth.

Some people are discovered or exposed for their enabling. They may be a person who only wants to give positive feedback or not say anything that may cause pain or discomfort to anyone else. The results of their kindness often deprive a person of the feedback they need to learn in order to have a better life. By avoiding the truth, they enable unhealthy behavior to continue indefinitely. Yet they see themselves as protective. They think there's something wrong with hurt feelings and they should be spared whenever possible, when hurt feelings are actually a part of growth.

Enablers are probably endeavoring to spare themselves the terror of confrontation or of possibly being disliked for a short excruciating time. They may have learned to fear negative feelings as a child when they were held responsible for their parents' pain. Even if they were not officially held responsible, their parents may not have let them off the hook.

Often in this world people don't tell the truth to one another. It's convention. In so doing, we keep each other blind by telling others our complaints and later exploding in anger. Enablers protect people from their karma, that is, the natural results of their actions. Enablers stand out as dishonest and would rather rescue than tell the truth. John Bradshaw tells the story of an enabler. While the enabler is dying, someone else's life flashes before him.

Confronting the Tarnished Mirror. There is a clear distinction between 'shoulding' on a person about how to live their life (country *vs.* city; saving *vs.* spending; working *vs.* going home; putting food away before eating *vs.* after eating; socializing with someone of the same religion *vs.* a different religion; proceeding through yellow *vs.* stopping on yellow; pruning at the leaf *vs.* away from the leaf; *etc.*) and expressing disagreement about immoral or unfair behavior toward others.

Failure to speak up can be an immoral act in that you might be choosing the easier path because it's more comfortable, despite the fact that a third party could fall victim as a result of your silence. If you know a priest is molesting a child, call the police. If you know with certainty that a therapist is having an affair with a client, write their licensing board and feel free to confront the therapist with how it affects you. If you know your priest is having an affair with a married person, you know your priest lacks integrity in his personal life and possibly with you. Tell him. If your friend wants to cheat on a licensing test, confront her.

Once you establish that someone is doing something unethical, tell them what you see and feel free to tell others who would be affected. If your friend is having an affair while engaged to be married you tell her that you will inform her fiancé if she doesn't stop. If you know for a fact (not by rumor) that someone who is in a position of leadership and authority does not follow their own advice or values, feel free tell the world. You may want to warn him first, but if he doesn't self-correct, tell others, please.

However, it is a grave assault to injure someone's reputation, so take care with your words. Give warnings and confirm the information thoroughly. If this is not possible, do not represent that the information is true. Be clear about what you don't know firsthand. Tell the therapist, priest or teacher what it looks like and see what they have to say.

If someone informs you that a third person has been unethical, harmful or, for example, racist and that has not been your experience, you may say, "Well I haven't seen anything like that," or, "That isn't my impression. Maybe you and I could check your information and I'll be open to revising my perspective too." If you have reason to believe someone is devaluing a third person recklessly, you'd do well to speak up. Their behavior is seriously wrong.

If you think someone is disregarding red flags, speak up. Often people marry someone, knowing they treated a previous spouse badly. How they treated the previous spouse could indicate how they'll treat others sooner or later if they don't get help.

It is wrong to gossip, but sometimes talking about others is not gossip; it's karma. Gossip is something people do when they enjoy having the goods on others because it makes them feel superior or in-the-know. It is without constructive intent. Assessment, however, including a willingness to test information or projections, is a valuable contribution to the truthfulness, honesty and safety of our environment. If we witnessed a teacher or friend of a friend call another person names without remorse, we have information about their character. Their reputation becomes their karma. We would ideally tell them they are creating their reputation by speaking that way. If they apologize, then we can forget it unless it continues. If they don't, that is a person whose reputation you may feel free to tell others about if they are considering this person for a teacher or a relationship. The most important people to mirror or chronicle are our leaders and teachers when their wrong behaviors are conspicuous.

We should always care how people treat and speak and require they treat others as well as they treat us. When we allow another to have a double standard in how they treat us *vs.* others, we may eventually be bitten by that same double standard.

The Role of Recognizing & Expressing Feelings. Expressing feelings is critical for healing, which is perhaps an understatement. In order to heal trauma and loss, one needs to cry, rage, scream or process whatever emotion the body was supposed to originally produce in response to trauma. In order to stay current with our feelings, we need to stay current with what triggers us in an issue. If someone talked down to you, perhaps you should have immediately said "Ouch." Sometimes it helps to discharge feelings, thus taking the bias or agenda out of one's position. This helps to address, correct and perhaps prevent misbehavior in the future. Feelings help identify the origins of misbehavior. Recognizing feelings may help us become conscious or self-aware of the impulses and drives behind our words and actions.

Feelings may inform the other person how you feel about something and whether you're repelled or attracted to it. Also, expressing reactions or responses through feelings often makes feedback more digestible.

When you're bothered by something and don't express that it's irritating or don't arrange to get away from it, you may eventually explode. In that case, it's your responsibility to not let your feelings build up so much that you over-react in the end. In that case, you will owe the irritant an apology for not speaking up sooner and then exploding. You might have simply said, "When you chew gum so loudly I start grinding my teeth." Probably the person would have simply thrown out their gum because your use of relationship skills would have helped them not feel too defensive. Instead you held back on expressing your growing irritation and then exploded on them out of the blue.

Thus, to reiterate, the best time to make social use of expressing feelings is when you are processing an issue with someone. It is easier for someone to hear how you feel than what you think when they do something that bothers you. By coming from your feelings you are less threatening and they will be able to hear you more easily.

That said, it is important that values (not feelings) instruct actions. Understanding feelings enlightens behavior, but it never excuses behavior. Once the sharing of feelings becomes more than information, you run the risk of being tuned out.

Unfortunately, some people believe they are supposed to be guided by their feelings and keep them on the table at all times. A person is always entitled to have and express their feelings, but that's not to say that feelings should direct and inform action, a seriously mistaken belief. Some people think feelings can excuse misbehavior or that their feelings are the only ones that count. Some people believe that the right to one's own feelings entitles them to wallow in them or to harangue others with them.

Some people believe they get to express their feelings all day long about everything and in large quantities because feelings are allowed. Lesser stimuli warrant smaller expressions. Reactions of overkill are inappropriate and become oppressive to the listener. If you overdo it, your feelings may become unimportant and your listener may start to think, "Who cares?" Worse, they may feel suffocated by you and wish to get away. The expression of feelings should be measured and should never overdose anyone.

Despite the intensity of a feeling, recovery and relationship skills both mandate that we make noble and heroic choices of integrity. The greatest heroics take place when we recognize our feelings and rise above them. In order to do this, we are forced to become self-aware. We will be rewarded with increased and well-earned self-esteem.

> Truth is like oxygen and water.
> – Esther Seznie,
> photographer and casting director

Yelling. Yelling makes it harder for people to hear you in general. You also might look out of control. Nevertheless, in this theory, there are no rules against raising our voices or yelling, especially because we don't believe in repression. Further, when someone does not recognize what you are saying, the natural response is to yell to be heard. It is karma for the listener, even though it still makes us look out of control.

Start softly and build up if necessary to be heard. As I have said, some people can be reached with feathers; others take boulders. Some people manage others arrogantly by drawing a line against yelling, yet they feel free to say inflammatory things. Sometimes, yelling is quite appropriate, especially if it keeps someone from exploding on the wrong person later on. A healthy person can sit comfortably and listen to someone yelling without feeling responsible for quieting the yeller.

There's no name-calling, judging or blaming allowed in this theory, but there isn't any rule against, "Fuck *you!*" It can be a way of non-violently giving back an offense or assault to the abuser. However, this response should not be commonplace in a family. If it is, the family needs treatment.

Feelings *vs.* Opinions ("I feel..." *vs.* "I feel that..."). Some people think that expressing their opinions about you is the same thing as expressing their feelings. This is loaded, especially since thoughts are often judgments or projections. People often say, "I feel that..." or worse, "I feel that you are..." By following the word "feel" with the word "that," they are actually expressing a thought disguised as a feeling. When told they're expressing a thought, not a feeling, they may look stumped. "What's the difference?" It's an important endeavor to identify the difference between a feeling and a thought. It's actually Self-Awareness 101. Further, to say, "I feel that you..." is loaded because it's an opinion that is shrouded in misleading language in order to sneak it in. Self-awareness mandates that we know the difference for our own sake as well as for others.

If you find yourself saying, "I feel that...," retrace your words and change them to, "I think...," or, "I'm having the thought that..." Feelings tend to be a vulnerable sharing that can be easy for the other person to digest. Thoughts tend to show up as judgments with an arrogant pretense. "Feeling that..." is an invisible mind trick.

Assessments *vs.* **Judgments.** Judgment is usually intended to write someone off or draw a long-term conclusion about them. It tends to have finality about it. One means to label someone's core identity or inherent worth. It is akin to the "bad seed" theory in that one person holds intrinsic superior disdain for another.

This theory prefers that you assume bad behavior is the result of unhealed childhood trauma, which you will choose to avoid unless the person is willing to do the healing work to self-correct.

A judgment is designed to hurt or bully someone into submission or even to meet your demands. It is mean-spirited as if inflicted for enjoyment. It strikes at a person's identity, intending to cripple or ridicule rather than raise up. It does not serve us to assert that anyone is beyond redemption, even if they threaten our lives.

Thus, if someone is judgmental of another in the context of our Relationship Skills Workshop, the facilitator may make an "arrest." That is, they may tell someone speaking to "Stop!" or, in some cases, they may even have to be more abrupt. The facilitator is responsible for protecting the membership in the group from being judged. A parent is responsible for protecting a child from being judged by a sibling. A partner is responsible for protecting their mate from judgment by their own extended family.

If we judge a child molester rather than assess them for their childhood and predictable actions, they, and we, become worse. We can see that the child molester needs to be removed from the community, most probably for life, but we don't benefit by writing them off as someone to be righteously despised. In so doing, we make things worse because it feels good to judge and it's a lot easier than correcting or understanding the origins of pathological behavior. We would think more clearly if we did not forget that no one rescued them or defended them when they were being molested as helpless little children. After their isolated and terrifying ordeal, they were doomed to grow up injured and destined to re-enact their experience from the other side by becoming offenders themselves.

From judgment, we opt for retribution rather than healing or prevention. Then we become just like the molester. Just like them, we become part of a chain reaction that opts to injure rather than heal or prevent.

Judging is for the judger. It doesn't make a person better. It's such a "high" that it can even become sexualized. It gives the injured person a sense of righteousness in their injury, perhaps even re-establishing their victimhood above their ability to survive and transcend. Judging becomes an opportunity to scapegoat our despised object with the volcanic fury we pent up from childhood and our original injuries. Judging is indulgent.

In the beginning it's often difficult to know the difference between an assessment and a judgment. All of us make assessments to survive intelligently, as we need to discern. We have to make value judgments too. We are not being asked to live blindly in order to give up judging. An assessment is simply more scientific. It sees and identifies a behavior and recognizes what needs to be heeded while appreciating its origins. It assumes that the behavior can be corrected or the drive can be transcended if the person chooses to do the therapeutic work. Assessment skills help one realize whether or not the behavior of another is personal so we don't have to get upset or offended unnecessarily. In any adversarial situation, one needs to assess their opponent. Judging them will do no one any good.

Value judgments are useful in setting personal standards for the people we bring into our lives. They expose or clarify choices that reveal willingness or unwillingness, if not inability, to do the work to meet these values. If we invest in someone who refuses to self-reflect and self-correct or suffer the discomfort of correct choices, then we will eventually have to absorb their karma. We will have invited in someone we can love to hate or blame for the way our life is going. Assessment skills and value judgments provide criteria by which we can determine whether we would do well to associate with such a person or not. Assessment skills and value judgments put the responsibility back on us for who we choose to be in our lives. The extra bonus is that when we make a choice not to associate with someone who exhibits destructive or self-destructive behavior, we may become the actual influence that causes them to work on themselves.

Projections vs. Perceptions. Just as some people do not know the difference between a thought and a feeling, some people don't know what a projection is and how deadly it can be to a person's original self or authenticity. Simply put, a projection is a belief about someone that forces them into an identity that's not theirs. In this way, a child can have a parent who chooses only to "see" him or her when the child accepts the projections. Attempts by the child to break away from the projection go unacknowledged, so the child gives up.

Like a radio, the parent is receiving only on a given frequency or station. In order to interact or exist in the eyes of her parents, the child has to tune into that station. For example, if the parent requires continuous deference, the child has to tune into deference at the expense of his own experience. If the parent thinks the child is just like his father who is in jail, he may have to become a bit of a criminal to be seen. If his father is an artist, he may not be validated for his love of science and math.

Projections are so deadly they may bring up violent internal feelings in a healthy adult. When we treat a person according to our judgment or projection, we force them to either react against us or respond as if it were true.

Dealing with projections can be crazy-making because it's like shadow-boxing. The projection is silent and invisible. When the person tries to deal with it, the projector can often prove that the subject has no right to make such a claim because there is no evidence. Often, there may even be evidence to the contrary. A mother who feels guilty about favoring one child over another may often make a point of always buying both children the same gift, announcing to all who will listen that she always treats her children equally.

If a parent denies their projections and never cleans them up, the child is forced to adopt a warped window through which to see and learns to doubt his or her own perceptions. Often a mate, friend, employer or even therapist may simply deny their projection.

One toxic variation would be the projector who believes he or she is right, but doesn't want to hurt anyone's feelings by telling the "truth" of what he "sees" and believes. Perhaps, he would rather take the offense and act offended than reflect upon whether he is, in fact, silently judging. In any event, when someone avoids owning their projections at all costs, they may be at a level of denial that is so extreme, it has evil dimensions. That is, they are willing to make another person feel crazy for their benefit rather than honestly own their own position, beliefs or thinking.

You may think it could be harmful to acknowledge a projection. For example, you may think a parent shouldn't say, "You're right. I favor your sister over you." That would be brutal honesty. However, the parent could say, "Oh my God, you think I favor your sister over you? I am so sorry. I will think long and hard about how I gave you that impression."

So it's difficult to unveil someone's projection. It's also difficult to discern our own projections. Most of us arrive into adulthood without the ability to distinguish between perceptions and projections because projections feel as real or true as perceptions, if not more so. Because projections feel so real, we assume they are and skills are needed to get a reality check. Those who don't check are at risk of becoming harmful if not delusional. (Failure to receive appropriate feedback in childhood contributes to bipolar disorder and when parents disavow projections they can lead their child to schizophrenia.)

Some people do not know how to deal with the perceived ulterior motives toward another person without accusing them. Again, I recommend the Change Model. Start with the assumption that you do not know how to tell the difference between a projection or a perception. Assume that whatever you see about another person could be a projection rather than a perception. You don't get to take what you see to the bank until you have asked questions. The way you discern is by checking and gathering information.

There is a woman I see every week who frequents the same place. She and I have nothing to talk about really and the environment discourages discourse. However, she seems to be hostile toward me. She seems cold. She asks harsh questions that seem to have judgments in them. I have to continually remind myself that until we have a moment for open dialogue, if ever, I must assume this is her personality for now, that she has had something difficult happen recently in her life, that I have done something unconsciously to offend her or that she is projecting something on me. I cannot simply assume she is a cold person or even that she has a Narcissistic personality based on what I see. I have to try to be nice to her to give her the benefit of the doubt. I also need to see her in more situations with other people. I find myself seeking her eyes to see who is in there and hoping for an exchange that will tell me more.

Who Can I Trust? A person you can trust is not someone who sees things your way. Only infants and small children get to have that luxury when the parenting is really good. The person you can trust is not someone who will defend you, right or wrong.

You can trust that no one is designed to make choices on your behalf. We are all designed to make choices on our own behalf. When people are thoughtful, it is something they can do somewhat regularly, especially if we are also equally as thoughtful. Some can do it regularly because they have been emotionally blackmailed to be thoughtful. Some people are charming and thoughtful in order to manipulate and that doesn't last. So, if you are looking for the ideal person to trust no matter how you act, you won't find him.

Even if you treat others perfectly, everyone will disappoint you sooner or later. That's why we have communication and skills. When someone disappoints you, you speak up. You at least say, "Ouch," or "Why?" A person who can be trusted will be the one who says, "Oh, I'm sorry." Or, maybe they might say, "Let me think about that" or "I am so sorry that I hurt your feelings, but it's what I have to do to be true to myself." A person you can trust will dialogue with you about what they can or can't do. They will look at their thoughtless moments and get back to you.

When I am speaking to paranoid types, I am amazed by this complaint. Often these people cannot trust me, yet they have people in their lives who are abusive or self-destructive.

People who ask who they can trust are often looking for loyalty, right or wrong. They want someone who has their back no matter what. What they really need to do is grieve the peril of their childhood. They will never get to have a safe childhood, but they can have a safe adulthood if they choose relationships with people who mutually self-reflect.

Loyalty is a very bad reason to trust someone. I don't want it because I would rather have honest feedback to know where I stand. I don't want someone who tells me what I want to hear. I want to live in a world where no one sacrifices themselves to meet my needs. I want to live in a fair world, not a world designed for me.

Of course I want the kind of loyalty where I am informed if someone is actually betraying me behind my back. If my husband was having an affair and someone knew about it, I would hope they would tell me because it's the ethical and right thing to do. I want to live in a world of good ethics.

The best conversations I've ever had have been with my team of protégés. My husband, son and daughter-in-law run a close second. I am sure it is because of the intense nature of our work that I find these dialogues consistently amazing. The honesty, openness and mutual commitment to ethics, clients and children is heaven for me. I don't think the heavenliness of our interaction results from loyalty, *per se*. I think it results from a commitment to good practices and good work. It ends up feeling similar to loyalty, only better. I am with people who see clearly, are willing to do the right thing when it is in front of them to do, who practice relationship skills, who will defend anyone who deserves defending and will question poor ethics and anyone who demeans or badmouths anyone else. I think that is as good as it gets.

From Judging to Choosing for Self. In the beginning of my workshop, some people do not realize the difference between judging and choosing what's right for oneself. People who resort to judgment and resist relinquishing it often think they need to judge in order to change the other's character. If they judge them harshly enough or try to fix them in earnest, maybe that person will change and they won't have to leave because they would rather judge than leave a person.

The focus becomes that of change-by-blaming rather than mustering the courage to make the right choices for one's self. A person who would rather judge than leave does not understand how toxic they are and how they may be part of the problem, if not the whole problem. Judged people rarely self-correct under the cloud of judgment or force of a negative projection; instead they rebel, either overtly or passively, creating a self-fulfilling prophecy or sometimes they just wither.

Thus, some people actually believe it's kinder to stay and judge a person than to leave them. This kind of thinking reveals difficulty having empathy or putting oneself in the other's place. If they did think back, they'd likely remember when they were surely judged with excruciating precision. Perhaps they'd remember what it did to them and how they wanted to rebel and it kept them from learning. Judgment is cruel; leaving is kinder in the long run.

A person who's been left due to their chronic behavior is more likely to self-correct. This is not a tactic to be used frivolously and is most effective when someone is hitting bottom. You will have to follow through and hold to your position until you are satisfied with the quality of the changes enough to return. Don't return prematurely because this is a tactic that usually works just once. If you return prematurely, you will not be believed or respected next time.

When one leaves after mirroring the other person at least three times already, they have more power of persuasion than at any other time. Of course this is contingent on your request being a necessary and correct one. For example, if you leave because someone drinks too much alcohol, you have power of persuasion in this moment more than any other time. If it's a new relationship, you may just want to say, "It's not for me because you drink too much."

You can live your entire life without judging, free of harmful relationships. You can give palatable feedback to well-intentioned people who unwittingly commit hurtful acts. In this way can you determine who is responsive to uncharged feedback and who, in fact, refuses or seems unable to self-correct at that time.

Only if your delivery is clean can you make this determination because even the best people and those most invested in self-improvement rebel against feedback that diminishes them or leaves them no dignified way to grow. Until you practice the skills, you cannot say what kind of person you're with or whether communication would have worked with them. When your skills have been clean and you can clearly see that the other person is bad for you, you need to leave for their sake as well as yours. If you stay with a person who obviously won't grow in the light of your good skills, then you are living like a professional victim. Of course, leaving follows several attempts to express one's feelings first. It's not acceptable to walk out every time you don't get your way. It's not acceptable to threaten to leave unless you mean it and it has to be done calmly because we never leave someone in the middle of an issue.

Sometimes people who have lived crippled with shame, judgment and self-judgment find enormous relief in letting go of judging others. By doing so, they get to let go of judging themselves. They can stand up straighter and be more invested in life and in their choices. They learn that their job is to self-correct and if they don't self-correct, natural consequences, not judgment, will get them. Further, impartial mirrors work better than judgment to reveal mistaken ways and can be used to head off natural consequences.

There is no need to be defensive, self-righteous or judgmental any more with others or one's self. We have become as forgiven as one who just left a confessional and as safe as one who lives in a sanctuary. We have come to realize that in taking moral stands for ourselves, others will want to measure up or need to leave. We can live in honor without being a tyrant to others or ourselves. Living in honor without fear of judgment or a need to judge is sweet. On the other hand, it's time to model and live with standards that are without hypocrisy and inspire self-reflection in others.

Lastly, to those of us who come from unhealthy backgrounds, I need to let you know that if you want to live this healthy lifestyle, sometimes it means you have to let others go. Not everyone is up for this way of living and relating. Weigh the choice before you make it and when you make it, make the choice yours, not mine.

Yes, If... I recommend to my clients not to tell someone no when asked for a relationship, arrangement, agreement or any otherwise mutual connection. I recommend they say, "Yes, if..." I believe this is a great clarifier. It is a perfect mirror. It reveals your criteria. It is educational and it puts the ball back in the other person's court.

I wish everyone would do this. I wish that when someone comes to look at office space for rent at our location they would say, "Yes if," rather than, "No," or simply disappearing. We have had a number of potential tenants look at our space to see if they would be interested. If they said "Yes, if...," we would know if the problem is the location, the layout, the size, the price or something else. Instead we are often left in the dark without a mirror.

If a nerdy guy wants to date you, say, "Yes, if you go to acting classes (to study how you come across), parenting and relationship skills classes (something I recommend for everyone), take karate (which tends to build a mystique), get a $100K a year job, pay a stylist to dress you and get contact lenses. Then I would date you." Or you could even say, "Yes, if you grow five inches." Now he has a choice. He understands what you require in a relationship. He won't take the mirror personally or have to guess what the reasons are. He can be on track in the real world. He can choose to modify himself or not and determine what he can't and won't change. Further, he can see how he barks up wrong trees. Of course my examples may be extreme, and you may choose to save "Yes, if..." for more reasonable situations.

If a serial killer wanted to be your friend, you don't say no. You say, "Yes, if you turn yourself in, do ten hours of therapy every day for the rest of your life, pay ten million dollars to each family member of everyone you have killed and then I will be your friend." Or you could say, "Yes, if you agree to turn yourself in, work with a therapist to get clear why you did what you did and accept a relationship of occasional correspondence only."

Actually, I know a woman who told her step-father she would forgive him for molesting her if he separated from her mother for a year, did intensive therapy with me, gave up his house and all his savings to her and lived in a humble trailer for the rest of his life. She was a therapist. I supported this demand of hers. Interestingly enough, he did it all. He and his wife sold the house and gave her about a million dollars, including his savings, holding on to enough money to pay for his therapy. He moved into the trailer and his wife stayed in a small apartment for a year so she was allowed to visit all her grandchildren. After that year she moved into the small trailer with her husband. Her son and daughter-in-law allowed the two of them to visit their children, although they were never left alone together. The daughter cut off contact with her stepfather and mother. He did all of this and she still refused to forgive him. I actually thought she was wrong. His family was so moved by his humility and taken aback by her inability to forgive that they ended up choosing him over her for family gatherings.

Living with Honor and Courage. Here are some myths some people believe when entering my workshop:

- We are entitled to our hypocritical point of view.
- We have the right to do what we want without consequence or judgment.
- If a feeling is strong enough, we should be allowed to follow it without consequence.
- To be true to oneself is primary in a relationship.
- Our only responsibility is to put out the fires within by finding ways to avoid our feelings and even to indulge them.

In the RSW, I ask students to live with courage and honor by doing the right thing no matter how difficult it seems. Such a path becomes the easiest way to live with others, but to get to that path is hard at first. Often what is required in order to come clean in a relationship is to privately go all the way into the original injury so it can be processed and done. It is common for big, brave men to fear going inside. Sometimes old traumas of childhood are more frightening than any present-day threats, but if that's true, these old demons will show up in current relationships and often take on scapegoating behavior. The honorable task is to go through it. In so doing, you'll find out that the idea of it and the dreading of it are far worse than the feelings of leftover denied pain. When you go in, wear the feelings and they will discharge before you realize you are crying or raging. You will just be expressing yourself and it will feel so good. As I wrote in Chapter 3: Healing, it is the resistance to feeling your emotions that is so emotionally painful. We can only keep our finger in the dyke for so long before it starts to swell, ache and hurt. Resisting the pain requires a fortress and repressing does us harm. Releasing heals. Expressing pain from trauma is like falling off a log once you let go. Before you know it, it's over.

Keeping Our Word. The most important aspect of our identity is the way we are known to others. We will be known, in large part, for how we keep our word. It is smart to promise nothing, but offer our intentions and keep the other apprised of our progress. If we promise at all, it is better to promise less than it is to agree to something we may fail to complete. People who make agreements that they treat lightly or don't keep can earn a great deal of contempt and even anger from those in their lives.

Ultimately, the best way to relate to this type of behavior is to treat the person with little expectation and relate to them minimally until they change and can be trusted to keep their word. For example, if someone tends to be late to pick you up, meet them there. If they cancel several times for reasons other than work or a sick child, then only make spontaneous dates at the last minute.

Right Actions, Wrong Consciousness. Some people have used skills to make others wrong and to avoid their own self-reflection. They have actually abused others with relationship skills. Some try to digest the skills so they can be more perfect and more correct, or perhaps to be superior to others. It won't work. If you use skills to have a leg up on others in order to get your identity needs met so you can play the role of the better person, you will not be in skill.

Forgiveness. I believe one should not forgive before they release their feelings. Alice Miller tells the story of a client who was persuaded by his therapist that it was time to forgive his parents, but he wasn't ready and he felt ashamed that he couldn't forgive them yet, so he went home and put a bullet through his head (1984).

After we have expressed our feelings and feel heard, at least by someone with empathy, we forgive naturally. If we don't forgive, then there may be something else at issue. Incidentally, when adults cannot get over the loss of a parent it is often due to Complicated Bereavement, wherein a person cannot complete with the deceased because they may still be angry or hurt.

Sometimes, we can't forgive because we hold a revenge ethic. Forgiveness is something that is for us, not for our offenders. It allows us to let go of the toxic feelings of resentment that take over our mind and our body. Forgiveness does not require us to renew a relationship and put ourselves at risk again. Forgiveness simply allows us to move on. Sometimes forgiveness is necessary for a relationship to continue. Sometimes it is necessary for a relationship to end. After emotions have been expressed and sincere apologies have been offered, forgiveness is the next necessary step. If it does not come, the contrite offender needs to exit the relationship for his own sake.

Lastly, some people seek forgiveness selfishly. If it seems that they want forgiveness before their victim has finished expressing her feelings, then they are still taking. I don't ask for forgiveness from people because it is a way of taking more and I don't want to run the risk of interrupting any more feelings that need to come out. A truly contrite person is interested in the other person's wellbeing, not their own. However, sometimes asking for forgiveness is intended to be a sign of pure humility. Sometimes it needs to happen after the offender has expressed deep remorse and the victim has voiced all her grievances. That is a good time to ask for forgiveness in order to punctuate an ending and a beginning.

Commitment. There seems to be an epidemic of commitment phobia running rampant with respect to marriage. I have heard it spoken of as if "it is just a piece of paper and some hocus pocus." The fear of commitment is one thing, but rationalizing the aversion to commitment is wrong. After a reasonable amount of assessment time if you can't decide or commit, set your partner free and perhaps consider therapy.

There are reasons for that piece of paper and the ceremony. The former gives a woman security and the latter gives her social dignity. Women are the vulnerable and dependent sex most of the time. It's actually in our sexual design. Without the ring, the ceremony and the piece of paper, she may feel used. If you are afraid of another failed marriage and monthly payments to follow, then get the two of you into a relationship skills workshops where you can get reassurance that each of you has the ability to fight cleanly, and both of you know your rights and responsibilities in a relationship.

You can also explore a reasonable prenuptial agreement. One can be written even for working class couples. You can write it so that assets you presently hold can be kept separate and private in case you have need for starting over. You can write it so that her contribution to the marriage and the care of your children are fairly considered. You can protect yourself against gold-digging if that's the issue. Perhaps you may want to discretely set up a savings account for her in case you ever need to set her free. I don't believe women get to become accustomed to a lifestyle a man must maintain if the marriage doesn't work out, but I do believe a man should leave her better than he found her, marriage or no marriage.

On the other hand, I have known women who are offended at the idea of a prenuptial agreement. Men are not in this world to give us free rides in life. This is an era when there are more divorces than there are lasting marriages, so marriage is a gamble, especially without the basis of good relationship skills and ethics. We need to have some compassion for the man's position if we want him to have empathy for ours. Take marriage as a statement of intentions and may both of you do your very best.

I have met so many couples where one, usually the woman, bears the respectfully passive role in hopes that some day she will experience the romantic surprise of her life when her man proposes to her. So important is this moment that she will not nudge or hint. The more I check in on these couples the more I find out that the man has no intention of proposing, at least not now or for some time to come. When I ask him about it he is surprised that anyone would push him to make a decision. He does not seem to have any empathy for the woman's need to be chosen. In the meantime he enjoys her company in bed. Because he has not chosen her, she secretly fights off feelings of worthlessness and feeling "cheap." As time passes and her childbearing years wane, this treatment begins to appear like theft to me.

Of course there are some good reasons to avoid commitment. If both parties are widowed and receiving pensions they may not be able to afford to live together if they married. Sometimes the parties are more roommates than lovers. Sometimes one of them is in an extended divorce and custody dispute, which suggests the need for a thorough self-reflection and correction before marrying again.

It is my general opinion that women in their prime should spend no more than two years under assessment with a man. If he cannot make up his mind in that time then move on. Do not let him take you for granted. You are worth a ring in the right man's eyes. If both parties are in therapy and your girlfriend has a violent temper, it seems reasonable to ensure that she no longer has a violent temper before proposing to her. Opt for an extended engagement while she works on herself.

If she lives with you, put a ring on her finger even if it is an engagement ring. I know that sounds old fashioned but some old fashioned notions were healthy, right and fair (such as moms staying home). Older individuals or couples that have no intention of having children can afford to take their time before deciding to marry. Older couples also experience less shame in living with someone out of wedlock as they are not under the same pressure. However, I would not give a man more than two years without a ring on my finger. It's a dignity thing.

If a man cannot afford to support a woman to stay home to raise children in the first three to five years, then don't date him. Don't fall in love with someone who will lead you into working while your child is in day care. Think ahead.

If you are a man dating a woman who will not commit and you want children, move on. Fair is fair.

Terminating

Your reputation will often grow out of your ability to keep your word and your ability to self-reflect. You may also be known by how you have an issue with people. I often share the sad and ironic insight that you never really know a person until you have an issue with them or come to a parting with them. Likewise, they may not know your true character until you part with them. How a person ends a relationship reveals so much of who they were all along.

Our ultimate coping mechanisms show up when we're in a heated issue and when we're leaving or being left. You can say that our personality disorders are full blown or exposed the most at this time. When you leave in anger, a lot of things finally become clear about you or them. Thus it's important to observe how a prospective mate chooses to end their relationships with others. <u>How a person terminates their workshop is critically important, especially whether they completed their work or are leaving in the middle of an issue.</u>

Often people sit in my skills workshop safely without presenting any problems or issues and then one day they announce that they are leaving because they aren't getting anything out of the workshop. Again, we cannot refine our ways of interacting without taking the risks of giving and receiving feedback with people who are on board to tell one another the loving truth. I have often found in the workshop that the point at which a person becomes disappointed with the process is when they have their first real issue to work on. To leave at the moment of their first real issue is to miss the work altogether. Leaving this way is an abdication of honor, honesty, courage or intimacy.

When my students have learned how to properly terminate my workshop, they also know how to end other relationships, including therapy, religious study, schools, jobs and friendships. They have learned that we explain why we are leaving, how we feel about going and what we have gained from the relationship to take with us. The students who are left then tell the person leaving how they experienced them, how they feel, whether or not they seem prepared to leave and maybe offer their blessings or wish they had worked harder on the relationship. This is termination of the highest order.

When books end, the author writes a conclusion. When people have an issue in or out of RSW, I ask them if they feel "complete" so I know if they are ready to move on. "Terminate" is a strong word; some people prefer closure. A relationship that ends is terminated and if it ended in a healthy way, the parties involved have that closure.

Summary of Relationship Skills

Beginning
- Get the lay of the land before jumping in (the best way to be "the new kid on the block").
- Leave your ego behind. Practice being at 6 o'clock. Don't spread your arms wide or put your hands in a tent unless you choose to look arrogant.
- Be prepared to speak in unfamiliar and unnatural words until you can use relationship skills in your own words.
- Be prepared to learn the hard way, asking for mirroring after an issue: baptism-by-fire.
- Begin all relationships in faith, never in suspicion or projections. In this way the other person's pathology is exposed more quickly and you do not contribute to a self-fulfilling prophecy.
- Do not dominate the air-time, give advice or talk down to people.
- Don't waste precious time thinking about what you should say to look good.
- There is dignity in owning mistakes and shame in covering them up.

Resolving Issues
- "Practicing" represents an issue from outside the conversation. Ensure you are preparing for the confrontation or clarification discussion, not gossiping or judging. Your listeners will not judge, but will expect you to take it to the person with whom you have your issue soon.
- "Live issues" are right now. They take precedence over everything else. Never let a live issue wait.
- There are two skills of disagreement: the Change Model ("When you...") and Mirroring. The former is subjective and said in vulnerable feelings. The latter is objective and said impartially. Neither is ever offered from a 12 o'clock position.
- Use the "Ouch!" template when someone hurts you. That is, "I feel... when you..." "When you..., I see...", "When you..., I have the thought that..." When at a loss for words, just say "Ouch," unless you just got a clean mirror. In that case, thank them for the mirror.
- Use the "Oops!" template when you hurt someone. That is, "I am sorry." "I'm sorry, what can I do to make it better?" "I'm sorry, I will take a look at that." "I'm sorry for hurting you, but this is my path." I'm sorry, generally speaking, is enough. Do not wallow in remorse.
- Never presume to know a person's motives, but you can check out an impression of motives by asking with "spacers": "Forgive me, but when you..., I have the thought that... Would you be willing to correct my impression?"
- If you don't know how to say something in skills when talking with a growing partner, frame it in words or a literal "air drawing."
- Focus on your part: Don't use "you" statements. Stick to "I feel... when you..."
- If someone offends you, figure out your part before complaining.
- No blaming or judging EVER. Prepare to be scorned for blaming or judging repeatedly if you are in training in a RSW. Mirroring and assessing is allowed (with objective feedback about how someone is coping or *seems*, but not *is*). Feelings are also allowed.
- No advice giving unless you are asked or you are a parent or designated teacher.
- Don't present or sneak in a thought or judgment as a feeling, *i.e.,* "I feel that…"
- Use feedback from others to see how you are coming across as opposed to who you are. That way there is nothing to defend, given you are exquisitely Divine. Only your ways of coping are off.

Standards and Values
- Assessing (*vs.* judging) is allowed and expected. Take a person's dysfunctional behavior as something they could change.
- Judging is not allowed. It sees their character as inborn.
- No enabling. If you accept or enable bad behavior, you are a co-conspirator.
- No projecting. If you have a projection, frame it and ask about it.
- No old mirrors allowed. People can change on a dime so only mention patterns (of three examples) that still exist.
- Never demand. When imposing on someone, always use "Would you...?" "Could you...?" Or "Please..."
- Keep your word. If you need to break your word, notify the person first that you are breaking your agreement and give your true reasons why.
- Don't do evil. Don't scapegoat. Don't harm someone else for your own end.
- Don't saddle someone with a secret. If you do, expect them to tell someone.
- Don't make choices, even romantic choices, out of feelings unless the choice is also correct or ethical.
- Do the right thing when it is in front of you to do.
- Act with courage, honor, love of truth and self-observation.
- When you own something and pass through the eye of the needle (by dropping your ego, going to 6 o'clock and recalling your original injuries), you heal and change then and there, earning the respect of everyone beholding.

Living
- Do not live a secretive or overly private life. To do so is indicative of someone who wants to act one way and get credit for another. Excessive privacy is unhealthy and usually harbors unethical secret choices or a false self. Make it a goal to live your life openly and authentically. When you do, you will be achieving your optimum in mental health and healthy relationships.
- Don't misuse skills theory to bully in an argument
- Pick relationships with people who live in skills whenever possible.

Group Etiquette for Those in RSW
- You may discuss lessons and stories from group, but not names.
- No secrets will be harbored within the group from anyone else in the group and no relevant issues will be hidden.
- We get to talk about you in your absence, in skills.
- Any public posts belong to the group.
- Any emails, voicemails or other communications about someone else in the RSW belong to the group.

Terminating Relationships
- We don't stay in a relationship with people who do evil things.
- It may be harmful to stay in relationship with someone who doesn't use or want to learn skills.
- Don't terminate a relationship by withdrawing without dialogue.
- Before quitting a relationship, at least three times, tell a person how you feel, how they seem and what you need in order to stay.

- Never terminate a relationship in the middle of an issue. Never offer new reasons for terminating a relationship into an agreement or disagreement that have not already been thoroughly processed or discussed.
- Don't terminate by devaluing the other person.
- If you want to terminate, go to the person calmly (or come to your workshop), give reasons and hear feedback openly. (Those who terminate a workshop must bring it up in the beginning of workshop or the meeting so people have time to process and respond.)

Endings

When I was about twenty, I dated a successful, charming young man, Brian Matosian. I had a motorcycle, so he bought one to ride with me. He also had a red sports car and drove me around some beautiful homes to tell me that if we worked out as a couple, this is where we could live some day. He also had a cabin in the mountains, to which he whisked me off one weekend to get to know me better. I was enchanted, but he eventually broke up with me. When I asked him why, he said, "You are the most boring woman I have ever met." It definitely stung a little, but he set me free. I learned in that moment that it didn't pay to be such a good girl as to have no opinion. After that, I began to really live.

Perhaps the most influence we have with someone and the most valuable thing we have to say is when we are leaving. I believe we should endeavor to leave people better than we found them, if we can, even if all we have to offer is clean feedback.

I discovered my husband while I was dating a radio talk-show host, Michael, whom I met while volunteering on the switchboards for a rock station in Los Angeles. After I dated my husband-to-be a few times, I thought it was time to choose. In one of the last conversations I had with my therapist, he asked me if I was just going to "dis" the talk-show host or if I intended to say goodbye. I said I didn't want to say goodbye and he asked why. I said I didn't want to hurt his feelings. My therapist then proposed that it was my feelings, not Michael's that I wanted to spare. He explained to me that I could handle anything anyone wants to tell me, which was an interesting concept in itself. I had thought until then that I couldn't handle hard words or harsh feedback, something I projected onto others as well. (I should have remembered how well I responded to Brian's feedback or the two times I wrote about in my Preface where I was purged from organizational memberships.)

My therapist prepared me for my last intimate conversation with Michael. He told me that I would have less guilt because I would hurt him less if I were willing to listen to his experience and feelings. This was amazing information. To help me out a little more, he offered a coping mechanism. "Throw up some white light around yourself and simply imagine that words can't hurt you. Then listen well."

When I got to Michael's place, I told him our intimate relationship was over while he was cooking dinner. When he sat down, he said, "Couldn't you have told me this last week before...?" And then he changed his mind, "No, it would have been a lot better if you told me next week..." Then he said, "There is no other time to tell me but now." It turned out to be a remarkably honest conversation. I did just fine. He genuinely wished me well with Ron and he subsequently found the love of his life too.

I moved many times in my childhood

and often pretended that I would still see my friends some day so I wouldn't have to say goodbye again. I didn't know that when you say goodbye properly, people don't feel as abandoned. When you disappear, they feel abandoned and you may feel closed off, guilty, lost or incomplete. I know mothers who duck out of day care while the day care worker distracts their child, thinking he won't notice. I also know day care workers who are trained to tell the parents that the child adjusted well after she left no matter how much he cried. People who experience being left "out of the blue" are hurt the most. I know it's a pain to have to say a complete goodbye because you will see and hear the other person's reaction, but it's worth it. It is how you will be remembered and how good you will feel about yourself for the years to come, having allowed them their say.

Dying and Death

From the time your child is small until the last time you see his face, it is important that you occasionally speak of death, as it's inevitable for all of us. Holding that awareness near and far gives us intelligence. We take nothing for granted. We may treasure every moment, even the ones we love to hate. The awareness that death takes us all at some point may give us a deep appreciation of every breath so we don't sweat the small stuff. From this we can perhaps see that when we were born we won the lottery.

When you sit at the bedside of your dying parent, spouse or best friend, you have a couple of ways to go. You can pretend nothing is happening and miss the best conversation of your life or you can ask them what's on their mind and tell them what's on yours. When a relationship ends, it is good to mention the best times, how you grew together and perhaps the worst times so you can discuss forgiveness. If there is something you have needed to say for years, say it unless it is hurtful.

I know a cop who volunteered for hospice duty or, perhaps, he was assigned the chore. He sat with a man dying of AIDS. The rapidly fading man looked at him, humbly asking, "Do you think God will forgive me for being gay?" The man answered honestly, "No." Needless to say, that is not the kind of honesty the world or dying people need. When I heard him tell this story, it was about all I could do to not fly across the table between us and strangle him.

On the other hand, I know a woman who told her dying mother, "I didn't feel loved by you. Did you love me?" Her mother nodded yes and then died.

If we are fortunate enough to spend precious time with someone who is dying, try not to pretend they aren't dying; it makes for bad company and you'd be silently asking them to be inauthentic in their last moments for your sake, which is a lot to ask. This is one good time to put your feelings aside. Someone else's feelings are more important.

See them as clearly as possible. Step out of your own emotions, fears of death and fears of loss. See if they feel complete. Are their affairs in order? See if there is anything you can do for them, without promising them something unreasonable or unethical, like you will marry their son who you can't stand. Do they have things they still need to say or do? Do they have regrets to express? Would they recall for you their sweetest moment? Is there a message they would like to dictate that you can deliver? Do they need to reflect aloud or is there something you need to say? Would they like their feet gently massaged, their hair brushed or their arms stroked lightly?

Their openness with you now is the greatest privilege of the deepest intimacy. Be aware that these are precious moments because when people lay dying, they tend to become holier on the way out. Take it in. If they won't go there, then that's interesting too, for we have the gift of beholding the steel of the very prison in which they lived.

When you are with someone in the final moments of their life, you need to reassure them that you see meaning in their lives and God in their eyes. You need to be there for them and not want them to be there for you unless you have important questions, of course.

For whatever it is worth, based on a few experiences of my own and reading some experiences of others, I believe that when we are dying all the deep questions of our lives become answered from within. We have stored the information of everything we ever learned, be it religious training or pure curiosity and observation, and when our brainwaves are slow enough, the answers come to our deepest questions. I believe our last seconds are filled with insight and awe, which is why I hope I am not asleep or drugged when the time comes. I wouldn't miss it for the world.

> Oh wow. Oh wow. Oh wow.
> – Steve Jobs' last words

Conclusion

The human being is a fragile thing and at our very core, we are all vulnerable and designed by a multitude of the smallest experiences, especially the repeating ones. If you can recall how sensitive you are to how somebody words things, especially if it is a way of telling you how they perceive your worth, that's how sensitive an infant is to every action: rough voice, rough wiping, preoccupation, scratchy beard, lack of eye contact, disappointed facial expressions, worry, leaving and so on. How we are reassured determines what we do with those fragile and vulnerable feelings.

I suspect one of the main reasons we are so susceptible to believing that genes, rather than our parents, shape our character is that we don't realize how fragile we began. We don't realize how every little nuance creates temperament and every major act creates personality. We look at a little baby as a thing doctors say won't remember the first years. As a matter of fact, doctors were doing heart surgeries on infants without anesthesia as late as the 1980s because they didn't think they could feel pain yet (Hall, 1992).

Even psychotherapists mostly believe you can't remember much of the first few years and our field interprets the infant's earliest moods as temperament rather than emotional responses to repeating experiences. We just don't seem to get that the child's right brain is fully online at birth and ready to perceive clearly (Siegel, 1999). She's all there and is taking in every experience as information about her new world, her parents and herself. This is fundamental information. Every tiny little thing that happens to a baby matters to him. All events of any size either reaffirm previous experiences to a baby or prove otherwise.

I am trying to drive home to you that a baby looks for the same experience you do when you choose someone to be in your life by what you feel in their presence: safety, acceptance, commitment, understanding, empathy, regard and awe. These are what the newborn baby seeks too.

Do you understand now that I am speaking of you when you were new to the world and that you were just as sensitive then, if not more so? Do you get that I speak of everyone you'll ever meet? If a baby doesn't find these safe experiential feelings, she goes inward and shuts down to some degree. She more or less becomes an island or she begins a life of second guessing her own feelings, perceptions or needs. Perhaps ironically, a child who is free to be vulnerable has the strongest constitution because she feels safe in the world. Anyone who fears vulnerability has lost part of her humanity, just as those who chronically fear loss have lost part of theirs.

Beyond quality of attachment, there is another major source of resilience. One of the most important things a person finds out is whether good times replace bad times. If Mommy is in a bad mood, will a good mood come soon? If I am kept from my Mommy, will she stay next time? If I am hungry, will Mommy feed me? If she goes out of the room, will she come back? If I cry, will she care? Will she understand? If I am hurt, can she help me? If she scolds me, will she forgive me? Later, during the process of separating and individuating, the child may wonder, if Mommy leaves, does she know how bad it hurts? Does she really love me? If I am being punished, will she ever forgive me? Am I still loved? Am I still good if I am punished? The answers to all of these questions help to determine resilience. Small children need to learn that the answer to these questions is undeniably YES. Resilience is not built in a day. Resilience is built over time and even over mistakes between parent and child.

We all began the same: fragile, seeing and seeking. From there, some of us got stronger as our emotional needs got met. Some of us got weaker the more we were left to fend for ourselves emotionally. Whatever adaptations we made, our parents got to think of our traits as inborn, which comforted them, not us. Actually, I think good parents know that good parenting is behind high character and high functioning. I have written all these pages to tell you that "bad," ineffective, inadequate and hurtful parenting comes from injured moms and dads in denial who have difficulty seeing their children, who lack empathy, who put their own needs over their children's and who repress their own feelings for their own parents' sakes. These caregivers need to believe in genes as the origin of personality to avoid inner conflict. To be fair, anyone who doesn't understand imprinting will also believe in gene association. Anyone who is afraid to hurt their parents' feelings with a complaint about how they were treated or who won't stop their parents from mistreating their own child will believe in gene association, that is until they read this book hopefully.

The wonderful thing about fragility and resilience is that one compensates for the other. We can make a lot of mistakes as parents if only we use the mirror of our child to self-correct. Recovering from bad times actually makes us stronger than if there had never been any bad times at all. If we feel hurt or sad and Daddy understands us, we get stronger. When Mommy leaves the room and comes back shortly, our child grows stronger. If Mommy has a bad mood, but a good mood follows shortly thereafter, he will become optimistic. If Mommy is mad at him, corrects him and forgives him, he will become someone who can learn and recover quickly. If he is scared and she understands, he will ultimately develop the ability to value, express and regulate his own emotions. If she harmed him and hears him out, he will believe in justice. Bad experiences and bad parenting followed by a mutual dialogue or correction, acceptance and forgiveness lead to self-control. They inoculate us from hard knocks and make us resilient. This manual is not about how to be a perfect parent because no one can do that. This manual is about how to be honest and self-correcting so your child can become the same. Now go be the parent you wish you had.

APPENDIX

References

Ainsworth, Mary D. Salter (1978). *Patterns of Attachment*. Hillsdale, New Jersey: Lawrence Erlbaum Associates, Inc.

American Psychiatric Association (2000). *Diagnostic and Statistical Manual of Mental Disorders Fourth Edition Text Revision (DSM-IV-TR)*. Washington, DC: APA.

Appelbaum, Paul S., Uyehara, Lisa A., & Elin, Mark R. (1997). *Trauma and Memory: Clinical and Legal Controversies*. New York: Oxford University Press.

Athens, Lonnie (1992). *The Creation of Dangerous Violent Criminals*. Chicago: University of Illinois Press.

Barker, Elliott (2000). The critical importance of mothering [Online]. Available: www.naturalchild.com/elliott_barker/mothering.html

Barkley, Russell (1997). *ADHD and the Nature of Self Control*. New York: The Guilford Press.

_____ (1999). *ADHD, Ritalin, and Conspiracies: Talking Back to Peter Breggin*. Plantation, FL: ChADD (Children and Adults with Attention Deficit Disorder).

Beck, Don (1996). Spiral Dynamics: Mastering Values, Leadership, and Change. Audio series.

Belsky, Jay (1986). Infant day care: a cause for concern? Zero to Three. Washington, D.C.: *Bulletin of the National Center for Clinical Infant Programs, VI*(5).

_____ (2006). Early child care and early child care development: Major findings of the NICHD Study of Early Child Card. *European Journal of Developmental Psychology*, 2006 3(1), 95-110.

Bentall, Richard P. (2009). *Doctoring the Mind: Is Our Current Treatment of Mental Illness Really Any Good?* New York: New York University Press.

Bowen, Murray & Kerr, Michael (1988). *Family Evaluation: An Approach Based upon Bowen Theory*. New York: Norton & Company.

Bowlby, John (1969). *Attachment, Volume I*. New York: Basic Books.

_____ (1973). *Separation, Volume II*. New York: Basic Books.

_____ (1980). *Attachment and Loss, Volume III: LOSS, Sadness, and Depression*. New York: Basic Books.

_____ (1988). *A Secure Base*. London: Basic Books.

Bradshaw, John (1988). *Bradshaw on the Family: A New Way of Creating Self-Esteem*. Deerfield Beach, Fla.: Health Communications Inc.

Brandtjen, Henry & Verny, Thomas. Short and Long Term Effects on Infants and Toddlers in Full Time Day Care Centers. *Journal of Prenatal and Perinatal Psychology and Health* 15(4). Summer 2001.

Brazelton, T. B. (1986, October). A speech to parents at the Auraria Higher Education Center, Denver, CO.

Breggin, Peter (1991) *Toxic Psychiatry*. New York: St. Martin's Press.

_____ (1998). *Talking Back to Ritalin.* Maine Common Courage Press.

_____ (2000). *Reclaiming Our Children. A Healing Plan for Nation in Crisis.* Cambridge, MA: Perseus Publishing.

_____ (2001). *The Anti-Depressant Fact Book: What Your Doctor Won't Tell You About Prozac, Zoloft, Paxil, Celexa and Luvox.* Cambridge, MA: Perseus Publishing.

_____ (2008). *Medication Madness: The Role of Psychiatric Drugs in Cases of Violence, Suicide, and Crime.* New York: St. Martin's Griffin.

Breggin, Peter R. & Cohen, David (1999). *Your Drug May Be Your Problem: How and Why to Stop Taking Psychiatric Medications.* Cambridge, MA: Perseus Publishing.

Brown, Daniel, Scheflin, Alan W., & Hammond, D. Corydon (1998). *Memory, Trauma Treatment, and the Law: An Essential Reference on Memory for Clinicians, Researchers, Attorneys, and Judges.* New York: W.W. Norton & Co.

Burlingham, D., & Freud, A. (1944). *Infants without families.* London: Allen & Unwin.

Bynum, W. F. (1964) "Rationales for Therapy in British Psychiatry: 1780-1835." *Medical History*, 18, p. 325.

Calfaro, John V. & Conn-Calfaro, Allison (1998). *Sibling Abuse Trauma:Assessment and Intervention Strategies for Children, Families, and Adults.* The Haworth Maltreatment and Trauma Press: Binghamton, NY.

Calhoun, J.F. (1977). *Abnormal Psychology: Current Perspectives.* New York: Random House.

Carlo, Phillip (1996). *The Night Stalker: The Life and Crimes of Richard Ramirez.* New York: Kensington Books.

Carmichael, Mary. "Growing Up Bipolar: Max's World". *Newsweek.* May 26, 2008.

Cermak, T. L. & Brown, S. (1982). "Interactional group psychotherapy with adult children of alcoholics." *International Journal of Group Psychotherapy, 32,* 375-389.

Cline, Foster W. & Helding, Cathy (1999). *Can This Child Be Saved? Solutions for Adoptive and Foster Families.* Franksville, Wisconsin: World Enterprises.

Colbert, Ty (2000). *Rape of the Soul: How the Chemical Imbalance Model of Modern Psychiatry has Failed Its Patients.* Tustin, CA: Kevco Publishing.

_____ (1997). *Broken Brains or Wounded Hearts: What Causes Mental Illness?* Tustin, CA: Kevco Publishing.

Cole, Michael, Cole, Sheila R. & Lightfoot, Cynthia. (2005). *The Development of Children.* New York: Worth Publishers.

Court TV, 1993. Trial of Lyle and Erik Menendez.

DeGrandpre, Richard J., & Hinshaw, Stephen P. (2000). "ADHD: Serious Psychiatric Problem or All-American Cop-out?" *Cerebrum: The Dana Forum on Brain Science,* 12-38.

DeGrandpre, Richard J. (1999). *Ritalin Nation: Rapid-fire Culture and the Transformation of Human Consciousness.* New York: W.W. Norton & Co.

Dreskin, William & Wendy (1983). *Day Care Decision: What's Best For You and Your Child.* New York: M. Evans and Co.

Dunstan, Priscilla (2006). Dunstan Baby Language: Learn the Universal Language of New Babies. Audio series.

Dutton, Donald G. (1995). *The Batterer: A Psychological Profile.* New York: Basic Books.

_____ (1998). *The Abusive Personality: Violence and Control in Intimate Relationships.* New York: The Guilford Press.

Ellenberger, Henri F. (1970) *The Discovery of the Unconscious: The History and Evolution of Dynamic Psychiatry.* New York: Basic Books.

Fancher, R.T. (2009). *Health & Suffering in America: The Context and Content of Mental Health Care.* New Brunswick, NJ: Transaction Publishers.

Fancher, R. T. (1995) *Cultures of Healing: Correcting the Image of American Mental Health Care.* New York: W.H. Freeman Co.

Fonagy, Peter, *et al.* (2002). *Affect Regulation, Mentalization, and the Development of the Self.* New York: Other Press.

References

_____ (2001). *Attachment Theory and Psychoanalysis*. New York: Other Press.

Forbes, Heather T. & Post, Bryan (2006). *Beyond Consequences, Logic and Control*. Orlando, FL: Beyond Consequences, LLC.

Frank, Justin A. (2004). *Bush on the Couch: Inside the Mind of the President*. New York: HarperCollins.

Freyd, Jennifer (1996). *Betrayal Trauma: The Logic of Forgetting Childhood Abuse*. Cambridge, Mass.: Harvard University Press.

_____ (1993). "Theoretical and Personal Perspectives on the Delayed Memory Debate. Proceedings of the Center for Mental Health at Foote Hospital's Continuing Conference: Controversies around Recovered Memories of Incest and Ritualistic Abuse," August 7, Ann Arbor, Mich.: Tape available from Sidron Foundation (410) 825-888.

Galves, Albert, *et al.* (2002). *"Debunking the Science Behind ADHD as a Brain Disorder"*, www.prozactruth.com/article_debunking.htm.

Gilbert, Roberta M. (2004) *The Eight Concepts of Bowen Theory*. Falls Church, VA: Leading Systems Press.

Giovacchini, P.L. (1990). "Regression, Reconstruction, and Resolution: Containment and Holding". *Tactics and Techniques in Psychoanalytic Therapy* (p226-263). Northvale, New Jersey: Aronson.

Gopnik, A. (2009). *The Philosophical Baby: What Children's Minds Tell Us about Truth, Love, and the Meaning of Life*. New York: Farrar, Strau and Giroux.

Grosskurth, P. (1985). *Melanie Klein: Her world and her work*. London: Hodder and Staughton.

Grossman, Gerry (1992). *Preparatory Workbook for the Standard Written Exam*. Santa Monica, CA: Gerry Grossman Seminars.

Guntrip, H. (1962)."The Schizoid Compromise and Psychotherapeutic Stalemate". *British Journal of Medical Psychology*, 35, 273-286.

Hall, Nancy (June/July, 1992). "The Painful Truth," *Parenting Magazine*.

Harlow, Harry F., & Zimmermann, Ronald R. (1959). "Affectional responses in the infant monkey". *Science*, 130, 421.

Harris, Sam (2010). *The Moral Landscape*. New York: Simon & Schuster, Inc.

Heinicke, C., & Westheimer, I. (1965). *Brief Separations*. New York: International Universities Press.

Herman, Judith (1992). *Trauma and Recovery: The Aftermath of Violence from Domestic Abuse to Political Terror*. New York: Basic Books.

Holtzworth-Munroe & Stuart, *et al.* (1994). Testing the Holtzworth-Munroe and Stuart batterer typology. *Journal of Consulting and Clinical Psychology*, Vol 68(6), Dec 2000, 1000-1019. doi: 10.1037/0022-006X.68.6.1000

Hubbard, Ruth & Wald, Elijah (1999). *Exploding the Gene Myth: How Genetic Information is Produced and Manipulated by Scientists, Physicians, Employers, Insurance Companies, Educators and Law Enforcers*. Boston: Beacon Press.

James, Beverly (1994). *Handbook for Treatment of Attachment-Trauma Problems in Children*. New York: The Free Press.

James, William (1902). *Varieties of Religious Experience*. New York: Simon & Schuster, Inc. Reprinted 1997.

Joseph, Jay (2004). *The Gene Illusion: Genetic Research in Psychiatry and Psychology Under the Microscope*. New York: Algora Publishing.

_____ (2006). *The Missing Gene: Psychiatry, Heredity and the Fruitless Search for Genes*. New York: Algora Publishing.

Kaplan, Stuart L (2011). *Your Child Does Not Have Bipolar: How Bad Science and Good Public Relations Created the Diagnosis*. Santa Barbara, CA: Greenwood Publishing Group.

Karen, Robert (1998). *Becoming Attached: First Relationships and How They Shape Our Capacity to Love*. New York: Oxford University Press.

Karr-Morse, Robin & Wiley, Meredith S. (1997). *Ghosts from the Nursery: Tracing the Roots of Violence*. New York: Atlantic Monthly Press.

Kelves, Daniel J. & Hood, Leroy (1992). *The Code of Codes: Scientific and Social Issues in the Human Genome Project*. Cambridge: Harvard University Press.

Klein, M. (1953). Some Reflections on the Ortesia, in *Envy and Gratitude and Other Works*, 1946-1963. New York: Delacorte Press/Seymour Lawrence.

Kring, Ann, Sheri Johnson, Gerald C. Davison, John M. Neale. (1992). *Abnormal Psychology*. Hoboken, NJ: John Wiley & Sons, Inc.

Koplewitz, Harold (1997). *It's Nobody's Fault: New Hope and Help for Difficult Children*. New York: Random House.

Kræpelin, Emil (1917). *One Hundred Years of Psychiatry*. New York: Citadel.

Kramer, Joel (1974). *The Passionate Mind*. Berkeley, CA: North Atlantic Books.

Ledoux, Joseph E. (1998). *The Emotional Brain: The Mysterious Underpinnings of Emotional Life*. New York: Touchstone.

LeDoux, J. E.; Romanski, L., & Xagoraris, A. (1991). "Indelibility of subcortical emotional memories." *Journal of Cognitive Neuroscience, 1*, 238-243.

Lehrer, J. (2009, April 26). Inside the baby mind. *The Boston Globe.com*. Retrieved from: http://www.boston.com/bostonglobe/ideas/articles/2009/04/26/inside_the_baby_mind/?page=full (2011 September 21).

Levine, Peter M. (1997) *Waking the Tiger: Healing Trauma, the Innate Capacity to Transform Overwhelming Experiences*. Berkeley, CA : North Atlantic Books.

Levons, Richard & Lewontin, Richard (1985). *The Dialectical Biologist*. Cambridge: Harvard University Press.

Levy, Terry M. & Orlans, Michael (1998). *Attachment, Trauma, and Healing: Understanding and Treating Attachment Disorder in Children and Families*. Washington, DC: CWLA Press.

Levy, Terry M. (2000). *Handbook of Attachment Interventions*. New York: Academic Press.

Lewis, Dorothy (1998). *Guilty by Reason of Insanity*. New York: Ballantine Publishing Group.

Lewontin, Richard (1991). *Biology as Ideology: The Doctrine of DNA*, previously *The Dream of the Human Genome*. New York: HarperPerennial.

_____ (2000). *The Triple Helix: Gene, Organism and Environment*. Cambridge: Harvard Press

_____ (2000). *It Ain't Necessarily So: The Dream of the Human Genome and Other Illusions*. New York: NYRB.

Lewontin, Richard; Rose, Steven; & Kamin, Leon J. (1984). *Not in Our Genes: Biology, Ideology, and Human Nature*. New York: Pantheon Books.

Lieberman, A.F. & Pawl, J.H. (1988). *Clinical Implications of Attachment Theory*. (J. Belsky & T. Nezworski, Eds.) Hillsdale, N.J.: Lawrence Erlbaum.

Lipton, Bruce (2001). "Nature, Nurture and Human Development". www.brucelipton.com.

_____ (2001a). "Evolution by BITs and Pieces: An Introduction to FractalEvolution." www.brucelipton.com.

_____ (2001b). "Insight into Cellular 'Consciousness.'" www.brucelipton.com.

Los Angeles Times, "McMartins Not Guilty." January 8, 1990.

Los Angeles Times (October 30, 1993). "Kitty Menendez Weighed Suicide." http://articles.latimes.com/1993-10-30/me-51371_1_Kitty_Menendez.

Loftus, E.F. (1995). (1995, March/April). Remembering dangerously, *Skeptical Inquirer*, 20-29.

Loftus, Elizabeth & Ketchum, Katherine (1994). *The Myth of Repressed Memory*. New York: St. Martin's Press.

Loftus, E.R., Polonsky, S., Fullilove, M.T. (1994). "Memories of childhood sexual abuse: Remembering and repressing". *Psychology of Women Quarterly, 18*, 67-84.

Leo, Jonathan (2000). "Attention Deficit Disorder: Good Science or Good Marketing?" *Skeptic, 8*(1), 63-69.

Lowen, Alexander (1990) "Why Are You So Angry With Me?" *Reclaiming the Inner Child*. Jeremiah Abrams, editor. Jeremy P. Tarcher, Inc.: Los Angeles. 183-188.

_____ (1972). *Depression and the Body: The Biological Basis of Faith and Reality*. New York: Penguin Books.

References

MacPherson, C. N. (1962). *The Political Theory of Possessive Individualism*. Oxford: Oxford University Press.

Magid, Ken & McKelvey, Carole (1987). *High Risk: Children without a Conscience*. New York: Bantam Books.

Main, Mary (1995). *Attachment Theory: Social, Developmental and Clinical Perspectives*. Hillsdale, NJ: Analytic Press.

Main, M. & Solomon, J. (1990). "Procedures for Identifying Infants as Disorganized/Disoriented During the Ainsworth Strange Situation." Greenberg, D. Cicchetti, and E. M. Cummings (Eds.), *Attachment during the Preschool Years: Theory, Research and Intervention*. Chicago, IL: University of Chicago Press.

Main, Mary & Weston, Donna R. (1981). *The Place of Attachment in Human Behavior*, eds. Collin Murray Parkes and Joan Stevenson-Hinde. New York.

Masson, Jeffrey Moussaieff (1986). *The Complete Letters of Sigmund Freud to Wilhelm Fliess: 1887-1904*. Cambridge, Mass.: Harvard University Press.

_____ (1984). *The Assault on Truth: Freud's Suppression of the Seduction Theory*. New York: Simon & Schuster.

McGraw, Phil (2004). *Family First: Your Step-by-Step Plan for Creating a Phenomenal Family*. New York: Free Press.

McHugh, P. (1993a). "Procedures in the Diagnosis of Incest in Recovered Memory Cases". *False Memory Syndrome Foundation Newsletter*. (May).

_____ (1993, October 1). "To treat." False Memory Foundation Newsletter. (October).

Miller, Alice (1981). *The Drama of the Gifted Child: The Search for the True Self*. New York: Basic Books.

_____ (1983). *For Your Own Good*. New York: Noonday Press.

_____ (1984). *Thou Shalt Not Be Aware: Society's Betrayal of the Child*. New York: Basic Books.

_____ (1990). *Banished Knowledge: Facing Childhood Injuries*. New York: Bantam Doubleday Dell Publishing Group, Inc.

_____ (1990). *Breaking Down the Wall of Silence: The Liberating Experience of Facing Painful Truth*. New York: A Meridian Book.

_____ (2001). *The Truth Will Set You Free: Overcoming Emotional Blindness and Finding Your True Adult Self*. New York: Basic Books.

Miller, Alice. "The Political Consequences of Child Abuse," *Journal of Psychohistory*, Volume 26, No. 2, Fall 1998.

Millon, Theodore (Nov. 12, 1993). "Understanding the DSM IV Personality Disorders: A Renaissance in Clinical Therapy Workshop". Ramada Inn, Sherman Oaks, CA.

Minuchin, Salvador & Fishman, H. Charles C. (1981). *Family Therapy Techniques*. Boston: Harvard College.

Monte, Christopher F. (1980). *Beneath the Mask: Introduction to Theories of Personality*. New York: Holt, Rinehart and Winston.

Molyneux, Stefan (2011). "But They Did the Best They Could: A Moral Examination of Historical Parenting," http://www.youtube.com/watch?v= 1x3eHt5hWuQ

Nance, R. D. (1970). "G. Stanley Hall and John B. Watson as Child Psychologists". *Journal of the History of the Behavioral Sciences*, 6(4), 303-316.

Norris, Joel (1992). *Jeffrey Dahmer*. New York. Shawn Lawn Press.

Parkes, Colin Murray, *et al.* (1991). "Attachments and Other Affectional Bonds Across the Life Cycle" by Ainsworth, Mary D. S. *Attachment Across the Life Cycle*. New York: Tavistock/Routledge.

Peck, M. Scott (1978). *The Road Less Traveled*. New York: Touchstone.

_____ (1983). *People of the Lie: The Hope for Healing Human Evil*. New York: Simon & Schuster.

Perry, Bruce (2000). "The Neuroarcheology of Childhood Maltreatment" [Online]. http://www.bcm.tmc.edu/cta/Neuroarcheology.htm

_____ (2000a). Traumatized children: How childhood trauma influences brain development [online]. Retrieved from 7/01/01 from http://207.235.43.156/CTAMATERIALS/TRAU_CAMI.asp.

_____ (2000b). *Biological Relativity: Time and the Developing Child.* http://teacher.scholastic.com/professional/bruceperry/biological_relativity.htm.

_____ (2000c). *Bonding and Attachment in Maltreated Children: Consequences of Emotional Neglect in Childhood.* http://teacher.scholastic.com/professional/bruceperry/bonding.htm.

Perry, Bruce D. & Marcellus, John (2000). The Impact of Abuse and Neglect on the Developing Brain. http://teacher.scholastic.com/ professional/bruceperry/abuse_neglect.htm.

_____ (1997). "Early Childhood Development and Victims' Rights" [Video]. Presentation to the National Governor's Association (February 4). C-SPAN.

Pezdek, K. (1995, November). "What types of false childhood memories are not likely to be suggesively implanted?" Paper presented at the annual meting of the Psychonomic Society, Los Angeles.

Piaget, Jean (1954). *The Construction of Reality in the Child.* New York: Basic Books.

Pincus, Jonathan H. (2001). *Base Instincts: What Makes Killers Kill?* New York: W.W. Norton & Co.

Pope, Kenneth S. & Vasquez, Melba J. T. (1998). *Ethics in Psychotherapy and Counseling.* San Francisco: Jossey-Bass, Inc., a Wiley Company.

Pope, H.G. & Hudson, J. L. (1995). "Can Individuals "repress" memories of childhood sexual abuse? An examination of the evidence". *Psychiatric Annals, 25,* 715-719.

_____ (1995). "Can memories of childhood sexual abuse be repressed?" *Psychological Medicine, 25,* 121-127.

Prescott, James (2000). "Birth and the Origins of Violence: Perspectives on Violence." http://www.birthpsychology.com/violence/prescott.html

Putnam, F. W. (1997). *Dissociative Disorder in Children and Adolescents.* New York: Guilford Press.

Read, John; Perry, Bruce; Moskowitz, Andrew; & Connolly, Jan. (Winter, 2001). "The Contribution of Early Traumatic Events to Schizophrenia in Some Patients: A traumatagenic Neurodevelopmental Model."

Reps, Paul & Senzaki, Nyogen (1957). *Zen Flesh, Zen Bones: A Collection of Zen and Pre-Zen Writings.* Vermont: Tuttle Publishing.

Rizzolatti, Giocomo (2006). *Mirrors in the Brain: How Our Minds Share Actions, Emotions and Experience.* Oxford: Oxford Press.

Roberts, Albert R. & Watkins, Julie M. (2009). *Social Workers Desk Reference, 2nd Ed.* New York: Oxford University Press.

Robertson, Brian C. (2003). *Day Care Deception: What the Child Care Establishment Isn't Telling Us.* San Francisco: Encounter Books.

Ross, Colin A. (2004). *Schizophrenia: Innovations in Diagnosis and Treatment.* New York: The Hayworth Maltreatment and Trauma Press.

Ross, Colin A. & Pam, Alvin (1995). *Pseudoscience in Biological Psychiatry: Blaming the Body.* New York: John Wiley & Sons.

Rothschild, Babette (2000). *The Body Remembers: The Psychophysiology of Trauma and Trauma Treatment.* New York: W.W. Norton & Co.

Ruskan, John (1993). *Emotional Clearing: Releasing Negative Feelings and Awakening Unconditional Happiness.* New York: R. Wiley & Co.

Santner, Eric (1966). *My Own Private Germany: Daniel Paul Schreber's Secret History of Modernity.* Princeton: Princeton University Press.

Schatzman, Morton (1973). *Soul Murder: Persecution in the Family.* New York.

Schore, Allan N. (1994). *Affect Regulation and the Origin of the Self.* Hillsdale, N.J.: Lawrence Erlbaum Associates, Publishers.

_____ (2001). "The Effects of Early Relational Trauma on Right Brain Development, Affect Regulation, and Infant Mental Health". *Infant Mental Health Journal, 22,* 201-269.

_____ (2002a). "Dysregulation of the Right Brain: A Fundamental Mechanism of Traumatic Attachment and the Psychopathogenesis of Post Traumatic Stress Disorder. *Australian and New Zealand Journal of Psychiatry, 36,* 9-30.

_____ (2002b). "Advances in Neuropsychoanalysis, Attachment Theory, and Trauma Research: Implications for Self Psychology". *Psychoanalytic Inquiry, 22,* 433-484.

References

_____ (2003a). *Affect Regulation and the Repair of the Self.* New York: W.W. Norton & Co.

_____ (2003b). *Affect Dysregulation and Disorders of the Self.* New York: W.W. Norton & Co.

Schreber, Daniel Paul (1955). *Memoirs of My Nervous Illness.* New York: New York Review of Books.

Schwartz, P. (1983). "Length of day-care attendance and attachment behavior in eighteen-month-old infants". *Child Development, 54.*

Scott, Timothy (2006). *America Fooled: The Truth about Antidepressants.* New York: Argo Publishing.

Siegel, Daniel J. (1999) The *Developing Mind: Toward a Neurobiology of Interpe*rsonal Experience. New York, London: Guilford Press.

_____ (2001). "Toward an Interpersonal Neurobiology of the Developing Mind: Attachment Relationships, 'Mindsight,' and Neural Integration". *Infant Mental Health Journal. 22*(1-2), 67-94.

_____ (2002). "Attachment and Self-Understanding: Parenting with the Brain in Mind." Conference on "New Developments in Attachment Theory: Applications to Clinical Practice." 2003 UCLA Extension and Lifespan Learning Institute.

Simons, D.A.; Wurtele, S.K.; Durham, R.L. Developmental experiences of child sexual abusers and rapists: Colorado Department of Corrections, Canon City, CO. *Journal of Child Abuse and Neglect,* 2008 May; 32(5):549-60.

Snyder, Ron (February, 1982). Conversation. Sherman Oaks, CA.

Society For Neuroscience (Nov. 7, 2007). "Mirror, Mirror In The Brain: Mirror Neurons, Self-understanding and Autism Research".

Solomon, Marion F. (March 8-9, 2003). "Treating the Effects of Attachment Trauma". Excerpted for: *New developments in attachment theory: Applications to Clinical Practice*, UCLA.

Solomon, Marion F. & Siegel, Daniel J. (2003a). *Healing Trauma: Attachment, Mind, Body, and Brain.* New York: W.W. Norton & Co.

Sonkin, Daniel Jay (2005). Attachment Theory and Psychotherapy. *The Therapist Magazine.* January/February, Vol. 17, 1, 68-77.

Spitz, Rene A. (1949). "The Role of Ecological Factors in Emotional Development in Infancy". *Child Development, 20*(3): 145-155.

Stacey, Judith & Biblarz, Timothy. "How Does the Sexual Orientation of Parents Matter?" *American Sociological Review* (Vol. 66, #2, April 2001).

Stern, Daniel. (2000). *The Interpersonal World of the Infant.* London: Basic Books. (Original work published 1985)

_____ (2003). Attachment and Intersubjectivity. Conference on New Developments in Attachment Theory: Applications to Clinical Practice. UCLA Extension and Lifespan Learning Institute.

Stosny, Steven (1995). *Treating Attachment Abuse: A Compassionate Approach.* New York: Springer Publishing Company.

Sullivan, Terry & Maiken, Peter T. (1983). *Killer Clown: The John Wayne Gacy Murders.* New York: Pinnacle Books.

Summit, Rolland (1994). "The Dark Tunnels of McMartin". *The Journal of Psychohistory, 21*(4, Spring), 397-416.

_____ (1983). "The Child Sexual Abuse Accommodation Syndrome". *Child Abuse & Neglect,* Vol. 7, 177-193.

Szalavitz, Maia & Perry, Bruce (2010). *Born for Love: Why Empathy is Essential and Endangered.* New York: Harper Collins.

Szasz, Thomas (1970). *The Manufacture of Madness: A comparative Study of the Inquisition and the Mental Health Movement.* New York: Harper and Row.

Taylor, Madeline S. (1996). Taboo On Tenderness: The Rise and Suppression of Relational Concepts in Early Psychoanalysis. Unpublished Dissertation, Ryokan College.

Teicher, Martin (2002, March). "Scars That Won't Heal: The Neurobiology of Child Abuse: Maltreatment at an early age can have enduring negative effects on a child's brain development and function". *Scientific American.*

Thomas, Nancy (1998). *Rebuilding the Broken Bond, Part I for Reactive Attachment Disorder* [video]. Glenwood Springs, CO: Nancy Thomas. *Timmons v. Indiana,* 584 N.E. 2nd 1108 (Ind. 1992).

_____ (1997). *When Love is Not Enough: A guide to Parenting Children with RAD-Reactive Attachment Disorder.* Glenwood Springs, CO.: Families by Design.

Turner, Erick H, Matthews, Annette M., *et al.* (January 17, 2008). Selective Publication of Antidepressant Trials and Its Influence on Apparent Efficacy. *New England Journal of Medicine* (Vol. 358, #3).

van der Kolk, Bessel, *et al.* (1994a)."The Body Keeps the Score: Memory and the Evolving Psychobiology of Post Traumatic Stress." *Trauma Information Pages*: http:\\www.trauma-pages.com.

van der Kolk, Bessel; McFarlane, Alexander; Weisaeth, Lars (eds.) (1996). *Traumatic Stress: the Effects of Overwhelming Experience for Mind, Body & Society.* New York: Guilford Press.

_____ (1994b). Childhood Abuse and the Loss of Self-Regulation. *Bulletin of Menninger Clinic*, 58(2), 145-167.

_____ (1995). "The Body, Memory, and the Psychobiology of Trauma". In Judith L. Alpert (Ed.), *Sexual Abuse Recalled: Treating Trauma in the Era of the Recovered Memory Debate.* Northvale, NJ: Jason Aronson Inc., 29-60.

_____ (1989). "The Compulsion to Repeat the Trauma:Re-enactment, Revictimization, and Massochism". *Psychiatric Clinics of North America, 12*(2), 389-411.

Valenstein, Elliot S (1988). *Blaming the Brain: The Truth about Drugs and Mental Health.* New York: The Free Press.

Vaughn, B. E., Gove, F. L., & Egeland, B. (1980). "The Relationship between Out-of-Home Care and the Quality of Infant-Mother Attachment in an Economically Disadvantaged Population". *Child Development, 51*

Vermeer, Harriet J. & van Ijzendoorn, Marinus. Children's elevated cortisol levels at day care: a review and meta-analysis. *Early Childhood Research Quarterly* 21 (2006) 390-401.

Wallin, D. (2002 August). Attachment and intersubjectivity in healing relationships. Cassedy Seminars. Skirball Center.

Watson, John (1928). *Psychological Care of the Infant and Child.* New York: W.W. Norton & Co.

Welch, Martha G. (1988). *Holding Time: How to Eliminate Conflict, Temper Tantrums, and Sibling Rivalry and Raise Happy, Loving, Successful Children.* New York: Simon and Schuster.

Whitfield, Charles L. (1995). *Memory and Abuse: Remembering and Healing the Effects of Trauma.* Health Communications, Inc., Deerfield, Florida.

_____ (1989). *Healing the Child Within.* Health Communications, Inc.: Deerfield Beach, Florida.

Whitfield, Charles L.; Silberg, Joyanna; Fink, Paul Jay (2001.) *Misinformation Concerning Child Sexual Abuse and Adult Survivors.* Haworth Maltreatment & Trauma Press: Binghamton, NY.

Whitaker, Robert (2002). *Mad in America: Bad Science, Bad Medicine, and the Enduring Mistreatment of the Mentally Ill.* New York: Basic Books.

Wilbur, Ken (1977). *The Spectrum of Consciousness.* Wheaton, Illinois: Theosophical Publishing House.

_____ (1981). *Up from Eden: A Transpersonal View of Human Evolution.* Boston: Shambala Publications.

_____ (1982) *The Holographic Paradigm and Other Pardoxes.* Boston: Shambala Publications.

_____ (1984). *Quantum Questions: Mystical Writings of the World's Greatest Physicists.* Shambala Publications.

_____ (2008). *The Pocket Ken Wilber.* Shambala Publications.

Winnicott, D. W. (1953). "Transitional Objects and Transitional Phenomena – A Study of the First Not-Me Possession". *International Journal of Psychoanalysis, 34,* 89-97.

_____ (1958). *Primary Maternal Preoccupation. Collected Papers: Through Pediatrics to Psycho-Analysis.* New York: Basic Books.

Wylie, Mary Sykes (2004). "The Limits of Talk Therapy: Bessel van der Kolk Wants to Transform the Treatment of Trauma". *Psychotherapy Networker, January/February,* 30-38.

Yogananda, Paramhansa (1998). *Autobiography of a Yogi.* Los Angeles: Self-Realization Fellowship.

Zametkin, Alan J. (1995). "Attention-Deficit Disorder: Born to Be Hyperactive". *Journal of the American Medical Association, 273*(23), 1871-1874.

Zeanah, C.H., Mammen, O.K. & Liebermen, A.F. (1993). "Disorders of Attachment". In C.H. Zeanah (Ed.), *Handook of Infant Mental* Health. New York: Guilford Press.

Glossary

12 o'clock: assuming power which, in a healthy scenario, could present as leadership but in an unhealthy scenario, presents as superiority, arrogance and abuse

6 o'clock: being out of power which, in a healthy scenario, presents as humility, learning and self-reflection, but in an unhealthy scenario, presents as shamed, devalued and diminished; often referred to as being "sixed out"

Attention Deficit Disorder (ADD): a developmental disorder characterized by difficulty focusing, specifically at school; see also Attention Deficit/Hyperactivity Disorder (Inattentive Type)

Attention Deficit/Hyperactivity Disorder (ADHD): a developmental disorder in children characterized by difficulty focusing and hyperactivity in a multitude of ways; now includes the former ADD diagnosis (Inattentive Type), Hyperactive-Impulsive Type and Combined Type

adhesive identification: a feeling of non-existence or porousness due to lack of touch and sensory deprivation in first years, leaving a person defenseless against projections

alogia: impoverishment of thought

anaclytic depression: depression in infant, which begins with inconsolable crying and progresses to head-banging, rocking, withdrawal, and self-stimulating behavior; results from a greater loss of parent figure than the child can tolerate

attachment: the long-term relationship between child and primary caregiver(s)

avolition: inability to set goals and pursue them

Asperger's syndrome: a developmental disorder characterized by loss of expressive or perceptive language, bowel or bladder control and play or motor skills; impairment in communication and/or social skills; repetitive restricted movements; stereotyped patterns of behavior and mannerisms

autism: a developmental disorder characterized by social impairment, communication delays, repetitious preoccupation with things, refusal to make eye contact, lack of spontaneous facial and body expressions, lack of sharing, lack of enjoyment

bonding: the initial relationship between infant and primary caregiver(s)

caregiver: one who parents with continuity

caretaker: one who enables pathological behavior of others by taking care of them

catharsis: releasing buried trauma, primarily by crying or raging

child speak: This term was coined as a result of my observations of how children speak versus when parents speak of the same experience. Child Speak is a way of evaluating and authenticating a child's report of an event as opposed to words children used when they have been coached by adults on what to say.

coach: a guide, often but not necessarily a therapist, with designated specialties not falling under any certifying board. Coaches work with people to achieve specified goals. Historically, coaches worked especially with athletes, executives and entertainers. More recently, they coach yoga, breath work and parenting. TIPP's coaches specialize in Causal Theory parenting, breath/couchwork and relationship skills.

countertransference: the personal feelings the therapist develops toward the client and the resulting responses upon which the therapist feels like acting. These feelings can be useful forms of information, especially if the client evokes these feelings in others, or these feelings may include expectations, projections, and learned responses from the therapists own childhood.

Conduct Disorder (CD): the diagnosis given to a child whose behaviors are prone to violence, vandalism, cruelty to people and animals, stealing from victims, purse-snatching, forced sexual activity, fire-setting, breaking and entering, lying to obtain goods or favors or to avoid responsibility, stealing expensive items, staying out significantly late, running away, truancy

dialectical: the tension, relationship or opposition between two interacting forces or elements; an interaction of opposites in which the action of one co-creates the action of the other; an integral part of The Way of nature; the "in-between", invisible or the energy passing between two things giving soul or essence to the relationship or dynamic; presumes energy never exists separate from matter

Diathesis-Stress Model: a psychological theory that attempts to explain behavior as a result of genetic vulnerability together with stress from life experiences

echolalia: involuntary imitation of the speech of another

echopraxia: involuntary imitation of the movements of another

encopresis: inappropriate passage and smearing of poop at age four or older

enlisted child: a child or grown child who accepts the proposition that parents must always be protected and represented above the child's needs, no matter what. It creates a blindness in the child for life.

enuresis: bedwetting after age five

existential: a philosophical interpretation of events in terms of the here and now, with a focus on irony, personal responsibility and the impact judgment has on an event in that judging it actually changes it and blinds us to what is really happening

Existential Dilemma: A dilemma, which by design, almost has no solution. Only higher consciousness can transcend such a problem. When two people have to resolve it, they both can achieve higher levels of self-awareness by committing together to achieving it.

framing: in general, the process of organizing experiences, thoughts and feelings into a context that makes sense; in the Relationship Skills Workshop, identifying a forthcoming statement as probably hurtful because it may lack relationship skills; usually done by newcomers in order to prepare the listener and be openly self-aware and sensitive to the feelings of the listener; implied is an intention to communicate and reduce pain as a result of open communication

holograms: four-dimensional representations which can be created scientifically and tend to look somewhat ethereal. When the brain records an image to represent something it has encountered or imagined, it utilizes four-dimensional representations.

imprinting: the process of digesting a treatment in a weaker or vulnerable state of 6 o'clock and storing it with the strong possibility that it will be delivered on another weaker person at a later date

imprint energy: the stored energy unloaded on an unsuspecting, possibly weaker or innocent person resulting from an interaction at an earlier or younger time with a parent, authority figure or dominant person

karma: In the purest sense of the word, karma refers to cause and effect. Some religions have extended the meaning of karma into previous lifetimes, where there is no evidence of cause and effect.

Master Parent: someone who has completed *The Miracle Child Parenting Series* four times

Master Teacher: a Master Parent who has completed the extensive written exam, has participated in the Relationship Skills Workshop to the degree that his or her peers acknowledge a high level of proficiency in the skills, has done sufficient couchwork to demonstrate a high degree of self-awareness, concurs with the content of the *Intelligence* and is approved by TIPP's certification committee

Miracle Child: children who were raised according to The Causal Theory, someone who has been raised in a healthy way and is thus resilient, good natured, confident, problem-solving, charismatic, ethical and low-maintenance

Miracle Child Parenting Series: the live parenting class based exclusively on The Causal Theory from which *The Manual* grew

maya: projections on and illusions about reality which are not recognized and are actually believed as true.

mirroring: in the Relationship Skills Workshop, the process of giving objective, thoughtful, diplomatic and uncharged feedback about how a person is coming across so they can better see themselves

misogynist: a woman hater

Obsessive Compulsive Personality Disorder (OC): a personality disorder, structure or trait characterized by control issues including the need to organize, clean, "should" or think technically (See Lecture 2)

Oppositional Defiant Disorder (ODD): a diagnosis given to a child who often loses his temper, argues with adults, refuses to take orders or follow rules, deliberately annoys people, often blames others for his mistakes or misbehavior, is easily annoyed, angry, resentful, spiteful and/or vindictive

perception: seeing or perceiving another person accurately

projection: seeing what one expects to see rather than perceiving a person clearly, which often feels disturbing to the object of the projection; experienced identically with perceptions, so investigation is required in order to distinguish between the two

projective identification: being the object of someone's projection, identifying with it as if it is true and defending it accordingly

Reactive Attachment Disorder (RAD): a disorder characterized by inappropriate social relatedness developing before age five, expressive inhibition (Inhibited Type) or indiscriminate sociability (Disinhibited Type), resulting from failed attachments with caregivers and leading to possible antisocial or sociopathic adult behavior

reframing: looking at material in discussion from another perspective, resulting in a different conclusion than originally found

scapegoating: exacting retribution on someone who unconsciously represents a parent or injurer, often while verbally maintaining there is no issue with the actual parent and asserting they did their best

separation anxiety: the fear that develops in a small child forced to separate too soon, often leading to general anxiety in the adult

Snyder Causal Theory & Treatment (SCTT): practice of The Causal Theory

socioeconomic status (SES): politically correct reference to one's socioeconomic level, as in lower-class or poor, middle-class or upper-class or rich (politically incorrect).

Stage One: an issue brought into Relationship Skills Workshop from outside the group to be studied for lessons

Stage Two: the highest priority issue that takes place in real time in Relationship Skills Workshop that can be witnessed, studied, and mirrored for corrections and lessons

Stereotypic Movement Disorder: mechanical behavior (*e.g.*, flapping, head banging, body rocking, hand shaking or waving, self-biting, self-hitting)

symbiosis: two people functioning as one; ultra-intimacy

thought broadcasting: a person's belief that they can either read other people's thoughts or people can read theirs; often experienced by schizophrenics

transcendent: refers to the achievement of having risen to another level. In Causal Theory, transcendent refers to a level of healing that includes significant insight.

Transcendent Child: an injured child with marked symptoms who has done the work to heal; displays honor, wisdom, self-discipline and radiance as a result, Transcendent Child: one who has achieved significant healing and insight

Glossary

transference: occurs when the client responds to the therapist as if she is the client's parent, especially involving projections, expectations, hopes and fears.

transitional object: the security blanket toddlers use to keep them company out of the home and away from their parents, reducing the impact of separation

trichotillomania: nervously pulling out one's own hair

The Way: reverent Buddhist reference to the laws of the universe

Name Index

Ainsworth, Mary, 4, 30, 200
Athens, Lonnie, 309–11
Baker Brown, Isaac, 15
Barker, Elliott, 6
Beck, Don, 41
Becker, Judith, 52, 115
Belsky, Jay, 4, 232
Bentall, Richard, 4
Benzer, Seymour, 278
Berkson, Gershon, 51
Biblarz, Timothy, 186
Bowen, Murray, 46
Bowlby, John, 4, 8, 30, 57, 282
Bradshaw, John, 182, 265, 347
Brandtjen, Henry, 229, 232
Breggin, Peter, 4, 17, 69, 165, 182, 232, 234, 235, 269, 279
Breuer, Joseph, 17
Brown, Daniel, 180
Brundige, Joe, 92
Buddha, The, xv, 66, 69, 78, 188, 271
Burt, Cyril, 284
Bynum, W.F., 14
Calfaro, John, 182
Calhoun, J.F., 13
Carlo, Phillip, 65
Carmichael, Mary, 210
Chad, Clayton, 6
Cline, Foster, 169, 182, 331
Clinton, Bill, 69
Colbert, Ty, 5, 13–17, 182, 282
Cole, Michael & Sheila, 6
Dahmer, Jeffrey, 52, 65, 68, 69, 115, 183, 255

Dahmer, Lionel, 52
Damon, Matt, 69
de St. Exupery, Antoine, 344
DeGrandpre, Richard, 4, 182, 233, 234, 282
DeLisi, Charles, 281
deMause, Lloyd, 1, 265
Donahue, Phil, 69, 78
Dreskin, William & Wendy, 209
Dunstan, Priscilla, 205
Dutton, Donald, 5, 50, 251, 266, 282
Dyer, Wayne, 154
Dylan, Bob, 69
Einstein, Albert, 10, 65, 69
Eisenhower, Dwight, 69
Ellenberger, Henri, 19
Fancher, R.T., 14
Ferenczi, Sandor, 20
Flechsig, Paul Emil, 17
Fliess, Wilhelm, 17
Fonda, Jane, 69
Forbes, Heather, 168, 331
Frank, Justin, 58
Freud, Sigmund, 17–21, 25
Freyd, Jennifer, 5, 179, 182
Freyd, Peter & Pamela, 179
Gacy, John Wayne, 69
Galileo, 19, 69
Galves, Robert, 281
Gates, Bill, 69
Goldwater, Barry, 69
Gorbachev, Mikhail, xv, 69, 78
Gottheiner, Karin, 32
Hall, Nancy, 15, 381

Harlow, Harry, 4
Harris, Eric, 232
Harris, Sam, 12, 69, 280
Helding, Cathy, 169
Hitler, Adolf, 20–21, 65, 69, 135
Hitler, Alois, 20
Houston, Whitney, 69
Hubbard, Ruth, 4, 182
Hussein, Saddam, 69
Jackson, Michael, 36, 69
James, William, ix, 154
Jesus, xv, 66, 69, 78, 188
Joan of Arc, 69
Jobs, Steve, 69, 381
Joseph, Jay, 4, 11, 281, 282
Julius, Mary Jane, 4, 211
Jung, Carl, 11
Kaczynski, Ted, 137, 313
Kallman, Franz, 284
Kaplan, Stuart, 4, 210
Kelves, Daniel, 281
Ketcham, Katherine, 180
Klebold, Dylan, 232
Klein, Melanie, 8
Knox, Amanda, 10
Kohut, Heinz, 30
Kræpelin, Emil, 15
Kramer, Joel, 39, 182
Kring, Ann, 53
Lady Gaga, 69
Lawe, Daren, 148
LeDoux, Joseph, 4, 50
Leo, Jonathan, 11, 278, 281, 282
Levine, Peter, 143
Levy, Terry, 26
Lewis, Dorothy, 182, 281
Lewontin, Richard, 4, 11, 182, 281, 282
Lilienfeld, Michael, ix, 153
Linehan, Marsha, 356
Lipton, Bruce, 4, 282
Little Albert, 22
Locke, John, 13
Loftus, Elizabeth, 180
Loughner, Jared, 69
MacPherson, C.N., 13
Madoff, Bernie, 69, 130
Mahler, Margaret, 182, 191
Main, Mary, 4, 200–202

Mandela, Nelson, 69
Manson, Charles, 50, 69
Mason, William, 51
Masson, Jeffrey, 18, 19, 27, 182
Masters and Johnson, 350
Matosian, Brian, 379
McGraw, Phil, 186, 303
Menendez, Lyle & Erik, 10, 46, 131
Michelangelo, 69
Miller, Alice, 5, 17, 18, 19, 21, 27, 51, 58, 143, 145, 163, 182, 265, 297, 374
Millon, Theodore, 73
Minuchin, Salvador, 46
Mother Teresa, 4, 67, 69, 234
Moya, Stacy, 289
Nance, R.D., 23
Norris, Joel, 65
Obama, Barack, 67, 69
Oprah, xv, 6, 69, 141, 150, 353
Orlans, Michael, 26
Orne, Martin, 179
Pam, Alvin, 4, 11, 182, 281
Peck, M. Scott, 45, 46, 130, 182, 250, 341
Perry, Bruce, 5, 4, 5, 17, 50, 135, 182, 278, 282
Piaget, Jean, 7
Pincus, Jonathan, 282
Pinel, Philipe, 13
Plomin, Robert, 281
Pope, Kenneth, 5, 180
Post, Bryan, 168
Prescott, James, 6, 51, 282
Ramirez, Richard, 64, 68, 69, 269, 277
Read, John, 17
Reich, Theodore, 25, 31
Reps, Paul, ix, 39, 174, 182, 277
Rizzolatti, Giocomo, 256
Robertson, Brian, 233
Roosevelt, Eleanor, 69
Ross, Colin, 4, 5, 11, 50, 64, 182, 281, 282
Rothschild, Babette, 182
Rumi, 156
Rush, Benjamin, 14
Ruskan, John, 182
Santner, Eric, 16–17

Index

Schatzman, Morton, 16
Schlessinger, Laura, 348
Schore, Allan, 4, 5, 17, 64, 192, 282
Schreber, Daniel Gottlieb Mortitz, 15–17
Schreber, Daniel Paul, 15–17, 19
Scott, Timothy, 11, 281
Seznie, Esther, 367
Siegel, Daniel, 4, 5, 45, 381
Simons, D.A., 134
Sinsheimer, Robert, 281
Sklar, Reenie, 4, 11
Snyder, Ron, ix, 148, 152
Snyder, Scott Clifton, ix
Solomon, Marion, 163, 182
Sonkin, Daniel Jay, 200
Spitz, Rene, 4, 30
Stacey, Judith, 186
Stalin, Joseph, 69
Stern, Daniel, 182
Stosny, Steven, 182
Super Nanny, 303
Szalavitz, Maia, 5, 182
Szasz, Thomas, 15
Taylor, Madeline, 30
Teicher, Martin, 4, 17, 50
Thomas, Nancy, 182, 331
Tuke, William, 13
Underwager, Ralph, 179, 181
Valenstein, Elliot, 4, 11, 182, 281, 282, 284
van der Kolk, Bessel, 4, 5, 8, 17, 50, 156, 157
van IJzedoorn, Marinus, 233
Vermeer, Harriet, 233
Verny, Thomas, 229, 232
Wakefield, Hollinda, 179
Wald, Elijah, 182
Waller, Joseph, ix
Wallin, David, 8
Washington, George, 14
Watson, John, 22–25
Weinberg, Robert, 281
Welch, Martha, 165, 182, 331, 332
Whitaker, Robert, 4, 5, 11, 281, 282
Whitfield, Charles, 5, 182
Wilbur, Ken, 41, 281
Winnicott, Donald, 30, 192
Wuornos, Aileen, 65, 259, 263
Wylie, Mary Sykes, 157
Yates, Andrea, 196
Yogananda, Paramhansa, 151–52
Zametkin, Alan, 278
Zeanah, C.H., 182

Subject Index

12 o'clock (power clock), 258
12 o'clock high vs. 12 o'clock fright, 168–70, 334
6 o'clock (power clock), 257
abandonment, 47, 70
abuse, 50, 70
   emotional, 55
   physical, 50, 266
   sexual, 245, 246, 329
abuse excuse, 9, 62
adapt, 5
adopted child, 330
Alcoholics Anonymous, 356, 357, 358
Alienated Child, 99, 106
American Medical Association (AMA), 37, 285
American Psychiatric Association (APA), 37, 285
American Psychological Association (APA), 37
American Revolution, 13
amygdala, 50
anger, 159, 167, 172, 265, 270, 306
anorexic, 88, 263
arrest, 160, 168, 358, 368
Aspergers Syndrome, 230
assessment, 149, 368–69
Association for Medical Superintendents of American Institutions for the Insane (AMSAII), 14
astrology, 38

attachment assessment (questionnaire), 202
attachment styles, 201
Attachment Theory, 30, 234
Attention Deficit Disorder (ADD) & Attention Deficit/Hyperactivity Disorder (ADHD), 229, 232–36
attune, 157, 190, 191, 205
autism, 50, 230
Babinsky Reflex, 6
Baby Mom, 82, 173
Baby Prince, 81, 173
bad seed, 1, 168, 278
bedwetting, 223, 245, 247
Behavioral Theory, 7, 22–25, 28, 30
bias, 9, 28, 31, 35
black box, 7, 25, 30
blaming, 264, 266, 268, 337, 348, 354, 358
blind spots, 311, 326
bonding, 48, 72, 188–94, 208, 229
Bored Child, 120
boundaries, 304
Bubble Child, 114
bulimic, 88
bullying, 274–76
California Board of Psychology, 28
castration, 115
catharsis, 17, 30, 142
Causal Theory, The, 1, 4, 31, 42–44, 236, 257, 352
Change Model (John Bradshaw), 347, 360–61

Children and Adults with Attention Deficit/Hyperactivity Disorder (CHADD), 234, 235
Christian parents, 12, 15, 20, 224
clinicians, 27
clitorectomies, 15
Cold Charming Child, 128
Columbine High School, 46, 193, 232, 272
commitment, 375–76
Complying Child, 86, 87
Conflicted Child, 111
Consciousness Ladder (chart), 338–39
containing, 165–67
   preparation checklist for, 167
Continuum of Potential, 207
controlling parents, 72
core self, 4, 38, 48, 131, 188, 227
corporal punishment, 15
corruption, xi, 13
couchwork, 153, 156–59, 162–64
countertransference, 295
courage, 148, 357
courtship disorder, 249
Coveting Child, 93, 97
critical period of development, 6
critical wiring period, 287, 288
curiosity, 10, 289, 326
currency, 323
Custody Child, 111
custody dispute, 71
dating guidelines, 346
day care, 37, 232–35
day care parenting, 312
death, 380–81
defensiveness, 61, 155, 175, 287, 356
Defying Child, 84
delusions, 38, 125, 143, 232, 252
Demeaning Child, 93, 96
denial, 47, 61, 143–44, 146, 182
depression, 2, 17, 143, 144, 146, 152, 213, 231
Diabolical Child, 129
Diathesis-Stress Model, 53, 285
Disengaged Family System, 46
dissociation, 16, 50, 51
Dissociative Identity Disorder, 139
divorce, 213–24

Divorce Act of 1857, 15
domestic violence, 266–69
Dominated Child, 99, 100
Double-Crossed Child, 124
double-damned, 267–69
Double-Damned Child, 136
drugs, 250–52, 329
Dunstan Baby Language, 204–5
ego, 149–50, 363
Electra Complex, 19
Emasculated Child, 134
enabling, 314, 365
enlightened witness, 51, 157, 170
enlightenment, 35, 41, 59, 147, 271
enlisted, 143, 259, 270
Enmeshed Family System, 46
Entertaining Child, 90
epiphanies, 38, 147
Episcopalians, 12
Erhard Seminar Training, 41
Ethereal Child, 116
ethics, 154, 182, 265, 365–76
Ethics of Personality Types (chart), 138
Evidence-Based Practice, 28
evil, 269–74
Exiled Child, 111
existential dilemma, 349–50
expression, 30, 158, 170, 204, 265, 302, 366–67
eye of the needle, 363–64
faith parenting, xv
Faking Positive Child, 94, 95
false memories, 5, 178–81
False Memory Syndrome Foundation (FMSF), 179
Family Projection Process, 46
Family Systems Theory, 31
feedback, 355–56
feminism, 32, 36, 215, 234
feral children, 6
fight or flight, 142, 143
forgiveness, 144–45, 172, 374–75, 380
Four Traits for Healing, 148–50
fragmentation of competency, 288
framing, 362
Freudian Theory, 29
gatekeepers, 7, 27, 280

Index

genes as the origin of personality, 1, 3–6, 35, 296, 382
genetics, 279–86
Got-It-Handled Child, 93, 98
hallucinations, 50, 125, 143, 152
Hanging Judge. *See* Schreber, Daniel Paul (Name Index)
Head-Tripped Child, 99, 104
healer, 31, 153, 162, 271
healing your grown child, 170
Health Maintenance Organizations (HMOs), 28
Here & Now, 38
hippocampus, 50
holding environment, 165
Holding Therapy. *See* containing
holograms, 300
Human Genome Project, 281
humility, 40, 43, 151, 337
identity, 48, 142, 181, 182, 191, 204, 244, 374
In Power, 258
inborn traits, 12, 23
inevitable learning, 7, 8, 11, 12, 278
Infantilized Child, 81
injury, 142–44, 146, 171, 209, 257
insane asylums, 13
instincts, 6, 24, 290
intelligence, 2, 10, 65, 190, 192, 278
Internal Drive Theory, 19, 263, 295
Interpersonal Therapy (IPT), 30
intrusive parenting, 16, 46, 71, 84, 232
Islam, 12
Isolated Mind Theories, 29
jealousy, 6, 312
Jews, 12, 20, 35
judgment, 6, 45, 148–49, 368–69, 371–72
karmic discipline, 289, 321
La Leche League, 193
Lamaze, 6
Landmark Forum, 41, 271
leave no trace, 241, 294, 318, 327
Leboyer Childbirth, 6
Little Man, 82
loitering, 153
madness, 14
magical thinking, 12, 51, 177

masturbation, 17, 23, 244
medication. *See* pharmaceuticals
meditation, 38–41
mental health, 2–3, 5, 192, 278
mind's eye, 11, 40
Mind-Raped Child, 118
Miracle Child, xv, 2, 35, 45, 206
mirror neurons, 4, 256, 278
moods, 5, 189
Moral Management, 13
morals, 78, 87, 90, 269, 359
Moro Reflex, 6
motives, viii, 29, 279–86
multiples, 197–200
Muslims, 12
National Alliance for the Mentally Ill (NAMI), 279
natural consequences, 31, 37, 43, 45, 289–90, 292–93, 305–7
nature vs. nurture, 34, 59, 278
Nazi Germany, 12
neglect, 47, 70, 236, 293, 311, 312
neural connections, 5, 227, 278
No-Mistakes-Allowed Child, 110
Novartis Pharmaceuticals, 235
Object Relations Theory, 30
Obsessive Compulsive Disorder (OCD), 117
Oedipal Complex, 19
omnipotence, 143
Orgone Box, 26
out of body, xiii, 16, 49, 230
Out of Power, 257
over-burdened child, 71
pacifiers, 25
paranoia, 296
Paranoid Judge. *See* Schreber, Daniel Paul (Name Index)
parent bashing, 62
parental alienation, 221, 316
Parentified Child, 82
perception, 10, 369–70
perpetrator, 5, 9, 143, 169, 259, 266, 363
Personality Diagnosis Charts, 77–137
    Antisocial, 126
    Approach-Avoidant, 111
    Avoidant, 109
    Bipolar, 121

Borderline, 99
Dependent, 81
Dissociative Identity Disorder (Multiple Personality Disorder), 122
Dysthymic or Cyclothymic Disorder, 120
Healthy, 78
Histrionic, 90
Mass Murderer, 135
Narcissistic, 93
Obsessive-Compulsive, 83
Paranoid, 123
Passive-Aggressive, 79
Psychopath, 132
Rapist, 134
Schizoid, 114
Schizophrenic, 118
Schizotypal, 116
Serial Killer, 136
Sociopath, 128
Personality Diagnosis Charts, Map, 74
pharmaceutical industry, 4, 37, 234, 279
pharmaceuticals, 4, 42, 60, 182, 233, 235–36, 278, 281–86
positive thinking, 38, 73, 145, 263
Post Traumatic Stress Disorder (PTSD), 28, 31, 50, 180
Postal Child, 135
postpartum depression, 70, 195–97
potty training, 238–40
predetermination, 55
prediction, 64, 352
predisposition, 1, 12, 64, 197, 278
Preventive Diagnosis Cheat Sheet, 75
pride. *See* ego
primary caregiver, 185, 187, 192, 196, 208, 216–18, 221
Princess Baby, 81, 173
principles of a healthy relationship, 347
processing, 153, 158, 171
pro-child, xi, 9–11, 26, 34, 279
projection, 8, 10, 39, 143, 146, 295–97, 369–70
projective identification, 143, 295–97
pro-parent, xi, 9–11, 26, 31, 34, 143, 208, 233, 279, 282, 307
pruning, 5, 278
Pseudo Mutuality vs. Pseudo Hostility, 46
psychobabble, xi, 9, 31
Psychogeneology, 31
Psychohistory, 31, 58
Quakers, 12
quitting, 79, 161, 378
Rage Reduction. *See* containing
rage work, 52, 159, 178, 259, 267, 334
ramifications, viii, 26, 29, 279
Reactive Attachment Disorder (RAD), 23
  adult traits, 232
  child traits, 230
  disciplining a RAD child, 330–36
  healing a RAD child, 167–73
re-bonding, 166, 232
recovered memories, 31, 178–81
re-enactment, 262
reflexes, 6
regression, 133, 175, 178
Reichian Therapy, 31
reincarnation, 37–38, 263
Relational Model, 30
relationship questions, 344
repression, 47, 71, 143, 263
Resiliency Spectrum, 54
resistance, 62–63, 144, 147
responsibility
  parental, 26, 43, 45, 52, 215
  teaching your child, 243, 246
retribution, 159, 259, 270, 358
rocking
  during attachment, 188, 193
  for healing, 51
  self-soothing behavior, 55, 228
Royal Child, 93
Royal College of Physicians, 14
Santa Monica Zen Center, 41, 271
scapegoating, 21, 123, 143, 146, 152, 159, 261, 269, 309
schizophrenia, 15, 232, 370
Secretive Child, 88
Secretly Angry Child, 79
secure attachment, 192, 206, 208, 222
Seduction Theory, 18, 19, 20

Index

Self Psychology, 30
Self-Controlling Child, 83
self-fulfilling prophecy, 263, 278
self-observation, 39, 148
Sensate Focus, 350–52
sensitive period, 6
sensory deprivation, 50, 116, 118, 232
separation, 49, 207–40
Separation Anxiety Disorder, 229
separation rituals, 227
Separation Schedules, 208–12
   Abandonment Schedule, 209
   Continuity-of-Care Schedule, 210
   Snyder Child Custody Schedule (SCCS), 211–12
separation-individuation, 206
Set-Up Child, 109
shadow, 146, 152–55
Shahzade v. Gregory, 180
Shocking Child, 91
Sickly Child, 83, 88
Side-by-Side Model, 348
skin issues, 192
Slovenly Child, 85
Snyder Causal Theory & Treatment (SCTT), 31
social awareness, 58, 63
sociopathic decision, 21
Somatosensory Affectional Deprivation (SAD), 51
Spiral Dynamics, 41
Stage Fearing, 262
Stage Fixation, 262
Stage One and Stage Two, 362
state of grace, 147, 154
stay-at-home moms, 55
Sudden Infant Death Syndrome (SIDS), 204
Suffocated Child, 99, 107
surrender, 43, 147, 153, 157, 158
   of ego, 149–50

symbiosis, 191
talk therapy, 155
tantrums, 236–38
tao, 11
temperament, 1, 5, 189–92, 278, 381
terminating, 376
Terrorized Child, 122
theoreticians, 27, 150
Tormented Child, 132
Torn Child, 111, 112
touch, 192
transcendence, 7, 44, 150
Transcendent Child, xv, 2, 35, 261
transitional object, 225
trauma, 43, 49–55, 157, 182, 302
   healing, 155–59, 366
Trauma Model, 50
Trauma Predictor Scale, 64, 66
Trauma Theory, 31
Tricked Child, 123
true parent, 51–53
truthfulness, 270, 366
Twice-Blessed Child, 78
Type A Thinkers. *See* pro-parent
Type B Thinkers. *See* pro-child
Unitarians, 12
Unprotected Child, 99, 102
Vagrancy Act, 14
Violated Child, 126
War of the Researchers, xi, 9, 34, 150, 178, 279
Way, The, ix, 11
weak parenting, 71, 302, 313
Western Association of Secondary Schools, 28
Wilderness Therapy, 207, 275, 330
Wishing-It Child, 121
workhouses, 13
yelling, 367
Yes, if..., 372
Zen student, 41, 42, 149, 152

www.ingramcontent.com/pod-product-compliance
Lightning Source LLC
Chambersburg PA
CBHW021351290426
44108CB00010B/193